Mississippi Writers

Reflections of Childhood and Youth

MISSISSIPPI WRITERS

Reflections of Childhood and Youth

Volume II: NONFICTION

Edited by
DOROTHY ABBOTT

UNIVERSITY PRESS OF MISSISSIPPI
Jackson and London

Center for the Study of Southern Culture Series

Manufactured in the United States of America

Library of Congress Cataloging-in-Publication Data
(Revised for vol. 2)
Main entry under title:

Mississippi writers.

(Center for the Study of Southern Culture series)
Contents: v. 1. Fiction—v. 2. Nonfiction.
1. American literature—Mississippi. 2. American literature—20th century. 3. Mississippi—Literary collections. 4. Children—Literary collections. 5. Youth—Literary collections. 6. Mississippi—Literary collections. 7. American literature—Collections. I. Abbott, Dorothy, 1944–
II. Series.
PS558.M7M55 1985 813'.008'09762 84-5131
ISBN 0-87805-231-3 (v.1)
ISBN 0-87805-232-1 (pbk: v.1)

CONTENTS

ACKNOWLEDGMENTS

THE EDITOR is grateful for the assistance given by consulting editors Samuel Prestridge, Ann J. Abadie, Sue Hart, and Janice B. Snook and by JoAnne Prichard, my editor at University Press. The editor also wishes to thank the following authors and publishers or magazines for permission to reprint the designated selections. Rights in all cases are reserved by the owner of the copyright.

"Have We Overcome?" by Lerone Bennett, Jr., first appeared in *Have We Overcome? Race Relations Since "Brown"*, edited by Michael V. Namorato. Published by University Press of Mississippi. Copyright © 1979 by the University Press of Mississippi. Reprinted by permission of the editor.

Excerpt from *Amazing Grace: With Charles Evers in Mississippi* by Jason Berry. Published by Saturday Review Press. Copyright © 1978 by Jason Berry. Reprinted by permission of the author.

"Eudora Welty's Jackson" by Nash K. Burger first appeared in *Shenandoah: The Washington and Lee University Review*. Copyright © 1969 by Washington and Lee University. Reprinted by permission of the editor.

Excerpt from *Brother to a Dragonfly* by Will D. Campbell. Published by Continuum Publishing Corporation. Copyright © 1977 by Will D. Campbell. Reprinted by permission of the publisher.

Excerpt from *A Highly Ramified Tree* by Robert Canzoneri. Published by the Viking Press. Copyright © 1971, 1973, 1976 by Robert Canzoneri. Reprinted by permission of Viking Penguin Inc.

"God and My Grandmother" by Charlotte Capers first appeared in *The Delta Review*. Copyright © 1982 by Charlotte Capers. Reprinted by permission of University Press of Mississippi from *The Capers Papers* by Charlotte Capers.

"Sunday Has a Different Smell" by Anne Carsley first appeared in *Mississippi*. Copyright © 1971 by Anne Carsley. Reprinted by permission of the author.

"Grandmother Was Emphatic" by Hodding Carter from *Southern Legacy*. Published by Louisiana State University Press. Copyright © 1950 by the Louisiana State University Press. Reprinted by permission of the publisher.

Excerpt from *My Life and The Times* by Turner Catledge. Published by Harper & Row, Publishers, Inc. Copyright © 1971 by Turner Catledge. Reprinted by permission of the publisher.

"A Personal View of the Mississippi Chinese" by Sung Gay Chow. Copyright © 1985 by Sung Gay Chow. Printed by permission of the author.

Excerpt from *A Feast Made for Laughter* by Craig Claiborne. Published by Holt,

Rinehart and Winston. Copyright © 1982 by Craig Claiborne. Reprinted by permission of the publisher.
"Recollections of a Mississippi Boyhood" by Thomas D. Clark. Copyright © 1985 by Thomas D. Clark. Printed by permission of the author.
Excerpt from *Where I Was Born and Raised* by David L. Cohn. Published by Houghton Mifflin Company. Reprinted by University of Notre Dame Press. Copyright © 1935, 1947, and 1948 by David L. Cohn and 1967 by University of Notre Dame Press. Reprinted by permission of Mrs. David L. Cohn.
"A Wop Bop Alu Bop A Wop Bam Boom" by Danny Collum. Copyright © 1985 by Danny Collum. Printed by permission of the author.
Choctaw Boy by Paul Conklin. Published by Dodd, Mead & Company. Copyright © 1975 by Paul S. Conklin. Reprinted by permission of the publisher.
Excerpt from *Families: A Memoir and a Celebration* by Wyatt Cooper. Published by Harper & Row, Publishers, Inc. Copyright © 1975 by Wyatt Cooper. Reprinted by permission of Gloria Vanderbilt Cooper.
"Harder Times Than These" by L. C. Dorsey first appeared in *Southern Exposure*. Copyright © 1982 by the Institute for Southern Studies. Reprinted by permission of the publisher.
"Reading and Writing: Beginnings" by Ellen Douglas first appeared as "Faulkner in Time" from *"A Cosmos of My Own": Faulkner and Yoknapatawpha 1980*, edited by Doreen A. Fowler and Ann J. Abadie. Published by the University Press of Mississippi. Copyright © 1981 by the University Press of Mississippi. Reprinted by permission of the publisher.
"The Search for Eudora Welty." by Charles East first appeared in *Mississippi Quarterly*. Copyright © 1973 by Mississippi State University. Reprinted by permission of the publisher.
Excerpt from *This Bright Day* by Lehman Engel. Published by Macmillan Publishing Company. Copyright © 1974 by Lehman Engel. Reprinted by permission of Phyllis L. Herman, Celeste L. Orkin, and Beatrice L. Gotthelf.
Excerpt from *Evers* by Charles Evers. Published by World Publishing Company. Copyright © 1971 by Charles Evers and Grace Halsell. Reprinted by permission of the author.
"Why I Live in Mississippi" by Medgar Evers was first published in *Ebony*, November 1958. Reprinted by permission of the publisher.
Excerpt from *For Us, the Living* by Mrs. Medgar Evers (with William Peters). Published by Doubleday & Company, Inc. Copyright © 1967 by Myrlie B. Evers and William Peters. Reprinted by permission of the publisher.
Excerpt from *My Brother Bill*. Published by Trident Press. Reprinted by Yoknapatawpha Press. Copyright © 1963 by Lucille Ramey Faulkner. Reprinted by permission of Lucille Ramey Faulkner and the publisher.
"And Now What's To Do" by William Faulkner first appeared in *Mississippi Quarterly*. Copyright © 1973 by Jill Faulkner Summers. Reprinted by permission of Jill Faulkner Summers and The University of Mississippi.
"Mississippi" by William Faulkner first appeared in *Holiday*. Copyright © 1965 by Random House, Inc. Reprinted by permission of Random House, Inc., from *Essays, Speeches, and Public Letters* by William Faulkner, edited by James B. Meriwether.
Excerpt from *Blues from the Delta* by William Ferris. Published by Anchor Press/Doubleday. Reprinted by DaCapo Press. Copyright © 1978 by William Ferris. Reprinted by permission of the publisher.
Excerpt from *The Civil War: A Narrative, Fort Sumter to Perryville* by Shelby

Foote. Published by Random House, Inc. Copyright © 1958 by Shelby Foote. Reprinted by permission of the publisher.

"The Three Kings: Hemingway, Faulkner, and Fitzgerald" by Richard Ford first appeared in *Esquire*. Copyright © 1983 by Richard Ford. Reprinted by permission of the author from *Esquire's Fifty Who Made the Difference*.

Excerpt from *The Making of Black Revolutionaries* by James Forman. Published by Macmillan Publishing Company. Reprinted by Open Hand Publishing Inc. Copyright © 1972, 1985 by James Forman. Reprinted by permission of the author.

"Three Journal Entries" by Ellen Gilchrist first presented on National Public Radio's Morning Edition of the News. Copyright © 1985 by Ellen Gilchrist. Reprinted by permission of Don Congdon Associates, Inc.

"Growing Up in Mississippi" by Loyle Hairston. Copyright © 1985 by Loyle Hairston. Printed by permission of the author.

To Praise Our Bridges by Fannie Lou Hamer. Published by KIPCO. Copyright © 1967 by Fannie Lou Hamer, Julius Lester, and Mary Varela. Reprinted by permission of the publisher.

"Fire Over the Town" by Barry Hannah first appeared in *Southern Living*. Copyright © 1982 by Barry Hannah. Reprinted by permission of the publisher.

"Memories of Fawn Grove" by Phyllis Harper. Copyright © 1985 by Journal Publishing Company. Reprinted by permission of the publisher.

"Growing Up Among the Soon-to-Be Rich and Famous" by Kenneth Holditch. Copyright © 1985 by Kenneth Holditch. Printed by permission of the author.

"The Afternoon of a Young Poet" by M. Carl Holman first appeared in *Anger, and Beyond: The Negro Writer in the United States*, edited by Herbert Hill. Published by Harper & Row, Publishers. Copyright © 1966 by Harper & Row, Publishers. Reprinted by permission of the publisher.

"The Best Advice I Ever Had" by Laurence C. Jones first appeared in *Reader's Digest*. Copyright © 1956 by The Reader's Digest Association, Inc. Reprinted by permission of the publisher.

Excerpt from *A Slaveholder's Daughter* by Belle Kearney. Published by Abbey Press. Copyright © 1900.

"By Love Possessed" by Don Lee Keith first appeared in *Courier*. Copyright © 1977 by Don Lee Keith. Reprinted by permission of the author.

"Knee-Pants and Parasols" by Don Lee Keith first appeared in *New Orleans Magazine*. Copyright © 1978 by Don Lee Keith. Reprinted by permission of the author.

"Growing Up in Mississippi in a Time of Change" by Edwin King. Copyright © 1985 by Edwin King. Printed by permission of the author.

"A White Girl Remembers" by Beverly Lowry. Copyright © 1985 by Beverly Lowry. Printed by permission of the author.

Excerpt from *Reminiscences of an Active Life: The Autobiography of John Roy Lynch*, edited by John Hope Franklin. Published by the University of Chicago Press. Copyright © 1970 by the University of Chicago. Reprinted by permission of the publisher.

Excerpt from *Witness in Philadelphia* by Florence Mars. Published by Louisiana State University Press. Copyright © 1977 by Louisiana State University Press. Reprinted by permission of the publisher.

Excerpt from *Three Years in Mississippi* by James Meredith. Published by Indiana University Press. Copyright © 1966 by James H. Meredith. Reprinted by permission of the author.

Excerpt from *Coming of Age in Mississippi* by Anne Moody. Published by The Dial Press. Copyright © 1968 by Anne Moody. Reprinted by permission of Doubleday & Company, Inc.
Excerpt from *North Toward Home* by Willie Morris. Published by Houghton Mifflin Company. Copyright © 1967 by Willie Morris. Reprinted by permission of the publisher.
Excerpt from *The Courting of Marcus Dupree* by Willie Morris. Published by Doubleday & Company, Inc. Copyright © 1983 by Willie Morris. Reprinted by permission of the publisher.
"Notes from a Voluntary Exile" by Linda Peavy. Copyright © 1985 by Linda Peavy. Printed by permission of the author.
"Introduction to *Lanterns on the Levee*" by Walker Percy. Published by Louisiana State University Press. Copyright © 1973 by Walker Percy. Reprinted by permission of the publisher.
Excerpt from *Lanterns on the Levee* by William Alexander Percy. Published by Alfred A. Knopf, Inc. Copyright © 1941 by Alfred A. Knopf, Inc.; renewed 1968 by LeRoy Pratt Percy. Reprinted by permission of the publisher.
Excerpt from *Black Rituals* by Sterling D. Plumpp. Published by Third World Press. Copyright © 1972 by Sterling D. Plumpp. Reprinted by permission of the author.
"Notes from the Laughing Factory" by Samuel Prestridge. Copyright © 1985 by Samuel Prestridge. Printed by permission of the author.
Excerpt from *Christmas Gif'* by Charlemae Rollins. Published by Follett Publishing Company. Copyright © 1963 by Charlemae Rollins. Reprinted by permission of the publisher.
Excerpt from *Mississippi: The Closed Society* by James W. Silver. Published by Harcourt Brace Jovanovich, Inc. Copyright © 1963, 1964 by James W. Silver. Reprinted by permission of the publisher.
Excerpt from *God's Step Chilluns* by Ann Odene Smith. Published by Harlo Press. Copyright © 1981 by Ann O. Smith McGee. Reprinted by permission of the author.
Excerpt from *Congressman from Mississippi* by Frank E. Smith. Published by Pantheon Books. Copyright © 1964 by Frank E. Smith. Reprinted by permission of the publisher.
Excerpt from "Emerging as a Writer in Faulkner's Mississippi" by Elizabeth Spencer first appeared in *Faulkner and the Southern Renaissance: Faulkner and Yoknapatawpha 1981*, edited by Doreen A. Fowler and Ann J. Abadie. Published by the University Press of Mississippi. Copyright © 1982 by the University Press of Mississippi. Reprinted by permission of the publisher.
"Newbery Award Acceptance Speech for *Roll of Thunder, Hear My Cry*" by Mildred D. Taylor first appeared in *The Horn Book Magazine*. Copyright © 1977 by Mildred D. Taylor. Reprinted by permission of the author.
Excerpt from *Smile Please* by Mildred Spurrier Topp. Published by Houghton Mifflin Company. Copyright © 1948 by Mildred Spurrier Topp. Reprinted by permission of the publisher.
"Mawmaw and Pawpaw" by Glennray Tutor. Copyright © 1985 by Glennray Tutor. Printed by permission of the author.
"Growing Out of Shadow" by Margaret Walker first appeared in *Common Ground*. Copyright © 1943; renewed 1985 by Margaret Walker. Reprinted by permission of the author.
"Mississippi and the Nation in the 1980s" by Margaret Walker first appeared in

The Inaugural Papers of Governor William F. Winter, edited by Charlotte Capers. Published by Mississippi Department of Archives and History. Copyright © 1980 by Mississippi Department of Archives and History. Reprinted by permission of the author.

"A Christmas Remembered" by Dean Faulkner Wells first appeared in *Parade*. Copyright © 1980 by Dean Faulkner Wells. Reprinted by permission of Raines and Raines.

Excerpt from *Crusade for Justice: The Autobiography of Ida B. Wells* edited by Alfreda M. Duster. Published by The University of Chicago Press. Copyright © 1970 by the University of Chicago. Reprinted by permission of the publisher.

"A Sweet Devouring" by Eudora Welty first appeared in *Mademoiselle*. Copyright © 1957; renewed 1978 by Eudora Welty. Reprinted by permission of Random House from *The Eye of the Story: Selected Essays and Reviews* by Eudora Welty.

"The Little Store" first appeared as "The Corner Store" in *Esquire*. Copyright © 1975; renewed 1978 by Eudora Welty. Reprinted by permission of Random House from *The Eye of the Story: Selected Essays and Reviews* by Eudora Welty.

Excerpt from *This Is My Country Too* by John A. Williams. Published by New American Library. Copyright © 1973 by John A. Williams. Reprinted by permission of the author.

"Facts About Me" by Tennessee Williams. Copyright © 1952 by Tennessee Williams. Reprinted by permission of New Directions Publishing Corp. from *Where I Live* by Tennessee Williams.

Excerpt from *Black Boy* by Richard Wright. Published by Harper & Row, Publishers, Inc. Copyright © 1937, 1942, 1944, 1945 by Richard Wright. Reprinted by permission of the publisher.

"Black, Brown and Beige" by Al Young. Copyright © 1981 by Al Young. Reprinted by permission of Creative Arts Book Company from *Bodies & Soul* by Al Young.

PREFACE

I WAS WRAPPING up the work on this, the second volume of *Mississippi Writers: Reflections of Childhood and Youth*, and someone, as a lot of people did during that time, asked me how it was going. I responded with an anecdote, not for the sake of being folksy, or more to the point, evasive, but because I was reminded of what these writers have already experienced, and having experienced, have honed into a skill—that the measure of their experiences is of greater metaphoric value (the big values being always the least articulated) than any sum of their conclusions. Or maybe—and more to the point—Mississippians just talk a lot.

I met a man from New York on his first trip down south. He wanted to know about the South, what it was like to be Southern, to be here. I thought, of course, of Shreve McCannon—"Tell about the South. What's it like there. What do they do there. Why do they live there."

I believe that it is best to give people who ask complex questions simple answers. So, I answered him: "Imagine having an unresolved Oedipus complex with an incredibly vast tract of land."

"You mean," he said, "like a love/hate relationship—an ambiguity created by the tension between the attraction of the mother, the land, the society that produced the individual, and the individual's recognition of the inequities inherent in the traditional values that the individual must reject in order to establish himself as a separate entity?"

"Yes and no," I said.

He nodded and seemed satisfied. I was off the hook. Evasions aside, I think the answer I gave is one I'd have to stick with if asked to give a central thematic concern of the essays in this book. The bitterness of the civil rights years stands in juxtaposition to the progress made toward racial equity. The accounts of individual estrangements are equaled by the remembrances of family, friends, and homes that provided sanctuary in times both economically and socially troubled. History meets apocrypha. Those who left the state are balanced by those who stayed. Poverty and elegance. Hope and despair. Grief and celebration. In short, these experiences are human accounts of what it was like to grow up in Mississippi in the decades that have lead us to this century's latest version of "modern times."

In my research for this book, I came across the word "microcosm" many times. It was, of course, used to describe Mississippi, both as a cultural representative of the South, and as a collection of humans representative of all humans. It could be argued that any collection of writers from any given state might be as expressive, as adamant, as introspective, as damning, and as eloquent in praise of the state that gave them their first years of life. Not being from any other region, I really can't assess whether that is true or not. Maybe such an assessment implies an objectivity akin to omniscience. Maybe after all the bother, the much vaunted "sense of place" is simply a matter of being closest to where you came from.

I can't say.

What I can say is that these are Mississippi writers and that the following pages are what they have to say about where they came from and what's happened while they were on the way.

Dorothy Abbott
The University of Mississippi

INTRODUCTION
Mississippi's Living Presence

MARYEMMA GRAHAM

WHEN WE VIEW the main body of Mississippi literature contained in this rich and diverse collection of nonfiction, we are made keenly aware of the contradictions inherent in the history of the state. These contradictions have to do, first and foremost, with the matter of race. For both black and white writers, the compulsion to confront the racial dilemma is ever present. In Mississippi, race is not only linked to a history of political and social conflict that its average citizen is still reluctant to discuss, but the Afro-American influence on Mississippi's folklore, language, and material culture has been of such a profound nature that it has become a principal research topic for scholars around the world.

As these scholars have realized, black people have greatly influenced Mississippi life, past and present. Mississippi is one of three states that had black population majorities for significant periods of time—Louisiana until 1890, South Carolina until 1921, and Mississippi until about 1940. In the 1980 census, Mississippi had a higher proportion of black citizens than any other state in the nation. Today, twenty-two of the state's eighty-two counties have black population majorities, mostly concentrated in the Delta region along the Mississippi River, a fertile and productive cotton-growing area.

Blacks who left the state during the great migrations that began in the 1920s carried Mississippi with them, transferring their religion, their blues and gospel music, and other forms of cultural expression to Memphis, St. Louis, Chicago, Detroit, and numerous other cities. Among the migrants were those who would synthesize the Mississippi experience into an aesthetic vision, making it comprehensible and accessible to the country and the world. The list of these writers—and they are all represented in this volume—reads like a Who's Who in Black America and in Modern American Literature: Richard Wright, Margaret Walker, John A. Williams, Al Young, Lerone Bennett, Loyle Hairston, Ida B. Wells. For some of these writers, Wright and Walker in particular, the Mississippi experience becomes archetypal or paradigmatic, deepening our understanding of the shape and character of black life in America.

Moreover, most of these writers exemplify the tendency in Afro-American writing to emphasize the treatment of explicitly social themes. For novelist Richard Wright this became more sharply defined as a literature of social protest. Wright was not only the most outstanding example of this school of literature, but was primarily responsible for shaping the direction of Afro-American fiction that followed.

By way of contrast, we might look at Mississippi's literary and historical culture from another angle. The movement of social protest literature coexisted with the Southern Renaissance in American literature, begun by such writers as William Faulkner, Tennessee Williams, and Stark Young and continued by Eudora Welty, Walker Percy, Shelby Foote, and numerous others. It is ironic that the leading figures in both movements—movements that are ideologically opposite, mainly because they were informed by a different set of assumptions, definitions, and experiences—were and are Mississippians. At the risk of oversimplification, we might say that, on the one hand, the Southern Renaissance was white, mostly male and generally conservative in tone and temper, with a certain romantic ambivalence for the agrarian way of life. As a movement, it was closely linked to the emergence of the New Criticism, a school of literary criticism that saw the validity of art as an autonomous object. On the other hand, the movement that brought social protest literature into being was identified with black people and the oppressed, linked closely to the emergence of radical ideas of social justice and to the interests of working class people. Mississippi is thus a common frame of reference for a certain dialectic that has been made operational not only in social and political history but also in American literary history as well.

From this vast body of expression, one that has been generally neglected by anthologists, emerges a dialectic of race, class, culture, and ideology. On the most immediate sensual level, Mississippi is a real "place" in writings represented in this volume. Its landscape, its agrarian appeal, its natural wonders that claim the body and spirit can seldom be denied by the Mississippi writer. More importantly, however, we become aware of the many issues with which Mississippians in this century have been confronted, issues so direct and immediate that we come readily to accept those forms of discourse that have not been regarded as the natural province of "creative literature." They are often more polemical than imaginative, and their appeal is sometimes less sensual than intellectual.

It is this form of discourse that dominates this volume. The selections here are mainly prose narratives or autobiographical essays in which both the well-known and the unheralded reflect upon the Mississippi they experienced during their formative years. To see the world of Mississippi from this perspective offers us a distinct advantage: it permits us insight into life at a time when perceptions of reality are automatically intensified. The period of childhood is also associated with storytelling, a device typically used to enhance the memory and to provide a way of expressing both the vitality and subtlety of a very complex culture. These impressions of childhood and youth by Mississippi writers can thus be an essential starting point for those who would come to know and understand all that is Mississippi.

Although the selections in this volume were written during the twentieth century, some of them focus on earlier experiences. One such work is an example of the formal slave narrative, a selection from *Reminiscences of an Active Life* by John Roy Lynch. Lynch, who was thirteen years old when the Civil War began, describes his childhood experiences as a house slave and comments on the immediate effects of Emancipation on both blacks and whites in Natchez. Shelby Foote's description of the youth of one of Mississippi's greatest heroes—Jefferson Davis—finds a discomforting presence beside Lynch's reminiscences. Yet in many ways Lynch and Davis are not unalike. Davis went to Washington to represent Mississippi in the House and the Senate before becoming President of the Confederacy. Lynch became Mississippi's first black member of the United States House of Representatives and helped engineer the passage of the 1875 Civil Rights Act. In addition to being prominent political leaders, both men were writers and noted public speakers. Davis became historian and apologist for the Confederacy; Lynch, who lived until the age of ninety-two, wrote a history of Reconstruction and was an advocate of black causes and racial integration.

Other nineteenth-century childhood experiences are related in the autobiographies of Ida B. Wells and Belle Kearney, both of whom were born in the early 1860s and became social rebels. In her excerpt from *A Slaveholder's Daughter* Kearney describes a youth concerned with dances, croquet, card parties, and other social activities—all of which were so unsatisfying to her that she defied customs of her class and established a private school in her parents' home. Wells, born a slave, also became a teacher, but as a means of supporting her brothers and sisters after the death of her parents during the yellow fever epidemic of 1878. Both women eventually gave up teaching in order to devote themselves to writing and speaking—Kearney for temperance and women's issues, Wells for racial justice as well as women's suffrage.

Mississippians' preoccupation with history is apparent in numerous selections contained in this volume, with author after author recalling childhood memories of stories about the Civil War. In an autobiographical account published in 1950, Hodding Carter describes how the Confederate legacy affected his generation:

> I was born forty-two years ago, just midway between the close of the War Between the States and the present. Similarly located in meaningful time are hundreds of thousands, even millions, of white Southerners of my age and older, who represent the thinking, the political directions, the economic attitudes of our badgered South. Almost every one of us, farmer, city man, mountaineer, teacher, preacher, poor white or so-called "Bourbon," was close to some fabulous father or grandfather, some remembering grandmother, to whom, in our childhood and even our young manhood, the war and its aftermath was a personal, bitter, and sacred reality. And if, in their declining years, they embroidered fact with fancy, our inheritance was no less real, our conviction of wrongful treatment no less strong, our resultant idealization no less significant.

The spirit of such stories would be merely naive, provincial, somewhat pathetic, and generally harmless, Carter says, were not the southern legacy exploited by unworthy politicians or used as "a tragically employed excuse for wrongs since committed and right things left undone."

Turner Catledge, one of the many sons of the South who grew up hearing Civil War stories, tells about going to Confederate reunions with one of his grandfathers. Catledge also notes that acceptance of this heritage and its related racial system had limits: "I grew up, of course, under a system of total segregation and it did not occur to me to challenge that system, nor did it to many people in that time and place. Yet I was always taught to treat Negroes with respect. If I used the word 'nigger,' for example, when I was playing with Negro children, I'd get a licking, and I was taught to regard whites who did use that word as themselves inferior."

Will Campbell had similar experiences, but the stories he heard from his grandfather were not romanticized:

> There were the times he told us of the violence of the Civil War. His first vivid recollection was seeing his daddy in a wooden box, placed in the doorway where the cool air would slow the decomposition of the body until the circuit-riding preacher got there to bury him. His daddy had run away from the Confederate Army at Shiloh because he was sick. Grandpa reported it with neither rancor nor judgment. And with no visible pride that his father had been a Confederate soldier. And such feeling as we had regarding the outcome of a nation divided we got elsewhere, never from him. He was not the Southerner one reads about in books.

This man, Campbell reports, also found an effective way of letting his grandchildren know that the Civil War was over. "There ain't any more niggers," he told them. "All the niggers are dead. All that's left now is colored people."

Not all Civil War stories were told by whites, as historian Thomas D. Clark reminds us in "Recollections of a Mississippi Boyhood." He grew up hearing men who had worn the gray tell sentimental stories about their war experiences, but he also notes that "just as mellow in their reminiscences were ex-slaves such as Aunt Betsy Harper who had been sold South by the famous distilling family of Frankfort, Kentucky, and Uncle Sam Metts who had ridden stirrup-to-stirrup with Captain Tom Metts throughout the war." Less mellow, of course, are the stories blacks recall hearing about the Old South.

Families, like history, are supremely important to Mississippians, and nearly all the works included here make constant reference to relationships, allegiances, and kinship ties. Selections that focus specifically on the role and significance of families include Walker Percy's Introduction to *Lanterns on the Levee,* Ellen Gilchrist's journal entries, Mildred Taylor's acceptance speech for the Newbery Award, Mildred Topp's *Smile Please,* and Wyatt Cooper's *Families: A Memoir and a Celebration.*

Charlotte Capers in "God and My Grandmother" combines the theme of family with another important theme found in this collection—religion. Capers recalls summer visits with her grandmother, an Episcopalian whose religious zeal was strengthened by a visiting evangelist and who thereafter required constant praying, Bible reading, and church going for all family members—including visiting granddaughters. Black families had similar experiences, as Charles Evers points out in his autobiography: "We were brought up in the Church of God in Christ, also called the Holiness Church, and they don't believe in smoking, drinking, gambling, chewing, playing cards or dancing on Sundays. As a kid I was in church so much that I don't go often today." Evers also reports that "besides going to church all the time" his family would have prayers and Bible study at home. In an excerpt from *Black Rituals* Sterling Plumpp explains his initiation into the black church, or how he got "'ligion," a tradition which has a mesmerizing effect upon most youth. In "Revival," an excerpt from *A Highly Ramified Tree,* Robert Canzoneri writes of a trip with his father, a Sicilian turned Baptist minister. Anne Carsley describes the atmosphere that made her childhood Sundays unique in "Sunday Has a Different Smell."

Music is also important to Mississippians. Barry Hannah gives us a hilarious account of his trumpet-playing days in Clinton's high school band; Lehman Engle reminisces about the piano teachers in Jackson who helped prepare him for his musical career; Danny Collum of Greenwood entertains us with descriptions of his first encounters with Little Richard, Elvis Presley, and the Beatles; and Kenneth Holditch shows how Tupelo, a "forgettable place," was changed by Elvis Presley. Also, Mississippi's rich musical heritage is examined in William Ferris's study of blues in the Delta and Phyllis Harper's account of Sacred Harp singing in Fawn Grove.

Nor is cooking forgotten. Many of the writers included here make passing references to Sunday dinners, picnics, and other meals, but food is central to Charlemae Rollins's *Christmas Gif'*, which offers recipes collected from the "big house" and the slave cabin and passed from generation to generation. Recipes are also included in *A Feast Made for Laughter,* Craig Claiborne's charming account of growing up in his mother's boarding house in Indianola. He notes that the food his mother served "fell into three categories—soul food, which is a blend of African and American Indian; creole cookery, which is a marriage of innocent Spanish and bastardized French; and pure French, desserts mostly, from the first edition of *The Boston Cooking-School Cook Book.*" Soul food was and is the favorite of the Mississippi boy who became one of the nation's leading chefs, but writer John A. Williams finds nothing to sing about in "the dark, greasy gravy, the greens cooked to a softness the consistency of wet tissue paper, the grits, the red-eye gravy, the thick, starchy rice" he knew as a child. Nonetheless, during a visit to his native Jackson after spending many years in New York, he decided to have some down-home southern cooking. "I ate breakfast, one of soul food," he tells us, "and then I took a Dexedrine tablet."

For many of the writers here, childhood memories focus on the quest for knowledge. It may be the knowledge that comes with a developing self-awareness as it is for Margaret Walker, whose "Growing Out of Shadow" details the discovery of her "blackness," or for Ann Moody, whose excerpt from *Coming of Age in Mississippi* describes her discovery of the meaning of "whiteness." M. Carl Holman's "Afternoon of a Young Poet" describes that writer's initiation into the white literary world. Frank Smith's first encounter with the "race problem" came after his father, a leading white proponent of racial justice, was killed by a terrified black man. Recalling this incident of his childhood, Smith says that "learning to live with the relationship between white man and black man was and is part of the experience of growing up in Mississippi. It leaves its imprint on us all, white and black, rich and poor."

In "A Sweet Devouring" Eudora Welty reminisces about trips to the library as a girl in Jackson, and in an excerpt from the classic *Lanterns on the Levee* William Alexander Percy recalls Caroline Stern, who nurtured his love for poetry and became his favorite teacher. Another influential teacher is described in Loyle Hairston's "Growing Up in Mississippi." Ophelia Lewis "wanted to fortify us against life's many disappointments," he recalls. She thought "education would liberate us from the thrall of ignorance, unleash the vitality of our dreams and free us from ever having to lick the boots of white supremacy. I am personally indebted to her for helping me discover my individuality, for helping me grasp more fiercely a sense of being a somebody."

Personal discovery can come through the discovery of or sometimes even the confrontation with one's literary ancestors, those who help to shape the artist's world. Richard Ford in "The Three Kings: Hemingway, Faulkner, and Fitzgerald," Charles East in

"The Search for Eudora Welty," Ellen Douglas in "Reading and Writing: Beginnings," and Elizabeth Spencer in "Emerging as a Writer in Faulkner's Mississippi," all discuss their coming of age in a fertile literary environment. These writers define their "sense of place" as Mississippians variously: the power and magnetism of Mississippi's greatest literary figures, the vitality of the physical landscape, the paradoxical nature of the Mississippi experience.

Growing up in a small town is a theme underlying the selections by Don Lee Keith. These selections reflect upon the richness of meaning of his simple childhood pleasures. Keith recalls how he and his best friend found far-flung diversions to relieve the boredom of small town summers.

Places associated with Mississippi writers are also examined in several selections. Tennessee Williams recalls the Columbus of his boyhood, William Faulkner's brother, John Faulkner, and his niece, Dean Faulkner Wells, write of youthful experiences in William Faulkner's Oxford, and Nash K. Burger describes Jackson, where he and Eudora Welty were schoolmates and where another prominent writer was also a student. "In 1921," Burger writes,

> the same year that Eudora and the rest of us left all-white Davis School to go to all-white Central High School, a Negro boy our own age entered Jackson's all-Negro Jim Hill School and went on to graduate from all-Negro Smith-Robertson School four years later, the same year we graduated from Central. He was Richard Wright, and he has told us he wrote his first story at that time. You can read his account of Jackson in those days in his *Black Boy.* I wonder if the school system of any small, provincial town has ever nourished at the same time two such remarkable talents as Eudora Welty and Richard Wright.

Welty and Wright did come of age at the same time in Jackson, but the selection from *Black Boy: The Record of Childhood and Youth* included in this anthology shows how very different were the experiences that nourished their literary talents.

Greenville, located in the legendary Delta, has also figured prominently in Mississippi's literature, having been the home of more of the state's writers and journalists than any other city. Beverly Lowry in "A White Girl Remembers" tells about growing up there in the 1950s and being constantly aware of the "beneficent shadow" of William Alexander Percy and the living presence of Shelby Foote, Ellen Douglas, and Walker Percy.

Perhaps the most important social and economic history of this area is provided by David L. Cohn, whose *Where I Was Born and Raised* has become a classic with its opening line: "The Mississippi Delta begins in the lobby of the Peabody Hotel in Memphis and ends on Catfish Row in Vicksburg." As Cohn suggests, the persistence of a rich and diverse folk culture in Mississippi's fertile Delta region is due to a complex of factors, not the least of which is the intensity of oppression and social isolation of the black population.

The stark reality of poverty, racism, and lawless violence encountered by black Mississippians growing up in the Delta is described in Fannie Lou Hamer's "To Praise Our Bridges" and L. C. Dorsey's "Harder Times Than These." For both these writers, born and raised in sharecropper's cabins, the childhood quest for knowledge became synonymous with a developing consciousness of economic and racial and sexist oppression.

The response to the economic and social conditions among the poor in Mississippi has led to a wide range of social actions within the state. One of these has been the continuing commitment of pioneering black educators to improve the method and delivery of education to black youth. Among these educators are Laurence C. Jones, who explains how his mother's words led him to found the Piney Woods School in 1909, and Ann Odene Smith, who in *God's Step Chilluns* details her early years as a rural school teacher.

The large selection of essays, speeches, and narratives that offer varying perspectives on the impact of the civil rights movement in Mississippi is a major contribution of this volume. As many of the writings collected here indicate, this broad-based social movement did not initiate the discussion of racism and segregation in the state. It did, however, greatly accelerate a process of confrontation and transformation, and it is this, more than anything, that has solicited a wide variety of responses. The civil rights movement was part and parcel of full-scale social revolution among black people in America, a revolution that began in the courts but proceeded to the streets.

The hardest battles were fought on Mississippi soil, where a series of cataclysmic events recalled the Civil War a hundred years earlier. In his excerpt from *The Making of Black Revolutionaries* James Forman depicts the scene of the new "war":

It was Mississippi: The state which had led the Southern drive to take back from black people the vote and other civil rights won during Reconstruction, the state which had reduced the number of registered black voters from 190,000 in 1890 to 8,600 in 1892, through a combination of new laws, tricks, and murder. It was Mississippi, with a larger proportion of blacks than any other state and the lowest proportion—only 5 percent—of eligible blacks registered to vote. It was Mississippi, birthplace of the White Citizens' Council—a white-collar version of the Ku Klux Klan. It was Mississippi, where years of terror, economic intimidation, and a total, grinding, day-in, day-out white racism had created a black population numb with fear and hopelessness—yet still able from time to time to produce individuals in whom the spirit of rebellion lived.

Forman goes on to describe the vehement resistance and violent confrontation that resulted from the voter registration drive organized in McComb in 1961 by leaders of the Student Nonviolent Coordinating Committee (SNCC). It was SNCC that provided the link between the civil rights movement and the more radicalized sectors of the society in the 1960s and 1970s. The transformation of this broad based movement is one of the best examples we have in this century of the merging of political and social ideas with youth culture. Other writers represented in this volume tell of the struggles that occurred in Jackson, Philadelphia, Oxford, towns throughout the Delta, and communities all over the state.

As the civil rights "war" escalated, Mississippians became more and more polarized over the racial issue. The anguish this caused black Mississippians is described in many selections, including the one in which James Meredith tells about returning home to Mississippi in 1960 after spending nine years in the United States Air Force. He describes his deep love for his native state and his fierce determination to fight for racial equality, which he did by integrating the University of Mississippi in 1962. Civil rights leader Medgar Evers, who was murdered in 1963, also knew that to be a native Mississippian is to be confronted with the desire to both celebrate and condemn one's heritage, to explain and to expose the inadequacies and imperfections, while at the same time clinging to the native soil, choosing not, as Evers says in an essay reprinted here, "to live anywhere else."

William Faulkner tries to come to terms with this paradox in his well-known "Mississippi," as does Myrlie Evers in *For Us, the Living*. She writes:

Much of the recent history of Mississippi could be told in the lives of these two men, my husband and his killer, the murdered and the murderer—one dead but free, the other alive and at large but never really free: imprisoned by the hate and fear that imprison so many white Mississippians and make so many Negro Mississippians still their slaves. . . . Medgar used to astonish Northern reporters who asked why he stayed in Mississippi by answering simply that he loved Mississippi. He did. He loved it as a man loves his home, as a farmer loves the soil. It was part of him. . . . I suppose the man who killed Medgar loved Mississippi, too, in his twisted, tortured way. He must have loved the Mississippi that divides whites from Negroes, that by definition made him better than any Negro simply because he was white. In a way, I suppose, he was a jealous suitor, seeking by his murder to eliminate a rival, for he loved the Mississippi Medgar sought to change. What Medgar loved with hope, his assassin loved with fear. And he killed, I suspect, largely out of that fear.

James Silver, an eyewitness of the Meridith riot at the University of Mississippi where he taught history for nearly three decades, attempts to put that intensely emotional experience into historical perspective. In his book *Mississippi: The Closed Society* he writes: "The point is that when people are told from every public rostrum in the state on every day of their lives—and such is the case with the undergraduates who assaulted the marshals—that no authority on earth can legally or morally require any change in the traditional terms of Mississippi social life, this very process generates conditions that will explode into riot and insurrection."

The civil rights movement polarized the races in Mississippi, but it also brought them together. Danny Collum, Edwin King, and Jason Berry are three white activists whose writings provide a glimpse of the movement that looms so large in the minds of the people of the state, the region, and the nation. Edwin King's "Growing Up in Mississippi in a Time of Change" recalls his own personal transformation and some of the most intense moments during the civil rights movement. And Jason Berry's excerpt from *Amazing Grace: With Charles Evers in Mississippi* tells of his experiences as press secretary for Evers during his gubernatorial campaign in 1971.

Other writers who comment on the civil rights movement describe changes in perception on the part of participants as well as the observers of this great human drama. Florence Mars opens her narrative with a description of what it was like to be a white person opposed to the Ku Klux Klan in her hometown of Philadelphia, where three civil rights workers were murdered in 1964. Two decades later Willie Morris examines this community in his story of Marcus Dupree, a nationally acclaimed football player whose high school graduating class was the first in which young whites and blacks had gone through school together since the first grade. About Dupree and Philadelphia Morris writes:

> His great-great-grandparents had been slaves, and he was born one month less a day before three young men, two New York Jews and a Mississippi black, were murdered seven miles from his birthplace and buried fifteen feet under an earthen dam. . . . Gradually, almost imperceptibly in the years which followed, something would begin to stir in the soul of the town. A brooding introspection, a stricken pride, a complicated and nearly indefinable self-irony, all but unacknowledged at first, would emerge from its dreadful wounds. A long journey lay ahead, marked always by new aggrievements and retreats, yet this mysterious pilgrimage of the spirit would suggest much of the South and the America of our generation.

The civil rights movement has changed life not only in Philadelphia but in thousands of communities throughout Mississippi, and it has helped increase sensitivity to social inequities in the society as a whole. For the Mississippi Chinese, says Sung Gay Chow, the American heritage must be viewed within the confines of southern prejudice. Denied other outlets and fleeing from the hard labor of the railroads, many Chinese settled in the Mississippi Delta, where they maintained close family ties and preserved traditional Chinese customs. The inclusion of one work by a Mississippian of Chinese ancestry is welcomed here but raises questions about an aspect of the state's heritage that needs further investigation.

Choctaw Boy by Paul Conklin is the single work representing Mississippi's Choctaw nation, another area that needs further investigation. The narrative illustrates the cultural traditions among the Choctaws, who have been victimized by the loss of land and rights but whose isolation from the mainstream of society is beginning to change. Conklin's story is typical of a special type of narrative that has emerged in the literature of American Indians, the ethnographic biography.

Since the 1970s writers and scholars have been seeking an even deeper understanding of those vital elements that have enriched Mississippi's heritage. The dichotomy of black-white relations in Mississippi is no longer excused. It is a historical fact, though not necessarily a confrontational issue. Further, a generation has emerged whose relationship to that history is not automatic, as indicated by Samuel Prestridge whose "Notes from the Laughing Factory" describes the first time he saw the Ku Klux Klan. For Prestridge, certain aspects of Mississippi's racial past are ridiculous—like a Klan protest over the use of the Confederate flag at the University of Mississippi. In Prestridge's opinion, this is too ludicrous an issue to become a matter for debate in the current decade.

There is, of course, much of the old rural life remaining, as Glennray Tutor recalls his own rural upbringing in the not too distant past in "Mawmaw and Pawpaw." Perhaps Al Young is typical of the contemporary writer whose search for his roots goes deep into the Mississippi soil, where there is such total integration of those spontaneous folk elements so many Mississippians have experienced as they have grown up. In his selection from *Bodies and Soul* Young suggests that the true artist is that person who understands the profundity of the structures and rhythms of black vernacular culture in Mississippi. It is a culture that translates experience through symbolic gesture, language, musical sound, and sometimes unexplained acts of human endeavor.

When the social movements of the last two decades are definitively summed up, perhaps it will be clear that events that occurred in Mississippi have had a significant impact on the country's awareness of social prejudice and injustice based on race, gender, and class. The experiences of black people in Mississippi serve to highlight this fact. That these events had to occur—the murders of Emmet Till, Andrew Goodman, James Earl Chaney, Michael H. Schwerner, Medgar Evers, and many others; the maiming of thousands of black Mississippians—is more than tragic. By giving attention to these events in the social histories that continue to be written and in the educational materials we prepare for our country's youth, we can help assuage the pain and guilt that we all bear. And we might reach that "promised land" that Lerone Bennett points us toward in his essay "Have We Overcome?"

The speeches, narrative histories, personal memoirs, and prose selections that are included here chart the course of Mississippi's development during a period of constant change. These writings serve as an intellectual and social barometer for those changes. Mississippi as the land of birth or residence profoundly affected the literary imagination and serves as an impulse for its many creative writers, journalists, and historians. When we view these writings as a whole, we can appreciate the directness and literalness and, above all, we can accept the paradoxical nature of the Mississippi experience.

While Mississippi is not a total picture of the universe, the writings in this volume encourage readers to see themselves in relationship to a particular set of forces, historical, social, or economic—in short, to become a part of the motion of history. Moreover, when this individual experience merges with the collective experience, as is done with so many whose voices we hear, we can begin to understand the preoccupation with the South and its distinct regions. This is the particular strength of the literature presented here. If Mississippi remains closer to its southern heritage than other states of the region, it is because of the mental attitudes and psychological responses that are deeply embedded in the fabric of its culture. Those attitudes and responses are presented to us in this volume.

An edited volume, like any collection of selected materials, bears the biases of its editor. We must commend Dorothy Abbott's single bias—her patriotic inclusiveness, to borrow a phrase from Louis Rubin. She has simply included so much of Mississippi's reality that is uncluttered that it is oftentimes painful. Yet it is a reality that has defined twentieth-century thought and experience for most of us. We should welcome that which Mississippians have to say about their own heritage, about who they are and what they have been. Perhaps no other heritage in this country is as distinctly a part of all of us as this one is.

Maryemma Graham
University of Mississippi

THE PHIL HARDIN FOUNDATION AND THE MISSISSIPPI WRITERS SERIES

IN 1964 Mr. Phil B. Hardin of Meridian, Mississippi, established an educational foundation. At the Foundation's organizational meeting, Mr. Hardin made the following statement:

> My material wealth has been principally acquired by the operation of my bakery business in the State of Mississippi and from the good people of that state. For a long time I have been considering how my estate could best be used after my death. I have finally conceived the idea of creating a charitable foundation through which the bulk of my estate can be used for furthering . . . the education of Mississippians.

Upon his death in 1972, Mr. Hardin willed a portfolio of stocks and bonds, as well as the bakeries, to the Phil Hardin Foundation. The directors of the Foundation use income from these sources to make grants intended to improve the education of Mississippians. Since the transfer of Mr. Hardin's estate to the Foundation in 1976, the Phil Hardin Foundation has distributed over 3.8 million dollars for this purpose.

In 1983 the Foundation directors authorized a challenge grant to support the publication of the series of anthologies entitled *Mississippi Writers: Reflections of Childhood and Youth*. This series recognizes the accomplishments of our state's authors. The series also introduces young Mississippians to their state's literary heritage, perhaps providing thereby a "shock of recognition" and the transmission of values revealed in that heritage: family, community, a sense of place and history, the meaning of justice and honor, the importance of enduring in the struggle for just causes, the significance as we live out our lives one with another of "courage . . . and hope and pride and compassion and pity and sacrifice." By so doing the series may help young Mississippians come to grips with the complexities of Mississippi culture and heritage and of the larger society that now more than ever impinges on this place. As importantly, the series may help forge a sense of common identity and interest.

The Phil Hardin Foundation is honored to join with other Mississippians to make possible the publication of the *Mississippi Writers* series. Mississippians can accomplish more working together than working alone.

C. Thompson Wacaster
The Phil Hardin Foundation

The Following People, Organizations, and Businesses Generously Contributed Funds to Match the Challenge Grant Awarded by the Phil Hardin Foundation

Dr. and Mrs. Joe Bailey
Mr. and Mrs. Charles G. Bell
Ms. Jane Rule Burdine
Mrs. Roberta J. Burns-Howard
Mrs. Betty W. Carter
Centennial Study Club (Oxford)
Mr. Henry Chambers
Coca-Cola Bottling Co. (Vicksburg)
Mr. and Mrs. Sam W. Crawford
CREATE, Inc.
Ms. Carole H. Currie
Mr. and Mrs. Glen H. Davidson
Mr. and Mrs. William Deas
Mr. and Mrs. Herman B. DeCell
Mrs. Keith Dockery McLean
Mr. and Mrs. Robert B. Dodge
Fortnightly Matinee Club (Tupelo)
Dr. and Mrs. Jan Goff
Dr. and Mrs. William Hilbun
Mr. and Mrs. Howard Hinds
Mrs. Mary Hohenberg
Mr. Irwin T. Holtzman
Mr. Stuart C. Irby, Jr.
Stuart Irby Construction Company
Dr. and Mrs. David Irwin
The Honorable and Mrs. Trent Lott
Mr. and Mrs. T. M. McMillan, Jr.
Miss Marjorie Milam
Mrs. Blewett Mitchell
The Honorable G. V. Montgomery
Mrs. Gaines Moore
Mrs. L. K. Morgan
R. R. Morrison and Son, Inc.
Mr. Richard A. Moss
National Association of Treasury Agents
Mr. William M. Pace
Mrs. A. E. Patterson
Dr. Max Pegram
Mr. and Mrs. Jack R. Reed
Dr. and Mrs. Pete Rhymes
Dr. Stephen L. Silberman
Mr. and Mrs. Bill Spigner
Mr. and Mrs. Landman V. Teller
Dr. and Mrs. P. K. Thomas
United Southern Bank (Clarksdale)
University Press of Mississippi
Mr. and Mrs. Harold Wilson
Mr. Sam Woodward

MISSISSIPPI WRITERS
Reflections of Childhood and Youth

Have We Overcome?

LERONE BENNETT, JR.

I HAVE BEEN AWAY from this state for a long time, and I hope you will permit me a personal remark or two. I grew up in this state in the thirties and forties when this institution was closed to me, and to my people, and when Mississippi occupied a position in the western world roughly equivalent to the position of South Africa today. And as I stand here tonight,* I am reminded of Richard Wright and the other great sons and daughters of Mississippi who were lost to this state and this region because of that situation. And I am reminded also of other great sons and daughters of Mississippi—the James Merediths, the Fannie Lou Hamers, the Aaron Henrys, the Margaret Walker Alexanders, the brave children of SNCC—who stayed here and fought the good fight in the hope that Mississippi would one day come into its own and recognize its own. And it seems to me that whatever the difficulties of the moment, or the magnitude of the obstacles, that we should always remember the brave and beautiful few who brought us thus far along the way. For if it was possible for them to change what they changed in Mississippi, then there is absolutely no limit to what we can dream and hope.

It is in this connection, and in the context of what has been done, and what remains to be done, that I am reminded of the story of a group of people who sought a great prize that was across a deep river, up a steep mountain, on the far side of an uncharted sea. The task before them was almost impossible, but they were a brave people, and history had given them big hearts. And so they embarked, in the white of the night, and reached the middle of the river, where a great storm arose. The storm lashed their little boat and washed many overboard, but they managed somehow to reach the other side, losing many of their friends on the way. When the boat touched dry land, they held a symposium of sorts, and a select group went to the captain and said: "We did a great thing in cross-

*Paper presented at the 1978 Chancellor's Symposium on Southern History at the University of Mississippi

ing that river, and we believe we will dig in and rest for a while in this new and desegregated place." And the captain said: "This thing that you did in crossing the river was splendidly done, and deserves praise. But there is no rest for us, or safety, short of the grail freedom. So sing, shout, and rap tonight, for tomorrow the journey continues. *We crossed a river, and now we've got to cross a sea.*"

The words speak to us all. They speak to white Americans, who crossed many rivers in the last two hundred years, and now face the necessary task of reinventing themselves in a world that is overwhelmingly red, brown, and black.

We crossed a river, and now we've got to cross a sea.

The words speak to black Americans, who crossed ten thousand Jordans in the years of the movement and who now face the necessity of dealing with the gravest crisis we have faced as a people since the end of slavery time.

We crossed a river, and now we've got to cross a sea.

The words speak to us all, and define us all. And it is within the context of these words that I approach the topic assigned me tonight:

"Have we overcome?"

I could, and should, say no and sit down and save your time. But this is a scholarly setting, and a scholarly no requires—I am told—at least one hour of disputation and on-the-other-handing. Let me try then to earn my keep, and let me begin by questioning the question.

The question is have we overcome?

And my question is how are we to understand that dangerous word *we?*

And what does it mean *to overcome?*

Well, in the context of the song and the struggle, *we* means black people and—watch this interpretation—white people who are committed to and involved in the struggle for equality and racial justice. And *to overcome,* again in the context of the song and the struggle, means the act of transcending and destroying all racial barriers and creating a new land of freedom and equality for all men, all women, and all children.

"Oh, deep in my heart I do believe we shall overcome," we shall overpass, triumph over mean sheriffs, robed riders, assassins of the spirit, segregation, discrimination, hunger, poverty, and humiliation.

Have we done it? No, a thousand times no.

We were there, some of us, and we sang the song, some of us, and saw the blood, some of us. And we know—deep in our hearts—that what the singers and dreamers and victims hoped for . . . what they struggled and died for . . . has not happened yet. Because of the passion and the pain of the singers and victims and dreamers, we have, in the past twenty-four years, crossed many barriers . . . but we are nowhere near the end of our journey, and we have miles to go before we sleep.

And so, it is necessary to say here, in the name of the dreamers and victims, that we have not yet started the process of grappling with the depth and the height of the dream. As a matter of fact, we haven't even defined what we must do in order to overcome. To cite only one point, the admission of a handful of gifted black students and athletes to a white university in which all the lines of authority and power are still controlled by whites is not—repeat—*not* integration. It is at best desegregation and a prelude, perhaps a necessary prelude, to that great American dream which was written down on pieces of paper, which was promised, and which has never existed anywhere in America, except in the hearts of a handful of men and women.

By any reasonable standard, then, we have failed to meet the goal. And to understand the magnitude of our failure, and the dangers that failure poses to all Americans, it would be helpful, I think, to go back for a moment to the beginning, to Monday, May 17, 1954, when some man believed the millennium was around the next turning.

According to news reports of that day, the Supreme Court decision was immediately hailed by a wide variety of black voices as "a second emancipation proclamation," which was, in the words of the *Chicago Defender*, "more important to our democracy than the atom bomb or the hydrogen bomb." In Farmville, Virginia, for example, a sixteen-year-old student named Barbara Trent burst into tears when her teacher interrupted class to announce the decision. "Our teacher told us," she told a reporter, "it may cost her her job . . . we went on studying history, but things weren't the same and will never be the same again."

There were, of course, cynics and dissenters, most notably Langston Hughes, who put the following words in the mouth of his fictional character, Simple:

> White folks are proud, but I don't see nothing for them to be proud of just doing what they ought to do. If they was doing something extra, yes, then be proud. But Negroes have a right to go to decent schools just like everybody else. So what's there to be proud of in that they are just now letting us in. They ought to be ashamed of themselves for keeping us out so long. I might have had a good education myself had it not been for white folks. If they want something to be proud of let them pay me for the education I ain't got.

Simple's views were shared apparently by many blacks, but in the first flush of victory most people focused on the silver lining in the cloud. The most widely quoted man of the day was the architect of the victory, NAACP counsel Thurgood Marshall. Here is an excerpt from an interview with Marshall that appeared in the *New York Times* on Tuesday, May 18, 1954: "Mr. Marshall, asked how long he thought it would be before segregation in education was eliminated, replied it might be 'up to five years' for the entire country. He predicted that, by the time the 100th anniversary of the emancipation was observed in 1963, segregation in all its forms would have been eliminated from the nation."

Not only Marshall but significant sectors of the white population said the struggle would soon be over. Earl Warren recalled later that it was suggested at the Supreme Court that the processes set in motion on this day would be completed by the centennial of the Fourteenth Amendment—1966.

Thus America, thus the petitioners and dreamers, on a day of hope and triumph and innocence!

How remote, how unimaginably distant and remote that May day seems in this October of our years. The events of the intervening years—Montgomery, the sit-ins, the freedom rides, the marches, and urban rebellions—came so suddenly, so dramatically, that our sense of time has been distorted and incidents and personalities of only a few years ago have been pushed into the distant past.

For this reason, among others, it is difficult to put this period into proper perspective. For this reason, among others, it is difficult to orient and situate the young. It is a fact, worthy of long thought, that there is a whole generation of young blacks and whites who have never seen a Jim Crow sign and who express astonishment when told that they once existed.

The Jim Crow signs are gone now. There are black mayors in Alabama and black representatives in the Mississippi legislature, and there are children, and even some adults, who seem to believe that it has always been this way. But it hasn't always been this way, and it would be well for us to remember tonight that this October and the Octobers of yesterday are linked and separated by a great crossing and a great hope. During that crossing, a revolution . . . it is not too strong a word . . . in the courts and a rebellion in the streets destroyed the legal foundations of segregation and moved the racial dialogue to a new level.

The internal and external changes flowing from this event have been profound and dramatic. So have the costs. Martin Luther King, Jr., is dead; Malcolm X is dead. Whitney Young, Medgar Evers, Fred Hampton, James Earl Chaney, Viola Liuzzo, Fannie Lou Hamer, the four Birmingham girls: they are all dead. And the movement they led and symbolized has foundered on new realities.

What makes this all the more disconcerting is that the gains for which they died are threatened by a new mood of "backism" and reaction in white America. And there is the further fact that the gains of the green years, important as they were, did not go to the root of the matter, the neocolonial relations between the black and white communities of America and the institutionalized unfavorable balance of trade of black America.

It is true, and important, that blacks are going places today they couldn't go twenty-four years ago. *Everything, in fact, has changed in Mississippi and America, and yet, paradoxically, nothing has changed.*

Despite the court orders and civil rights laws, blacks are still the last hired and the first fired. They are still systematically exploited as consumers and citizens. To come right out with it, the full privileges and immunities of the U.S. Constitution do not apply to blacks tonight, in Mississippi or in Massachusetts, and they never have. You want to know how bad things are? Listen to the facts cited by Robert B. Hill of the National Urban League in a recent booklet, entitled *The Illusion of Black Progress.*

> Contrary to popular belief, the economic gap between blacks and whites is widening. Between 1975 and 1976, the black to white family income ratio fell sharply from 62 to 59 percent.
>
> Not only is black unemployment at its highest level today, but the jobless gap between blacks and whites is the widest it has ever been. . . .
>
> The proportion of middle-income black families has not significantly increased. In fact, the proportion of black families with incomes above the labor department's intermediate budget level has remained at about one-fourth since 1972.
>
> The proportion of upper-income black families has steadily declined. Between 1972 and 1976, the proportion of black families above the government's higher budget level dropped from 12 to 9 percent.
>
> The two black societies thesis of a widening cleavage between middle-income and low-income blacks is not supported by national income data. The proportion of black families with incomes under $7,000, as well as those with incomes over $15,000, has remained relatively constant in recent years.
>
> The statistical evidence strongly contradicts the popular belief that high unemployment among black youth is primarily due to their educational or skill deficiencies—when job opportunities are greater for white youth with lower educational attainment. White high school dropouts have lower unemployment rates (22.3%) than black youth with college education (27.2%).

These figures are terrible, and the reality is worse. How did this happen? How is it possible for black America to be in so much trouble after all the demonstrations, and marches, and court orders? What is the meaning of this terrible indictment?

The short answer to these questions is that we stopped marching too soon. The long . . . and scholarly . . . answer is embedded in the history of our journey.

We started out, twenty-four years ago, in the white of night. We crossed large bodies of water, marched day and night, were pushed back and advanced again, singing and shouting and stepping over the bodies of our brothers and sisters. By these methods . . . and others . . . we arrived, after indescribable anguish and pain, at this place.

But where precisely are we? What have we gained and lost? Did we go wrong somewhere? Or is this a necessary historical detour leading to a higher level of development. What, in short, is the meaning, the sense, the signification, of the twenty-four years of the great crossing struggle?

There can be no easy answer to that question, for we are too close to that event to situate it globally. But it is possible, indeed likely, that the post-*Brown* struggle, despite its limitations, was a necessary stage in the social maturation of black people. And there can be little doubt that it created black America's finest hours and one of the finest hours in the history of the republic.

It is fashionable nowadays to heap scorn on the old civil rights movement and the so-called "Hamburger War." But this is a misreading of the historical process that advances on the crest of succeeding waves, which rise and fall, over and over again, with the ebbing and flowing of the energies of the people. From this vantage point, history is a dialogue, and the movement of the last twenty-four years was a vast and leaping wave in a continuous flow of energy that started with the first revolt on the first slave ship and will not end until America deals with the revolutionary mandate of its birth.

Because of that struggle, we have made significant gains on the political front and in the middle sectors. The movement changed, destroyed, wiped out the visible and dramatic signs of racism, but it did not and perhaps could not at that time deal with the subtle forms of institutional racism. Nor did it change or even make a dent in the economic inequities of a society that can make work for black men inside prisons after they commit crimes but cannot find work for black men outside prisons before they commit crimes.

And so, as a result of the failure of the movement to make a total breakthrough on the racial front, we find ourselves tonight in the postrevolutionary phase of a revolution that never happened, the postrevolutionary phase of a revolution that turned sour because it could not be accomplished historically at that particular time under the prevailing ratio of forces.

Does this mean that the movement was a failure? By no means. As a result of that struggle, one-third of this nation—the South—was changed, perhaps forever, and the rest of the nation made its first tentative steps toward democracy. Beyond all that, the movement created the foundations for future departures, which will depend on the maturation of social forces and the courage, vision, and perseverance of black people.

The important point here, as elsewhere, is that the movement was historical. It had historical roots, its direction and limitations were historically determined. It rose and fell according to the laws of motion . . . I almost said . . . the laws of being of the political economy of blackness.

One way to avoid the implications of this fact is to focus, as so many people do, on ephemeral aspects of the movement, such as the personalities. And so we find people saying almost everywhere that the main problem was leadership. Or we find them saying—and you've heard them say it—that the movement failed because the leaders were integrationists or separationists or because they didn't brush with Crest. This is a Walt Disney approach to the historical process. The leaders didn't start the Montgomery boycott: the people started it. The leaders didn't start Watts: the people started it. And when the energy of the people ran out, when they had tried everything, or almost everything, when they had demonstrated, petitioned, rioted, prayed, and consulted astrologers, and when every new advance revealed a new all, the people withdrew to retool and rethink. And what we've got to understand tonight is that this temporary withdrawal was and is natural under the circumstances. The law of history is that people cannot live forever on the heights. The law of history is that a people advance and retreat, advance and retreat, advance and retreat, until they reach a collective decision to go for broke.

Since 1900, the black movement in America has been characterized by this rhythm of advances and withdrawals. And this entitles us to say, I think, that if the sun continues to shine and the wind continues to blow, the movement of the sixties will reemerge in America on a higher level of development.

And the task we face tonight is the task of consolidating our gains and preparing the ground for the next departure which will come, as surely as night follows day, if we stop cursing history and learn from history how to make history.

One of our problems in the sixties—certainly one of my problems—was that we underestimated the resiliency of the system. For a moment there, we thought we had the cat. For a moment there, we thought the promised land was around the next turning. But that was an illusion, and the mandate we have tonight from the dreamers and victims is to learn from our illusions and prepare ourselves for a long-range struggle for the transformation of this society.

This, in my opinion, was one of the four great lessons of the sixties, which taught us, in many a hard classroom, that the struggle to overcome is not a hundred-yard dash but a long-distance run involving phases and characteristics that have no precedent and cannot be predicted. We must prepare, therefore, for the long haul. We must prepare for a struggle of five, ten, fifteen, or even fifty years.

The second lesson, growing out of the first, is that people change only when they have to change, and that it is the task of the oppressed to do whatever is required to force change. The lesson of the sixties, and of this hour, was anticipated more than one hundred years ago by Frederick Douglass, who said:

> Let me give you a word of the philosophy of reform. The whole history of the progress of human liberty shows that all concessions yet made to her august claims, have been born of earnest struggle. If there is no struggle, there is no progress. Those who profess to favor freedom and yet deprecate agitation, are men who want crops without plowing up the ground, they want rain without thunder and lightning. They want the ocean without the awful roar of its many waters.
>
> This struggle may be a moral one, or it may be a physical one, and it may be both moral and physical, but it must be a struggle. Power concedes nothing without demand. It never did and it never will. . . . Men may not get all they pay for in this world, but they must certainly pay for all they get.

Struggle: that's the second lesson, and the third is that we cannot overcome and the gains of the post-*Brown* years cannot be preserved without a total struggle for a fundamental transformation of institutional structures. It should be clear by now, to almost everyone, that the white problem cannot be solved and black America cannot be saved without a total struggle for a fundamental transformation of American society, without real changes in the tax structure and the relations between the private and public sectors, without a redefinition of values, and a redistribution of income.

This need is particularly acute in the South. In my travels through the land of my birth, I have been struck repeatedly by the gains white southerners have made in the areas of personal relations. I have also been struck repeatedly by the same structural faults that led to the failure of the First Reconstruction. It is admitted now, by almost everyone, that the First Reconstruction was doomed from the start by the failure to provide blacks with economic as well as political votes. If we hope and intend to overcome, and if there is still time, somebody, somewhere is going to have to come up with the twentieth-century equivalent of forty acres of land and a mule.

Finally, and most importantly, the white South and white North are going to have to deal with themselves. The great lesson of the sixties, a lesson heeded almost nowhere, is that there is no Negro problem in Mississippi and in America. The problem of race in Mississippi, and in America, is a white problem, and we shall not overcome until we confront that problem. Somebody, somewhere is going to have to tell poor whites the truth about their lives. Somebody, somewhere, is going to have to assume responsibility for educating white people about the political, economic, and social realities of the twentieth century.

This is the challenge, this is the danger, this is the hope. It is the next great barrier, the sea beyond that we must cross together, before we can reach a place of safety where we can speak, with truth, to our graves and say: "You did not dream or die in vain, for we have finally and at long last overcome."

The whole wide world around, the whole wide world around, the whole wide world around someday.

FROM

Amazing Grace

Jason Berry

I

MY EARLIEST MEMORY of southern politics is still vivid. When I was ten years old my father called me into the living room to see the late news. "Son," he said, "I want you to watch history-in-the-make. Look at that man—he's your governor. His name's Earl K. Long. Look out, now! Three men are holding him down in a wheelchair. Can you believe that? They're dragging him into a mental hospital and Channel 6 is beeping out his curse words!"

Old Earl was a year out of the Governor's Mansion and three months dead when I graduated from the sixth grade. Forgetting him was easy, but as more southern politicians came along I grew bewildered. Their vocation had a flexibility to it which was much like that of the deceased governor himself: it was never tied down by sanity, and rarely did the man holding the job appear to employ reason on purpose. But Long, at least, was a legitimate madman. That cannot be said of the rest of the southern leadership.

Through all of its years of insanity and fury, the South has been a region of sharp contrasts. The state with the starkest contrasts, the quintessential southern state, is Mississippi. Mississippi is the original Cotton Kingdom, and today in the Delta that crop is the major economy. Tarpaper shacks totter in the wind less than a city block from palatial homes. Mississippi was the second state to secede from the Union. Jefferson Davis, the President of the Confederacy, once lived along the banks of the great river for which the state is named. His home, Le Beauvoir, stands as a museum on the Mississippi Gulf Coast. His birthday is a legal holiday for state employees.

With notable exceptions, most of Mississippi's figures of prominence have left: B. B. King, Willie Morris,* Richard Wright, Stark

*Willie Morris has since returned to live in Mississippi.

Young, Bobbie Gentry, James Silver, Elvis Presley, Tennessee Williams. Those who stayed—William Faulkner and Hodding Carter (now both deceased), Charles Evers and Aaron Henry—are themselves testimony to the clash of emotions of the land. Mississippi has had more recorded lynchings than any other state, is considered the state most brutal in opposition to civil rights legislation and its implementation, and has an unparalleled history of racist demagoguery. Mississippi is the land where Pulitzer Prizes are anathema and where the nation's fourth Nobel winner in literature, William Faulkner, was hated even after he won the prize.

Mississippi is nevertheless a state of rare beauty. Springtime is a glorious experience, especially in the Delta, with its brilliant green kudzu, the ivy-vine enmeshing landscape and water; it is a sight of pure metaphysical wonder. Yet the beauty of Mississippi only underscores the terrible poverty of the state. Today Mississippi is the rock-bottom state in per capita income, and it pays less in taxes than it receives in federal aid. While bellies of black children swell with hunger each Delta winter, Senator James Eastland receives an average $150,000 in federal payments for not farming cotton on his vast acreage, which is part of perhaps the richest land in the hemisphere.

Mississippi is a state of diametric oppositions: black and white, rich and poor, quarterbacks and sorrow, misery and beauty queens. Even the word "Mississippi" evokes widely varied reactions from people who hear it:

Xenophobia, from 46,000 race-crazed fans at the Ole Miss vs. Kentucky football game in 1962 when Ross Barnett was introduced after he had blocked James Meredith from registering at the university.

A *shudder* from President Kennedy one night later, after he was forced to call out federal troops to maintain order on the rioting Ole Miss campus.

A *song*—"Mississippi Goddamn!"—from black entertainer Nina Simone, who understands what the word means to her people.

Silence, from my father, sitting in the den of his New Orleans home twelve years after he "introduced" me to Earl Long, as he listened to me on the telephone. I sat on the floor of my Washington apartment, letting the word sink in.

"*Mississippi!*" he said. "Of all the God-forsaken places to work for a black man runnin' for governor!"

"Dad, how can I explain it? What's the sense of going back South if I can't do something . . . well, just do something that I haven't done before? Something meaningful."

"Hell, I'm the first to admit *Mississippi* needs to be changed! I just don't like the idea of you doin' it. You could get your head shot off!"

"This isn't civil rights work . . . it's politics. And they haven't had anybody killed in five years."

"That doesn't mean they're finished shootin'."

His breath was heavy. "Son, I'm sure Charles Evers is a remarkable man. And you know your mother and I are opposed to racism. But we've got property in Mississippi . . ."

"The campaign office is in Jackson. That's over a hundred and fifty miles from our farm in Poplarville. You can't even get Jackson stations on the TV cable at the farm. Nobody'll know."

He breathed again. "When did you get the letter from his secretary?"

"Day before yesterday."

"She says they want you?"

"She said they're assembling a staff in Jackson and they need all the help they can get. I'll be going as a volunteer. I don't even know if I'll get a salary."

"It'll be dangerous over there, son."

"Maybe. Maybe not."

"But why in hell do you want go *go?*"

"Because I *like* Mississippi," I said blandly.

The conversation remained mutually unproductive and so we agreed not to talk about it until after commencement exercises, which he and mother were coming up for at the end of the week. On May 23, 1971, I was graduated from Georgetown *cum laude,* but it wasn't the most joyous of occasions. None of us talked much about Mississippi until they got ready to leave. Mother hinted at a trip to Europe, and then all three of us had a big argument.

The next day I went to Mississippi.

Eudora Welty's Jackson

Nash K. Burger

Eudora Welty's English and German-Swiss ancestors, in their migration through 18th-century Virginia crossed trails with my own for a generation or two down there in the Shenandoah Valley. Neither Eudora nor I knew that or cared anything about ancestors when we met in the first grade at the buff-brick Jefferson Davis School in Jackson, Mississippi. A world war had just begun, but it was a long way to Sarajevo; and the small-town capital of Mississippi was quiet, peaceful and largely oblivious to Europe's guns of August.

Davis School faced west, toward the town's Greenwood Cemetery a block away, with its Confederate dead and its monument to the Episcopal rector from New York who died ministering to yellow-fever victims in antebellum times. A short distance up a low hill to the north was Fortification Street, where fortifications had indeed been erected in 1863 and Joseph E. Johnston's hard-pressed Confederates had lobbed shells at Grant's Yankees approaching from Raymond and Port Gibson.

Atop another small hill to the south sat the large, handsome New Capitol building, not unlike the one in Washington and so named to distinguish it from the Old Capitol, some blocks away, where Andrew Jackson, Henry Clay, Jefferson Davis and other notables had spoken and where, in 1861, the Ordinance of Secession was passed. On the Capitol grounds, when not chased off, we played baseball and football after school and on Saturdays, and both boys and girls roller-skated on the vast stretches of concrete walks and esplanades.

The Weltys lived in a comfortable, low, white frame house almost across the street from Davis School. Like most Jackson homes of that time, the Welty's house was neither new nor old. Antebellum Jackson had been pretty well destroyed during the Yankee occupation, and the area around the school was made up of postwar houses set in the midst of ample yards. I remember Mrs. Welty often at the door or on the porch, smiling and speaking as I went to and from school and Eudora emerging on some mornings to share pomegranates or persimmons before school. Whether these fruits were purchased or grew in the yard, I don't know; they are remembered because they were not everyday fare.

Around the corner from the Welty's was a little grocery store where, before school, Eudora and the rest of us bought Red Bird tablets, penny Tootsie-Rolls, little chocolate-flavored candies called "nigger-babies" and other essential items. Our textbooks themselves were bought at a store downtown. This was before the days of "free" textbooks, and the books were, I would say, the more appreciated and used, the money to buy them having come directly from the family purse.

Before school and at recess, boys and girls played in carefully separated parts of the school yard until time to line up, boys on one side of the building, girls on the other. Boys and girls were considered different orders of beings in those days—as indeed they are. We marched to our rooms while one of our classmates (for years it was the same pretty girl with long, brown hair) played "The National Emblem March," "Dixie" and other lively airs on a piano in the main hall. I don't recall too much about what went on in those classrooms except that we were exposed to what would be called today a traditional curriculum: the old math (the kind one actually uses in life), spelling as old as Webster, geography full of capitals, and history full of heroes and patriotism.

Once, in about the sixth grade, students who volunteered to learn to write the names of all 82 counties of Mississippi and spell them correctly were promised a full day's holiday; those who could name them all but misspelled one or two were promised one-half day off. It was characteristic that Eudora was one of the few who received the full day off and I managed only half a day. (I bumbled over the spelling of Oktibbeha.)

Other memorizing (an educational tool and discipline more popular then than now) that I recall was of Psalms from the King James Bible. We would read a Psalm aloud together every morning for several days until it became fixed in the memory—then move on to another. The students would usually decide which one. I am sure there was much benefit—spiritual, moral, rhetorical—in getting those splendid phrases and concepts into our growing minds and psyches.

That, of course, was a time when education, according to the

10th Amendment, was one of those powers reserved to the states, and the State of Mississippi in its wisdom considered prayer and Scripture essential elements of a sound and civilized education. The state also thought racially separate schools beneficial to whites and blacks, and so decreed. At that time Jackson was about half white and half Negro, and I don't believe the Negro half felt any more unequal in separate schools per se than the whites did.

Perhaps the education at Davis and other Jackson schools is better now that it is no longer racially separate. But it was very good then, it seems to me. And it was good then for the colored students, too, though their schools were certainly not equal in terms of physical plant.

Yet in 1921, the same year that Eudora and the rest of us left all-white Davis School to go to all-white Central High School, a Negro boy our own age entered Jackson's all-Negro Jim Hill School and went on to graduate from all-Negro Smith-Robertson School four years later, the same year we graduated from Central. He was Richard Wright, and he has told us he wrote his first story at that time. You can read his account of Jackson in those days in his *Black Boy.* I wonder if the school system of any small, provincial town has ever nourished at the same time two such remarkable talents as Eudora Welty and Richard Wright.

About the end of our seventh and last year at Davis a photographer came up and took a class picture. I still have my copy. There we stand, 23 boys, 14 girls. One of the boys is barefooted—it was that far South and that long ago. Eudora, in a middy blouse, is in the second row, one of three girls with hair-ribbons, her hair in braids around her head, large-eyed, smiling, then as now.

I had forgotten the class was so large, but I remember it was orderly—a little corporal punishment now and then in the cloakroom took care of that. And besides it was a time when all were agreed that teachers knew more than students and that young people adapted themselves to the adult world rather than the other way around.

Soon after our class moved on to Central High, the Jackson city fathers decreed that, beginning in 1925, an additional and 12th grade should be added to the 11 that heretofore had sufficed for the town's public-school scholars. This would have meant that in 1925, the year we were to complete the 11th grade, there would be no graduating class, no senior pictures in the yearbook, no commencement oratory, no awarding of diplomas—unthinkable. So a sizable proportion of the graduates from the town's several grammar schools were selected to take a little extra work each year at Central, the town's one high school, and accomplish five years' work in four. Eudora, of course, was one so chosen, and I somehow was also included.

From those four years at Central I remember especially our Latin classes—Caesar, Cicero, Virgil—because they baffled me, and the English classes—especially the literature and composition (oral and written)—because I liked them. Latin, for Eudora, was a breeze, and in Virgil particularly I recall her smoothing out many a complication in the day's assignment for me before class.

In English we made book reports, some on assigned books, "classics," considered needful for young readers, others on books of our choice. But all of Eudora's reports were on the better books—George Eliot, Jane Austen, Scott. Once when a teacher complained of my unvarying selection of Zane Grey and Edgar Rice Burroughs, I reported on an entirely imaginary book and author. This nonexistent author (we had just been reading "L'Allegro" and "Il Penseroso") was named Milton C. Milton. The title and subject of his book escapes me, but the report (which I read aloud), complete with plot summary, characters, setting, etc., was enthusiastically received, especially by those students who knew the true identity of Milton C. Milton. Eudora, who was aware of the hoax, raised her hand and said she would like to read that book if I would bring it to school. I promised to do so. For several days she publicly repeated her request in class, but I always pleaded forgetfulness. So the matter has rested for more than two score years.

Several times a year we were asked to write stories of our own for English class. Eudora's were invariably smooth, beautifully, painstakingly written. Even then, there was evidence of her special talent for describing a character or a scene, for the quietly humorous turn of narrative that mark her adult stories—or so I remember it. We all listened when Eudora read her stories, and we all marveled—the teacher no less than the rest of us.

After Central most of the Class went on to college: some to nearby Millsaps, Belhaven or Mississippi College, others to the University of Mississippi, Mississippi State or, as in Eudora's case, to Mississippi State College for Women. One student even went to far-off Princeton, considered the most Southern and therefore most respectable of Ivy League schools. Eudora found the M.S.C.W. of those days too confining and was soon off to the University of Wisconsin.

She wrote back enthusiastic letters about her writing, her drawing and painting, and she drew a cover for a short-lived magazine, *Hoi-Polloi,* which some of us tried to start as a statewide college literary magazine. *Hoi-Polloi* was to include material from Negro colleges as well as white, and I remember the cautious but pleased response we received from officials at Jackson College (for Negroes) when we visited them and told of our plans. In our youthful innocence and enthusiasm we didn't realize what an innovation we were attempting—which is probably the best way to innovate.

Eudora and I were back in Jackson in the Thirties and early Forties, the Depression and early World War II years. She had a venture at the Columbia Graduate School, and I the same at the University of Virginia (after Sewanee). Her stories began to be published soon after college, and she worked in journalism, radio and with the Federal Writers' Project. Mississippi was poorer than usual in those years; jobs were scarce; salaries were infinitesimal—but there were compensations.

For Eudora there was time to look at people and places, to see them in depth, and to put them in those wonderful stories that make up her collections, *A Curtain of Green, The Wide Net,* and time to fabricate out of her imaginings and the Mississippi past that finest of tales, *The Robber Bridegroom* (one of the few books by a contemporary that William Faulkner ever singled out for praise). I remember the day, driving up into the Yazoo hills from the Delta, we saw the sign beside a ramshackle store: "If you're so smart, why ain't you rich?" A very sensible question. You can see it today, preserved as the last line of Eudora's famous story, "Petrified Man."

While many of Eudora's stories originally appeared in such nationally known publications as *Harper's Bazaar, The Atlantic* and *The New Yorker,* others were generously offered to the little magazines and quarterlies in which she has always been interested. These included such tiny and forgotten publications as *River* at Oxford, Miss., and Hubert Creekmore's gallant little *Southern Review* at Jackson that preceded L.S.U.'s prestigious quarterly of the same name.

Eudora's work with the Federal Writers involved the taking of photographs of Mississippi people and scenes, and you can see some of the results in *Mississippi: A Guide to the Magnolia State*—and more in a forthcoming volume of her photography. For the Federal Writers' Project she was all over the state; into the Delta, into the hills of what Faulkner called Yoknapatawpha, into the piney woods, to the Gulf Coast and the old haunted towns of the Natchez district. (You can discover the spell of some of these places in her fine 1944 essay, "Notes on River Country.")

The large Welty home on Pinehurst, which had succeeded the earlier house near Davis School, became the center of a swarm of local writers and would-be writers, journalists, painters, practitioners in all the arts and just plain friends and disciples. All were attracted by Eudora's unflagging interest, hospitality, humor and often long-tried good manners. Nor was the swarm only local.

As Eudora became known and praised in megalopolis, a succession of writers and others, encouraged by publishers, acquaintances, acquaintances of acquaintances or by no one, appeared on the Welty threshold, curious to see her and have a look as well at Mississippi, which many of them considered one of the world's quaint, undeveloped regions. Eudora suffered all such visitors gladly. It is her way.

I recall one such visitor, the American expatriate novelist, Henry Miller, whose fondness for physiological explicitness in his prose and for four-letter words kept him for some time off American bookstore shelves except in expurgated form. When Eudora phoned me and said she, Hubert Creekmore and I were to take Henry Miller to Natchez, I hurried right over. I expected to see a raffish, dissolute roué, spouting flamboyance and double-entendres. Instead I found a quiet, soft-spoken, middle-aged man who had little to say and might well have been a grocer.

We had a very pleasant day exploring the Natchez Trace, visiting Port Gibson (the town Grant said was too beautiful to burn), the old houses of Natchez and the Mississippi River bluffs. Afterward we sat at a little sidewalk cafe (Mississippi was officially dry at that time, but Natchez paid no attention) and had vermouth-cassis or something, while Henry Miller, like any tourist, wrote ten or twenty postcards to persons scattered over the globe. I can't recall a thing he said except that he told Eudora he admired her stories but didn't think she was very good at titles—a peculiar and libelous observation I thought, then and now.

Time marched on. World War II came, and Robert van Gelder, editor of The New York *Times Book Review,* prevailed on Eudora to join his staff. Van Gelder had interviewed Eudora for *The Times* some years before and had long been one of her most enthusiastic supporters in the East. No stranger to New York, Eudora has always enjoyed the contact here with other writers, with editors and, of course, the museums, restaurants, concerts and theater. Especially the theater. I believe she received more pleasure from the successful run of the play *The Ponder Heart* in the fifties than from all the critical acclaim for the book.

Anyway, she entered into the hurly-burly of New York publishing and the *Book Review* with enthusiasm and conspicuous success. She searched out many new names for the reviewing staff, suggested and obtained fresh, new articles, edited manuscripts beautifully (I speak with authority; her renovation of my own reviews, sent up at that time from Mississippi, made them fit to print), and she wrote many fine reviews of her own on all sorts of books.

At that time books from the war front were numerous; and, although the only battlefields Eudora had probably ever seen were at Vicksburg and Shiloh, she turned out splendid reviews of World War II battlefield reports from North Africa, Europe and the South Pacific. When a churlish *Times* Sunday editor suggested that a lady reviewer from the Deep South might not be the most authoritative critic for the accounts of World War II's far-flung campaigns, she switched to a pseudonym, Michael Ravenna.

Ravenna's frequent and perceptive reports on the literature of the war were well received and frequently quoted in the publishers' ads. Invitations from radio networks for Michael Ravenna to appear on their programs were perforce declined with the statement that Mr. Ravenna was extremely busy.

When Eudora finally decided that the hectic pace of New York journalism was interfering with her own major interest, fiction writing, and left the *Book Review,* I became Ravenna. His well-known byline continued to be seen until the war's end. I daresay his name has already appeared, as it should, in more than one scholar's bibliography—a critic of perception and authority.

Eudora has spent most of the postwar years in Jackson. She has found time for some lecturing in the East, for appointments at Bryn Mawr, Smith, Vassar and Millsaps. Her writing has continued strong and true, marvelously catching the special regional characteristics of Mississippi and its people and yet revealing in them the life that is universal. Just as, for example, her deceptively simple story, "A Worn Path" (the 1941 O. Henry Memorial Award winner), caught the essence of the Mississippi Depression years (including the paradoxes and subtleties of Negro-white relations), so her story "The Demonstrators" (1968 winner of the same award) reveals with no less power and authority the ferment of the state's postwar years (including its changed, yet not so changed, race relations).

When I begin to think of the quality of Eudora's achievement, I always recall V. S. Pritchett's comment about *The Robber Bridegroom:* "There is not a mistake in it." And I remember the frustrated remark of Charles Poore, *Times* daily book critic as he sat down to write his review of *Delta Wedding;* "How can you review a book there's nothing wrong with?"

Meanwhile, there at the house on Pinehurst Street, Eudora remains what she has been: Jackson's best-known, most accessible, celebrity and the Deep South's most distinguished writer in residence.

FROM

Brother to a Dragonfly

Will D. Campbell

No, it's further down the path. I know it's further down the path." Joe was looking for something but had not told me what it was. So I couldn't help him find it. He said he would tell me when we got there.

We were walking down a path, through the woods behind our house, in the direction of Grandpa Bunt and Grandma Bettye's house which stood a few hundred yards away. A spring branch flowed directly behind their place and we could hear the rushing waters from the heavy rain of the night before. Joe was seven years old and I was five. And Joe was the leader.

He said we were looking for an experiment. That was all he would tell me. Whatever it was, I knew that it would be successful. Sawbriars, those thin, spindly vines with spines like fish teeth, were reaching out to take hold of whatever piece of clothing or skin they could hook themselves into. I do not know if sawbriars still exist. In 1929 they covered the south Mississippi hills, springing out of the red clay like so many tiny quills, hostile toward everything around them. They were considered a part of the curse, a curse we grew up believing was somehow a part of the Adam and Eve story. We defended ourselves against them with both hatred and reverence. We hated them because one was supposed to hate evil. We revered them because the Bible taught us that it was a part of what we had coming to us on account of someone's long ago sin—sin which was passed on to us and which became our own. Perhaps the sawbriars are all gone and do not exist anymore.

And "stickers" too. Those almost invisible needle points rooted in the ground which had no height at all but spread themselves upon lawns and grassy places like a carpet. They, too, were related somehow to the curse—humanity's sinful condition and history.

As we walked along, bradding the stickers with our bare feet and avoiding the sawbriars as best we could, Joe kept repeating, "I know it's further down the path, I know we didn't pass it yet."

It was early summer and our feet had not become toughened as they would be later on. We stopped occasionally to pull the stickers out, scratching and rubbing where they itched. Joe said this was good training for the "sticker races" which would take place later in the summer.

Sticker races were a frequent game for the dozens of Campbell cousins who gathered at Grandpa Bunt's house on summer Sunday afternoons. They required no equipment and could be played by every size. Training for the races began on the day we began to go barefooted. I do not recall any criteria, such as how many days from the last frost, but somehow it became known that on a particular day all boy chaps would take their shoes off. On that day the tender feet of winter began their perilous journey into spring and summer. First in the yard only. Then timidly onto the stomp—that area between the scraped, packed dirt yard surrounding the house, swept clean with dogwood brooms, and the edge of the fields—and finally into the field, woods, riverbanks and graveled roads. It was not that shoes were looked upon with scorn. We looked forward to the time, generally in late adolescence, when we would wear them all year. It was a symbol of manhood. (Joe would one day have twenty pairs of shoes in his closet and under his bed at once.) Shoes were, in fact, one's most prized possession. They alone separated a man from what was at once his best friend and worst enemy—the earth. Best friend because it produced the corn and potatoes to eat, the cotton to try to pay off the mortgage. And worst enemy because it harbored the cottonmouths and rattlers, the sawbriars and stickers, and snow and ice of winter. The earliest songs we sang had to do with shoes:

Mamma, soon I'll be an angel.
By perhaps, another day.
Give them all my toys, but Mother,
Put my little shoes away.

And years later Carl Perkins and Elvis Presley, swinging, gyrating, twisting, rejoicing to the music and lyrics of "Blue Suede Shoes," a song not about a rich dude from the city who impressed the girls with his daily change of shoes, but a story written in the cotton fields of west Tennessee by a poor boy who saved enough money to pay for the coveted suede, and served notice on the world that it could do anything it would to him but, "Stay off my blue suede shoes!" The wearing of shoes was a luxury dreamed of. The taking them off in spring an occasion which might as well be celebrated as lamented.

The Sticker Race was no more than a contest to see who had the toughest feet. The winner was the one who could run the length of Grandpa's Stomp and "brad" the most stickers. The race was run in groups of four, lined up by age or size. "Bradding" meant that the needle points were broken off by the leather-like soles of the feet with no penetration into the "quick." One was disqualified if he had to stop to pull one out. Those finishing the course were inspected to see if any stickers were present. A tie in the number of stickers went to the one who crossed the line first. When four boys finished a race the winner stepped aside to compete in the finals and four more began. There was never any tangible prize, just the satisfaction of having the toughest feet in the Campbell community.

Joe kept whispering my name. "Dave. Dave. Dave." My name was Will Davis but Joe, and most everyone else, called me Dave until I was seventeen and left home to go to college and announced that I wanted then to be called Will. Joe was the first to make the change saying, "A *man* ought to be called what he wants to be called." Joe was first to declare me a man.

"It's got to be further down the path. I know we didn't pass it yet, Dave." Each time he called my name he whispered it.

I had just returned home that morning from "across the river"—Grandpa Will and Grandma Bertha's house. I stayed with them often when I wasn't needed in the fields at home. I was Grandpa Will's namesake and he made no secret of the fact that I was his favorite. For the favors I had to suffer the taunts and jeers of "Grandpa's little pet" from numerous cousins and even aunts and uncles who were offended at such favoritism. If it offended Joe we never discussed it. His only resentment was that he wanted me at home with him. I had come home that morning because Mamma had been sick the night before and had sent for me.

Before we left the house to look for Joe's experiment, we sat for a long time on the back steps and Joe told me how he had thought

Mamma was going to die and how she had made him promise that he would get word to Uncle Boyce to bring me home on his way to McComb where he worked in the Illinois Central Railroad shops.

Suddenly he found what he was looking for. In a clearing in the weeds and briars beside the path there was a tiny mound of clay. I stooped down and started to dig it up.

"No, waitaminit, Dave. Don't dig it up yet." He had to explain what it was about.

"I caught a 'skeeterhawk Sunday and buried it alive in a Bayer aspirin box. I said I was going to dig it up on Wednesday and if it was alive that would mean you were coming home that same day. If it was dead that would mean you would be gone for a long time."

We had gone up and down the path several times looking for the grave. The heavy rain had settled the earth and washed some leaves over it. In his haste to show me his experiment he had walked past it. When we saw the water in the branch he knew that we had gone too far and when we turned back the last time he walked directly to it.

He had dug the hole in the ground with the blade of his barlow knife and the actual exhuming was brief. We stood touching each other in the damp, eleven o'clock heat of a June, Mississippi morning. The ceremony was not to be rushed, and he must be certain that I understood what was happening.

"I betcha that 'skeeterhawk is alive." 'Skeeterhawk was what we called dragonflies. They had something to do with luck, both good and bad luck. If you were fishing and one lit on the end of the pole, it meant you were going to catch a fish. If one paused, hovered nearby but then darted away, you might as well go to the house. It was bad luck. Someone had told us they caught and ate mosquitoes. We imagined they did it like the big, wide-winged chicken hawks which swept down from the sky and grabbed young chickens from the yard in the spring. We had watched the giant bird soar around and around the chicken pen, stopping dead still in the air. Then, rolling his body into a ball, looking to us like the big steel balls we had seen chain gang prisoners pulling along behind them, he would drop straight to the earth with a force and speed far beyond what its body weight could create. His aim was always perfect, his work quick. With the chicken knocked down from the fall upon it, his beak was sunk into the chicken's head like a flashing spike, killing it instantly. Just as quickly he was gone with his prey. We used to watch a dragonfly to see if he killed a mosquito that way.

"You can't chase a 'skeeterhawk and catch him. They fly all the time. You just have to wait till they light, when they're all tuckered out. Then you can slip up on him and grab him by the tail. Not by the wings though. By the tail. That's the way I caught him."

He held the aspirin box in the palm of his hand.

"I betcha he's alive. I betcha anything he's alive, Dave. I said to myself when I buried him that I was going to dig him up on Wednesday. And if he was alive that meant you were coming home. And you're already home. I betcha he's alive."

Slowly, deliberately, he unsnapped the aspirin box with his thumb nail. The lid was gently raised open. Two brothers stood as close as two brothers could stand, beholding the proof of one brother's experiment.

It did not, could not, have occurred to me that the fluttering of the transparent, gauze-like wings might have been caused by the wind. Joe had buried the dragonfly on Sunday and said that if it were alive on Wednesday I would come home and we would be together. And the wings had fluttered.

He snapped the lid shut, ran quickly and dropped the aspirin box into the rushing and muddy waters of the spring branch.

"Didn't I tell you!"

And two brothers tried to outrun each other, and tried harder not to outrun each other, back to the yard. For there was no thought of ascendancy.

Joe had climbed up a small ladder built along the wall of the corncrib, looked down at us from the hayloft, and finally made his way to the highest cross piece at the top of the gable of the barn. Aunt Susie's boys, Vernon and Prentiss, were with us and Joe had insisted to us all that he could fly.

"I tell you, I can fly. I've watched buzzards and hawks, the way they do it. All they do is spread their wings out and let the wind blow them along. I can do it too." As he climbed the thirty or forty feet to where he was sitting he kept shouting down to us that he was going to show us he could fly.

It was drizzling rain outside and we had been sitting on a pile of cottonseed in the barn, telling ghost stories. Joe had read Edgar

Allan Poe stories and had mastered the telling of many of them: "The Pit and the Pendulum," "The Premature Burial." Later he would memorize and recite—generally only to me—some of Poe's poems: "Annabel Lee," "The Raven."

The old barn was a special place. Not because it was our barn and we knew our Daddy had built it but because it was headquarters for so much learning. And because Joe and I spent so much time together there, usually just the two of us. Joe was the leader here as everywhere.

Once our barn had become infested with large packrats, some of them, tail and all, fifteen inches long. A favorite sport was to take a long handled pitchfork and, as dozens of them lay sleeping where the roof came together forming a sharp gable, go down the line sticking them through the belly with the fork, hearing them squeak and watching them scatter for cover. On one day Joe suggested that instead of stabbing them we try to catch one. I don't recall if we planned to try to make a pet of it or throw it into the pond as we sometimes did 'possums we caught. We would throw the 'possum to the middle of the water and wait on the bank until he swam out, throw him in again and again. Each time he was a little more weary and finally he would be so tired that he couldn't make it out, would sink to the bottom and drown.

His plan to catch the rat was simple. And soon successful. He told me to stand in the corner of the corncrib where there was a hole in the floor. He said that when he bumped on the roof the rats would run for the hole. I was to catch one and not let go. I was not long in waiting. As one ran for the hole in the floor I grabbed him by the stomach. He jerked his head to my left index finger, ripping it from the outer edge of the nail, down and across to the first joint. Blood spurted and the rat, his mouth, eyes and body covered with the salty warm claret, let go. Though he had let go of me I did not let go of him. Joe had said to hold it until he came down and that was what I intended to do. Joe came tumbling down, yelling for me to let go as he fell beside me. But in my confusion I understood him to mean that I should hold on. He grabbed my arm and shook it so hard the rat landed against the far wall, momentarily stunned. The moment was long enough. Joe stomped and cursed and kicked it and finally ground its head to a pulp with the heel of his shoe. Revenge over, he turned quickly to me. The bone could be seen through the flow of blood. Tearing off the tail of his shirt he wrapped and pressed the wound until it stopped bleeding. Several stitches would be required to close such a wound in other days. But then, several weeks of time and healing did as well. The long scar remains as a monument to obedience, trust, love and leadership. Things like that happened in the barn.

Now perched high above us in that same barn, having looked down to the ground and deciding against flying, Joe was telling Vernon and Prentiss a scary story which had really happened and which we had heard Mamma and Daddy tell many times. When school was in session we could get books to read. At other times we had stacks of magazines given to us by Uncle Boyce and various girl cousins. These were always either *Smith and Street Westerns* or *True Romance.* Other forms of entertainment were simply not available to us. So, idle time was passed by listening to stories of the early childhood of our parents.

The one Joe was telling now had happened when Mamma was four or five years old. She and one of her sisters, Aunt Dolly, were playing in front of their house when they heard yells and screams and pleas for help from the field across the road from their house. Even before they came into sight they knew that it was their neighbors, Mr. Lum Cleveland and his wife, called by Mamma, and thus by us, Aunt Stump. They were both old.

Joe was embellishing the story by making the sounds he supposed each of them was making, dropping his voice as low as a little boy could to imitate Mr. Lum's voice, and raising it as high as he could for Aunt Stump's screams.

"YE—OOOW!"

"*ye—oow!*"

"HELLP!"

"WHE—OOOW! HELP! HELP!"

Now Mr. Lum and Aunt Stump came into vision from the woods that surrounded their house, several hundred yards north of Grandpa Will's house. Running after them, a shotgun in his hands, was a much younger man. The two little girls, frozen in terror, recognized him too. It was Allen Westbrook, son-in-law of the two old people. He was screaming incoherent sounds as loudly as the two he was pursuing. Joe imitated his sounds, or what he imagined his sounds to have been, flailing one arm around, holding onto his perch with the other hand to keep from falling.

Then we heard the shots, Joe pausing after each two volleys to allow time for reloading.

"BOOM! BOOM!"

"POW! POW!"

"BAM! BAM!"

Mr. Lum dropped to the ground and did not move. The screams of Aunt Stump continued. No longer hearing the calls of her husband, she hesitated. Glancing back over her shoulder to look for her husband, she tripped and fell. Now another shot rang out.

"BOOM!"

Aunt Stump did not get up.

Vernon and Prentiss had not heard the story before. I had heard it many times but sat in the same rapt attention as they, beholding now with them two old people lying bleeding on the ground.

The story continued from the lofty roost.

Mamma and Aunt Dolly went screaming to the house, seeing as they did their daddy running in the direction of the cries of his neighbors, his own shotgun in his hands. He had heard their calls from the field where he was working. But he was too late. Both lay dead in the sun a few yards apart. Allen Westbrook was gone.

The two bodies were brought across the road on a mule-drawn ground slide and placed on the back porch beside the water shelf. Most rural porches had such a water shelf. A cedar bucket was there, a stainless steel or gourd dipper beside it, and a wash basin. Beneath the shelf would be elephant-ear plants, those stout stem plants with leaves looking like their name. Water used for washing hands and faces was always poured onto the elephant ears, the soap and dirt and moisture making them grow to mammoth size as the summer advanced to fall and winter. The first frost would bring them to the ground. Joe continued to garnish the tale, telling us how the blood of Mr. Lum and Aunt Stump dripped onto and around the elephant ears, and how they grew so big and so tall that they had to be cut down with an ax. He told us how the doctor, summoned to pronounce them dead, had washed the brains of Aunt Stump before placing them back in her head, and how Uncle Boyce, older than Mamma and Aunt Dolly, already a young man, had walked across the field with a piece of head bone to be placed with the body of Mr. Lum.

Vernon and Prentiss thought it was time for them to go home. But the story was not finished. Joe told them there was more, and so they stayed.

The story to that point was what we had heard Mamma tell. She would usually include some speculation as to why the murders were committed, but always leaving something to the imagination.

"The daughter was to blame. She's the hussy who should have been punished. She's the one who always kept things stirred up between them, tattling first to one and then the other. It was her fault." And Mamma sometimes used the story to explain why her nerves were so bad, and why she was sick a lot.

Daddy's part of the story had to do with the punishment of Allen Westbrook. He was soon captured, or turned himself in, and the trial followed. He was found guilty and sentenced to death by hanging. It was to that event that Joe turned next.

"They killed him on a gallows. Made him climb up this big, tall scaffold, and I'll bet he was as high up as I am now."

He imagined, and passed on to us as fact, that when Allen Westbrook climbed up there he could see all over the town of Liberty.

"Yea, that was the last thing he saw before they put that black hood over his face. He could see the church houses, the school house, Dr. Quin's office and both drug stores. That's what he saw. Everything. He was so high up he could see everything in the world."

And our daddy had been there. The account as it was told to us, and as it was then being told by Joe, began in early morning, before daylight the day of the hanging. Grandpa Bunt got up real early and got his five boys up to go with him. They ranged in age from nine to fourteen years. He already had the mules hitched to the wagon when they got up. They drove the ten miles to Liberty, the county seat of Amite County. It was almost noon when they got there, and that's when he was going to be hung. At exactly dinnertime.

Wagon teams, buggies, and saddled horses were already tied under every shade tree. Allen Westbrook's mother, father and sister waited under a tree far to the left of the jail and courthouse, far enough away that they could neither see nor hear what was taking place. But a clear lane had been considerately left through which they could drive their wagon bearing the casket to the courthouse to claim his body when it was over.

"They told Allen Westbrook he could have whatever he wanted for his last meal. And you know what he asked for?" I knew, of course, but all three of us shook our heads. "No."

"He got fried chicken, rice and gravy and biscuits. He wanted some ice tea too. And some blackberry pie. But they said he didn't eat the pie. But he ate all the chicken and stuff."

He climbed the steps of the scaffold without assistance. The sheriff, a short, fat man named Mann Causey, whom we knew for he had been sheriff again in our time, asked him if he had any last words. He said that he did.

"He made a little speech. He told everybody that if he had listened to his mamma he wouldn't be there on that scaffold. He told everybody to listen to their mamma and they wouldn't ever get in any trouble. He thanked the sheriff and the jailer, said they had been real good to him. That's what he said, and it was the last thing he ever did say."

The traditional black hood was placed over his head. The rope, properly knotted for public display several days in advance, was placed around his neck. Daddy, the youngest of the boys, milled around the courtyard with his brothers and the hundreds of others who had come. Mann Causey pulled a lever which released the trapdoor upon which Allen Westbrook was standing and he came plummeting to justice, stopping short of the ground by not more than a yard. A bubbling, gurgling sound, a few feeble kicks of the feet and legs, feet searching for something stationary in the final moments of consciousness, and then the heavy twisting and turning.

The body was lowered gently and tenderly to the ground and taken inside as if the whole thing had been an accident. Dr. Quin, standing by all the while with stethoscope in hand, leaned over and listened to his chest. Daddy and Uncle Bill, little boys, peered through the window. The doctor said something to the sheriff who then made a circular motion with his arm, motioning to another man stationed midway between the scaffold and the waiting wagon. He in turn made a similar motion in the direction of the wagon, cue to the parents that they could come and take their son home.

The people of Amite County had been heard. Justice prevailed. Grandpa Bunt and his five boys got back on their wagon and went home. Grandpa had said nothing to his boys about why he was bringing them to witness the hanging as they came. He said no more about it as they returned.

Joe, his story finished, climbed slowly and silently down to where we were and sat down beside us. Vernon and Prentiss, heirs to the same genes as Joe and I, wondered why Grandpa Bunt took his boys to the hanging.

"What'd he do that for?"

Their mother was our daddy's youngest sister and was just a baby when it happened. But she wouldn't have been taken anyway. Only the boys. Vernon and Prentiss kept asking, "What'd he do that for?" As if we knew something they didn't know. We agreed that he had taken them as a sort of lesson against a life of crime.

Later, when we were grown, and the exposure to the man who was Grandpa Bunt was complete, we knew that we had been wrong. We came to know him as a man who opposed violence in any form and for any reason, no matter the justification or provocation. More likely he was saying, "The world is this way but it should not be." He was too gentle a man to have said otherwise.

He was no stranger to either tragedy or violence. In his middle twenties he had buried his entire family of children within a two week period. Little Sophia died. Then Myrtis a few days later. And finally Claudie. Bleeding Flux they had called it, an intestinal disorder which could be cured today with one injection. But one by one his children had died of it until they were all gone. He would describe to us the building of the boxes in which they were buried, how, on each occasion, he insisted upon being the one who would lift the tiny coffin to his own shoulder and carry it the hundred yards from the wagon to where it was to be planted. It was his sorrow, his burden, grievous to be borne. He knew, and passed on to us, that some journeys had to be made alone.

Like the day he died. Near ninety, he had been bedridden for weeks. That very afternoon he had said to all of us gathered, "Y'all have chairs." It was his usual greeting when anyone entered his house. As we were leaving he had asked his lastborn son, our Daddy, not to leave him. But in a few hours he said to him, "Well, Son, you have gone as far as you can go." And the son knew that he was free to leave and did not hesitate nor feel guilty in leaving. In less than an hour Grandpa Bunt was dead.

But as four little boys sat on the cottonseed out of the rain, that day was far in the future. Grandpa would live to see all of us grown, and both Vernon and Prentiss would die before he did. We were just trying to figure out why he took young boys, some of whom were no older than we, to see a man die. We did it in the form of "Remember the time Grandpa . . ." anecdotes.

There were the times he told us of the violence of the Civil War. His first vivid recollection was seeing his daddy in a wooden box, placed in the doorway where the cool air would slow the decomposition of the body until the circuit-riding preacher got there to bury him. His daddy had run away from the Confederate Army at Shiloh because he was sick. Grandpa reported it with neither rancor nor judgment. And with no visible pride that his father had been a Confederate soldier. And such feeling as we had regarding the outcome of a nation divided we got elsewhere, never from him. He was not the Southerner one reads about in books.

It was, in fact, from him that we learned for sure that the war was over and done with. A dozen or more of us were playing on his stomp and had hollered at a black man who was walking down the road.

"Hey, nigger. Hey nigger." The man, John Walker, had recently been beaten by some men for stealing a sack of roasting ear corn. We had heard older boys laughing at the way he told about it.

"Yessuh. Dey got me nekked as a jaybird. Took a gin belt to me. Whipped me 'til I almost shat." We saw no harm in the taunting.

But Grandpa did. Yet he did not scold. Instead he called us all around him. Sitting on a huge tree stump he explained that there were no more niggers.

"Yessir, Grandpa. There's still niggers. We just saw one go down the road. John Walker's a nigger. We saw him."

"No, hon. There ain't any more niggers. All the niggers are dead. All that's left now is colored people."

He knew how to tell a group of his grandchildren in rural Mississippi that the Civil War was over. And some of us never forgot it.

Eventually we tired of telling Grandpa stories and trying to figure out his reason for doing what he did, and turned to other things. Vernon and Prentiss had recovered from the fright of seeing Allen Westbrook hang and no longer wanted to go home. The rain had stopped and Joe began insisting again that he could fly. He wanted to bet us a dime that he could fly from the highest peak on the barn to the ground. None of us had a dime so all of us took the bet. Then he said, "Now I didn't say *how* I was going to do it."

We didn't know what he meant by that, but however he could get from the top of the barn to the ground without climbing down we would accept as flying and we helped him carry out his scheme.

A half-inch cable had been left at the house by someone and Joe went and got it. He also had with him when he returned a pulley from a well windlass and a short piece of rope. By now we were beginning to understand how he was going to fly but continued to do his bidding. The cable was more than a hundred feet long. He climbed back to the top of the barn and fastened the cable to the top rafter under the overhang, letting it drop to the ground. Next he stretched it as far as it would go away from the barn, the slant of the cable forming about a forty-five degree angle with the ground. The pulley was placed on the cable and the cable was then secured to a heavy iron stake driven in the ground. A short piece of rope to hold onto was tied to the pulley. Then there was the problem of how to get the pulley from the ground end of the cable to the starting place at the gable of the barn. This was accomplished by tying two plowlines together and pulling the pulley up the cable after he climbed to the top of the barn.

After the hour of preparation, the flight was about to begin. But first he decided to have a test flight with a burlap sack filled with cottonseeds to see just how fast the pulley would come down the cable. From his perch at the top of the barn he pulled the sack up to him, then released it. The sack came down with such speed and such force that it split open when it hit the ground, scattering cottonseed all over the barn lot. The rest of us joked and laughed about how Joe's seeds were going to be scattered when he came down just like the seeds from the sack. But he had bet us he could fly and it was obvious that he intended to do it, scattered seeds or not. First the iron stake had to be driven deeper into the ground so that he wouldn't hit it for he said that was what had busted the sack. Then he determined at what point his feet would first touch the ground as he approached the end of the cable from the top of the barn. He said if he hit the ground running, and let go of his grip on the pulley rope there would be no sudden stop and he could make it.

Back at the top of the barn he pretended to be Allen Westbrook.

"If I had listened to my mamma I wouldn't be here today. You boys always listen to your mammas and you won't ever be in any trouble."

And then, imagining, I suppose, that he was seeing what he had imagined Allen Westbrook saw from the gallows, he spoke again as he took his grip on the pulley rope, speaking in a shout. "I can see all over the world from up here. I can see everything in the world.

I can see Mr. Scott Nunnery's store and all the way to Uncle Bill's house. I can see to East Fork! *I can see all over the world!"* Then with a wild scream he kicked his body away from the roof of the barn and in not more than two seconds the pulley brought him down the cable to the ground. Rolling over several times as the force of the flight continued to carry him forward, he bounced quickly to his feet and bowed politely to each of us, holding his hand outstretched for the dimes he knew did not exist.

"I told you I could fly!"

FROM

A Highly Ramified Tree

ROBERT CANZONERI

REVIVAL

I USED TO HOLD my mother's hand mirror flat under my nose so that the hanging light fixture rose like a glass flower up to my waist; then I would turn with great care, step over the top of the door into the hall, and walk through the house on the quaking plaster of the ceiling. Or I would face the hand mirror to the larger mirror over the dresser and watch precise frames swing into an infinite corridor of empty doorways.

What flat silvered glass could do to a familiar scene fascinated me. A rectangle of sunlight across the quilt on my parents' bed would be the brightest spot in the reflected room. The colored patches looked richer in the mirror, perhaps, but in that world of mere light nothing could release the warm smell of cotton cut and sewn by my grandmother's hand. Move your head and perspective would strike you like a catch of the breath: the chair would slide across a couple of inches of bed; the bedpost edge over to show the corner of the door frame; the door frame shy aside just enough to reveal a tall sliver of dining room, seen clearly through the dark hall.

When nobody else was around, how could I resist trying to find out what I looked like? Except the mirrors turned me left-handed, shifted the mole to the other cheek. Abraham Lincoln had a mole there, but the face with it was craggy. The way my hair fell across one eye, I could hold the end of a comb under my nose and look more like Adolph Hitler. The only thing I could really watch myself do, anyway, was watch myself. The face around those eyes that I could never catch off guard is, at least by now, a blur.

What image I have of the boy I was is recalled from snapshots: big eyes, wide ears under the turned-up flaps of an aviator cap, skinny legs sticking out of short pants, mouth quirked as though trying not to break into a laugh—he is one of six or eight kids standing in the yard at home, with the edge of the gravel driveway at their sneakered toes, the front porch behind them.

The Word

Sometimes the boy would sit with his father behind the unfolded morning paper and read the funnies, except he would be through and waiting by the time his father's eyes moved from Dick Tracy down to Little Orphan Annie. If his mother passed by on her way from making up the beds to cleaning up the breakfast dishes, she'd stop in the wide doorway to the dining room and look at them there on the wicker davenport. "I declare, Joe; you can waste half a day reading the comic strips." His father would not hear her. "Waste," she'd say. "Total and absolute waste. What could you possibly get out of those things? You'd think you were studying the Scriptures." His father did study the Bible the same way, only with his finger moving from word to word."Well, they're not the Scriptures," she'd say, "and they're not the garden that ought to be hoed before the heat of the day." His father would be reading Sandy's balloon, saying it slowly to himself as though letting all its significance sink in: "Arf."

"Joe!" His mother's voice would come so sudden and loud that he would jump. "Joe Canzoneri!"

His father's eyes would pull slowly from the page the way you stretch bubble gum out with your fingers. "Had what?" It was what he always said when he realized somebody was talking to him.

"You haven't heard a word I've said. You'd do better to hoe those beans before it's too hot to breathe."

His father's eyes would still not have lost their absorption in Little Orphan Annie. "Bob and I just read the funny paper."

His mother had a way of setting her jaw. "Just read the funny paper," she'd say, mocking his father. "Then it'll be the crossword puzzle till I've got dinner on the table." And this time she went on to say, "You have to write that letter to Richmond, too, if you're going to do it. You can drag that out for the rest of the day."

"Oh," his father said. "Yeah," eyes pulling back to the paper. "I better do that."

She stood there a minute longer. Finally she just shook her head. "If you're right, the Lord sure enough does work in mysterious ways. And he'd better perform some of his wonders pretty soon."

He knew what his mother was talking about. They needed

money to make the payment on the house, to buy cowfeed, cornmeal, sugar. His father had been in a revival meeting up in the delta, but he'd led the singing, not preached, and they split the offering so the preacher got sixty percent and he got forty. He'd come home Sunday for a week off, which meant no money. Every morning except this one he had worked in the garden till his overalls were soaked and dripping, and then he'd rest flat on his back on the kitchen floor. He was lying there Monday so quietly that he heard the mailman all the way from the highway. "I get it," he said, hurrying to his feet. He came back up the driveway with a handful of letters. "If only I'd beat you to the mailbox that one time," his mother had said over and over since. The first letter his father opened was an invitation to preach and sing for two weeks at Wanilla, a little church in the country out from Brookhaven. The next was an invitation for the same two weeks at the First Baptist Church of Richmond, Virginia. The rest were bills.

His mother had sat down at the kitchen table and sighed. "Richmond. Thank the Lord. That'll just about get us through the summer."

His father had stood there, still dripping wet. "I go to Wanilla," he said.

"Wanilla. Have you lost your mind?"

He sat down, too, and picked up the letters, one and then the other. "The Lord lead me to open this letter first."

"The Lord didn't stack the mail. Mr. Rochester did that."

He shook his head slowly and said nothing.

"If the Lord hadn't wanted you to go to Richmond, why did he lead them to invite you?" She put her head in her hands. "You're not the only one the Lord deals with. What if he leads me to say take Richmond and cash money instead of a handful of change and a couple of gallons of molasses?"

"I have to do what God say."

"The only reason you're free to 'do what God say' is that I keep up your house and garden and four children, not to mention two cows and a yardful of chickens and that useless dog. But that doesn't count for anything."

He spread his hands. "The Lord take care of us, Mabel."

"He takes care of you, all right. But why does it always have to be through the sweat of my brow?"

Half the afternoon his father sat in front of the portable Royal at the dining room table. Now and then he'd stiffen one finger on each hand and poke three or four keys in succession. Then he'd peer at what he'd written, sit a while longer, strike again. The typewriter keys were round, the kind with rims holding circles of glass over the letters. If you stood near the china cabinet, the light through the side door blanked them out.

He stood there till his father pulled the paper out, read the couple of lines with long deliberation, signed his name. Then he moved to his father's side. "I'll go to Lena, I guess."

His father put his arm around him. "Good. We have a good time." He folded the letter carefully and ran a blunt thumbnail down the crease. He rolled a small envelope into the typewriter, moved the carriage back and forth slowly, checking to see that it was straight. "I don't use typewriter like you sister," his father said. She took typing in school; her fingers hovered over the keyboard, rattling out the letters like hail. "Somebody say I use method he call . . . H. F. C.? Something like that."

"H. P. C.," he told his father.

"Yeah." His father laughed. "Stand for Hunt, and . . . something he say. . . ."

"Hunt, Peck, and Cuss."

His father laughed again. "Hunt, Peck, and Cuss, somebody say. I do that, sure 'nough, only the Lord help me not cuss." He shook his head. "I declare, if the Lord didn't give me sense of humor, see the funny side of thing, I don't know what I do."

"You want to go Lena with me next week," his father had asked him at dinner, "or wait and go to Wanilla?"

"I'm going where they've got a pickle factory," his younger brother said.

"You went there last year," his older brother said. They had all driven down to get his father and younger brother and got to go through the pickle factory too. It was just an old tin-roofed shed; they climbed up onto the high wooden walkways between huge vats of brine. "Don't fall in," his younger brother told him; you'd think he owned the pickle factory.

"I'm going again." His younger brother poked out his bare stomach and rubbed it. "I'm going to eat a hundred pickles."

"And die with a bellyache," his older brother said.

"Don't say that," his mother said.

"Why not? That would give anybody a bellyache."

"Say stomachache."

"If I said stomachache, they'd laugh me off the school bus."

His sister got up from the table. "They'd do that just from looking at you."

"Well, you don't have to worry. Nobody'd look at that face of yours."

"Where are you going?" his mother asked his sister. "You haven't eaten enough to keep a bird alive."

"Make him leave me alone. He makes me sick."

"You started it," his brother said. "So quit your bellyaching."

"Be ashamed, both of you," his mother said. She turned to his father. "Can't you tend to your children just once?"

His father looked up, a forkful of peas halfway to his mouth. "Had what?"

The Tree

After dinner, when his father took the typewriter from its case, the boy went outside to think. The sun was very hot on his bare shoulders, and the ground was so packed and dry where he went through the pasture fence that it burned his feet. He hurried toward the clump of oaks; the cows were standing in the shade, tails switching. He stopped to pat old Blackface, and she swung her head aside to nuzzle him. Fenwick tossed her horns; she was younger, and sometimes on cool days she would run and buck just for the fun of it. In the winter he enjoyed milking old Blackface while his older brother milked Fenwick across the stall. He would put his head against the warm flank, smell the warm milk, listen as his brother sang hillbilly songs through his nose or preached crazy sermons in a voice like a radio preacher, making them up as he went. Sometimes Kaiser would bark at the stall door, and his brother would squirt milk through the crack and tickle his nose.

The tallest of the half dozen oaks was his tree. He took hold of the bottom limb he used to have to jump for, walked up the trunk until he could swing a leg over, and climbed slowly to the top. The next tree, nearly as tall as his, was his younger brother's. Sometimes they pretended they were in the crow's nests of old sailing ships, shouting to each other over a heavy sea. Sometimes they just talked. This was the only place they really talked to each other, high in their separate trees, across the empty space where the limbs didn't quite touch.

He had been to Wanilla with his father before. You went on the G. M. & N. railroad, on the one-car Doodlebug that was kind of like the Toonerville Trolley; the streamlined Rebel didn't stop there. The town was only the depot, a store, a couple of houses, and the white church in sight down the road. Maybe you could count the nearest farm, where a boy about his age lived; he bragged that his birthday was January 19, the same as Robert E. Lee. He had gone swimming with that boy's family in the creek behind the church, where they baptized people, and then he had walked by himself all the way out to the Edwards' farm, where he and his father were staying. But his father wasn't there; he had gone, Mrs. Edwards told him, to the house near the depot, for supper. He trudged the dusty road back. When he got there they were already eating. "I thought they bring you here," his father said. The boy sat down, took one bite, and without knowing he would do it, started to cry. "He's just exhausted," his father said. It was the first time he'd ever heard the word.

A slight breeze swayed the tree, and he held tightly to the trunk. He could feel the rough bark printing itself into his side.

He did not want to go to Wanilla, to the dim church with the slatted pews where his father once preached so late that the Rebel came through before he finished, long blasts of the whistle shattering toward them and rushing away in the night. But he did not want to go to Lena, either, to unknown people and a strange house to sleep in. It was the only time he hadn't wanted to go with his father since he first went to Utica when he was three years old. They'd held him up to pull the bell rope hanging through a little round hole in the ceiling, and he would cry when his father got up to lead the singing.

There was always something he did wrong. Up at Catchings, his father had to get after him for giggling in church every time the boy in front threw his thumb out of joint. At Carthage, he got sick and had to be driven home. At Hickory, he couldn't bring himself to ask the people where the bathroom was and wet his pants.

His father wanted him to go again this year, anyway, and he could imagine how hurt his father would look if he said no. He might as well go on to Lena and get it over with. You went there on the G. M. & N. too, he knew, only you went north instead of south. The phrase struck him: north instead of south. He looked at the house, the gray roof shingles, the brick chimneys, the front porch facing the same way he was facing, toward the highway. In his mind Wanilla had been in front of him, but that was north, and Wanilla was south. He closed his eyes and hugged the tree trunk. You'd think anybody would know the directions where he had lived ever since he could remember, but he kept getting them backward, as if somebody had stuck a pin right where the house was and had turned the map around it so that all the words were upside down. He had to force the world back around in his head until what the house faced was north, until Wanilla was behind him and Lena swung into place ahead—northeast, really—off to the right a little, out of sight beyond the highway, the trees.

It made him dizzy, the way he had felt the night he'd looked out the car window and realized that there must be something past the stars, and something past whatever was past the stars, and something past that, and on and on forever. The same dizziness he felt every time his thoughts got too near the dark emptiness inside that was like a black hole in his mind.

Chorus

The sun slanted in the open window, lighting the pews on the other side of the church. It was not hot yet; morning services would start in half an hour, when the pastor led the visiting preacher in and they sat solemnly in the high-backed chairs. Now his father was standing in front of a handful of kids; a woman in a thin flowered dress waited at the piano.

"I love children," his father said. "You see, Jesus say, 'Suffer the little children to come unto me. . . .' "

He looked away. You don't say, "I love children" to a bunch of kids, he wanted to tell his father. But he knew it didn't matter; people liked his father so much they didn't care when he said things like that.

"I may not sing ver' good," his father was saying with a little laugh, "and maybe I say words funny, but I try do what the Lord say and make a joyful noise."

The preacher who was here for the revival seemed more like what a preacher was supposed to be. "Just call me David," he'd said when they met; "I'm a preacher's kid too." Some of the older men said he had great promise, the Lord would use him in a big way, as he had David in the Bible. He was just out of college, slender, tall, slightly pale. He wore a white suit and white shoes, and out of doors a straw hat; from under the stiff brim his blue eyes looked upon the world as if in judgment.

"Listen," his father was saying. His face clouded. His face and his voice changed, his hands, shoulders, body moved with everything he said. "'Let no man despise thy youth.' Paul say that to Timothy, but God mean it for you too."

He focused on the hymnal in the rack before him. In a while his father would get around to the singing, to the choruses he taught all his junior choirs. The first one would be "In the Sweet Bye and Bye," and when he got to the line

Won't it be glorious when I get there,

his father would say it like a cross between won't and wouldn't:

Wunt it be glorious when I get there;

and all the kids, hanging onto every word, every note, would sing it the same way:

Wunt it be glorious when I get there!

The boy loved maps, had loved them since Mrs. Lasseter taught them geography in the fourth grade and they had had contests, trying to be the first to point to whatever city or state or river she called out. He always thought of the United States as it was on the map that pulled down in front of the blackboard, right where during recess one day somebody had drawn a circle and beside it what looked so much like a banana that it took him a minute to understand why some of the kids snickered and the teacher was upset. Now on that map in his mind he could mark off the whole Southland his father had traveled, a vast slab of land from New Mexico nearly to Maryland, from above the Ohio River all the way down to Florida, the Gulf, the Rio Grande; he could remember the colors of the various states, imagine the line of mountains where Kentucky and Virginia, Tennessee and North Carolina came together, the hills of pines and oaks through Alabama and over to the flat black Mississippi delta shoulder-high with cotton, and on across to the dry open plains of Texas spreading westward to the Rockies. He could see sprinkled over this expanse the dots, the tiny circles, the stars that stood for towns and cities and state capitals, each with at least one Baptist church his father had been to—white plank churches among scrub oaks; low brick churches with painted palm trees and a blue River Jordan snaking down into the baptistry; massive stone churches with huge windows of stained glass, with cushioned pews and aisles thickly carpeted. Hundreds of churches holding thousands of children, faces scrubbed and eyes alight, all singing,

> I'll have a mansion so bright and so fair,
> Wunt it be glorious when I get there!

The Ministry

"He's ver' young," his father was saying, "but the Lord use him. He learn. Gotta few craz' notion from some postmillennialist book, but I try show him what God say."

Mr. Davis nodded. He never said much. They were in the Davises' breakfast nook, drinking coffee as they did every night after services.

"And I try say a few things to the people, in song service, not be confused what God say. And when I tol' my experience tonight."

The boy's eyes were tired and hot. As long as his milk had kept the glass cold, he would hold it tight and then put his hand over his eyes, but now he had drunk all the milk. "I think I'll go on to bed," he told his father.

"You go by you'self?" His father opened his arms; he got up and hugged him goodnight, kissed the whiskery cheek. "Goodnight, Kerflumox. I be there in a minute."

"Night," he said. "Night, Mr. Davis." He did not look at Mr. Davis. Why did his father have to call him Kerflumox in front of somebody? He went through the dining room with the fine china and silver shining from the polished cabinet, into the living room with its heavy drapes and soft carpet, up the silent stairs past the closed door where Mrs. Davis was already asleep, probably.

The light in the bedroom was on. If it hadn't been, he'd have reached around the door frame to find the switch, risking only his hand and arm. At home he would force himself to go into the bedroom before turning on the light; sometimes if his hand didn't touch the switch first thing, he would jump back through the door in spite of himself. Once, without even trying to turn on the light, he had made it almost to the middle of the room before he couldn't stand it, and then he held himself almost to a walk going back to the hall.

The pillow felt cool to his face, but too soft and smooth, too full. It was Thursday, a whole week after he had decided to come, and he had to spend tonight and tomorrow night here, and then they'd take the Rebel back to Jackson. His mother would meet them at the station near the Old Capitol, and they'd drive all the way out Capitol Street past the zoo and cross over the bridge beside the woods where he could feel by the cool air he was getting toward home.

Kaiser would jump up on him and bark, waggle around so that he could scratch his ears and just above his cutoff tail at the same time. He missed Kaiser more than anything. He had spent the whole afternoon out in the country with Herbert, shooting his Benjamin air rifle that you could pump so hard the BBs would bury themselves in a fence post, but even then he'd rather have been playing with Kaiser, chasing each other around the yard and tumbling together. When the sun went down, he'd go to the little coop for baby chickens and Kaiser would jump up on it and sit there beside him watching the colors spread over the whole western sky, with the one tall hickory tree down beyond the sloping pasture like a finger touching the edge to see if the paint was wet. Kaiser would turn to lick his ear and then look back at the sunset.

He had to quit thinking about that. He ached all down through his chest, already. He ought to go to sleep. It was very late. His father had told the story of his conversion tonight and it took a long time. David had sat out in the front pew. "Let me tell you something," his father had said, "I'ma not got religion, and I'ma not got theology, I'ma got life, new life, not something put on outside." David said Amen. "Inside. Jesus give to me when I trust him, there in that li'l barber shop in Purvis, Miss'ippi, when I try learn a li'l English by read the Bible, look in dictionary every word, near 'bout."

He had told about being afraid to go into a Baptist or Methodist church because the floor was supposed to open up and devils take you down to hell. "I love the people in the Catholic church, God love them too, but I'ma tell you one thing, I don't need priest or some pope talk to God for me, I talk to God myself, you talk to God you'self." Amen, David said. "I don't call any man father but my own father, live in Sicily still. God is the Father, not somebody in a collar turn 'round, say hocus pocus you don't even know what is. Listen, I don't wanta be call reverend, li'l peanut like me. You calla just plain Joe Canzoneri, or Brother Joe, or craz' mutt, maybe you want to."

Other people kept saying Amen, too; the pastor and old Brother Nutt and some of the deacons. Afterward everybody crowded around his father and kept telling him that it was the best sermon they'd ever heard, but his father would say, "Well, that's not a sermon, just try to tell my experience with the Lord." David stood by, nodding. When nearly everybody had gone, David grasped his father's hand and looked straight into his eyes. "Brother Joe," he said, "the Lord moved me tonight like I have never been moved since the day he saved me."

"I 'preciate you give up you time to preach," his father said.

"Not at all. Not at all. No sermon of mine could ever be as dramatic as the way you tell of your conversion. Not at all. Not at all."

Go to sleep, he told himself. But things kept coming into his head, like the young bluejay Herbert had shot out of the chinaberry tree, lying there with black glassy eyes, feet folded. Think about something funny, he told himself.

The only thing really funny all week happened the first night. After the song service and the offering, his father had said, "My wife go to school here, high school, you see. Boarding school. Then go down to Hillman College, where I meet her. And you know something, we get married right here in Lena. We come over from Standing Pine, on eleventh of July 1918, and Brother Nutt marry us. So this ver' special place to me, glad to be here."

Everybody looked around at Brother Nutt, and he nodded a little, like taking a bow. He was very old and hadn't preached for a long time.

"Now I gonna sing a solo, one my favorite song I hope the Lord use." When his father glanced at the pianist and she started playing, the boy tried to sit farther down in his seat. People said his father had a beautiful voice, that he could have been in opera, but lately all he could hear was the wavy sound running through it. Vibrato, his father called it. And he would sing each word separately, to get the message across, holding onto a note so long sometimes that the pianist would be left with her hands high above the keys, waiting for him to go on.

> I am a poor wayfaring pilgrim,
> Wandering through this world below.
> There is no sickness, toil, nor danger
> In that bright world to which I go.
>
> I'm going there to see my father,
> I'm going there no more to roam.
> I am just going over Jordan.
> I am just going over home.

When the song was over, nobody even fanned for a minute, although it was a hot, still night. His father stood and let the sound all die out, then he bowed his head and started to the steps down to the front pew, where he always sat and listened to the sermon. But Brother Nutt stood up and said, "Joe?"

His father stopped and looked out into the congregation at him. "I heard my grandmother sing that forty years ago," Brother Nutt said, "and she beat you all holler." He sat back down. His father laughed about it later, but then he just stood there with his mouth open.

Preachers, he thought. If they were right and if there was only one right way, then shouldn't they all be just alike? When God called them to preach, why didn't he make them perfect? Make them all like the Apostle Paul or like George W. Truett, in Dallas, that people said was the best one now. His father had worked with Dr. Truett a long time ago, and he had written the boy a letter congratulating him on being born. His mother kept it in the box with the pictures. Maybe preachers ought to be what his father called scholarly, like Dr. Purser, the one who gave him the nickname Kerflumox that only his father ever called him. Or maybe quiet and gentle like Dr. Lovelace, who was dead now. The boy had seen his coffin let down in the ground. He jerked his mind away from that. Some of them were funny, he thought, like Dr. Patterson, who went hopping and gulping at the air in the middle of a sermon, saying some people were like a pullet chasing a grasshopper. He and Billy Rogers had laughed so hard they got down under the pew, and his mother had to pull them out.

He turned over on his stomach, put his head between the sheet and the cool underside of the pillow. The funny preachers didn't bother him, but some others did, like the one who had been at Hickory when they were; and then when they went to hear him at a revival in Jackson, he told exactly the same boiled okra jokes. His favorite song was "That Will Be Glory for Me"; he'd have the congregation sing it while he whistled the tune to himself, rocking from heel to toe.

David. The day they had chicken pie for dinner he wouldn't let the lady cut into it. "I can hit the gizzard every time," he said. He dangled his fork back and forth over the crust, stuck it through, and pulled out the gizzard. Everybody laughed but the boy was not sure what to think about it.

He heard his father come into the room, heard him getting a coat hanger out of the closet. He moved his head from under the pillow and rolled over.

"You not asleep?" his father said. He sat down on the edge of the bed. "You know, son, I think I tell you about Baptist World Alliance meet in Atlanta, and I like to go, but cost too much? Mist' Davis want to pay my way, he say, want me to go. Preachers from all over the world be there."

He roused himself. "Dr. Truett?" It was the only thing he could think of to say.

"Dr. Truett, R. G. Lee, everybody. Preachers from all different countries in the world. I try to tell Mist' Davis he shouldn't do that but he insist."

He tried to imagine preachers from all over the world. The nearest thing to it he had ever seen was the convention last year at the First Baptist Church in Jackson. He and his friend Atley had stood in the wide vestibule just to hear the preachers come out and blow their noses. "Why do they sound like that?" he whispered after one preacher had given a long honk—like something his brother might do on his trombone—then folded his handkerchief over, and honked again. "I don't know," Atley said, "but if it hadn't been so much I'd have thought it was his brains." He nearly died before they could get outside and laugh. It still made him want to laugh; so why, he wondered, did tears fill his eyes and spill down across his temples?

"Son? What's the matter?"

He could only shake his head.

"You be all right," his father said. "It's ver' late. You go sleep, we talk about it tomorrow."

The Book

The next day they had dinner at Dr. Lyle's house and were supposed to stay all afternoon, but his stomach began to cramp, and his father said, "I better take him back to Mist' Davis, let him lie down."

"He can lie down here," Dr. Lyle said. He was a dentist, not a medical doctor. "We've got plenty of beds."

It must have shown on the boy's face that he did not want to stay, because his father said, "I s'pect he feel better there." And as soon as they got to their room and his father pulled the bedspread down he was crying again.

"I declare, son. Can't you tell me what's wrong?"

He shook his head. He did not know either, not all of it. That morning after breakfast was cleared away, his father had spread out his timetables and studied them for a long time. Finally he said, "Look like no way to make it if I go home first. Have to go on to Meridian and make connection with Southern to get Atlanta on time." He picked up his coffee cup, put it down, looked at the boy. "You think be all right to ride down Jackson by you'self? You be on Rebel. You mother meet you at the station."

He had not answered. He had never been anywhere by himself, and the thought of it scared him.

"I have to leave early in morning. Mist' Davis take you to train couple hours after." He waited again. "If I go." It would be his only chance; usually the World Alliance met in foreign countries, his father had said, like England and Brazil.

He licked his lips. "I want you to go," he said.

His father rumpled his hair. "That's the ticket."

He turned away, his jaw tight. ". . . go brush my teeth," he managed to say, and hurried upstairs.

In church that morning he had kept touching the pew, pulling his fingers slowly away from the thick varnish to feel the pull, the letting go, the lingering invisible residue. Anywhere he touched, a detective could sprinkle powder and see the lines and whorls that were like nobody else's in the world.

"Whatever you do today," David was saying from the pulpit, "is written minute by minute in the Book of Time forever. And when you come before God Almighty in that last judgment day, you will see it whole, like a story written, like a map of where you've been, like a moving picture used for God instead of the devil, flashed up on a screen as big as the sky. Your dark, secret, sinful pleasures will shine out bold for all to see—your lust, your greed, your gossiping and backbiting, your selfishness and pride. And, oh, my friends, do you realize you hang over an open pit of eternal fire and damnation?"

David stepped to the side of the pulpit stand, held up a hymnal for everybody to see, thrust it out in front of him like a platter. "Only God holds you safe, as I hold this book. Only the mercy and forgiveness of God sustains you. Oh, you may be held so high, my friends, that you do not feel the awful fires of hell leaping toward your feet. But they are there. Fire and darkness and eternal torment. And once it's too late, once God lets go, you will fall endlessly into the pit, never, never, never to return. Never, never, never to reach the bottom, my friends, because God is the only foundation and without Him there is nothing."

He stood holding the book, sweat beading on his forehead. "Falling forever, lost, burning with unquenchable fires through the long endless night of eternity. And God will let you go, my friends. God will let you go. Unless you trust him now, God . . . will . . . let . . . you . . . go." For a moment David stood motionless, and then the book hit the floor with a sound like a shot.

After the service, the people lined up to shake David's hand. "Powerful sermon," an old man said. "Powerful."

The boy stood close by his father; he felt that he could still hear the slam of the book, the reverberations through the whole church.

"We're going out to Dr. Lyle's for dinner," the pastor had said finally. "We can all go in my car."

They had walked down the aisle and out the door. When they stepped into the blinding sunlight, David slowed down to let the older men walk on ahead. "How'd you like that?" he whispered. "I really turned that ole songbook loose, didn't I?"

The Known World

"We s'posed to go back for supper," his father said. He could not say anything. "I declare, I don't know what to do with you, son. You cry last night. I bring you back from Dr. Lyle's, you cry all afternoon. Don't have fever, I don't think you sick. I go craz', you keep this up."

He lay there looking up at the light fixture, a glass bowl with faint white flowers all over it. If he concentrated on that, he could be quiet for a while. The light was not on. When he would glance aside at the venetian blinds, he could see strips of green where the tree in the front yard was, and strips of blue diminishing above it.

"Got to take the car back, anyhow." His father stepped over to the window, and the blind made bars of light and dark across his face. "You say you want me to go to Atlanta, but I guess you don't want stay here, do you? Don't want go home by you'self." He was silent a moment, looking out toward the tree. "Is that what the matter is?"

He cleared his throat, but he did not know what to say, even if he could talk.

"Don't you think God take care of you?"

The only thing that would come into his head was his Sunday School teacher telling how she prayed when her chickens got out and God helped her find them.

His father turned to him, shook his head. "I thought you big boy now."

He tried to say that he wanted to be, but his throat knotted up. He could see exasperation in his father's face, in the way he took a deep breath and pressed his lips tightly together. He flopped himself over and crammed as much of the pillow as he could into his mouth, into the sockets of his eyes. He heard his father let the breath out with a hollow sound, a sound that seemed to come from the gray puffed cheeks and rounded lips of the North Wind drawn on some old map of the known world, with its warped chunks of land and its blank expanses of ocean where legendary monsters swallowed those who might otherwise sail off the edge.

"All right." He felt the bed sag as his father sat beside him, felt the strong hand on his shoulder. "Daddy not goin' leave you. We go home together."

FROM

The Capers Papers

CHARLOTTE CAPERS

GOD AND MY GRANDMOTHER

WHEN MOTHER AND I got to Columbia every summer, Grandmother would be on the front porch, waving and crying. The crying was because she was so happy to see us. If she had not been crying, I would have been disappointed.

We usually left Jackson for Columbia the last week in June, and Father joined us in August if nobody in the congregation at St. Andrew's was seriously sick. Somebody was always sick, as I remember it, and it seemed to me that all Episcopalians appointed to die did so in August. As pastor, Father saw his sheep in or out of the Valley of the Shadow, and thus was often late for his vacation. Mother and I went on ahead, and had most of the summer in Columbia, Tennessee, where her parents lived.

When I was nine or ten Columbia was heaven to me. This attitude was due in large part to Grandmother, who was in close touch with the Almighty and made heaven seem a very attractive place.

Our summer pleasure began when Moses met us at the C.M.A. station in the old Essex, and drove us home. My grandparents lived in a two-story brick house on the Mt. Pleasant Pike. The house, built in the 1880s, was late Victorian in style, and was set far back from the Pike. A gravel driveway led through stone gate-posts to the house. It had a fine tin roof, on which the rain drummed marvelously. It had a cupola, with a lightning rod rampant. And it had heavy wooden shutters at the windows, which were closed every afternoon at naptime by Moses, with the aid of a broom-handle with a hook on the end of it. The shutters were closed from the outside, of course, and they were very effective. I remember the dim cool of the library, produced almost the instant the shutters closed. The front door was half-glass, at the top, framed in little squares of stained glass.

Middle Tennessee had more than its share of rip-roaring windstorms and thunder storms, and when a storm was brewing, Grandmother and I would go to the front door and watch the trees toss wildly in the wind. Grandmother would tell me about storms that blew cows up into trees, and houses off their foundations. We looked at the storm through the red glass and the blue glass and the yellow glass, and this gave a weird, other-worldly glow to the scene as the trees bent to the wind and the lightning flashed. The limbs twisted and snapped, and sometimes there was a tearing, cracking noise as a tree went down. Then Grandmother and I would dash from the front door and take refuge in the bathroom, which for some reason she thought was safest in storms.

This bathroom had been added on with the advent of plumbing, and it was a funny little room painted bathroom blue and smelling of strong blue carbolic acid soap. The pipes made strange sounds when the water was drained out of the wash basin, and one of the Negroes had told my brother that this was the plumber, coming to get him. He passed this bit of folklore down to me, and I was really more frightened of the bathroom than I was of the storm, when the gurgling of the pursuing plumber was heard in the pipes.

Anyway, Grandmother and I huddled in the bathroom and she prayed until the storm passed. Grandmother was very religious, and I thought she always had been. But Father said, "No, she took a turn in her early married life when some evangelist came to town." Before that she had been an Episcopalian in a relaxed sort of a way, but the evangelist really got to her. She didn't leave the Episcopal Church, but she tightened up on some sins that hadn't worried her before. She made Granddaddy stop betting on harness races, and when Uncle Stith, Granddaddy's younger brother, made the long trip from Brooklyn, New York, to visit them, she found a bottle of whisky in his room and forthwith poured it down the toilet. Uncle Stith never returned, understandably enough, and Grandmother's religious turn continued to her life's end.

By the time I was old enough to hear and receive the Word, Grandmother had mellowed considerably, but I still got a stiff course in the Bible every summer. We had Bible reading every morning, and Grandmother was such a good reader I looked forward to these sessions, as well as to Family Prayer at night. I knew also that I had to read the Bible before I rode the pony, and I accepted this sequence of events as Virtue and Its Own Reward. I could not ride until Joshua had fought the battle of Jericho, or made the sun stand still. When I was excused by Grandmother and left for the latticed back porch and the pony standing hitched to the acting bar in the back yard, I was often worried about what was going to happen to Joshua next.

There were no children near to play with, so the days were pretty much spent in reading and horseback riding, and sometimes croquet with the grown people in the late afternoon. At night we had Family Prayer, and Grandmother was in charge of this operation, too. After she and Granddaddy had played checkers or euchre or High-Low-Jack in the library, and Father and Mother had come in from supper with friends or the picture show, and the grown people had run through a game of riddles or conundrums with me, it was time for Family Prayer. We had it from the Prayer Book, and we had Evening straight through. Then if there were any special problems, we did Additional Prayers to cover them.

Additional prayers were usually for my brother, Walter, who was sixteen or seventeen and seemed to be always standing in the need of prayer. He was full of all sorts of natural juices, and he had discovered Nashville, forty miles away, and girls. So he was not with us much at night, but Grandmother always remembered him in our prayers. She prayed for him to be healed of whatever accident had recently befallen him. I remember one summer we prayed for Walter's foot, when he cut it with an axe, and we prayed for his head, when he jumped a horse over a stone fence and was thrown, and we prayed for him to recover from typhoid fever, which he contracted at summer camp. We also prayed regularly for him to get home from Nashville safely. In the mornings we did not see him, for he was asleep. Grandmother spoke of him as King Agrippa—I don't know why unless it was because Herod Agrippa was such a high-riding king, and Grandmother's orientation was so Biblical. She would say, "Sh-h, King Agrippa's still asleep," and everyone would tip-toe around and sympathize with the poor tired boy who had danced all night.

Walter was very charming and pretty spoiled, and Father complained about it a good deal. "These women are ruining Walter," he would say, "they won't let me make him work." They really wouldn't, because Walter was so good-looking and so polite, and wherever my mother and Grandmother went ladies told them that he was Prince Charming and Lord Chesterfield, and they believed them. Add King Agrippa to this, and he could have been a real mess, but somehow he wasn't. In the winter Father tried without success to get Walter to help around the house, and he would say, "I can bring the coal in and make the fires without losing my religion, but I cannot make Walter bring the coal in and make the fires without losing my religion." Which is to say that Walter was seventeen, and I did not see much of him in the summer.

When special supplications or additional prayers were over, we had the Aaronic blessing. Grandmother preferred this one to "the grace of our Lord Jesus Christ, the love of God, and the fellowship of the Holy Ghost," though she was all for the Trinity. Aaron is said to have said, "The Lord bless us and keep us. The Lord make his face to shine upon us and be gracious unto us. The Lord lift up his countenance upon us, and give us peace, both now and evermore." I liked that too, not for any special reason or because we were stronger on the Old Testament, but because the words were so pretty.

When the blessing was said Grandmother kissed Granddaddy on the cheek and said, "God bless you, Mr. Woldridge," and Granddaddy kissed Grandmother on the cheek and said, "God bless you, Miss Liza," and we all went to bed. I got to sleep in Grandmother's room.

She had a white iron single bed put up beside her bed, next to the old walnut wardrobe. When I had bad dreams I thought the heavy old wardrobe was a monster. I have seen ghosts come out of it, as a door creaked heavily open on its hinges. Before we went to sleep we named all of the oceans of the world, and we imagined a voyage on one of them which we were to describe to each other the next morning. We named the corners of the room for sweethearts, of which I had none, and the corners of the bed for saints.

Then Grandmother might be moved to tell me about the beaux she had before she married Granddaddy, or of the little baby whose crib stood in the corner of that very room, who died before she was six weeks old, or of the visions she had seen. Father would have thought she was crazy, so I never discussed the visions with him. But Grandmother told of climbing a high white mountain, with mists swirling about the top, and stumbling, and falling back, and stumbling again, and falling back, and being about to plunge to the rocky depths below, and then a hand, which was the hand of God, reached out from the top of the mountain, through the mists, and clasped her hand, and brought her home. I thought this was a very nice vision, and it was Grandmother's type.

She liked her religion dramatic and she was High Church, as opposed to Father, who was Low. Grandmother liked everything mystical, and all the bells and incense and genuflections in the world would not have seemed too much to her, to worship the King, all glorious above. Father, on the other hand, was a South Carolina low country low churchman, and he had gone to Seminary in Virginia besides. He had little traffic with visions or the visionary.

He was fond of the old story about the man in the field who saw the writing in the sky, "G. P." and thought it meant "Go! Preach!" After a miserably unsuccessful ministry he found that the message was really "Go! Plough!" So much for visions, Father would say, and then he would press on to tend his sheep. So I certainly didn't bother him about Grandmother and God.

We were involved with the Church always. Father met Mother when he was rector of St. Peter's in Columbia, where Granddaddy was senior warden. Later we moved to New Orleans, where Father was rector of Trinity, and then he was called to St. Andrew's, Jackson, where he spent the rest of his ministry. Despite their differences in churchmanship Father and Grandmother were great friends. Grandmother often reminded us that we had the best father in the world. We did not question this, and we also thought we had the best grandmother. So as a courtesy to both of them I would be Low all winter with Father and High all summer with Grandmother, and we got along just fine until we began to argue about Mr. Norman.

We called him Mr. Norman but Grandmother called him Father Norman and that is what he called himself. He was an Anglo-Catholic priest who was trying to establish a religious community of some sort near Columbia, and having a tough go of it. His work was never clearly defined in my mind, but he called on Grandmother constantly for help and he always stayed for dinner. He had no sense of humor and he was not good with children, but he did wear interesting clothes and ornaments. Father's attitude toward Mr. Norman was uncharitable, to say the least, and this got on Grandmother's nerves. Father teased her about Mr. Norman, and wondered how he could keep his mind on the Lord when he was so busy changing his clothes in the chancel. Mr. Norman had services at St. Peter's occasionally when the rector was out of town, and he did put on quite a show. Grandmother was fascinated by him, and he couldn't change his clothes too often to suit her. He brought Grandmother books of devotions and Anglo-Catholic literature, and she added these to our daily Bible sessions. She learned a good deal that was not in the Prayer Book and she taught a lot of it to me. She set me to memorizing the Three Theological Virtues, the Four Cardinal Virtues, and Seven Gifts of the Holy Spirit, and a good deal more, in mathematical progression.

I was delighted with the Seven Stages of Sin, and I was very pleased with a Form of Confession, but I hadn't been confirmed yet and I wasn't quite ready to think of Holy Communion as the Mass. Father complained a good deal about Mr. Norman, who was always around the house, and pointed out to Grandmother that he didn't seem to work at all. They got a little tense about Mr. Norman, but Grandmother didn't get too mad at Father because she really loved him very much, and then he fussed about Mr. Norman in a joking way and she would have to laugh. Grandmother and Father made it through August, and then Mr. Norman, being a little ahead of his time in this part of the country, went on off in search of the Liturgical Revival.

After Mr. Norman's departure there was nothing to argue about, and our summer routine continued until September. Nights were especially nice when everybody was home. That is, everybody but Walter, who was never home. On an August night we would finish supper and Grandmother and Granddaddy, Mother and Father and I would go out on the front porch and talk and watch the cars go by. The road in front of the house was not paved, but it was being surveyed for paving. The cars left plumes of dust behind them, and their headlights were pale yellow in the dust. The grown people would comment on the increase in automobile traffic on the Mt. Pleasant Pike in the last few years. Granddaddy and Father would light their El Roi Tan cigars, which were not permitted inside. The smoke from their cigars would drift slowly in the summer night, and when they drew on their cigars the ends glowed redly. They talked about when they were boys, the ladies talked about when they were girls, or about people they knew in Columbia or Nashville, and often a car would crunch up the drive and company would come in. Once the company told a thrilling tale about a prominent married man in Nashville who was in a wreck with some woman, not his wife. His wife threatened to shoot them both. I don't believe she shot anyone, but this was exciting word from the outside world, and the chairs rocked faster as the story was told. One night Grandmother and Granddaddy told about the dances they used to go to, and then they got up and did a polka by the light of the moon. Anyway, the cigars would glow, the rocking chairs would creak, lightning bugs would venture up on the porch and wink, a mourning dove would call from the fence, and sometimes the old owl in the dead tree in the Grant's yard would hoot. Much as I wanted to chase the lightning bugs, I would not leave the talk. The laughter was pleasant to hear, and usually somebody would ask Father to tell a story.

One of his favorites was about Willie May Loflin and her baptism. When Father was rector of St. Peter's in Columbia, a lady called on him to ask a special favor. She wanted to come into the Episcopal Church, and she had not been baptized. She believed that the only valid baptism was by immersion. She wanted to be baptized, she wanted her three children to be baptized, and she would like for Father to do the job. But she wouldn't feel right if she wasn't immersed. She firmly believed that only thus could she be sure of the authenticity of her regeneration, according to Scripture.

Father was very broad-minded about everything but Anglo-Catholics, and he thought that if Mrs. Loflin would feel better about being immersed, he would try to accommodate her. Immersion is permissible in the Episcopal Church, though affusion or sprinkling has long been the custom.

Father went to his friend Mr. Legion, the Baptist preacher, and asked to borrow his baptismal pool. Mr. Legion, a hearty fat man, agreed, and said he would be glad to lend Father his rubber undersuit. Father was tall and at the time slim, and there was a good deal of difference in his girth and in Mr. Legion's girth. The appointed day came, and Father, his convert, her husband, who was uneasy about the whole thing, and the three children presented themselves at the pool in the First Baptist Church. Father had on his vestments over Mr. Legion's baptizing suit. He began to read the Ministration of Holy Baptism, and got along fine with it until he got to the part having to do with water. Mrs. Loflin had renounced the devil and all his works, the vain pomp and glory of the world, and had promised to obediently keep God's holy will and commandments all the days of her life, when they got to the place in the service where Father asked the witnesses the name. Mr. Loflin named his wife Willie May, which had been her name all the time, Father took her by the hand, and the two of them processed into the pool, where Father was, according to the rubric, to "dip her in the Water discreetly."

When Father entered the pool the extra space in Mr. Legion's pants began to fill with air. Father grasped Willie May more firmly by the hand, and pressed on into deeper waters. The airy suit, now buoyant, floated upward, and Father floated with it. He lost his footing. He lost Willie May at the same time. Panic seized them both. Discretion was out of the question. The issue was survival, regenerate or not. When Father fought to get his feet on the bottom of the pool, the inflated rubber suit bore him up like water wings. He lunged toward Willie May, got her by the neck, and gasping for breath forced her head under, sputtering, "Willie May, I baptize thee in the name of the Father and the Son, and the Holy Ghost." By this time Mr. Loflin was about to come in after them, Mrs. Loflin had gotten over any reservations about the validity of sprinkling, and Father had nearly drowned. He and Mrs. Loflin bobbed to the surface, and worked their way to the edge of the pool, coughing and choking. As they reached shallow water and Father got a firm footing, Mrs. Loflin, her hair and eyes streaming, and fear written all over her face, gasped: "Mr. Capers, I want you to sprinkle the children!"

This always brought the house down on a summer evening long ago. Grandmother laughed until she cried. Soon it was time for bed. If the stars were out, Grandmother and I would go out in the yard for a last look at the night. "The heavens declare the glory of God," said Grandmother, "and the earth sheweth his handiwork." The next day I would read and ride and say my memory work, High or Low. In the afternoon I could play in the tree house or bury treasures in a Whitman's candy box. There would be long conversations and tall tales on the porch at night. We would pray for Walter to get safely home from Nashville. September was in the air. Vacation time would soon be over. When we left, Moses took us to the C.M.A. station in the old Essex. Grandmother was on the porch, waving and crying.

Sunday Has a Different Smell

Anne Carsley

I DO NOT RECALL that all the Sundays of my childhood differed. To remember one is to remember them all in an endless circle of dappled light, slow moving and serene.

I woke that Sunday morning shivering in the first faint coolness of the coming fall and reached for the sunny smelling sheet on the floor where I had kicked it during the night. The chill that drifted with the early haze would melt at the first touch of sunlight; later the day would be blaring and brilliant, stapled in brass and edged with blue. I lay back for a long moment, hugging the crisp whiteness to my shoulders, and watched the flickering patterns of light and shadow on the bare, cool floorboards. Breakfast smells mingled with the chickens' cries of accomplishment from below. From the hall where it was enthroned in massive doily draped pride came the sounds of the radio mourning the sorrows of the chosen people and the triumphant glory of faith tested in the fiery furnace. I savored the sense of anticipation, late breakfast and newness that was and is ever Sunday to me—a timeless moment to hold against all the years.

The tempo increased: A pot lid clattered; the kettle sang; I heard the slap and thwack of my father's razor; the ice box door slammed repeatedly; my aunt cried daintily from the kitchen and it was breakfast time. We three ate, spreading the Sunday paper between the dishes, each to his own island of interest. My aunt sipped dark coffee, commenting on the possible circumstances of each obituary. Second only in her fascination was the wedding section. Curious, this mingling of death and beginnings. My father hunched over the same dire headlines that, he often remarked wryly, used to infuriate his own father in his day. I sprawled over peaches and cream with the funnies, half listening, sniffing the warm, dark scent of sun bleached paper and reading large-eyed of the escapades of the Katzenjammer Kids and the perils of Little Orphan Annie who was to me in those days as Deirdre of the Sorrows. In the silence that sometimes fell I could hear the distant clang of a cow bell and the small birds twittering in the purple flowers at the window.

Invariably the blare of the alarm startled us and the rush to get ready for church began. My father snarled amiably over the set of his tie, I turned over the only bottle of white shoe polish, the car fought all attempts to start it. When finally I stood ready in starchy, crimped glory, my aunt eyed me dubiously between pokes at the simmering roast and remarked hopefully that at least I ought to get to church clean—to stay that way would be beyond us both. My father, half out the door, pulled uneasily at his coat and adjusted the band of his summer straw under the admonishing eye. We moved carefully, feeling the responsibility of this day. I thought that he, no less than I, was hearing again the commands of his mother. My aunt never went with us. Prayer meeting was her forte for she had not missed a Wednesday night in ten years. She preferred to rock by the radio, raising her voice with the hymns, drink innumerable cups of scalding coffee, and slowly prepare the ritualistic Sunday dinner. We envied her as we drove stiffly, itchily, up the dirt road between the sweet glimmering fields, past the slow train with its sad little hoot, to the small church of uncompromising red brick and white boards set in a clump of shade trees. Neighbors and relatives stood talking until the first authoritative organ peal summoned them into the dim interior with the slow moving overhead fans and dusty odor of velvet.

We settled into the hard pew just as the first long Bible reading began. The begats had a rhythmic swing that made my eyelids droop. It grew stickily hot as the sun poured through the yellow, green and purple glassed windows that some contended were "Popish." I glanced up at the weatherbeaten face of my father, his eyes the same faded hazel as the deepest pool of our creek on a hot day, red knuckled hands still in his lap. Starch pricked my damp legs and I reached furtively to scratch, trying to avoid his impaling glance that could cure the fiercest itch. It was a relief to rise for the hymn, the call of longing for the River Jordan flowing deep. The choir was enthusiastic and off; the voice of old Mrs. Benton who knew everything that happened in the county—sometimes even before the participants—rose in a penetrating soprano that her detractors said could give the Lord himself an earache.

Our preacher introduced a visiting brother who would "bring the message." The people sat back as he crossed the mundane flatlands and soared toward the theological mountains. Old ladies nodded in the warmth, chins sinking lower and lower into lace collars. Farmers mopped wet brows. Their wives sat upright assessing the dress and righteousness of each other while the roses of their hats jounced emphatically with the movements of the fans. Small boys sat decorously under vigilant parental scrutiny. If that eye shifted, they made horrible faces—tight shut eyes, mouths down, tongues out—snapping back to angel smoothness in a trice. Teenage girls in fluffy dresses sat delicately straight with new dignity that could melt quickly into nervous uncertainty. Here and there a big boy snatched heavy fingered at an unfortunate fly. A baby whimpered and was quickly hushed.

Time drowsed by as the visitor rolled grandiloquently along. Mr. Jonas, a recent and fervid convert, muttered, "Amen, Brother, amen." Across the aisle, Mrs. Simms, who had four children under six and a mother-in-law who was all tongue, slept unabashedly on her husband's shoulder as she did each Sunday morning. My stomach growled; I put an elbow in it, thereby making it growl all the more. There was a thud as Ella Mae Robbins removed the high heels that were my envy. Her feet hurt, so the ladies in our parlor whispered, from dancing all Saturday night out at "that dreadful place on the highway." Portly Mr. Stevens, owner of the biggest hardware store in town, drew out his huge gold watch and fixed a sharp eye on the preacher. Heads inclined knowingly; Mr. Stevens was a surpassing good Christian but he liked his dinner on the dot of twelve thirty—two wives had been trained to that.

Sweat trickled down my back as I gazed cautiously at my father's watch. It was twelve forty-five. My stomach snarled again and I twisted uneasily. I caught the eye of my best friend, Ruth, and we engaged in one of those staring contests dear to the hearts of children. Minutes ticked away and our lips began to quirk; I felt a horde of giggles rising. There was a click as Mr. Stevens peered incredulously at his watch, then sharply up at the preacher who took it for rapt attention and boldly launched his eleventh premise. Our own preacher, who knew his congregation, stirred nervously in his chair, thinking no doubt, of his annoyed wife and the drying roast, not to mention the possible—often threatened—departure of Mr. Stevens, a generous giver, to the Methodists across the street who at least knew when to stop. They had long since left. We had heard their good-byes, swishing tires and the bell clap as one of the boys yanked the rope in passing. Beside me a little boy punched his mother, demanding in a carrying whisper, "How much longer?" Quickly, I turned from Ruth's convulsed face, trying to suppress my giggles as the pew shook and several ladies craned their necks in well bred surprise. I felt the flick of my father's birch switch look while the sonorous voice rolled over us, inexorable as Jordan. It was no use, I could not stop. My father correctly judged the situation to be hopeless; he lifted me out of the pew, propelling me toward the door, murmuring about "something she ate" to the blur of faces as we moved.

Once out in the blasting heat under the shade trees, their drying leaves rattling in the little wind, I laughed helplessly until my sides ached and the hiccups came. When the paroxysm subsided, I looked apprehensively up at my stern faced father who smiled in spite of himself. We hung suspended, the mood broke and we roared with laughter in a camaraderie not of age.

We were just about to get in the car when the limp congregation emerged and several concerned ladies rushed over to us. By this time I was so pale and shaky that they could not doubt the fact that I had been suddenly "taken." What they did doubt was the kind of ailment. But, as my father wore his most resigned look and I one of imminent regurgitation, they hovered for one last minute and wisely retreated. We took the high road for home.

The cool house was hung round with Sunday smells. Roast and gravy, dumplings floating in a blue bowl, giblet gravy with egg whites, yellow cornbread, rice, peas, tomatoes, warm cake drowning in chocolate ice cream, a moisture beaded pitcher of tea. When my father regaled my aunt with the morning's happenings, he did not mention the shared time under the trees, but she looked benignly at us and I knew that she understood. I gulped tea, curling my toes and spreading them wide over the worn linoleum, contentment deep and solid in my stomach. Meaningful words sometimes came hard with us; they were as unyielding as the steel pipe I used to "skin the cat" on. Now the air lay smooth and fair between us.

After the opulence of Sunday dinner we slept amid the morass of the paper until company time—a stylized ritual. On most Sundays we dressed in our second best and waited for them to arrive. Rich cakes and tea were served in the dim, quiet parlor where shades were drawn to protect the carpet and the ancestors glared sternly down while the visitors sat uneasily on the prickly couch or precise chairs. Conversations were balanced as precariously as the cups, as delicately as the grandfather clock which struck the quarter hours.

The Sunday afternoon before, I had been fetched down from the fig tree, thrust into a pink party dress, my hastily scrubbed ears still flaming, and coerced to recite "something pretty" for the assembled ladies of my aunt's sewing circle. My face had brightened; I knew just the thing. The ladies waited, smiling and breathless, with coos of "How sweet." My aunt, suspicious of such alacrity, viewed me darkly as it occurred to her, belatedly, that it might have been better to specify a child's poem or a short Psalm. But I had my own ear for words and sonance. I launched into a perfect rendition of several choicely explicit sentences used by my father's cronies as they sat on the porch one evening. There was total and complete silence for a full minute; then a concerted screech, a gasp or two, and a look of downright fascination on several faces as my aunt, who was nothing if not a quick thinker, jerked me away, remarking as she did so on the possible morals of old Mr. Latham across the road who had recently acquired a bride half again his age. I was, naturally, soundly spanked, but some things are worth the price.

On the third Sunday of each month, which this happened to be, we usually went to visit Cousin George and his wife, Viola, who lived on a farm not far away. They were not really cousins, but in the vast, interlocking circles of relatives where precise relationships were sometimes obscure—"second cousin twice removed on your great grandmother's side"—we tended to call people in all degrees of kinship "Cousin" or, in our soft elision, "Cun." Cousin George was a passionate hunter who thought only of guns, dogs, and hunting plans. Cousin Viola was soft and fidgety; her speech was interspersed with "Dear" and "Honey" as she reached out vaguely patting fingers.

Cousin George, lured from his gun polishing, and my father sat in the yard under the shade trees, watching the smoke from their cigars spiral on the air, sipping bourbon, talking of hunting and the war. My aunt and Cousin Viola sat in the most comfortable chairs the parlor could boast, chatting in low voices that rose magically over the rattle of the fan blades when I came near. I sat covertly listening but soon grew bored with bean staking and a whiter wash.

Finally I wandered away to tour my favorite spots. I passed the stable where the amiable old horse nickered a lazy welcome, along the path where blackberries and honeysuckle had lifted their June profusion, to the clearing in which a house had once stood. Now only a blackened chimney remained near a huge cedar. Nearby a straggling rose bush was brave with late roses. There was no air of desolation; I knew that, whoever they had been, they had been happy here. I scratched idly in the loose earth as I always did in hopes of finding something that would tell me what they had been like. Perhaps they had buried their cherished treasures during the Civil War and had been unable to return.

The wash of moist air from the creek lifted my hair. I ran past the pine grove and the little garden to sit, by ritual, on the silvery old log at the edge. My questing fingers touched the curious roughness of the gray-tendrilled moss which fell, curtainlike, from the trees. Sounds from the droning afternoon penetrated my little cave: A jay cried raucously; a fish plopped in the purling water; in the distance a dog yapped steadily. Out in the bottom the grass parted before a snake's stealthy glide. High in the blue sweep of sky a lone buzzard circled. A bright, humming quiet hung over all.

I went up to the crown of the hill which overlooked the green-gold fields, the browning corn patch, red roofed house and barn, on to the distant band of dust that was the road to home. Here were three ancient mock orange trees which grew so closely that they could have been one. I stared up into the endless caverns of twisted branches and trembling leaves that melted into secret greenness, thinking with a sense of trepidation that they might reach up to the land of giants. They were titans, those trees; several times, in tears over some small thing or large, I had clung to their rough bark, feeling a form of comfort at their height and strength in a shifting world. I stood for a long moment, looking at the panorama, then I fled down the long sweep of hill with the doleful hound dogs baying at my heels, the mad summer ecstasy upon me.

The afternoon was shading softly toward evening as I reached the house and slithered in the screen door, for once without banging it. The tea glasses sat in a neat row on the drainboard and the cake plate stood almost empty on the table. I popped a forgotten morsel in my mouth and started on noiseless bare feet for the parlor. I was stopped by the sound of Cousin Viola's voice as I had never heard it, full of tension and pain, hard at the edges, each word etched in vitriol. The fluttery manner, blurriness, genteel sweetness—all were gone.

"I tell you, Edna, I've stood it just as long as I can. George doesn't even see me any more. I'm just a thing to cook, wash, iron, and feed those everlasting hound dogs. Maybe if there'd been children . . . We're getting old now. There's more tenderness in the way he pats those animals than there ever was with me, even years ago."

A palpable sense of disaster came over me as I peeped around the door in curiosity and horror. She sat in a disconsolate lump on the couch, clenched hands shaking, lips twitching. She was not crying; that would have been bearable. Her sad middle-aged face, so carefully rouged and powdered, was blotchy and streaked. She rushed on.

"It wouldn't do any good to leave. Where would I go? The awful thing is, George wouldn't know what I was talking about if I tried to tell him. When we were younger it didn't matter that we couldn't talk too much, but it matters now. God! How it matters!"

I felt cold at the long anguish in her voice. So that was what it was like to be grown up. Goosebumps stood out on my arms and my usually volatile stomach recoiled as I looked again, unable to turn away. My always positive aunt put her arms around Cousin Viola and made the sensible, soothing sounds she did so well. She had routed many a green peach stomach ache for me. But Cousin Viola jerked away furiously and her face ran together in little lines.

"There's just nothing. Nothing." The words hung there in that dim parlor that I would hate from this time on. I have remembered that tone and have heard it but few times since—matter of fact, devoid of life and hope, paralyzing. I could bear it no longer; the world that had been so right was suddenly awry and faintly sickening in the way that it sometimes was when we played "Swing the Statue" and I whirled too long. I was afraid of that which had no name. My hand was heavy on the door knob and my voice seemed to come from a distance; it was high, trembling, with the sheen of tears on it.

"What's the matter?"

Cousin Viola was once more soft as pigeon down. "Nothing, dear. Nothing at all. Your auntie and I have just been having a nice chat. Now, honey, just run and find your daddy. I expect he'll be getting ready to go."

I stared at her, knowing that I disliked her. Her face still shook but her mouth said things were all right. Wrongness was a miasma in the air. There was desolation behind the words. I recognized it because I felt it when I woke sometimes in the depths of night when the morning is years away and saw strange shapes in my room. Cousin Viola and I seemed the same age then. But she said one thing and meant another. What was real? I issued my own defiance of fear.

"No. I don't want to. I won't."

I chewed my thumb end and dug my big toe deep in the patterned carpet. Cousin Viola sank back on the couch, her fading hair tangled in the fringed cover. My aunt stood up, slapping her knee. The birch switches swished in her eyes. Her voice was that of authority and certainty.

"Go do what Cousin Viola says. This very instant. Don't let me have to say it again."

I saw her strength and my own was renewed; the rock to which I held was still sure and steady. I ran and was glad to run. It was ridiculously good to see the tall, spare form of my father coming up the steps, draining his glass, remarking irritably that it was past time to go and what were we doing anyway?

Our goodbyes were quick. Cousin Viola handed me a jar of plums, smoothing my hair with nervous fingers. She appeared not to see my instinctive move backward but her eyes were empty above the smile. Cousin George lifted an abstracted hand in farewell; his attention never left the gun he was readying for the morning's hunt.

Going home I lay on the back seat of the car with my head pushed down into the mustiness, letting the bumps and jerks lull me. For once I did not listen to the murmured conversation from the front. The strangely bruising afternoon had rendered me vaguely unhappy for things I could not understand and the tears ran warm and salt over my dirty fingers.

Never had home been so welcome. We sat rocking on the porch in the paling evening with the trees limned dark against the saffron sky. A cricket rasped hesitantly. The fireflies flickered on in the hedge. The old green swing creaked back and forth companionably as the dog snuffled in her sleep. Mist rose white in the hollow; a bird call came round and delicate in the twilight.

Slowly the knot in me lessened and peace settled on my shoulders. The calm and comfort of sure things was all about; even if the world appeared strange and hurting this remained. We smiled at each other in a tenderness as real as the tension had been. This day bound us in a circle all our own, in a kindness and warmth that was a seal against the inexplicable. So my world came right as we sat there in the calm of the Lord's day, in the warm coming darkness, yawning, commenting, slapping a stray mosquito, touching the velvet ears of the dog.

Sunday has a different smell.

FROM

Southern Legacy

HODDING CARTER

WHEN I WAS a brash youngster of seventeen, with a year in a Yankee college behind me, I visited my maternal grandmother in Concordia Parish, Louisiana, across the river from Natchez.

She was a dainty little lady, given to delicate scents and a hairdo that displayed her white curls to advantage; but her femininity was no more pronounced than was her domination over the conglomeration of daughters, nephews, nieces, and grandchildren who surrounded her as permanent guests or occasional visitors.

There were eighteen of us thus gathered together at midday dinner on a summer day of my visit back in 1924. Grandmother presided at the head of the table. I sat midway at her left and, in the hubbub of unrelated conversation, I was learnedly holding forth to a cousin on the evils of the resurgent Ku Klux Klan. I had just said that the Klan was a rotten, no-good, and un-American organization, or words to that effect, when I became conscious of frightened signals from my cousin and a sudden, awesome hush. I looked toward the head of the table. Obviously grandmother was about to speak to us.

But grandmother's words were for no one but me. She had heard only my concluding comment on the Klan, and her failure to understand that it was not *the* Klan I was castigating, but only a spurious, latter-day imitation thereof, was my undoing.

"Stand up, young man," she said. She had a flair for the dramatic. I stood up.

"Your year up North seems to have disagreed with you," she began. "Did they teach you to say what you have just said about the Ku Klux Klan?"

It was too late to rectify her error or mine. For a long five minutes grandmother retold the warm, familiar story. With her own hands she had made my grandfather's Klan robes. Practically singlehanded, though with some minor assistance from a legendary Captain Norwood—"the second most handsome man in the Confederate Army"—grandfather had saved a large section of the South through some well-timed night riding and an unerring aim. Had it not been for grandfather and a few lesser giants in the land, no man's life and no white woman's virtue would have been safe. I had heard the story since childhood, loved it, believed it, believe some part of it even today. But I had gone back on my raising. I had denounced the Klan. I was a traitor to the South, thanks to my parents' grave mistake in permitting me to go to college in Maine.

I tried once, but only once, to interrupt with an explanation. My cousins were giggling. One or two aunts were nodding ready approval of grandmother's fury. I was hopelessly lost.

"Leave the table, young man," grandmother concluded. "You may apologize to me when we have finished dinner."

Later, of course, I received a qualified pardon after grandmother finally came to understand that I meant no sacrilege. But thereafter, in her presence, I kept my thoughts on the Klan, past, present, or future, to myself.

I have told this story many times since that uncomfortable dinner hour, as an amusing anecdote of my youth. I did not understand its implications for a long time, nor, I suspect, did many who heard the tale. For it seemed to be simply one of those incomprehensible Southern incidents, having no reference to things as they are and altogether out of place in the world today.

But this interpretation is wrong.

I was born forty-two years ago, just midway between the close of the War Between the States and the present. Similarly located in meaningful time are hundreds of thousands, even millions, of white Southerners of my age and older, who represent the thinking, the political directions, the economic attitudes of our badgered South. Almost every one of us, farmer, city man, mountaineer, teacher, preacher, poor white or so-called "Bourbon," was close to some fabulous father or grandfather, some remembering grandmother, to whom, in our childhood and even our young manhood, the war and its aftermath was a personal, bitter, and sacred reality. And if, in their declining years, they embroidered fact with fancy, our inheritance was no less real, our conviction of wrongful treatment no less strong, our resultant idealization no less significant.

For, in folk history, the eighty-four years since Appomattox is a short span, especially for people who were on the losing side. I remember bicycling through Ireland once, in the mid-twenties, and stopping for a cup of water at a peasant's hut. Rebellion was unusually rife in Ireland then, and the old woman with whom I chatted had nothing good to say for the English. Just four miles up the road, she told me, the English had tied 200 God-fearing Irishmen to stakes and burned them. I was incredulous, for I had not come across this grim tale in any reports of the Black and Tan or rebel excesses.

"My God," I exclaimed, "when did they do that?"

"It was Cromwell," she said. "The dir-r-ty dog."

The South is scarcely less persevering in remembering its dirty dogs, in bedaubing some who were not dirty, and in discrediting what might be offered as the other side of the story. Did we not have our grandfathers and grandmothers as proof? Do we not remember the old men from the Confederate home, men still hale in 1916, whose rebel yells turned the first showings of *The Birth of a Nation* into emotional pandemonium and who assured the children of nine and ten that life had been just like that, only worse? It was as true as gospel itself that Ben Butler had stolen spoons and ordered his troops to despoil the women at New Orleans; that Sherman was Satan incarnate who laughed at his bummers' toll of starving women and children along his line of march, and that Thaddeus Stevens took a Negro wife, and sought to provide white Southern wives for his Negro cohorts.

Profane history has not triumphed over such articles of faith. And, as a corollary, some of the bittersweet morsels which fed our minds have not themselves been made more savory by actual history. While in school in the East, I met and liked a student of considerable means. His grandfather, who shall be nameless here, actually gave the family fortune its sizable start by dishonest trafficking in federally seized cotton. About the time this Eastern fortune was being accumulated in the immediate wake of the war, my greatgrandmother, whose husband had been mortally wounded at Shiloh, journeyed to Washington to seek a presidential pardon for herself so that she could regain her modest properties in New Orleans. We have that pardon, signed by Andrew Johnson. In it the engraved descriptive phrase, "the late traitor," was amended in ink, with the word "traitress" scrawled above the scratched-out "traitor," and her name following thereafter. And speaking of contraband-cotton fortunes, my mother's family dreamed for years of the windfall that would come our way when Congress approved the Southern cotton claims. Only Congress never did.

These unseparated truths and fantasies did strange things to those of us who stand midway in the eighty-four-year time span. They explained inertia and genteel poverty too well. My Ku Klux grandfather, I was convinced, would have left unnumbered acres to his widow had it not been for war and Reconstruction; and I still remember my shocked disbelief when my wryly humorous mother once suggested that another reason was his postwar inability to fill inside straights when the chips represented cotton land. They provided a background which gave approval to a childish game of draping ourselves in white sheets and chasing Negro children through the woods with guns. They gave sanctity to the pronouncements of our Episcopal rector's son, who would argue with the high-school history teacher and declare baldly that Abraham Lincoln was an atheist and the illegitimate brother of Jefferson Davis, and that slavery was the foreordained and natural state of Africans.

Every now and then since those earlier days, I remind myself hopefully that, after all, these determining factors were waning even in my childhood. My own three sons would not be thus conditioned by any past. We would see to it, my wife and I, that their pride in the South and its past would be balanced, as they grew up, with proper emphasis upon the new South and the nation of which it is an irrevocable and generally wholesome part. None of that ancestor-worship business for them, no sir. And this shaping would be easy, because they had lived away from the South for almost five years during the recent war: the oldest from his sixth to his eleventh year, the second from his first year to his sixth. Even the baby, born in Washington, had been almost a Northerner for a year.

I am not so sure about that now. In June, 1946, after only a year of being home in Mississippi, we started out for our annual summer in Maine. The first night's stop was at Chattanooga, and that meant a trip to the top of Lookout Mountain and considerable, if improvised, emphasis upon a long-ago battle among the clouds. The end of the second day brought us to Lexington, Virginia. We left Lee Chapel at Washington and Lee University, laden with Confederate flags, our minds past-haunted with the words of the soft-spoken curator, whose first assumption that we were "non-Southern" I had corrected hastily and almost indignantly. Later in the morning, the older boys became starry-eyed and silent at VMI before the proud canvas that depicted the charge of the boy cadets of VMI at New Market; and we left Lexington with the Stars and Bars waving wildly from the windows of the car. In the late afternoon of that day we reached Gettysburg, and that was our undoing. First, we visited the sad, majestic battlefield, and then the ghost-ridden museum, in whose amphitheater one can look down upon an electrically controlled topographical map of Gettysburg, where changing battalions of red and blue lights illustrate the lecturer's account of the bloody campaign. When the lecturer finished, the two older boys were disconsolate.

"That was a tough one for us to lose," Hodding III said moodily. "Anyhow, we killed more of them than they did of us, didn't we?"

I roused myself from inwardly cursing at Longstreet and wondering where in hell Stuart could have been all that time, to remind him that it all happened for the best, and, anyway, where would we be today if we weren't a united country?

So there it is, this persistent initial legacy. Play "America" or the "Star Spangled Banner" before a Southern audience, and it will stand at required attention. Play "Dixie" and you had better stick cotton in your ears.

Let alone, the spirit of which these stories are symbols is harmless enough; a little pathetic perhaps, and naïve and provincial. Let alone, it will, of course, wear itself out someday. Not tomorrow or next year or the next. But someday. But it is not let alone by those least worthy to capitalize upon it, the politicians who subvert the Southern legacies to confuse their constituents and perpetuate themselves, though it can be said honestly that such instruments are losing their effectiveness.

Meanwhile, let us see this stubborn legacy for what it is. A defensive thing which stiffens the spine of the colonially exploited and prideful and poor against the urban and sophisticated and economically entrenched. A rallying point for conservatism against the impact of change and of ideas. A shared past, drawing together a long-related folk against the newcomer and the alien. A shield against the constant thrusting from the outside. And a tragically employed excuse for wrongs since committed and right things left undone.

This emotional heritage is difficult of understanding for the detached, present-minded, and amiable non-Southerners to whom that war of our grandfathers is a struggle happily over, properly won by the side which should have won, and now properly relegated to the limbo of the past. It is even more difficult of understanding for those new, zealous historians who take as a starting point the assumption that the South deserved whatever it got; that, in fact, its Bourbons came off too lightly; and that the war and Reconstruction were essentially a struggle between the submerged classes—black and white in the South lumped carefully together—on the one side, and on the other, the spirit of reaction so oversimply represented by a diabolical figure, the ante- and post-bellum Southern Planter.

Nevertheless, the stories told by aging men and women to young boys persist, and there is more than legend to them. What my grandmother remembered in microcosm represented a macrocosm of disaster whose material and spiritual effects are as readily recognizable to the psychologist as to the historian. The South's wealth was as completely gone at the close of the Civil War as is that of any postwar European country today, and there was no Marshall Plan. Its banks were closed, its currency without value, its bonds and insurance worthless too. Its principal single item of wealth, two billion dollars' worth of slaves, was destroyed. The South's largest cities were ravaged by bombardment and fire, many of its smaller towns were desolated, and the scorched-earth technique had left its countryside, where the Union armies had passed, a desert. Two thirds of its railroads were in ruins. Land dropped in value from $50.00 to as low as $3.00 an acre and was sold for taxes, and at the close of 1865 an estimated 500,000 people in three states alone existed at starvation levels. Returning Confederates, with no clothing other than their ragged uniforms, were forced to remove the military buttons—or have them forcibly removed by Negro troops. Those among them who had been veterans of earlier American wars were stricken from the pension lists. Though courts still functioned, military commissions tried defendants in cases far removed from their ordinary jurisdiction, and the longest military occupation in modern history was accompanied by a political vengefulness that healed no wounds.

These things, however vaguely identified, were in my grandmother's mind as she lectured me there at the dinner table. Secondhand, they have persisted in the memory of many others and they cannot be shrugged off.

And I am thereby reminded of another story which, better than any other I have heard, illustrates this Southern legacy of resentment over the outcome of an ancient war. The story's heroine is in her eighties, the daughter of one of Stonewall Jackson's bodyguard, and indomitably Virginian. Not so many years ago, at an age when few of us would be interested in further pursuit of learning, she enrolled in a university summer course in the history of the South. One day during the session, the lecturer made the usual comment, namely, that it was best that the war had ended with a Northern victory. Later on during his talk he made the same apologetic interjection. The smoldering little lady could stand his treason no longer. She rose from her chair and interrupted him.

"Professor," she challenged, "you keep saying that it was best that the North won the war. But how do you know? We didn't get a chance to even *try* it our way."

FROM

My Life and "The Times"

TURNER CATLEDGE

A YOUTH IN MISSISSIPPI

I WAS BORN ON MARCH 17, 1901, on my Grandfather Catledge's three-hundred-acre farm near the little community of New Prospect, in Choctaw County, in central Mississippi. My parents lived there until I was three, when we moved to Philadelphia, Mississippi, and thereafter I would often return for visits to the farm. As a boy, it seemed to me that I knew two very different and distinct worlds. One was my Grandfather Catledge's farm, where I felt free and independent, where I could do as I pleased with no one looking over my shoulder. The other world was Philadelphia, where, as part of a small Southern community and of my mother's large, closely-knit family, I was subject to influences that did much to make me the man I became.

My parents were Lee Johnston Catledge and Willie Anna Turner. I was their second child; my sister Bessie preceded me by about eighteen months. My parents had been married in 1898, when my father was twenty-seven and my mother thirty-one. I am almost certain my parents met at church, there in the New Prospect community, for both were quite devout. It happened that he was a Baptist and she a Presbyterian, and they might never have met except that my father sometimes "crossed over" and attended the Presbyterian church because his mother was one.

Both my grandfathers served in the Confederate Army as very young men. My mother's parents were James Andrew Turner and Mary Hanna Turner. They were married while still in their teens, soon after he returned from the war. At age fifteen or so he had joined General Nathan Bedford Forrest's Third Army, taking with him his own horse, a saber he had forged in his father's blacksmith shop, and two sides of salt pork. His mother, my great-grandmother, used to tell how Jimmy rode off to war, his legs sticking out over the two sides of bacon.

Jim and Mary Turner had fourteen children, all of whom survived to a ripe age. My mother was their first child, and in time she became a kind of "deputy mother" to her thirteen younger brothers and sisters. This responsibility was one reason she did not marry until she was thirty-one.

My Grandmother Turner's people, the Hannas, had been small slaveholders; she inherited several slaves just before the Civil War began, but they were soon freed by proclamation. My Grandfather Catledge's people were farmers but not slaveholders. Thus, in the community where my parents lived, there were several Negro families named Hanna and Turner, but none named Catledge. My Grandfather Catledge was what was called a subsistence farmer, which meant that his farm produced almost everything he needed. He slaughtered his own meat, grew his own fruits and vegetables (he was noted for his fruit, especially his peaches and watermelon), produced his own soap and sugar, even operated his own blacksmith shop. He was contemptuous of money; if he couldn't produce something himself, he didn't want it. He had, to my knowledge, only three indulgences, roasted peanuts, chewing tobacco, and stick candy.

My father grew up on the farm, but he didn't like farm work. He attended only a small church college, but he was a sensitive and well-read man, and had an abiding interest in politics and public issues. He taught school for a few years before his marriage, and he had several types of jobs throughout his life, but he never really found his niche. I think this was due partly to ill-health and partly to his temperament. Several times in his early years, when some venture had not worked out, he would return to the security of his father's farm as he did at the time of my birth.

When I was three, our family moved to Philadelphia, where two of my mother's brothers were opening a hardware store. Two other Turner brothers had successfully operated a hardware store in the little town of McCool, in Attala County, so two younger brothers decided to try their luck in Philadelphia. It was then a community of less than a thousand people, and because it was on a new railroad line, the town was expected to boom.

The Turner brothers offered my father a job as clerk and bookkeeper in their new store, primarily because they wanted their beloved older sister with them. My father accepted the offer and we set out by horse and wagon on the two-day trip to Neshoba

County. We camped at night beside a stream and set lines to catch fish for breakfast. We had plenty of fresh milk on our journey, because we'd brought our cow with us.

The Philadelphia we had moved to was a rough, raw town. A few wooden houses were perched up on a red clay hill, and down by the new railroad tracks was a Negro section called Froggy Bottom. There were no sidewalks, nor water nor sewage system, and pigs roamed the streets. Yet Philadelphia was growing; my mother would recall that when we first arrived she could hear a constant beat of carpenters' hammers throughout the town. In addition to my father's job in the hardware store, it had been arranged that we would live in, and my mother operate, a small boardinghouse. It would cater to the swarms of salesmen, politicians, merchants, and other travelers who we thought would be coming to Philadelphia.

Neither the boardinghouse nor my father's job in the hardware store worked out as anticipated. The boardinghouse didn't succeed because there simply weren't as many travelers as we'd hoped. My father's lack of success at the hardware store is more complicated.

The muted conflict between my father and my uncles, the Turner brothers, was an important influence on my youth. They were very different sorts of men. The Turners were hard-working, tight-lipped, frugal men, men who knew what they wanted and how to get it. My father was not like that. My uncles regarded him as a ne'er-do-well and some of them were bitter that he didn't provide better for their beloved sister. They were fine men, and I respected them, but they were not tolerant or always tactful and I often overheard their scathing remarks to one another about my father. It was a hard position for a young boy. The Turner brothers prospered while my family stayed poor. All this, combined with my mother's high hopes for my future, early instilled in me an intense desire to prove myself, to show the Turners that a Catledge could succeed as well as they had.

My mother, I hasten to say, always stood by my father in our muted family disputes. She said that ill-health was the cause of his difficulties, and it is true that he died of a heart disorder at age fifty-two, and his six brothers also died at relatively early ages—two in infancy.

My father was a tall, thin, handsome man who always wore a mustache. He and his brothers were quite musical, and the Catledge Brothers Quartet was well known in our community's churches for its gospel singing. I don't know where he acquired the talent, but he was somewhat of a tap dancer; at my Grandfather's farm the few Negroes who lived around would often plead, "Mr. Lee, show us some steps," and he would oblige them with the few steps in his routine. But that was about as close as he got to frivolity. He was a religious man and served as superintendent of the Baptist Sunday school in Philadelphia. He rarely took a drink and I never heard him utter a word of profanity.

He was one of the two or three best-informed men in our town. He read the Memphis *Commercial Appeal* every day to keep abreast of current issues and he discussed politics with anyone who'd take him on. None of these qualities, however, helped him succeed in my uncles' terms and in a short time he withdrew from the hardware store.

After that, for some years, he often wasn't working. He spent a lot of his time at the courthouse, talking politics with the other men who hung out there. Before his marriage back in Choctaw County, he had worked as a deputy sheriff and had run unsuccessfully for sheriff. When I was about six he was elected the first mayor of Philadelphia. Besides prestige, the job provided a $25-a-month salary, which the Catledge family was glad to have. He was elected to a second term but for some reason—I never knew the story—he resigned before the term was up. As mayor he was the town's chief judicial officer, and on Monday mornings he'd hand out $2 and $5 fines to all the Negroes and poor whites who'd been tossed in jail on Saturday night for drinking or brawling. As mayor, he was empowered to perform weddings; I remember going with him one Sunday morning to a Negro wedding for which he received the grand fee of fifty cents.

After he quit as mayor, he continued to spend most of his time at the courthouse, talking politics, sometimes working in the courthouse offices. He was quite an expert on deeds, property records, and other courthouse affairs. He could add two rows of figures at the same time. During the First World War, he went to work as a clerk at the railroad station. He became a fervent union member, and he stayed at that job until ill-health forced his retirement. He died in 1924.

My mother was very unlike my father. As the oldest of fourteen children she learned at an early age to be a leader. She was a tireless worker. After our boardinghouse ceased to make much money she took in sewing—for she was an expert seamstress. We were poor people but my mother substituted pride for money—in that sense, there was no one richer than my mother.

She dominated my father and, by her force of character, she became a leading figure in the community. She was always heard from when a family or community decision was being made. She was a sentimental woman, quick to shed tears about other people's troubles, but rarely about her own. A strict Presbyterian and a firm believer in predestination, she believed that everything in her life had been written in the Book at the beginning of time. Among other things, this made her entirely fearless; if a cyclone came through the town, as they often did, she would simply ignore it. If the Lord wanted her, he would take her, and His will was not to be challenged. One of her favorite hymns began, "What a friend we have in Jesus," and she meant that literally, for she considered the Lord a close personal friend.

As more and more of my mother's younger brothers and sisters moved to Philadelphia, she remained the center of Turner family life. She was always on call during births and sicknesses, and she was as free with her advice as with her assistance. In later life, she raised the children of three of her brothers whose wives had died. I suppose some of her in-laws resented her, but her own kin loved her and were in awe of her. I remember when my Uncle Joe Turner, then a middle-aged man, took up smoking, he'd always dispose of his cigarette if my mother was coming. Once she appeared unexpectedly and he stuck his burning cigarette into his pocket and set his pants afire.

My mother thought her family could do no wrong, and few outsiders could, in her mind, measure up to our standards. She could be highly critical of other people and, for all her goodness, she was lacking in tolerance. She had little use for people who indulged in drinking, smoking, gambling, or idleness. Dancing to her was a mortal sin, at least so far as it involved the body contact of opposite sexes.

In the years after 1903, Philadelphia began to fill with Turners. Eventually, all of my mother's five sisters and all but one of her eight brothers settled there—and the missing brother settled in a nearby community. All of them married except one sister, and I was one of forty-two first cousins, some thirty of whom are still living. In 1912, my Grandmother and Grandfather Turner moved over from McCool, officially making Philadelphia the family base of operations.

My mother and her brothers and sisters had grown up poor and they yearned for financial security. Unlike my father—or me—the Turners were not interested in politics, only in the church and material success. They achieved it. All of the brothers, as they arrived in town, worked in the hardware store—for a time they even operated two hardware stores, across the street from each other. Then, as they became settled, most of them branched out into other businesses. My Uncle Jim owned a drugstore, Homer and Joe ran a grocery. Sam had the Ford agency. Homer, after returning from World War I, branched out into the lumber business with his father-in-law.

To this day, the Turners are prominent people in Philadelphia. I have kept in close touch with many of them over the years, although my career has taken me far from Mississippi. Perhaps I got to know them better in 1963, when our little town attracted worldwide attention because some of its Ku Klux Klansmen murdered three civil-rights workers. At that time, I was shocked and saddened to see that the good people of Philadelphia, certain members of my family included, did not step forward to condemn the murderers. I felt that I had misread their natures, that I had changed but they had not, and that in many ways I had romanticized the little town where I grew up. As I wrote then to a friend in Philadelphia, Florence Mars, one of the few citizens who was carrying the banner of decency, "Where oh where are those decent people I used to know? Most, of course, are over there on the hill, but where are their descendants?" And yet, in honesty, I had to ask myself what I would have done in their place, under the same pressures, and sometimes I'd almost break into a cold sweat thinking about that question.

I grew up, of course, under a system of total segregation and it did not occur to me to challenge that system, nor did it to many people in that time and place. Yet I was always taught to treat Negroes with respect. If I used the word "nigger," for example when I was playing with Negro children, I'd get a licking, and I was taught to regard whites who did use that word as themselves inferior. We were taught to call older Negroes "uncle" and "aunt"; that sounds paternalistic today but we meant it as a sign of respect and affection. We considered many Negroes our friends. They were as poor as we, as Southern as we, as religious as we, and we valued them despite the great social barrier between us.

The Negroes were subject to terrible cruelty from what we called the white trash. To these poor, ignorant whites, it was a sign of manhood to mistreat helpless Negroes. In the twenties and later, the Negroes' greatest fear was of course the Ku Klux Klan. My father always despised the Klan and the politicians who catered to it—in our house the name of Bilbo, then a state politician and later the famous racist Senator, was a dirty word. I remember once when a pro-Klan preacher came to town for a revival meeting, and during the service six Klansmen walked in dressed in their full regalia and made a contribution. My father stood up and walked out and about half the congregation followed him.

I am not by nature a crusader. I thought very little about the plight of Negroes during my early newspaper career. Separate but equal was the law of the land and it did not occur to me to challenge it. My thinking changed slowly, as did the nation's. When the great Supreme Court decisions of the 1950s came down, outlawing various forms of segregation, I realized that they were right, that segregation in public institutions and facilities cannot be tolerated.

I served as managing editor and executive editor of the *New York Times* in 1951–64, some of the most turbulent years of the Negro revolution. Other men wrote the editorials, but I saw it as my job to ensure that the *Times* printed the fullest possible presentation of the facts about the racial situation in America. But I will say more about that later.

When I look back on my boyhood, it is the good memories I recall, not the problems. I was a poor boy but I didn't know it. There were people in our town who owned big houses or automobiles but I didn't think much about that or ever feel resentful. Even though we were poor my mother's standing in the community made us "quality folk." The church was a great leveler in small Southern communities; rich and poor stood the same there. The church was also a great disciplinary force. If I missed church, I felt terribly guilty about it. Our community churches were active in the prohibition cause, and I must have signed the temperance pledge a dozen times before I was twelve years old, but I fear that all these vows of sobriety only made me all the more curious about that forbidden fruit called whiskey.

I remember the first time I got really drunk. I was home on a college vacation and had gone over to the Neshoba County Fair where I ran into some fellows who had a fruit jar of moonshine liquor. I don't know what an LSD trip is like, but it can't be much more debilitating than a young man's first encounter with corn whiskey. My uncles later found out about my spree but they never told my mother about it.

When I was ten or so, I started working at part-time jobs. That was one way my uncles would help my mother indirectly, by seeing that I had a job on weekends and in the summers. So I skipped around from the grocery store to the hardware store to the drugstore to the automobile agency. Few of the Turners ever worked for anyone else; it was a sort of tribal system with the family determined to take care of its own.

Most often I worked at the grocery store owned by my uncles Homer and Joe. They were the youngest of the brothers and the ones I was the closest to. Uncle Joe never went past the seventh grade in school but he became the wealthiest of the Turners. I remember when I eventually left Philadelphia, to start my newspaper career, Joe took me to the station, and as the train came in he handed me a checkbook. "Don't ever borrow money," he said. "If you need money, write a check on me." That was the way it was with him and his brothers: each one took care of the others. I often needed money in the next few years but I never wrote that check. My uncles Joe and Homer were as good friends as I ever had, but I was finished with living off my uncles.

My schooling, by Mississippi standards, was quite good. Schools then were entirely autonomous; whether they were good or bad depended on the quality of the teachers the community could attract. Fortunately, the Philadelphia high school in my time was one of the best in the state. The principal was a man named Orvis Van Cleave, a graduate of Columbia, and he had assembled an excellent faculty, most of them college graduates. Thus, in high school I was able to study Latin, German, physics, and other courses that might not have been available elsewhere. My father always encouraged me to take the hardest courses they offered. Latin was a must.

I was always a good student. I had a quick and retentive mind and I was a hard worker. I enjoyed school, particularly English composition, in which I made my best grades, but I must admit that I was driven less by a pure quest for knowledge than by a desire to please and be praised by my teachers, my family, and our friends. I could never forget how my mother was counting on me. My success would compensate for my father's failures. I was her pride and joy, her hope of security in years to come.

My obligation seemed even greater after an eye disease struck my older sister, Bessie, when she was twelve, leaving her nearly blind. She had to go to the state institute for the blind, in Jackson, to continue her schooling. She was, like our mother, a brave and religious person, who never complained or showed self-pity. Eventually her eyesight improved and she married and bore two children.

I had to drop out of school and work one semester when my father was ill and make up the lost courses by taking a double load the next year. And in my senior year my Uncle Homer was drafted into the army and I was "drafted" to do the bookkeeping at his grocery store, but I managed to juggle that job and my schoolwork too. I was helped by the fact that I was never an athlete, so if I wasn't working I could spend my time studying.

There were, of course, many hours in my childhood when I was neither working nor studying—hours I spent enjoying the wonderful variety of people in that little town. As a storyteller, which I've been accused of being, I got a lot of mileage out of Philadelphia. There were an abundance of colorful characters and memorable events there, or so it seemed to a boy who had never known any other world.

Because of my father, I grew up interested in politics and I liked to spend my spare time at the courthouse watching trials; before I was bitten by the newspaper bug, I thought I would become a lawyer. Sometimes at the courthouse I would encounter a boy of about my age named Jim Eastland, the future Senator, who would be with his father, Woods Eastland, the district attorney for our area. Besides the trials, I remember vividly the scene twice each year, at the opening of the court terms, when the traveling horse traders came to town with long strings of horses to trade and sell. We called the traders "gypsies" because they camped on the outskirts of town, and everyone was suspicious of them. The horse trading often led to angry words and fights. Yet almost everyone was lured on by the hope of a bargain. Mississippi's greatest storyteller, William Faulkner, captured the flavor of these events perfectly in one of his most famous stories, "Spotted Horses."

One of the great heroes of my youth was a man named Adam Byrd, a successful lawyer who later became a Chancery Court Judge and after that a Congressman. Byrd lived for a while in our boardinghouse and I first came to admire him one day when my father was about to give me a licking for something and Byrd talked him out of it—in fact, he simply ordered him not to whip me.

He was a large, fine-looking man with a reddish complexion and high cheekbones that bespoke his Indian blood—his mother was one-fourth Indian. Philadelphia was in the heart of the old Choctaw nation. Most of the Choctaws had gone to Oklahoma under the terms of the Dancing Rabbit Treaty, but some had stayed behind and others returned and Byrd was their champion. Quite a few white families in that area had Indian blood and they made no attempt to hide the fact. They hoped (vainly, it turned out) that the federal government would repay the Choctaws for the lands taken from them by the Dancing Rabbit Treaty.

I loved to watch Adam Byrd defend his Indian friends in court. He seemed to me the most exciting man in our community; when I was ten or twelve he was my idol of greatness. When I prayed—as I did every night and at least twice Sundays—the visage of God I saw in my mind's eye was not the white-robed, bearded Deity of the Sunday-school books, but the ruddy Choctaw face of Adam Byrd.

My friend Byrd impressed me a great deal more than the first President of the United States I ever saw. That was in 1908 when my father took me to Jackson to see President William Howard Taft, who was visiting the state fair. My father was invited because he was mayor of Philadelphia. On the train ride to Jackson, people kept telling me, "Young man, you're going to see the President." Finally I asked my father what a President was. Knowing I enjoyed fairy tales, my father told me that a President was the same as a king.

I couldn't sleep that night thinking I would see a king the next day. The next morning my father took us up on the top floor of the tallest building in Jackson, an insurance-company building that was three stories high. From that vast height we watched out a window as the parade started up Capitol Street. I was looking anxiously for the king—a man with a gold-and-diamond crown on his head and a scarlet, fleece-lined robe.

I didn't see him, although there was a fine parade in progress, with marching soldiers and a band and horse-drawn carriages, as automobiles could not be trusted in parades at that time. But where was the king? I kept asking my father until finally he pointed and said, "There he is—that big fat man." I saw the man he meant—for President Taft was very fat—in an open carriage waving to everyone. And I was crestfallen. According to my father, I said disgustedly, "Ah, shucks, he's just a man," and crawled down out of the window.

Years later, in Washington, I told that story to President Taft's son, Senator Robert Taft, and he often asked me to repeat to his friends—"Ah, shucks, he's just a man."

Sometimes I think that encounter when I learned the President was just a man may have left a mark on me, for throughout my newspaper career I was never much awed by great political figures. I tried to treat them with respect, as I did everyone, but I kept in mind that they were just men like me, and I think that attitude helped me along as a Washington correspondent. After all, I had known Adam Byrd.

My Grandfather Turner was an extraordinarily silent man. He could go days hardly uttering a word. On many Sunday afternoons my sister and I were made to share in his meditation. We would sit with him as he rocked in his rocking chair, chewing tobacco but rarely speaking. I hated those silent Sunday afternoons, but looking back I guess the discipline did me no harm.

There were many stories about my grandfather's odd ways—I think today we would call him alienated. When one of his daughters was being married at his home he refused to join the ceremony; he just sat on the porch until it was over. At church he used to terrify visiting preachers by sitting in a corner pew and staring them down. What he was thinking as he sat so silently, we never knew. He never told us.

We older grandchildren were often terrified of him; our parents used to warn that if we weren't good they'd send us to have a talk with Grandpa. Yet I have some happy memories of him too. He used to love to go to the Confederate reunions that would be held in the summers throughout our region of Mississippi, and one summer he took me along as a companion and errand boy. I loved hearing the old-timers describe their exploits in battle, although I sensed that many of the tales were imaginary. My grandfather never told a single story, although he would grin with delight whenever an eyewitness would explode someone's tall tale. It was wonderful listening to those old men, especially when someone would break out a jug of liquor and they would laugh and sing as they recalled the distant battles of their youths.

My grandfather never took a swig with the others. That was another of his peculiarities. He only drank on one day of the year, Christmas. Then he would allow one of his daughters to mix him some eggnog. He would give a nip of it to his sons-in-law, but never to his own sons. Apparently he was willing to corrupt other men's sons but not his own.

One character in my home town was our lone Republican, whom I'll call Mr. Eustace Eubank. Mr. Eubank was an odd individual in many ways. For one thing, he always attended strictly to his own business, which quickly set him apart in our community. But the oddest thing about this old man was his being a Republican. He never admitted being a Republican, but every four years one Republican vote would turn up in the local ballot box and we never doubted who had cast it. And in those days, in Philadelphia, Mississippi, a Republican was as much an oddity as a Communist would be today.

He had other peculiarities. He read books, quoted Shakespeare, and discussed poetry with Brother Arnett, the Presbyterian preacher, and politics with my father. My father respected Mr. Eubank's learning but had some reservations about him because he took a nip now and then.

Mr. Eubank lived over west of the railroad tracks in a little unpainted house with his second wife and three daughters. One of his daughters was in school with me. She was very smart and I'm certain she won most of the literary contests we had at school. But she never got the prize, because the teachers didn't think it would be right to give prizes to a Republican's daughter. Eubank's only work was his gardening, and he grew the biggest tomatoes in Philadelphia. They would slice out as big as saucers. My Uncle Homer used to sell those tomatoes in his grocery store, but he never told customers who'd grown them, as he figured no one would want to eat a Republican tomato. Eubank walked with a limp which, the town legend said, was because he had a wooden leg. The story went that Eubank had been a Union soldier at the battle of Shiloh and had his leg shot off. His fellow Yankees—as we told the story—had run off and left him, but he had been so fortunate as to survive and make his way to our compassionate little community. And yet he'd repaid us by casting that lone Republican vote every four years!

Such was the situation one hot summer, when Eustace Eubank's saga came to a close. That summer my uncles Homer and Joe had bought a Ford car and converted it into a truck. They'd taught me to drive and I was having a wonderful time delivering groceries in it. One hot July day, about noon, I was out in front of the grocery, polishing the Ford, when a Negro boy who worked for us said that my Uncle Joe wanted to see me. I went inside the store and found a gathering of the local power structure: the town marshal, the county sheriff, the owner of the furniture store, a livery-stable keeper, our leading physician, and my Uncle Joe.

I took one look at this assembly and decided they were going to arrest me for speeding. The marshal, Lon Welsh, had been after me several times about exceeding the ten-mile-an-hour speed limit around the courthouse square. So I was ready for the worst when my Uncle Joe put his hand on my shoulder and said, "Turner, Mr. Eubank was found dead in his bed this morning, and I want you to take the truck, go over to his house, get the remains and take them out to the cemetery."

Suddenly the reason for this assembly became clear. The town elders wanted to ensure that our lone Republican was properly laid to rest; they wanted it done promptly, for it was a ghastly hot day. I felt proud to be part of this ceremony, which combined civic, political, and religious significance. A younger boy, Clifford Sanford, was to assist me, and two Negroes from his father's livery stable would dig the grave, but I was in charge. Clifford and I jumped into the Ford, went by Mr. Spivey's furniture store for a coffin, and then I drove us out to the Eubank house. His family led me into a little front room, where a body was lying on a bed under a heavy quilt. I lifted the quilt and there he was, our lone Republican, stiff and cold. I had been born and bred a Democrat, and I couldn't suppress a moment of triumph at the sight.

Our first problem was that Mr. Eubank's body was longer than our coffin, but finally we were able to bend his legs enough to get the lid screwed down. But when we got the coffin out to the Ford truck, I faced another problem. The Eubank family would be coming to the cemetery in a wagon drawn by little mules. Should I drive the Ford slowly, so the mules could keep up in a funeral procession, or should I hurry on to the cemetery and let the family follow as best it could? It was Philadelphia's first motorized funeral, so I had no precedent to follow.

I decided to respect tradition and have a funeral procession. So I drove very slowly, and soon the Ford began heating up. I had to stop every five or ten minutes and run into someone's house for water. Then the fanbelt broke. Meanwhile, I was wondering what sort of religious ceremony would be held. Mr. Eubank had never been seen in church, and we assumed that, being a Republican, he was bound to be an atheist too. So, as our little funeral procession approached the graveyard, I wondered if Mr. Eubank would be laid to rest in the respectable part of the graveyard or across a little gravel road in the Potter's Field. I was pleased to find the mourners waiting around a newly-dug grave in the respectable part of the cemetery, although only three feet from the gravel road.

Standing at the head of the grave was Brother Arnett, the Presbyterian preacher who'd liked to talk about poetry with Mr. Eubank. Brother Arnett led us in a hymn, and read from the Psalms, and then read Tennyson's "Crossing the Bar." Then we lowered the coffin into the grave and everyone present helped shovel dirt onto the coffin. It was a sort of community project. Finally there was the question of a headmarker for the grave. No one seemed very worried about it, now that Mr. Eubank was underground, so I made a marker out of a couple pieces of wood that were in the back of the truck and wrote his name and dates on it, and stuck it in the dirt at the head of the grave.

Then I drove the Ford back to the grocery store, where a lot of people came around to congratulate me on a job well done. A great sense of relief came over the entire community. The Lord had taken away our Republican, and we were pure again.

Thus things stood until November of that year, when the balloting was held in the Presidential election. The balloting was held under a chinaberry tree in the courthouse yard. Not many voters turned out for the general elections, because all the important decisions were made in the Democratic primaries. But the election that fall was important to the Catledge family because my father was earning a dollar and a half as one of the election judges.

I was standing in front of my uncles' grocery, eating some of their cheese and crackers, when I noticed a commotion in the courthouse yard. In those days, when you heard shouting at the courthouse on election day, you waited for the shooting to begin. I was worried about my father's safety. Then, suddenly, I saw the chancery clerk break out of the crowd, race across the courthouse yard, jump over the fence, and come running into my uncles' store, waving his arms and shouting.

"My God, my God," he cried, "that Republican vote has showed up again!"

We had buried the wrong man. Forever after, the community had to live with guilt and shame. The Republican, whoever he was, was not our departed friend Eustace Eubank. He was still in our midst, and we would never know who he was, and everyone was suspected.

There was never any doubt in my mind that I would go to college. I had done well in high school, and I had set my sights on being a professional man, a doctor or a lawyer. My father wanted me to be a lawyer, and I'm sure my mother wanted me to be a Presbyterian preacher. But there was the question of money. The state's finest university, Ole Miss, at Oxford, was too expensive for me. My Uncle Joe would have readily loaned me the money, but I didn't want to be that much in debt to anyone. So I chose Mississippi A & M, now known as Mississippi State University, which was located sixty miles from Philadelphia on a beautiful two-thousand-acre campus near Starkville.

At A & M rooms were free and I could earn my meals by working in the dining hall. It was a military school and I would not have to worry about buying clothes because everyone wore a uniform, supplied from World War I surpluses. I arrived on campus in September, 1918, and went right to work in the mess hall. My job was to serve the food to two tables of twelve boys each; I did this three times a day, seven days a week, for two years. By then I had learned touch-system typing and was able to trade the mess-hall job for one as secretary to one of the deans.

I was just getting settled in my dormitory, an old building known as Polecat Alley (because skunks sometimes occupied its basement), when the great influenza epidemic of 1918 struck the campus. I was among the first to catch the flu and luckily I got over it quickly. But the epidemic spread fast among the three or four thousand students and soon some were dying.

One day an army sergeant rounded up several of us freshmen for emergency duty in the school hospital. We knew boys had been dying there, for we had seen the coffins coming out. The sergeant took us to a big first-floor ward. A nurse was trying to hold down a delirious patient on a bed near the door. "Hold that man," the sergeant ordered me and Peter Minyard, who became my close friend. "He won't last long." The man was a regular soldier, perhaps twenty years old, and even sick and delirious he was strong as a bull. We held him for about an hour until his struggles began to weaken and he died.

Peter and I were quickly assigned to another patient. There was only one doctor in the place; a local veterinarian was helping him. I saw three men die that day. They wouldn't let Peter and me leave. We had gained too much needed experience. After three days I was assigned to be assistant to the undertaker. By then I wanted out of there, so I faked a faint. I didn't know how people fainted so I fell to the floor and kicked my feet. The undertaker reluctantly released me.

Fifty-two people in the college died in that epidemic and by then I was ready to end my college career before it got started. But there was no way to leave; a military school during wartime was like a prison; we couldn't even use a telephone, much less go off the campus. So I went back to waiting tables. There was little academic work that fall, because of the epidemic, the war, and finally the Armistice on November 11. Another unpleasant factor was the hazing that was common in military schools then. The upperclassmen beat us with big saber belts. I hated that—but I did my share of the whipping the next year.

Hundreds of students didn't return to A & M after that awful fall semester, and I was almost one of them. But I knew my parents would be heartbroken if I quit, and I knew it would be wrong for me in the long run, so I went back.

A & M was a land-grant college—a "people's college"—with stress on agriculture and engineering courses. It had four schools: agriculture, science, business, and engineering. While I was there, however, a professor began an "academic course," stressing literature, history, government, and languages, and I took all of those courses I could, although technically I was a business major. Eventually I graduated with honors and an average above 85; much of the credit for my record goes to the instruction I had received in the Philadelphia school.

Being able to type got me a job as secretary to Fitzjohn Wadell, the head of the academic department. He then helped get me a job as assistant to the school's agricultural editor, who sent bulletins on agricultural topics to the state's farmers. I helped write, edit, and distribute these bulletins. It was valuable experience for me and, even more important, in my senior year my classmates elected me editor of the college yearbook.

I think that one reason for my election was that the editorship was a moneymaking post and they knew I needed the money. The editor and business manager got to keep whatever profits they might make from the yearbook, so my senior year was a financial success. I had entered college with $90 loaned to me by my Uncle Joe; I graduated in 1922 with $300.

I was a campus politician from my first day at A & M. The mess-hall job was no fun, but it did help me get to know a lot of people. By the time I became an upperclassman, if a student wanted to be elected to anything at A & M, he was wise to have a talk with four young men: Turner Catledge; Jimmy Ewing, who later became president of a junior college in Mississippi; John Stennis, the future Senator; and Stennis Little, John's cousin, who was captain of the football team.

I was not surprised when John Stennis entered politics and became a Senator. He was an outstanding student, a persuasive speaker, and a born politician even at age seventeen. It happened that John had the best wardrobe of civilian clothes on the campus. Many of us, when we had dates with girls in nearby towns, would borrow John's clothes, and this generosity didn't hurt his popularity.

When I graduated from college I was not prepared for any particular line of work, and there were no corporate recruiters clamoring to hire me. I thought I wanted to go on for further education, preferably in law. The most important thing I had learned in college was simply that, even away from the Turner clan, I could get along with people and usually get them to like me and listen to me.

But there remained the matter of making a living. My uncles assumed I would follow them into business, and they arranged a job for me with a large wholesale hardware firm in Memphis. This was agreeable with me, for I had it in mind to take the job and study law at night. But a depression struck the South that year and one of its casualties was my job in Memphis. After a brief and unsuccessful fling as a door-to-door salesman of aluminum pots and pans in Middle Tennessee, I was back in Philadelphia working for my uncles and wondering if I would spend the rest of my life there. That was what my mother was counting on. My father had by then retired from his railroad job because of his health, and was bedridden most of the time. I was restless and uncertain; I wanted to get out of Philadelphia but I didn't know how to break away. It was then that Clayton Rand, the publisher of our little county paper, the *Neshoba Democrat*, offered me the job that started me on my career as a newspaperman.

A Personal View of the Mississippi Chinese

SUNG GAY CHOW

AS A CHINESE who grew up in Mississippi, I have as an initial impression that my childhood wasn't that bad. Although I was born in China, Cleveland has been my home since I was less than a year old. I don't remember feeling different. I don't even remember experiencing any prejudice as a child. But then I begin to remember bits and pieces of stories that my father once told me about the way it was for his generation, who came primarily in the 1920s and 1930s to the Mississippi Delta as poor immigrants from a rural part of China. And long forgotten words, images, and actions come rushing back.

"Why did Chinese come to Mississippi?" I asked my father. I was fifteen or sixteen then, and I knew many Chinese lived in towns throughout the Delta, the northwest corner of the state. I was trying to understand—as much as I could then—my heritage or what it meant to be Chinese in a region whose cultural divisions included only black and white and whose social structure was firmly fixed by race and class.

"I don't really know," he replied in Chinese. He could tell me that there had been Chinese in the Delta as early as the late 1800s. He could explain that his father—my grandfather—and a nephew had come to the Delta in the 1920s and opened a grocery store in Boyle. And like most Chinese immigrants they couldn't speak English very well. My father could tell me how our family along with three or four others lived in the same house and worked in the same store in Cleveland. But he couldn't tell me why these immigrants chose Mississippi, of all places, as their Promised Land.

At one time, perhaps 3,000 to 4,000 Chinese lived in that corner of Mississippi. There aren't as many now, but I still wonder why so many Chinese came to a state with a history—a tradition—of prejudice and with a society closed to all who were seen as different. Perhaps the climate was suitable. Maybe life in a rural area was more appealing than the crowded slums of San Francisco or

New York City. Maybe these early Chinese immigrants felt life was less expensive here. Some scholars and journalists have written that the early Chinese who settled here were initially hired in the latter half of the 1800s to replace the blacks as field hands. And when these Chinese, who had come in pursuit of the American Dream, realized they were being exploited, they left the cotton fields and moved into the small Delta towns. While this is probably true, Chinese of my father's generation don't remember anyone who picked cotton.

At any rate, these Chinese opened little grocery stores in the black section of the communities, where it was cheaper for them to build and where good English wasn't a priority. Living in rooms at the back of the store, the Chinese did well, and as business increased, so did the size of their stores. Even today, many Chinese have stores with a large percentage of black customers. And anyone who lives in the Delta knows of at least one store owned and operated by a Chinese family. Indeed, at one time you could find a grocery on practically every corner along a single street in Cleveland's black community. Some are still there.

Imagine how hard it must have been for the first ones who came to Mississippi: strangers in another land; separated from wife, family, and home; and isolated by race, culture, and language. Nevertheless, they managed to make enough money in order to live modestly or to return to China and live prosperously. My father knew of a Chinese who owned a grocery store so small that all the canned goods were stacked on shelves behind the counter. Because he neither spoke nor understood English well, he kept a stick that his customers used to point out the items they wanted to buy. When he had to restock his shelves with a particular item, he would take that one remaining item off the shelf and put it under the counter. He would then show it to the salesman, thus indicating what he needed to order.

Many of the Chinese who immigrated to Mississippi in the years before World War II have stories like those told by my father. They are proud of what they have accomplished in building a home and raising a family. They are proud of the success they have made of themselves. If coaxed, they will tell you so.

However, we who came of age in Mississippi in the 1960s and early 1970s know there is more. We know there are other stories about the life of the Chinese in Mississippi, stories perhaps a little more painful in the telling. They aren't told with a hint of pride or with a sense of nostalgia. Instead, they're told with less expression, with a lower voice. But never with anger. That's because for them it's over and done with. They've done what they set out to do, no matter what anybody else said or did to them. Nothing and no one can take away the success they have achieved.

But for us adolescents, we were sensitive to the fact that we were different and that we were considered second-class citizens, more or less. The social status of the Chinese, I think, has always been low (although not as low as that of the blacks). In the years before World War II, Chinese in Mississippi were classified as black. My father said that in some Delta communities we were not admitted to white hospitals. We weren't even allowed in public schools in Bolivar County until the early 1950s.

And my father also noted that when he first came to Cleveland, only one doctor and one dentist accepted the Chinese as patients. We were also denied homes in the white residential areas of some communities. Consequently, the Chinese who lived in the Delta built living quarters behind their stores. (There were economic reasons as well, since most Chinese couldn't have afforded to build both store and house at that time.)

However, the Chinese soon gained an acceptable social image through their hard work and frugality. This rise in social status was due to their economic success, which can be indirectly attributed to the white community. Because a person's social standing within a community is largely dependent upon his occupation, no white was willing to do business with blacks unless he had to; Chinese grocers were thus literally given the black customer. And once it was realized that the Chinese proved to be no threat, either economic or social, the whites removed the black classification and allowed them into the public schools and other institutions. After this occurred, my generation had more contact with the white community than our parents ever did.

The generation of my father had paved the way, so we children had it much easier. We were born into families that were financially secure, and those of us who could bought houses. We had all the material possessions which any middle-class family sought to own.

My generation learned early how fixed the racial and social boundaries were. We soon understood that there were rules—most of them unwritten—that required everyone to toe the line. The

Chinese in Mississippi have always been situated between a white majority and a black minority. We were neither a part of the white community nor a part of the black one. It was as if we occupied a narrow strip of ground between two high fences, one with white people on the other side and one with black people on the other side.

As children, some of us had been able to crawl underneath both fences and see what each society was like. We could even play with the other kids. But as we grew older—it was the seventh grade for me—these kids, now teenagers, began to ignore us. Now, we had to be content just to look through the cracks of the fence and see what white society was doing that we couldn't participate in any longer. Ironically, we treated blacks the same way. We thus made our way down a narrow path between two fences, one which kept the blacks apart from us and another which kept us from the whites.

One should understand, too, that many Chinese prefer life that way. All three races are different, they say, and it's futile trying to integrate them. Sure, you might be able to do it to a certain extent, but never, ever, fully. Not yet anyway. You can do business with each other. You might be able to exchange pleasantries with each other on the street. But you won't have the kind of relationship that is indicative of people who truly interact. The majority of people in Mississippi, I think, accept this coexistence without question.

My generation was the first to have an opportunity to go to college, and our parents urged us to do so. Chinese highly value education, and we have always been told to apply that deeply instilled work ethic to our studies. Our parents insisted that we had to be educated in order to make money. That meant majoring in a technical field or in the sciences. We listened to our parents and studied engineering or pharmacy, even though some of us preferred English or history. "It is all right for your sister to major in the humanities, but as the husband and father of your family you will need a job that pays well," said our parents.

To be sure, we wanted to make money, but I never thought that we were as driven to succeed economically as our parents were. Instead, we were more interested in becoming part of the mainstream, part of the class with power. To the despair of our parents, we aspired to be assimilated into white society.

What we learned and what we became during and after college

distanced us from our parents and our heritage. We formed certain perspectives, held different interests, and had conflicting attitudes which set us apart from the previous generation. After college, some of us did return to the Delta and worked in the family store. Others also stayed in Mississippi but worked in occupations unrelated to the grocery business. But some also left the state after finding the gap between Chinese and white society too wide to bridge and realizing that they would never be accepted fully in white society. As one of my friends, who grew up in Greenville and lives now in San Francisco, says, "When I worked in Mississippi, I was always made aware that I was different, that I was the exotic one. In San Francisco I don't have that problem."

Those who continue to live in Mississippi have tried hard to become part of the white community. Being upwardly mobile, some have left the small stores in the black neighborhoods and have opened larger ones on the other side of town. Others, having left the grocery business to their fathers, have become pharmacists, computer programmers, and engineers. Still others have their own businesses, such as gift shops, restaurants, and television repair shops. They have joined civic organizations and have become members of churches. They do charity work, host parties, and give dinners. Some even have an interest in local politics. An increasing number have married members of the white community.

I question, though, whether my generation has really "made it." It is a delusion to think that just because we have gotten out of the store and into pharmacy or engineering we have been accepted into white society. True, the fact that we are economically successful does count for something, but money is only one measure of power and only a minimal means of entrance into white Mississippi society. I think the members of my generation understand that, although they may not admit it.

Take, for example, the occupations some Chinese choose. While they may be employed in high-paying jobs, it is doubtful if any will rise to high management positions that require decision- or policy-making, which is an expression of power in any level of society. Moreover, it seems to me that Chinese know or anticipate risks (such as discrimination) involved in desiring to move upwards in white society. They thus choose disciplines such as engineering and accounting, where they can keep a low profile. The fear of discrimination, too, perhaps accounts for the rarity of Mississippi

Chinese in law and medicine, which are socially prestigious professions within the community. In addition, some Chinese may see themselves as too passive or acquiescent to deal directly with patients and clients.

In considering what it meant to grow up as a Chinese in Mississippi, I have probably stressed too much the differences among the races. Yet, for all the problems concerning ethnic differences and assimilation the Mississippi Chinese have encountered, I find it ironic to think that we have a culture not unlike the rest of Mississippi. To me, what is clearly analogous between the Chinese and Mississippi society is the emphasis placed on family ties and traditional values.

Within the Chinese nuclear family, children still demonstrate their respect for their elders. They grow up working in the grocery store, and at home they help with the housework. We listen as our parents insist we enter a particular discipline of study, even though we might not really want to. And while the father may be the head of the family, it is usually the mother who runs it. In addition, a strong network of relatives exists in most families. Any important occasion, such as a wedding, a birth, or a Chinese holiday, calls for a gathering of relatives to celebrate with a banquet. Such events are very similar to family reunions.

Like the rest of Mississippi, the Chinese are pretty conservative in their lifestyle and politics. Because they are slow to accept change, they prefer to maintain the status quo. Instead of being vocal or assertive, they remain passive and pragmatic. Instead of forcing the issue, they wait for the opportunity for change to present itself. They would rather work within the system than outside it.

Of course, one can say people in other sections of the country also emphasize family, tradition, and a conservative way of life. True, but these traits are more closely identified with the South. One can also say that such traits are characteristically Chinese. However, these attributes are even more strongly reinforced in the Chinese who live in Mississippi. None of the young Mississippi Chinese act like their counterparts elsewhere. For example, the Chinese in California, especially in San Francisco, act more assertively and are more aggressive in their ethnicity. And in the Chinatowns of other cities like San Francisco, street gangs thrive.

With the South as a region changing so rapidly, it is interesting to note that Mississippi Chinese in some ways show more resistance to change, and in this respect they are perhaps more traditionally southern than many southerners.

I suggest that environment has a lot to do with those similarities between the Chinese and the prevalent culture. It is a sense of place—and that place being Mississippi—which reinforces our cultural values and ideals. And while the Mississippi Chinese seem to be disowned or dislocated, we are certainly not detached. We have roots embedded in this place as well.

FROM

A Feast Made for Laughter

CRAIG CLAIBORNE

THERE IS ONE AROMA that, more than any other, rekindles concrete thoughts of my mother in the kitchen. This is the smell of chopped onions, chopped celery, chopped green pepper, and a generous amount of finely minced garlic. This was the basis for, it seems to me in recollection, at least half of the hundreds of dishes that she prepared, and it is a distinctly southern smell. (A great southern chef, Paul Prudhomme of New Orleans, once told me that in Cajun and creole kitchens, chopped onions, celery, and green peppers are referred to as the Holy Trinity.)

And there is one dish, her own creation, and using this base, that I recall most vividly. This was chicken spaghetti, which she almost invariably made for special occasions—birthdays, holidays, Sundays. The boarders and her own family loved it and it has remained throughout my many years in the world of food a special favorite.

There were two holidays each year—Christmas and Thanksgiving—when my mother stipulated that meals would not be served to boarders, all of whom went to visit relatives or friends anyway.

I remember one nonturkey Thanksgiving that came about because the three children in the family announced that they were bored with a daily diet of poultry. A vote was taken. Almost in unison we asked for Mother's baked spaghetti. On that day we had it fresh from the oven for the midday Thanksgiving dinner; reheated for supper.

When the vegetables were cooked (they always remained al dente) a little ground beef was added and a tomato sauce containing cream, Worcestershire sauce, and Tabasco sauce. Worcestershire sauce and Tabasco sauce were primary ingredients in my mother's kitchen. Once the meat and tomato sauce were finished, the time came for the assembly of the dish. A layer of sauce was topped with a layer of cooked spaghetti or vermicelli, a layer of shredded chicken, and a layer of grated Cheddar cheese.

The layers were repeated to the brim of an enormous roasting pan, ending with a layer of cheese. The pan was placed in the oven and baked until it was bubbling throughout and golden brown on top. The spaghetti was served in soup bowls with grated Parmesan cheese and two curious, but oddly complimentary side dishes—sliced garlic pickles and potato chips.

My Mother's Chicken Spaghetti

1 (3½-pound) chicken with giblets
Fresh or canned chicken broth to cover
Salt
3 cups imported Italian peeled tomatoes
7 tablespoons butter
3 tablespoons flour
½ cup heavy cream
⅛ teaspoon grated nutmeg
Freshly ground pepper
½ pound fresh mushrooms
2 cups finely chopped onion
1½ cups finely chopped celery
1½ cups chopped seeded green pepper
1 tablespoon or more finely minced garlic
¼ pound ground beef
¼ pound ground pork
1 bay leaf
½ teaspoon hot red pepper flakes, optional
1 pound spaghetti or spaghettini
½ pound Cheddar cheese, grated (about 2 to 2½ cups)
Freshly grated Parmesan cheese

1. Place the chicken with neck, gizzard, heart, and liver in a kettle and add chicken broth to cover and salt to taste. Partially cover. Bring to the boil and simmer until the chicken is tender without being dry, 35 to 45 minutes. Let cool.

2. Remove the chicken and take the meat from the bones. Shred the meat, cover, and set aside. Return the skin and bones to the kettle and cook the stock down for 30 minutes or longer. There should be 4 to 6 cups of broth. Strain and reserve the broth. Discard the skin and bones.

3. Meanwhile, put the tomatoes in a saucepan and cook down to half the original volume, stirring.

4. Melt 3 tablespoons butter in a saucepan and add the flour, stirring to blend with a wire whisk. When blended and smooth, add 1 cup of the reserved hot broth and the cream, stirring rapidly with the whisk. When thickened and smooth, add the nutmeg, salt, and pepper to taste. Continue cooking, stirring occasionally, for about 10 minutes. Set aside.

5. If the mushrooms are very small, leave them whole. Otherwise, cut them in half or quarter them. Heat 1 tablespoon of butter in a small skillet and add the mushrooms. Cook, shaking the skillet occasionally and stirring, until the mushrooms are golden brown. Set aside.

6. Heat 3 tablespoons of butter in a deep skillet and add the onion.

Cook, stirring, until wilted. Add the celery and green pepper and cook, stirring, for about 5 minutes. Do not overcook. The vegetables should remain crisp-tender.

7. Add the garlic, beef, and pork and cook, stirring and chopping down with the edge of a large metal spoon to break up the meat. Cook just until the meat loses its red color. Add the bay leaf and red pepper flakes, if desired. Add the tomatoes and the white sauce made with the chicken broth. Add the mushrooms.

8. Cook the spaghetti in 3 or 4 quarts of boiling salted water until it is just tender. Do not overcook. Remember that it will cook again when blended with the chicken and meat sauce. Drain the spaghetti and run under cold running water.

9. Spoon enough of the meat sauce over the bottom of a 5- or 6-quart casserole to cover it lightly. Add about one third of the spaghetti. Add about one third of the shredded chicken, a layer of meat sauce, and a layer of grated Cheddar cheese. Continue making layers, ending with a layer of spaghetti topped with a thin layer of meat sauce and grated Cheddar cheese.

10. Pour in up to 2 cups of the reserved chicken broth or enough to almost but not quite cover the top layer of spaghetti. At this point the dish may be left to stand, covered, for up to an hour. If the liquid is absorbed as the dish stands, add a little more chicken broth. Remember that when this dish is baked and served, the sauce will be just a bit soupy rather than thick and clinging.

11. When ready to bake, preheat the oven to 350 degrees.

12. Place the spaghetti casserole on top of the stove and bring it just to the boil. Cover and place it in the oven. Bake for 15 minutes and uncover. Bake for 15 minutes longer, or until the casserole is hot and bubbling throughout and starting to brown on top. Serve immediately with grated Parmesan cheese on the side.

YIELD: 12 or more servings.

In my childhood, it would never have occurred to anyone to analyze or categorize the kind of food we dined on from my mother's kitchen. It was simply "southern cooking." In retrospect, it fell into three categories—soul food, which is a blend of African and American Indian; creole cookery, which is a marriage of innocent Spanish and bastardized French; and pure French, desserts mostly, from the first edition of *The Boston Cooking-School Cook Book.* To my mind that book was, in its original concept, the first great cookbook in America. For years it had no peer (Mrs. Rorer's works notwithstanding) and it was my mother's kitchen bible.

My mother had an incredible aptitude in her ability to "divine" the ingredients of one dish or another. She could dine in New Orleans and come back to reproduce on her own table the likes of oysters Rockefeller, oysters Bienville, the creole version (so different from the original French) of rémoulade sauce with shrimp.

There was another advantage to the old-fashioned southern kitchen: the talent and palate of the American Negro. I am convinced that given the proper training in the kitchen of a great French restaurant, any American black with cooking in his or her soul would be outstanding.

With rare exceptions, all the servants in our kitchen arrived with a full knowledge of soul cooking, which is broad in scope. Essentially it encompasses the use of all parts of the pig, more often than not boiled, plain, or with other ingredients. Pig's feet, pig's tails, hog jowl, and that most soul of all foods, chitterlings, the small intestines of pigs. It has always amused me, since I first encountered the regional cooking of France, to know that one of that nation's most prized and delectable of sausages—called andouille or andouillettes—is nothing more than chitterlings blended with various spices, onions or shallots, white wine, and so on, and stuffed into casings. For what it's worth, a New Year's party without grilled andouillettes in my house is as unthinkable as an absence of at least a couple of bottles of champagne. Once a year in my childhood home, Mother had a chitterling supper. Chitterlings, cooked and served with vinegar and hot pepper are, to some noses, a bit odoriferous. Therefore, the boarders were advised that they were invited to the chitterling supper, but if they found the aromas less than fastidious, they were cordially invited to find another place to dine.

The standard items of soul food that appeared almost daily at my mother's table were one form of greens or another, always cooked with pieces of pork, the feet, hocks, belly, and so on, sometimes salted, sometimes smoked. The greens were of a common garden-variety, such as mustard greens, collard greens, and turnip greens. These would be put on to boil with a great quantity of water and salt and allowed to cook for hours. Once cooked, the liquid is much treasured by southern palates. It is called "pot likker" and you sip it like soup with corn bread. If you want to be fancy, you can always make corn meal dumplings to float on top of the greens. Black eye peas are also a regional treasure, some people think the finest of all staples. These, too, are cooked for a long while (preferably from a fresh state; if not, frozen; if not frozen, dried; and if none of these, canned).

One of the most distinguished roomers and boarders in my mother's house was a scholarly gentleman, well known in academic circles, the late Dr. John Dollard, a highly praised Yale psychologist and social scientist. Dr. Dollard had come to Indianola to do research on a book called *Caste and Class in a Southern Town* and with what might have been an uncanny sense of direction or perception, had chosen my house as his base of operation.

Dr. Dollard, a patient, kindly, amiable man was, of course, a Yankee and thus had a "funny accent." The other boarders did not take kindly to him for no other reason than that he was an "outsider." In the beginning he criticized the cooking of the greens, complaining that there was not a vitamin left in the lot. And as a result of his well-intentioned explanations and at the base encouragement of the other boarders, my mother willingly committed one of the most wicked acts of her life. Dr. Dollard was placed at a bridge table, covered, of course, with linen and set with sterling, and he was served a mess of raw greens that he ate with considerable and admirable composure and lack of resentment. Always the detached and critical observer, I found my mother's role in this little game almost intolerable, although I said nothing.

Odd coincidences have occurred often in my life. One day, a decade or so ago, I wandered into the photographic studio where portraits bearing the title *New York Times Studio* were taken. I glanced at an assignment sheet and saw the name John Dollard, Yale.

As I walked out, John walked in.

"John," I said, "I'm Craig Claiborne."

"How's your mother?" he asked. "She's a great woman."

With one possible exception, the dishes prepared by my mother that I liked best were the creole foods. As I have noted, to this day, like the madeleines of Proust's childhood, I can smell chopped onions, celery, and green peppers, cooking together in butter or oil. This, to my mind, is the creole base, and it is a combination that often perfumes my own kitchen.

My mother would purchase one of Mr. Colotta's (Mr. Colotta was the only fish dealer for miles around) finest red snappers from the Gulf Coast brought in that morning, encased in ice, and weighing almost twenty pounds. A fish that size would barely fit in the oven. It would be baked and basted with oil and the creole base and it was as succulent and tender as anything I ever tasted here or abroad. Her shrimp creole with the same base was robust and glorious.

It would be easy to recite the entire roster of her creole and other southern specialities. A remarkable Brunswick stew, an incredibly good barbecue sauce with tomato ketchup, Worcestershire sauce, and vinegar as a base. She made a delectable assortment of gumbos—crab, oyster, and plain okra. (The word gumbo, I was to learn in later life, derived from the Bantu word for okra.) Her deviled crab was spicy, rich, and irresistible.

There were two specialties of my home kitchen for which my mother made only the final preparation. In my earliest years, my father cured his own hams and sausages in the smokehouse out back and these she prepared with expert hands. On occasion she made country sausages, fiery hot and spiced with red pepper flakes before smoking, but more often than not she bought these from a neighbor. These sausages, for which I have developed a formula as closely paralleling the original as possible, I prepare today in a small portable smoker. Southern to the core, my mother frequently prepared beaten biscuits, one of the most curious of southern kitchen or back porch rituals.

Beaten biscuits are a blend of flour, lard, and butter that is worked together by hand. You then add enough milk to make a stiff dough, which is rolled out and literally beaten with any handy sturdy instrument. It might be a rolling pin, a shortened broom handle, even a hatchet or ax. You beat the dough, folding it over as you work, for the better part of an hour until it blisters. The dough is then rolled out, cut into small round biscuits, and pricked in the center with a fork. There are beaten biscuit cutters that cut and prick at the same time. And there are, or used to be, special beaten biscuit machines with rollers through which you roll the dough until it blisters, not unlike the old-fashioned clothes wringer.

There are dozens of dishes that come to my mind when I think of my mother's kitchen—fantastic caramels, divinity fudge, a luscious coconut cake with meringue and fresh coconut topping, the best, richest pecan pie in the world, incredible fried chicken, great shrimp rémoulade, chicken turnovers in an awesomely rich pastry served with a cream sauce—but two of the dishes that she made for very "party" occasions had a curious appeal for my childhood palate. Sunday dinner, which was served at twelve-thirty in the afternoon, was always paramount among our weekly meals and if she wished to offer the boarders an uncommon treat she would serve them as a first course toast points topped with canned, drained white asparagus spears, over which was spooned a hot tangy Cheddar cheese sauce. This dish was generally garnished with strips of pimento.

Another for which she was renowned was a three-layered salad composed of a bottom layer of lime gelatin chilled until set, a middle layer of well-seasoned cream cheese blended with gelatin and chilled until set, and a top layer of delicately firm tomato aspic. The salad was cut into cubes, garnished with greens, and topped with a dab of mayonnaise.

Years later, when I was working for the American Broadcasting Company in public relations, I knew a reporter for the old, once thriving monthly called *Liberty* magazine. Her name was Beulah Karney and she was food editor of that journal. She once asked me casually if I could name the best cook in the South and I specified my mother. Beulah traveled to Mississippi and interviewed "Miss Kathleen." In the May 1948 issue there appeared an article entitled "The Best Cook in Town" and it described my mother's boardinghouse. Pursuant to a good deal of recent research, I found that issue in the New York Public Library.

One sentence stated "the six paying guests, all bachelors, said there wasn't much point in getting married when Miss Kathleen's food was so good." Four recipes were printed, including one for Miss Kathleen's Party Salad, that three-layered affair.

After World War II when I had settled in Chicago, my mother wrote in a school child's composition book a collection of her favorite recipes. They are in her own handwriting. There are recipes for Karo Caramels (The Candy You All Liked and All the Others So Much), Galatoire's Trout Marguery, Oysters Rockefeller, Mrs. Robert Johnson's Rice Pudding (Do You Remember The Lovely Meal We Had With Them In Chicago), Great Grandmother Craig's Grated Potato Pudding, Italian Ravioli, Grand Hot Cakes, Sister's Sausage, Charlotte Russe, and a Craig Wedding Punch, the recipe for which was more than two hundred years old.

To say that in my childhood I considered my mother to be a "blessed damozel," does not mean that in my early youth I was unaware of a few peccadilloes in her make-up. She was vain and I was aware of her vanity. She taught me—as she taught my brother and sister—that we were of noble blood and to the manor born.

"Never forget," she would admonish me almost daily, "that you are a Craig." Oddly perhaps, she never said, "Never forget you're a Claiborne." She practiced *noblesse oblige* with her servants but with her peers she was arrogant and imperious.

Because of the blue blood that I was assured coursed through my veins, there was a certain dichotomy in my ego and self-esteem. And I was subjected to countless humiliations, which I suffered meekly, because of my ennobled vision of my mother.

My greatest humiliation—and it occurred daily—was to be sent to the grocery store for provisions, a pound of butter, five pounds of sugar, a sack of flour, or whatever. In my mind I *knew* that we perennially owed the grocery store hundreds and hundreds of dollars. And the fact that the owners of the store, a couple of bachelors, lived in my mother's rooming house and admired her did not lessen my lacerations as I entered their business domain.

I was not a robust child. I had an extremely delicate nature and I was often on the verge of tears as I made that trek over the bridge to the store. As my mother acted out her role as a grande dame, I suffered in silence in my family's poverty.

Her friends and their children rode in automobiles and we had none. Taking a ride in an automobile was what one did to while away the hours in that small town. Some of the inhabitants would get in their cars and drive for only a block to visit a neighbor or drive two blocks to get to church. An automobile was the ultimate status symbol in that town.

I was aware that for the most part I had a gloomy, downtrodden look about me. My mother, misinterpreting this for boredom, would further humiliate me by calling up a neighbor and asking if he or she would not like to take me for a ride.

There is a condition that is known as childhood amnesia that stems from feelings of desolation, loneliness, and deprivation in the formative years of life and, although I have a fairly keen and vivid memory of the situations that caused these things in my own person, I am confused as to the precise dates of certain acts that caused uneradicable scars on my spirit and well-being.

Since I first learned to read I have had a phenomenal ability to spell. It was partly this ability, I believe, that motivated my earliest teachers and my mother to let me "skip" a grade, namely the first. I went from kindergarten directly into the second grade, a decision that I came to regret in my later years of schooling.

When I was probably seven or eights years old, I was chosen to compete in a county-wide spelling bee to be held in a small college in a neighboring town, Moorhead, Mississippi. I was not terribly ambitious or impressed that I had been chosen for that competition, but I was keenly anxious to win for the simple pleasure that it would give my family and friends.

As it happened, I placed second and I was not dismayed at my standing.

When I returned home that afternoon, my mother was in the living room with acquaintances and my sister, Augusta.

"How did you place?" someone asked.

"Second," I answered.

"You should be ashamed," my mother told me, and I was chilled with a distinct feeling of alienation.

Had she slapped me in the face, it could not have disturbed me more. Gradually and guardedly I started to cry. My sister put her arms around me and led me from the room while my mother picked up the thread of her conversation with her guests. I brooded on this for a good long while.

Quite early in my childhood I had been taken to Greenville to see the family doctor, Hugh Gamble, whom my mother idolized. It often occurred to me that had she been given the choice, Dr. Gamble would have made a fine husband for her. On one of my many visits to him, he diagnosed one of my small illnesses as a slight heart murmur and advised my mother that I should avoid strenuous exercise.

From that moment on she started to treat me with excessive concern, reminding me relentlessly that I was "fragile." Whenever I left her presence she would admonish me, "Don't hurt yourself." She often referred to me as "delicate" and took uncommon pride in advising friends and neighbors of my condition, not as though I were ailing but as though I had been given a major award.

It is true that I was never an athletic child and when I ran only a short distance I was afflicted with a stitch, a very real and stabbing sensation in my right side. At times, I was bent over double because of it, but I was loathe to discuss this with my family or anyone else because of a fear that it might be serious. I did not want to become a burden.

In Indianola, it was taken for granted that if you were male, you would quite naturally become a member of the football, baseball, and basketball teams, but I was not of that persuasion. I was convinced that I was "fragile," that I was incapable of developing muscles, and, besides, there was that pain in my side. It came on with any mode of roughhousing.

I was engulfed with childhood feelings of self-doubt and inadequacy. I felt that if my fellow townspeople were kind to me, it was out of sympathy. It was customary for most of the other children in school to be driven back and forth from their homes to the school building in the morning, at lunch, and in the afternoon. I walked for want of a family conveyance. I dreaded the moments when somebody would stop and ask, "Would you like a ride?" I'd turn my head and shake my head sheepishly. I loathed their magnanimity.

On the first morning of one fine school term, I do not remember the grade in junior high school in which I was enrolled, but I was seated in an arithmetic class that was taught by a supposedly grown man named Joe Green. Joe was the school athletic coach.

On that first morning, he passed out sheets of paper and asked us to write down the name of the sport in which we would participate. I returned mine with my name on it but with no indication of a sport.

On the second day, I returned to the class and, when it was called to order, the instructor had roll call.

When he got to my name he smirked.

"I see," he said, "we've got a sissy in the class."

To this day, in all my life, I have rarely known a more stunning and vivid pain. I have never known a moment more devastating or emasculating. The blood ran from my face and I was frozen with a kind of panic. It created a scar from which I never recovered and to this day I cannot add, multiply, divide, or subtract with anything remotely resembling facility. My life was colored from that moment on. I have never in all my life seen, start to finish, a football, baseball, or basketball game either in person or on television.

From that day on in junior high and high school I felt like a leper and I became the victim of a bunch of childish thugs who took delight in tormenting me, in pinning my shoulders to the ground while shoving their hands in my face.

One of my favorite lines in contemporary literature occurred some years ago in an essay by Woody Allen. He noted that as a child he was a nonphysical, vulnerable youth whose mother appended a note onto the back of his shirt whenever he walked out of the house. It read, "Do not fold, spindle or otherwise mutilate."

In my childhood I was very much a victim of my playmates' wrath and torture. The perfect target because I simply refused to fight back. Even had I felt myself physically able to resist the barbaric taunts of my assailants, I seriously doubt that I would have done so. In my adulthood, I have developed my own weapons of revenge, and these weapons consist almost exclusively of silence in the face of hostility and personal outrage. Mine enemies lose nothing more serious than my respect and friendship. That is why I consider my favorite and most consoling poem that of Emily Dickinson. I might even consider it the most fitting for my tombstone if it were not my wish to be cremated and have my ashes scattered to the wind; or, preferably perhaps, thrown into the sea, the better yet to feed the mouths of the progeny of all those fish and sea creatures that nourished me in my days on earth.

It dropped so low—in my Regard—
I heard it hit the ground—
And go to pieces on the Stones
At bottom of my Mind—
Yet blamed the Fate that flung it—less
Than I denounced Myself,
For entertaining Plated Wares
Upon my Silver Shelf—.

Recollections of a Mississippi Boyhood

THOMAS D. CLARK

COMING OF AGE IN another time and in an emerging region one gathered a mixture of memories and awarenesses, if not an understanding of influences which became crowded into a cherished pattern of realities and sentimentalities. These things linger in mind and heart throughout a lifetime of recalling the turnings of the land and seasons, of revered old landmarks, the bending of roads and the bridgings of streams, of weather-beaten houses and barns, the now vanished homesteads of good neighbors, of drab rainswept country school and church yards, the deep fishing and seining holes in moccasin-infested creeks, of ancient sentinel trees which by some quirk of nature or man survived storms and timber harvest, swamp woodland trails, the whereabouts of chinquapin trees and muscadine vines, and of blackberry patches. Then there is the nostalgia for sign-cluttered country stores sheltering their helter-skelter assortment of merchandise, and the blended aroma of kerosene, chewing tobacco, axle grease, cloth glaze, fat back, plow gear, Christmas apples and oranges, of customers and the store cats.*

Centerpiece in this collage of memories is the gallery of faces which stared out from ready-print pages of the weekly paper, and which ranged from matronly Lydia E. Pinkham to Woodrow Wilson. Of home origins were the likenesses of governors, United States Senators, congressmen, judges, and the endless procession of local office-seekers. None, however, stimulate so pleasant a memory as the rough plank tables off to the side of the church where following special Sunday meetings country wives spread bounteous dinners, or the Fourth of July picnic grounds where oratory and food were equally as bountiful. Then there were the Confederate reunions with all the speaking and yelling, and the almost continuous hustings where candidates for every office in the gift of the people so successfully dodged cardinal issues. There

An excerpt from an address delivered in 1983 at the annual meeting of the Mississippi Historical Society were the clay-stained streets of country towns with their Saturday melanges of red-necked farmers, candidates, medicine men and peddlers, and the frequent fist fights. These are only a few of the scenes etched in the memory of a rural Mississippian growing up in the early decades of this century.

What was once accepted as a matter of fact in the course of rural life now seems but a remote fantasy. On every hand in earlier years there remained a full complement of men who had worn the gray, and who had become reminiscent about their battle experiences at Shiloh, Bryce's Crossroads, Vicksburg, and in the retreat to Atlanta, then finally in the grecian-like tragic end of escorting Jefferson Davis on his flight through the Georgia woods. Just as mellow in their reminiscences were ex-slaves such as Aunt Betsy Harper who had been sold South by the famous distilling family of Frankfort, Kentucky, and Uncle Sam Metts who had ridden stirrup-to-stirrup with Captain Tom Metts throughout the war. Then there were Silas and Jeremiah Miller who were among the last African slaves to make the middle passage to North America.

Still active in the opening decades of this century was that generation of Mississippians who recalled with considerable bitterness the excesses of Radical Reconstruction. Some of the ones I knew had ridden with the knights of the old Ku Klux Klan, or engaged otherwise in the intimidating activities which resulted in immortalization of sorts on the pages of the *Report of the Committee of the House of Representatives in the Late Insurrectionary States.* In my early years of growing up these men of the past crowded onto the Mississippi scene in a final moment of glory before their enfeebled hands loosened their grasp on the past in surrender to bolder and younger ones to reach out to an uncertain future.

Like every moment of human renascence, Mississippians in their formative years stumbled toward a regional destiny burdened by history as they sought to determine whether or not present events portended a brighter future or further frustrations. I can think of few times in American history when a youth came of age so intimately between two worlds, both ladened with an imperishable sense of the past. An only present regret must be the lack of maturity to comprehend the salient forces of the changing times.

My generation of Mississippians was comprised predominantly of yeoman subsistence farmers whose mores were shaped by geography, economics, faltering political systems, and social environment. A million and a half of us lived on the land, while only 120,000 more lived along dusty main streets, streets which actually were little more than knotted junctures in country roads leading past general furnishing stores, cotton warehouses and gins, courthouses and jails, and political stamping grounds. Editors of country papers and regional farm journals scolded us perpetually for living, if not in economic carnal sin, then for being obstinately wedded to one-crop cotton culture, buying the necessities of life from outsiders, and thus living away instead of on the land.

If we had read the reports of the decennial United States *Census* for the first three decades of the new century, or could have accurately interpreted the statistical implications, then our pride would have been injured further by the fact that no Mississippi urban center even approached 50,000 souls. We could have salved our pride somewhat with the knowledge that 99.5 per cent of the population, white and black, sprang from native stock. Whites, however, were statistically the minority race, divided 641,200 whites to 907,630 blacks in 1900, and this disparity bore down upon us in every aspect of our lives.

Never for one moment did Mississippians of either race forget that most of us lived in communities and a state where social conditions were so fragile that an explosion could occur at any time. I saw, for instance, Negro tenants gathered in my grandfather's farm kitchen as frightened as whites by rumors of a race riot, and they hoped to place themselves above implication. Mississippi's whole social and economic being was bonded to its disparate statistical image. Perhaps no historian can ever fully interpret the impact of racial history in basic human terms on Mississippians. In the economic area alone the racial imbalance bore heavily on the instability of everyday life. The gulf between homeowners and tenants, for instance, vividly revealed the cancerous condition of the old agrarian system for its servitor yeoman farmers. Though a fair number of delta and prairie farms could be called plantations, predominantly the pattern among the 220,000 existing farmsteads in 1900 was small, less than a hundred acres, and combined farm property was valued at a fraction over two hundred million dollars. Less than half the landed area was developed, and scarcely half of that in cultivation, according to the United States Soils Survey of selected counties in 1912, was suited for sustained row-crop cultivation.

Few settled areas of the United States could exhibit so intense a cultural pattern of rurality as Mississippi, 1900–1920. Preponderantly the state's population in these decades lived in severely isolated geographical and social worlds. Countrymen functioned largely within folk and fixed social patterns which their forbears had transported overland from the older culture regions of the Upper South, and even from the British Isles. Our speech pattern and accent was reflective of seventeenth century English derivation, and our food tastes were set largely by Virginia and Carolina standards, varied with a few regional adaptations. The Mississippian's traditional fondness for hunting and taste for wild game and fish was comparable to that of Prince Edward County, Virginia, and Chester and Fairfield counties in South Carolina.

Our pioneer Mississippi ancestors brought to delta and Indian hill country the folk ways, superstitions, home remedies, and patterns of social behavior of the older Atlantic coastal South. Packed away in their mental cultural baggage were memories of old folk tales to be told and retold by countless Mississippi hearthsides, and which were of Carolina and old world origins. Along with these came one of the state's most distinctive personal traits, enjoyment of folksy and humorous stories. Elements of these are laced throughout the literature of the state like golden threads. Never in our most darkening moments have we been so bound down in despair that we could not laugh at ourselves and our neighbors, often this was our saving grace.

In 1900 a southern Baptist congregation in Winston County, or anywhere else in Mississippi, could have annexed itself to one in Chester County, South Carolina, without having to modify the surnames on its roster or having to chisel new ones on tombstones in the adjoining graveyards. No matter how sophisticated some Mississippians wished to appear their pride was dampened by the eternal multitude of country cousins. Most of us were entangled in the intractable net of folkways and attitudes whose antecedents reached back well beyond our ken. Like Hindus hoping for reincarnation in pleasanter forms in the next cycle of life, there persisted among Mississippians an evergreen hope that someday our lives would be transformed from one of servitude along weedy cotton rows and heart-crushing low prices into one of celestial ease in eternal shade and succor of pastoral bliss. Without sensing the broad implications of progress, we put our faith in social and economic salvation in changes without comprehending the emotional costs and disruptions which it would bring to our way of life.

From the circumscribed perspective of Mississippi rurality in the early part of this century our lives reflected little of the excitement and sophistication of rapidly emerging America. Nevertheless, viewed from a broader perspective of time and changing conditions in national society this, paradoxically, was an exciting era of social shock, transitions, of institutional searchings for new directions, and for more decisive leadership in all areas. This was an era which made heavy demands on moral and spiritual resources to deal with staggering problems in the fields of economics, education, politics, race relations, and personal improvements.

I think none of the above challenges outweighed the pressing need for responsible political leadership. Andrew H. Longino ushered in the present century as Governor, and he seems to have been the last of the old-line courteous victorians who had the confidence of supporters and the central political powers. During his administration the New Statehouse was completed and dedicated, the insurance laws were revised, the direct primary law was enacted, and the State Department of Archives and History was established, all landmark accomplishments. The primary was used during my first year of existence, and throughout the rest of my life in Mississippi we were subjected to what seemed an almost uninterrupted seige of electoral campaigning.

In the gubernatorial race of 1904 voters were aroused to a high pitch of excitement in Louisville and Winston County by the daylong visit of James Kimball Vardaman. He had stirred large gatherings of red-necked voters in neighboring Attala and Choctaw counties, and word of this had preceded him to Louisville. On hand to meet him was a throng of countrymen who came to shout hosannas loud and clear. Vardaman rode through the streets atop a log wagon with his bold Choctaw-like profile and wondrous shock of shoulder-length black hair in full view. He hypnotized the audience with his illiterative descriptions of his racial attitudes and opposition to educating the Negro. In Ackerman he had inflamed his hearers so much that a mob rushed the county jail and lynched a Negro boy charged only with theft. Vardaman's opponents supported educational advantages for both races. This at a time when the South was emotionally aroused over the ill-founded gossip that

President Theodore Roosevelt had entertained Booker T. Washington at a formal dinner in the White House. Racial anger was stirred further by the appointment of Effie Cox, a black, to be postmistress at Indianola.

Succeeding Vardaman was one of America's rarest collection of governors, including "Granny" Edmund F. Noel, Earl Brewer, Theodore G. Bilbo, and Lee M. Russell. The Noel-Brewer-Sisson-Thomas-Truly-Scott campaign in 1907 became deeply impressed upon my mind. A nosey neighbor asked me how my father was going to vote, and in some foggy way the word Republican had become impressed upon my childish mind, and I answered Republican. I learned my first lesson in practical political science without benefit of classroom.

In a backward glance I marvel that my generation of Mississippians had any respect at all for the so-called democratic process. We were bombarded with charges, and often facts, of thievery, bribery, libel, adultery, and most every other sort of indiscretion of our elected officials. There were times when one would have been justified in thinking that we had in Jackson as state officials either recent graduates of Parchman or prime candidates for the institution.

On home grounds our neighbors never went half-hog into politics, they were either rampant and blind Vardaman-Bilbo rednecks, or supported their uncompromising opponents. These partisans flocked about green lumber stands to hear their idols, and then rushed home to beget sons to bear their favorites' names, and when they ran short of sons there were always dogs and mules to bear the honor.

The last vote I cast in a Mississippi election was against a Bilbo partisan in the election of 1930, but nevertheless I am now glad that I heard many of the old timers speak. Attending a Vardaman or Bilbo rally was as exciting as going to a W. I. Swain show. Of all the demagogic propositions ever offered a benighted American electorate Bilbo's brick road bubble must be considered a classic.

By a lucky circumstance I believe I heard what may have been Bilbo's last campaign speech which he made in Fayette in the fall of 1946. He was warring with Old Lady Roosevelt, Old Lady and Old Man Luce, *Time, Life,* and *Look* magazines, and a host of other absentee devils. I stood near him under a shade tree listening to

John Bell Williams tear into his collection of evil forces with neophytic zeal, and I heard Bilbo mutter under his breath, "Aw hell, he knows the words but he doesn't know the music yet." In his time Bilbo had mastered these arts as well as having an understanding of the turn of mind of a host of Mississippians.

My richest memories of rip-snorting-barnburning political oratory, however, is not that of the state-wide masters, but of those humbler yeomen who labored at the foot of the political ladder seeking the offices of justice of the peace and constable. Even Bilbo could not out promise these ignoramuses who yearned to shoulder the onerous burden of maintaining law and order in a neighborhood which was at peace. Never were we short of political grist to enliven crossroads and front gallery arguments. Somehow Mississippi muddled along. Turning back through the pages of contemporary newspapers one wonders how real the state's fiscal woes really were, and how much of the news was sheer political bombast? One thing can be documented, the social and economic challenges of these years were genuine and pressing.

Correctly state and regional historians have described the first quarter of this century in Mississippi as a progressive era, even though a reluctant one. This was an age of startling and unsettling discoveries in every aspect of life in the state. At times it seemed that every seam in the fabric of Mississippi civilization was about to come undone. Old concepts and approaches proved either inadequate or false, and all the old standby values had to be reappraised.

No economic fact in the early decades was more disturbing than the clear observation of government forestry statisticians that the Mississippi stand of virgin timber would be largely exhausted by 1930. People would then become dependent upon a less plentiful and inferior second-growth supply of wood products. Actually the report was more accusative; its implications were that Mississippi would be without sufficient forest products to sustain its then modest industrial economy. Another and somewhat unsettling fact was that every discernible indicator seemed to show that the older agricultural age was easing rapidly into the closing phases of an agrarian revolution. The rapidity with which the antiquated credit system disintegrated, the appearances of the boll weevil and the Texas fever tick, and sagging prices for farm products within the first decade and a half combined to bring about a revolution which endless country newspaper and farm journal articles had been unable to achieve. Mississippi editors, state officials, and concerned commercial groups began searching for some hopeful indications of changes in both agriculture and new industries. Location of even the most modest kind of a manufacturing plant generated editorial and official joy.

In our section in Winston County it was the arrival of the large sawmills. As a youth I witnessed and participated in the harvest of the magnificent stands of hill-country shortleaf and loblolly pine. Some of the hoary old loblollies had towered above the land for a century or more, and their stately boles shaded their lesser neighbors with the majesty of undisputed monarchs. Somewhat like the coming of the boll weevil and fever ticks, the big mills moved in and gobbled up prime virgin timber with an insatiable appetite. In less time than a human generation the virgin forest in my section was raped and pillaged by mills and fires, and the people left little if any better off economically and socially. Again, I retain a vivid memory of a grand horizon outlined with the domes of great trees one month, and left gapped and disheveled the next. Almost within days the soul-lifting timber line had fallen victim to the saw.

By 1912 the commercial mills had moved into our section of central eastern Mississippi, and the editor of the *Winston County Journal* welcomed them as though they were the arrivals of guardian angels. One yankee millmaster was introduced as the epitomy of gentility and a rare human addition to the community. Apparently the editor was uninformed about Captain Shryver's operational slogan, "Kill a nigger, hire another'n, kill a mule, buy another'n." Perhaps the editor never visited the slab-sided filthy sawmill camps or villages, or had he stood by the roadside to watch the endless procession of galled mules and oxen slogging through mud and dust dragging overloads of lumber to railway sidings. Then there were the "dummy" or mud railway lines which thrust their tentacles deep into backcountry woods to bring out millions of feet of prime logs, and to set wildfires from one end of the lines to the other. Between 1900 and 1930 Mississippi sawmills harvested from the state's forests approximately 70,000,000,000 board feet of lumber, leaving in their wake perplexing problems of human readjustments, and of recovering the land itself.

The big sawmills had an inestimable impact on the rural way of life in many parts of Mississippi. They drew away from the farms surplus laborers, and introduced to many of the intensely rural areas a somewhat higher rate of wages. One of their greatest social influences was the process of separating people from the land, and, maybe, inducing the great out-migration of these early years.

When the big mills ceased operation their woodlands were left to the mercy of the jackal peckerwood mills which cut out the remaining two-by-four stand, and left the woods to be further ravished by wildfires. We fought those fires in desperate efforts to save cotton fields, rail fences, houses, barns, and livestock. Remarkably one searches in vain through the columns of contemporary papers for some true sense of the waste caused by wanton forest fires; they were so frequent as to be unnewsworthy.

In the management of the forests as in that of their farms, Mississippians of my generation remained bound by their ancestral folk beliefs. Annual woods burnings not only were viewed as a matter of course, but so long as fire was kept away from buildings and fences, were justified on the grounds they hastened the greening of spring grass, destroyed ticks, boll weevils, snakes, and mosquitoes. They were also an effortless way to get rid of old field pines and persimmon sprouts. Then there were those reckless rabbit-hunter incindiaries who scorched sage fields to flush game. I am certain few, or, perhaps, none of us reckoned the losses caused by the raping of our woods in terms of the long-range future. If the true costs had been reckoned in terms of support of schools, universities, and hospitals, I am certain concerned Mississippians would have disavowed them.

Mississippi's road to progress in these earlier decades was strewn by tremendous obstacles, obstacles growing out of human conditions. Topping the list was an underdeveloped and poorly directed public school system incapable of training youth beyond the minimal needs of a rural agrarian society. Just as deterrent to progress was lack of a connected and modernized system of all-season highways. These advances were delayed, if not absolutely defeated by small bore name-calling, mud-slinging factional politicians at all levels. There was an ingrained folk resistance to change and acceptance of improvements over the old ways, especially if they involved increased taxes. These plus the traditional way of the land obscured a certain unhappy fate and held the state's social and economic systems in a thraldom of one-mule staple crop subsistence agriculture. This land-bound-mindedness created a state of myopia too dense for the mass of Mississippians to interpret the obvious and ominous signs of the time.

As a lad growing up in this era of change, I think I sensed vaguely the undercurrents of human uncertainties and defeats from our out-moded farming practices, and at the same time experienced some of the gestation pains of spawning a new system. Perhaps I never heard the names of Seaman A. Knapp, Frank Lever, W. H. Smith, or A. J. Holmes. If I did I must have thought they were running for state office, nor had I heard of the demonstration project introduced in Holmes County in 1906. Nevertheless my life was influenced by these men and their crusade. I was both a corn and pig club member, and gloried in the fact that my modest forty bushel an acre of corn, grown from a peck of improved seed, was the best on the farm which seldom exceeded twelve to twenty bushels an acre. Likewise my pure-bred duroc jersey pig gave promise of stocking the family smokehouse in the future. These boyish demonstration projects were practical applications of the doctrine of living at home preached so fervently by our local editor and the *Progressive Farmer* to which we subscribed.

Even the most devout in the first quarter of this century must have felt that nature and nature's God were in concert by inflicting upon Mississippians one more burden of intolerable woes. Among my vivid early memories are of the furious swathcutting cyclones which roared over us from out of the Gulf to lay waste life and property. There was imprinted on my childish mind fright akin to undergoing a bombing raid. To be rudely awakened in the night and hustled off to safety in a damp road-side clay storm pit and there await the certain approach of a roaring thunderstorm which lashed across the land with the fury of hell's angels was to get a taste of judgment day itself. Yet we lived through the storms with the complacency of countrymen who had no place but the storm pit to flee.

Turning back through the files of contemporary newspapers it now seems hardly a spring season passed without stories of devastating floods. Then there were the drives to collect money and supplies for the sufferers in the Yazoo and Pearl river valleys.

Occasionally some of these straggled to our farm begging aid. Hill Mississippians responded almost as a matter of course to these drives, but no individual was more generous of heart than my aged Scotch grandmother who busied herself crocheting dresser doilies for victims of the flood in 1914 or 1915. . . .

Mississippi rural life three quarters of a century ago had both simplistic pleasures and standard of values, the essence of which now sweeten the memories. The warp and woof of humanity in that other era may have been coarse textured, but formed the backdrop against which the state's authors cast their stories and books, and with which they stroked the responsive chords of global humanity.

Writers in Mississippi's renascent years came to maturity in an age when most of the rest of America had drifted into a monotonous state of urban-industrial sterility. Much of their writing delineated more precisely than is possible for the historian the essential inner human impact of the closing of the great frontier which had lingered on the land for so long. In their golden age the local authors created new literary dimensions not only in the field of southern genre literature, but for universal mankind struggling against the forces of a technological age. The rich strand of folk commonality woven into the writings of Young, Percy, Faulkner, Welty, and all the others could have sprung from no other soil, time, or plights of humanity.

FROM

Where I Was Born and Raised

DAVID L. COHN

THE DELTA LAND

THE MISSISSIPPI DELTA begins in the lobby of the Peabody Hotel in Memphis and ends on Catfish Row in Vicksburg. The Peabody is the Paris Ritz, the Cairo Shepheard's, the London Savoy of this section. If you stand near its fountain in the middle of the lobby, where ducks waddle and turtles drowse, ultimately you will see everybody who is anybody in the Delta and many who are on the make.

Memphis is the metropolis of the Delta. It is its financial, social, and cultural capital. Many of its citizens grew wealthy by lending money at exorbitant rates of interest to Delta planters. When a gentleman of the old school needed a loan he did not quibble about the cost, especially if there had been a disastrous stud-poker game the night before. Other Memphians founded their dynasties in lumber. They leaped from cypress to Cézanne in one generation. Some of them brought fortunes to Memphis from Arkansas. They had lived on land which "wasn't fitten fur a houn'dawg." But oil spouted underneath their feet. On the whole, however, Memphis draws its sustenance from its immense surrounding territory, and the Delta is one of its richest tributary provinces.

Culturally, Memphis is to the Delta what Paris is to Toulouse. One day I wandered into a bookshop there. I asked for a book by William Faulkner. The clerk, a fragilely lovely woman of the old régime, flew into a rage. "That man!" she said. "He ought to be run out of the country, writing about the South the way he does." I retreated rapidly to my second line of defense. "Have you anything by Thomas Wolfe? Isn't he one of your famous Southern writers?" "Well, he might be, but we don't approve of him, either." Finding that both my authors were on the Index, and that I had been mistaken for an upstart Yankee, I browsed among the shelves for a while, quietly licking my wounds. Then I asked delicately whether books were not at least a minor passion of the people of Memphis. "No, people don't read many books here. Do you live in town?" I regretted profoundly that I did not. "Then," she said, in a sudden burst of confidence, "I'll tell you the truth. We don't have any real culture in Memphis. We have culturine. You know, like oleomargarine. Looks like butter but isn't."

That may or may not be true. There are many cultures in the world composed of many things ranging from sauces to symphonies. I do know that Memphis has beaten biscuit, rambler roses, and luscious lawns. To Delta citizens in search of light it glows with the beauty of the honey-colored pile of the Erechtheum seen at sunrise from a high Athenian hill. Here they all come in good time to see the occasional flesh-and-blood actors who appear upon its stage, to hear the rare symphony orchestra that straggles down from the north like a lone lost wild duck, and to dance to the music of some radio band advertising the virtues of a genteel purgative.

Here, too, come the businessmen of the Delta to make loans, sell cotton, buy merchandise, and attend conventions. For a day or two the lobby of the Peabody is filled with ice-cream men and their ice-cream wives. They suddenly melt into nothingness and are succeeded by ant-exterminators bent upon destroying the termite, which, like the politician, is blind but destructive. Then the undertakers appear. They discuss embalming by day. By night they dance delicate dances macabre with their necrophilic ladies under the scared and disapproving eyes of the Negro waiters. Finally they vanish into the outer darkness from which they came, giving way to hay-and-feed men who year long have cherished harlequins in their hearts now to be released in this place of bright carnival. Month after month come the conventions. The banners of business adorn the railings of the mezzanine, songs and resounding speeches come like the roar of the distant sea to lesser citizens as they sit at lunch or dinner in the hotel dining-rooms, and town competes with town for the honor of entertaining the carbonated-beverages men next year. During these periods the panoplied life of the sixteenth century guilds is created anew. The lobby glows briefly with the glory of the vanished Cloth Hall of Ypres.

The Delta, however, loves life as well as art and profits, and in Memphis the stern businessman shows the world his other soul-side. Here he meets his inamorata, come up from his home town to sit for a little while together under a mango tree and lose the noisy sentient world. Here he goes in search of frail women, human, all too human, who live in houses with shades perpetually drawn, or he stumbles perhaps with a sudden gasp of delight upon some peripatetic beauty strolling sloe-eyed and lost in the soft darkness of the hotel mezzanine. Sin, a hydra-headed monster at home, becomes in Memphis a white dove cooing in the shade of tall cathedral columns.

Women of the Delta pass transiently through the lobby of the Peabody as they go to buy clothes or to get a permanent wave. A trip of two hundred miles is but a pilgrim's tribute to loveliness. Or sometimes they track culture to its lair in the recesses of a metropolitan woman's club where the nineteenth century in Europe is taken up intact at three o'clock and set down in fragments among the tea things at four.

Here the young men and young women of the Delta stop between trains en route to schools and colleges. Everybody in the area is whole-heartedly for what is vaguely called "education," but the reasons for it are always a little dim. For a while they fill the lobby with their laughter, and suddenly, like migratory birds, are gone, to come again at Christmas and in June.

All in all, at one time or another, everybody passes this way, and here one begins to glimpse the civilization of the Delta and to bruise his perceptions on the jagged points of its paradoxes.

Catfish Row, far to the south in Vicksburg, is a typical gathering-place of Negroes. Here are no marble fountains, no orchestras playing at dinner, no movement of bell-boys in bright uniforms. Tumble-down shacks lean crazily over the Mississippi River far below. Inside them are dice games and "Georgia skin"; the music of guitars, the aroma of love, and the soul-satisfying scent of catfish frying to luscious golden-brown in sizzling skillets. In Vicksburg Negroes eat catfish as catfish at fifteen cents a plate. In the cities white folks eat it as filet of sole at a dollar a portion. Negroes are realists and purists. They are satisfied with the catfish as God made it without benefit of the expensive euphemisms of a white *maître d'hôtel.*

Racially the white of the Delta are largely Anglo-Saxon. Religiously they are Protestant. The Episcopalians are smallest in numbers and largest in membership of old families. Baptists are myriad. They assail the ear of heaven with stentorian voice on

Sundays. There are a few Catholics. They walk alien ways lighted by tall candles and perfumed with incense redolent of Rome, intent upon their own purposes, seeking salvation with Latin incantations. But they are lost in the Protestant mass.

This is a church-going and whisky-drinking society. That which is due to the church and to the bootlegger is offered up with such smooth harmony that the life of the body and the life of the spirit go happily in mystic marriage. Mississippi is legally dry, but the liquors of Louisiana are brought across the river, and potent brews are distilled in the swamps. The Delta has indeed the distinction of having created its own *vin de pays,* the corn whisky of one of its towns being famous for hundreds of miles around.

The churches of the Delta are not content merely to assure the salvation of their own members. The woes of the world impinge upon them and they mourn for the lost of Africa and of China. Bazaars, dinners, and "socials" are held continually for the purpose of raising money for foreign missions. Occasionally the bread cast upon the waters returns tenfold when a missionary comes from overseas to report how the sweating heathen of Africa have been taught, in the midst of a thousand false gods worshiped in a thousand false ways, to render homage to the one true God in the one true way which is the sole possession of his sect. Then there ensues a great feasting and communion of souls mystically joined in the common task of bringing light into the darkness of hearts which God for some strange reason failed to illuminate with the brilliance of God-head. Amid music and song eyes are lifted on high in gratitude. If they are blurred by a myopia which reveals the plight of Bechuanaland blacks ten thousand miles away, and obscures the fate of poor whites nearby as they descend from degradation to degradation, who shall question the wisdom of God's plan and the works of his appointed ministers on earth?

The civilization of the Delta is on the surface simple and almost naïve. Actually it is filled with complexities, with clashing contradictions and irreconcilable disharmonies. In its tolerance it shelters without hindrance every sect and creed within its borders. In its fanaticism it has descended to the hatreds and bigotries of the Ku Klux Klan. Devoting large sums to secondary education, it scarcely considers that literacy has profounder meanings than the ability to read and write. College-going, its students largely miss the point. They rarely return with a passion for truth, with an intellectual curiosity aroused and a desire to pursue beauty and wisdom for their own sakes.

Culture is distrusted. One who bears it or seeks it is regarded as being unfitted for the stern struggle of life. If a man should collect Byzantine textiles or Persian ceramics, his business ability would be discounted and serious doubts thrown upon his sexual virility. It is suspect to read good poetry and catastrophic to one's reputation as a normally functioning male to write it. Red-blooded men simply do not do that kind of thing. Fine distinctions are, however, drawn and exceptions made. A man may with impunity collect firearms, stamps, daggers, and stuffed birds. These are protoplasmic. He may like bird dogs, but not Persian cats. Coffee, but not tea. Whisky, but not wine. The Delta, in the midst of a Western civilization, cherishes taboos as rigid and as all-inclusive as may be found in a Melanesian village.

The field of intellectual culture is matriarchy ordered and preempted by women. This is done with the cheerful consent of the men, who feel that the manifestations of culture are things with which their wives may harmlessly amuse themselves in the long afternoons. And they do.

It is no feat at all for a study club to toss off the Periclean age of Greece in an hour and send its members away in plenty of time to get the dinner going before their husbands come home. The jump from Aristotle to trailing arbutus is easily made because there is a magnificent indifference to relevancy and continuity. Subject matter is not of much importance provided that it be non-controversial and delicately ladylike. Shelley is a favorite. Little essays on religious leaders are always welcome. Marie Antoinette, gentle, fragile, beautiful, and queenly, dies a merciful death just before the ice-cream and cake are served. Napoleon, torn without benefit of anaesthetic from the encyclopaedia, collides with the tea and comes out second best. The veil is torn from the mysteries of ancient Egypt by a member just returned from a cruise, while the audience sinks into a mood sweetly-sad as another plays *Humoresque* on the violin. Sometimes poets read original poems. Virgin brides entangled in disappointment and false rhyme die in the white moonlight. Gallant youths stammer of undying love in metaphors hopelessly mixed. Mockingbirds sing among the poison ivy. For poetry, too, is the company of the seven arts and every member must have her fling.

The pursuit of knowledge is not, however, the sole diversion of the Delta. The people are kind, gregarious, and genuinely hospitable. Isolated from theaters and night clubs, few in number in the towns and fewer in the country, they visit and are visited by innumerable friends and relatives throughout the year. The length of visits is usually vague in the minds of both host and guest. Hospitality is not chilled by the blight of a parsimonious invitation for a weekend, and if the visit of days lengthens into months the host is usually pleased. A gracious elderly woman of the old régime told me, without sense of the unusual, that "Mary Bruce came to stay for six weeks and remained eight years." So hospitable indeed are these people that if you are at all presentable and have any charm—fortunately for civilization charm remains here the passport to all homes and all hearts—you will be passed on from family to family in the Delta for as long as you like. When you leave one town in the Delta to go to another, your host insists upon telephoning his Aunt Clara to meet you. You stay then at her house. She in turn passes you on to her Uncle Fred who lives on Swan Lake plantation, and thus you may go on for years moving from one house to another, paying for your keep in the bright coin of chatter and conversation.

Summerlong, when the crops are growing, the youngsters are at home from school, and there is little business to be done, the roads are alive with automobiles, and the nights are merry with the music of dance orchestras. Everybody within a radius of fifty or a hundred miles knows when a dance is to be held, and neither heat, perspiration, nor rutted roads keep them away. Often these gatherings are held in the courthouse. Then one may see girls in bouffant frocks of organdie powdering their noses in the jury-box or nursing their weary feet on the judge's rostrum, while a sweat-bedrenched Negro orchestra hurls jagged bits of jazz into the heavy heated air.

At rare intervals a large steamboat built solely for dancing comes up the river from New Orleans. The old-fashioned "floating palace" or showboat has vanished. The drama has given way to the dance. The huge boat glows with light, and its orchestra, through amplifiers, hurls its music out upon the river, against the banks of the levee, high up to the unblinking swarming stars of summer. Its searchlights play upon the streaming crowds as they ascend the hill of the levee and march over the gangplank to fairyland within. On the crown of the levee stand or sit hundreds of Negroes, their ears wooed by the music, their eyes enchanted by the myriad lights, their souls weary in the presence of this other-world beauty suddenly come within their view but beyond their grasp. Crowds stream down to the river's edge, and when all those who are going have finally been assembled after repeated hootings of the whistle to warn the lagging, the boat shoves off downstream.

The dance floor is thick-clotted with people moving to the music of a Negro orchestra whose members are resplendent in uniforms which are a doorman's dream of heaven. There are loud laughter, shouts of recognition, tilting of bottles, and hurried introductions. The dancing is energetic. In it is a bit of Saint Vitus and the movements of standing upon a hot stove. Dark splotches soon appear upon the white linen suits of the men. On the faces of the women the make-up runs in tiny rivulets. The rich voice of a Negro baritone floats above the heads of the dancers. He recalls the sadly voluptuous fortunes of that

> St. Louis woman with the diamong ring,
> St. Louis woman with that man tied to her apron string.

The close-packed mass of humanity pillows itself upon the soft bosom of a waltz. It becomes excited by the hot staring eyes of jazz. It oscillates a bit wonderingly to the alien rhythm of the rumba. The night slips by.

Outside on the top deck there is darkness. Restless breezes of the river come coolly blowing. There is no sound save the far-away murmur of the music, the muted voices of lovers, and the drip, drip, drip of water on the paddlewheel. The boat is suspended between river and sky. Its fingers of light search the nether banks both sides. Green willows of Arkansas suddenly appear out of the black night. Shantyboats of fishermen pop up shining white out of the dark waters. The lanterns of the aroused occupants glow like insect's eyes for a moment and vanish. It is nearing midnight and the boat slowly turns to begin its homeward voyage.

When the passengers disembark the moon has risen. The land lies drowned beneath a flood of silver. Cows lie sleeping on the levee, resting heavily upon their folded feet. Mules move about, cropping grass, looking like questing creatures out of a dream. Negroes gaze at the incredible blaze of the steamboat's lights, and watch the white folks as they get into their automobiles and go away. Over the levee's rim the town lies sleeping and the roads that lead to plantation homes far away shine in the white moonlight. The air is alive for a little while with the coughing of motors and the shouts of good-bye. Then there is stillness. The lights of the boat go out. Only the beams of its searchlight are alive now as they search the shores. Its paddlewheel makes silver circles as it slowly turns and goes downstream to bring beauty and enchantment to another river town. Far off there is the baying of a dog. A mockingbird essays a fugitive note or two from the top of a tree. Silence then. The Delta sleeps the hot night through.

A Wop Bop Alu Bop A Wop Bam Boom

DANNY COLLUM

The Great Awakening

IT'S 1964. There's a pudgy ten-year-old white boy sitting in the living room of a rundown old Mississippi town. It's Saturday afternoon. And suddenly there's a crazy man on TV. At least they say he's a man. He calls himself Little Richard and he's got greasy, sculpted ringlets of hair piled a foot high on his head. It looks like a slick pompadour that grew like cancer into a crazed, decadent bouffant. And, oh my God, he's wearing make-up. Not just the usual TV pancake but garish lipstick, silver mascara and little penciled-in eyebrows. He's wearing this slicky, shiny, cool-drape suit that shimmers and radiates even through the grainy Zenith black-and-white video and he's *standing* at a piano banging away like a jackhammer. While he plays he's also writhing and thrusting his pelvis around in a manner that is absolutely, cathartically abandoned, but somehow kind of delicate too.

Behind him there's a drummer, a bassman and a guitar player blaring out this heartbeat/heart-attack rock and roll music that sounds like a 40-yard dash to hell. Out front the wildman is shrieking a chorus of sanctified-demonic nonsense syllables (a wop bob alu bop a wop bam boom) and a series of sure-as-hell-ain't-no-nursery-rhyme verses about a gal named Daisy who almost drives him crazy and another one named Sue who knows just what to do.

And, oh yeah, the guy is black.

Now the white boy is sitting there taking this all in, but he most certainly doesn't know just what to do. This kid is a Cub Scout, a PeeWee football/Little League jock, and a born-again and baptized-already member of the First Baptist Church. And, yes, he's already a died-in-the-wool little racist. He doesn't throw rocks at black kids or anything but he knows who belongs where and so on. And he knows that this raving weirdo on the TV embodies everything that he is supposed to be shocked, nauseated and repulsed by. And the boy is a little shocked. But for some reason he is not the least bit nauseated or repulsed. He doesn't run from the room in horror or call for his little brother and yell, "Hey, look at this monkey," and he doesn't switch the channel to the Game of the Week. Instead he just sits there a little bit scared but completely fascinated.

Well, he's not just fascinated. If the truth were told, he's actually drawn to this bizarre spectacle. Something mysterious clicks inside him. He has felt something a little like this once before. It was during revival week at church when that little Mexican evangelist in the red suit had made him feel the fires of hell, the blood of Jesus and the glory of heaven all running around inside him at once. That time he'd risen in a semi-trance, walked down the aisle, shook the preacher's hand and let Jesus into his heart to stay. But this time he didn't dare tell anyone what had happened. There was no aisle to walk and he still wasn't sure he could shake that crazy person's hand if he tried. But all the same some strange, powerful, nameless thing had come into his heart to stay. And he'd never be the same.

Origin of Species

This kid was born way back in 1954 in the wintertime desolation of the Mississippi Delta. And by some strange coincidence two other things happened just weeks later in 1954 that drew the map for this white boy's life while he was still in a cradle spitting up on himself.

One of those things happened 1,000 miles away in Washington, DC when the U.S. Supreme Court decided that a little black girl in Topeka, Kansas must be allowed to go to school with the white kids of that prairie outpost. The other thing happened just 90 miles up Highway 51 in Memphis, Tennessee when a poor white teenager from Tupelo named Elvis Presley walked into the Sun Records studio and invented rock and roll as we know it.

Elvis and the dull old men of the Supreme Court never met each other. They wouldn't have known what to say if they had. But together they turned America, and especially Mississippi, upside down. What the Supreme Court did was finally take a long, hard look at the system of segregation that helped keep black people in near-slavery and say it all had to go. They laid down the law. That law has been working for 30 years now and still hasn't finished its job. But that's the way the law is, it's quiet and timid and slow.

On the other hand, our man Elvis had a kind of magic that could make the law run and hide. He had the beat. It was a big, black beat and, unlike the law, it was loud, reckless and fast. It was the beat black people had used for centuries to dance, pray, curse the white man, praise Jesus and generally keep themselves sane through slavery, segregation, poverty, lynchings and all the rest. Our homeboy Elvis had absorbed some of that beat. He had fallen in love with the power, passion and sheer joy of it and he revealed some of its mysteries to all the other bored and restless white kids of America.

While the law was taking apart the wall between black and white people one brick at a time, Elvis just rammed through it with a big four-on-the-floor bulldozer. After that it all started to break loose everywhere. Some of those white kids even started listening to real black music and once that happened it was going to be very hard to make them good do-as-you're-told Americans again. Once they'd been hit with something that real, everything else was bound to seem a little bit phony. That white boy in the rundown old living-room didn't know it yet, but that was what had happened to him.

The Second Great Awakening

Now it's 1968. The white boy is 14 and that strange rock and roll thing inside him is getting mixed together with all the other juices that start to run in a boy that age. He starts acting differently. He's always been a smart aleck kid, but now he's aggressively so. He doesn't want to go to church anymore. He's stopped doing his homework and the monthly fight over haircuts has escalated into total war. The boy doesn't know what he wants. But he knows that his tidy little white Baptist world isn't it. And the wild, propulsive roar of the music keeps telling him he doesn't have to settle for it either. It's telling him that schools are prisons, and teachers, preachers, politicians and parents are all liars. At the same time the Beatles are singing something about, "turn off your mind relax and float downstream." He doesn't know exactly what that means yet, but it sounds like more fun than football practice or debate club. But if you listened closely (and our boy did) you could hear that the music wasn't just about escape or rebellion-for-the-hell-of-it anymore. The descendants of Elvis were starting to actually try to live in the wide-open, free, multi-colored world he had opened to them.

Around this time there was another flamboyantly overdressed black rock and roll preacher named Sly Stone. The whole country was dancing to his black and white, rock and soul music. He had one song in the Top Ten that said whether you were black, white, brown, yellow or red; rich or poor; skinny or fat; hip or straight you were still just "Everyday People." Sly's gospel was "we got to live together" and when he preached it you could not only imagine heaven on earth, but even believe that everyday people could make it come true. And if you had any doubts, his band, The Family Stone, was the living proof. They were black, brown, white and yellow men and women all making that beautiful noise together. And they were an equal opportunity band with a white boy drummer and a woman playing the horns.

The Hour of Decision

Having been so imbued with a healthy instinct for rebellion and a vision of an interracial utopia of equal rights and equal fun, it is no surprise what happened to our white boy when the Supreme Court's law finally came to his town. Starting in 1968 there were black kids in his school. Some of his white friends left for an expensive private school where blacks weren't allowed. Some of those who stayed made a sport of seeing how much they could harrass the black kids without actually starting a fight. But most of the whites just kept their heads down and pretended the black kids weren't there. As for our boy, he, for once in his life, knew just what to do. He thought of Little Richard and Aretha Franklin and Otis Redding. He meditated on the gospel according to Sly. And he even remembered, "Red and yellow black and white, they are precious in His sight" from somewhere. So he knew it was time to join the other side.

Joining the other side meant a lot of things. First it meant crossing the invisible line and finally getting to know some black people as individuals instead of radio icons. Then it meant learning that he had only skimmed the surface of Afro-American life and that led to finding out just how wide the gulf between black and white Americans really is. But after a while crossing the line came to mean that now and then a few black and white kids could decide to be friends and allies in spite of everything.

In addition to crossing the color line, joining the other side meant that our boy found himself thrown in with other white rock and roll rebels and rejects that he hadn't known were there. He found out that they were all stumbling down that path to the other side together. None of them really knew the way, but there were clues on the radio that kept getting stranger, wilder and more glowing with promise. And the white boy kept following them.

The dark, warm, narcotic American night . . .

It's sometime in May 1971. It is almost midnight but you could still strangle on the heat and humidity. The white boy is sitting on the hood of a car outside the American Legion Hut. Inside a local band called The Candy Shoestring is taking a break. Our boy is drifting. He's drifting in the crowds, the sweat, and the lingering shell-shocked ear-ringing of the music. But he's drifting inside his head too. He's feeling strange feelings and thinking strange thoughts. A fire engine races by with sirens blaring and our boy makes a startled leap, except it somehow turns into a slow-motion, mid-air float. At the peak of his levitation he turns and sees that the fire engine has turned across the bridge and is almost out of sight. It is one of those nights. But which one? Is it the night with that stuff the guy said was concentrated THC, or is it the night of the innocent looking joint that had been treated with something strange? No, it is probably just one of those rubbery, elongated cough syrup nights.

Later that night, or perhaps another, the white boy is back in the Legion Hall sitting off on the side of the stage. Some trio of frizzy-haired, psychedelicized farm boys from up the road is working its way through one of the more obscure Grateful Dead jams, or maybe it was Mountain Jam. Anyway the white boy is in the flow, swaying along with his eyes closed when he starts seeing this movie projected on the back of his eyelids. It's like a dream except he knows he's awake. But still he can't open his eyes or stop the pictures. He notices that the movie is showing a panoramic view of his car making a wide flat curve out on Highway 7. He watches transfixed as his car begins to cross a bridge then goes through the rail and over the edge. The car falls in slow motion for several minutes then bursts into flames and disappears. The movie's over. The white boy finally opens his eyes. He's still there, but different.

Life During Wartime

There was a war on. Of course there was the war against the blacks that went on all the time. But further away there was another war on against some other colored people called the Vietnamese. In both of these wars our white boy found himself becoming a conscientious objector with not-so-secret treasonous sympathies. In 1972 his time has come to register for the draft. The student deferment is about to end so his call-up could be as little as a year away. He's started thinking of how he's going to escape it. Small town Mississippi draft boards don't hand out many conscientious objector passes and he's not sure he'll qualify for 4F. Our boy thinks about Canada and even prison. He thinks about the flaming death of Vietnam and about the kids who've been killed right here in the U.S.A. while protesting the war. He thinks about that little midnight epiphany of his own flaming death. He's 18 years old and he's scared.

For two years now he and his friends have been wearing black armbands to school on the national days of anti-war protest. But now schooldays are almost over. So one fine spring afternoon our boy and three comrades stand in front of the local federal building handing out mimeographed leaflets about the bombing of Vietnamese civilians and collecting signatures on a petition to their congressman. The good citizens of the town, many of them friends of the young protesters' parents, walk past. Some gape in amazement, more glare in disgust. A few keep their eyes glued to the pavement in embarrassment while they grab a leaflet and endure the brief rap about the number of civilian dead and the cost in American lives. But much to their surprise a number of black passers-by stop to sign the petition and offer words of encouragement. Through all this our white boy is standing there with his leaflets feeling very foolish and full of fear. But he also feels very free and full of life. He's singing to himself under his breath, "Imagine there's no countries, I wonder if you can. . . ."

And the Beat Goes On . . .

It is now about ten years later. The white boy is a man. At least they say he's a man. He still feels a lot like that scared clumsy high school kid, but he's almost 30 years old. He lives in Washington, D.C., now in a mostly black neighborhood. He makes his little living working against war and racism. He often remembers that day he made his first real stand at the federal building because every time he makes another stand he still feels very afraid but very free and alive. He still sings "Imagine" for courage. But John Lennon is dead now.

Tonight our boy has gone dancing with a woman friend at a seedy punk/new wave club in downtown Washington. The club is less than a mile from the Supreme Court building. He's there because he's found out that he is still a rock and roll rebel after all these years. In fact the punk explosion has made him realize that he is more committed to rock and roll rebellion than he was at 14. He's beginning to think that maybe you can make a life out of what was once considered an adolescent fad.

Anyway, he and his friend are out on the floor dancing to the music that the DJ plays. It's a white British punk band doing a fair facsimile of Afro-American funk. The lyrics are a New York ghetto-style rap calling for working-class revolt. The version is one of those long dance mixes with lots of electronic effects. As the record hits one of the percussion breaks the white boy looks around at the other people on the dance floor. There are black people and white, kids not old enough to drink at the bar and people who look to be near 40. There are people in the most outlandish array of costumes from punks in torn T-shirts and black leather to out-and-out drag queens to people (like our boy) dressed in a marginally normal style. All around him there are women dancing with women and men dancing with men scattered casually among the more orthodox couples. There are also several interracial couples of all sexual varieties. And it's all ok. They are all everyday people. They are all, our boy included, rebels and rejects saying, in their different ways, "I am somebody." And because they're doing it together, it becomes, at least for a while, "We are somebody."

It may not last, but the white boy now knows for sure that it will not fade away.

. . . and the Beat goes on . . .

It's 1984. Somewhere out there in America, maybe even in a small town in Mississippi, there's another bored young white boy staring at the TV. Then suddenly this crazy black man, at least they say he's a man, appears on the screen. He's wearing a gold lamé overcoat and red bikini underwear and he calls himself Prince. He's just finished a song about nuclear war and now he's singing one he calls "D.M.S.R.". It's about Dance, Music, Sex, Romance. In the middle of the percussion break he points out at the audience and sings, "All white people clap your hands on the floor now . . ."

Choctaw Boy

Paul Conklin

The ball was made of thongs of deer hide. It was small and when it was flung across the Mississippi sky it looked like a brown bird in flight. It went higher and higher and Clifton Henry, sitting on the sidelines, followed it with his eyes until he lost it in the sun.

The ball fell to earth again. With a raucous shout of "*Kil abi!* Let's win!" a Bogue Chitto player scooped it up with his two sticks and began zigzagging down the field toward the Conehatta goal. He didn't get far. At midfield half the Conehatta team swarmed over him, knocking him flat and jarring the ball loose. A wild melee developed as both teams flailed away at the ball with their sticks.

At that moment a stranger to the Choctaw Indian fair might have thought—and who could blame him—that a battle was taking place on the field and that thirty men armed with sticks were trying to kill one another. The stranger would have been wrong. What was actually taking place was the final game in the stickball tournament the Choctaws hold every summer at Pearl River in central Mississippi.

If the game was unusually rough and if the players were whacking each other with great gusto, it was because the rivalry between the Choctaw communities of Bogue Chitto and Conehatta is intense and goes back so far that nobody can remember when it started. At the very least, the grandfathers of these same players, and their grandfathers before them, joyously gave each other bruises.

It was the middle of July and it was hot. Even though the sun was aslant in the sky—already it had started to drop behind the rim of Choctaw Stadium—its heat still hit the parched grass on the field and the spectators in the stands with the force of a hammer stroke. A trickle of sweat ran down between Clifton's shoulder blades. He dug into his pocket to see if he had enough change to buy another bottle of pop. He didn't. He was a nickel short.

A voice came over the public address system. "Ladies and gentlemen, you are watching America's oldest game. And probably its roughest. It has been called 'the little brother of war.' As you can see, the players wear no helmets, masks, or padding of any kind. Many do not even wear shoes. In the old days Choctaws often settled their serious differences with stickball games instead of fighting. The games were bigger then, with as many as seven hundred men on each side. The goals were usually out of sight of one another and the players had to run through woods to reach them."

Stickball players are not exactly weighed down with rules. There is very little in the freewheeling game which is forbidden. Nobody cries foul if you tackle an opponent, trip him, grab him in a wrestling hold. Each stickball player is armed with two *kapuchas*. The *kapucha* is a slender hickory stick, about as long as a baseball bat, with a small pocket of thongs attached to one end. A player uses his *kapuchas* for carrying and throwing the ball, as well as for fending off opponents. The only rule of much importance in stickball is that a player cannot touch the ball with his hands. Goal posts are located at each end of the playing field and points are scored by hitting the enemy goal post with the ball.

The championship game was well into the last period, and after almost an hour of sweaty struggle neither team had scored. Clifton's throat felt as though it was filled with cotton and he wished the game was over so he could go find something to drink.

To his right, a few feet away, was an inviting shadow cast by one of the stadium light towers. He moved over to it. That was better. His brown face expressionless, he continued to watch the game, but not as intently as before. His mind strayed. Stickball is part of his life. It should be. He is Choctaw and his ancestors were playing stickball in this part of Mississippi hundreds of years before Columbus' tiny fleet approached the New World. But there are other things to claim an eleven-year-old boy's interest these days. Football is one. His brother Dalton, who is now in junior college in Kansas, was the best running back ever to play for Choctaw Central High School. Clifton cannot count the number of frosty autumn evenings he sat in this very stadium, filled almost to the bursting point with pride, while Dalton ran around and over enemy tacklers on his way to the goal line.

Baseball is another thing Clifton likes. Mississippi does not have a major league team. The only games Clifton has seen are those that are played Sunday afternoons on the Bogue Chitto diamond located a quarter of a mile down a dusty road from his house. People come from all around to watch the games, sitting on the ground in the shade of pines, or driving their cars close to the field and leaning on them. Baseball excites Clifton. At that very moment he had three dog-eared cards with Johnny Bench's picture on them in his back pocket. The Cincinnati catcher, himself part Indian, is as close to a hero as Clifton has. Johnny Bench catching and Clifton Henry pitching. Wouldn't that make a great combination? He could see old Johnny now, squatting behind the plate, sending him a signal for a fast ball high and tight under the batter's chin—Henry Aaron's chin.

The boy's dark eyes focused again on the field. There was a big pile-up in front of the Bogue Chitto goal. By this time the players were too exhausted to shout at one another and the only sound on the heavy afternoon air was the crack of hickory stick hitting hickory stick. Suddenly, like a watermelon seed squirted between slippery fingers, a Conehatta player darted from the struggling mass and dashed the ball against the Bogue Chitto goal. The game was over and for the thirteenth straight year Conehatta was Choctaw stickball champion.

Fingers clamped on Clifton's ear and gave it a sharp tweak. He looked around into the grinning face of his cousin, Travis Wallace. Travis is in the fifth grade with Clifton at Bogue Chitto and during the school year he spends much of the time with the Henry family. The two boys are inseparable.

"Hey, *kil ia*—let's go," Travis said.

"What do you want to do?" But even as he spoke, Clifton knew exactly what he wanted to do. The creaky, old ferris wheel had started to turn at the far end of the field. He could hear the muffled thudding of colliding dodgem cars, and along the midway lights were winking on in booths where there was row upon row of stuffed animals and other prizes waiting to be won. But all that would require a little money. Clifton knew his father would help. As the two boys went off to find Dolphus Henry, the cheerful refrains of "Choctaw Saturday Night" sounded across the fair grounds:

Down in Mississippi in ol' Bok Chitto
Saturday night I won't forget-O—
Holhponi cookin', everybody lookin' for a girl.
Folks comin' down from Conehatta—
Wish you'd look at what they gotta,

Choctaw baby, I don't mean maybe,
Choctaw Saturday night!

It was evening. Lightning forked from a pile of thunderheads west of the stadium. The Yockanookany River country was catching a hard rain. Clifton was afraid the storm would wash out the pageant if it moved in the direction of Pearl River. He didn't want that to happen. He was too comfortable sitting in the darkened stands. His stomach was full and in his pockets were the trophies of the afternoon: a rabbit's foot, a pair of dice on a key chain, and a rubber dagger. Travis had fared even better. He sat next to Clifton with a velvet green and yellow snake draped around his neck.

It was a relief for Clifton just to be able to sit in the warm darkness and do nothing for a change. His weary legs needed a rest. This was the best fair he had ever been to and for three days he had been a perpetual motion machine.

It had all started Monday afternoon with the parade in Philadelphia, which is the county seat of Neshoba county and located eight miles east of Pearl River. During the parade Clifton carried one side of the Bogue Chitto Development Association banner.

It was the first time he had ever been given an important job like that. The banner was made of canvas and stretched almost across the street. Behind the banner came the Bogue Chitto dancers—the men in black hats and bright shirts and the women in equally bright dresses aflutter with ribbons and wearing tiaras in their long hair—chanting as they went and stepping along to the sound of Gibson Bell's drum.

Bogue Chitto was in the middle of a long procession of dancers, stickball teams, floats, and pretty girls riding on the tops of cars from the other parts of the Choctaw nation—or the Mississippi Band of Choctaws, as they call themselves. The parade wound its noisy, exuberant way through Philadelphia's streets, past the courthouse and its Civil War statue, past the Ellis Theater, past the Ben Franklin store and the Rexall drug store, down by the post office and the bank, and back by the courthouse again.

Thick crowds lined the curbstone. They became a blur of faces for Clifton as he walked proudly along, making sure that the banner stretched out all the way so that everybody could read it. The excitement didn't end with the parade. On its heels came two hours of suspense in the high school gym when his sister Pamela was chosen as second runner-up to the Choctaw princess. Waiting for the judges to make up their minds was an ordeal he wouldn't soon forget.

On Tuesday morning, while the sun was barely up and the grass was still heavy with dew, Clifton had been out in the garden helping his father select the peppers, cabbage, kale, and wax beans that would go, accompanied by jars of his mother's pickles, canned peaches, and raspberries, into the Bogue Chitto fair booth.

By now everything connected with the fair had become a pleasurable blur in Clifton's mind. He was worn out. But there was more. The darkened stage at the edge of the field sprang into life, revealing an old Choctaw village. It was a busy, cheerful scene. A brave sat on a log repairing a bow. Another practiced with a blowgun. Beside him sat a basket weaver with a pile of cane at her feet. Women leaned over fires as they stirred kettles of hominy. From where Clifton sat the fires looked real, but he knew they were only light bulbs shining through red paper. His sister, DeLaura, was pageant director this year and she had told him what a problem they had had during rehearsals, making the fake fires look genuine.

A spotlight framed a young woman at one side of the stage. It was DeLaura. She wore a brilliant red dress which reached down to her ankles. Over the dress was a ruffled white apron. Reflected light danced from the bespangled tiara-like comb in her hair. This was the traditional Choctaw costume. Until the 1950s Choctaw women, even school girls, wore similar clothes. Now, except for special occasions, only old women dress this way. The red dress, which Choctaws called *iluka,* requires six yards of cloth. It is intricately decorated, and it had taken DeLaura and her mother weeks of patient hand stitching to put it together. Clifton thought she looked beautiful in it. He was accustomed to seeing his sister in her usual garb of blue jeans and sneakers.

DeLaura was going to narrate the pageant. She began to speak. "Many years ago the ancestors of the Choctaws lived in the Northwest. In time, the population became so large that life there was difficult. The tribal wise men announced that a land of fertile soil and abundant game lay to the southeast, in what is now called Mississippi. The people could live there in peace and prosperity forever."

Forever! The word had a bitter sound for every Choctaw in the audience.

The pageant with its sad story of the Choctaw past was not new to Clifton. He had heard it often, but each time in some mysterious way he did not understand, he was deeply touched by it. Slowly, as the story unfolded, he was drawn into it again, until he was no longer aware of his aching legs and all the people sitting around him in the dark. Even Travis and his stuffed snake were forgotten.

When this continent was still entirely the home of the Indian, there were more than seventy-five tribes living in the area that later became the states of Florida, Alabama, Mississippi, Louisiana, the Carolinas, Virginia, and Tennessee. The tribes had beautiful, melodic names such as Chitimacha, Opelousa, Chawasha, Catawaba, and Apalachicola. The Choctaws were one of the largest and most powerful of these tribes. At the peak of their power they numbered 30,000 and ruled a vast domain of 26,000,000 acres. The Choctaws were a proud and prosperous people who lived in harmony with the pine forests and red clay hills of Alabama and Mississippi where they hunted and fished and raised food in such abundance they were able to sell a surplus to their neighbors.

And then the first white man came. He was Hernando De Soto. As the Spanish explorer prowled around the Southeast looking for gold and silver in 1540, he burned a Choctaw city and left 1,500 Choctaws slain behind him. That bloody moment was the beginning of a great change for the Choctaws and their Indian brothers. Slowly at first, but then faster and faster, the fabric of their lives unraveled completely over the next four hundred years, until today, the Indians who survive in the southeastern United States bear little resemblance to their proud forefathers. Some of the tribes have disappeared entirely.

After the De Soto expedition, a hundred and fifty years passed before the next white men appeared in the land of the Choctaws. They were traders. After the traders came settlers, who wanted to clear the forests, plant crops, and settle down. At first a trickle and then a flood, the settlers put great pressure on the government to make the Indians leave their ancient hunting grounds. The government surrendered to this land hunger, and in 1805 forced the Choctaws to sign a treaty in which the Indians gave away 4,000,000 acres. Other treaties followed and, piece by piece, the Choctaws saw their beloved hills and forests taken from them. Each time the government demanded land from the Choctaws, it promised it would not ask for more. The promises were never kept.

The Choctaws remained loyal to the young American nation, despite its treachery to them. They refused to join the Shawnee chieftain, Tecumseh, in his campaign to drive the colonists from Indian soil. The Choctaws even shed blood for America when Pushmataha, their greatest leader, took 750 warriors to join Andrew Jackson in his war against another Indian tribe, the Creeks, in 1813. Choctaw warriors also helped Jackson thrash the British in the last battle of the War of 1812. Their blood and their loyalty earned the Choctaws very little—not even a rest from the persistent land-grabbers who continued to swarm into the South. The government promised—again, the promises—that if the Choctaws would leave their shrunken homeland in Mississippi it would give them much fertile land in Oklahoma in exchange.

Finally, by the 1830s, the Choctaws were exhausted. No longer able to resist the pressure on them, some of their leaders signed the Treaty of Dancing Rabbit Creek. It was the death knell for the Choctaw nation in Mississippi. While a stubborn handful remained behind, most of the tribe trekked westward to Oklahoma. Their "trail of tears" was a terrible ordeal for the Indians. Many perished along the way of cold, hunger, sickness, and broken hearts. But life was not much better for those who stayed in Mississippi.

DeLaura Henry continued the story. "Today's Mississippi Choctaws are the great-great-grandchildren of nearly 1,000 Choctaws who retreated into the swamplands of east central Mississippi where they wandered homeless in a country once their own. For them there was no fixed home; they camped near the school and within the sound of the church bell, but their children were never taught.

"We, the Choctaw Nation of Mississippi, descendants of these strong people, are proud of the legacy of their courage, and we welcome you to our nation with the Choctaw warrior's proudest boast: *Chahta siah hoke*—I am a Choctaw."

Then DeLaura brought the pageant to an end by singing a song she had written. It was beautiful but filled with sadness, Clifton thought.

This was the home
Of my people long ago
Settlers came one day
And told my people go.
They promised—better land,
They promised—better grass,
We want to stay here, we want to stay
Where our people rest.

Trouble came
To this peaceful tribe.
Settlers asked, either
Leave or die.
We were called drunkards,
We were called thieves.
We asked for help but
No one listened to our pleas.

We are the children
Of our people long ago.
They who have fought
For the land they loved so.
They who had suffered much,
But they've never lost their touch.
Now we are proud to say
We are Choctaws.
Chahta siah, Chahta siah hoke.

The Choctaw fair was over. Clifton was so tired he felt like a marionette with its strings cut. On the drive home, wedged in between Pam and his mother on the back seat, he fell asleep long before they reached Bogue Chitto.

Once the domain of the Choctaws stretched unbroken from horizon to horizon and even beyond—a vast green carpet of pine cut through by swift, clear rivers. That was four hundred years ago. Today the Choctaw homeland has been reduced to a few square miles of poor soil in central Mississippi. The Choctaws live in seven widely scattered rural communities located within fifty miles of the town of Philadelphia. One of the communities is Bogue Chitto. The other six are named Pearl River, Bogue Homa, Standing Pine, Red Water, Tucker, and Conehatta.

The Henrys and about a hundred other families live in Bogue Chitto, which means "Big Creek" in Choctaw. Bogue Chitto has no street lights, no paved streets, no filling stations, and no stores. What it does have is several small churches and an elementary school where Clifton and Travis are students.

If you want to get to Bogue Chitto, you drive northeast from Philadelphia for fifteen miles along a paved road and then turn off to the south along a dirt road. A ribbon of red mud in the winter and a ribbon of red dust later in the year, the dirt road leads past played-out cotton fields, tenant farmer shacks, and the shallow waters of Owl Creek where Choctaw families fish for mudcats and bass in the twilight of summer evenings. Some new houses that look as though they might have been transplanted from the suburb of a big city begin to appear among the pines. One of these belongs to the Henry family.

Dolphus Henry is a medium-sized, friendly man with thinning black hair. His weathered face is brown, partially because it has been exposed to the fierce Mississippi sun so many years, but mainly because of the pure Choctaw blood flowing through his veins. A small tattoo on his right arm is a souvenir of the days when he was a rifleman in World War II, following General Patton's tanks through Europe. Now he is the janitor at Bogue Chitto's school. He is also a leader in the Bogue Chitto Baptist Church and from time to time is a member of the Tribal Council which governs the reservation. He is also Clifton Henry's father.

It was Saturday morning in Bogue Chitto. It was winter, too, and the pale sun was not warm enough yet to soften the brittle frozen grass beside the Henry's back door. Smoke came from the chimney. Inside a fire of white oak logs blazed cheerfully in the living room. A TV was turned on in one corner of the same room but nobody was watching it. Clifton's mother was in the kitchen singing to herself as she made biscuits for breakfast. She was very pleased with her kitchen. Three years earlier when the Henrys' old house was badly damaged by fire, Dolphus borrowed money and built a ranch-style house with four bedrooms, two bathrooms, and a kitchen so modern that it has taken all the drudgery out of cooking for Inez Henry.

There was some strenuous activity going on in one of the bedrooms at that very moment. Clifton and Travis were tussling. The room was quiet except for bursts of muffled giggling. At this time of year, when it often was bleak and cold, they didn't get outside as much as they wanted, and excess energy was like a great tickle down inside them. The day before it had been warm enough at recess time, and all the boys in the fifth grade burst out of their prison and wrestled on the partially thawed ground of the schoolyard. When the bell rang they were muddy from head to toe. The mud was pretty well dried by the time Clifton got home, and he was able to brush some of it off. When his mother saw him, though, the expression on her face could hardly be described as happy.

Finally the boys hit the floor with a thump. "I won!" Clifton shouted.

"*Kiyo*, no! You didn't, I did," Travis replied, jabbing his cousin in the ribs. Clifton retaliated. The battle started anew.

"Boys! Boys!" It was Pam. "Do you want to eat breakfast, or do you want to tear this room apart? Come on."

The boys untangled themselves, pulled on their tennis shoes, and went into the kitchen. The table was already crowded. Even though three of the six Henry children no longer live at home, the house is usually full. The Henry family tree has many branches in Bogue Chitto. Clifton's mother seldom puts a meal on the table without setting an extra place for an aunt or an uncle or a cousin or two.

Today Uncle Bob was sitting there at the end of the table covering a fresh biscuit with blackberry jam. Clifton was delighted to see his uncle. Bob Henry is his father's oldest brother. He lives just a bit down the road, but had not been feeling well that winter and had been an infrequent visitor. Sickness had lined his face and it seemed to Clifton as though the old man's hair was whiter. But there was a twinkle in his eye and Clifton knew a story was on the way. His uncle is an endless source of Choctaw stories. Some of the stories are funny, but some are frightening enough to raise goose pimples.

Between bites of fried egg and hominy, Clifton persuaded his uncle to tell about Kashe-ho-ta-pa-la, the ugly creature with the head of a man but the body and legs of a deer, who roams the woods frightening Choctaw hunters. Kashe-ho-ta-pa-la gets its name from its cry which sounds like an old woman in distress.

A long time ago, Uncle Bob began, there was a Choctaw boy named Hatak moma-In-kana, which means "man who is friendly to all." The boy loved animals. In order to avoid hurting them, he wandered in the woods by himself much of the time, so that he wouldn't have to join the other braves in their hunting parties. For this he was mocked and made an outcast. One day when he was by himself he came upon a deer which had been wounded and was dying of thirst. To Hatak moma-In-kana's great surprise the deer spoke to him and begged him to bring it water. The Choctaw youth found a nearby spring. The deer gratefully drank the cool water and then, before it died, it granted Hatak moma-In-kana one wish. The boy knew right away what he wanted to do with his wish. He wanted an ugly face, the body and legs of a deer, and the voice of an old woman so he could frighten hunters away from wild animals. And thus it was that Kashe-ho-ta-pa-la was born.

Even though Clifton had heard the story of Kashe-ho-ta-pa-la so many times he knew it by heart, he never tired of hearing his uncle tell it. Mrs. Henry began to clear away the breakfast dishes. As Clifton sat in the warm, cheerful kitchen a shadow passed over his mind. He thought of the half-man, half-beast roaming the woods out there, maybe even in the pines behind the house. He shivered. He tried to imagine what Kashe-ho-ta-pa-la's strange cry would sound like. It must be terrible, and he knew if he ever heard it behind him in the woods he would jump out of his skin.

Uncle Bob had another talent besides storytelling. When he was younger he was Bogue Chitto's most respected *alikchi*, or Choctaw doctor. For years people came to him with their aches and pains, and he prescribed medicines made from Sampson's snakeroot, Jerusalem oak, rabbit tobacco, the mayapple, the pottage pea, and other roots and barks which he collected from the fields and woods around his house. Sometimes he helped his patients by placing the tip of a cow horn over an infection and drawing out the poison through a small hole drilled in the end.

Almost always Uncle Bob's patients felt better after taking his remedies. He had learned the secrets of Choctaw medicine from his father, who learned them from his, and so on for many generations into the past. But times have changed and it is unlikely that there will be any more doctors in the Henry family. Today when Choctaws get sick they usually go to a fine hospital which the government built for them in Philadelphia. Bob Henry is left with his memories and the piece of cow horn which he pulls out and looks at every now and then.

After breakfast Clifton and Travis carried a heavy bucket of slops out to the tough, sinewy pigs rooting around in the pen behind the house. The pigs were the family meat supply and as soon as they added enough weight to their scrawny frames, they would become bacon, sausage, ham, and lard. The boys poured the slops into the trough and then, after watching the pigs fight for it, got to work. The small pigs were not getting their share and Dolphus had decided it would be better if they were penned by themselves.

For an hour the boys chased the elusive animals. One by one, they caught the pigs and dragged them by their hind legs, as they squealed with indignation, to the new pen. Clifton's old black dog, Herman, didn't help because he kept nipping at the pigs' heels, making them run faster.

After that chore was done the boys found a basketball and, even though it needed air, they began to shoot baskets through the battered iron hoop at the side of the house. Travis tried to guard Clifton, but Clifton twisted free and shot one-handed. Swish! The ball went through the basket just as the game ended. Clifton Henry had won another one for Choctaw Central. Clifton wins many games for Choctaw Central in his backyard.

When the boys returned to the house, Mrs. Henry was sitting alone in the kitchen. The breakfast dishes were done and she was sewing the final bit of decoration on Clifton's new purple dance shirt.

In the old days dancing was an important part of Choctaw life. Choctaws danced before they went to war, and at weddings, and to celebrate the ripening of crops and the change of seasons. They danced when they were sad and when they were angry and when they were pleased with life. Slowly over the years Choctaws forgot the dances, until finally it was something that only a few old people knew how to do. It got so that when young Choctaws wanted to dance they went to Choctaw Central and gyrated to the rock of the Flaming Arrows. This bothered the parents and they were quietly pleased when one of Clifton's teachers went to the tribal elders and learned *ok fochush hitha,* the duck dance, *ittibi hitha,* the fast war dance, and three or four others, and taught them to her students.

In the beginning Clifton and his friends went to the dance class as gingerly as a cat approaching a tub of soapy water. It was something that was all right for girls, but certainly not for boys. Imagine their surprise then when they discovered that Choctaw dancing is fun. And much more difficult than it appears. Most Choctaw dances are not rapid, but the feet have to follow intricate patterns and the dancer has to concentrate.

Clifton watched his mother finish his shirt. It was a pretty shirt. He put his arm around her shoulders as she worked.

Dolphus had a couple of errands to do that morning and on his way out the door he asked Clifton and Travis if they wanted to go with him. The three piled into the Henrys' rusted old Dodge, with its red peace symbol on the rear windshield. The boys sat in back and immediately began to shuffle through their baseball cards. The boys are great patrons of the bubblegum industry. Except at school, where they are not allowed to indulge, they usually have a mouthful. As a result, their supply of cards is large. Their trading was spirited and was done in Choctaw. Choctaws love their language and when they are by themselves they almost always speak it instead of English.

As they bumped down the red road through a forest of pine and oak and past the withered strubble of last year's cornfields, Dolphus told the boys how it was when he was their age. His father had been a tenant farmer who worked his land "on halves," which meant that he had to give half of every cotton crop to the man who owned the land. Rural Mississippi was bone poor in those days, and the man who had to work for somebody else couldn't count on getting more than fifty cents a day for his sweat. In 1929 a bumper cotton crop enabled Dolphus' father to buy a second-hand 1927 Chevy truck. That was a good deal better than the wagon and mules the family had used to take them into Philadelphia. The mules were ploddingly slow and sometimes it was late at night and pitch dark—except for the coal-oil lantern swinging on the back of the wagon—before they made it home again.

Dolphus was twelve before his father could spare him for school, and then he had time to go only through the sixth grade. It wasn't like it is today, when most young Choctaws go at least through high school. Dolphus' father had taught him how to hunt with a blowgun. A Choctaw blowgun, a *uski thompa,* is made of a hollow, fire-hardened length of swamp cane from six to eight feet long. The darts, or *shumatti,* are usually sharpened splinters of twisted cane with a tuft of cotton tied to one end, although sometimes an umbrella rib is used. Up to thirty paces, the swift, silent darts can be deadly.

On more than one night Dolphus and a companion had crept through thickets and briars, trying hard not to think of the rattlers that might be underfoot. Then one would light a torch of pine knots and hold it up, being careful to keep it behind the shooter's head so the light would not get in his eyes. The idea was to blind whatever might be in front of them—a roosting dove, a fat squirrel, or maybe a cottontail sitting frozen except for its quivering ears. If the marksman's aim was true, there would be fresh meat on the table the next day. That kind of hunting was part of the Choctaw past. Today the .22 rifle has replaced *uski thompa,* which is regarded by Choctaw boys more as an interesting toy than as a serious weapon. Clifton had tried using a blowgun, but he wasn't very good at it.

Dolphus stopped the Dodge in front of a crossroads general store. The boys hunted up the pop cooler and Dolphus went to buy a bag of groceries. His eye fell on a shelf of boxes of powdered soap. It wasn't too long ago that Choctaw women made their own soap in the backyard over an open fire by cooking a mixture of lye and wood ashes. That soap sure was strong! It would almost take the paint off a board.

The three left the store and drove down the road to see if Ary Willis had finished preparing the corn for Sunday's *tanchi labona.* Ary Willis was standing beside her front steps pounding the corn when they arrived. Grains flew in all directions, sending the chickens fluttering at her feet into ecstasies.

Tanchi labona is the Choctaw name for hominy with chicken necks. Choctaw women make the thick, nourishing dish by pouring dried corn into the end of a partially hollowed log and pounding it vigorously with a stick until the outer layers of the corn fall off. Then they soak the soft, inner kernels for half a day, add the chicken, and let it all simmer in a big, black kettle over a wood fire for four or five hours. That is the way Choctaw grandmothers still do it. Their granddaughters more than likely make *tanchi labona* in a pressure cooker on a gas range—if they make it at all.

Tanchi labona is so delicious, its fragrance is such when it is steaming hot, that it is beyond the power of an eleven-year-old boy to resist it. As soon as he saw Ary Willis pounding the corn, Clifton's stomach started to make hungry noises. In his mind he could see in glorious detail what was going to happen the next day. His Aunt Sally Henry would take the corn, when Ary Willis was through with it, and, starting about an hour before Sunday school began, have her massive black kettle bubbling in front of the Baptist Church. By noon, when church was out, everything would be ready. His mother and the other women in the congregation would unwrap their dishes of pigsfeet, fried chicken, cornbread, biscuits, catfish, and pies and cakes of every description, and place them on a long wooden table near the church. The table would almost break beneath the weight of all the dishes. There would be a blessing, and then the dinner-on-the-grounds would begin. It would be a feast!

When Ary Willis finished with the corn, Dolphus put it in the car. The boys were behind the house throwing pine cones at each other. He whistled for them, and then remembered that DeLaura had asked him to be sure and pick up Ary Willis' latest beadwork while he was at her house. Ary brought out a belt, some pendants, and a brooch. She laid them on the hood of the car where they stood out like bright butterflies against the faded green paint.

There are not many such butterflies on the Choctaw reservation any more. At one time Choctaw women were renowned for their beautiful baskets and pots and beaded objects. Now the ancient secrets are found largely in the arthritic fingers of old women. When these women are no longer around, their skills will be gone forever. The tribe has asked DeLaura to work with the older women, encouraging them to make more of their wares and at the same time to teach their art to younger women so that it will be kept alive. There is not much time to spare. Only a few women on the entire reservatiion still remember how to make a double-weave basket.

One of them is Rosie Amos, who lives a short distance from Ary Willis. Dolphus and the boys found Rosie Amos sitting in her living room. The house was chilly and she was close to a gas heater. She kept one eye on a television set in front of her and the other on the basket that was taking shape in her lap.

Rosie's face, brown and seamed with wrinkles, broke into a smile when she saw them.

"*Hailito. Chim achukma?* Hello. How are you?" she said, picking up another piece of Calcutta cane from the pile beside her. "Sit down."

She had gathered the cane the summer before in a swamp in Bogue Homa. It is not easy for Rosie, who is sixty-five and bent with arthritis, to go into a swamp where mud sucks at her feet and where she must keep her eyes open for cottonmouths. Rosie goes herself instead of having somebody else do it for her, because she is the only one who knows exactly when the cane is the right size. She cuts it with a sharp knife, puts it on her shoulder, and carries it out of the swamp. Later, at home, she dries the cane and slices it into narrow strips. In the old days she made natural dyes from berries and wild roots which she dug up and boiled. The stooping and digging are too strenuous for her now and she uses store-bought dyes, which suffice but are not as good.

A few minutes later Dolphus and the boys were bumping down the road again. Beside Dolphus on the front seat were three of Rosie's baskets, which DeLaura would sell in a crafts store operated by the tribe in Philadelphia. The trading market for baseball cards was reopened on the back seat. Choctaw words flew back and forth until, finally, just before they got home, Clifton grudgingly gave up one of his precious Johnny Benches for a Tom Seaver, a Pete Rose, and a Willie Mays.

Just like most boys his age, Clifton has an internal motor which keeps his gears and wheels turning constantly from the time he gets up in the morning until at night when he tumbles into bed. Remaining in one spot for long is hard for him. It is against his nature. And yet as he leaned against a rough-barked hickory in front of the Baptist Church, he was so still he almost seemed to be part of the tree. It was Sunday afternoon. After the dinner-on-the-grounds was over, Choctaws came from all parts of the reservation to Bogue Chitto for a hymn-sing. Their cars and pickups surrounded the church. The weak, winter sun found its way through the bare branches of the trees and warmed the back of Clifton's neck. There were lots of times during Sunday school when the hard-backed benches and long sermons made him restless. His mind would wander then and he wished he were some place else. But there was something within him that always responded to these old, sweet songs he had been hearing as long as he could remember. "What a Friend We Have in Jesus," "O, Master, Let Me Walk with Thee," "The Old Rugged Cross." He listened raptly.

Sunlight filtered in through the leafy roof of the forest and dappled the path beside the creek. Dolphus walked ahead. He carried a cane fishing pole in one hand and a can of worms in the other. Accompanied by the dog Herman, Clifton and Travis dawdled behind, each carrying his own pole. Their bare feet were tender after a winter of wearing shoes, and they walked carefully so as not to step on anything sharp. Once the creek area was known for its shards of hard yellow flint which suplied Choctaw hunters with their arrowheads.

It was early and the air was still cool. All was quiet except for the gurgling of the current and the occasional call of a cuckoo somewhere in the shadowy depths of the forest. The swift, dark water swirled and eddied around roots of cypress trees that looked like gnarled fingers.

They crossed the creek on a footbridge which swung gently to and fro while they were on it. Once across, they found their favorite fishing place. Dolphus threaded a worm onto his hook and plopped it into a quiet patch of water behind a cypress stump. His red and white bobber floated for a minute and then suddenly disappeared. Dolphus jerked the pole upward, and laughed because he knew he had a fish. It happened so quickly that the boys were open-mouthed with surprise. Before they had even gotten their lines untangled, there was a goggle-eye flopping on the grass between them, its silvery sides gleaming in the sun.

"How's that?" Dolphus asked. "If we get a mess of these, we'll have them for supper. But you boys will have to help." He gently put the goggle-eye on a stringer and dropped it back into the creek.

The fish didn't cooperate with their supper plans. A chunk of the morning slipped by and there were only two more goggle-eyes on the stringer. Dolphus caught them both. Clifton didn't mind. He sat in a patch of sunlight slapping mosquitoes as they lighted on his arm. He counted them for a while and then lost track. "I wonder what they eat when I'm not here," he said to himself, and glanced over at Travis to see if some of the pesky things had found him too.

As he watched his bobber in the water, Clifton thought how pleasant life was, now that it was June and school was out. For boys, summer is a time of idleness when nothing is ever very pressing. Get up about 8 o'clock. Eat breakfast. Feed the pigs. Hoe a row of corn in the garden. Help his father tinker with their ancient tractor. Knock down mud dauber nests in the old barn. Have a water fight with his cousins. Eat some more. Watch TV.

Clifton's daydream was interrupted by old Herman, who chose that moment to jump into the creek and paddle about. Fishing was finished for the day.

"Let's take a walk," Dolphus said, getting up.

They followed the path deeper into the woods. As they skirted a swampy place, Dolphus pointed out a deer track in the damp earth. By this time the boys knew where they were headed. The path led to higher ground. The trees thinned out and they found themselves at the edge of a cotton field.

Two hundred yards on the other side of the field was Nanih Waiya, for a long time revered by Choctaws as the most important place in their world. A legend about Nanih Waiya says it was the Mother Mound which the Choctaws built when they first arrived in Mississippi after traveling from much farther west. After completing the mound, according to the story, the Choctaws spread out in all directions, building their villages and clearing fields for farming.

At the high-water mark of Choctaw power, long before the white man set foot in North America, Nanih Waiya was a large, fortified city. The mound was eighty feet high and its base was longer than a football field. Earthen walls encircled the city at a distance of two arrow flights. The Choctaw nation was governed by its wise men, who sat around the Nanih Waiya council fire. It was the mighty capital of a mighty people.

Today, Nanih Waiya is simply a low hill with a few trees on it. Mississippi made it into a state park, but then neglected it. The tribe does not own the land and cannot care for the Mother Mound. Paint peels from a wooden marker which tells passing motorists about the golden age of the Choctaws. Steps leading to the top of the mound need repairing. Everything is overgrown by weeds.

Dolphus and the boys climbed the steps to the top of the mound and looked about. What they saw was very familiar to them—the green expanse of forest, the red earth, the blue vault of the sky. Except for the ripening cotton, it was the same view that a Choctaw would have had as he stood on the top of the old Nanih Waiya many centuries ago.

High overhead Sheki, the buzzard, wheeled on motionless wings. The clear, sweet note of a bobwhite came from the field. A breeze tugged at Clifton's hair. He fidgeted, and put his hand in his back pocket to see if his baseball cards were still safe. His thoughts began to drift and he saw Johnny Bench, squatting behind the batter, cock his wrist and, without even getting up, throw out a base stealer by ten feet. Old Johnny has an arm like a slingshot. At that moment baseball was much more important than the past glories of the Choctaw tribe. And more important than the indignities and wrongs that the Choctaws had suffered, and continue to suffer.

Life was cruel for the thousand or so Choctaws who remained in Mississippi instead of following the bitter trail to Oklahoma. The government still gave them no rest, and to escape, the Mississippi Choctaws fled into the swamps. This ragged band of men, women, and children were all that remained of a once large and prosperous tribe. Years passed. The Civil War flared and went out. The Choctaws lived in the shadows, strangers in their own homeland. They had no schools. The crops from their wretched land were meager. They often went hungry.

It was not until a flu epidemic in 1917 killed many Mississippi Choctaws that their plight became known and the government was shamed into doing something for them. It bought land around the Choctaw villages and gave it back to the Indians. It built a few small schools on the reservation. Gradually, life improved a little.

But only a little, for the Choctaws found themselves locked into a different kind of prison. It was a prison with invisible walls, but a prison just the same. It was the prison of their skin color. Minorities in the South have had their lives hemmed in and limited by racial prejudice. This is still true for the Choctaws, although here and there the invisible walls have been knocked down. The first hole appeared in 1964 when Congress passed a Civil Rights law, forcing Southern businesses to open their doors to workers of all races. Now Choctaws work side by side with whites and blacks in factories throughout central Mississippi.

Other changes have been slower in coming. It was not until just recently that Choctaws could own homes in Philadelphia and send their children to its schools. Choctaws still are not welcome in many of Philadelphia's restaurants, and if they go to a movie they still have to sit in the balcony. It is hard to find barbers who will cut their hair.

The Choctaws are a proud people. They do not go where they know they are not wanted. They prefer to eat at home rather than go to a restaurant which they know does not want to serve them. They prefer to drive forty miles to a larger city for a haircut rather than be offended in Philadelphia. Over the years, the Choctaws have drawn into themselves and have used their language, which few outsiders understand, as a shield against the hostility of the surrounding white world.

Sometimes in the evening after supper, when there is still light in the sky and swallows zigzag through the air in their pursuit of insects, Dolphus and Inez Henry talk about their children's future. Like most parents, they are concerned about the kind of people their sons and daughters will become.

The Henrys have watched four of their children grow up and leave home. Darry Lee lives in Texas where he works as a welder. Dallas works with a construction company in California. Both are married and both bring their families back to Bogue Chitto for brief visits. Probably neither will ever live in Bogue Chitto again. Dalton is finishing college. What he will do after he graduates is uncertain, although he thinks about playing professional football. DeLaura went to Mississippi State University—in fact, she was the first Choctaw woman to attend that school—and then for a few months she had a job on another Indian reservation. She returned to Bogue Chitto because she wanted to help her tribe. Pamela is still in high school and will live at home for another year. And then there is Clifton.

Clifton's parents sense that it is not easy these days to be young and to be an Indian. It is not easy to grow up caught between the old and new ways of doing things—between the healing methods of Uncle Bob and his piece of cow horn and the methods of a modern doctor at the hospital with his gleaming instruments. For some young Indians the choice between old and new is almost impossible to make. They may spend their entire lives wondering who and what they are.

Dolphus and Inez want there to be no doubt in the minds of the Henry children as to exactly who they are. They want their sons and daughters always to remember the warrior's proud claim: "*Chahta siah hoke*. I am a Choctaw."

It was getting on toward noon when the old Dodge pulled back into the front yard in Bogue Chitto from the fishing expedition. By that time Clifton and his father and Travis were starved. They found Dalton in the kitchen sitting at the table telling his mother about Baton Rouge. He had just finished cutting the grass in the backyard with the power mower. Beads of sweat stood out on his forehead and the front of his T-shirt was wet. Dalton's strongly muscled arms looked like brown cypress roots.

Clifton watched his brother enviously. Would he ever be as big and as strong? Dalton had a summer job in Baton Rouge and was home for the weekend. He was describing some of his adventures in the big city. This made Clifton's envy go up another notch. Would he ever be old enough to have adventures of his own away from home? The only city he had ever seen was Jackson, and that was when his class visited the Dixie National Livestock Fair. That was fun. He could see all the cows now, lying in their beds of fresh hay as their jaws worked rhythmically. And that bull covered with soapsuds. Clifton couldn't believe it when he first saw it. He thought that kind of disaster happened only to boys. The memory made him laugh out loud. His family looked at him curiously.

Dalton grabbed him in a sudden bear hug.

"Hey, kid, you get bigger every time I see you. Maybe I'd better beat you up now while I can still do it."

Clifton squirmed happily. Jackson—that wasn't much. He wanted to go further away than that. Baton Rouge sounded like a lot more fun. Would it be hard to wait and grow up? Maybe. In the meantime the fair at Pearl River was coming up again next month. And right now they were going to eat. There was a tantalizing smell coming from the pot of stew which his mother had warming on the stove. He remembered he still had not shown her their string of fish. He gave Dalton a jab in the ribs with a sharp elbow and wriggled free. Then he ran out to the car to get the fish.

FROM

Families: A Memoir and a Celebration

WYATT COOPER

GOING HOME

THOMAS WOLFE wrote a book and called it *You Can't Go Home Again*. That is a catchy title and it caught on. It caught on with people, even, who know nothing of the great autobiographical novel that went with it. One often hears it quoted, repeated with the half-jocular, half-embarrassed shrug that accompanies axioms from the Bible, Shakespeare, or *Poor Richard's Almanac*. As is usual with such popular utterances, it caught on precisely because it is part profound truth and part arrant nonsense.

We recognize the truth of it because each of us has at one time or another undertaken that almost mythical journey back to the familiar landscape that used to be home, to confront, instead, a land that is foreign and unfamiliar. That this is so is, of course, not the fault of the place. A place, after all, is only trees, ground, water, soil, and the uses men have put them to. We must credit it, instead, to the heavy burden we lay upon the trip. We go encumbered by an unreasonable demand, unspoken and not even totally formed, that in some mysterious way the questions of a lifetime should be answered there, the hungers of a lifetime assuaged. We hope, perhaps, that we will be able to reach back in time and correct something in our shaping that needs correcting. I dream from time to time that I am making improvements on the house I grew up in, though this house has not existed for ten years. We take with us a troubling sense of longing and of loss. We travel with a haunting mixture of memory and desire. We set out on the nostalgic road with the hope and faith and expectation of the child that once was, with the child's tenderness and innocence, which are not only not what they were but perhaps never even existed as they are recalled, and which are, in fact, an adult's poignant, reconstructed, partly calculated, and carefully nurtured idea of what he himself has been.

He expects to see the giants of this childhood and to know once more those towering and superhuman parents and teachers, neighbors and friends who gave form and shape to his youth, who seemed to move in a world of assurance and competence, and whose eyes were the mirrors in which he first formed images of himself. He expects or hopes to find them not the ordinary mortals they are, with limited knowledge, primitive notions, and narrow interests, complaining about the rising cost of meat and boasting about the town's recent erection of a power plant, but the concerned, judicious, all-knowing authorities he remembers, who once gave him answers and quieted his fears.

He expects to find intact and unchanged the church and the school that helped to mold him, which were so much more than wood and stone and once seemed absolute and everlasting and immovable, guardians of all the certainty in the world, where the depth and breadth of his thoughts, feelings, and impulses were first plumbed.

He finds that they have vanished. If they are physically there, unchanged even, they have become somehow shrunken, diminished, flat, and devoid of any life he recognizes, peopled by strangers of a smaller and lesser race, a company now of dwarfs whose comings and goings have nothing of the burning passions, swelling ambitions, consuming thoughts, raging fears, strange intensities, compelling laughter, or vexing tears that he remembered in them and in himself.

And he expects to come upon himself: to see the towheaded youth, all eager eyes and lengthening bones, with fair freckled skin under a frayed straw hat, barefoot and in overalls, climbing the red clay hill with the distracted air of the born daydreamer, the pale, lonely prince somehow disguised as the farmer's son.

But he is not there. Instead, there are ghosts, glimpses, and hints that tease and tantalize. While he was not looking, life went on. Faces, minds, bodies have altered. The very look of the land has changed. Where once there were hills, there is flat land. It is all gone, washed away by a thousand rains. During the decades it has flowed across the fields, along the ditches, and down the little river, on to bigger rivers, and eventually out to the great uncaring sea. It seems so simple but so unlikely that so much could flow so surely away on such a little stream, that little stream with the Indian name that sits now, hardly moving, evaporating under a hot summer sun.

But so it is, and, instead, he comes upon himself as a middle-aged man with a tiring body, a declining spirit; he is thrown back upon the person he has become.

He sees people. He is hailed by those he knew. He is recognized and remembered. His hand is shaken and his back is slapped, and he in his turn shakes hands and slaps backs. Smiles and hearty remarks are exchanged, but they know nothing of what the years have been for him, little of his dreams for himself or of his place in the world. As he knows nothing of them and of theirs. Together they recall the past; they compare dates and occurrences; they shake their heads over those who have died or been ruined; they smile with pride over childen who have become doctors or salesmen or computer scientists or housewives or mothers, and they joke about the improbable presence of a generation of grandchildren. Photographs are displayed. Cheerfully they deny in each other the evidence of graying or vanishing hair and withering flesh. Then they go their separate ways, making promises that will not be kept, wearing a glow that will last for a little, relishing for a time the tender residue of that reaching out, that tentative touching of another familiar life, cherishing the moments of sweet reunion with someone who is not quite a stranger, someone with whom there is something of a shared past, but afterward feeling more lonely, more alone, and more mortal, feeling somehow disturbed, somehow at a loss, somehow less enlightened, and altogether more puzzled about the meaning in it all.

That much, then, of Thomas Wolfe's title is true. But in another sense there is foolishness in it because, as no one knew better than Thomas Wolfe, we go home in our thoughts all the time, sometimes when we have no idea we are doing it. We have in truth never left home, for we carry it around with us. It is a part of our dreaming and our waking. It is a part of our breathing. It is a part of all we have been, all we are, and all we shall ever be. I doubt that there is a day in my life in which some fleeting image of that treasured country does not cross my inner eye. I will suddenly become aware that I have been standing beside the path that led down to the pump behind the schoolhouse, or I will for a moment see clearly the two giant hickory trees beside the road to Grandma's. I will remember the pervading smell of new overalls on the first day of school or the act of lighting the kerosene lamps in the kitchen and the comforting aroma of the biscuits a busy mother made for our supper. I remember driving the cows home from the pasture in the late afternoons, under the red sky of sunset, moving slowly and lazily, striking with my stick at weeds along the path, dreaming hazy dreams of glory, watching out for snakes and stinging nettles, avoiding the cows' droppings. I can close my eyes and know once more the lurking sense of terror as twilight faded and darkness gathered in clumps at the edge of the woods. I can hear the wail of the congregation singing at night in the church nearby, the collective sound of it floating mournfully through the still mystery of a starlit world, riding on the air with the scent of honeysuckle or crabapple bloom, and mingling in my ear with the cries of crickets, of frogs, of whippoorwills, and the rhythmic creaking of the porch swing I sat in. I recall the novelty of an airplane passing overhead and my sister Janice, who had never seen one on the ground, speaking both our thoughts when she said, "I don't want a plane to fall, but if one is going to fall, I wish it would fall near here so we could see it."

Sometimes walking and talking with my sons, I will hear in my own voice the voice of my father echoing from all those years ago, and I will know once again the strange fascination his mysterious presence held for me. I hear his rich voice vibrate against the trees we move among, and in it I can now hear something of pain, something lost and lonely, I was then too young to recognize or suspect in others.

I remember the sights and sounds and smells of home because the memory of home is the thing that never leaves us.

There is a familiar old saying, "You can take the boy out of the country but you can't take the country out of the boy," and, whatever your country has been, however alien it may have seemed to you at the time, or however alien to it you may have felt, it is forever a part of what you are, what you become, and what you mourn for.

And the core of it, the center around which all revolves, is the family: the father that was, the mother that was, the brothers and sisters, the uncles, aunts, grandparents, friends and neighbors—all exist forever in some part of what you are and what you do. They are as inescapable as life, as inevitable as death, and even if you somehow shut them out of your waking mind, they remain a part of everything that moves, molds, and renews you. You live with them and they with you.

Harder Times Than These

L. C. Dorsey

I WAS BORN SOME 42 years ago in the Mississippi Delta on a plantation. The plantation was in Washington County and called Tribbett. I was the eleventh of 13 children; only seven of us survived the first year of life. The reason for that, of course, is poverty.*

My mother was a native of Alabama, who moved early to Mississippi. She only finished the third grade, but could read and write fairly well. My father couldn't read and write at all. The Xs on pieces of paper, and quite often not even Xs on pieces of paper, were the way that we were committed to bondage.

Plantation workers very seldom lived on the same plantation all of their lives, and by the time I was grown I had lived on four. The owners of the plantation I was born on, the Walkers, were considered good boss people. They were considered good boss people because they didn't employ Klan tactics to control people. They didn't come to your house in the middle of the night to beat you up or kill you. They had a school for the "colored" people. They had houses that would leak, but you were allowed to patch them up. You were allowed some time off in the summer to cut wood for the wintertime. If you were really sick and not just pretending, Mr. Walker would allow you to see the plantation doctor.

Now growing up I never knew we were poor. One of the things that poverty does is isolate you. I thought all black people lived as we did, all over the country and all over the world, because our world was that plantation. We were one of the few families who didn't have any folks in Chicago. They never got out of Mississippi.

I didn't really understand racism. My earliest memories are of fear and it was only after I was grown that I understood the relationship between racism and fear. Two kinds of fear, I might add: the one that we carried around that dictated we could survive if we understood our places and stayed in those places; and another

*Address delivered in Atlanta at the 1981 Campaign for Human Development Conference

kind, a nameless, senseless kind that poor whites and well-to-do whites had of us.

I remember fear being very much a part of the plantation life. If a person mysteriously disappeared, who I later learned had been killed or lynched, the fear was so great that even at night with everybody at home in their own houses, nobody talked about this occurrence or this incident out loud. They would whisper. Fear so great until people walked around with their heads hanging down so they would not have the appearance of being uppity. Fear so great that people didn't look white folk in the eye because that was a no-no. Fear so great that all the black men I knew, when in the presence of white ladies, removed their hats and stepped off to the side so as not to brush against them accidentally. Fear so great that you call a little boy that you had raised "Mister," and little girls "Miss," because not to do so was an impudent, arrogant act that could get you in trouble.

We didn't know poverty or understand poverty as you understand poverty and as I grew to understand it later. It is a relative term really. We had enough to eat, and it didn't really matter that the three meals you had might be fatback and corn bread, not even biscuits sometimes, but cornmeal that we grew and ground ourselves. But, if you had those three meals, you don't understand what people are talking about by growing up hungry. You ate the fatback and in the summertime if you were fortunate and lived on a good plantation like we did, you had a little garden spot so you had the vegetables. In the wintertime you had wild greens and rabbits and squirrels and fish from the lake. My father was a proficient hunter and fisherman. We had a good realtionship, and we would go hunting and fishing together. We have eaten everything from turtles and birds to possums. I never liked possums—they said they ate out of the graveyard—but folks ate them. So, we never understood poverty and hunger in the sense that you hear talked about.

My father, who had never known education, was sure that all the problems he suffered and the things that he was not able to give his family were the result of not being educated. And, in a time when it was mandatory that all members of a household who were old enough to chop or pick cotton be in the field by order of the plantation owner, my younger sister and brother and myself went to the school. My father carried his gun to the field wrapped in a cotton sack and laid it under the cotton to enforce that decision. And when men drove by and said, "Will, where are your children?" he said, "They are in school." I didn't understand when I was young the courage it must have taken for him to say that and to back it up. I understand now that was why we had to move so frequently, why we couldn't stay on the plantation until we grew up. And that was a big dream: to grow up on the same plantation and not to be the new kid on the plantation or the new kid in the little one-room school.

I decided that part of my father's reasoning was correct when I was 13 years old, that the reason black people on plantations were so poor was because they didn't have the education to keep records. They really didn't keep account of how much they owed a man, how much the cotton sold for and how much they should get for their part. So I decided when we moved to a new plantation that we were going to do something different this year with the crop. I would keep records because my father had been sending me to school so I could help us do better. He bought me a blue composition book, and with my little learning I got in these country schools, one-room church places, I learned how to set up bookkeeping records. I put down all the little things that we got, and Daddy cooperated by telling me. Beginning in March, you get a "furnish," a little amount of money from the owner of the plantation and you get that for six months. That is to help you with food and stuff until the cotton crop comes in and you start to harvest. Well, I put down all the things that we got that whole year. All the money we had to borrow before the furnish started in March, all the money that we had to pay to the previous plantation owner so we could move off his place, so you never get out of debt. We had a radio by this time and every day at 12:00 the radio would broadcast what cotton was selling for. With my arithmetic, we would figure up how much we owed.

We knew we had to give the man half of all the bales we picked. Cotton sold for a good price that year—40 cents a pound. We added up all the extra pounds; bales are generally figured at 500 pounds a bale, but there were some bales that weighed 600 pounds. All this extra money the white man usually just takes. We figured up plantation expenses because that is the catch-all—when you paid everything else and there was nothing else they could legitimately add to your debt, they added plantation expenses. When all this division and multiplication and subtraction was over, by my set of books our share should have been $4,000, and we should have at least gotten $1,000. I did know there was no fairness in this system. Well, settling day finally came and my father had to go up to the house for the settlement. This is in December. I went off to school, but all day long I was anxious to know what was happening at this house when my father pulled out his set of figures and gave them to the man and said, 'Now listen, you have to deal with me honestly because here is what I owe you, here is what the cotton sold for, here is my part." I don't know what really happened at the house that day. I don't even know if my father brought out this composition book with all my figures neatly entered. But what we cleared out of that crop—and this is the first time we had ever cleared any money—was not the $1,000 that I thought we would clear, but $200, which was just a token. It wasn't what we were due, but it had a lot to do with "coming of age" in the sense of how little control black people have over their lives.

When I got home and found out what the settlement had really been, there was another coming of age—people were locked into this system, and the fear and lack of control made them take that. There was no protest. There was no saying I'm not going to take that. There was nobody else you could appeal to. *Nobody else*. That did something for my whole life from that point on. Maybe if I was white I would have become a Klansman. But what it made me was a very angry person who spent the next 20 years using that anger against unfair systems.

I said 20 years because I'm still dealing with stuff, but it is no longer from a base of anger. A long time ago anger got to be a burden—it grows and feeds on itself and it gets to a point where it is almost uncontrollable. And then it becomes very, very destructive. I think you have to have it so it molds you into something that is a lot more manageable.

You see, I never thought all those years that it was fair for things to happen like this, but I could never find a way to deal with it. When I was 11 years old, a little girl—my classmate—was slapped by a white lady in the 10-cent store for not saying "Yes, ma'am." I knew that wasn't fair. But I didn't know how you deal with it. I told my mother how I would have dealt with it: I would have hit her back, but I know that would have brought a lot of pain to the family.

So I started the cycle that my parents had been in, dropping out of school when I was 17 and getting married to a man on a plantation. We started having babies that we could not afford, and we kept on until we had six—four girls and two boys. You have the same cycle of poverty continuing. We were getting the exact same set of experiences that my father had gone through, with a different plantation owner and a different plantation, but the same system being in place. And we probably would have been there until now, with my children on somebody's plantation doing something, except for the Civil Rights Movement and except for chemicals and except for the mechanization of picking cotton, all three of which worked independently to put us off that plantation.

We began to hear about the Movement on the radio and in black newspapers. Let me tell you about my father. My father would walk 10 miles into town to the black barbershop that sold black newspapers—the *Chicago Defender* and the *Pittsburgh Courier*—and he would bring those newspapers home on Saturday evening and my momma would spend the weekend reading that paper to all of us. You began to hear a little bit about that struggle from those papers. The radio stations didn't broadcast a lot about that. We didn't have televisions, and the local paper wasn't carrying that stuff. People used to come out to our house at night from the NAACP—whatever they say about it now, in the old days it had some courageous warriors. They drove down the turn road with their lights out so that the white folks wouldn't know that they were coming. They would get the word on the grapevine about what movement was going on where, what progress was being made, how many folks were being registered and if you wanted to register, how to go register. They would come to my folks' house and they would talk and I would listen and I soaked it all in.

When the Movement started moving closer, we would get together on the ends of the cotton rows in the morning and we would whisper about it. If we heard something we'd pass it on to everybody else. We were a people who were sitting, waiting for the Movement to come and help us with all these things that we were struggling against all of our lives, that we couldn't ever get a handle on, that we couldn't ever figure out how to deal with. We felt the Movement would offer a way out.

Let me tell you, when it got to Mississippi, where I was living then, having been forced off a plantation because the machines could do it better, I was waiting for it. When the word went around through town that the Freedom Riders were here, we said "Where?" When we found out where they were, we were there. The fear that our folk had known, the fear that kept a lot of people quiet when abuses were being made not only to them but to their families, sort of fell by the wayside because there was this unified group of people, black and white, who had come into town to say we are here to work with you against this system of oppression and hatred. We got involved in that and just kept going from that point through the economic movement with the Federation of Southern Cooperatives, where you had to realize that the right to vote, the right to go into any cafe or restaurant or hotel was really kind of empty without a job for all of us who were moved off those plantations, without the money to eat.

From then on we've worked on other human-rights struggles—the Vietnam War, the oppression by the Klan, more sophisticated, much more organized, the police brutality where you have your policemen using the color of law to abuse and oppress people in the black community and in the poor communities. And we've been able for the first time to really deal with white people on a human basis. You know what poverty and racism do to us; it also dehumanizes you white folks because we don't see white folks as people, we don't see them as folks that you can sit down with. Until this day I haven't gotten to the point where we can sit down in church with whites because I find myself looking at them and wondering if they are Klan or this or that. It cripples all of us.

As black and white together, we have seen harder times. Much of my life has been so apart from white folks in terms of understanding how they perceive hard times and how they deal with them. But, as black people, I don't know that we have seen any harder times than we see now. Let me tell you why. We have more property—no, we don't, we have more houses that we own with FHA mortgage companies—we have more color television sets, we drink more cognac, we have more Brooks Brothers suits and more things, so that if you look on an acquisition basis, maybe we have had harder times. But we have less love.

On those plantations, when times were really tough, there was a sense of oneness. Oneness and the fact that even in our oppression we were brothers and sisters, with love for each other and concern for each other, and if in fact I had no cornmeal in my house I didn't have to worry, because down the street there was meal and a house for me and my kids.

I have had no experience worse than—I've only had it once and I hope none of you ever had it—the experience of having your kids cry themselves to sleep because there was no food in the house. That is a miserable thing that I never intend to go through again. I would rob a bank, break into a store or anything because I am never going through that again. I had that experience from being in a new community in an isolated place and being a part of all the foolishness of protecting black men's dignity and not letting people know that you are hungry because the man is out someplace. I've lived with that nonsense and I am not going through that again.

If I had said anything to anybody when those kids were hungry, nobody in the black community would have suffered them to go hungry. I've left my little kids at home to go to the field to chop cotton and not even worried about it, because I knew black neighbors who were too old to go to the fields anymore were taking care of them. They took care of the whole community. It was more like what I have seen in some of the other countries I have traveled in where our problems were community problems, our strengths were community strengths, and when we went off to school or when we went off to get a skill, it was a skill that was an investment in the total community. So that when you learned how to write, you wrote letters for everybody on the plantation. You didn't charge anybody for writing those letters and reading the letters they got back, and you kept their business in those letters. You didn't tell nobody what was happening.

As I move across the country now, I don't see that unity in the black community. It worries me that these are the hardest times we have ever seen. It worries me that these are the times when we might not survive as a group. The strong always survive so a few individuals will survive, but at what cost? I worry that this man who we've got in the White House now, who's got the greatest script he has ever had in his whole life, that he is going to do things to us that further divide us. I worry about the impact that the media has on defining issues for us, on shaping our perception.

I worry that we look at the ills of this society and we do not address the causes. We look at crime that makes us all fearful, and we decide that because people are stealing and shooting and killing that it is alright to fill up the prison predominantly with black people although we represent only 11 percent of the total population, that it's okay if 48 percent of the people on death row are black. I'm talking to black folks now. We have decided that these kinds of inequities in a society are all right. We have decided to become aligned with those who we have called oppressor and have failed to deal honestly with what threatens our survival.

We have become fragmented and changed our personal values away from our commitment to the community. Most churches are no longer a part of the community or concerned about the community as a whole. The family, even the family, has changed. We no longer set forth the values of where we want out children to go. Nor do we make sure they get there. There is a falling away of that sense of togetherness, of belonging, of having meaning and purpose, of having your life be a part of a group of people who depend on you, who seek love and comfort from you. It's not enough to say we're too busy, because if we don't pay attention to our family and our community, we can't build anything.

With some creative energy, we can make the meal, clean up the house and still listen to our children. It may mean we have to involve them in that process of making the meal and talk to them while we're doing the housework, but that's what we have always had to do. I don't want to come off sounding like the Moral Majority, but we have to also let our children know they are important by being an authority figure in their lives. One of the things that has happened in our desire to be good parents is that we have abandoned some basic tried-and-true principles, and we've been very uncertain about what we should be doing. We have gone through a period as parents—and particularly mothers—of being told by experts about how bad our influence on children is, and that has made many of us very timid about asserting our authority or relying on our experiences in rearing our children. As a result of our uncertainty and our failure to give guidance and discipline, we have children relying on their own, taking wild directions from their peers, and winding up seeking someone that can give them direction, discipline and the love they never had.

The churches have failed to give that direction, too. People throng to churches every Sunday morning because there is an absolute emptiness in their lives that they recognize and they're going to the place where they think it can be filled. Pastors who know how to put away the mystique of saints walking across hell on spider webs and who can reduce the born-again experience to the Here and Now, they could be a powerful force in bringing families together, making the church a meaningful forum for people to deal with issues in the community, and filling the void that is causing people to search in the church in the first place.

We have lost so many of these basic things that kept us together on the slave ship, that kept us together after we were over here, the whole business of getting back to our country and determining our culture, determining our future, the whole nation vision that we shared that kept us through all these hard times. We survived slavery and the Klan and the plantation system because we all had a unified vision and if we stuck together we could make it. Somehow, somebody decided in the '60s, after the Movement, that the best way to deal with us was to get a few individuals and say you are better than the rest. You deserve this and you deserve that. And you'll get it if you forget about the rest of those people. Because of that attitude, because of the absence of the strong family structure, because of the failure of the Church to take its rightful place and tell us about living here instead of heaven, I am not sure that we are going to survive these hard times as a people.

We will not survive if we depend on Washington to solve our problem, or if we talk ourselves into thinking we are helpless to do anything about the powers around us. At some point, we must recognize that all we have now and all we ever had was each other. The cutbacks or new legalized powers of the FBI and CIA are nothing new; there was a long period of our history when we had *no* social programs, when the KKK and FBI were oppressing people openly. There is nothing new about today except *us*.

Before, when we had nothing, we were more prepared to struggle. Now, we let ourselves think that if we don't speak up, if we don't take the risk, then maybe we can hold onto what little we've been able to get through our new alliances with the power structure—whether that's being able to attend a meeting with the governor or hold a job that somebody else gave us. We'd like to forget about our part in the community's struggle, to just hope that somehow other folks will get by without us. But the key to anything we had or will ever have lies in our ability to accept the reality that to keep together, to get by, to hold onto what is ours and what we've won, to survive, to have meaning in our lives, will always require that we continue to struggle together, with creativity and with commitment to build our community and move forward as a people.

Reading and Writing: Beginnings

ELLEN DOUGLAS

IT IS DIFFICULT, but not, I think, impossible to shovel away the sediment laid down by forty years of reading, writing, and experiencing the world and go back to one's early adolescence, the Eden of one's adult reading—to re-imagine first the child, then the emerging adult.*

I had read obsessively, uncritically, from my seventh year. I believe a child reads as he runs and swims, because he can, with compulsive joy in the act. I remember that by the end of the first few weeks of a school year I would have read through all my textbooks and would be frantic for more books, more texts, more stories, more printed words. I had a curious habit when called on in class to read aloud, of reading to myself a paragraph ahead, simply because I couldn't talk as fast as I wanted to read. I remember an almost unconscious immersion in language, sensation, emotion, make-believe—the *story.* I remember sitting down, plunging into a book, hearing nothing, aware of no one for hours at a time.

The kinds of books I liked best to begin with were fairy stories—Anderson and Grimm; then later the adventures and travail of heroic children and princes and outlaws—Elsie Dinsmore, Oliver Twist, Robin Hood; and later still, savage tales of the jungle, Gothic ones of ruined houses, tortured heroes and heroines—Edgar Rice Burroughs and Poe. Sometimes—often—I would be trapped in the house of one of my grandparents whose library was—in my terms—disgracefully limited. To feed my habit, I read Foxe's *Book of Martyrs* and all four volumes of *The Rise of the Dutch Republic.*

Reading was like playing. I plunged into it and was wholly taken up with the make-believe. In short, it was very close to being a function of the unconscious. But, just as, in the tree where I was hiding from a pack of savage head hunters, I heard and finally responded to the call to supper, so I roused reluctantly from my

*From paper presented at the 1980 Faulkner and Yoknapatawpha Conference at the University of Mississippi.

reading and took a bath or did my homework or went off to Sunday school with my sisters and my brother. That is, without difficulty or even thought, I separated the make-believe from the real world.

It goes without saying that I was always writing too. I suppose I wrote my first poems at the age of seven or eight. They were based on ballad form or on the hymns I sang every Sunday in church. I wrote plays for my sisters and friends to act and stories that I read aloud to my mother. Like reading, like play, this too happened mostly at the unconscious level. Never mind parsing sentences, organizing paragraphs, or learning to "speak the king's English," as my mother put it. Inside my head the language box was humming like a powerful transformer, pouring dreams and fantasies into the forms and language furnished me by Poe and Burroughs and Dr. Watt.

Then, in adolescence, something happened to the language-and-myth-and-make-believe-smitten child. It happened abruptly, immediately, and specifically in relation to two things I read, things so disparate that they serve to illustrate not only the kind of change I am talking about, but also the relationship of the emerging adolescent to the world of literature. As a child, of course, I had not read "literature." I had absorbed myth, adventure. I had no tools to make even the most rudimentary literary judgments. I was at the very beginning of becoming a human being.

At fifteen I read one day Milton's "On His Blindness." I suppose I must have had to read it for a high school English class—along with "Thanatopsis" and "The Legend of Sleepy Hollow" and *As You Like It* and Gray's "Elegy," none of which moved me deeply at the time. They couldn't compare with *John Carter, Warlord of Mars.* But the Milton sonnet hit me like a ton of bricks. I don't know why. I sometimes think it may have been because my mother was deaf and I lived every day a witness to her stoicism and resourcefulness. But I don't remember thinking of her at the time. What I thought was: Milton was a *man.* He was blind. This marvelous poem is about what it is really like in the real world to be blind. It is about human fate. Tarzan and John Carter and "For-the-love-of-God, Montresor," the Little Mermaid, and Robin Hood receded into the mists of childhood.

Not long afterwards I read what is probably a fairly light-weight book (I don't know. I haven't seen it again in the intervening forty-odd years), a memoir by a leftist American journalist, Vincent

Sheean, called, I think, *Personal History.* (Was it a Book-of-the-Month Club selection? I remember at the same time the appearance on our book shelves of *Kristin Lavransdatter,* and I can't believe my mother bought either out of genuine interest.) In any case I read it and the same insight moved me: This man is writing about the struggles of real people in the real world, about the real effects on their lives of political and economic systems.

So that's what writers do! welled up like a shout, broke over my horizon like the rising sun. Books, the books that I love above all else to spend my time with, are the great tools for understanding one's life and the lives of other people.

It was not long after this, after I had consciously made this first adult discovery, that I wrote my first "real" story and that I read my first book by Faulkner. My story, I remember, although I had not yet read Faulkner, had a sublime disregard for probability that would have done him proud. It was about an old black man whose place in the world is defined by his mystical, almost magical ability to predict the rises and falls of the river; who, when his prediction proves wrong, walks into the flood and drowns himself, singing the while, "Ole Man River, He don't say nothin. . . ."

Now, as I begin to talk about how the first reading of Faulkner affected me, you should put out of your minds two orders of thinking and feeling: first, what the scholar and critic, the teacher, looks for when he is reading, and second, what the general reader looks for. Beginning writers are not beginning critics and they are not beginning general readers. The critic and teacher look for ways to fit a writer into his tradition, ways to locate and analyze him for the student. They identify trends and map literary landscapes. The general reader looks first for entertainment, then (if the writer is lucky) for aesthetic pleasure and stirred emotion, finally, for insight into the human condition. But obsessively, selfishly, single-mindedly, again, almost unconsciously, the beginning writer *uses* other writers—just as I unconsciously used hymns and fairy stories, *imitated* them. He says, "What's in it for me?"

He may not even ask that question, but he absorbs and uses, must use, other writers to become himself, to find his own window in the house of fiction, his own focus and frame for the world of his art, to learn to hear his own voice. He precariously clings, at the beginning, like a small new leaf to the top of a supporting tree whose branches are the giants of modern literature and whose roots reach back to Homer and Vergil and the Old Testament prophets. He must read to hear the voices of his tradition and to find where he belongs in it, where he may be fortunate enough to move it and to contribute to it. He reads to learn the great questions. His reading gives him his language and his grasp of form. It gives him something else as well: It contributes, along with his own experience of the world to the unique ordering of his experience, to his moral and ethical vision.

How fortunate and at the same time how overwhelming, indeed, almost paralyzing for a young Southern writer, sixteen years old in 1938, to lay her hand on a book by William Faulkner, the man whose voice was that very moment in the act of shaping the modern perception of the world she lived in. Doubly, triply fortunate and overwhelming. In every way I felt the joyous sensation of *coming home.* Here were my outlaws, my heroic children, my heroines riding—oh, joy!—into battle with their lovers, my good witches and bad witches, even a jungle! And here, simultaneously, was the adult world I had begun to grope toward, not as it had been for Milton in seventeenth-century England or Sheean in New York or in Russia, but *here, now,* the very streets, the very houses, the very people by whom I was surrounded. And all in a language more seductive, more powerful than any Edgar Rice Burroughs ever dreamed of.

The book was *The Unvanquished,* published early that same year. I am not sure now who directed me to it, but I think that out of my own random reading I directed myself. I did not get it from a library. I went out and bought it. At the time Faulkner would never have been mentioned in a high school literature course in a small town in the South. We were taught, not the people who were making American literature—Hemingway or Fitzgerald or Dos Passos—but those who had once made it and were thoroughly and safely dead—Hawthorne and Irving and Longfellow and William Cullen Bryant.

In any case, I bought *The Unvanquished* and read it and I remember how peculiarly it suited my needs. Put together from half a dozen or so stories which had been separately published in magazines, it was not in any finished, structured sense of the word, a novel at all. In terms of Faulkner's highest standards it was a pot boiler. But that did not trouble me. It was accessible to my uneducated adolescent mind. It was romantic and sentimental. It was about the world I sprang from, and it dealt with the questions that loom all through Faulkner's work and that I would soon begin to address myself to. That is, under the treacle I lapped up so readily were the moral issues that Faulkner had from the beginning heroically addressed: the temptation to violence, the nature of heroism, the indissoluble marriage of love and hate between white and black, the pernicious nature of respectability, the obligations of the individual to society—and everything laid out in that rolling, hypnotic, irresistible language. Like the glittering lure that the young and reckless bass snaps at without thought, the stories, to begin with, caught my eye. The hooks caught me.

The following winter, as a freshman in college, I read *Light in August.* I had read the first book as scarcely more than a child. I read the second as the adult world began to open out before me. Here was no potboiler, but a novel whose power seemed to me unquestionable. It moved me from where I was to some place else. Again, I go back and try to shovel away the intervening layers of experience and remember what it was like to be what I then was—seventeen, an upper middle class Southern girl from an unusually pious radically sheltering family, a freshman in one of those colleges for young ladies in Virginia, struggling frantically, almost hysterically to escape the rigid world in which I was expected to function happily.

At first thought, it seems to me now that the unbending character, the terrible suffering, the crucifixion of Joe Christmas would have been so utterly foreign to me that I would have been unable to grasp their significance. The monstrous McEachern, the insane Hightower, the sex-obsessed Joanna Burden—what had these people to do with me? No one had ever struck me with anything heavier than a fragile chinaberry tree switch. I thought *whore* was pronounced *wore* because I had only seen it, not heard it spoken. And then I remember that at sixteen and seventeen I was not so sheltered as my parents might have wished and believed me to be. I was observant and I listened. I knew well enough that a black man had been lynched the year we moved into the little central Louisiana town where we lived. I had seen the hungry faces of beggars at the kitchen door, the ragged tenant farmers riding into town on Saturdays in their wagons. I was already in love. I knew how important sex would be to me. And more. I could take these characters in, not only in their relation to the real world I knew, but in relation to the world of myth and fairy tale from which I was emerging. And it is true, too, that I had learned from my first day in Sunday School that moral meanings, ethical meanings were a reality in that sheltered, rigid Presbyterian world.

And what spun like a tornado into my life, all indissolubly one—language, form, and story—was the product of one man's moral vision, moral obsession. Faulkner, I saw, wrestled titantically with that threatening, fascinating, complex, confusing world into which I had begun a puny struggle to make my way. He was obsessed with what it was at that moment essential for me to be obsessed with. The questions that every writer must in some fashion face, he faced in terms of the world that I looked out at from my window in the dormitory at Randolph Macon Women's College, asking: What does it all mean? How can I write about it until I understand what it all means?

I did not know then that what I have called "process"—the process of making something—is the way the artist *finds out* what he means, that what he means is the work of art. But I have only to check my preoccupation with Faulkner against my other preoccupations at the time (I had begun to read Conrad and Dostoyevsky) to recognize that in every case it was the problem of the moral order of the world that obsessed *me.*

The Search for Eudora Welty

CHARLES EAST

THERE IS A GAME I sometimes play—a test of memory. But more than that. A reconstruction of something in the past. A particular house (where we lived when I was twelve). A particular room (the marble-top table was *there,* and the sofa *there,* on the wall nearest the window through which one of us accidentally pushed Elbert Jacobs). Close your eyes and try to remember now: all that happened in that room.

I have been playing that game with the name Eudora Welty. An unusual name, even for someone growing up in my section of the country. Janula Poitevent, Narcissa Cruise, Fern and Dixie Pattie . . . all names that, forty years and more later, hang in the memory. But Eudora Welty? When did I first hear it? Who, of all those people in my past, first called her to my attention? I have narrowed the possibilities. First Effie Glassco, my high school English teacher. It is 1941 (my junior or my senior year) and we are seated in that classroom on the second floor and she is telling us of a writer from Greenville named William Alexander Percy and a book he has written. *Lanterns on the Levee.* We are intrigued by the title (ours is a levee world). She opens the book, reads pages from it. Did she also mention Eudora Welty?

Now it's another day. She is introducing the aunt of a girl in our class who will next year be valedictorian. The aunt lives in New York. She was the founding editor of the O. Henry Memorial short-story volumes, and Eudora Welty's stories have begun to appear in the O. Henry volumes. One has been (or is about to be) awarded a prize. But we don't know that. The aunt's name is Blanche Colton Williams and she wears a fur collar. What is it she is saying? I can remember the name Willa Cather. I don't remember Faulkner. Yet the best of Faulkner's work is behind him. I don't remember Eudora Welty. Still, it's possible. Could Blanche Colton Williams come back to Mississippi in 1941, the founding editor of the O. Henry Memorial short-story volumes, to this second-floor room in this consolidated school one hundred miles from Oxford and one hundred and fifty from Jackson, and mention only Willa Cather?

Where, indeed, would we have gone if we had suddenly been told: "Read Eudora Welty"? To the library upstairs, past the bust of Caesar, to the shelves well stocked with *Lorna Doone* and *Ivanhoe* but almost certainly barren of O. Henry volumes? Outside the O. Henry volumes, outside the pages of the literary quarterlies and one or two of the monthlies, where in 1941 (before the publication late that year of her first collection) would one have read the stories of Eudora Welty?

One thing I can be sure of: I did not read Eudora Welty in 1941 (I did read *Lanterns on the Levee*). And it is in fact possible that I had not heard the name until sometime in 1946, after the appearance of *Delta Wedding.* But there is another possibility and that is that it was sometime in 1943 or 1944, and that the person who spoke of her was the person who told me of Carson McCullers and *The Heart Is a Lonely Hunter.* By then three of Miss Welty's books had been published: *A Curtain of Green* (1941), followed by *The Robber Bridegroom* (1942), and *The Wide Net* the year following. It is *The Robber Bridegroom* that I connect (subject to all the tricks of memory) to my friend James Garrett.

I have, oddly enough, no memory of the moment I first read something by Eudora Welty, the way I can remember reading Eliot for the first time in the barracks at Great Lakes in 1945, when I was in the Navy, or that evening in New York (later the same year) when I saw *The Glass Menagerie. Delta Wedding* was published in the spring of 1946. I think it was in the summer of that year that I read brief passages from the novel in the weekly newspaper column written by Effiie Glassco, my old teacher, by now friend and surrogate mother. *The Key Hole.* What an injustice that name does it, and yet, on the other hand, how appropriate. It had a sophistication and knowledgeability which commanded the attention of those who wanted to know not only who was summering where but what books one should read and what plays one should see on the New York stage, or even at Ellis Auditorium in Memphis.

Surely for everyone young and with the ambition to write and a vision of a larger world there must be an Effie Glassco.

I had not, however, outside her weekly newspaper column, read Eudora Welty until sometime the following year when, off at college in Louisiana, I came under the tutelage of a teacher and poet named George Marion O'Donnell. O'Donnell is today no more than a footnote: one of the first (in 1939, in a *Kenyon Review* essay) to divine what Faulkner was doing. At the time I knew him, he was in his early thirties, younger than he looked, years out of Belzoni, Mississippi, by way of Nashville and Vanderbilt, in transit between Harvard, where he had taught for a time during the war, and a small college in Atlanta. The promise of the late thirties and early forties (New Directions included him in a 1940 volume of Young American Poets, alongside Jarrell and Berryman) was an unfulfilled promise. But there was still much that he could impart to students: more than the lesson of great talent wasted . . . more than the knowledge that he had been there, if only for a time, and that he had had an acquaintance with people like Ford Madox Ford and Auden and Allen Tate and Caroline Gordon.

Those evenings when he played Eliot on his phonograph—and a record of O'Donnell himself reading his own work—he sometimes talked of Eudora Welty. There was of course a double bond of kinship: they were not only writers but Mississippians. More than that: Deltans. Though Miss Welty has lived all of her life in Jackson, which lies outside that legendary section of the state which geographers call the Yazoo-Mississippi Delta, she is familiar with the Delta, has used it as the setting for several of her stories, and—most important—is thought of as a Deltan by Deltans, even those who know better. It is not simply a matter of distance: Faulkner, who lived no farther from the Delta than Miss Welty, has never been mistaken for a Deltan.

O'Donnell had the most Southern of voices, and when he spoke the name Eudora it was with an intonation and cadence that conveyed the greatest affection. Once, I remember, he rummaged (was it in that trunk where he kept the unfinished manuscript of the novel he would never finish?) for pictures that had been taken on a visit to Jackson. O'Donnell and a friend and Eudora Welty. Snapshots. Gag poses. Miss Welty is mugging for the camera. Or do I merely imagine it?

O'Donnell was the faculty advisor of LSU's student literary magazine which I edited and which we decided to call *Delta.* He suggested that we solicit Miss Welty for a congratulatory quote that we could use in our promotion, and she responded graciously.

Meanwhile, I bought all of the Welty I could get my hands on. The gummed labels inside the front covers help to reconstruct the story. The first, *A Curtain of Green,* I remember, came from Nelms & Blum's Book Nook in Greenville, sold to me by Faulkner's friend and one-time literary agent, Ben Wasson, who in addition to presiding over the book department edited the Sunday book page of the *Delta Democrat-Times* for Hodding Carter. I had come to buy Welty, but Ben Wasson also sold me, that day, *The Member of the Wedding* and the *Collected Poems* of Eliot. Also, on a later visit, *Music from Spain,* a Welty story published in a limited edition by The Levee Press of Greenville (Wasson, Carter, Kenneth Haxton).

Something happened when I read those stories—something that has never happened before or since, and never, by way of contrast, when that same year I sat down to read Faulkner. I admired Faulkner. I was frequently amazed by his powers as a writer—by the sheer range of the man. But I was never moved in just the same way that I was by Eudora Welty. I wanted to meet her. Once, in the days when she was still listed in the Jackson telephone directory, I drove past her house, and then back past in the opposite direction. Once, on the Panama Limited (or was it the City of New Orleans?), I thought I saw her: she was in the lounge car when I boarded south of Memphis and she left the train there in Jackson. I even drove past that big rambling house in Baton Rouge, long since torn down to make room for an expressway, where one hot midsummer, as Katherine Anne Porter tells us in her introduction to *A Curtain of Green,* she and the quiet young girl from Jackson "spent a pleasant evening together talking in the cool old house with all the windows open."

But it was in the early sixties before I finally saw her—a meeting of the Southern Literary Festival on the Millsaps campus in Jackson—and suddenly there she was, those marvelous eyes, that smile, and the tranquility that Katherine Anne Porter had spoken of in her introduction. *Had she really intended this . . . was her purpose here . . . did she mean to say. . . ?* Those questions from teachers and students who would reduce "A Worn Path" or "Livvie" to point of view and metaphor and symbol. And she smiled and sat down on the edge of the table and answered, "I just wanted to write a story." So deceptively simple.

Then I spoke to her for the first time and the memory comes back of the Garbo-watcher who has followed his Goddess from one side of Manhattan to the other and who suddenly, come face to face with her at a street corner, finds that he has nothing to say. Miss Welty is my Garbo. The idea is not so preposterous. I have waited these years. So I ask her about the story "Asphodel." Is she aware of certain connections to the 1932 events near Natchez—Dick Dana and Octavia Dockery living in the ruins of what came to be known as "Goat Castle"? Especially the similarity between Dick Dana, "the wild man of Natchez," and Miss Welty's Pan-like Mr. Don McInnis. Would "Asphodel" have been written, or would it have been the same story, if she had never heard of "Goat Castle"? The question interested her, but no, she had never connected the two, though she had of course followed the story of "Goat Castle." But the idea for her story came, she recalled, on a picnic at the ruins of a great plantation house near Port Gibson known as "Windsor."

Afterward I talked to her briefly, and at a subsequent literary festival held in Oxford I had an opportunity to talk with her at greater length and to observe what I had only glimpsed earlier: a warmth, an openness, above all a lack of affectation—she is what we used to call a genuine person. I suspect it has not been easy for her to retain her privacy. Yet over the years she has somehow surrounded herself with the protection that has enabled her to survive the ordeal of being a writer. During the course of the evening I brought up the subject of George Marion O'Donnell and her face lit up as she recalled those visits that George made to Jackson in the late thirties or early forties. I remembered the affection in O'Donnell's voice. Yes, she said, he brought all the literary gossip.

Still later, at home one night in 1965 reading proofs on my collection of short stories which Harcourt was about to publish, it suddenly occurred to me that the names of two of the characters in one of my stories might have been subconsciously picked up from Welty. The son, Troy. The mother, Deedie Fairchild. I went to the bookcase and pulled down *Delta Wedding.* Found Dabney Fairchild and Troy Flavin. That night Deedie Fairchild in my story "The Rarest Kind of Love" became, in proof, Deedie Ringgold. Whatever happened of course happened in a season of dreams.

Under the influence of Eudora Welty? Certainly. We have all, I think, all of us who wrote in the fifties and sixties and who wanted to write short stories more than we wanted to write novels, been influenced by her. Over the years I have read some of her stories five . . . six times, each time with some new discovery and with admiration and astonishment.

I would like to be able to remember who it was that first spoke her name. I would like to remember exactly which of those incredible stories I read first, what it was that triggered a search which has never ended. For the search for Eudora Welty is, after all, for each of us who read her, the search for ourselves. And so I play that game. I am in that room on the second floor of that school that long ago burned, or in that high-ceilinged house out toward the Bogue where James Garrett told me of *The Heart Is a Lonely Hunter*, or in Effie Glassco's living room, or the room where O'Donnell lowers the arm of the phonograph and Eliot begins speaking . . . It is the beginning. Nothing is ever quite the same again. The light itself seems to take on a new intensity. Like the light in *Delta Wedding:* "The sky, the field, the little track, and the bayou, over and over—all that had been bright or dark was now one color." Eudora Welty is that kind of beginning.

FROM

This Bright Day

LEHMAN ENGEL

THIS WAS FALL. And it was the time of goldenrod bright in parched fields. Goldenrod announced school, which was preceded by shopping trips and the pulling out of last winter's clothes, long laid away in camphor balls, the odor of which continued to permeate them for months. I dreaded the shopping because it was Mama who had to be pleased. She never asked me if I liked something because she alone knew best.

Pecans fell in the back yard; crisp leaves crunched noisily underfoot. Odor of chrysanthemums rose out of the damp dead leaves and the smoking leaf piles. Summertime barefoot boys and girls covered their feet. The school bell rang.

Even when the temperature is well above freezing, Mississippi in winter is damp and cold. It is even cold when narcissus, jonquil, and hyacinth bloom in the yard. Our large white house was heated by coal-burning gratefires, but many rooms were closed in winter except for sleeping because they were not heated. It was usual to get up out of a warm bed and race into the next room to dress by a sputtering fire. The coal crackled and banged. Facing the fire, our fronts burned while our backs froze. In winter I used to dress by the light and heat of the fire in Tatsie and Aunt Flo's room, which had once belonged to Grandma.

I accepted school without question. At noon recess, as I ate dinner (my mother sitting with me), Tatsie would cross into the schoolyard carrying a large pot of freshly made soup. The cook would follow her with bowls and spoons and a large basket of crackers. Tatsie sold the soup to the children, most of whom were poor, for five cents, and many of them came to depend on it. Just as often, the soup was given without charge.

Often during the winter afternoons, Mama sat at home in the half-light of the fire, sewing or reading a book—always compulsively occupied. She would urge me to do my homework or (later) practice the piano. She discouraged me from going out to play with other children, partly because she felt that they were "roughnecks" and I might get hurt. They were also "beneath" me—the leftovers in a rapidly deteriorating neighborhood. But mostly it was Mama's fear. I could not ride a bicycle or a pony because I might break my neck. (She had a repertoire of broken-neck incidents she could recite in the rare event of an argument.) And the fears were not limited to bicycles and ponies but included "taking colds," upsetting my stomach, not dressing warmly enough, getting blood poisoning from a scratched knee, contracting fevers, being killed crossing the street, offending an aunt, failing to remember a birthday, not visiting an old lady, being impolite, soiling my clothes. The fears, easily communicated, were incessantly fed and cataloged.

Being younger, less robust, and conspicuously cleaner than the boys I went to school with, I found coming home a lonely if welcome escape from what particular horror I never thought to ask. After all, I seldom knew any of these boys. Arrival at school coincided with the ringing of the morning bell. Lunch recess was spent at home. The dismissal bell propelled me once again through the dividing hedge into our own yard—two feet ahead of the Kanes.

I remember standing before a frosty window, my nose pressed against the glass, looking out at nothing, hearing faintly the distant jagged sounds of children's high voices, designless in play. In the house everything was silence and waiting.

Many of these afternoons were spent in making "scene boxes," for which I used large cardboard cartons. With a knife I would gouge out one end of a box, which thus became the proscenium of a stage. Across the box top, I carved out narrow slits for letting in scenery consisting of pictures cut from magazines and pasted on cardboard. There was always a curtain (usually a handkerchief pinned around a stick) and sometimes a flashlight to provide illumination. I never meant to give a "show." These scene boxes were made only for myself.

During these days, I also began to play the piano "by ear" but was not given lessons until I was ten because my parents thought my interest was merely a whim they could ill afford.

I saw whatever shows came to town. Al G. Field's Minstrels was an annual event. Fritz Leiber brought us tattered grandeur in Shakespearean repertoire. There were Walker Whiteside, *May-*

time, Blossom Time, The Student Prince, Chu Chin Chow, the St. Louis Symphony Orchestra, Paderewski, John McCormack, Galli-Curci, and Sousa's Band, and the Redpath Chautauqua, which brought smiling culture in a large tent for five full days each spring.

But my most profound experiences were in the Majestic Theatre, the local moviehouse: the Griffith pictures, Gish, Nazimova, and Chaplin. A small orchestra presided over by Sara B. McLean at an upright piano accompanied the pictures. Mrs. McLean would lean far back in her swivel chair peering at the screen over the top of her nose-glasses. The "score" consisted of bits and pieces taken from movie-music albums: "hurries," romantic melodies, marches—primitive music whose dramatic intentions were clear to all. The music changed as abruptly as the film frames, and Mrs. McLean would indicate these changes with a sudden jerk of the head, cutting off the orchestra often after she had already plunged ahead. (The music always warned of approaching danger.)

When I was ten, I began to take piano lessons with an aristocratic southern lady who had her pupils do a variety of things: we played duets and trios, learned rudimentary harmony and history of music, and had "scrapbook parties," at which we pasted pictures of musical artists, composers, and operatic scenes, from phonograph record catalogs and music journals, in blank books.

Almost immediately after my lessons commenced, I began to compose. There were several short scraps of things, then *The Scotch Highlander* for piano, my first complete "piece." Charles Wakefield Cadman came to Jackson to give a recital of his compositions, and I was able to meet him. He was gentle and enthusiastic and the only composer I had ever met: indeed, the only one (I thought) who was not dead. He heard me play, saw my single composition, and was encouraging. We began a correspondence that continued until his death more than twenty years later. And years before his death, his letters ironically became pleas for me to arrange New York performances of his compositions!

Soon after this meeting with Cadman, I decided to write an opera. I had never heard one, but I was fascinated by photographs in the *Victor Book of the Opera.* I began by drawing and coloring a title page: *Alfred.* An Opera in One Act by A. Lehman Engel. The characters were A Lady; Her Suitor, a Knight; The Lady's Maid; and The Lady's Father; and the scene, a castle tower during the

Middle Ages. I wrote words and music for a solo, a duet, and a recitative, then abandoned the project only (!) because the words were too much trouble to write.

My second piano teacher, Miss Emma Manning, scheduled my lessons at 8:00 A.M. in the summer nonschool months. I would ring her doorbell, then see her through glass panels sleepily descending the stairs while fastening her corset. After lessons—half an hour later—I went next door to the beautifully kept house of my cousins, the Loebs, for breakfast.

Saturday was, especially in summer, farm-folk day in town: the day for greeting friends, exchanging news, selling produce, buying supplies. I would wander out on our front porch in my pajamas in the early morning and see the caravans of wagons already crawling slowly by. I always found Mama sitting there as Grandma had done; Tatsie was often with her. They sat partially shielded from view and the rising summer sun by a thin vine of large purple morning glories that had replaced Grandma's long-dead Marachel Neil. They sat in their "wrappers" rocking, their hair piled unsteadily on the tops of their heads.

The caravan had to pass our house between the Pearl River Bridge and the business section, which was rapidly encroaching upon us. Most of the farm-folk rode in long unpainted wagons drawn by a pair of horses. Others squatted on the wagon's floor with the farm produce, while sometimes women sat with extraordinary dignity on straight rush-bottom chairs placed without anchorage on the wagon's floor. A few men rode on horseback. From dawn until noon this caravan plodded slowly in; from noon until sunset it passed in return. All of the people (seeing us on the front porch) nodded their heads in greeting whether they knew us or not, and they never seemed to be talking among themselves.

Some stopped their wagons. Little barefoot boys, women with small girls, men in fraying sombreros peddled produce from door to door: eggs, cantaloupes, blackberries, figs, squash, beans, tomatoes, chickens. Tatsie or Mama bought while planning meals, and often a vegetable woman had to hear creation, revision, and re-creation of an entire week's menus before knowing whether or not she had sold ten cents worth of snap beans.

On summer Sundays I rode with Mama and Aunt Flo to collect their rents, for each of them had borrowed money to build a row of two-room shacks for colored occupancy similar to the ones

Grandpa had owned. Each rented for fifty cents weekly, and although the collections from twelve houses in two districts could have been accomplished in half an hour, it took half a day by the time Mama and Aunt Flo heard each family's personal history and in turn dispensed lengthy, and often merely tolerated, advice.

Poor as these shacks were, most had been transformed by their occupants into homes. Brilliant red cockscomb grew tall out of the parched earth before nearly every house and vegetables filled the yards in the rear.

The side yards of flowers at our house, and the garden of weeds behind, more and more tended to separate us from our neighbors. Our friends increasingly moved to the north end of town. Uncle Isy sold his beautiful bungalow at a loss in order to rear his children in a "better" environment. In our old neighborhood, filling stations replaced corner homes. A hamburger stand pushed one house half a block behind it. Two houses gave way to an overall factory; another was demolished to make room for a tombstone display yard. The remaining homes, vacated by their original tenants who had once been our friends, were now operated as cheap rooming houses. We no longer had any life in our neighborhood outside the borders of our property. Mama wanted us to move away also, but Aunt Flo, for sentimental and financial reasons, steadfastly refused, and she continued to refuse for nearly fifteen years after I left home.

When we had visitors during the summer evenings, my mother used to entertain the women on the wide front porch, where, in spite of the mosquitoes, they sat talking and gossiping in shrill voices. Every bull's-eye they scored produced resounding laughter. The husbands, led by my father, would go indoors to play cards. The children who had been brought along and I would play out on the infrequently night-traveled street under an overhanging arc light. An almost solid mass of flying insects attracted to the lamp made a frantic perpetual circle-tour of it, somewhat resembling the rings around Saturn.

When visitors left—always many hours later—my mother kept them standing, talking, never *seeming* to want them to go. Often nearly half an hour passed in drawn-out leave-taking and at last when the visitors had resolved to break away, my mother's almost pathetic question came.

"Well, you all call that gone?"

In spite of her many and obvious faults, which included garrulousness, she was attentive to everyone. It can easily be argued that she was generous because she hoped her generosity would be reciprocated. Nevertheless, no one of even her most distant friends ever left Jackson on a trip without her sending a "going-away" present. This was of necessity inexpensive, but I was embarrassed to hear her extol its pathetic virtues.

"You know this bath-powder is *very* fine, although you may never have heard of it."

Well, no one ever *had* heard of it because it was Liggett's forty-four-cent "special" for the week, but this advertised fact never fazed her.

When relatives of friends died, she was the first to send mountains of superb food on decorated silver trays to the mourners. This was also, of course, a general custom, and the result was that a house of mourning suddenly became a banquet hall. However, it will always be a mystery to me and to my then-remaining Aunt Gussie that when Mama herself died, only her doctor and his wife sent a platter of food. There was so little in the house that Sister, Phyllis, and Beatrice were forced to go shopping on the morning of my mother's funeral.

One summer evening when my family and I were sitting on the front porch and speaking quietly among ourselves, an incident occurred which at the time I could only feel but did not understand. About ten o'clock a young colored girl on her way home from work neared our house as a flivver occupied by two stalwart young white men drove up quickly and squealed to a sudden stop. One man hopped out and blocked the path of the girl. He spoke to her. She refused. He became insistent. She tried to run away. The other young man joined his friend. The two of them carried her, screaming, into their car and drove quickly away across the river bridge into the night. I was emotionally upset, not understanding anything except that the girl was being forced to do something against her will. I yelled at my uncle and my father, who did nothing. They said simply that I did not understand. Then I peered up and down the dimly lit street, and as far as I could see, other men sat on other front porches. All were rocking peacefully, some fanning themselves.

During the afternoons of the late summer, not many hours before sunset, from the days of my earliest recollections until I left home when I was fifteen, I often found myself behind our house in the wilderness that had been my grandmother's garden. There was wild, crawling, lush ruin everywhere: green, heavy, pathless. I would stand in the midst of it for hours, facing the sun, inhaling the warm, heavy jungle fragrance of the high grasses and weeds. Overhead and behind me the branches of the now overwhelmingly high pecan trees spread immovable. Before me, tall sunflowers oozed thick honey for swarms of bees. Wild vines curled sturdily, clutching, jealously squeezing tall flowering weeds. Lazy sounds coming from distant chickens going to roost and slow, far-off train whistles alternated with one another. Sometimes the faint yells of another little boy, bringing his cow home from a nearby pasture, drifted into the garden and mingled with the other sounds. Then as the setting sun filled my staring eyes, I would be roused out of my real, though solitary, world by the clanging of supper bells.

This was my garden—not that anyone else wanted it or that anyone had ever given it to me, but it was my one place of refuge and mine alone. Only my grandmother, of all the others, had ever stood silently with me in its high damp grasses. Now I was alone with the garden and the aroma of her love, which would continue for me to pour out of every flowering weed. For it was now more than a garden: a shrine, a temple, the only true place of mystery and worship I would ever comprehend. The undulating *Sanctus* of the crickets sang the praises of heaven and earth, and I was continually renewed in faith and spirit, given fresh promise again and again (as when I gazed down the slope in the park or dreamed through the willow branches at the river), fresh promise of a world in which I would shed my loneliness and become completely and only myself, and it would be all right. More than the crickets sang it. The mystery in the pathless temple would continue for me not merely for as long as I could attend but when in the future I would go away forever and when the house would be demolished and the garden-temple smothered under concrete, I would be able to summon it again intact wherever I was. The promise, the song, the distilled dream have never failed me even in the roar of the life I never envisioned there in the garden.

During these years at home, I outgrew music teacher after music teacher. My entrance into high school at twelve in another end of town was fraught with increasing terrors. The old and by now deeply embedded fears were hard at work. I was projected into a class of strangers who seemed hostile. Now—far from home—I was obliged to mingle, for I no longer enjoyed the protection of the nearby family house. I was still the youngest in my class and still the smallest, the only one to continue (at my mother's insistence) wearing short pants and long black stockings. In my mind's eye, I was still an infant. The other boys were bigger and rougher—or so they seemed. I was a Jew and still frightened of the old battle cry. I also played the piano, a thing which boys simply did not do.

Inside the cafeteria, I ate alone. I felt that all eyes watched me and I was fearful of blunders, of dropping things, or of any slight fault. If I finished lunch quickly, I returned to the study hall in order to avoid playground encounters.

In class I was tense and self-conscious and could do nothing well: I merely got by. I made two friends, and in my final year I was invited to a few parties by the girls and boys who came (probably) to know that we had things in common. But to me, these parties—given by boys and girls who lived in the best part of town in fine, aristocratic houses, non-Jews, people with a lifetime of growing up together—held their own terrors. I was unused to them, their houses, their ways of life. I felt merely tolerated, a visitor on probation, one who must behave better than the rest, not merely as well. The end of the party was a blessed relief. I had again gotten by, but there was never any pleasure, and there would surely be another party and more terror.

At my mother's insistence, I had become a member of the Boy Scouts but had, of course, failed miserably at being transformed suddenly through it into a different kind of boy. I was the compulsory member of some unfortunate sports team at each weekly Scout meeting. That team always lost the game, and the reasons were not mysterious. When attendance at summer camp was proposed, I violently opposed it. I had never slept away from home except on trips with my parents, because I was still plagued with nightly bedwetting. The thought of the helpless days at sports and the even more helpless nights after which I would suffer the pain of being laughed at struck me with new horror. My mother insisted that I go to camp. The first night there, I deserted—a full pack on my back—and walked home in the friendlier dark, alone.

I graduated from Central High School, wrote an alma mater song, led the school orchestra at the graduation exercises in

Schubert's "Marche Militaire" and the *Aïdi* "Triumphal March" and did not otherwise distinguish myself.

Once during that last summer I went swimming in the municipal lake at Livingstone Park, where I ran into Frank Lyell. I had known him slightly in school (he was in the class with Celeste, a year behind mine) and he also had studied with my first piano teacher. We swam out to an anchored raft where I was introduced to a girl in the class ahead of mine. I knew her by sight as the daughter of the owner of Jackson's first skyscraper, an eleven-story insurance-company building, and gradually we became lifelong friends, with more in common than I could have ever dreamed anyone might have had. She was Eudora Welty.

During that final year, I gave a solo piano recital in the Episcopal Parish House. It must have been a grim affair, but all the friends of my family came, sent expected baskets of flowers, and applauded loudly. No one there knew how really badly I played. But I did.

In spite of my piano playing—and playing did seem to be what I was to do—I easily persuaded my parents to allow me to go all the way to the Cincinnati Conservatory the following fall. (All music students in the South went to Cincinnati.) As I look back on my leaving, I recognize the utter flimsiness of the line that led me to do the most important thing in my life. My piano playing certainly did not warrant my being sent to a conservatory in a distant city. My parents made financial sacrifices to accomplish it and in turn expected that music must become my profession. Once they had accepted the idea, a great responsibility fell on me. If I had been taught by a discriminating teacher, he would have argued against a musical career. As it was, nobody knew better, and I left home.

FROM

Evers

CHARLES EVERS

DECATUR, MISSISSIPPI, 1922–30

MY MOMMA WAS strong and my Daddy was strong, and they influenced my life the most. I got my religion from my Momma, and my Daddy taught me not to be afraid.

Daddy was a mean man. He couldn't read or write, but he didn't back off of any man—white or black. His name was Jim Evers, he was tall, over six feet, like me. He didn't have the kind of trouble that many blacks had, because Daddy was so mean. He'd just raise all kinds of problems. He worked hard, but he wasn't a bit scary. He taught me that most white folks are cowards. If they haven't got you outnumbered, you can back 'em down. So I've always thought I could outwit most white folks. Being black, you gotta learn that, just to survive. The only thing I didn't agree on with my Daddy was when he'd say, "That's a white man's job." There's no such thing. But he still had that belief that the white folks had indoctrinated all the Negroes with: "All the good jobs are for white folks, and the hard, menial jobs are for black folks." And he believed that. I guess he did the best he could, though. I don't know how he lived through what he did, standing up to the white man as much as he did, because back in those days to kill a Negro wasn't nothing. It was like killing a chicken or killing a snake. The whites would say, "Niggers jest supposed to die, ain't no damn good anyway—so jest go on an' kill 'em."

My Daddy's father was Mike Evers. He wasn't a slave but a free man. He had 200 or 300 acres of land in Scott County, and he raised his own corn, potatoes and peanuts; he had peach trees, pecan trees, fig trees, and apple trees. He was independent, but it must have made the white folks very unhappy, because they took away that land from him, illegally. (And I'm going to look into that one of these days.) My Daddy's mother was named Mary, and she was part Creole Indian. She had long, straight hair and high cheekbones.

Most black people can go back only to their grandparents. No one kept records. We didn't have birth certificates. Each family had a big old Bible, and usually the momma would put in there when each of the children was born.

I don't really remember much about my grandparents. They all died when I was just a kid. And we don't have any long livers in our family. Most of our people die young. My father was a sawmill man; he stacked lumber. And he'd always follow those mills around. That's how we were over at Decatur, in Newton County, when I was born. Momma had been married before—and had children named Eva, Eddie and Gene. Then they had four more children. I was born in 1922, September 11th, then Medgar, Liz and Ruth. I was two years older than Medgar.

My Momma was a bright woman, and she wanted the best things in life for her children. After I got elected Mayor of Fayette, I had one thought: *I wish Momma was here.*

She read the Bible a lot and had an understanding about it. She knew the time was coming when we were going to have to have an education. She just pounded it into our heads. She was shorty-short, about five-two, and when she was young she must have been a real doll, but later on in life she got stout. She had tiny feet, about a size four. She was part Indian and went barefoot most of the time. Her maiden name was Jessie Wright.

My great-grandfather on my Momma's side was half Indian. He was a slave, but from what I've heard he was one of the worst slaves they'd ever had. He'd just cause trouble and he just wouldn't take any abuse. His name was Wright—Medgar Wright. Medgar was named after him.

My Momma's father had a black mother and a white father. That's fairly common in the South, and that's why you see so many light-skinned Negroes. My half-sister Eva told me once about when she was just a kid and saw our grandfather for the first time. She was visiting at my Aunt Dora's in Forest, Miss. He came up to the front door and she ran to the kitchen. "Aunt Dora!" she said. "There's a white man at the door." My aunt laughed and said, "Eva, that's your grandfather." He looked just like any white man when you'd see him coming down the street. That's just how white he was. After 30 years up North, Eva's come back to Mississippi to help me run my restaurant. Eva's one sweet woman.

This half-white grandfather would stand up to any man, white or black, and he always carried a gun. Once a white man called my grandfather a "half-assed mulatto" and my grandfather shot at him. He didn't kill the man, but he had to leave town in a hurry.

Momma made all her clothes and all the clothes for my sisters. She'd make them out of gingham cloth and old fertilizer sacks and flour sacks. We didn't know anything about silk panties and things like that. They had cotton drawers and petticoats.

Momma would make us pants. She'd buy blue denim and cut out pants and coveralls for Medgar and me—no pockets—and she'd be up all night sewing. She sometimes slept only two or three hours. I don't know how she arranged to get things done. But she's typical of the average black mother when it comes to working. I can just name you thousands of black women in those days who had to do the same thing. They'd get up about five in the morning, cook the breakfast for the husband and then go out and wash a big washing. They'd go to the field and chop cotton or plow, leave the field about eleven in the morning, walk all the way in from the field, sweaty and dirty, then cook dinner for the whole family, the white folks, too; and when they'd get through eating they'd have to wash the dishes up. Then they'd go back to the field about one-thirty or two o'clock, work till five or six. Then, in the evening, they'd have to milk the cows and feed the chickens before cooking supper.

Where'd they get all that strength? They had no choice. God's been good to us. He kept our black women strong and healthy.

We were all very close, our whole family was very close. But Medgar and I were together most of the time. You know girls are girls, what can they really do with boys? Just sort of be around and annoy them all the time. And our two sisters, Ruth and Liz, were very close. And Liz, she's not afraid of anything. She has her own grocery store now, in Chicago. So we all scratched together.

I may be even closer to Medgar now than when he was alive, if that's possible. He was the saint of our family and I cherished him. I didn't want him to leave Mississippi as I had, because I knew how much he was needed here. So whenever he needed money, I'd send him down some.

Medgar never really knew how I earned my money in Chicago,

and neither did Momma. I guess my Daddy sort of suspected. He could never figure out where I got all the money to pay their bills. He once asked me if I was bootlegging. I said, "Dad, you know I'd never bootleg." Of course, I was bootlegging, and right under his nose.

I was sort of fatherly with Medgar. Took care of him. We went to school together, always slept together. God, I remember us kicking each other out of the bed. But I always warmed it for him, because, man, was that bedroom cold, especially between those old sack sheets of ours. So I'd get a spot warm, then move over and let him have it because he was the baby. I remember putting my legs on him to keep him warm.

He was so clumsy. When we'd go fishing together I'd help him across the log bridge. But strong. We'd wrestle and box. Sometimes I'd let him take me, and sometimes he'd really take me. He was bookish, very sharp and very lovable. He never wanted to hurt anybody. All the battling and beating we got into, that was my doing, not his. I wasn't cruel or bitter, but I could be mean.

Momma used to say to me, "You're different. Medgar's sweet. But you're always in trouble." And Medgar used to say to me, "Charley, you're going to get into trouble." And I said, "I was born in trouble. Being a Negro, you're automatically in trouble."

As far as our girls went, Medgar and I had completely different types. On account of growing up in the Holiness Church, we never confided in each other about what we were doing to the girls. But I know he liked young, sweet, untouchable, frail little things, who'd never give him anything. That is, they never became intimate with him. When he got a bit older, he became more aggressive.

I couldn't stand those young gals. For me, young gals are nothing but trouble. I liked older women who were able to do something for me. Young girls could do nothing but go to bed. I didn't need to go to bed. I needed protection. I was poor, had nothing. I wanted a woman who could at least buy me a shirt once in a while.

As boys, Medgar and I hated it when Momma or Daddy sent us into Decatur to a community store to buy flour or sugar. Soon as we'd go in the white men standing around there would start picking on us and trying to make us dance. "Dance, nigger!" The owner of the store was the worst of them all.

I used to swear to Medgar afterwards that some day I'd have a store and make white folks dance to my tune. Now I have a store, a couple of them, in fact, but I've never made anybody dance in them.

Usually, Daddy bought groceries on credit at the sawmill commissary. "Charge it," he'd say. Daddy would buy everything, even a box of snuff, on credit, and then every Friday or Saturday he'd pay. The store was run by a dirty white rascal named Jimmy Boware. This Jimmy knew that Daddy couldn't read or write, but Daddy was shrewd with figures. He could add and subtact and multiply in his head faster than you could with a pencil. And no one ever cheated him. One Saturday, Medgar and I went with Daddy to the commissary to pay his bill. I must have been about nine and Medgar about seven. When Daddy looked at the bill he told Jimmy Boware he'd overcharged him by $5 and something.

"Nigger," the white man shouted, "don't you tell me I'm tellin' a lie!"

Everybody knew how bad Jimmy Boware was. He beat Negroes, kicked Negroes, and this Saturday there must have been about ten or fifteen whites in the community store.

"Mr. Boware, you're just wrong," Daddy said. "I don't owe that much."

"You're callin' me a liar, nigger?"

Then Daddy said, "Well, I don't owe that, and I'm not going to pay it."

Jimmy stepped behind the counter to get a gun and Daddy grabbed a Coke bottle, broke it, pointed the jagged ends at him, and stood in his path. "If you move another step I'll bust your damn brains out."

Now there must have been about twenty whites who had gathered there. Medgar and I reached and got us a bottle each. Dad turned and said, "Get outside, boys," but we said, "No, Dad, we're not gonna leave you in here."

Boware said, "I'll kill you, you black sonofabitch!" and Daddy said, "You better not move. You better not go around that counter."

Daddy had nothing but a Coke bottle, but Boware was afraid to move, and we could see he was shaking like a leaf on a tree. Daddy kept his eye on him and backed us out of there. He'd bluffed every one of them, but when we were outside we thought they'd come after us and whip our daddy. We wanted to run, but Daddy said, "Don't run, don't run. They're nothing but a bunch of cowards."

We walked toward home, down along the railroad tracks, Medgar on one side of Daddy and me on the other. And we put our arms around him and he put his hands on our heads, and he told us, "Don't never let anybody beat you. Don't never let any white folks beat you." He said, "If anyone ever kicks you, you kick the hell out of him." It's because of my father that my nonviolence movement goes only so far.

White folks are always asking blacks, "When did you first realize you're black?" You know you're black from the day you're born. From the time your mother spits you out of her womb, you know you're different. We were born in our homes, in some old bed with some old woman midwife who pulls the baby from the mother's body. White boys and girls of my age were born in a nice clean hospital with sanitation. I was born in a house with flies.

The question "When did you know you were black?" is unfair. There is no black man in this country who'll tell the truth, who won't say he has known he's been black all his life. He has been mistreated like he's inhuman. I don't like to talk about it, because I get very upset—the way Momma had to wash and iron, and the way the children had to carry the clothes to the white man who'd send Momma a lousy 50¢ for her service. If a Negro tells you some little story about the moment he realized he's black, he's telling you a lie.

Being black is part of the air you breathe. Our mothers began telling us about being black from the day we were born. The white folks weren't any better than we were, Momma said, but they sure thought they were. When we'd ask why we couldn't do something or other, often she'd just say, "Because you're colored, son."

Our own people have been taught to believe that white is right and black is wrong. A lot of black parents would tell their children, "It's a white man's world, and you just happen to be here, nigger."

Medgar and I, right from the start, when we were little kids, were determined to prove that this wasn't a white man's world—or if it was, we'd at least get our share of whatever there was worth getting and see that some other black folks could, too.

Sometimes it was just no fun growing up black, like when we got it hammered into us to watch our step, to stay in our place, or get off the street when a white woman passed by so as not to brush up against her accidentally. To be black in this country is miserable more often than it's not.

We were brought up in the Church of God in Christ, also called the Holiness Church, and they don't believe in smoking, drinking, gambling, chewing, playing cards, or dancing on Sundays. As a kid I was in church so much that I don't go often today. In fact I got so much church thrown at me then, I wonder if some of the wilder things I did later weren't just to fill up on things I was told to stay away from as a kid.

The deacon of my Momma's Holiness church was Will Loper, and I'd tell Medgar, "You're just like ol' Brother Loper," but Medgar resented this guy, because he was always up shouting, dancing, twisting and carrying on. Every Sunday, ol' man Loper would get happy and dance. Medgar'd get fighting mad when I'd call him Loper, and he'd take off after me, and I'd take off running. Then we'd be sitting around talking and I'd say, "You know, Lope—" and he'd look a snap right quick, and then sort of grin. The name just stuck, and I kept calling him Lope after we got bigger.

My Daddy was not as religious as my Momma. He'd go to her church, but he kept his own religion. He was Baptist. We used to have to go to church three times a week (all day Sunday). On Sunday morning it was Sunday school nine to eleven, and at eleven we'd get out about five or ten minutes and go right back in for church service. And we'd stay in there for the singing and praying and dancing till about one. Then the preacher would come on about one. He'd preach until about three. We'd get out about three or three-thirty, rush home and eat, and come right back at six o'clock for YPWW—the Young People's Willing Workers. We'd stay there until seven or seven-thirty and prayer service would begin at seven-thirty. And we'd pray until about eight-thirty and then start the testimonials. That's when all the members got up and testified. Can you imagine that! And after every testimonial we'd sing a song.

Today all my civil rights meetings and business meetings are very religious. If I run for governor the campaign will be run the same way. Church became a part of me. And we still sing those good ol' Christian songs. Anyway, after the testimonials they'd take up collection. And then we all go outdoors and up the street asking everybody to give money to help pay the preacher. About nine-thirty or ten the preacher comes in to the pulpit. You've been there since nine that morning and about twelve hours later the preacher is getting up again to preach the second time, and he would preach *and* he would preach, and you'd get home about twelve midnight, and you'd just *done had it.* And a lot of times it'd be hot and you had to sweat and fight those mosquitoes and try to go to sleep, and you couldn't sleep, and the next morning you had to get up and go to work or to school.

Tuesday night was prayer meeting. This would start about seven-thirty and last a couple of hours. On Friday nights you would have prayer meeting plus business meeting.

We had about three months out of a year going to revivals. Medgar, me and all of us had to go to my mother's church's revival—that lasted about two weeks—and my Dad's church's revival, and some of the other church's revivals. Preachers came from all over, and they would preach and preach, and everybody was "saved." This meant that we were "saved by grace," because we had testified, and we were going to heaven and be with Jesus when we died. We called those revivals our soul-saving meetings. Every night you had to go and sit on that front seat, and you'd better not talk. All Momma would do was just look at you and you'd know, brother, she's gonna tear your fanny up. She wouldn't wait to get you home. Well, I don't object to that either. I'm proud my mother was like that because whatever we are, Momma and Daddy made us know right from wrong.

The big revivals, or tent meetings, opened with a picnic where everybody would bring their dinner and spread it all over tables, out in a pasture. People would come from miles around, and everybody seemed to be a kissing cousin. Everybody was getting saved and happy, they were shouting and they were kissing. Right now I kiss almost everybody I see. And it's because of my training. It's not that I'm being fresh. My Momma's people and all my people, everybody, we'd kiss each other when we saw each other. But a lot of people get the wrong impression of me, and I really wasn't aware of that until a couple of times women went a little too far about kissing. You know, they'd kiss back. So now I sort of lay my cheek against people's faces. But Momma always told us to kiss. She said. "It's showing that you care. It's affection that you show people, it's the concern." And when you're close to someone and kiss them on the cheek, it means you're not afraid of them. It means they're no different from you; and that we're all the same people. Caressing and comforting people is part of my life. That's what kissing means.

But I found that many people think I'm being fresh. And I'm only doing what Momma and Daddy, what all of us did. And most country people are that way, very affectionate. They hug you and kiss you. Aaron Henry and I, every time we meet, we hug. We embrace each other, and it's just a matter of being glad to see each other. Muhammed Ali and I once embraced right in the street. Because we hadn't seen each other in a long time; because we're friends and we're brothers—and that's the way it should be.

Besides going to church all the time we'd have prayers at home. We'd all get down on our knees and pray—every Sunday morning, and every night before we'd go to bed. In the prayers, Momma would say certain things out loud. She was talking to God, telling Him to help her take care of her children and help her sons to grow up to be men that the world would be proud of and not to be lazy rogues, haters or alcoholics. She'd just talk to Him, and we'd listen. And after we'd get through praying, my daddy would say, "You're goin' to church today, and after that you come on home. I don't want you gettin' into no trouble. But if anybody bothers you, you knock their ass off." So it was a combination of spiritual and natural teaching that we got.

Momma's old raggedy church leaked, so we didn't go when it was raining. Instead she'd read the Bible to us, and Daddy would always have something to do outside, and Medgar and me would say, "Daddy, Momma's gonna read the Bible," and he'd say, "Yo'll go on, listen to your Momma read the Bible. Get your Sunday school lesson," and he'd go out in the yard to take some snuff. Then he'd ease back in and we'd go up in his lap and he'd rock us to sleep.

On Sunday afternoons Daddy would tell us stories about when he was a boy, and we loved that. About how he used to steal watermelons and go swimming, buck naked, and how some white boys came and stole all their clothes, and how he and his friends had to make skirts out of pine branches to hide themselves. And Medgar and I'd sit there listening, wide-eyed, and we'd ask, "Did you, Daddy? Did you do all those things when you were a boy?"

I remember Daddy telling me a story about the evils of whiskey. As usual, he'd been drinking up a storm, raising sand, jumping onto tables and clearing them with his feet. Finally, he got to one table where there was "this little bitty old nigger," as Daddy called him. Couldn't have been much over five feet tall, probably weighed 130 pounds. My Daddy, remember, was big and mean and weighed over 200. Well, this little fellow said to him, "If you git up on that table I'll whup yo' big ol' ass." So Daddy jumped up on the table, kicked up his heels and began cussing him out. Without any warning at all, that "little nigger" just snatched the table out from under him and Daddy hit the floor with a plop.

"He beat me, he stomped me, he kicked me all over," Daddy said. "Then he snatched that half pint of whiskey I had in my pocket and busted it clean over my head. Why that little bitty old nigger like to beat me to death." That really broke him up about drinking. Never did drink much after that, my Daddy didn't. Sure didn't walk on any more tables, for sure.

He told us all kinds of stories. About parching peanuts, roasting potatoes, and rabbit and 'possum hunting. Old folks never did give him a gun. "Y'ain' gwine have no gun, bo' . . . You'd shoot somebody." So old Daddy'd take out after the rabbits on foot. He'd find their sinkhole, wait there quiet-like, and send the dog on out after the rabbit. Sure enough, pretty soon the rabbit would come back and Daddy'd clobber him over the head with a stick. Said he used to catch enough in one day to last the year.

As Medgar and I grew older we became more sensitive about his taking all the money we earned. He'd hire us out to an old farmer. I made about $15 a month, which Daddy'd promptly snatch from me, and return maybe $2. His theory was, you don't need anything anyway, since I'm taking care of you and feeding you.

One day Medgar and I sat down with him and complained about handing over the money to him. "Listen," he said, "you think you can take of yourself, you don't need to be in my house."

"Dad," I said, "It ain't *your* house. It's *our* house."

Whop! Bang! Daddy slammed me clean off the old bench we had, right onto the floor. Momma heard the racket and came in. She thought he was going to kill us. "Now Jim, honey . . ."

"Shut up, Jessie," he said. "Can't be but one Daddy in this house. When they get where they're telling me what to do, they better get out of this house."

Oh, we were smartass kids and Daddy knew just what to do with us. Seems we were always in the burial business. Medgar and I'd complain about the rickety old hearse we had. We called it the ambulance. And Daddy said to us: "Can you go buy 'nothern?"

"No."

"Then shut up talkin' 'bout this'n. Gotta' use what we got. Dead folks don't want to be toted away in this'n, let 'em find something better. Don't give a damn nohow."

We were the most comical family. Always had something going on in our house. Daddy used to chew Tuberose dip. When he'd come home, he'd make Momma a present of the coupon on the back. When she got 200 or 300 coupons, I think she could turn it in for an old dish. Every now and then Daddy'd roll his old lip, swish around some dip and let fly on the floor of the house. Medgar and I'd wait a minute, then we'd jump up and one of us'd say, "Looky here, Daddy, right here on the floor. Somebody's spit on the floor." "Shut yo' mouf' boy," he'd say, "know damn well who spit on that flo'." We never gave them a moment's peace.

Momma always cooked a big Sunday dinner, and some old rascal preacher would come eat with us. Medgar and I'd go out early Sunday to catch chickens and start ringing their necks, and Momma'd shout for us to ring 'em two at a time. Now, the average white person who kept chickens had nice chicken houses and kept the chickens away from where they were living, because a chicken is the filthiest thing you can get, but ours lived all around our shack and all we had to do was go out in the yard or on the porch to catch them. I'd ring one head off with my right hand and be killing another with my left hand, and those chickens would be gushing blood and flopping all over the place. Then Momma'd dump them in a tub of hot water and we'd all dive in to pick the feathers. Liz'd be shucking corn and Momma'd be frying chicken and baking good juicy sweet potato pie, or maybe pecan pie or blackberry pie or peach cobbler. We'd half-starve for the rest of the week, but that preacher had to have the best.

All the grownups sat down with the preacher, and he'd pray for about half an hour, then they'd dive in. The reverend liked Momma's white biscuits and her white gravy and her cornbread dressing, and he'd keep taking second helpings. And oh, he'd just eat and talk, eat and talk, eat and talk. And me and the rest of the kids would be outside sitting and waiting, and peeking in, watching them eat and just hoping they'd leave us some of the chicken.

One Sunday Medgar and I decided we'd get us some of the drumsticks and thighs, so I said, "Momma, come on out here, something's going on out in the yard!" Then Medgar slipped into the kitchen to steal some parts, but clumsy as Medgar was, he dropped them on the floor.

"Reverend," Momma shouted, "come look what these mean boys are up to!" And the mean ol' preacher came running and got a long peach switch and whipped us all around the house, and Momma was chasing after us, too, and the reverend was telling Momma, "That's right, Miz Evers, you gotta break 'em from stealing. 'Cause if they steal chickens they'll be goin' downtown and stealin'."

Momma tithed as best she could, which wasn't much. Maybe she'd give 50¢ or a dollar a month to her church. And she tried to teach us to tithe. I don't give 10 percent of my earnings right to a pastor, but maybe I pay someone's light bill or water bill, and maybe if someone dies and the family can't bury them, I bury them. Or someone gets stranded and needs help, I help them. Or some wino gets in trouble, I use a little money to help him. I always figure this is the way to help—without any thought of repayment.

Today I know a lot of young people resent the church because it's always promising heaven in the sweet by-and-by and lulling black people into accepting a subhuman way of life here on earth. But Momma was a different kind of religious person. She wasn't the kind who just believed in praying and sitting down. She taught us: "You pray—then you get up and go after it." She believed in prayer, and I guess I really believe in prayer, too. Because it does something to you. It may be all in your mind, but certainly it does something. Every time I get in a tight fix, I go off just for a minute. If I can pray just for a minute I'll be all right and can come out and meet it all head-on.

And I still say the Lord is up there and He hears you—if you believe in Him. You just got to believe in Him. It's like anything else, if you *believe* in something or other, that's what it's going to be. And before I make any speech I always ask the Lord to help me. "Now, You know I don't know what to say," I say. "You just tell me what to say and I'll say it." She always believed that prayer would get you through anything if you'd do your part. And I do, too.

Every spring and summer, Medgar and I and all the children were in our bare feet. We'd get briars stuck in our feet and we'd have to sit down and pull them off. Once every two years in the fall, Daddy used to carry us to town to buy us shoes. We'd get two pairs of shoes every two years. He'd buy us a pair of Sunday shoes—we called them our "slippers." We'd wear them to church and to funerals. And they'd always get them big enough for growth; if we wore size eight they'd get us ten so we could wear them two years. The minute you got out of church you pulled those slippers off and you went in your bare feet.

In the wintertime we had heavy, lace-up brogans for everyday wear. We had to put our brogans on when we got in from church in the wintertime. If Daddy caught us playing in our Sunday shoes he'd whip us good. "You'd better not be scuffin' in them Sunday shoes, son," he'd warn. And then just for the hell of it we'd go and do something in them—run around in the pasture and chase the cows out and get manure on our slippers. Then Daddy would beat the tar out of us.

We'd have to go pull off our Sunday clothes, too. We had one pair of green tweed pants for Sunday, and we'd pull them off as soon as we came back from church or come from a funeral. We'd put on coveralls, Medgar and me; or an old pair of blue jeans. And blue jeans, even to this day, remind me of how poor we were. It's a personal thing now. I just can't put blue jeans on to save my life.

But we were always clean. I remember Daddy wore coveralls all the time. And Momma could iron them better than anybody. Still, no matter how hard Momma worked and how much she prayed, we had a rough time. It's been no flowerbed for us, never was. No white person would take for one hour what most black people take all their lives. We didn't really go hungry, but we hardly had a change of clothes. I know this is why my half-sister Eva ran off and got married when she was sixteen. Marriage to her was having a pair of pretty new shoes.

At church the preacher was always talking about how "We're all God's children" and "No man is different from anybody else," so I'd ask Daddy, "*Why* are we different? The preacher don't say we *gotta* be different."

And he'd say, "Well, son, that's the way it is. I don't know what we can do about it. There ain't nothin' we can do about it. Because if we do anything about it, they kill you."

Why I Live in Mississippi

MEDGAR EVERS

MY PARENTS WERE POOR, but not destitute. I grew up with a white playmate, a kid next door who practically lived at my house. In the long, hot summers we would do all the things that kids do—play hide and seek, talk about our big plans for growing up, swap the little personal treasures that boys grow friendly over, and argue over his double-barreled stopper gun. Then, one day, my friend stopped coming by. In a little while, he began to get nasty. Finally, out in the street with a group of his friends, he called me "nigger." The split had come. The lines were drawn, black on one side and white on the other. I guess at that moment I realized my status in Mississippi. I have lived with it ever since. . . . But this is home. Mississippi is a part of the United States. And whether the whites like it or not, I don't plan to live here as a parasite. The things that I don't like I will try to change. And in the long run, I hope to make a positive contribution to the overall productivity of the South.

In Decatur [Mississippi] where there were 900 white voters and no Negroes even registered, I went with [my brother] Charles, and four others [in 1946] to register at the clerk's office. I never found out until later that they visited my parents nightly after that. First, it was the whites and then their Negro message bearers. And the word was always the same: "Tell your sons to take their names off the books. Don't show up at the courthouse voting day." Then, the night before the election, Bilbo came to town and harangued the crowd in the square. "The best way to keep a nigger from the polls on election day," he told them, "is to visit him the night before." And they visited us. My brother came from Alcorn College to vote that next day. I laid off from work. The six of us gathered at my house and we walked to the polls. I'll never forget it. Not a Negro was on the streets, and when we got to the courthouse, the clerk said he wanted to talk with us. When we got into his office, some fifteen or twenty armed white men surged in behind us, men I had grown up with, had played with. We split up and went home. Around town Negroes said we had been whipped, beaten up and run out of town. Well, in a way we were whipped, I guess, but I made up my mind then that it would not be like that again—at least not for me.

It may sound funny, but I love the South. I don't choose to live anywhere else. There's land here, where a man can raise cattle, and I'm going to do that some day. There are lakes where a man can sink a hook and fight the bass. There is room here for my children to play and grow, and become good citizens—if the white man will let them. . . . The youth have a definite responsibility to help, because much of what we are struggling for now will benefit them directly ten years from now—will open up opportunities that were not open when I came along. . . . Violence, certainly, is not the way. Returning physical harm for physical harm will not solve the problem. And one of our strongest appeals to the conscience of southern whites is that the NAACP has never been linked to violence.

FROM

For Us, the Living

Myrlie Evers

I

Somewhere in Mississippi lives the man who murdered my husband. Sometimes at night when my new house in Claremont, California, is quiet and the children are in bed I think about him and wonder how he feels. I have never seriously admitted the possibility that he has forgotten what I can never forget, though I suppose that hours and even days may go by without his thinking of it. Still, it must be there, the memory of it, like a giant stain in one part of his mind, ready to spring to life whenever he sees a Negro, whenever his hate rises like a bitterness in the throat. He cannot escape it completely.

And when that memory returns to him, I wonder if he is proud of what he did. Or if, sometimes, he feels at least a part of the enormous guilt he bears. For it is not just that he murdered a man. He murdered a very special man—special to him, special to many others, not just special to me as any man is to his wife. And he killed him in a special way. He is not just a murderer. He is an assassin.

He lived in a different world from the one Medgar and I shared for eleven and a half years, though all three of us must have spent most of our lives within a few miles of each other. And those different worlds we inhabited had been there, side by side in Mississippi, all along. When they collided, finally, my husband lay dying outside the door of our home, his key clutched tightly in his hand, a trail of his blood bearing witness to his struggle to reach safety inside. And as his life's blood poured out of him, his assassin dropped his weapon and slunk away through the underbrush of a vacant lot, hidden by the darkness of night. What were his feelings then? Joy? Fear? Triumph?

What are his feelings now?

I wonder if he has told others of his act that night, if, perhaps, he brags about it. And if he does, I wonder how those awful boasts are received. Do the other white men who hear his confession congratulate him? Do they laugh and slap him on his shoulder as though to share in his deed? Or do some, at least, stir uneasily at his tale? Do they, perhaps, even turn their backs on him, blotting him out, unwilling or unable to be a part of his murder even after it is done?

Much of the recent history of Mississippi could be told in the lives of these two men, my husband and his killer, the murdered and the murderer—one dead but free, the other alive and at large but never really free: imprisoned by the hate and fear that imprison so many white Mississippians and make so many Negro Mississippians still their slaves. Medgar and his assassin shared not only a state but a time; they grew up and lived in the same years, subject to the same influences. They breathed the same air, may have even brushed shoulders on the street or in a store.

Surely they heard the same speeches about the question that was central to both of their lives and yet moved them in such profoundly different directions. And that, too, is a strange thought: that there were times when both men sat by radios or television sets hearing the same news, the same words spoken about the racial crisis in Mississippi. But, oh, what different thoughts they must have had!

Medgar used to astonish Northern reporters who asked why he stayed in Mississippi by answering simply that he loved Mississippi. He did. He loved it as a man loves his home, as a farmer loves the soil. It was part of him. He loved to hunt and fish, to roam the fields and woods. He loved the feeling that here there was space for him and his family to grow and breathe. He had visited many other places. He had served in the Army in England and France; he had worked summers in Chicago during his college years; but always he came back to Mississippi as a man coming home.

Chicago held no appeal for him; he called life there a "rat race," and he was puzzled and a little resentful that all the Negroes from his part of Mississippi seemed to live in the same area of Chicago's South Side—the same block, almost; often the same buildings. He would say with disgust that Negroes who left his home town of Decatur, Mississippi, for the North all ended in the same neighborhoods of either Chicago or Flint, Michigan. He didn't like the dependence that implied, and he didn't like the Negro ghettos either. Both offended his sense of freedom. Chicago to him was a place to work, a place where you could earn better wages. Mississippi, with all its faults, was a place to live.

Medgar, of all people, was not blind to Mississippi's flaws, but he seemed convinced they could be corrected. He loved his state with hope and only rarely with despair. It was his hope that sustained him. It never left him. Despair came infrequently, and a day of hunting or fishing dispelled it. The love remained.

I suppose the man who killed Medgar loved Mississippi, too, in his twisted, tortured way. He must have loved the Mississippi that divides whites from Negroes, that by definition made him better than any Negro simply because he was white. In a way, I suppose, he was a jealous suitor, seeking by his murder to eliminate a rival, for he loved the Mississippi Medgar sought to change. What Medgar loved with hope, his assassin loved with fear. And he killed, I suspect, largely out of that fear.

But knowing this, thinking about it, wondering at it in the stillness of the night these many months after that act of horror cannot change the emptiness of life without my husband. There are times when I pause in a busy day and realize with surprise that I survive, that I am continuing, that my life goes on. For a long time after that shot rang out in the darkness and put an end to my life with Medgar, it seemed impossible to go on. And yet I do; the children eat and sleep and go to school, their lives almost complete; day follows night; and emptiness is, if not filled, at least ignored a little more each day than the day before.

But there are moments when it all comes back, when the warmth of those years with Medgar floods in on me, when I live again those shattering moments after the crack of the rifle. And then I wonder about the man who saw my husband's back in the sights of a high-powered rifle and coldly squeezed the trigger. What kind of man could that be? What kind of life brought him to that clump of bushes where he hid and waited? What can he be thinking now that the act is committed and he has escaped its legal consequences?

They are all questions I cannot answer in any sure or final sense. I can only speculate out of an intuitive knowledge of what hate can do to the human soul. For I, too, have been tempted to hate. It has been difficult, living in Mississippi, not to. Hate is one of the rare commodities whites and Negroes are permitted to share equally in that state. It is one of the few things in more than adequate supply for all.

But if I cannot know what brought my husband's murderer to that awful, final moment, I can at least hope to understand what brought my husband there. It may even be that the answer to both questions is the same, for Medgar, too, grew up in Mississippi, the same Mississippi that produced enough hate in one man to bring him to kill in the night. Medgar, too, was subject to the same forces that drove his assassin toward that desperate, fanatical moment. They affected Medgar differently, of course, for he lived at the other end of those forces, even as he died at the other end of that rifle.

But surely there must be in Medgar's life and mine at least a mirrored reflection of the life that produced his killer. Surely what Mississippi made of us should provide a clue to what it made of him. It is not so strange, when you think of it, to hope to learn something about a killer by an examination of his carefully chosen victim. And of one thing I am sure: Medgar was carefully chosen. No other victim would have served at that moment in time. Medgar was killed specifically because of what he represented, of what he had become, of the hope that his presence gave to Mississippi Negroes and the fear it aroused in Mississippi whites.

In many ways, the act of murder that deprived me of a husband was an official act, for Medgar's energies were all directed against the official state of things in Mississippi: against official positions of the state, official proclamations, official regulations relegating Negroes to an official status of inferiority. It is almost as though the assassin had been appointed by the state to carry out the execution of an enemy of the state, an execution that the state could not, in all good public relations, openly carry out itself.

And yet, as time goes by, I think that official view will change. There will, I believe, be a day when Medgar Evers will be remembered, in Mississippi as elsewhere, as a true friend of his state. Surely the day must come when his assassin and people like him will be remembered in Mississippi as the state's real enemies.

II

I was seventeen and had never been away from home when I went off from Vicksburg to Alcorn A & M College in Lorman, Mississippi. It was just a forty-six mile drive in a friend's car, but I saw it as the beginning of a new life. Squeezed in the back seat between my grandmother and Aunt Myrlie, the two people who had raised me and surrounded my childhood with adoration, protection, and towering hopes, I tried hard to conceal the pride, the nervousness, the joy and the fear that fought for possession of me.

My pride was of two sorts; first, in the certainty that by going off to college I was fulfilling ambitions both of these strong and loving women had held for me almost since I was born. Both, being teachers, were strong believers in higher education, and both had sacrificed to achieve at least part of a college education for themselves. In a way, I suppose, I represented their hopes and ambitions for themselves, and in any case I was carrying on an important tradition.

But there was a more personal kind of pride as well, and I confess to a certain vanity in the picture I had of myself that day: grown up, mature, a college coed dressed in a bright, new cotton print and my first pair of really high heels. A snapshot reveals today what an exaggeration this was, and I can see what others must have seen: a tall, very thin young Negro girl, wide-eyed and innocent-looking, with long hair worn page-boy style. But though I wobbled awkwardly on my new high heels, my uncertain steps were that day transformed in my mind into stately strides, and I remember seeing myself as an arresting figure that soon would be strolling under giant oaks along the campus paths that led from one exciting class to the next.

My sense of nervousness was that of any girl going off to college for the first time, but it was magnified in my case by a childhood well laced with often-expressed fears of what the outside world might do to me once I left the shelter of my aunt's and grandmother's protectiveness. I had always rejected these fears of theirs, mostly in annoyance at the restrictions they placed on me; yet now, suddenly, so near to being on my own, I began to doubt my complacency. I had been warned all my life about the dangers particular to whatever I was doing, and going off to college was no exception. This time, I had been told, the major menace was involvement with an older, wise and worldly veteran, for the year was 1950, and Alcorn was coeducational, and it was known that there were young men returned from the debauching experiences of the Army stalking the campus in search of innocent young girls from Vicksburg.

I don't know what I expected, but as mile followed mile and we finally reached the point at which we turned off the main highway to drive the last seven miles through piny woods and scattered cotton fields, I scanned each turn of the road for the sight that would tell me I had arrived at the place where I would be tested. In the end, there was sheer joy, for Alcorn was beautiful, set back in the woods with enormous old trees studding the sprawling campus. The outstanding building was the chapel, built entirely without nails by slaves more than a hundred years earlier. For Alcorn, like virtually everything else in Mississippi that had been set aside for Negroes, was a hand-me-down. It had been built originally as a white military school.

Parting with my aunt and grandmother an hour later heightened both my fears and my excitement, but it was quickly done with appropriately renewed warnings of the dangers of the big new world of the college campus. Then they were gone, and I was on my own. Two hours later, gathered in front of the college president's house with a group of other freshman girls, I met the older, wise and worldly veteran my aunt and grandmother had warned me about. His name was Medgar Wiley Evers.

Looking back now, I can see that it was indeed the beginning of a new life. What I saw then was a well-built, self-assured young man, a junior, an athlete back on the college campus early for football practice. We met—the football team and the freshman girls—in what seemed a casual way. I am sure now that it was carefully planned by both groups. We spent most of that first afternoon looking each other over, fencing, probing, pairing off and then regrouping. I was intrigued by what I saw. Although for a week I thought his name was Edgar Evans, there was to me something special about Medgar almost immediately. It was not until later that I learned he was, indeed, a veteran, that he was a football star, the president of the junior class, a campus leader. All I really knew at the time was that he was different from the boys I had known. There was something in the way he spoke, the way he carried himself, in his politeness, that made him stand out even from the others I met that day.

Though I had mistaken his name, he remembered mine, and he spoke each time we met. The more I saw of him, the more interested I became. He had a certain refinement, the air of a gentleman, and I learned that unlike many of the younger men he neither smoked nor drank. He was known on the campus as a hard worker, not only in his studies and athletics but in the many part-time jobs he held. He had a reputation for being stingy with money for dates and, paradoxically, for being something of a Don Juan. I was told by girls who knew him that he never went out with the same girl for more than a month.

The other college men knew him as an intellectual because he read a good deal and was serious about his studies. They said he never let his hair down, rarely clowned, and yet it was obvious just from knowing him slightly that he had a quiet sense of humor. The more I heard, the more fascinated I became. The more I saw him, the more I wanted to know him better.

I was accustomed to boys my own age, a happy-go-lucky crowd interested mostly in having fun, and the freshman boys at Alcorn were much like those I had known in high school in Vicksburg. Medgar, being a veteran, was older than most of the juniors, but it was maturity more than age, his air of having a goal and knowing precisely how to reach it that made him stand out. It was well known that he had refused to join a fraternity because he thought them somewhat childish, and this did not make him popular with some of the more typically carefree college men; yet even they respected him for his leadership in college activities.

I saw Medgar several times in those first few days at college. I used to go with a group of freshman girls to watch the football team practice, and my eyes were always drawn to him. As the rest of the student body arrived and classes began, I saw him around the campus, and we always spoke in passing. For a while, that was all.

Then, late in the fall, two months after I had first met him, Medgar took to walking past the music studio when I was practicing piano. At first I would notice him passing by, stopping, looking in at me, and I would nod and go on playing. Then, more and more, he would stop by the open window and wait, and we would exchange a few words when I had finished. Once he explained that he enjoyed hearing me play, and it was only much later when I learned that he really didn't think much of classical music that I realized this had simply been an excuse to explain his presence. More and more, I found myself bumping into him, and eventually I knew he was searching me out deliberately.

We began having lunch together, and sometimes we'd see each other after dinner. Several nights a week he would walk me back to the dormitory after our choir practice, where I played the piano to earn money for school expenses. We talked mostly about school, though he seemed amazingly up-to-date on current events, and I found myself reading newspapers more carefully in order to keep up with him. Eventually he asked me for a date. We went to the Saturday-night movie. I didn't tell him I had seen it a year before in Vicksburg.

But even after we began to have dates, Medgar remained slightly aloof. I knew that he liked me, though he was never one for saying so. He didn't go in for holding hands or other demonstrations of affection; he didn't even try to kiss me until we had been out together a number of times. He was friendly, but he kept his distance, and after all the talk of his being a Romeo, I was puzzled. Eventually I asked if he really liked me at all, and his reply was typical. He said he thought his actions ought to tell me, that I shouldn't have to ask. I was hurt, though I tried not to show it. I couldn't understand how anyone could be so businesslike about his emotions.

Toward the end of the year, it was generally assumed on campus that Medgar and I were getting serious about each other. I guess he and I assumed it, too, though it could hardly have been proved by anything he had said to me. He had still not said he loved me, though he had told me he would never say that to anyone unless he really meant it. Somehow, that both disturbed and reassured me. And, meanwhile, we had developed a crazy pattern of arguments that threatened to put an end to everything once each week.

Medgar liked to argue with me anyhow. He was forever telling me I was too timid, that I'd been too sheltered, that I should stand up and fight for what I believed. I knew in my heart it was true, but I conceded nothing. We were usually friendly all week, and then on Friday night we would almost always find something to disagree about. Saturday night would come, and with it the weekly campus movie, the only social event of the college. Medgar would either go alone or take another girl. I would accept a date with another boy and then try to make sure Medgar saw us together. Then, on Sunday afternoons, we always managed to find each other and make up. That, at least, was great fun.

I had been warned by a number of upperclassmen to watch my step with Medgar because he was known to change girls frequently. People said I should beware of falling in love with him because he always dropped the girls that did. I knew by this time that I had certain advantages over at least some of these former girl friends. Medgar liked girls with long hair, and I wore mine long. He used to say he liked girls who could do something more than just grin up in his face, and I had managed to make the honor roll at every grading period. I had even achieved a modest celebrity on the campus by winning second place in a state-wide oratorical contest sponsored by the Negro Masons, the prize a scholarship of $650 toward my college expenses.

He had clear-cut ideas about the girls he took out, and he made no secret of them. Even before our first date, he had told me he expected his girl friend not to go out with other boys. Since he made no such rule for himself, I thought it quite unfair and said so. And after we started dating, I made it a point to continue going out with other boys whenever he took out another girl. I think he both resented and respected it.

He had a sharp picture of the girl he wanted to marry, and he spoke about it openly. She must be well educated, friendly, neat and clean, he said, and she must love children. He hoped to have four. And the woman who would someday become Mrs. Medgar Evers, he said, would be completely devoted to him. There could be no question about that.

At the end of my first year at Alcorn, Medgar finally told me he loved me. It was a glorious moment, though we were both still hiding how deeply we felt about each other. There was still something tentative, something indefinite, something withheld. I wonder now how I managed to do so well in my studies when my emotions were in so constant a state of turmoil. Medgar was so intelligent and kind, so irritating and confusing and lovable all at the same time, that I think back on those first months of knowing him today with some of the same jumbled emotions I felt then.

In a way, I think we were attracted to each other largely because of our differences. He was right in saying I had been sheltered. And he had been raised with a certain independence. He was eight years older, had served with the Army in England and France during the war. I had never been anywhere. He came from a large family, with brothers and sisters. I was an only child, raised by a grandmother and an aunt. He grew up in the country on a farm. I was a city girl.

But the greatest difference between us, I think, was in our attitudes toward life itself. I was an accepting person, willing to deal with problems within the framework of the small world I knew, never really questioning that framework. Medgar was a rebel, ready to put his beliefs to any test. He saw a much larger world than the one that, for the moment, confined him. And he saw a place in that larger world for himself.

There was nothing on the surface in Medgar's childhood and family to account for the sort of man he was when I met him. But the explanations were there, and slowly, over the years, I found them. His father, James Evers, did not seem an unusual man. Quiet, stern, hardworking, he was a Baptist, a deacon of his church, a man who believed in work almost as an end in itself.

The family lived in a frame house on the edge of town in a Negro section of Decatur, Mississippi. They had enough land to farm, and James Evers kept cows, pigs, chickens, and a pair of mules for plowing. He grew vegetables for the table and cotton for cash. But, like most Mississippi Negroes, he could not survive on what he made from one job. He worked at times in a sawmill and at others for the railroad. Over the years he built two small houses on his property to rent out. Even before that, his wife, Jessie, rented a room in the main house to teachers to bring in additional income.

Jessie Evers did not share her husband's Baptist religion. She was a member of the Church of God in Christ. But she shared with him a belief in hard work, and besides running the house and caring for the children, she did housework for a white family and took in ironing. The children, from the time they were old enough, worked around the house and farm. As the girls reached an appropriate age, they too worked out in white homes. The boys did odd jobs for white families in town.

They were a poor family in spite of all the work, but they were never destitute, and they managed to take care of themselves without help from anyone. They took pride in that and in the respect in which they were held by the community generally, both white and Negro. Jessie Evers was a deeply religious woman, a leader of her church, a woman who kept an almost fanatically neat house and raised her children to be well mannered and clean.

She was proud of her mixed heritage. One grandmother had been an Indian; her father had been half-white. But it was the Negro half of her father's ancestry that she spoke of with fire and flashing eyes. As a mulatto, he had spent most of his adult life getting into and out of scrapes having to do with race. Once he had shot two white men and left town in the dead of night. It was a story that was told in later years to explain that the Evers fighting spirit had origins on her side of the family as well as her husband's. For there was never any question about James.

James Evers was paid on Saturdays, and with his money he did the week's shopping for staples in Decatur on Saturday night. It was a ritual on these trips for him to buy a big, round peppermint stick to be broken up at home and divided among the children. Medgar loved these trips to town with his father, but the candy was only a secondary reason. It was the obvious respect of the townspeople for his father and the way his father accepted this respect as his due that made those weekly trips really memorable. It was more than a custom, it was unwritten law that Negroes leave the sidewalks of Decatur for approaching whites. James Evers was one of the few Negroes that refused to do it. On the contrary, he behaved as though he had never heard of such a custom. "He stood up and was a man," was the way Medgar put it years later.

There was a frightening incident of his father's refusal to bow before the white man and his customs, and on one of those trips to town Medgar and his older brother, Charles, were witnesses to it. The arrangement with the stores was for credit all week with a final cash settlement on Saturday. One Saturday there was a dispute in a store. The argument over James Evers' account led to insults, and Medgar heard his father called "nigger" by two white men. When they advanced on him with the obvious intent of beating him, James Evers picked up a bottle, smashed the end of it over the counter, and held it in front of him as a weapon.

He told the boys to leave, to go home without him, and at their hesitation he made it an order. As they scampered out of the store, their last sight of their father was of a calm, grim man retreating slowly toward the door, holding the advancing white men at bay with the jagged glass of the broken bottle. He arrived home soon after the boys, unhurt, the bottle still in his hand.

But there were limits to what any Negro could do and get away with. It hurt Medgar to hear his father called "boy" by white men, and as he grew older, he began himself to experience racial incidents. For years he went with his mother on occasional days to the home of the white family where she worked. He played with white children both there and on the white fringes of the neighborhood where he lived. As he grew older, the white boys played less and less with him, and in the end there was a day of racial insults and the rupture of all friendly childhood relationships.

Race was a constant fact of Medgar's life; it was not something he had to ask his parents about. The only things to learn were the boundaries within which your race restricted you, and you learned these early and well from watching those around you.

It may have been the example their father set that led Medgar and his brother, Charles, constantly to test these boundaries, to push against them, to attempt to widen them, for there is evidence that they both did. There was the time that Mississippi Senator Theodore Bilbo, perhaps the most vicious racist of modern times to serve in the United States Senate, spoke in Decatur. Medgar and Charles went to hear him. The speech was given in the town square, and the two boys, sitting on the grass at one side, were the only Negroes in sight.

In the course of his usual racist speech, Bilbo warned the local whites of the dangers of educating Negroes, of associating with them, of letting down even slightly the bars of complete segregation. As he warmed to his theme, he pointed to Medgar and Charles at the edge of the crowd. "If we fail to hold high the wall of separation between the races," he shouted, "we will live to see the day when those two nigger boys right there will be asking for everything that is ours by right." The crowd turned to stare at Medgar and Charles. The two boys stared right back. They remained at the edge of the crowd until the end of the speech.

But the rules of racism were not just learned from speeches. Medgar must have been about twelve when a Negro man, accused of leering at a white woman, was snatched by a mob and dragged through town and out the road that led past the Evers' house. In a near-by field he was tied to a tree and shot dead. It was an event that Medgar recalled with horror, but his special revulsion was reserved for the Negro men who slunk from the sight of the mob without lifting a hand. The sickness he felt returned again and again in the months that followed, for when the lynching was over, the white mob stripped the Negro and left his bloody clothes at the foot of the tree. Medgar would pass the spot while hunting, drawn against his will to see the rotting clothes with their blood stains turning slowly to rust.

Within the larger world dominated by an obsession with race, though, was the smaller world of Medgar's family, and here was a world of warmth and closeness, of discipline and family pride. Jessie Evers had been married once before, and her older children, two sons and a daughter, were part of Medgar's family. The oldest, a son, died, but there was a daughter, Eva Lee, and a second son, Gene. Medgar was the third of James and Jessie Evers' four children. The oldest, Charles, was three years Medgar's senior. Then came Elizabeth, a year older than Medgar. Medgar was born on July 2, 1925. Two years later, the fourth child, Mary Ruth was born.

In a family that large, with both mother and father often working out of the home, there was inevitable delegation of authority to the older children. Medgar writhed under the demands of his older sisters, frequently setting out deliberately to irritate them. The arguments that followed were invariably reported to their mother. Punishment for serious breaches of the rules consisted of a number of strokes across the legs and thighs with a peach tree switch administered by his mother, and no one who has not felt the sting of a supple peach tree switch can guess at the effectiveness of such a penalty. Once Medgar's mother started after him with one of these switches, and he ran under the house. His father took over, pulling him from his sanctuary and spanking him with a leather belt. It was a spanking he never forgot, and it was the last time he ever ran from his mother.

Jessie Evers often entertained. She was an active church worker and her door was open to anyone that came by. It was a tradition for ministers to take their Sunday meal with members of their churches, and there were always church meetings that required the feeding of guests. People were constantly dropping in, and it was nothing for Jessie to get up in the middle of the night—or anytime, really—and prepare a meal. Jessie Evers' meals were famous, not only with her family but throughout the Negro community of Decatur. She was a marvelous cook, and the taste she left with Medgar for large and excellent meals was to make the early years of our marriage something of a trial for both of us. The only food that was a rarity in the Evers house was candy. Candy had to be bought for cash.

If the Everses ate well, they all worked hard enough to account for their appetites. Three times a year, a truckload of wood was delivered at the house, and Medgar and Charles had the job of cutting it into sticks of a size for the wood stove on which their mother cooked her magnificent meals. From an early age, it was Medgar's job to bring in firewood for the fireplaces and start fires before the rest of the family arose in the cold mornings. He mended fences, milked the cows and drove them home from the pasture at night. And in the fall it became a specialty of his to range the neighborhood killing pigs at hog-killing time. It was a thing he had to force himself to learn, for at first it had seemed a cruel and bloody occupation, and Medgar shrank from cruelty. But he learned the necessity for hog-killing in his family's smoke house, where he helped smoke hams and bacon, and at the table, where he helped to eat them.

Medgar and Charles were especially close, and they spent much of their youth together. They built scooters from skate wheels and boards, hunted squirrels and rabbits and possum and coons, went fishing in the many creeks and streams near the Evers' farm. Medgar learned to swim when Charles pushed him into a swimming hole far over his head.

The Evers children went to a one-room school heated by an old-fashioned potbellied stove, and here, too, it became Medgar's job to cut wood and make fires. Charles had a way of promoting fights between his younger brother and other boys, and for years the two brothers would range the countryside for miles around to carry out one of these arrangements by Charles. Medgar must have had a distinctive gait as they moved along the roadside, for he picked up the nickname "Lope," and it stuck.

It was a busy childhood, what with school and work, yet somehow Medgar left with his mother an impression of a boy who played often by himself. After he started school, he spent hours reading. Medgar himself later recalled a frequent solitary pastime that gives a picture of him as a quiet, reflective child. When something bothered him, he would leave the house, taking an empty tin can from the kitchen, and start off down the road kicking it ahead of him. Miles later, he would leave the road for the woods to find a place to sit and think. His thinking done, he would kick the can all the way home again.

When he was old enough for high school, Medgar left the one-room elementary school and began walking twelve miles each way to the Negro high school in Newton. James and Jessie Evers were both strong believers in education, and while many of the Negro children of Decatur never went beyond the small grade school, the Everses pushed their children to stay in school as long as possible. In the end, Elizabeth had some high school before she married, Mary Ruth finished high school, and both Charles and Medgar finished college. It was an unusual record for Negro children in Decatur.

The long walk to Newton was something Medgar resented, knowing as he did that the white children of Decatur had their own high school right in town. There was, of course, nothing he could do about that, but by working summers at cutting lawns and painting for white families, Medgar saved the money for a bicycle that made the long trip easier. He was an average student with no special interest in any subject, but he knew that getting an education was the only way he would get a better job than his father had at the sawmill. Both he and his father wanted that.

There was little in the way of entertainment to amuse a Negro boy growing up in Decatur, and what there was cost money. There was a small motion-picture house with a balcony known as the "buzzard's roost" reserved for Negroes. Occasionally Medgar saw a matinee on Saturday. But the big social events nearly all had something to do with church.

There was, each August, something called a tractor meeting, and after we were married, Medgar took me to one. It was held on a Sunday at the picnic grounds of a church far out in the country, and from just after dawn families would begin to arrive from all over that part of the state. It seemed to me that all of the families were huge and that somehow all were related, for nearly everyone you met was introduced as a cousin. Each family brought with it what seemed a ridiculous amount of food, and what developed was a sort of all-day picnic, with preaching and singing groups from different churches competing with one another.

A family would set itself up at a picnic table and spread out its food: three or four different kinds of cake, meats, vegetables, everything imaginable. During the day, whole families or groups of two or three would drift from table to table, from family to family, carrying baskets of food, sampling the delicacies of others and leaving something in return to be sampled. I never quite understood how it worked, for in spite of the enormous quantities of food consumed on the spot, everyone seemed to take home more food than he brought.

The primary reason for the success of the affair was that it served as a sort of reunion. This was where you found relatives and friends seen only once a year. It was where you learned who had married whom, who had died, who had graduated, and who had had another child. It was where the men discussed their crops and their jobs and the price of cotton and the impossibility of making a living cropping shares. It was where the women compared recipes and children and the white families they worked for and, I suppose, their husbands. It was where the ministers looked over one another's congregations and choirs and preaching techniques, and where the teachers talked about their schools and their students. Above all, it was where the genealogists in each family spent a happy day untangling the exact relationships of sixth cousins four times removed.

In a way these tractor meetings were both a time of renewal of bonds and a release from the drudgery of a year of hard work. They were the only real means of communication among the Negro families in that part of Mississippi. They represented the only large social gathering of the year, and there was a special sadness in going home when they were over.

In a smaller way, the various churches in each community filled many of the same needs throughout the year. Medgar's mother never missed a Sunday, and there were services all day long. With the older children, she would set off for Sunday school, which ran from nine to eleven, stay for church from eleven until two, and then break for two hours to visit and eat until four, when the young people's meeting would begin. At six o'clock the young people's meeting would end, and after supper, at seven, the evening service would begin. For years Medgar went to all of these, and it was only when he was old enough to assert himself that he managed to convince his mother that one, or at most two services each Sunday would satisfy the Lord.

Jessie Evers carried her devotion to God into her home with family prayers involving each member of the family on Sunday mornings. No meal was begun without the saying of grace, and a longer than usual blessing was said at one meal each day. Medgar's mother would tolerate no alcohol or tobacco in her home, and wearing of make-up by the girls was forbidden. She prayed on rising and before bed, and she sang hymns as she worked around the house. She was an indefatigable woman, a warm and loving mother.

Like many Southern Negro men, Medgar's father was sometimes out of work. His mother saw the family through these times, and the children never lacked for food or clothing and a warm house. She made sure that they stayed in school throughout the entire term, rather than quit during the harvest season as so many Negro children did. But, in spite of the occasional periods when James Evers could find no work, when the cash income came solely from his wife's earnings, Medgar's father was seen by all of his family as its indisputable head.

Medgar was sixteen and a sophomore at Newton High School when the United States entered World War II. Within a year he had quit school and followed his brother, Charles, into the Army. Eventually he wound up in a segregated port battalion that saw service in England and, after the Normandy invasion, at Le Havre, Liège, Antwerp, and Cherbourg. It was a rugged unit and a rough bunch of men, most of them considerably older than the seventeen-year-old lad from Decatur, Mississippi. Though Medgar neither smoked nor drank, his language was strongly influenced by the men around him. Obscenity must have seemed incongruous in one so young, and one day a white lieutenant took him aside.

"You're too intelligent to talk that way," the lieutenant said. "You have a good vocabulary. You can say what you want without swearing every other word. Some of these men can't. They don't know any better. You do. You can go a long way if you use the intelligence you've got."

There were other talks after that, and Medgar slowly realized that the lieutenant was right. As the war ended, the same lieutenant urged him to go back to school, to improve his mind, to finish his education, to make something of himself. He proved an important influence in Medgar's life.

Medgar had had no close friends among whites since his childhood, and I have no doubt that at first he regarded the lieutenant's interest in him with suspicion. But the whole experience of the Army was a new one, a broadening one, and it opened up new worlds to a young Negro boy from rural Mississippi. The fact that his unit was segregated, that its officers were white, would not have seemed strange to Medgar. That was the way his world had always been. But the trip by troop ship across the Atlantic was straight from a storybook, and though Medgar was seasick most of the way, the body's misery could not dampen the spirit's sense of adventure. In such an atmosphere, even a deeply ingrained suspicion of white men had to be questioned.

In France he found a whole people—all of them white—who apparently saw no difference in a man simply because of his skin color, and this was perhaps the greatest revelation of all. In time, he came to know a French family near where he was stationed, and they accepted him as one of them. A romance with a daughter developed, and nobody flinched. Before it could amount to much, the battalion was moved.

And yet even here, in France, where the French accepted both white and Negro American troops simply as American soldiers, the long arm of racism intruded. For white American soldiers brought their prejudices with them and imposed them wherever possible on the French. The white troops whispered stories about the colored troops, and more than once Medgar was asked by a naïve French girl if it were true that Negroes were some kind of monkey whose tails came out at night. There was embarrassment and shock when the lies were exposed, and there remained, for the French, wonder at what lay beneath the lies. Why should Americans hate each other? Why should they separate their troops according to color? There had to be reasons.

And so, in the end, even the openness and friendliness of the French were tainted by the presence of American racism. There was apparently no escape from it. And even the pleasant memory of Medgar's romance with the young French girl was later spoiled when, after the war, his mother pleaded with him to end his correspondence with her for fear that whites in Decatur would find out and take offense. Negroes have been lynched in Mississippi for less.

The war was liberating to Medgar in several ways. Both he and his brother, Charles, saved money from their army pay and sent it home to their parents. With some of it, Jessie and James Evers modernized their house, replacing the wood stove and bringing plumbing inside. Four rooms were added, and by the time the two boys came home, the family's living conditions were much improved.

There were many times during Medgar's army service when he felt how impossible it would be to return to Mississippi and settle down to the life he had known before the war. For if Mississippi hadn't changed, he had. He had a whole new vision of what life could be like, of the way it was lived in other places by other people. The simple fact that he had helped earn money that had done so much to improve his parent's home was an indication of the possibilities of life outside his native state.

And yet, when the war was over, back to Mississippi he went, along with Charles. Charles, who had finished high school, enrolled at Alcorn Agricultural and Mechanical College on the G.I. Bill. Medgar took a job while he decided what to do. But the changes wrought in both young men by their years outside Mississippi were not long in asserting themselves. In the summer of 1946, Medgar turned twenty-one. He and Charles rounded up four other young Negroes and went to the county clerk's office to register to vote. It was not such an innocent venture as it might seem. All of them knew that of the 900-odd voters on the rolls in Decatur none were Negroes. And all of them knew why.

A small crowd of whites gathered when the word went out that Negroes were registering. For the moment, that was all. "I never found out until later," Medgar said afterward, "that they visited my parents nightly after that. First, it was the whites, and then their Negro message-bearers. And the word was always the same: 'Tell your sons to take their names off the books. Don't show up at the courthouse voting day.' Then, the night before the election, Bilbo came to town and harangued the crowd in the square. 'The best way to keep a nigger from the polls on election day,' he told them, 'is to visit him the night before.' And they visited us. My brother came from Alcorn College to vote that next day. I laid off from work. The six of us gathered at my house and we walked to the polls. I'll never forget it. Not a Negro was on the streets, and when we got to the courthouse, the clerk said he wanted to talk with us. When we got into his office, some fifteen or twenty armed white men surged in behind us, men I had grown up with, had played with. We split up and went home without voting. Around town, Negroes said we had been whipped, beaten up, and run out of town. Well, in a way we were whipped, I guess, but I made up my mind then that it would not be like that again—at least not for me."

It may have been this incident, along with the memory of that white army lieutenant, that helped Medgar decide to return to school. Alcorn, where Charles was already enrolled, had a laboratory high school as part of its education department, and Medgar enrolled there as a high school junior in the fall of 1946. He was years older than most of the high school students, though there were other veterans completing high school, too. It did not bother him at all. For suddenly he had purpose and direction, even if it was nothing more than completing his education, and he plunged into it as he was to plunge into nearly everything he did from that time on. It was during that first year at Alcorn's laboratory high school that Medgar really began enjoying learning for its own sake.

There was an English teacher, Mrs. John H. Jackson, who gave Medgar his first real knowledge of how to study. Under her guidance, he began to develop a tremendous vocabulary, one that in later years often sent me to the dictionary to look up a word he had used. But while Medgar liked Mrs. Jackson and admired her, he had no desire himself to become a teacher. He regarded the teaching profession for Negroes as something close to an insult, because it was the one profession Negroes were encouraged by whites to aspire to. While most Mississippi Negroes reacted too little to the deprivation of segregation and racism, Medgar had a tendency during those years to over-react. Were the whites for it? Then he was against it. Did the whites approve? Then it was suspect.

This was, I think, the basis for his refusal even to consider a teaching career. He did not yet know what he wanted to do, but he was sure he would never teach. Looking back today, there is a certain irony in this, for Medgar undoubtedly turned out to be one of the more important teachers his people have ever had in Mississippi. But I suppose Medgar could say, with justice, that he taught in a way that Mississippi whites certainly did not approve.

If Medgar came alive as a student at Alcorn, he also found himself as an athlete. He had always loved sports and participated in them where he could, but Newton High School had had no organized teams. Now he made the first team in football and went out for track as well. These were interests he was to continue all through college.

With the G.I. Bill behind him, there was no real doubt that Medgar could finish high school and go on to college, but he was never one to waste either time or money—or the time to make money. Beginning that first summer after his junior year in high school, he and Charles began going to Chicago for summer jobs. Their half-sister, Eva Lee, had moved to Chicago's South Side, and each spring as soon as school was out, the two brothers would go home to Decatur, pick up some friends, and set off for Chicago in a rattle-trap car that always threatened to break down along the way but somehow never did. Medgar held a number of different jobs over those summers, usually doing manual labor on some construction job.

There was little about Chicago that Medgar liked except the higher wages. He always said he'd hate to live there. I think this was a reaction mostly to the ugly Negro ghetto on the South Side where first one sister and then eventually all three moved. It annoyed Medgar that the three of them—Eva Lee, Elizabeth, and finally Mary Ruth, toward whom Medgar had always felt particularly close and protective—all settled in the same neighborhood of that vast slum, the same neighborhood in which one could find hundreds of other Negroes from Decatur. He was constantly urging them to move, to spread out, to try something different and new, but they, like their friends and neighbors from Decatur, found it easier, friendlier, and perhaps even safer to stay together.

Many white people had pointed to this tendency of Southern Negroes to cluster together in Northern cities as proof that Negroes prefer segregation—that they really want to live among themselves. I think it was his knowledge of this charge, as much as anything, that disturbed Medgar about what he saw in his sisters' neighborhood in Chicago. In fact, of course, there is nothing about Negroes from the same places in the South living together in small neighborhoods in Chicago that differs very much from the clusters of European immigrants that for generations settled in small sections of our Eastern cities on their arrival in the United States. And the reasons are much the same. New arrivals in any strange place tend to seek out friends and relatives, to settle near them and depend on their experience for help in getting started. The only real difference is that, for Negroes, the opportunity to escape these ghettos once this original purpose has been served has always been much more difficult. It remains that way today.

But if Medgar disliked Chicago, he nonetheless took advantage of some of the things it offered that were new and different. He swam at the lakefront beaches, visited museums and libraries, and luxuriated in the sense of freedom it gave him to enter such places with no thought to race or color. Strangely, his reaction to all of this was not that of many Southern Negroes: a desire to remain in the North. Instead, he would begin to talk about what a wonderful place Mississippi would be if it could only rid itself of racism, how much better, really, than Chicago.

Medgar knew, of course, that there was racism to be found in Chicago, too, but at least there were no desperate problems in Negroes and whites mixing freely at beaches, in school, on buses and trains, in the libraries and museums and restaurants and shops and movies and at work. All of this he took as proof of how easy it really ought to be to convince white Mississippians of the error of their traditional views, if only they could see how it all worked. Rather than incline him toward staying in the North, Medgar's enjoyment of the North's extra freedoms always seemed to send him hurrying back to the South with new hopes of changing it.

One of Medgar's greatest pleasures during those summers in Chicago was the chance to explore the suburbs. Whenever he could, he would borrow a car and drive out of the city to wander up one street and down another looking at houses. He had a dream of the sort of house he hoped someday to live in, the kind of street and neighborhood and town where he might raise a family, and the white suburbs of Chicago seemed to him right out of that dream. He would spend whole days just driving slowly through the suburbs of Chicago's North Shore, looking at the beautiful houses and wishing. Years later, when we were in Chicago together, he took me on these drives, and by that time he had picked out specific houses that came closest to the dream.

One of them was in Evanston, a two-story house with tall shade trees and shrubbery neatly placed throughout the green yard. It was an older house with a settled look about it, and as we sat in the car across the street, Medgar began to dream out loud.

"Listen," he said suddenly, and I did, "Do you hear how quiet it is? This is the kind of neighborhood to raise children in. Look at that lawn, like a carpet almost. And those big old trees. Wouldn't you like to just lie down under one of them?"

I suppose that Medgar's dreams of what America might be were derived, as many of our dreams are, from what he had seen in the movies. No one who saw the Andy Hardy pictures in the 1930s and '40s and drank in the warmth of that small town and its life could help identifying with it. No one, that is, except a Negro who knew that there was no place for him in that America. And that, in a sense, is what has been wrong with American movies: that white Americans could sit through them week after week, year after year, and never realize how distorted they were. For if Andy Hardy's town was anything like Evanston, Illinois, in the years that Medgar used to park on its streets and admire its houses, then fifteen per cent of its population was Negro, and they lived in a segregated ghetto that was never seen on the screen. If Andy Hardy's town was like Evanston, it had both a white and Negro YMCA; its public high school had no swimming pool because that would mean whites and Negroes swam together; and its hospital did not admit Negroes as patients. I don't know that Medgar knew these facts; I myself learned them only recently, and some of them have changed in the years since then; but Medgar would not have had to know specific facts about Evanston—or any other white suburb—to know the truth. The truth is concealed from whites, not from Negroes.

It was this kind of knowledge, I think, that drove Medgar to try to change his world and his place in it. It is the same drive that moves millions of Negroes today to demand at least a chance at some of the good things in life. Nearly any movie, almost any page of *Life* magazine, the advertising on the billboards and in the newspapers, most of what we see each day on television—all of these constitute a kind of torture to many Negroes. For they know that this, or something like it, is what awaits the American who is willing to work for it—unless he is a Negro. American advertising is responsible for much of the Negro's current demand that he, too, be allowed to participate in the fulfillment of the American dream.

In the fall of 1948 Medgar entered Alcorn College as a freshman majoring in business administration. It was a compromise, I think, between his refusal to become a teacher and his determination to go to college. He used to talk vaguely about someday having a business of his own, though he never indicated just what kind of business it would be. I know that the idea of being his own boss appealed strongly to him, and he had, of course, seen Negroes in white collar jobs during his summers in Chicago. He may even have met some Chicago Negroes who owned their own businesses, though I never heard him mention it. But certainly Medgar, whatever he knew to be possible in Chicago, was enough of a realist to know that few Negroes in Mississippi owned their own businesses, and he never spoke seriously of leaving Mississippi.

Medgar was not a student at Alcorn College long before he had made a name for himself on the campus. He was a member of the debate team, the college choir, and the football and track teams. For two years he was the editor of the campus newspaper, and in 1951 he edited the yearbook. As a business major, he joined the business club on campus, and through his activity in the campus YMCA he had an opportunity to travel to Millsaps College, a white school in Jackson, where every month campus "Y" groups from the two schools met together for panel discussions on world affairs. By the time Medgar was a senior, his leadership on the Alcorn campus was such that he had been chosen for listing in the annual publication of *Who's Who in American Colleges,* quite an honor for a rural Mississippi Negro at a segregated Mississippi college.

FROM

My Brother Bill

JOHN FAULKNER

WHEN FAIR TIME CAME the county pitched canvas display booths where our farmers could show their prize produce. These tents were backed against the hitch chain around the courtyard. Here the farmers placed their best ears of corn and biggest potatoes, and their wives displayed cakes and jars of jelly and preserves.

The merchants believed carnivals were good for business. They would bring crowds to town with fall money in their pockets. The carnival pitched their tents with their backs to the line of elm trees at the edge of the sidewalk. There was always a lady snake charmer, and a wild man from Borneo, that some English explorer had caught in a net. The scene of his capture was always depicted on the front of his tent. We stared at it and believed and paid our dimes to go inside and stare at the wild man, seated in a cane-bottomed chair with one leg chained to the stand on which he sat, and gnawing at the bones scattered about him.

There were games too, where you won things by pitching rings over numbered pegs, or covering a painted circle with five disks you got for ten cents. The man who ran the booth could easily fan the disks out and cover the circle. We tried but couldn't. Jack and I tried several times. Bill tried once. I did win a dollar watch by fishing for toy fishes in a canvas trough, though. It didn't run good but then time didn't mean much to us, at least the time we kept ourselves. Mother saw to it that we got off to school on time and we knew better than to be after dark getting home to do our chores.

Anyhow, I broke the crystal on my watch on the acting bar at school the first day I carried it and twisted the hands together trying to get it out of my pocket. I was disappointed for a while but not for long. Time didn't make that much difference.

Bill didn't go in all the side shows and try every game like Jack and I did. He would listen to the barkers and try a game every now and then but that was about all. Dad gave us money for the carnival but Bill always had something else to do with his. Whatever he came by, he always saved some. I never knew him not to have a hoard tucked away somewhere when he came across something he really wanted.

They always had a special children's day, usually on Wednesday, and school would close. Then we'd go back to school for two days until Saturday came, when we had a whole day for the fair's closing. Saturday was the highlight of the whole week—the balloon ascension. We called the man a "balloonitic" and wanted to be sure to be there if he fell.

All airmen of that day were looked on as lunatics. Our papers always pictured them with Death riding by their sides. We knew one of them would fall and be killed sooner or later, and many of them were. We believed any man was a fool if he got both feet off the ground at the same time. If he insisted on being a fool we wanted to be there and see him when he got what was coming to him.

About eight o'clock in the morning the balloonist and his helper, a Negro, would appear with a great pile of dirty canvas loaded in a wagon. With curses and grunts they would dump this into the widest part of the midway at one of the corners. A frame would be erected and the mouth of the great bag would be draped over it and pulled down close to the ground. Then the Negro would bring the man a five-gallon can of coal oil, a dipper and an iron skillet full of hot coals. Soon we would see a tiny flame in there, then a gush of flame as the balloonist would fling coal oil on the coals.

Throughout the day he would feed the fire and the bag would begin to swell with hot air. During those hours we would stand there and watch, Bill most steadfast of all. Other children would come by to watch with us. Their pet dogs would be with them. Most of us would wander off, to come back later, but not Bill. The only time I remember him leaving was to hurry home to dinner so he could come right back.

Although it would take nearly all day to fill the bag with enough hot air and smoke to whisk the man aloft, by about ten o'clock it would begin to take a flabby, wrinkled shape above the framework. Soon he would step out from under the frame, dirty and smoke-grimed and with his eyes reddened from the fumes, and pitch us ropes to hold. These were mooring ropes, attached to the reinforced top of the bag, and there were about a dozen of them. We would spread out in a circle around the inflating balloon. Each of us would take an end as they were pitched to us and stand there till three-thirty or four in the afternoon, watching the bag swell, grow taut and sway above us.

Along about noon, with the bag swelled enough for the man to stand erect within the smoothing canvas, we would see him in the glare of each flung dipper of coal oil. He would stand back against the canvas wall and we'd see him raise a bottle to his lips. As time wore on and the moment of ascent came closer and closer, we would see him raising the bottle more and more often. Usually one bottle wasn't enough. He'd emerge from his canvas igloo and send his Negro for another one. And soon he would have drunk that one too.

By three or four o'clock in the afternoon the bag would be tugging at our hands. It was time to go. The man would come out from under the bag for the last time. He'd be almost black from oil fumes and smoke and his eyes would be red and streaming. But he would be as coldly sober and as steady as anyone I had ever seen. Glaring at us, he would say, "Move in a little now," and wave us closer with his hands.

We would step forward slowly, moving in toward the balloon, and as we advanced it would rise until a bar, like a trapeze bar, fastened by two ropes to the bottom of the bag, would rise from the ground to knee height. At that point he would stop us. "Hold it now." Tensely we would hold, staring at him, readying our muscles to be sure and let go when he said so.

As we watched he would fasten his parachute harness on, flexing his legs and arms to seat the straps. The parachute itself was packed in a crokersack, tied end-down to the horizontal bar on which he would sit to go aloft. The sack was laced with grocer's string so it would rip out as he fell away from the balloon. Trailing the risers behind him, he would seat himself carefully on the bar, making sure the risers were free. He would settle himself, reach up and grab the ropes leading to the balloon with clenched hands and, with his feet placed firmly upon the ground, stare at us with the fever-ridden eyes of Old Nick and say, with the most tragic voice in the world, "Let her go, boys."

We would release our grip and jump back, craning our necks upward to follow the smoke-filled bag's flight, to see which way the wind would drift the balloon as soon as it cleared the elm trees. As soon as we did, we would begin running, to be near where the man jumped, to see him land in his parachute or to watch him fall if his chute failed to open.

Bill always gave us the signal to start and though we could see as well as he could which way the balloon was drifting, we always waited for him to tell us which direction to run. He knew more about aircraft than we did. He had read about them in the *American Boy.*

We never got there in time to see the man actually land in his parachute, nor did we ever see one fail to open, though we chased the balloonitic each year. The bag rose swiftly. It didn't take it long to get high enough for the man to tumble backward from his roost and jerk the chute from its bag and float down to earth. We would watch as we ran, and shout and point as the gas-filled bag swept away, then a small dot would appear below it and a long white ribbon would flower out behind the dot and we would shriek again. There would be fifty to a hundred of us in the pack, all running toward the descending toadstool.

The balloon, free of the man's weight, would turn upside down and trail a long black smear of oily smoke across our autumn sky. The bag itself would always land not too far from where the man came down.

We watched this too as we ran, but we kept our eye on the man. We never did beat him to the spot where he landed. He always got there first. Yet we usually arrived while he was still in his harness, staggering around, cursing, trying to free himself from the straps. By then he would be too drunk to know what he was doing. Once back on the ground, the liquor seemed to hit him all at once. He would be higher than the balloon from which he had just jumped.

I remember Bill leading us into a thicket in which he had landed one day, and trying to help him free from his straps, but he flailed us away with his hands. Always, soon after we got there, there would come some carnival men in a buggy with the Negro helper. They would gallop up and subdue him, get his harness off and him into the buggy and away before the law came and arrested them for disturbing the peace. The Negro helper would be left to gather up the parachute and roll the balloon, so they could be picked up later after the balloonitic had been taken somewhere and sobered up.

One day the parachutist came down in our lot and the balloon fell on our chicken house. It caved the roof in on our chickens, who had already gone to roost, and caused Dad to shoot a pig right between the eyes.

It had been still the day when the balloon left the Square. There was almost no wind and the sky was gray and overcast. It took several seconds to tell which way the balloon was going to drift and then we took off. It seemed to be drifting toward South Street, toward our house. We saw the man had come down in our lot and the balloon not far behind. As soon as he had left it, it had turned bottom side up and plummeted to earth.

By the time we began pouring over our fence he was already on the ground, staggering around and cursing. It was almost dark. The balloon had hit the hen-house roof and caved it in and our chickens were squawking indignantly and running around every which way. We never did find some of them. Others were two or three days getting over their fright enough to come back home.

Where the man had landed was right in our pig lot. It was fenced off from the rest of the property and we had several shoats in there waiting for first frost to be butchered. They ran and squealed and bunched up in the far corner.

Dad had just come home from work when he heard the disturbance out back. He ran out the kitchen door in time to see the thirty or forty of us swarming over the fence and knotting up against the hog pen, where the man was stomping around trying to get himself out of his harness. The hens were sailing around, screeching, and the pigs were squealing and the man was cursing. Dad shouted at him to stop, that Mother could hear him from inside the house. The man paid no attention. So Dad turned and ran back to the house and came out this time with his pistol.

It was a silver-plated Colt, a .41 single-action, and with the longest barrel I ever saw on a hand gun. It was dusk by then but you could see the pistol shining in Dad's hand as he strode across the back yard and into the lot. A man from the carnival had got there by then and was stripping the harness off the balloonist and trying to calm him down. He went to Dad to try to pacify him while the Negro, now that the parachutist was free of his harness, tried to lead him away to the wagon. Of the boys there, all of us stood still at the sight of Dad with his pistol, watching the carnival man talking to him.

In the carnival buggy the balloonist quietly went to sleep. By that time Dad had sort of calmed down, especially since the man talking to him promised to pay damages if Dad would agree to let the matter rest there.

The Negro helper hung around outside the gate. He didn't like the look of Dad with his pistol. Now he came in and began working at the balloon, trying to get the one corner off the chicken house so he could fold it. The rest of the balloon was spread over the hog lot but that one corner was caught on the roof. Finally Dad called one or two of our Negroes to help and they got the balloon rolled up and loaded in the wagon and hauled it away.

All the other boys who had chased the balloon with us left then and in our darkening lot was left only Bill and Jack and me and Dad. Dad was standing there with his arm hung down, the pistol in it and cocked. He stood there glaring about the lot, at the caved-in chicken house, a few white feathers strewn over the ground, and the pigs huddled in the far corner of the pen. Bill and Jack and I sort of huddled together, quiet, looking.

Just then one of our smaller pigs came up behind Dad and raised his snout and said, "Unh!" Dad whirled, and leveling his pistol, shot that pig right between the eyes. He stood there looking down at the pig a few moments, then told us to get Jessie. He wanted Jessie to come dress the pig out before it spoiled. Then he turned and strode off toward the house, the pistol still swinging from his hand.

I'll always remember three little boys standing there wide-eyed in the deserted gloom of that empty autumn lot, watching Dad with that long shiny pistol in his hand, cocked, his anger at the boiling point, and nothing to shoot at. When that pig grunted right behind him, it was more than he could stand. He simply raised his gun and shot it between the eyes.

And Now What's To Do

William Faulkner

"And Now What's To Do" came to light when a box of forgotten Faulkner papers was found in an understairs closet at Rowan Oak, Faulkner's Oxford home, in 1970, as the University of Mississippi began restoration work on the house. Written in an early version of Faulkner's neat and stylized hand, the two-page uncompleted manuscript appears to be extremely autobiographical, though it may well move toward fiction as the narrative proceeds. Faulkner's great-grandfather, grandfather, and father very closely resembled the portraits here, to judge by both Faulkner's biography and his fictional treatment of the family in such works as *Flags in the Dust* and *The Sound and the Fury*. The charming picture of himself in the livery stable, diminutive and with a "shrill cricket voice," and the touching revelations about adolescence and coming of age also have counterparts in his fiction—for example, *Elmer, Light in August*, and *The Hamlet*, among other works—and in other autobiographical writings and interviews. The tone of the piece prefigures by almost 30 years the lovely essay he would be asked to write for *Holiday* magazine in 1954 when the Mississippi writer James Street, himself ill, turned down the assignment and strongly recommended Faulkner; as Street would say later in a letter to a kinsman in Mississippi, explaining why Faulkner was the only man to take on the job: "You don't pinchhit for Babe Ruth." Probably written in the mid-1920s, "And Now What's To Do" is a fitting prelude to "Mississippi," both examples of a "chronicle voice"—one can hear it also in *Requiem for a Nun*—that Faulkner might have used if he had ever written his "Golden Book of Yoknapatawpha." "And Now What's To Do" was first published by Professor James B. Meriwether in the Summer 1973 issue of the *Mississippi Quarterly;* that transcription of the text is followed here. The original is in the University of Mississippi Library.

Tom McHaney

His great-grandfather came into the country afoot from the Tennessee mountains, where he had killed a man, worked and saved and bought a little land, won a little more at cards and dice, and died at the point of a pistol while trying to legislate himself into a little more; his grandfather was a deaf, upright man in white linen, who wasted his inherited substance in politics. He had a law practice still, but he sat most of the day in the courthouse yard, a brooding, thwarted old man too deaf to take part in conversation and whom the veriest child could beat at checkers. His father loved horses better than books or learning; he owned a livery stable, and here the boy grew up, impregnated with the violent ammoniac odor of horses. At ten he could stand on a box and harness a horse and put it between runabout shafts almost as quickly as a grown man, darting beneath its belly like a cricket to buckle the straps, cursing it in his shrill cricket voice; by the time he was twelve he had acquired from the negro hostlers an uncanny skill with a pair of dice.

Each Christmas eve his father carried a hamper full of whisky in pint bottles to the stable and stood with it in the office door, against the firelight, while the negroes gathered and rolled their eyes and ducked their gleaming teeth in the barn cavern, filled with snorts and stampings of contentment. The boy, become adolescent, helped to drink this; old ladies smelled his breath at times and tried to save his soul. Then he was sixteen and he began to acquire a sort of inferiority complex regarding his father's business. He had gone through grammar school and one year in high school with girls and boys (on rainy days, in a hack furnished by his father he drove about the neighborhood and gathered up all it would hold free of charge) whose fathers were lawyers and doctors and merchants—all genteel professions, with starched collars. He had been unselfconscious then, accepting all means of earning bread as incidental to following whatever occupation a man preferred. But not now. All this was changed by his changing body. Before and during puberty he learned about women from the negro hostlers and the white night-man, by listening to their talk. Now, on the street, he looked after the same girls he had once taken to school in his father's hack, watching their forming legs, imagining their blossoming thighs, with a feeling of defiant inferiority. There was a giant in him, but the giant was muscle-bound. The boys, the doctors' and merchants' and lawyers' sons, loafed on the corners before the drug stores. None of them could make a pair of dice behave as he could.

An automobile came to town. The horses watched it with swirling proud eyes and tossing snorts of alarm. The war came, a sound afar off heard. He was eighteen, he had not been in school since three years; the moth-eaten hack rusted quietly among the jimson weeds in the stable yard. He no longer smelled of ammonia, for he could now win twenty or thirty dollars any Sunday in the crap game in the wooded park near the railway station; and on the drug store corner where the girls passed in soft troops, touching one another with their hands and with their arms you could not tell him from a lawyer's or a merchant's or a doctor's son. The girls didn't, with their ripening thighs and their mouths that keep you awake at night with unnameable things—shame of lost integrity, manhood's pride, desire like a drug. The body is tarnished, soiled in its pride, now. But what is it for, anyway?

A girl got in trouble, and he clung to boxcar ladders or lay in empty gondolas while railjoints clicked under the cold stars. Frost had not yet fallen upon the cotton, but it had touched the gum-lined Kentucky roads and the broad grazing lands, and lay upon the shocked corn of Ohio farm land beneath the moon. He lay on his back in an Ohio hay stack. The warm dry hay was about his legs. It had soaked a summer's sun, and it held him suspended in dry and sibilant warmth where he moved unsleeping, cradling his head, thinking of home. Girls were all right, but there were so many girls everywhere. So many of them a man had to get through with in the world, politely. It meant tactfully. Nothing to girls. Dividing legs dividing receptive. He had known all about it before, but the reality was like reading a story and then seeing it in the movies, with music and all. Soft things. Secretive, but like traps. Like going after something you wanted, and getting into a nest of spider webs. You got the thing, then you had to pick the webs off, and every time you touched one, it stuck to you. Even after you didn't want the thing anymore, the webs clung to you. Until after a while you remembered the way the webs itched and you wanted the thing again, just thinking of how the webs itched. No. Quicksand. That was it. Wade through once, then go on. But a man wont. He wants to go all the way through, somehow; break out on the other side. Everything incomplete somehow. Having to back off, with webs clinging to you. "Christ, you have to tell them so much. You cant think of it fast enough. And they never forget when you do and when you dont. What do they want, anyway?"

Across the moon a V of geese slid, their lonely cries drifted in the light of chill and haughty stars across the shocked corn and the supine delivered earth, lonely and sad and wild. Winter: season of sin and death. The geese were going south, but his direction was steadily north. In an Ohio town one night, in a saloon, he got to know a man who was travelling from county seat to county seat with a pacing horse, making the county fairs. The man was cunning in a cravatless collar, lachrymosely panegyric of the pacing of the horse; and together they drifted south again and again his garments became impregnated with ammonia. Horses smelled good again, rankly ammoniac, with their ears like frost-touched vine leaves[.]

Mississippi

William Faulkner

Mississippi begins in the lobby of a Memphis, Tennessee hotel and extends south to the Gulf of Mexico. It is dotted with little towns concentric about the ghosts of the horses and mules once tethered to the hitch-rail enclosing the county courthouse and it might almost be said to have only those two directions, north and south, since until a few years ago it was impossible to travel east or west in it unless you walked or rode one of the horses or mules; even in the boy's early manhood, to reach by rail either of the adjacent county towns thirty miles away to the east or west, you had to travel ninety miles in three different directions on three different railroads.

In the beginning it was virgin—to the west, along the Big River, the alluvial swamps threaded by black almost motionless bayous and impenetrable with cane and buckvine and cypress and ash and oak and gum; to the east, the hardwood ridges and the prairies where the Appalachian mountains died and buffalo grazed; to the south, the pine barrens and the moss-hung liveoaks and the greater swamps less of earth than water and lurking with alligators and water moccasins, where Louisiana in its time would begin.

And where in the beginning the predecessors crept with their simple artifacts, and built the mounds and vanished, bequeathing only the mounds in which the succeeding recordable Algonquian stock would leave the skulls of their warriors and chiefs and babies and slain bears, and the shards of pots, and hammer- and arrow-heads and now and then a heavy silver Spanish spur. There were deer to drift in herds alarmless as smoke then, and bear and panther and wolves in the brakes and bottoms, and all the lesser beasts—coon and possum and beaver and mink and mushrat (not muskrat: mushrat); they were still there and some of the land was still virgin in the early nineteen hundreds when the boy himself began to hunt. But except for looking occasionally out from behind the face of a white man or a Negro, the Chickasaws and Choctaws and Natchez and Yazoos were as gone as the predecessors, and the people the boy crept with were the descendants of the Sartorises and De Spains and Compsons who had commanded the Manassas and Sharpsburg and Shiloh and Chickamauga regiments, and the McCaslins and Ewells and Holstons and Hogganbecks whose fathers and grandfathers had manned them, and now and then a Snopes too because by the beginning of the twentieth century Snopeses were everywhere: not only behind the counters of grubby little side street stores patronised mostly by Negroes, but behind the presidents' desks of banks and the directors' tables of wholesale grocery corporations and in the deaconries of Baptist churches, buying up the decayed Georgian houses and chopping them into apartments and on their death-beds decreeing annexes and baptismal fonts to the churches as mementos to themselves or maybe out of simple terror.

They hunted too. They too were in the camps where the De Spains and Compsons and McCaslins and Ewells were masters in their hierarchial turn, shooting the does not only when law but the Master too said not, shooting them not even because the meat was needed but leaving the meat itself to be eaten by scavengers in the woods, shooting it simply because it was big and moving and alien, of an older time than the little grubby stores and the accumulating and compounding money; the boy a man now and in his hierarchial turn Master of the camp and coping, having to cope, not with the diminishing wilderness where there was less and less game, but with the Snopeses who were destroying that little which did remain.

These elected the Bilboes and voted indefatigably for the Vardamans, naming their sons after both; their origin was in bitter hatred and fear and economic rivalry of the Negroes who farmed little farms no larger than and adjacent to their own, because the Negro, remembering when he had not been free at all, was therefore capable of valuing what he had of it enough to struggle to retain even that little and had taught himself how to do more with less: to raise more cotton with less money to spend and food to eat and fewer or inferior tools to work with: this, until he, the Snopes, could escape from the land into the little grubby side street stores where he could live not beside the Negro but on him by marking up on the inferior meat and meal and molasses the price which he, the Negro, could not even always read.

In the beginning, the obsolescent, dispossessed tomorrow by the already obsolete: the wild Algonquian—the Chickasaw and Choctaw and Natchez and Pascagoula—looking down from the tall Mississippi bluffs at a Chippeway canoe containing three Frenchmen—and had barely time to whirl and look behind him at a thousand Spaniards come overland from the Atlantic Ocean, and for a little while longer had the privilege of watching an ebb-flux-ebb-flux of alien nationalities as rapid as the magician's spill and evanishment of inconstant cards: the Frenchman for a second, then the Spaniard for perhaps two, then the Frenchman for another two and then the Spaniard again and then the Frenchman again for that last half-breath before the Anglo-Saxon, who would come to stay, to endure: the tall man roaring with Protestant scripture and boiled whiskey, Bible and jug in one hand and like as not an Indian tomahawk in the other, brawling, turbulent, uxorious and polygamous: a married invincible bachelor without destination but only motion, advancement, dragging his gravid wife and most of his mother-in-law's kin behind him into the trackless wilderness, to spawn that child behind a log-crotched rifle and then get her with another one before they moved again, and at the same time scattering his inexhaustible other seed in three hundred miles of dusky bellies: without avarice or compassion or forethought either: felling a tree which took two hundred years to grow, to extract from it a bear or a capful of wild honey.

He endured, even after he too was obsolete, the younger sons of Virginia and Carolina planters coming to replace him in wagons laden with slaves and indigo seedlings over the very roads he had hacked out with little else but the tomahawk. Then someone gave a Natchez doctor a Mexican cotton seed (maybe with the boll weevil already in it since, like the Snopes, he too has taken over the southern earth) and changed the whole face of Mississippi, slaves clearing rapidly now the virgin land lurking still (1850) with the ghosts of Murrell and Mason and Hare and the two Harpes, into plantation fields for profit where he, the displaced and obsolete, had wanted only the bear and the deer and the sweetening for his tooth. But he remained, hung on still; he is still there even in the boy's middle-age, living in a log or plank or tin hut on the edge of what remains of the fading wilderness, by and on the tolerance and sometimes even the bounty of the plantation owner to whom, in his intractable way and even with a certain dignity and independence, he is a sycophant, trapping coons and muskrats, now that the bear and the panther are almost gone too, improvident still, felling still the two-hundred-year-old tree even though it has only a coon or a squirrel in it now.

Manning, when that time came, not the Manassas and Shiloh regiments but confederating into irregular bands and gangs owning not much allegiance to anyone or anything, unified instead into the one rite and aim of stealing horses from Federal picket-lines; this in the intervals of raiding (or trying to) the plantation house of the very man to whom he had been the independent sycophant and intended to be again, once the war was over and presuming that the man came back from his Sharpsburg or Chickamauga majority or colonelcy or whatever it had been; trying to, that is, until the major's or colonel's wife or aunt or mother-in-law, who had buried the silver in the orchard and still held together a few of the older slaves, fended him off and dispersed him, and when necessary even shot him, with the absent husband's or nephew's or son-in-law's hunting gun or dueling pistols,—the women, the indomitable, the undefeated, who never surrendered, refusing to allow the Yankee *minie* balls to be dug out of portico column or mantelpiece or lintel, who seventy years later would get up and walk out of *Gone with the Wind* as soon as Sherman's name was mentioned; irreconcilable and enraged and still talking about it long after the weary exhausted men who had fought and lost it gave up trying to make them hush: even in the boy's time the boy himself knowing about Vicksburg and Corinth and exactly where his grandfather's regiment had been at First Manassas before he remembered hearing very much about Santa Claus.

In those days (1901 and -2 and -3 and -4) Santa Claus occurred only at Christmas, not like now, and for the rest of the year children played with what they could find or contrive or make, though just as now, in '51 and -2 and -3 and -4, they still played, aped in miniature, what they had been exposed to, heard or seen or been moved by most. Which was true in the child's time and case too: the indomitable unsurrendered old women holding together still, thirty-five and forty years later, a few of the old house slaves: women too who, like the white ones, declined, refused to give up the old ways and forget the old anguishes. The child himself remembered one of them: Caroline: free these many years but who had declined to leave. Nor would she ever accept in full her weekly Saturday wages, the family never knew why unless the true reason was the one which appeared: for the simple pleasure of keeping the entire family reminded constantly that they were in arrears to her, compelling the boy's grandfather then his father and finally himself in his turn to be not only her banker but her bookkeeper too, having got the figure of eighty-nine dollars into her head somehow or for some reason, and though the sum itself altered, sometimes more and sometimes less and sometimes it would be she herself who would be several weeks in arrears, it never changed: one of the children, white or Negro, liable to appear at any time, usually when most of the family would be gathered at a meal, with the message: 'Mammy says to tell you not to forget you owe her eighty-nine dollars.'

To the child, even at that time, she seemed already older than God, calling his grandsire 'colonel' but never the child's father nor the father's brother and sister by anything but their christian names even when they themselves had become grandparents: a matriarch with a score of descendants (and probably half that many more whom she had forgotten or outlived), one of them a boy too, whether a great grandson or merely a grandson even she did not remember, born in the same week with the white child and both bearing the same (the white child's grandsire's) name, suckled at the same black breast and sleeping and eating together and playing together the game which was the most important thing the white child knew at that time since at four and five and six his world was still a female world and he had heard nothing else that he could remember: with empty spools and chips and sticks and a scraped trench filled with well-water for the River, playing over again in miniature the War, the old irremediable battles—Shiloh and Vicksburg, and Brice's Crossroads which was not far from where the child (both of them) had been born, the boy because he was white arrogating to himself the right to be the Confederate General—Pemberton or Johnston or Forrest—twice to the black child's once, else, lacking that once in three, the black one would not play at all.

Not the tall man, he was still the hunter, the man of the woods; and not the slave because he was free now; but that Mexican cotton seed which someone had given the Natchez doctor clearing the land fast now, plowing under the buffalo grass of the eastern prairies and the brier and switch-cane of the creek- and river-bottoms of the central hills and deswamping that whole vast flat alluvial Delta-shaped sweep of land along the Big River, the Old

Man: building the levees to hold him off the land long enough to plant and harvest the crop: he taking another foot of scope in his new dimension for every foot man constricted him in the old: so that the steamboats carrying the baled cotton to Memphis or New Orleans seemed to crawl along the sky itself.

And little steamboats on the smaller rivers too, penetrating the Tallahatchie as far up as Wylie's Crossing above Jefferson. Though most of the cotton from that section, and on to the east to that point of no economic return where it was more expedient to continue on east to the Tombigbee and then south to Mobile, went the sixty miles overland to Memphis by mule and wagon; there was a settlement—a tavern of sorts and a smithy and a few gaunt cabins—on the bluff above Wylie's, at the exact distance where a wagon or a train of them loaded with cotton either starting or resuming the journey in the vicinity of Jefferson, would have to halt for the night. Or not even a settlement but rather a den, whose denizens lurked unseen by day in the brakes and thickets of the river bottom, appearing only at night and even then only long enough to enter the tavern kitchen where the driver of the day's cotton wagon sat unsuspecting before the fire, whereupon driver wagon mules and cotton and all would vanish: the body into the river probably and the wagon burned and the mules sold days or weeks later in a Memphis stockyard and the unidentifiable cotton already on its way to the Liverpool mill.

At the same time, sixteen miles away in Jefferson, there was a pre-Snopes, one of the tall men actually, a giant of a man in fact: a dedicated lay Baptist preacher but furious not with a furious unsleeping dream of paradise nor even for universal Order with an upper-case O, but for simple civic security. He was warned by everyone not to go in there because not only could he accomplish nothing, he would very likely lose his own life trying it. But he did go, alone, talking not of gospel nor God nor even virtue, but simply selected the biggest and boldest and by appearnace anyway the most villainous there and said to him: 'I'll fight you. If you lick me, you take what money I have. If I lick you I baptise you into my church': and battered and mauled and gouged that one into sanctity and civic virtue then challenged the next biggest and most villainous and then the next; and the following Sunday baptised the entire settlement in the river, the cotton wagons now crossing on Wylie's handpowered ferry and passing peacefully and unchallenged on to Memphis until the railroads came and took the bales away from them.

That was in the seventies. The Negro was a free farmer and a political entity now; one, he could not sign his name, was Federal marshal at Jefferson. Afterward he became the town's official bootlegger (Mississippi was one of the first to essay the noble experiment, along with Maine), resuming—he had never really quitted it—his old allegiance to his old master and gaining his professional name, Mulberry, from the huge old tree behind Doctor Habersham's drugstore, in the gallery-like tunnels among the roots of which he cached the bottled units of his commerce.

Soon he (the Negro) would even forge ahead in that economic rivalry with Snopes which was to send Snopes in droves into the Ku Klux Klan—not the old original one of the war's chaotic and desperate end which, measured against the desperate times, was at least honest and serious in its desperate aim, but into the later base one of the twenties whose only kinship to the old one was the old name. And a little money to build railroads with was in the land now, brought there by the man who in '66 had been a carpet-bagger but who now was a citizen; his children would speak the soft consonantless Negro tongue as the children of parents who had lived below the Potomac and Ohio Rivers since Captain John Smith, and their children would boast of their Southern heritage. In Jefferson his name was Redmond. He had found the money with which Colonel Sartoris had opened the local cottonfields to Europe by building his connecting line up to the main railroad from Memphis to the Atlantic Ocean—narrow gauge, like a toy, with three tiny locomotives like toys too, named after Colonel Sartoris's three daughters, each with its silver-plated oilcan engraved with the daughter's christian name: like toys, the standard-sized cars jacked up at the junction then lowered onto the narrow trucks, the tiny locomotive now invisible ahead of its charges so that they appeared in process of being snatched headlong among the fields they served by an arrogant plume of smoke and the arrogant shrieking of a whistle—who, after the inevitable quarrel, finally shot Colonel Sartoris dead on a Jefferson street, driven, everyone believed, to the desperate act by the same arrogance and intolerance which had driven Colonel Sartoris's regiment to demote him from its colonelcy in the fall elections after Second Manassas and Sharpsburg.

So there were railroads in the land now; now couples who had used to go overland by carriage to the River landings and the steamboats for the traditional New Orleans honeymoon, could take the train from almost anywhere. And presently pullmans too, all the way from Chicago and the Northern cities where the cash, the money was, so that the rich Northerners could come down in comfort and open the land indeed: setting up with their Yankee dollars the vast lumbering plants and mills in the southern pine section, the little towns which had been hamlets without change or alteration for fifty years, booming and soaring into cities overnight above the stump-pocked barrens which would remain until in simple economic desperation people taught themselves to farm pine trees as in other sections they had already learned to farm corn and cotton.

And Northern lumber mills in the Delta too: the mid-twenties now and the Delta booming with cotton and timber both. But mostly booming with simple money: increment a troglodyte which had fathered twin troglodytes: solvency and bankruptcy, the three of them booming money into the land so fast that the problem was how to get rid of it before it whelmed you into suffocation. Until in something almost resembling self-defense, not only for something to spend it on but to bet the increment from the simple spending on, seven or eight of the bigger Delta towns formed a baseball league, presently raiding as far away—and successfully too—for pitchers and short-stops and slugging outfielders, as the two major leagues, the boy, a young man now, making acquaintance with this league and one of the big Northern lumber companies not only coincidentally with one another but because of one another.

At this time the young man's attitude of mind was that of most of the other young men in the world who had been around twenty-one years of age in April, 1917, even though at times he did admit to himself that he was possibly using the fact that he had been nineteen on that day as an excuse to follow the avocation he was coming more and more to know would be forever his true one: to be a tramp, a harmless possessionless vagabond. In any case, he was quite ripe to make the acquaintance, which began with that of the lumber company which at the moment was taking a leisurely bankruptcy in a town where lived a lawyer who had been appointed the referee in the bankruptcy: a family friend of the young man's family and older than he, yet who had taken a liking to the young man and so invited him to come along for the ride too. His official capacity was that of interpreter, since he had a little French and the defuncting company had European connections. But no interpreting was ever done since the entourage did not go to Europe but moved instead into a single floor of a Memphis hotel, where all—including the interpreter—had the privilege of signing chits for food and theatre tickets and even the bootleg whiskey (Tennessee was in its dry mutation then) which the bellboys would produce, though not of course at the discreet and innocent-looking places clustered a few miles away just below the Mississippi state line, where roulette and dice and blackjack were available.

Then suddenly Mr Sells Wales was in it too, bringing the baseball league with him. The young man never did know what connection (if any) Mr Wales had with the bankruptcy, nor really bothered to wonder, let alone care and ask, not only because he had developed already that sense of *noblesse oblige* toward the avocation which he knew was his true one, which would have been reason enough, but because Mr Wales himself was already a legend in the Delta. Owner of a plantation measured not in acres but in miles and reputedly sole owner of one of the league baseball teams or anyway most of its players, certainly of the catcher and the base-stealing shortstop and the .340 hitting outfielder ravished or pirated it was said from the Chicago Cubs, his ordinary costume seven days a week was a two- or three-days' beard and muddy high boots and a corduroy hunting coat, the tale, the legend telling of how he entered a swank St Louis hotel in that costume late one night and demanded a room of a dinner jacketed clerk, who looked once at the beard and the muddy boots but probably mostly at Mr Wales's face and said they were filled up: whereupon Mr Wales asked how much they wanted for the hotel and was told, superciliously, in tens of thousands, and—so told the legend—drew from his corduroy hip a wad of thousand dollar bills sufficient to have bought the hotel half again at the price stated and told the clerk he wanted every room in the building vacated in ten minutes.

That one of course was apocryphal, but the young man himself saw this one: Mr Wales and himself having a leisurely breakfast one noon in the Memphis hotel when Mr Wales remembered suddenly that his private ball club was playing one of its most important games at a town about sixty miles away at three oclock that afternoon and telephoned to the railroad station to have a special train ready for them in thirty minutes, which it was: an engine and a caboose: reaching Coahoma about three oclock with a mile still to the ball park: a man (there were no taxis at the station at that hour and few in Mississippi anywhere at that time) sitting behind the wheel of a dingy though still sound Cadillac car, and Mr. Wales said:

'What do you want for it?'

'What?' the man in the car said.

'Your automobile,' Mr Wales said.

'Twelve fifty,' the man said.

'All right,' Mr Wales said, opening the door.

'I mean twelve hundred and fifty dollars,' the man said.

'All right,' Mr Wales said, then to the young man: 'Jump in.'

'Hold up here, mister,' the man said.

'I've bought it,' Mr Wales said, getting in too. 'The ball park,' he said. 'Hurry.'

The young man never saw the Cadillac again, though he became quite familiar with the engine and caboose during the next succeeding weeks while the league pennant race waxed hotter and hotter, Mr Wales keeping the special train on call in the Memphis yards as twenty-five years earlier a city-dwelling millionaire might have hacked a carriage and pair to his instant nod, so that it seemed to the young man that he would barely get back to Memphis to rest before they would be rushing once more down the Delta to another baseball game.

'I ought to be interpreting, sometime,' he said once.

'Interpret, then,' Mr Wales said. 'Interpret what this goddamn cotton market is going to do tomorrow, and we can both quit chasing this blank blank sandlot ball team.'

The cotton seed and the lumber mills clearing the rest of the Delta too, pushing what remained of the wilderness further and further southward into the V of Big River and hills. When the young man, a youth of sixteen and seventeen then, was first accepted into that hunting club of which he in his hierarchial time would be Master, the hunting grounds, haunt of deer and bear and wild turkey, could be reached in a single day or night in a mule-drawn wagon. Now they were using automobiles: a hundred miles then two hundred southward and still southward as the wilderness dwindled into the confluence of the Yazoo River and the big one, the Old Man.

The Old Man: all his little contributing streams levee-ed too, along with him, and paying none of the dykes any heed at all when it suited his mood and fancy, gathering water all the way from Montana to Pennsylvania every generation or so and rolling it down the artificial gut of his victims' puny and baseless hoping, piling the water up, not fast: just inexorable, giving plenty of time to measure his crest and telegraph ahead, even warning of the exact day almost when he would enter the house and float the piano out of it and the pictures off the walls, and even remove the house itself if it were not securely fastened down.

Inexorable and unhurried, overpassing one by one his little confluent feeders and shoving the water into them until for days their current would flow backward, upstream: as far upstream as Wylie's Crossing above Jefferson. The little rivers were dyked too but back here was the land of individualists: remnants and descendants of the tall men now taken to farming, and of Snopeses who were more than individualists: they were Snopeses, so that where the owners of the thousand-acre plantations along the Big River confederated as one man with sandbags and machines and their Negro tenants and wagehands to hold the sandboils and the cracks, back here the owner of the hundred or two hundred acre farm patrolled his section of levee with a sandbag in one hand and his shotgun in the other, lest his upstream neighbor dynamite it to save his (the upstream neighbor's) own.

Piling up the water while white man and Negro worked side by side in shifts in the mud and the rain, with automobile headlights and gasoline flares and kegs of whiskey and coffee boiling in fifty-gallon batches in scoured and scalded oil-drums; lapping, tentative, almost innocently, merely inexorable (no hurry, his) among and beneath and between and finally over the frantic sandbags, as if his whole purpose had been merely to give man another chance to prove, not to him but to man, just how much the human body could bear, stand, endure; then, having let man prove it, doing what he could have done at any time these past weeks if so minded: removing with no haste nor any particular malice or fury either, a mile or two miles of levee and coffee drums and whiskey kegs and gas flares in one sloughing collapse, gleaming dully for a little while yet among the parallel cotton middles until the fields vanished along with the roads and lanes and at last the towns themselves.

Vanished, gone beneath one vast yellow motionless expanse, out of which projected only the tops of trees and telephone poles and the decapitations of human dwelling-places like enigmatic objects placed by inscrutable and impenetrable design on a dirty mirror; and the mounds of the predecessors on which, among a tangle of moccasins, bear and horses and deer and mules and wild turkeys and cows and domestic chickens waited patient in mutual armistice; and the levees themselves, where among a jumble of uxorious flotsam the young continued to be born and the old to die, not from exposure but from simple and normal time and decay, as if man and his destiny were in the end stronger even than the river which had dispossessed him, inviolable by and invincible to, alteration.

Then, having proved that too, he—the Old Man—would withdraw, not retreat: subside, back from the land slowly and inexorably too, emptying the confluent rivers and bayous back into the old vain hopeful gut, but so slowly and gradually that not the waters seemed to fall but the flat earth itself to rise, creep in one plane back into light and air again: one constant stain of yellow-brown at one constant altitude on telephone poles and the walls of gins and houses and stores as though the line had been laid off with a transit and painted in one gigantic unbroken brush-stroke, the earth itself one alluvial inch higher, the rich dirt one inch deeper, drying into long cracks beneath the hot fierce glare of May: but not for long, because almost at once came the plow, the plowing and planting already two months late but that did not matter: the cotton man-tall once more by August and whiter and denser still by picking-time, as if the Old Man said, 'I do what I want to, when I want to. But I pay my way.'

And the boats, of course. They projected above that yellow and liquid plane and even moved upon it: the skiffs and skows of fishermen and trappers, the launches of the United States Engineers who operated the Levee Commission, and one small shallow-draught steamboat steaming in paradox among and across the cotton fields themselves, its pilot not a riverman but a farmer who knew where the submerged fences were, its masthead lookout a mechanic with a pair of pliers to cut the telephone wires to pass the smokestack through: no paradox really, since on the River it had resembled a house to begin with, so that here it looked no different from the baseless houses it steamed among, and on occasion even strained at top boiler pressure to overtake like a mallard drake after a fleeing mallard hen.

But these were not enough, very quickly not near enough; the

Old Man meant business indeed this time. So now there began to arrive from the Gulf ports the shrimp trawlers and pleasure cruisers and Coast Guard cutters whose bottoms had known only salt water and the mouths of tidal rivers, to be run still by their salt water crews but conned by the men who knew where the submerged roads and fences were for the good reason that they had been running mule-plow furrows along them or up to them all their lives, sailing among the swollen carcasses of horses and mules and deer and cows and sheep to pluck the Old Man's patient flotsam, black and white, out of trees and the roofs of gins and cotton sheds and floating cabins and the second storey windows of houses and office buildings; then—the salt-water men, to whom land was either a featureless treeless salt-marsh or a snake- and alligator-infested swamp impenetrable with trumpet vine and Spanish moss; some of whom had never even seen the earth into which were driven the spiles supporting the houses they lived in—staying on even after they were no longer needed, as though waiting to see emerge from the water what sort of country it was which bore the economy on which the people—men and women, black and white, more of black than white even, ten to one more—lived whom they had saved; seeing the land for that moment before mule and plow altered it right up to the water's receding edge, then back into the river again before the trawlers and cruisers and cutters became marooned into canted and useless rubble too along with the ruined hencoops and cowsheds and privies; back onto the Old Man, shrunken once more into his normal banks, drowsing and even innocent-looking, as if it were something else beside he who had changed, for a little time anyway, the whole face of the adjacent earth.

They were homeward bound now, passing the river towns, some of which were respectable in age when south Mississippi was a Spanish wilderness: Greenville and Vicksburg, Natchez and Grand- and Petit Gulf (vanished now and even the old site known by a different name) which had known Mason and one at least of the Harpes and from or on which Murrell had based his abortive slave insurrection intended to efface the white people from the land and leave him emperor of it, the land sinking away beyond the levee until presently you could no longer say where water began and earth stopped: only that these lush and verdant sunny savannahs would no longer bear your weight. The rivers flowed no longer west, but south now, no longer yellow or brown, but black, threading the miles of yellow salt marsh from which on an off-shore breeze mosquitoes came in such clouds that in your itching and burning anguish it would seem to you you could actually see them in faint adumbration crossing the earth, and met tide and then the uncorrupted salt: not the Gulf quite yet but at least the Sound behind the long barrier of the islands—Ship and Horn and Petit Bois, the trawler and cruiser bottoms home again now among the lighthouses and channel markers and shipyards and drying nets and processing plants for fish.

The man remembered that from his youth too: one summer spent being blown innocently over in catboats since, born and bred for generations in the north Mississippi hinterland, he did not recognize the edge of a squall until he already had one. The next summer he returned because he found that he liked that much water, this time as a hand in one of the trawlers, remembering: a four-gallon iron pot over a red bed of charcoal on the foredeck, in which decapitated shrimp boiled among handsful of salt and black pepper, never emptied, never washed and constantly renewed, so that you ate them all day long in passing like peanuts; remembering: the predawn, to be broken presently by the violent near-subtropical yellow-and-crimson day almost like an audible explosion, but still dark for a little while yet, the dark ship creeping onto the shrimp grounds in a soundless sternward swirl of phosphorus like a drowning tumble of fireflies, the youth lying face down on the peak staring into the dark water watching the disturbed shrimp burst outward-shooting in fiery and fading fans like the trails of tiny rockets.

He learned the barrier islands too; one of a crew of five amateurs sailing a big sloop in off-shore races, he learned not only how to keep a hull on its keel and moving but how to get it from one place to another and bring it back: so that, a professional now, living in New Orleans he commanded for pay a power launch belonging to a bootlegger (this was the twenties), whose crew consisted of a Negro cook-deckhand-stevedore and the bootlegger's younger brother: a slim twenty-one or -two year old Italian with yellow eyes like a cat and a silk shirt bulged faintly by an armpit-holstered pistol too small in calibre to have done anything but got them all killed, even if the captain or the cook had dreamed of resisting or resenting trouble if and when it came, which the captain or the cook would extract from the holster and hide at the first opportunity (not concealed really: just dropped into the oily bilge under the engine, where, even though Pete soon discovered where it would be, it was safe because he refused to thrust his hand and arm into the oil-fouled water but instead merely lay about the cockpit, sulking); taking the launch across Pontchartrain and down the Rigolets out to the Gulf, the Sound, then lying-to with no lights showing until the Coast Guard cutter (it ran almost on schedule; theirs was a job too even if it was, comparatively speaking, a hopeless one) made its fast haughty eastward rush, going, they always like to believe, to Mobile, to a dance, then by compass on to the island (it was little more than a sandspit bearing a line of ragged and shabby pines thrashing always in the windy crash and roar of the true Gulf on the other side of it) where the Caribbean schooner would bury the casks of green alcohol which the bootlegger's mother back in New Orleans would convert and bottle and label into scotch or bourbon or gin. There were a few wild cattle on the island which they would have to watch for, the Negro digging and Pete still sulking and refusing to help at all because of the pistol, and the captain watching for the charge (they couldn't risk showing a light) which every three or four trips would come—the gaunt wild half-seen shapes charging suddenly and with no warning down at them as they turned and ran through the nightmare sand and hurled themselves into the dinghy, to pull along parallel to the shore, the animals following, until they had tolled them far enough away for the Negro to go back ashore for the remaining casks. Then they would heave-to again and lie until the cutter passed back westward, the dance obviously over now, in the same haughty and imperious rush.

That was Mississippi too, though a different one from where the child had been bred; the people were Catholics, the Spanish and French blood still showed in the names and faces. But it was not a deep one, if you did not count the sea and the boats on it: a curve of beach, a thin unbroken line of estates and apartment hotels owned and inhabited by Chicago millionaires, standing back to back with another thin line, this time of tenements inhabited by Negroes and whites who ran the boats and worked in the fish-processing plants.

Then the Mississippi which the young man knew began: the fading purlieus inhabited by a people whom the young man recognised because their like was in his country too: descendants, heirs at least in spirit, of the tall men, who worked in no factories and farmed no land nor even truck patches, living not out of the earth but on its denizens: fishing guides and individual professional fishermen, trappers of muskrats and alligator hunters and poachers of deer, the land rising now, once more earth instead of half water, vista-ed and arras-ed with the long leaf pines which northern capital would convert into dollars in Ohio and Indiana and Illinois banks. Though not all of it. Some of it would alter hamlets and villages into cities and even build whole new ones almost overnight, cities with Mississippi names but patterned on Ohio and Indiana and Illinois because they were bigger than Mississippi towns, rising, standing today among the tall pines which created them, then tomorrow (that quick, that fast, that rapid) among the stumpy pockage to which they were monuments. Because the land had made its one crop: the soil too fine and light to compete seriously in cotton: until people discovered that it would grow what other soils would not: the tomatoes and strawberries and the fine cane for sugar: not the sorghum of the northern and western counties which the people of the true cane country called hog-feed, but the true sweet cane which made the sugar house molasses.

Big towns, for Mississippi: cities, we called them: Hattiesburg, and Laurel, and Meridian, and Canton; and towns deriving by name from further away than Ohio: Kosciusko named after a Polish general who thought that people should be free who wanted to be, and Egypt because there was corn there when it was nowhere else in the bad lean times of the old war which the old women had still never surrendered, and Philadelphia where the Neshoba Indians whose name the country bears still remain for the simple reason that they did not mind living in peace with other people, no matter what their color or politics. This was the hills now: Jones County which old Newt Knight, its principal proprietor and first citizen or denizen, whichever you liked, seceded from the Confederacy in 1862, establishing still a third republic within the boundaries of the United States until a Confederate military force subdued him in his embattled log-castle capital; and Sullivan's Hollow: a long narrow glen where a few clans or families with North Ireland and Highland names feuded and slew one another in the old pre-Culloden fashion yet banding together immediately and always to resist any outsider in the pre-Culloden fashion too: vide the legend of the revenue officer hunting illicit whiskey stills, captured and held prisoner in a stable and worked in traces as the pair to a plow-mule. No Negro ever let darkness catch him in Sullivan's Hollow. In fact, there were few Negroes in this country at all: a narrow strip of which extended up into the young man's own section: a remote district there through which Negroes passed infrequently and rapidly and only by daylight.

It is not very wide, because almost at once there begins to the east of it the prairie country which sheds its water into Alabama and Mobile Bay, with its old tight intermarried towns and plantation houses columned and porticoed in the traditional Georgian manner of Virginia and Carolina in place of the Spanish and French influence of Natchez. These towns are Columbus and Aberdeen and West Point and Shuqualak, where the good quail shooting is and the good bird dogs are bred and trained—horses too: hunters; Dancing Rabbit is here too, where the treaty dispossessing them of Mississippi was made between the Choctaws and the United States; and in one of the towns lived a kinsman of the young man, dead now, rest him: an invincible and incorrigible bachelor, a leader of cotillions and an inveterate diner-out since any time an extra single man was needed, any hostess thought of him first.

But he was a man's man too, and even more: a young man's man, who played poker and matched glasses with the town's young bachelors and the apostates still young enough in time to still resist the wedlock; who walked not only in spats and a stick and yellow gloves and a Homburg hat, but an air of sardonic and inviolable atheism too, until at last he was forced to the final desperate resort of prayer: sitting after supper one night among the drummers in the row of chairs on the sidewalk before the Gilmer Hotel, waiting to see what (if anything) the evening would bring, when two of the young bachelors passing in a Model T Ford stopped and invited him to drive across the line into the Alabama hills for a gallon of moonshine whiskey. Which they did. But the still they sought was not in hills because these were not hills: it was the dying tail of the Appalachian mountain range. But since the Model T's engine had to be running fast anyway for it to have any headlights, going up the mountain was an actual improvement, especially after they had to drop to low gear. And coming from the generation before the motor car, it never occurred to him that coming back down would be any different until they got the gallon and had a drink from it and turned around and started back down. Or maybe it was the whiskey, he said, telling it: the little car rushing faster and faster behind a thin wash of light of about the same volume that two lightning bugs would have made, around the plunging curves which, the faster the car ran, became only the more frequent and sharp and plunging, whipping around the nearly right-angle bends with a rock wall on one hand and several hundred feet of vertical and empty night on the other, until at last he prayed; he said, 'Lord, You know I haven't worried You in over forty years, and if You'll just get me back to Columbus I promise never to bother You again.'

And now the young man, middleaged now or anyway middleaging, is back home too where they who altered the swamps and forests of his youth, have now altered the face of the earth itself; what he remembered as dense river bottom jungle and rich farm land, is now an artificial lake twenty-five miles long: a flood control project for the cotton fields below the huge earth dam, with a few more outboard-powered fishing skiffs on it each year, and at last a sailboat. On his way in to town from his home the middleaging (now a professional fiction-writer: who had wanted to remain the tramp and the possessionless vagabond of his young manhood but time and success and the hardening of his arteries had beaten him) man would pass the back yard of a doctor friend whose son was an undergraduate at Harvard. One day the undergraduate stopped him and invited him in and showed him the unfinished hull of a twenty-foot sloop, saying, 'When I get her finished, Mr Bill, I want you to help me sail her.' And each time he passed after that, the undergraduate would repeat: 'Remember, Mr Bill, I want you to help me sail her as soon as I get her in the water:' to which the middleaging would answer as always: 'Fine, Arthur. Just let me know.'

Then one day he came out of the postoffice: a voice called him from a taxicab, which in small Mississippi towns was any motor car owned by any footloose young man who liked to drive, who decreed himself a taxicab as Napoleon decreed himself emperor; in the car with the driver was the undergraduate and a young man whose father had vanished recently somewhere in the West out of the ruins of the bank of which he had been president, and a fourth young man whose type is universal: the town clown, comedian, whose humor is without viciousness and quite often witty and always funny. 'She's in the water, Mr Bill,' the undergraduate said. 'Are you ready to go now?' And he was, and the sloop was too; the undergraduate had sewn his own sails on his mother's machine;

they worked her out into the lake and got her on course all tight and drawing, when suddenly it seemed to the middleaging that part of him was no longer in the sloop but about ten feet away, looking at what he saw: a Harvard undergraduate, a taxi-driver, the son of an absconded banker and a village clown and a middleaged novelist sailing a home-made boat on an artificial lake in the depths of the north Mississippi hills: and he thought that that was something which did not happen to you more than once in your life.

Home again, his native land; he was born of it and his bones will sleep in it; loving it even while hating some of it: the river jungle and the bordering hills where still a child he had ridden behind his father on the horse after the bobcat or fox or coon or whatever was ahead of the belling hounds and where he had hunted alone when he got big enough to be trusted with a gun, now the bottom of a muddy lake being raised gradually and steadily every year by another layer of beer cans and bottle caps and lost bass plugs—the wilderness, the two weeks in the woods, in camp, the rough food and the rough sleeping, the life of men and horses and hounds among men and horses and hounds, not to slay the game but to pursue it, touch and let go, never satiety—moved now even further away than that down the flat Delta so that the mile-long freight trains, visible for miles across the fields where the cotton is mortgaged in February, planted in May, harvested in September and put into the Farm Loan in October in order to pay off February's mortgage in order to mortgage next year's crop, seem to be passing two or even three of the little Indian-named hamlets at once over the very ground where, a youth now capable of being trusted even with a rifle, he had shared in the yearly ritual of Old Ben: the big old bear with one trap-ruined foot who had earned for himself a name, a designation like a living man through the legend of the deadfalls and traps he had wrecked and the hounds he had slain and the shots he had survived, until Boon Hogganbeck, the youth's father's stable foreman, ran in and killed it with a hunting knife to save a hound which he, Boon Hogganbeck, loved.

But most of all he hated the intolerance and injustice: the lynching of Negroes not for the crimes they committed but because their skins were black (they were becoming fewer and fewer and soon there would be no more of them but the evil would have been done and irrevocable because there should never have been any); the inequality: the poor schools they had then when they had any, the hovels they had to live in unless they wanted to live outdoors: who could worship the white man's God but not in the white man's church; pay taxes in the white man's courthouse but couldn't vote in it or for it; working by the white man's clock but having to take his pay by the white man's counting (Captain Joe Thoms, a Delta planter though not one of the big ones, who after a bad crop year drew a thousand silver dollars from the bank and called his five tenants one by one into the dining room where two hundred of the dollars were spread carelessly out on the table beneath the lamp, saying: 'Well, Jim, that's what we made this year.' Then the Negro: 'Gret God, Cap'n Joe, is all that mine?' And Captain Thoms: 'No no, just half of it is yours. The other half belongs to me, remember.'); the bigotry which could send to Washington some of the senators and congressmen we sent there and which would erect in a town no bigger than Jefferson five separate denominations of churches but set aside not one square foot of ground where children could play and old people could sit and watch them.

But he loves it, it is his, remembering: the trying to, having to, stay in bed until the crack of dawn would bring Christmas and of the other times almost as good as Christmas; of being waked at three oclock to have breakfast by lamplight in order to drive by surrey into town and the depot to take the morning train for the three or four days in Memphis when he would see automobiles, and the day in 1910 when, twelve years old, he watched John Moissant land a bicycle-wheeled aileronless (you warped the whole wing-tip to bank it or hold it level) Bleriot monoplane on the infield of the Memphis race-track and knew forever after that someday he too would have to fly alone; remembering: his first sweetheart, aged eight, plump and honey-haired and demure and named Mary, the two of them sitting side by side on the kitchen steps eating ice cream; and another one, Minnie this time, grand-daughter of the old hillman from whom, a man himself now, he bought moonshine whiskey, come to town at seventeen to take a job behind the soda counter of the drug store, watching her virginal and innocent and without self-consciousness pour Coca-Cola syrup into the lifted glass by hooking her thumb through the ring of the jug and swinging it back and up in one unbroken motion onto her horizontal upper arm exactly as he had seen her grandfather pour whiskey from a jug a thousand times.

Even while hating it, because for every Joe Thoms with two

hundred silver dollars and every Snopes in a hooded nightshirt, somewhere in Mississippi there was this too: remembering: Ned, born in a cabin in the back yard in 1865, in the time of the middleaged's great-grandfather and had outlived three generations of them, who had not only walked and talked so constantly for so many years with the three generations that he walked and talked like them, he had two tremendous trunks filled with the clothes which they had worn—not only the blue brass-buttoned frock coat and the plug hat in which he had been the great-grandfather's and the grandfather's coachman, but the broadcloth frock coats which the great-grandfather himself had worn, and the pigeon-tailed ones of the grandfather's time and the short coat of his father's which the middleaged could remember on the backs for which they had been tailored, along with the hats in their eighty years of mutation too: so that, glancing idly up and out the library window, the middleaged would see that back, that stride, that coat and hat going down the drive toward the road, and his heart would stop and even turn over. He (Ned) was eighty-four now and in these last few years he had begun to get a little mixed up, calling the middleaged not only 'Master' but sometimes 'Master Murry', who was the middleaged's father, and 'Colonel' too, coming once a week through the kitchen and in to the parlor or perhaps already found there, saying: 'Here's where I wants to lay, right here where I can be facing out that window. And I wants it to be a sunny day, so the sun can come in on me. And I wants you to preach the sermon. I wants you to take a dram of whiskey for me, and lay yourself back and preach the best sermon you ever preached.'

And Caroline too, whom the middleaged had inherited too in his hierarchial turn, nobody knowing anymore exactly how many more years than a hundred she was but not mixed up, she: who had forgotten nothing, calling the middleaged 'Memmy' still, from fifty-odd years ago when that was as close as his brothers could come to 'William'; his youngest daughter, aged four and five and six, coming in to the house and saying 'Pappy, Mammy said to tell you not to forget you owe her eighty-nine dollars.'

'I wont,' the middleaged would say. 'What are you all doing now?'

'Piecing a quilt,' the daughter answered. Which they were. There was electricity in her cabin now, but she would not use it, insisting still on the kerosene lamps which she had always known.

Nor would she use the spectacles either, wearing them merely as an ornament across the brow of the immaculate white cloth—headrag—which bound her now hairless head. She did not need them: a smolder of wood ashes on the hearth winter and summer in which sweet potatoes roasted, the five-year-old white child in a miniature rocking chair at one side of it and the aged Negress, not a great deal larger, in her chair at the other, the basket bright with scraps and fragments of cloth between them and in that dim light in which the middleaged himself could not have read his own name without his glasses, the two of them with infinitesimal and tedious and patient stitches annealing the bright stars and squares and diamonds into another pattern to be folded away among the cedar shavings in the trunk.

Then it was the Fourth of July, the kitchen was closed after breakfast so the cook and houseman could attend a big picnic; in the middle of the hot morning the aged Negress and the white child gathered green tomatoes from the garden and ate them with salt, and that afternoon beneath the mulberry tree in the back yard the two of them ate most of a fifteen-pound chilled watermelon, and that night Caroline had the first stroke. It should have been the last, the doctor thought so too. But by daylight she had rallied, and that morning the generations of her loins began to arrive, from her own seventy and eighty year old children, down through their great- and twice-great-grandchildren—faces which the middleaged had never seen before until the cabin would no longer hold them: the women and girls sleeping on the floor inside and the men and boys sleeping on the ground in front of it, Caroline herself conscious now and presently sitting up in the bed: who had forgotten nothing: matriarchial and imperial, and more: imperious: ten and even eleven oclock at night and the middleaged himself undressed and in bed, reading, when sure enough he would hear the slow quiet stockinged or naked feet mounting the back stairs; presently the strange dark face—never the same one of two nights ago or the two or three nights before that—would look in the door at him, and the quiet, courteous, never servile voice would say: 'She want the ice cream.' And he would rise and dress and drive in to the village; he would even drive through the village although he knew that everything there will have long been closed and he would do what he had done two nights ago: drive thirty miles on to the arterial highway and then up or down it until he found an open drive-in or hot-dog stand to sell him the quart of ice cream.

But that stroke was not the one; she was walking again presently, even, despite the houseman's standing order to forestall her with the automobile, all the way in to town to sit with his, the middleaging's, mother, talking, he liked to think, of the old days of his father and himself and the three younger brothers, the two of them two women who together had never weighed two hundred pounds in a house roaring with five men: though they probably didn't since women, unlike men, have learned how to live uncomplicated by that sort of sentimentality. But it was as if she knew herself that the summer's stroke was like the throat-clearing sound inside the grandfather clock preceding the stroke of midnight or of noon, because she never touched the last unfinished quilt again. Presently it had vanished, no one knew where, and as the cold came and the shortening days she began to spend more and more time in the house, not her cabin but the big house, sitting in a corner of the kitchen while the cook and houseman were about, then in the middleaging's wife's sewing room until the family gathered for the evening meal, the houseman carrying her rocking chair into the dining room to sit there while they ate: until suddenly (it was almost Christmas now) she insisted on sitting in the parlor until the meal was ready, none knew why, until at last she told them, through the wife: 'Miss Hestelle, when them niggers lays me out, I want you to make me a fresh clean cap and apron to lay in.' That was her valedictory; two days after Christmas the stroke came which was the one; two days after that she lay in the parlor in the fresh cap and apron she would not see, and the middleaging did indeed lay back and preach the sermon, the oration, hoping that when his turn came there would be someone in the world to owe him the sermon which all owed to her who had been, as he had been from infancy, within the scope and range of that fidelity and that devotion and that rectitude.

Loving all of it even while he had to hate some of it because he knows now that you dont love because: you love despite; not for the virtues, but despite the faults.

[*Holiday*, April 1954; the text printed here has been taken from Faulkner's typescript.]

FROM

Blues from the Delta

WILLIAM FERRIS

LEARNING THE BLUES

MANY MISSISSIPPI blues singers began to play music with a homemade instrument known by some as a "one-strand on the wall." Children who could not afford a guitar took a wire from the handle of a broom and stretched it on the wall of their home. A hard object such as a stone raised and stretched the wire at each end to its proper tone, and as one hand plucked a beat, the other slid a bottle along its surface to change the tone. The result was a haunting sound which strongly influenced the blues style known as "bottleneck" guitar.

One-stringed instruments are common in both West Africa and Brazil, and Mississippi examples are usually nailed on the wall of a home which serves as a resonator for the instrument. Sometimes groups of musicians string several wires on the same wall and play in unison for dancers. As a child, B. B. King built and played a one-strand.

I guess that was kind of like a normal thing for the average kid to do because instruments wasn't very plentiful in the area where I grew up. When we felt a need for music, we'd put the wire up. We usually would nail it up on the back porch. Take a broom wire.

They had a kind of straight wire wrapped around that straw that would keep this broom together. So we'd find an old broom or a new one if we could get it without anybody catching us. You'd take that wire off of it and you'd nail that on a board or on the back porch.

Once you nailed this nail in there, put that wire around these two nails, like one on this end and one on the other and wrap it tight. Then you'd take a couple of bricks and you'd put one under this side and one under that one that would stretch this wire and make it tighter. And you'd keep pushing that brick, stretching this wire making it tight until it would sound like one string on the guitar. Like that.

Louis Dotson has played the one-strand for fifty years and nails his instrument to his home's front wall. He compares his house to a guitar body in that both serve as a resonator.

When you put it up side the wall, it'll play. I'd say the house must give a sound to it. Just like a guitar.

When I started I didn't have no radio and I had to have some music some kind of way. So I put me up a one-strand and made my own music.

The way I decided to do, I said I'll put me a brick and a staple up there at the top and one at the bottom to pull it tight, just as tight as I can git it.

The brick at the bottom, that's where you git your tightening, from the bottom. Knock it down till you git it real tight. When you git it real tight, you go to picking and she'll play good then.

When a guitar could be found, aspiring musicians often played it secretly when its owner was not around. The young musician listened carefully to older performers and imitated their notes and chords. James Thomas talked about how he began to play blues on his uncle's instrument.

I learned from my uncle. He showed me two or three chords and he would charge me to play his guitar. But after he'd leave home his wife would let me play and I didn't have to pay nothing.

I'd play till noon when he come in for dinner. Then at one o'clock he'd go back to work and I'd play till night. That's how I began to learn how.

Then after I learnt I used to go and play for dances with my uncle. He'd pay me a dollar a night. Oh, I had a hard time learning. I've got some work tied up in it.

Instruments were so high that it was a long time before I could get an electric guitar. When you're playing for a big crowd of people you needs an electric guitar because with a regular guitar you've got to work too hard. The electric is to help you out and give you more rest so you don't have to play so hard.

The evolution from one-strand to standard guitar to electric guitar was a familiar pattern in many communities. Musicians began with the simplest instrument, later acquired standard and electric guitars, and the early sound of the one-strand endured as these six-string instruments were played in a "bottleneck" style. Using an "open" turning the musician often slides his bottleneck along one string just as the bottle had been used on the one-strand. Elmore James, the acknowledged master of bottleneck blues, first played on a one-strand and James Thomas began his blues career by secretly playing with him.

FROM

The Civil War: A Narrative

SHELBY FOOTE

HE WAS BORN IN Christian County, Kentucky, within a year and a hundred miles of the man whose election had brought on the present furor. Like that man, he was a log-cabin boy, the youngest of ten children whose grandfather had been born in Philadelphia in 1702, the son of an immigrant Welshman who signed his name with an X. This grandfather moved to Georgia, where he married a widow who bore him one son, Samuel. Samuel raised and led an irregular militia company in the Revolution. After the war he married and moved northwest to south-central Kentucky, where he put up his own log house, farmed six hundred acres of land by the hard agronomy of the time, and supplied himself with children, naming the sons out of the Bible—Joseph, Samuel, Benjamin, and Isaac—until the tenth child, born in early June of 1808, whom he named for the red-headed President then in office, and gave him the middle name Finis in the belief, or perhaps the hope, that he was the last; which he was.

By the time the baby Jefferson was weaned the family was on the move again, south one thousand miles to Bayou Teche, Louisiana, only to find the climate unhealthy and to move again, three hundred miles northeast to Wilkinson County, Mississippi Territory, southeast of Natchez and forty miles from the Mississippi River. Here the patriarch stopped, for he prospered; he did not move again, and here Jefferson spent his early childhood.

The crop now was cotton, and though Samuel Davis had slaves, he was his own overseer, working alongside them in the field. It was a farm, not a plantation; he was a farmer, not a planter. In a region where the leading men were Episcopalians and Federalists, he was a Baptist and a Democrat. Now his older children were coming of age, and at their marriages he gave them what he could, one Negro slave, and that was all. The youngest, called Little Jeff, began his education when he was six. For the next fifteen years he attended one school after another, first a log schoolhouse within walking distance of home, then a Dominican institution in Kentucky, Saint Thomas Aquinas, where he was still called Little Jeff because he was the smallest pupil there. He asked to become a Roman Catholic but the priest told him to wait and learn, which he did, and either forgot or changed his mind. Then, his mother having grown lonesome for her last-born, he came home to the Mississippi schoolhouse where he had started.

He did not like it. One hot fall day he rebelled; he would not go. Very well, his father said, but he could not be idle, and sent him to the field with the work gang. Two days later Jeff was back at his desk. "The heat of the sun and the physical labor, in conjunction with the implied equality with the other cotton pickers, convinced me that school was the lesser evil." Thus he later explained his early decision to work with his head, not his hands. In continuation of this decision, just before his fourteenth birthday he left once more for Kentucky, entering Transylvania University, an excellent school, one of the few in the country to live up to a high-sounding name. Under competent professors he continued his studies in Latin and Greek and mathematics, including trigonometry, and explored the mysteries of sacred and profane history and natural philosophy—meaning chemistry and physics—with surveying and oratory thrown in for good measure. While he was there his father died and his oldest brother, Joseph, twenty-four years his senior, assumed the role of guardian.

Not long before his death, the father had secured for his youngest son an appointment to West Point, signed by the Secretary of War, and thus for the first time the names were linked: Jefferson Davis, John C. Calhoun. Joseph Davis by now had become what his father had never been—a planter, with a planter's views, a planter's way of life. Jefferson inclined toward the University of Virginia, but Joseph persuaded him to give the Academy a try. It was in the tradition for the younger sons of prominent southern families to go there; if at the end of a year he found he did not like it he could transfer. So Davis attended West Point, and found he liked it.

Up to now he had shown no special inclination to study. Alert and affectionate, he was of a mischievous disposition, enjoyed a practical joke, and sought the admiration of his fellows rather more than the esteem of his professors. Now at the Academy he continued along this course, learning something of tavern life in the process. "O Benny Haven's, O!" he sang, linking arms and clinking tankards. He found he liked the military comradeship, the thought of unrequited death on lonely, far-off battlefields:

> *To our comrades who have fallen, one cup before we go;*
> *They poured their life-blood freely out* pro bono publico.
> *No marble points the stranger to where they rest below;*
> *They lie neglected—far away from Benny Haven's, O!*

Brought before a court martial for out-of-bounds drinking of "spirituous liquors," he made the defense of a strict constructionist: 1) visiting Benny Haven's was not *officially* prohibited in the regulations, and 2) malt liquors were not "spirituous" in the first place. The defense was successful; he was not dismissed, and he emerged from the scrape a stricter constructionist than ever. He also got to know his fellow cadets. Leonidas Polk was his roommate; Joseph E. Johnston was said to have been his opponent in a fist fight over a girl; along with others, he admired the open manliness of Albert Sidney Johnston, the high-born rectitude of Robert E. Lee.

Davis himself was admired, even liked. Witnesses spoke of his well-shaped head, his self-esteem, his determination and personal mastery. A "florid young fellow," he had "beautiful blue eyes, a graceful figure." In his studies he did less well, receiving his lowest marks in mathematics and deportment, his highest in rhetoric and moral philosophy, including constitutional law. But the highs could not pull up the lows. He stood well below the middle of his class, still a private at the close of his senior year, and graduated in 1828, twenty-third in a class of thirty-four.

As a second lieutenant, U.S. Army, he now began a seven-year adventure, serving in Wisconsin, Iowa, Illinois, Missouri, where he learned to fight Indians, build forts, scout, and lead a simple social existence. He had liked West Point; he found he liked this even better. Soon he proved himself a superior junior officer, quick-witted and resourceful—as when once with a few men he was chased by a band of Indians after scalps; both parties being in canoes, he improvised a sail and drew away. In a winter of deep snow he came down with pneumonia, and though he won that fight as well, his susceptibility to colds and neuralgia dated from then. He was promoted to first lieutenant within four years, and when Black Hawk was captured in 1832, Davis was appointed by his colonel, Zachary Taylor, to escort the prisoner to Jefferson Barracks.

Thus Colonel Taylor, called "Old Rough and Ready," showed his approval of Davis as a soldier. But as a son-in-law, it developed, he wanted no part of him. The lieutenant had met the colonel's daughter, sixteen-year-old Knox Taylor, brown-haired and blue-eyed like himself, though later the color of his own eyes would deepen to gray. Love came quickly, and his letters to her show a man unseen before or after. "By my dreams I have been lately almost crazed, for they were of you," he wrote to her, and also thus: "Kind, dear letter; I have kissed it often and often, and it has driven away mad notions from my brain." The girl accepted his suit, but the father did not; Taylor wanted no soldier son-in-law, apparently especially not this one. Therefore Davis, who had spent the past seven years as a man of action, proposed to challenge the colonel to a duel. Dissuaded from this, he remained a man of action still. He resigned his commission, went straight to Louisville, and married the girl. The wedding was held at the home of an aunt she was visiting. "After the service everybody cried but Davis," a witness remarked, adding that they "thought this most peculiar."

As it turned out, he was reserving his tears. The young couple did not wait to attempt a reconciliation with her father; perhaps they depended on time to accomplish this. Instead they took a steamboat south to Davis Bend, Mississippi, below Vicksburg, where Joseph Davis, the guardian elder brother, had prospered on a plantation called The Hurricane. He presented them with an adjoining 800-acre place and fourteen slaves on credit. Davis put in a cotton crop, but before the harvest time came round they were both down with fever. They were confined to separate rooms, each too sick to be told of the other's condition, though Davis managed to make it to the door of his bride's room in time to see her die. She had been a wife not quite three months, and as she died she sang snatches of "Fairy Bells," a favorite air; she had had it from her mother. Now those tears which he had not shed at the wedding came to scald his eyes. He was too sick to attend the funeral; the doctor believed he would not be long behind her.

The doctor was wrong, though Davis never lost the drawn, gaunt look of a fever convalescent. He returned to the plantation; then, finding it too crowded with recent memories, left for Cuba, thought to be a fine climate and landscape for restoring broken hearts. The sea bathing at least did his health much good, and he returned by way of New York and Washington, renewing acquaintances with old friends now on the rise and gaining some notion of how much he had missed on the frontier. Then he came home to Mississippi. He would be a planter and, at last, a student.

He found a ready tutor awaiting him. Joseph Davis had got a law degree in Kentucky, had set up practice in Natchez, and, prospering, had bought the land which in that section practically amounted to a patent of nobility. By now, in his middle fifties, he was the wealthiest planter in the state, the "leading philosopher"—whatever that meant—and the possessor of the finest library, which he gladly made available to his idolized younger brother. Davis soon had the Constitution by heart and went deeply into *Elliot's Debates,* theories of government as argued by the framers. He read John Locke and Adam Smith, *The Federalist* and the works of Thomas Jefferson. Shakespeare and Swift lent him what an orator might need of cadenced beauty and invective; Byron and Scott were there at hand, along with the best English magazines and the leading American newspapers. He read them all, and discussed them with his brother.

Also there was the plantation; Brierfield, he called it. Here too he worked and learned, making certain innovations in the labor system. The overseer was a Negro, James Pemberton. No slave was ever punished except after a formal trial by an all-Negro jury, Davis only reserving the right to temper the severity of the judgment. James was always James, never Jim; "It is disrespect to give a nickname," Davis said, and the overseer repaid him with frankness, loyalty, and efficiency. Once when something went amiss and the master asked him why, James replied: "I rather think, sir, through my neglect."

Davis gained all this from his decade of seclusion and study; but he gained something else as well. Up to now, his four years at West Point, brief and interrupted as they were, had been the longest period he had spent at any one place in his life. His school years had been various indeed, with instructors ranging from log-cabin teachers to Catholic priests and New England scholars. When a Virginian or a Carolinian spoke of his "country," he meant Virginia or Carolina. It was not so with Davis. Tennessee and Kentucky were as familiar to him as Mississippi; the whole South, as a region, formed his background; he was thirty before he knew a real home in any real sense of the word.

The Three Kings: Hemingway, Faulkner, and Fitzgerald

RICHARD FORD

SOME BOYS, ALAS, do not come to serious reading, nor God knows to serious writing, precisely like hounds to round steak. Though, then again, special boys sometimes do.

I remember a few years ago reading in *Exile's Return,* Malcolm Cowley's wonderful book on the Twenties, the teenage correspondence between Cowley and Kenneth Burke. It is pretentious, chin-pulling stuff sent from Burke's parents' apartment in Weehawken to Cowley's house in Pittsburgh, dwelling chiefly on whatever were the palmy literary aspirations just then dawning on those two little booksniffs. It was 1915. Cowley was just leaving for Harvard, having already, he boasted, banged through Kipling, Congreve, and Conrad, plus a dozen other of the greats. Burke—poet and teacher to be—was contemplating his first grand tour of France, rhapsodizing about how much he loved the moon and all those things that didn't fit him out for literature, while advertising himself as "somewhat of an authority on unpresentable French novels" and the lesser Chopin—altogether things that they must both blush at now. But still, I thought: What smart boys they were! And what remarkable letters! They had already read more, I realized, digested it better, gotten it down for quicker recall, and were putting it to fancier uses at seventeen than all I'd read, understood, remembered, or could hope to make use of to that very moment. Or maybe ever. And my hat was, and continues to be, off to them.

Until I entered college at Michigan State, where I'd come from Mississippi in 1962 to learn to be a hotel manager, my own reading had been chiefly of the casual drugstore and cereal box type. Whatever came easy. And what I was doing when I wasn't reading Congreve or Kipling or Faulkner, Hemingway, or Fitzgerald at an early and seasoning age was whirling crazy around Mississippi in a horrible flat-black '57 Ford Fairlane my grandparents had bought me; fecklessly swiping hubcaps and occasionally cars, going bird hunting on posted land with my buddy-pals, snarfling schoolgirls, sneaking into drive-ins, drinking, fighting, and generally entertaining myself fatherlessly in the standard American ways—ways Cowley and Burke never write about that I've seen, and so probably knew little about firsthand.

Though, in truth, my "preparation" strikes me as the more usual American one, starting off from that broad middle ground between knowing nothing and knowing a little *about* something. Conceivably it is the very plane Faulkner and Fitzgerald and Hemingway themselves started out from at my age, or a couple of years younger—not particularly proud of their ignorance, but not sufficiently daunted by it to keep them (and me) from barging off toward appealing and unfamiliar terrains. They were novelists, after all, not experts in literature. And what they wrote about was people living ordinary lives for which history had not quite readied them. And it is, I think, a large part of why we like them so much when we read them. They were like us. And what they wrote about reminded us of ourselves and sanctioned our lives.

Reading was, in truth, my very problem in Mississippi. While I always read faster and with more "comprehension" than my school grade was supposed to (I used to pride myself, in the tenth grade, that I could read as well as any Ole Miss Freshman), I was still slow, slow. Slow as Christmas. And I am still slow, though more practiced now. I have thought that had I been evaluated by today's standards, I'd have been deemed a special student and held back. Whereas in Mississippi, 1960, I was decidedly college prep.

I have also realized, since then, that I am well and only have changed from hotel management to the study of literature in college not so much because I loved literature—what did I know?—but because it was a discipline for the slow (i.e., careful). And I'll admit as well that at Michigan State knowing about Faulkner, Hemingway, and Fitzgerald, which I began to do that first year, was a novelty to set one comfortably and creditably apart from one's fraternity brothers from Menomonie and Ishpeming, who by that time were already sunk greedy-deep into packaging engineering, retailing theory, and hotel management—all those necessary arts and sciences for which Michigan State has become justly famous.

I remember very distinctly the first time I read anything by F. Scott Fitzgerald. I read the story "Absolution," in my first English literature class at MSU. It was 1962. And I remember it distinctly because it was the first story assigned for class, and because I didn't understand anything that happened in it.

"Absolution" was written by Fitzgerald in 1924, when he was twenty-seven, hardly older than I was when I read it. In it, a fantasizing little Minnesota schoolboy lies in Holy Confession, then gets mistakenly forced to take Communion with an impure soul. Later, and in a state of baleful terror, the boy—Rudolph Miller—confesses what he's done to the same priest, who absolves him peevishly, only then promptly and in Rudolph's presence suffers his own spiritual crack-up, giving up his senses to a giddy rhapsody about glimmering merry-go-rounds and shining, dazzling strangers—all, we suppose, because he'd done nothing more venturesome than be a priest all his life. Little Rudolph sits by horrified. But in his wretchedness he has figured out already that private acts of pride and comfort matter more than public ones of abstraction and pretense. And while the priest writhes on the floor, howling like a lunatic, Rudolph slips away, having acknowledged something mysterious and consequential that will last him all his life.

End of story.

It is one of Fitzgerald's very best; youthful innocence brought into the alembic of a tawdry, usurping experience. A genuine rite of passage. Real drama.

I did not understand it because even though my mother had been a convent girl in Ft. Smith, still occasionally sat in on masses, and, I believe, wished all her life and secretly that she could be a Catholic instead of a married-over Presbyterian, I did not know what absolution meant.

That is, I did not know what the word meant, and indeed what all the trouble was about. A considerable impediment.

Nor was I about to look it up. I was not big on looking things up then. It could've been that I had heard of F. Scott Fitzgerald before. Though I don't know why I would have. He was not from Mississippi. But you could argue that Americans up to a certain age, and at that particular time, were simply born knowing who F. Scott Fitzgerald was. Ernest Hemingway and William Faulkner, too. It's possible they were just in the American air. And once we breathed that air, we knew something.

It is also true that if I knew *about* F. Scott Fitzgerald—likewise

Hemingway and Faulkner—before I knew them hands-on, through direct purchase of their published work, say for instance, as I had read hungrily through some Mississippi dowager's private stacks, opened to the bookless boy who craved to read and to learn (the way it happens in French biographies, though not in mine), it is because by that time, 1961-62, all three were already fully apotheosized; brought up to a plane of importance important Americans always seem to end up on: as celebrities, estranged from the rare accomplishments that first earned them notice.

What I didn't know, though, was what absolution meant, nor anything much of what that story was about. If I had, it might've changed my life, might've signaled me how to get along better with my own devious prides and festerings. But I was just too neck-up then in my own rites of passage to acknowledge anybody else's. And while I may even have known what that expression meant, I couldn't fathom the one Fitzgerald was writing about.

So my first experience with him gave me this: Puzzlement. Backed up by a vague, free-floating self-loathing, I was, after all, not very studious then, and I balanced that habit with a vast ignorance I was not aware of. I was pledging Sigma Chi at the same time.

I know I knew who William Faulkner was by at least 1961. He *was* from Mississippi. Though I had not read a word he'd written about it. When I got to Michigan State, though, he immediately became part of the important territory I was staking out for myself. He, and Ross Barnett, and a kind of complex, swinish liberalness I affected to keep black guys from stomping on me on general principle.

I *had* laid eyes on William Faulkner. At the Alumni House at Ole Miss in the fall of 1961. Or at least I remember thinking I had. And in any case I certainly told people at Michigan State I had—tightening my grip on things rightly mine. But I know I had never read anything of his, or even of Eudora Welty's—who lived only a few blocks from me and whom I used to see buying her lunch at the steam table at the Jitney Jungle grocery, where our families shopped, but never bothered to inquire about, though her niece, Elizabeth, was in my class.

I had, by the time I left high school, strangely enough, read Geoffrey Chaucer. He was unavoidable in senior English. I could (and still can) recite from memory the first fourteen lines of the

Prologue to *The Canterbury Tales*, in Middle English, without giving one thought to what any of it signifies.

I had also "written" a term paper on Thomas Wolfe by then, though I hadn't read a word he'd written either. I had been given Andrew Turnbull's biography of Wolfe and had boosted most of my text straight from there, verbatim and unconsidered. I got a B.

I do remember, somewhere in this period, noticing that a friend of mine, Frank Newell, had a copy of *The Wild Palms*. It was on his bookshelf at home, in the old green-tinted and lurid Random House dust jacket with the pastel wild palms on it. I thought that Frank Newell's family were literary people because of that. And I thought *The Wild Palms* was probably a novel about Florida. In a year I would read my first Faulkner, in the same English class in college: "A Rose for Emily." And I liked it immensely. But I was surprised to know Faulkner wrote some scary stories. Somehow I had expected something different from a man who'd won the Nobel Prize.

As for Hemingway, I remember that best of all. I knew who he was by at least 1960, when I was sixteen, because my mother liked him. That is, she liked *him*.

I, of course, had not read a word, and I can't be absolutely certain my mother had, though she was a reader. Books like *The Egg and I* and *Lydia Bailey* went around our house in Mississippi, and we both had put in a lot of time in the Jackson Public Library, where it was either cool or warm at the right times of the year and where I would browse in comfort through the *National Geographics*.

What she liked about Hemingway was, I think, the way he looked. His picture had been in *Life* or *Look* in the Fifties, looking about like the Karsh photo that's still sometimes seen in magazines. A rough yet sensitive guy. A straight-talking man of letters in a fisherman's sweater. The right look.

She also liked something he'd said in public about dying, about how dying wasn't so bad but living with death till it indignified you was poison, and how he would take his own life when that happened to him, which I guess he did. That my mother liked, too. She kept the quotation on a three-by-five card, written in her own hand, stuck inside the phone book, where I would occasionally see it and feel craven embarrassment. She admired resolution and certainty about first principles. And so, I suppose, did I, though not with enough interest to hunt up a novel of Hemingway's and see what else there was to it. This was about the time my father died of a heart attack, at home, in my arms and in her presence. And we—she and I—became susceptible to certain kinds of rigor as stanches against grief and varieties of bad luck. For a while during this period she kept company with a big, burly-bluff guy named Matt, who was married and drove a powerful car and carried a .45 caliber pistol strapped to the steering column (I liked him very much) and who growled when he talked and who might've seemed like Hemingway to someone who knew absolutely nothing about him, but who had a notion.

In any case, though, my mother, who was born in northwest Arkansas, in a dirt-floor cabin near the Oklahoma line and the Osage Strip, and who has now died, was, importantly, the first person I knew of who was truly Hemingwayesque. And that included Ernest Hemingway himself.

These, then, were the first writers' names to be chalked, if obscurely, onto my remarkably clean slate, a fact vouched true to me by my ability to remember when I knew of them and by my dead reckoning that before that time I knew of no writers at all—except Geoffrey Chaucer and a part of Andrew Turnbull that I stole. I arrived at 1962, the year I would first read William Faulkner, Scott Fitzgerald, and Ernest Hemingway, remarkably ignorant for a boy of eighteen; as unlettered, in fact, as a porch monkey, and without much more sense than that idle creature of what literature was good for, or to what uses it might be put in my life. Not at all a writer. And not one bit the seasoned, reasonable, apprentice bookman customary to someone who before long would want to be a novelist.

For these three kings, then, a kingdom was vacant.

And so I read them, badly. At least at first.

It was in the dog days of the New Criticism that I read *The Sun Also Rises*, *Absalom, Absalom!*, and *The Great Gatsby*. We were being instructed to detect literature's most intrinsic worth by holding its texts aloof from life and history, and explicating and analyzing its parts to pieces. Close reading, this was known as. And my professors—one, a bemused, ex-second-string football player from Oregon; and the other, a gentle, strange-suited, bespectacled man with the picturesque, Hemingway name of Sam Baskett—put us through our formalist/objectivist paces like dreary drill sergeants. Point of view. Dramatic structure. Image. Theme. Hemingway and Faulkner were still alive at that time, and Fitzgerald managed somehow to retain his contemporariness. And there was, among us students, a fine, low-grade brio that here we were reading new work. Probably my teachers admired these men's writing. Generationally they were much more under the thumb of their influence than I could ever be, and possibly they had wanted to be writers themselves once. (One told me that people who wanted to be writers should take jobs as fire watchers and live alone in towers.) But they still chose to teach literature to satisfy a weary system, and in any case it was in these dry classroom anatomies that I first learned exactly what meaning meant.

Symbols, I remember, were very much on my teachers' minds then, and so on mine. I was not yet *reading like a writer.* Indeed, I was just learning to read like a reader—still slowly—so that I never really got onto the symbol business as straight as I might've. But we Jessie Westoned the daylights out of poor Hemingway and Fitzgerald; unearthed wastelands, identified penises, fish, and fisher kings all over everywhere. From my sad underlinings and margin notes of that time, I can see that Dr. T. J. Eckleburg, the brooding, signboard optometrist, was very important to my reading of *The Great Gatsby.* He meant God, fate, decadence, evil and impotence, and was overlord of the wasteland—all qualities and identities I could not make fit together, since they seemed like different things, and since my sense of meaning dictated that assignments only be made one to one.

Jake Barnes's mystery war wound likewise supplied me no end of industry. For a time everyone in that book was wounded, or at least alienated very badly. Many things are marked "Ironic." Many things are marked "Imp." And everywhere I could I underlined *rod, bull, bandillera, worm,* and noted "Symb."

Of course, I paid no special attention to the lovely, lyrical celebration of comradeship among Jake and Bill and the Englishman, Harris, there on the Irati—a passage I now think of as the most sweetly moving and meaningful in the novel. Nor to the passage in *Gatsby* where Nick tries to say how Gatsby must've felt at the sad end of things, when he had "paid a high price for living too long with a single dream." I suppose I was just too young for all that, too busy making things harder, getting my ducks set in a straight row.

This, as I've said, was around the time I read "Absolution," and was completely puzzled by it. I was not, however, puzzled by Faulkner, whose gravity and general profusion so daunted the Michiganders I sat beside in class, since he resisted our New Critical shakedown like a demon. There was really just too much of everything in *Absalom, Absalom!* Life, in words, geysering and eddying over each other, so that just being sure what was what and who was who became challenge enough to make you beg off choosing among what things might formally *mean*—a valuable enough lesson, certainly for anyone who wants to learn about anything, ever.

Faulkner dazzled me, of course, as his writing inevitably will. But being from where he was from, I was already acquainted with the way the white man's peculiar experience in that particular locale over time begot the need to tell; to rehearse, explain, twist, revise, and alibi life clear out of its own weirdness and paradox and eventually into a kind of fulgent, cumulative, and acceptable sense. Begot, in fact, so much larruping and fabricating that language somehow became paramount for its own sake (a fresh idea to me) and in turn begot its own irony, its own humors, and genealogy and provenance.

That, I came to understand, was meaning too.

For me, reading Faulkner was like coming upon a great iridescent glacier that I had dreamed about. I may have been daunted by the largeness and gravity and variety of what he told. But he never puzzled me so as to make me feel ignorant, as I had been before I read him, or when I read "Absolution." To the contrary. When I read *Absalom! Absalom!* those years ago, everything came *in* to me. I got something. Somehow the literal sense of all I did and didn't understand, lay in the caress of those words—all of it, absolutely commensurate with life—suddenly seemed a pleasure, not a task. And I loved it.

Before, I don't believe I'd known what made literature necessary; neither what quality of life required that it be represented, nor what quality in literature made such abstractings a good idea. In other words, the singular value of written words, and their benefit to lived life, had not been impressed on me. That is, until I read *Absalom! Absalom!*, which, among other things, sets out to testify by act to the efficacy of telling, and to recommend language for its powers of consolation against whatever's ailing you.

I point this out now because if anything I read influenced me to take a try at being a writer—even on a midget scale—it was this pleasure I got from reading Faulkner. I wrote my first story about this time, a moody, inconclusive, not especially Faulkner-like domestic minidrama called "Saturday," which I liked. And putting those events together makes me understand now how much the wish to trade in language as a writer traces to a pleasure gotten from its use as a reader.

Not that it has to be that way. For some writers I'm sure ideas come first. For others, pictures. For others, probably symbols and Vico. But for me it was telling, in words. I don't think I ever read the same way after that but began to read, in my own way, like a writer. Not to satisfy a system, but to take whatever pleasure there was from language, no matter what I understood or could parse. And that, I am satisfied now, is the way one should always read. At least to start.

In the spring of 1964, my wife and I—barely not children and certainly not yet married—drove in an old Chrysler north from East Lansing up into the lake counties where most of Hemingway's Michigan stories are set—Charlevoix, Emmet, Mackinac. The two of us hiked around sunny days through East Jordan and Petoskey, picnicked on beaches where the rich Chicagoans used to come summers, boated on Walloon Lake, staying in a little matchstick motel across the straits in St. Ignace just to say we'd been there and seen the bridge that wasn't there when Hemingway wrote about the country.

Though I was there to get a closer, more personal lowdown on those stories; stories I had been reading that spring, had loved on instinct, felt intensely, but that had also sparked my first honest act of literary criticism; namely, that I felt they never *ever* quite said enough. They forbore too much, skimped on language, made too much of silences. As if things were said only for the gods, and the gods didn't tolerate that much. And I was there, I suppose, curious and nervous about silences, to tune in on things with some experience of my own. It seems romantic now. And it probably *was* silly. But it was my way of taking things seriously and to heart. My way of reading.

What I didn't understand, of course, and certainly didn't learn marching around those woods fifty years too late, was that these were a young man's stories. And their severe economies—I think of "Indian Camp," because it was my special favorite—were the economies and silences of a still limited experience, an intelligence that wasn't finished yet, though certainly also a talent masterful at mining feeling with words, or at least at the nervy business of stripping words in such a pattern as to strand the feelings nicely inside the limits of the story.

It was a young man's aesthetic, and ideal of impressing another young man.

But I wanted badly to know why that Indian had killed himself! And I did not understand why Nick's father wouldn't just come out, while they were heading home in the boat, and say it. Tell us. Telling was what writing did, I thought. And I wasn't savvy enough myself *not* to be told. Faulkner would've told it. He'd have had Judge Benbow or Rosa Coldfield spill it out. Fitzgerald would've had somebody try to explain later on, in another city in the Middle West.

Hemingway, though, was after something he thought was purer. Later, I read in *Death in the Afternoon* that he aimed for the "sequence of motion and fact which made the emotion." Whereas, if you said a thing—explained it—you could lose it, which is what Jake Barnes says. And indeed what you lost was the feeling of the thing, the feeling of awe, terror, loss. Think of "Hills Like White Elephants," a story I admire and that students love because it seems so modern. No one says abortion in it. Yet the feeling of abortion—loss, puzzlement, abstraction—informs every slender, stylized gesture and line, and the story has a wonderful effect.

But the embryo writer in me, even then, wanted more. More language spent. More told so that I could know more of what went on there and feel it in the plush of the words. A man had died. And I wanted the risk the other way, risking the "blur" Hemingway so distrusted—an effect caused by a writer who has not seen something "clearly," yet who still needs to get at a truth by telling it. The world, for me, even back in 1964, seemed too various, too full, and literature too resourceful to draw such rigid lines about life just to preserve a feeling.

To me, Hemingway kept secrets rather than discovered them. He held the overcomplex world too much at arm's length either because he wouldn't on principle or couldn't say more. And for that reason I distrusted him. He valued accuracy and precision over truth, and for that reason, despite his effects, he seemed a specialist in what he himself called "minor passions." Even today, when I am always surprised at how much broader a writer he is than I remember, he still seems a high school team captain with codes, a man who peaked too early and never went on to greater, harder feats.

Not, of course, that I didn't take with me something valuable from Hemingway, namely a deference for genuine mystery. I may now know what absolution means and why the Indian kills himself—too many doctors, too much pain and indignity. I may know beyond much doubt what was Jake Barnes's wound. But I also learned that for anyone, at any time, some things that matter can't be told, either because they're too important or too hard to bring to words, and these things can be the subject of stories. I think I learned that first and best reading Hemingway, learned the manners and protocols and codes a story observes when it comes round something it thinks is a consequential mystery. I may still prefer that mystery, once broached, be an inducement, not a restraint, to language, a signal to imagination to begin saying whatever can be said. But to have learned of that mystery at an early age is no small thing. And my debt for it is absolute.

From this highly reactive time, my memories of Fitzgerald are, at best, indistinct. I made my way through *The Great Gatsby*, exclusively settling matters of point of view and Dr. Eckleburg's significations. Then I simply left off, my memory retaining only the faraway beacon light on Daisy Buchanan's boat dock (it was "Imp."), and Gatsby floating dead in his swimming pool, a memory I soon confused with the beginning of the movie *Sunset Boulevard*, in which the corpse played by William Holden, not Nick Carraway, tells the story.

What I *was* attentive to, though, in my bird dog's way, were the subliterate runs and drumbeats of words, their physical and auditory manifestations, the extremes of utterance and cadence, what Sartre called the outside of language. It is undoubtedly one reason I liked Faulkner best, since he offers so much to the poorly educated but overly sensitized.

And my belief was that these etherish matters were matters of literary style. And like all novices, I became preoccupied with that.

What followed, then, was a partitioning up of literature into Faulkneresque and Hemingwayesque, leaving a kind of stylistic no-man's-land for all the other people. To me, Fitzgerald, by having the softest drumbeats, the fewest linguistic extremes and quirks, the rarest ethers, didn't really seem to have much of a style, or if he did he had a poor, thin one.

It seems feasible that one could think that putting Fitzgerald midway between the great putter-inner and the great taker-outer casts a kind of convenient cosmos map of the male soul and its choices. Though what I was doing twenty years ago, when I was almost twenty, was just confusing style with idiosyncrasy and making myself its champion.

Not that it was entirely my fault.

My ex-quarterback of a professor (we'd heard he'd played behind Terry Baker, and so had had plenty of time for reading) had assigned us all to write a paragraph in either "the style of Hemingway" or the "the style of Faulkner"—a miserable, treacherous task to assign any student, but particularly to one who had begun to write. (Though I now understand it was designed chiefly to kill class time.)

But we all wrote. And when we read our paragraphs aloud, mine produced the profoundest response from my instructor. He stopped me three sentences in and complained to all that my Hemingway sounded like everybody else's Faulkner, and that I clearly was not much good for this kind of thing.

I was badly stung. I liked style, whatever it was. And I believed I could be its master. Only I saw I needed to study it harder—Hemingway and Faulkner in particular, and what was so odd about them that I couldn't imitate them separately.

Nobody, though, was asking me to write a paragraph in the style of Fitzgerald at this time. *Fitzgeraldian* was not a word. And so for this reason he fell even more completely below my notice.

It is notable to me that somewhere in this period someone placed in my hands, for reasons I do not remember, a copy of Arthur Mizener's gossipy, pseudo-scholarly biography of Fitzgerald, *The Far Side of Paradise,* the edition with the Van Vechten photo on the front, a smiling, wide-faced Fitzgerald practically unrecognizable from the Princetonian-Arrow shirt profile on the Scribner's books.

Reading Mizener was a big mistake for me. His biographer's interest was the archly antinew critical one of mutually corroborating art and life. And since Fitzgerald, at least for a time, had lived a very, very *rich* life, there set on for me a long period in which I could not distinguish accurately all he'd done from all that he'd written: the profligacy, the madness, the high style and helling around, ruinous wives, prep schools, the Plaza, Princeton, New York, Paris, Minnesota, Hollywood. I read the other novels, the stories and notebooks. And though I didn't exactly forget them, they just fell to his life. *He* seemed smart and too clever and poignant and overweening. But the books almost always faded back into Fitzgerald myth, into imputation, half-fact, lie, remembrance, and confession—annals where even now for me they have their truest resonance.

Today, I still believe it's as much his failure as mine that I remember as much about him as I do, but can sort out so little of his work. And that his life—vulnerable, exemplary, short writer's life—save for a brilliant novel and a few excellent short pieces, makes a better story. It is tempting to think that, like Dick Diver and Amory Blaine and Anthony Patch, he represents some promising but spoilable part of our American self-conception. And since that is not exactly tragic, it is maybe more appealing and exemplary to us as biography than illusion.

Recently I read *The Great Gatsby* again, for possibly the fourth time (I know people who brag they read it every year). Fitzgerald wrote it before he was thirty, and as I get older it only gets better. I believe it is one of the maturest, more sophisticated and seamless books I have read, and I don't fault myself for not getting it back in 1964, since it has, I think, more to teach an older man than a young one.

And I have found its style: its elegant economies and proportionings, the sleek trajectory of its complex little story, the strategy of withholding Gatsby until his place is set, Fitzgerald's certain eye for the visual detail and, once observed, for that detail's suitability as host for his wonderful, clear judgment about Americans and American life—a judgment, Wilson said, "saturated with twentieth-century America."

The essence of Fitzgerald's style finally was that he itched to say something smart on the page, and made his novels accommodate that. It is why as a young man he was always better in shorter, manageable forms, and why a savvy young man might've learned plenty from him without ever having to mimic. And it is why I had such a hard time at first, my own ear then being chiefly to the ground.

Faulkner, of course, was the best of all three, and the very best of any American writing fiction in this century. It is not even discredit to Hemingway and Fitzgerald to say so. Liking Faulkner or not liking him is akin to liking or not liking the climate in some great territorial expanse. It seems like tautology. Whereas Hemingway and Fitzgerald, I sense, come to our affections more like the weather does, passingly.

No writer, including Henry James, minted more robust characters freshly and indelibly into our American literary memory. All those Snopeses, Temple Drake, Thomas Sutpen, Benjy Compson, Dilsey. A bear. No writer has exceeded his own natural regionalism (that dark American literary peril), or survived the codification of his style, or confessed apparently less of his personal life as grandly as Faulkner has. No one braves as much in a sentence. No one is as consistently or boisterously funny as Faulkner while remaining serious and dramatic. And, of course, no American writer this century has been so influential—impressive is the best word—both in the restraining effects of his work on other writers, and in the most generous ways as well: his work always urges all of us if not to be more hopeful, at least to be more various, to include more, see more, say more that is hopeful and surprising and humorous and that is true.

I loved Faulkner when I read him first. He stumped the symbolizers, the mythologizers, the taxonomists, the *pov* guys dead in the brackets in East Lansing. He would not reduce so as to mean more. And that I liked.

Though it seemed to me, then, as it did ten years later when I was writing a novel set in Mississippi—my home too—that that was because he'd appropriated everything there was. It was even possible to want to write like Faulkner without knowing you did; to want to put down some sense of a life there without realizing it existed first in his sentences. Until the end of the Fifties—1963—I am convinced, a large part of *everybody's* idea of the South came from William Faulkner, whether they'd read him or not. He was in the American air, as I said before. And that went for the air southerners breathed too, since we could see how right he'd gotten it, and since, of course, he was ours.

How can I measure what it was worth to read Hemingway, Fitzgerald, and Faulkner back then in the Sixties? Influence on a writer is a hard business to assess, and I'm not sure I would tell the truth if I could, since real influence means being affected by the weather in another writer's sentences, sometimes so much that you can't even imagine writing except in that weather. And no one who's any good ever wants to write like anyone else.

One truth is that my generation of writers—born mostly in the Forties—has not lived "the same life, the generic one" that Lowell speaks about in his elegy for his friend John Berryman. We have not all prized or even read the same books. We have not all had or aspired to teaching jobs. We do not all know one another. Lowell, of course, was probably wrong about his generation, since, from what I can tell of his thinking, it included only about fifteen people. But of my own, I am sure we are too many, too spread out and differently inclined ever to have been influenced similarly by another generation's writers.

Another truth is that I don't remember a lot of those books anymore. And I never read them all to start with. A fellow I met recently, who had spent time in a North Vietnamese prison, asked me if I thought Francis Macomber's wife shot him on purpose. And I had no idea. In my mind I had confused that story with *The Snows of Kilimanjaro*, and when I went back to figure out the answer, I was surprised. (Of course, Hemingway being Hemingway, I'm still not 100 percent sure what happened.)

Likewise, when I began to think on this essay, I chose a Faulkner novel just to graze over for atmosphere, one I thought I hadn't read—*Sanctuary*—but knew to be easy because of what Faulkner had written about it. Only now that I've finished it, I really can't be certain if I'd read it years ago or not. Odd. But there you are.

Still, as a little group, they seem to have traversed the Sixties and Seventies intact, despite the fact of a unique and intense war's being on then, and of immediate life's altering so rapidly and irrevocably. To me, they seem far away, their writing become *literature* finally. But that is only because I don't read them so much, and when I do it is usually to teach readers who were being born just when Hemingway and Faulkner were dying.

Though *their* pleasure seems certain.

I have always assigned classes to read "Babylon Revisited," Fitzgerald's bitter, touching story about Charlie Wales, the man who comes to Paris to reclaim his daughter, lost to him by the calamities of the Twenties, and the Crash, and by his own bad luck and improvidence. It is one of my favorite stories. And there is always a sentiment among students that it keeps its currency because of the Thirties' similarities—at least in my students' minds—to those years since the Sixties were over.

Faulkner still seems to excite the awe and affection he excited in me, though no one—correctly—wants to write like him. Only Hemingway, I detect, can occasionally exert a genuine and direct influence on young writers' "style." His old, dour, at-war-with-words correctness seems to ride the waves of austerity, ascending in tough, Republican times, and declining when life seems abler to support grand illusions.

As writers whose work taught me serviceable lessons about writing at a formative age, all three get high marks for mentorship—a role Hemingway cared much to fill, and that Faulkner, if we take to heart the sarcasm of his Nobel address, probably thought was ridiculous.

By 1968, when I had started graduate school in California, people were still talking about Faulkner, Hemingway, and Fitzgerald, though primarily just as Dutch uncles to our own newborn artistic credos. We were all tiny savages then, trying on big boys' clothes. Though it was still good to be able to quote a particular novel—*As I Lay Dying* was popular—or to own something specific one of them had reportedly said and be able to unsheathe it fast. *The Crack-Up* was highly prized as a *vade mecum*, along with the *Paris Review* interviews and *A Moveable Feast*.

Anyone who actually *wrote* like Faulkner or Hemingway was, of course, thought to be washed up from the start. But with their books, others' faults could be neatly exposed, crow and humble pie served to order. We were being read to by Richard Brautigan, taught by E. L. Doctorow, and imitating Donald Barthelme. But we were still interested in how those older men got along in the world where there were no grants or teaching jobs, and how they acted out their parts. One fellow in my class actually asked us all to call him Papa. And when I remember that, I need no better proof that they were in our lives, still behind us all, like Mount Rushmore in the Santa Ana Hills.

Speaking selectively, I know I learned from the economies of *The*

Great Gatsby how to get on with things narrative; how to get people in and out of scenes and doors and sections of the country by seizing some showy detail and then going along to whatever was next.

From Hemingway I learned just how little narrative "intrusion" (we talked that way) was actually necessary to keep the action going, and I also learned to value the names of things, and to try to know how things worked as a way of dominating life and perfecting its illusion. There was, as well, the old workshop rapier that said Hemingway's famous dialogue, when actually spoken aloud, sounded like nothing more than an angry robot on Valium, and not like real talk. Yet locked within is the greater lesson that the page is officially different from the life, and that in creating life's illusion, the page need not exactly mimic—need not nearly mimic, really—and, moreover, that this very discrepancy is what sets art free.

From Faulkner I'm sure I learned that in "serious" fiction it is possible to be funny at the expense of nothing—a lesson also discernible in Shakespeare; that it is sometimes profitable to take risks with syntax and diction, and bring together words that ordinarily do not seem to belong together—the world being not completely foregone—and in this small way reinvent the language and cause pleasure. And finally, from Faulkner, that in representing life one needs to remember that many, many things do not stand to reason.

They were all three dead, of course, before I had written a word. Already kings. But still, I and my generation might have learned from them just what time in life our words could start to mean something to someone else—nervy business, when you think of it. They all wrote brilliant books in their twenties. We might also have learned that great literature can sometimes be written by amateurs who are either smart enough or sufficiently miscast to need to take their personal selves very seriously. In this way we might've learned some part of what talent is.

And last, we might've learned from them that the only real *place* for a writer in this country is at the top of the heap. That the only really satisfactory sanction available, the one our parents could appreciate as happily as the occupations they wanted for us—the law and banking—is success and the personal price for success is sometimes very high, and is almost always worth it.

What I remember of them, though, is something else again, different from what they taught me. Though by saying what I actually remember, or some of it, I may say best why for me and possibly for people like me, they are three kings.

I remember, for instance, what Nick Carraway said about all our personalities, and Gatsby's in particular: that they are only "an unbroken series of successful gestures."

I remember that Hemingway gave up his first good wife, and never forgave himself for it, and that Fitzgerald kept his until she helped ruin him. (On the eve of my marriage I remember asking my soon-to-be-wife to please read *The Beautiful and the Damned*, and to promise not to ruin me in that particular way.)

I remember Hemingway saying, "It is certainly valuable to a trained writer to crash in an airplane that burns."

I remember Darl Bundren in *As I Lay Dying*, describing his sister Dewey Dell's breasts as "mammalian ludicrosities which are the horizons and valleys of the earth."

I remember Horace Benbow saying to a man already doomed, "You're not being tried by common sense. . . . You're being tried by a jury."

I remember where I learned what a bota bag was and how it was used—important gear for a fraternity man.

I remember where I learned what it meant to have *repose*—*Tender Is the Night*—and that I didn't have it.

I remember that dead Indian very distinctly.

I remember what Fitzgerald said—sounding more like Hemingway than our version of Fitzgerald, but really speaking for all three writers—that "Life was something you dominated, if you were any good."

And last, I remember what Fitzgerald wrote in his notebook about Dick Diver: "He looked like me."

This is important stuff of my memory: objects, snapshots, odd despairs, jokes, instructions, codes. Plain life charted through its middle grounds. Literature put to its best uses. The very thing I didn't know when I started.

These men were literalists, though they could be ironic. They were writers of reference. They were intuitors and observers of small things for larger purposes. They were not zealots, nor politicians. Not researchers nor experts nor experimenters. They seemed to come to us one to one. And though Faulkner could seem difficult, really he was not if you relented as I did.

Their work, in other words, seemed like *real* work, and we gave up disbelief without difficulty and said willingly, "This is our writing." They wrote to bring the news. And they were wondrous at that task. They wrote a serious, American literature that a boy who had read nothing could read to profit, and then read for the rest of his life.

"You've got to sell your heart," Fitzgerald said, and write "so that people can read it blind like braille." And in a sense, with their work they sold their hearts for us, and that inspires awe and fear and even pity. Reverence suitable for kings.

FROM

The Making of Black Revolutionaries

JAMES FORMAN

MCCOMB, MISSISSIPPI

BOB MOSES WROTE, in a field report from McComb:

On Tuesday, Aug. 29, 1961, we made our third attempt at registration in Amite County. I accompanied two people down to the registrar's office . . . we were to meet Alfred Knox on the courthouse lawn. However, Knox was not there and we had to walk through town looking for him. We found him at the east end of town, by the post office, and were walking back to the registrar's office when we were approached by three young white men.

They came up, stopped, and the fellow who was in the lead asked me what I was trying to do? Before I could answer he began to beat—hit at me. I covered my head and I was kneeling on the ground with my head covered and he was beating me for I don't know how long.

He finally stopped and I got up and walked over to the registrar's office, to the sheriff's office, and asked the sheriff if he couldn't swear out a warrant against him. He said that he couldn't since I wasn't sure whether or not he had an instrument that he was using to do the beating. . . .

The registrar had left. So we came back to Steptoe's where I had the wounds cleaned. (My shirt was very bloody and I figured that if we went back in the courthouse we would probably frighten everybody, so we went to Steptoe's). Then we went over to McComb where the doctor had to take nine stitches in three different places in the scalp.

Two days later we went back to press charges. The State of Mississippi had to prosecute, and that day they had a very quick six-man Justice of the Peace jury. Dawson and Knox and myself all testified, but the white defendent was found innocent and the case was dismissed.

This report by Moses is a brief one but it suggests all the major elements of SNCC's struggle in Mississippi:

The denial of voting rights, so flagrant that people with master's degrees in political science and even Ph.D.s were turned down in the same automatic way as all other black people.

The violence and terror waiting for anyone who challenged that denial.

The conspiracy of law enforcement and the courts with their "white only" justice.

It was Mississippi, that's all—for some, just to say the name of the state is to tell the whole story.

It was Mississippi: The state which had led the Southern drive to take back from black people the vote and other civil rights won during Reconstruction, the state which had reduced the number of registered black voters from 190,000 in 1890 to 8,600 in 1892, through a combination of new laws, tricks, and murder. It was Mississippi, with a larger proportion of blacks than any other state and the lowest proportion—only 5 percent—of eligible blacks registered to vote. It was Mississippi, birthplace of the White Citizens' Council—a white-collar version of the Ku Klux Klan. It was Mississippi, where years of terror, economic intimidation, and a total, grinding, day-in, day-out white racism had created a black population numb with fear and hopelessness—yet still able from time to time to produce individuals in whom the spirit of rebellion lived.

It was to Mississippi that Bob Moses, then a twenty-six-year-old Harlem schoolteacher with a master's degree from Harvard, had come after working for a period in the New York office of SCLC and in the Atlanta SNCC office. While in Atlanta, Moses had been sent out to get people from Deep South areas to attend a full SNCC meeting in the fall of 1961. On that field trip, he talked with Amzie Moore of Cleveland, Mississippi, one of those individuals who had survived and defied tyranny. Amzie Moore felt that a campaign to register black voters could break the isolation of black Mississippians, replace the brokenness with a fighting spirit, and even possibly win a local political voice which would lead to further change. He convinced Moses of this, and together they laid plans for a voter registration drive to begin that summer.

But, when Moses had returned to Cleveland, he found it impossible to get the project going—no location, no equipment, no funds became available. Meanwhile, however, a man named C. C. Bryant—head of the NAACP chapter in Pike County, where McComb is located—had learned of the proposed registration project and written to Moses, inviting him to come to McComb to start a similar project. Amzie Moore and Moses traveled to McComb and found that it had better facilities. It was decided to make the experiment in that town.

McComb was Mississippi, no doubt about it: A village sitting down there in the southwestern part of the state, Klan country, with a long history of violence and oppression. In Pike County, two hundred of about eight thousand eligible blacks were registered in 1960; in nearby Amite, out of nearly five thousand eligible blacks, there was exactly *one* registered. And in Walthall County, out of three thousand blacks over twenty-one, *none* was registered.

During the first week of August Moses was joined by John Hardy and Reggie Robinson. Hardy was a small, muscular fellow from Nashville who had just finished a jail term resulting from his participation in the Freedom Rides, and Reggie Robinson was from Baltimore, Maryland, where he had been directing a voter registration project. Both students were among the sixteen who had decided to drop out of school for a year to work for SNCC. Together these three started traveling the dirt roads, going into the old, broken-down houses, talking the language and living the life of the oppressed people, and trying to persuade them to face the trials of registration.

On August 6 or 7, 1961, this small group opened SNCC's first voter registration school in Mississippi. The school operated in a two-story, combination cinder block and paintless wood structure which housed a grocery store on the street level and a Masonic meeting hall above it. It was located in Burglundtown, the black section of McComb. There, from 9 a.m. to 9 P.M., people could learn to fill out the intentionally difficult voter registration form. This meant having people read and interpret different sections of the Mississippi Constitution and describe the duties and obligations of a citizen. After doing this every day for two weeks, the workers finally started to get results. People began to go down to Magnolia, Mississippi—the seat of the Pike County—to register.

This sudden stir of activity in McComb interested people in Walthall and Amite counties, who then asked the registration workers if they would start schools in their counties. Moses was at first critical of going into such "tough" counties so early in the game; however, he decided to proceed for two reasons: First, because the people had asked for help and were anxious to try to register; second, SNCC couldn't take the position of turning down areas on the basis of difficulty, because the people would then lose confidence in us.

Around the middle of August, John Hardy and two other SNCC workers went into Walthall to start voter registration activities.

They also made the first attempt to take people down to the courthouse in Liberty—the seat of Amite County—to register. This is Bob Moses's report on that experience:

> I [Moses] accompanied three people down to Liberty in a first registration attempt there. One was a very old man and two middle-aged ladies. We left early the morning of August 15th. It was a Tuesday. We arrived at the courthouse about 10 A.M. The registrar came out. I waited by the side—waiting for either the farmer or one of the two ladies to say something to the registrar. He asked what they wanted; what were they here for, in a very rough kind of voice. They didn't say anything; they were literally paralyzed with fear. So, after awhile, I spoke up and said that they would like to try and register to vote. So, he asked, "Who are you and what do you have to do with them? Are you here to register?" I told him who I was and that we were conducting a school in McComb, and that these people had attended the school and they wanted an opportunity to register. "Well," he said, "they will have to wait because there is somebody else filling out the form." Well, there was a young white lady with her husband and she was completing the forms. When she finished, our people started to register—one at a time.
>
> In the meantime, a procession of people began moving in and out of the office—the sheriff, a couple of his deputies, people from the Tax Office and Driver's License Office—looking in, staring, moving back out, muttering. A highway patrolman finally came in and sat down in the office and we stayed that way in sort of uneasy tension all morning.
>
> The first person who filled out the form took a long time to do it, and it was noontime before he finished. When we came back after lunch, I was not permitted to stay in the office, but had to leave and sit on the front porch—which I did. We finished the whole process about four-thirty. All of the three people had had a chance to fill out the form. This was a victory because they had been down several times before and had not had a chance even to fill out the forms.
>
> On the way home we were followed by the highway patrolman who had spent the day in the Registrar's Office. He tailed us for about ten miles very closely, twenty or twenty-five feet behind us, all the way back to McComb. At one point we pulled over and he passed us and circled around and came back. We pulled off as he was passing us in the opposite direction and he turned around and followed us again. Finally, he blew us down and I got out and asked what the trouble was. The people in the car, by that time, were very, very frightened. He asked me who I was, what my business was, and told me I was interfering in what he was doing. I said, "I simply wanted to find out what the problem was and what we were being stopped for." He told me to get back into the car, and as I did so, I jotted his name down. He then opened the car door and pushed me and said, "Get in the car, Nigger," and slammed the door after me. He then told us to follow him in the car, and took us over to McComb where I was placed under arrest.

They called up the County Prosecuting Attorney, and he came down. He and the patrolman then sat down and opened the law books to find a charge. They charged me with interfering with an officer in the process of arresting somebody. When they found out that the only person arrested was myself, they changed the charge to interfering with an officer in the discharge of his duties.

Moses was found guilty and received a ninety-day jail sentence. It was suspended, probably because in jail he had telephoned the Justice Department (collect, and the call was accepted), told an official there that he was being intimidated simply because of trying to help people register, and the powers of McComb realized that they had something a little hot on their hands. Bob left jail—it had been his introduction to Mississippi jails—and returned to the tedious routine of canvassing.

The group was severely handicapped because they had no transportation and the farms in the area are far apart. Finally they got help from E. W. Steptoe, a local NAACP president who lived in the southern part of Pike County and who had already helped the voter registration workers—feeding them when they had no money for food. Steptoe made plans to set up a school near his farm, and Bob Moses, together with a local worker, went to live there for a week. The voter registration project had now spread to encompass the counties of Pike, Amite, and Walthall, with McComb as a sort of headquarters. Other workers came South to help. Hollis Watkins and Curtis Hayes, high school students who were both from McComb originally and who later became full-time SNCC workers, set up the Pike County Nonviolent Movement and served as its president and vice-president respectively.

On August 22, four more blacks went into Liberty to register and this time there was no trouble at all. People felt encouraged and another group planned to go on August 29. This was the day that Bob Moses was viciously beaten.

By this time, McComb had become a hotbed of activity. There was not only a voter registration effort in progress on August 29, but also direct action. Young people in McComb, eager to help in the canvassing, also wanted to engage in something more visible. Marion Barry had come down from Nashville and, with the help of Dion Diamond and Charles Sherrod, conducted workshops in the community on nonviolence and other direct action tactics.

The students decided they wanted to move and they chose as their first target the McComb Library, which did not admit blacks.

They first negotiated with the head of the library, who wouldn't budge and then, on August 29, headed down to demonstrate. But the whites had seen them coming and a sign was up on the library saying, "We are closed today." After a quick conference, they headed for the Woolworth's store to demonstrate there against the lunch counter for whites only. The manager refused to yield, they had a sit-in, Hayes and Watkins were quickly arrested and sentenced to six months with a five hundred dollar fine. Both served over thirty days. Hollis Watkins describes their time in jail:

We remained in the city jail for about two days, then we were transferred down to the county jail. When we first got to the county jail they placed us in the drunk tank, the place where they keep the drunkards. There was nothing in there but concrete, to sit or lay on. We remained in the drunk tank for about eight hours. After the eight hours had expired, they carried us upstairs to a better cell, which was not too good. We remained in jail for about thirty-four days, in the county jail that is.

During the time we was in the jail, the food that they would give us was very poor, didn't have any seasoning in it at all and at this time they wouldn't allow anyone to bring us things, such as seasoning, or anything. And when they would bring us breakfast it would be cold, which every morning would be grits and egg, maybe about half an egg, and the grits would be cold.

During the time when we was in McComb the police, as they would question us, would carry us into a room by ourself. And at one particular time they carried me into a room and after entering the room I found about twelve men sitting in the room which seemed to have been just off the street. And as I would answer the questions, yes and no, the officer told me to say yes sir and no sir, but I refused. And by refusing, the men that were in the room, they gathered round me, very close, as if to hit me or beat me if I continued to say yes and no.

So therefore I became very afraid, and at this particular time I decided the best thing for me to do was to make a sentence out of my answer, to keep from saying yes sir and no sir.

And another particular time when the officers carried me into a room to question me, he would look at me and try to frighten me, say bad remarks, call me all different kinds of names, and after all this, he carried me into a room by myself and left me. I didn't know what was going to happen and about five minutes later the police came through and he looked at me for about a minute and then he went into a little room which looked to be like a closet and he got a grass rope out.

After getting this rope he came in front of me and stopped. And he looked at me as I was looking at him, and he said to me, "O.K., nigger, get up, let's go, we're going to have a hanging here tonight and you're going to be first." I became very frightened at that moment, because I didn't know what to expect, but instead of showing my frightenedness, I crossed my legs and reared back in my chair and smiled at him. And he just looked at me for a moment, after which he walked out.

It was that spirit of defiance and determination that kept the local people moving despite the repression, that brought more SNCC workers down as things got tougher, that has sustained black people all over the country. On the night of August 29, after the arrest of Hayes and Watkins, there was a mass meeting attended by two hundred blacks—such a tremendous sight for McComb that the local *Enterprise-Journal* warned that this was no momentary "fussing," that the blacks were serious. At the meeting people decided they would keep on sitting-in and going down to the courthouse.

Two days later there were more sit-ins in McComb and three arrests of high school students including a sixteen-year-old girl named Brenda Travis. In Liberty there was a new registration attempt made in one room of the courthouse while Billy Jack Caston was being "tried" in another room for assaulting Bob Moses. The whites from all over the surrounding area had poured into the courthouse with their shotguns to witness the incredible spectacle of a black challenging the white man's right to hit him whenever he felt like it. The air was heavy with their lust for blood and the sheriff warned the SNCC people to get out of the courtroom while the jury met briefly to find its verdict.

Moses left the courtroom with the two witnesses for his case and went over to the registrar's office to join Travis Britt, a newly arrived SNCC staffer who was down there with the people trying to register. But Britt had been told to get the hell out of the office and went to wait outside the courthouse. As Moses approached him, two shots rang out. Fortunately no one was hurt and the source of the gunfire remained unclear. But the office was closed for the rest of the day and none of the black applicants were registered.

A first attempt at registration was made in Walthall County on August 30, and again two well-qualified applicants, including a senior political science major, were found "unsatisfactory." But the surge of activity mounted and continued into September. By this time almost the entire SNCC staff was in McComb. Then, on September 5, Travis Britt was the target of a new white attack when he again went to the registrar's office. He reported:

There was a clerk directly across the hall who came rushing out while we were waiting, and ordered us to leave the hallway. He said he didn't want a bunch of people congregating in the hall. So we left and walked around the building to the courthouse, near the registrar's window. By the time we reached the back of the building, a group of white men had filed into the hall in about the same spot we had been congregating. They were talking belligerently. Finally, one of the white men came to the end of the hall, as if looking for someone. He asked us if we knew Mr. Brown. We said we didn't. He said "You boys must not be from around here." We told him he was correct.

This conversation was interrupted by another white man who approached Bob Moses and started preaching to him—how he should be ashamed coming down here from New York stirring up trouble, causing poor innocent people to lose their jobs and homes, and how Bob was lower than dirt on the ground for doing such a thing. Bob asked why the people should lose their homes just because they wanted to register and vote. The white gentleman did not answer the question, but continued to preach.

At this point, Bob turned away and sat on the stoop of the courthouse porch, and the man talking to him took a squatting position. Nobody was saying anything. I reached in my pocket and took out a cigarette. A tall white man, about middle-age, wearing a khaki shirt and pants, stepped up to me and asked, "Boy, what's your business?" at which point I knew I was in trouble. The clerk from the hallway came to the back door leading to the courthouse with a smile on his face and called to the white man: "Wait a minute!" At this point, the white man hit me in my right eye. Then, I saw this clerk motion his head—as if to call the rest of the whites. They came and all circled around me, and this fellow hit me on my jaw, then on my chin. Then, he slammed me down. Instead of falling, I stumbled onto the courthouse lawn. The crowd followed—making comments. He was holding me so tight around the collar, I put my hand on the collar to ease the choking.

The clerk hollered, "Why don't you hit him back?" This set off a reaction of punches from this man. He was just hitting and shouting, "Yes, why don't you hit me, nigger? Yes, why don't you hit me, nigger?" I was beaten into a semiconscious state; my vision was blurred by the punch in the eye. I heard Bob tell me to cover my head to avoid any further blows to the face. Then, this fellow yelled, "Brothers, should we kill him here?" I was extremely frightened by the sincere way he said it. No one in the crowd answered the question, and the man released me. Moses then took me by the arm and took me to the street—walking cautiously to avoid any further kicks or blows.

The Travis incident was the beginning of a series of blowups.

On September 7, John Hardy accompanied two persons to the registrar's office in Walthall County. The registrar refused the people the right to register. Said Hardy:

I entered the office to ask, "Why?" The registrar, John Woods, had seen me on one other occasion—the 30th. After telling him my name, he came out—very insultingly and boisterously—questioning my motives and reasons for being in Mississippi, and said I had no right to mess in the "Nigger's" business, and why didn't I go back where I came from. He reached in his drawer and ordered me out at gunpoint. As I turned to leave, he struck me over the head with the pistol.

I staggered out into the street and walked about a block. I decided to go to the Sheriff's office to report the assault and, possibly, make charges. But this was not necessary, because the sheriff found me. He told me to come with him or he would beat me "within an inch of your life." After being put in jail [the charge was resisting arrest and inciting a riot—and later disorderly conduct] about 7:30 that night, after being interrogated at length by a city attorney, and later by the district attorney, I was taken to Magnolia Jail for "your own protection."

The Justice Department entered, immediately, on John Hardy's case. They filed a suit in the Federal District Court in Jackson, asking that a temporary injunction be issued stopping Hardy's trial, which was to take place on September 10. Judge Cox, who was the first appointee of President Eisenhower and a longtime friend of Senator Eastland, refused to give them a favorable hearing. It was probably a victory that he heard it at all. The Justice Department representatives then flew to Montgomery and woke up Judge Reeves in Montgomery, Alabama, at midnight to get a temporary injunction, overruling Judge Cox.

John Hardy was scheduled to be tried in Walthall and Bob Moses went with him. It was announced that the Justice Department had obtained a stay from Judge Reeves in Alabama and that the trial would be held over. As Moses and Hardy tried to leave, the white mob that had gathered grabbed John by the shirt-sleeves and threatened to kill him. They finally got out to their car, at which point a door of the vehicle stuck. A local policeman warned them that he couldn't hold the whites back any longer. The door finally opened and they got away.

Meanwhile, the three high-school students, including sixteen-year-old Brenda Travis, were still in jail with five thousand dollars bail on each for sitting-in. Money had to be raised to get them out. But even under this and all other pressures, the project managed to keep operating; workshops in nonviolent and direct action were being held, while canvassing and citizenship school activities continued in the rural areas.

Behind the scenes, the whites of McComb were moving in a very organized fashion. Bob Moses reported in a confidential memorandum to SNCC:

The Justice Department began a detailed investigation during the week of September 11th. They dug out information about meetings between the whites which were taking place regularly during the last week of August, beginning Aug. 28th, and the first week of September. We believe that as a result of the meetings, the beatings of Aug. 29th and Sept. 5th occurred; a list was circulated with the names of the people who had attended the voting schools; another list was circulated for white people to sign to effect the cutting off of Negroes and whites from the commodities; systematic pressure was put on Negroes connected with the schools to pay their bills.

The next day, September 25, Herbert Lee was killed. Herbert Lee of Liberty, black, age fifty-two, father of ten children, active in the NAACP and then in the voter registration project, was killed with a .38 pistol by Eugene Hurst, white, a state representative.

Hurst was never arrested, booked, or charged. A coroner's inquest ruled that the killing was in self-defense and he walked out free forever.

Three years later, on January 31, 1964, Lewis Allen, one of the key witnesses in the killing of Herbert Lee, was planning to leave Mississippi the next morning and look for work in Wisconsin. That night they found him dead in his front yard. He had been shot with a shotgun three times.

In a society where such things as the killings of Lee and Allen were not the unusual but the expected occurrence, it seems incredible that the spirit of McComb continued to burn as long as it did. It was the high school students who kept on pushing, the students and the SNCC workers. People sometimes said, "You have to be crazy to walk into the face of death like that—on purpose." But they did, and with not much for support except an anger rooted in centuries of oppression and a sense of common cause.

At the Burglund High School, the principal—Commodore Dewey Higgins—indicated that the students who had been jailed for sitting-in would not be able to reenter school for the fall semester. A number of their classmates took the position that, if this happened, they, too, would not attend classes. On October 4 a total of 118 students walked out of school and marched downtown in protest. They marched to City Hall, headed by the three students and the two SNCC workers—Curtis Hayes and Hollis Watkins—who had just been released from jail. Curtis began to pray from the steps of City Hall; a policeman asked him to move along. He refused. And refused again, and again. The police blew their whistles, a mass arrest followed. Bob Zellner, a SNCC worker who had arrived the day before and the only white person on the march, was jerked aside and choked by a white man. Two black SNCC workers threw themselves around him, to protect him with their bodies. The entire group was soon herded up the steps and thrown into jail. They were quickly released, with trial set for October 31.

The students were suspended for three days and then allowed to go back to school—on condition that they signed Commodore Higgins's affidavit acknowledging that they would be expelled if they participated in such a demonstration again. About eighty decided not to sign and many had their parents' strong support. They went to school carrying their unsigned affidavits, expecting expulsion. That afternoon more than a hundred students walked out again. This is the statement they issued:

We, the Negro youth of Pike County, feel that Brenda Travis and Ike Lewis should not be barred from acquiring an education for protesting an injustice. We feel that as members of Burglund High School they have fought this battle for us. To prove that we appreciate their having done this, we will suffer with them any punishment they have to take. In the schools we are taught democracy, but the rights offered by democracy have been denied us by our oppressors; we have not had a balanced school system; we have not had an opportunity to participate in any of the branches of our local, state, and federal government; however, we are children of God, who makes the sun shine on the just and the unjust. So, we petition all our fellowmen to love rather than hate, to build rather than tear down, to bind our nation with love and justice with regard to race, color, or creed.

SNCC workers set up a freedom school, "Nonviolent High," to provide some education to the expelled students. Chuck McDew took charge of history, while Dion Diamond handled physics; Moses took care of math and English, and a little French was also taught. Eventually Campbell College in Jackson said that they would accommodate the students, immediately, and within a short time everyone was back in school.

On October 31, a dozen high school students, along with Moses, McDew, and Zellner, were sentenced to four months in jail each. Robert Talbert, Ike Lewis, and Hollis Watkins, who had organized the walkout, were given six months. Brenda Travis was sent to reform school for a year. The students remained locked up until December 6, when thirteen thousand dollars in appeal bonds was finally raised. It was during this jail term that Moses wrote a moving letter which would become well known in the movement:

November 1, 1961

I am writing this note from the drunk tank of the county jail in Magnolia, Mississippi. Twelve of us are here, sprawled out along the concrete bunker: C. Curtis Hayes, Hollis Watkins, Ike Lewis, and Robert Talbert, four veterans of the bunker, are sitting up talking—mostly about girls: McDew ("Tell the story") is curled into the concrete and the wall; Harold Robinson, Stephen Ashley, James Wells, Lee Chester Vick, Leetus Eubanks, and Ivory Diggs lay cramped on the cold bunker; I'm sitting with smuggled pen and paper, thinking a little, writing a little; Myrtis Bennett and Janie Campbell are across the way, wedded to a different icy cubicle.

Later on Hollis will lead out with a clear tenor into a freedom song. Talbert and Lewis will supply jokes, and McDew will discourse on the history of the black man and the Jew. McDew, a black by birth, a Jew by choice, and a revolutionary by necessity, has taken the deep hates and loves of America, and the world, reserved for those who dare to stand in a strong sun and cast a sharp shadow.

In the words of Judge Brumfield, who sentenced us, we are "cold calculators" who design to disrupt the racial harmony (harmonious since 1619) of McComb into racial strife and rioting; we, he said, are the leaders who are causing young children to be led like sheep to the pen to be slaughtered (in a legal manner). "Robert," he was addressing me, "haven't some of the people from your school been able to go down and register without violence here in Pike County?" I thought to myself that Southerners are exposed the most, when they boast.

It's mealtime now: we have rice and gravy in a flat pan, dry bread and a "big town cake"; we lack eating and drinking utensils. Water comes from a faucet and goes into a hole.

This is Mississippi, the middle of the iceberg. Hollis is leading off with his tenor, "Michael row the boat ashore, Alleluia; Christian brothers don't be slow, Alleluia; Mississippi next to go, Alleluia." This is a tremor in the middle of the iceberg—from a stone that the builders rejected.

Bob Moses

That was the purpose of SNCC—to create tremors in icebergs. And we were succeeding.

Three Journal Entries

ELLEN GILCHRIST

Journal Entry, January 2, 1985, New York City, New York.

I AM HEAVILY under the influence this morning of a movie called *The Gods Must Be Crazy,* about a family of African bushmen in Botswana. These bushmen never say a cross word to their children and the children grow up to be the sweetest, gentlest, most light-hearted people in the world. Sir Laurens Van Der Post writes about these people, in books with wonderful names like *A Mantis Carol,* and *The Lost World Of the Kalahari* and *The Heart Of the Hunter.*

I'm a sort of bushman. My mother never said a cross word to me. Even when she would pretend to discipline me, when she would knit her brows together and screw up her lips and try to bring a little order into the chaos of my passionate response to life, I knew she didn't have her heart in it. I knew she thought it was funny as all get out when I was wild and crazy. She still thinks it's funny.

She'd fit right in with those bushmen. She's got this gift of knowing that life is supposed to be a happy outrageous business. Let's go shopping, that's her idea of how to discipline an unruly child. I think you need some new shoes. Let's go to lunch, let's go over to Heather's and see her toys.

I almost never went to school. That's why I'm a writer. Anytime I wanted to I could wake up and say I was sick and she'd let me stay home and read books. If she came into my room I'd start turning the pages real slowly like I was barely able to lift the book or I'd clutch my stomach or my head. She would bring me cool drinks and bathe my face with a warm cloth and around noon she'd show up with a sickbed tray, chopped steak and mashed potatoes and baked apples dyed green, one of her specialties.

Then, when it was afternoon and too late to get sent back to school I'd recover and get dressed and go outside and get in my treehouse and finish my book. I was reading about ten or twelve a week at that time. The stars on my reading chart fell off the board and dripped down onto the floor.

I really think this bushman stuff has a lot to do with my being a writer. I'm doing the same thing right this very minute that I did in the third grade. I'm all alone in a bedroom with some cookies and a drink, surrounded by books.

When I get through for the day, when I recover, I'll get dressed and go down to town and see what's going on.

Why have I been doing this? What have I been trying to find out all these long years of my extended bushman childhood? What am I hoping to learn from all this character and scene and plot? I don't know. All I know for sure is that by this means, ever since I was a small child, every now and then I'd get a glimpse, like a shiver, of what's underneath the illusion, and its the promise of another look at that which drives me to do this absurd thing for a living. An intimation of something wonderful and light, a chance to see what's really going on, stars and sub-atomic particles and so forth.

That's the thing that wakes me at dawn and keeps me in this room while everyone else is out in the real world making deals and talking on the phone and running the place.

We live at the level of our language. Whatever we can articulate we can imagine and understand. All you have to do to educate a child is teach him how to read. The rest is brainwashing.

Journal Entry, February 27, 1985, Fayetteville, Arkansas

I found a note to myself on the back of a tablet this morning. Get back to that happy child lying on the yard listening to China, the note said. What it meant was, go back into the self, not the thousand masquerades I am so adept at assuming. Back to that warm fat little girl lying on the grass in front of my grandmother's house, with the grass scratching my legs and the smell of the earth and its incredible richness.

The bayou was going by not a hundred yards away but I was not listening to the bayou. I was listening to China. Right underneath me were thousands of Chinese people hurrying through the streets of their crowded cities, carrying marvelous paper umbrellas, pulling each other in carts, endlessly polite and smiling.

Meanwhile, right there in Issaquena County I was in a houseful of white and black people who were also being very polite to each other, on the surface, but underneath was China, exciting undercurrents, alliances, power and usurpations of power, statements and allegations and rumors. This was not black against white or anything as mundane as that. No, this was Onnie Maud in Glen Allen having allegedly made the statement that Miss Teddy was grieving too long over her dead husband and visiting his grave too often. Onnie Maud and Miss Teddy were sisters.

My great-grandmother, Babbie, and Eli Nailor, the cook, were staying in the kitchen trying to keep out of it, but they kept being drawn into the fray. I hung out in the kitchen all I could in those days, as close as possible to the pantry where they kept the pinch cakes, long trays of yellow cake that we were allowed to break pieces off of in between meals, so I was spending a lot of time on a stool by the pantry anyway and got to hear everything that was going on.

There were German prisoners of war working the fields of Hopedale Plantation that summer and there was fighting in Europe and the Pacific and we heard reports of that every day at noon on the radio. But the war that interested me was the one that was raging between the big house and the house on Lake Washington where Onnie Maud lived with her husband, Uncle Robert, who was the only doctor for miles around.

Onnie Maud was supposed to have said that about Teddy and a cousin in Rolling Fork had reported it to her and Teddy wanted to go up to Glen Allen and confront Onnie Maud and get it over with, but my grandmother was against it and thought they should let sleeping dogs lie. The reason Miss Teddy's husband had died in the first place was because he was trying to save the levee, and she was only twenty-six years old when he died and pregnant and she thought she should get to grieve as long as she wanted to. Who was Onnie Maud to criticize her grief, up there in Glen Allen with her doctor husband in perfect health?

All that summer they would come into the kitchen one at a time and try to get my great-grandmother and Nailor to take sides but they wouldn't do it. Neither would I. I just kept on getting all the pinch cake I could and Nailor kept on sitting in his chair saying this too shall pass away and my great-grandmother kept on making the mayonnaise. She would drop the Wesson Oil one drop at a time into the lemon and the egg, then beat it with the whip.

"What makes it mayonnaise?" I would ask.

"It's a colloid," she said. "Doctor Finley says its called a colloid."

I would stare off into the pantry, filled with the mystery of mayonnaise. Of course, this was a long time ago when people lived in houses where a lot was going on, and China was only the speed of dreams away.

Journal Entry, March 26, 1985, Fayetteville, Arkansas

My cousin, Bubba Finley, was a genius. He was the first boy in Washington County to build a radio that could talk to foreign countries. He talked to England and Australia and France and Mexico and the Caribbean Islands.

Picture a frame house beside a lake. There is a huge magnolia tree in the middle of the front yard and screened in porches around three sides. There is a parlor as big as a dance hall but no one ever goes in it except Bubba's twin sister, Laura, who goes in to practice the piano. Many rooms surround the parlor, going out in all directions, bedrooms, kitchens, halls. My Aunt Roberta and Cousin Nell are out in the yard practicing cheerleading in their heavy white wool sweaters. On the front is a huge green R for Rolling Fork High. It is the middle of August and hot as the gates of hell but they have to wear the sweaters to get used to them for fall. I want to be them more than anything in the world but I am not. I am ten years old and I'm spending the week at Onnie Maud's house as a reward for being reasonable about my typhoid shot. Life is good.

It is midmorning, let us say, and Laura is in the parlor playing "Clair de Lune." Across the road is Lake Washington, the biggest natural cypress swamp in the world, mysterious and wide, beautiful in the morning sun. It is a lake left behind when the Mississippi River changed its course and went to Greenville.

Onnie Maud's husband, Doctor Finley, is in his brick office across the street giving shots and showing his skeleton to children and waiting for an emergency. At any moment a mule will step on someone's foot or someone will break a bone or get bit by a dog or step on a rusty nail and need tetnus. I have seen them drag suffering victims up onto Onnie Maud's porch right in the middle of Doctor Finley's Sunday afternoon nap. The atmosphere was hushed and dangerous and afraid. He would rise from his bed. It seemed as if he slept in his suit. He would take the victim into his hands. No wonder his son turned out to be a mechanical genius. Not that the radio was the only way Bubba's genius manifested itself. He also had an unbelievable tenor voice with a huge range. He would lie out in the backyard sunning his lungs, then rise up and go about the halls, singing, Figaro, Figaro, Figaro, at the top of his voice. I adored him. I adored him more than his piano-playing sister, Laura, or his wonderful older sister, Nell. I adored him more than I did Onnie Maud herself, with her unerring ability to make a ten year old girl look like a princess by the skillful application of a curling iron and Laura Finley's beautiful hand-me-down pinafores and dresses. Talk about genius! How those women could sew.

The first time I made one of these broadcasts for National Public Radio I thought of Bubba. I was in New York City wearing earphones and talking to Bob Edwards, who was in Washington, D.C. A wonderful redhaired girl named Menoli Wetheral was in the control booth. There were soft white things on the walls, reminiscent of the egg cartons Bubba used to line his room with. I was enormously at home in that room. I trusted it to be a place where people were on a quest for truth, the only journey I am interested in going on. This is a writer's journal. You must understand how significant these relationships and correspondences seem to me. How I rely on them to tell me where to go and what to do and who to trust in the world.

Growing Up in Mississippi

LOYLE HAIRSTON

WHEN I ENTERED the United States Navy during World War II, I told everybody that I was from St. Louis, Missouri, which was where I was living when drafted. I did this because I didn't want anyone to know I was really born and reared in Mississippi. By claiming a "Northern" city as home—I had only been living there a few years—I was attempting to erace all traces of my deep South origins. I hated Mississippi. I had no desire to ever return there, even to visit relatives or childhood friends in my old hometown, Macon, a particularly dreadful place for blacks to live.

It was a time when Senator Theodore Bilbo reigned supreme as Mississippi's champion of white superiority. For me Mississippi stood for degradation, brutality, inferiority, exhausting poverty—an aggregate of human horrors inlaid with a venomous white supremacy. I despised its smug backwardness, its fundamentalist pieties, its arrogant presumptions about race and patriotism. Even as a child these conceits affected me deeply, leaving me with a kaleidoscope of bleak remembrances stained with fear, loneliness and frustration.

I remember never having felt safe in my hometown; Macon never allowed the likes of me to feel really at home. My mother did not enjoy the protection of the law; she didn't have access to the justice system the city fathers claimed to uphold according to the laws and principles of the U.S. Constitution. Indeed, when I later learned about German *Master Race* theories and fascist crimes, it occurred to me that I had grown up under a similar terror. (Even the infamous Nuremberg Laws borrowed from the South's Jim Crow laws!)

Thus having grown up under its subjugation, I summarily rejected the South's creed and values. I didn't want to be identified as one of her sons. It seemed a gross insult. I felt that to even admit I once lived in Mississippi would somehow stigmatize me in some awfully embarrassing way. Wouldn't people conclude that I was ignorant, backward, illiterate or in a word—*stupid?*

And as for my hometown, Macon, I saw its very existence as a blight on the human experience. The worst features of Southern society seemed magnified and intensified in this proud old "capitol" of Noxubee County. Being a thriving county seat steeped in antebellum myths, Macon epitomized the celebrated Southern way of life, its very layout reflecting the town's social, class, racial mores. Whites lived on one side of town, blacks another.

I remember vividly the handsome white houses and wide green lawns and the clean, tree-lined paved streets that criss-crossed the white sections of town. A small elite even lived in stately Southern mansions complete with columned fronts, shuttered windows, flagstone walkways and lush flower gardens. The people living in these prosperous surroundings owned and worked in the shops and stores on Main Street. Though they lived within walking distance, many of them drove to work. Always they seemed smartly dressed, even during depression years, in suits and white shirts and ties and stylish "store-bought" dresses.

And well they might, the town's economy being heavily "subsidized" by the cruelly exploited labor of beleaguered blacks who lived, for the most part, at the sufferance of the white folk. This was during the period in the South when White Supremacy reigned with a vengeance, embracing all aspects of social life. The fundamentalist God had deemed the "colored race" the squalid imp of the human family, destined forever to be the "hewers of wood" for their white betters. Law and social attitude ruthlessly enforced the judgement.

Thus the black workforce was relegated to drudgery. The white households described above flourished in prosperity because the ingenius social arrangement provided them with an unlimited source of cheap labor. Blacks cooked their food, cleaned their houses, washed and ironed their clothes, nursed their children, kept their lawns and gardens flourishing. On Main Street blacks served as janitors, porters, delivery boys, chauffeurs, service station attendants—any menial job whites would not perform themselves.

Needless to say, the fruits of this labor and blacks' social status were harshly reflected in the way they lived. Our streets were not paved and when it rained they were turned into quagmires of mud, sluiced with deep, water-filled ruts carved by wagon wheels. Rows of mostly unpainted clapboard houses looked wearily out on those streets and the world, their dilapidation lessened somewhat by the starched curtains brightening the windows; by beds of flowers and rose bushes in the wire-fenced yards. I lived in one of those houses. Ours was a small three-room shotgun-styled "bungalow" on Green Street, part of the "better" section of the black quarter.

The inhabitants of this section of town were hard-working, God-fearing, church-going folk who prayed trustingly to an Almighty God. Six days a week most of them toiled like beasts of burden—but to little avail. Their lives did not change materially; they simply got older, grew weary, took sick and died. There were many funerals during those halcyon days, including the one that saddened me most—the death of my dear grandmother. Though she was a devout Christian, God failed to grant her the alloted "three-score and ten."

Nevertheless, my grandmother, Dicey Ella Dunn left the imprint of her personality on our unhappy world. Tough, iron-willed, possessing a kind of haughty dignity, she raised six children and filled the hearts of two little grandsons with moments of consummate love and joy. And she buried two husbands. Indeed, the home I remember best (and with deep affection) was the one built by my mother's father, Grandma's first husband. (He was handed down to us through stories as simply, "Mr. Johnson.") This gracious place was four long blocks from the home I described above.

Mr. Johnson's house was a double-winged unpainted shingle-roofed building with five large, drafty rooms and front and back porches. A basket-weave porch swing hung from the rafters of the front porch, screened from the scorching rays of summer sun by a lattice of honeysuckle runners. Beds of flowers and scattered rose bushes softened the scruffiness of a large front yard overgrown with crab grass. A small cluster of scrub peach trees blossomed cheerfully every spring in a corner of the yard but disappeared every summer.

This was more than a front yard. Through my grandmother's tales and recollections and commentaries, it was transformed into a gateway to the world, an outpost of the vast and mysterious heavens, a bridge into the awesome depth of the universe. Yes, Mr. Johnson's house was the place where my first remembered dreams were born; the launching pad of my earliest fantasies about the world and its wonders and trepidations. How my brother and I loved cuddling up on either side of Grandma in the cushioned porch swing to listen to her wondrous stories. She told us about the "old days," the time of her youth which to us seemed incredibly fascinating, mysterious and alluring.

On warm summer nights she introduced us to her mother and father and brothers and sisters, to all of our progenitors within the scope of her recollections and imagination. And like warm, friendly ghosts they would come and sit with us in the haunting night quiet under a star-filled heaven, reassuring us that we sprang from a vigorous, enduring lineage. These tales comforted me, made me feel strong and confident. Grandma and my mother tried to shield us from the harshness of the real world; or rather they sought to instill in us the fortitude to weather its blows without wavering in confidence or determination.

Taking refuge in religion, they taught us to believe in God; that faith in Him was the ultimate wisdom and thus the guarantor of the realization of our hopes and dreams. Their God too was a "merciless God." He demanded total submission to His will lest one is prepared for an eternal roasting in *fire and brimstone!* To them the Church was the center of gravity, the Altar upon which God judged the worthiness of human flock. Only those baptised "in the name of the Father and Holy Ghost" could possibly gain entrance into an eternal after-life in "His Kingdom."

Lying, cheating, stealing, deceit, adultery, fornication, drinking and gambling were the recurring themes of preachers' sermons. They trivialized sin and magnified its consequences, condemning lust and ignoring greed, while the larger crimes of war and tyranny and colonialism and the senseless brutalities of rampaging racism neatly escaped scrutiny by these righteous men. Apparently, neither God nor His earthly emissaries dared intrude the wicked domain of wealth and power and white supremacy.

Long before the power to reason found clarity in my young mind, I began to feel uncomfortable in church. I used to listen to the grand singing of the choir and congregation. I listened to the pulsating words of the preacher's sermon and often felt strong inexplicable emotions stirring in my young bosom, emotions that were at once moving and baffling. What did it all mean? In my youthful innocence, I pondered this Almighty God's awesome powers and wondered if He always used them well.

Why didn't He heal the sick, reward goodness and give a moment's respite to the weary downtrodden. The model was my dear grandmother who lay buried in a cold, lonely grave. She prayed to God every day and night, trusting her soul to be placed in the vault of His care. And I don't remember Grandma ever having time to sin, for she worked all the time. After burying her second husband, she was reduced to a drudge by a seemingly pitiless providence. Having no skills as a cook or a servant for whites, she was compelled to "take in washings" for a living. I have vivid memories of the long, grueling hours she spent over the zinc washtub in the backyard; and even longer hours ironing huge piles of (white people's) clothes with a flat-iron that was heated by the hot coals of the open fireplace. Grandma died penniless, broken in health and spirit.

On Green Street we flourished in impoverished middle-class respectability. Mother had also become a home-owner and to own property translated into social status. This elevated Mother to my grandmother's prominence as a member of A.M.E. Methodist Church. She was now entitled to a pew! Though I was unconscious of it at the time, these subtle changes had a decided influence upon my life, my sense of self-esteem and the way I observed the world around me. I became vaguely suspicious that I was important, that I cast a shadow in the world and deserved recognition for it.

And when it was not granted—either at home or abroad—I became rebellious. Like the great Russian writer, Maxim Gorky, I too believed I came into the world to protest. Against what I wasn't quite certain at the time but I began summoning the necessary indignation for the moment. In short, I was proud, sensitive, headstrong. Though I disputed it at the time, people always said that "you take after your mother"—meaning I resembled her in temperament, sensibility and intelligence.

My mother was indeed a woman of keen intelligence, a living refutation to white supremacy notions of the innate dimness of the "nigger" mind. Despite a punitive Jim Crow system that deprived black children of a decent education (few got beyond the fifth or sixth grade) she graduated from high school, valedictorian in her class. A quick, decisive, resolute manner set her apart among most black townsfolk as an "unusual" person, a personality few wished to challenge. In fact, a rather fierce integrity made her somewhat more feared than admired. But most agreed that in a sane and decent society she would have made a contribution worthy of her talents, vitality and creative energy.

But white supremacy scorned such qualities in blacks. From its viewpoint their claims to a sense of dignity simply meant a "spoilt, impudent nigger!" Such people must be compelled to submit, to play the role dominant white society had assigned to them. The South had a heritage to attend—defending the superiority of the white race! The very presence of "free niggers" in its midst was repugnant to its values, a desecration of reclaimed antebellum traditions. Was the blood of Confederate soldiers spilled for such a travesty? Thus, Appomattox jettisoned the full fury of the white South's hatred for the ex-slave. A war of vengeance was declared. The "nigger" would pay in blood for this monstrous humiliation. He would be made to pay in even more devastating terms—by lynching his will and spirit.

My mother grew up in this social climate, with its pervasive terrors swirling round every corner of her life. Still she plunged willingly into the storm, bravely facing down the racist winds buffeting her spirit and determination. She weathered all its lashing blows, never veering from her charted course—to hold her head high above the wicked tides. She never foundered in this resolve. But the course of human events having no moral impulse, life would extract its toll in denial and abuse.

Unable to live with my father she bundled me and my brother off to set up a household independent of the emotional and material spoils of a loving husband. It was a turbulent venture and I don't think it was a rousing success. Though she kept us fed and clothed and housed, we grew up in a home environment somewhat lacking in the embracing warmth of a loving, happy family. Still we prevailed, persevered, thrived and even prospered on the strength of Mother's industry and remarkable energy. Moreover, she found time to nurture and cultivate our active young minds and to instill in us a positive view of ourselves and the world. Perhaps she even succeeded in imbuing us with some of the spiritual vitality that fueled her dynamism.

But the Southern gods were merciless, invoking severe penalties upon those who refused to abide the will of such demons. Mother, however, worshiped no secular deities, a disposition that cost her a chance to teach at the local Jim Crow school, the best job for black teachers in the county. Macon's all-white Board of Trustees could find no fault with her academic credentials. They were excellent and were backed by strong community support. But she refused to open a charge account at any of the uptown department stores—stores owned by our worthy Trustees. Such temerity enraged their free enterprise sensibilities. My poor mother's career was promptly relegated to teaching in country schools!

That year we trundled off to the country for a five-month school year, sandwiched between harvest and spring planting time. It seemed that every year we found ourselves in a different place. The schools were one-room structures with no interior walls or ceilings, crude wooden benches, plank blackboards and a potbellied wood-burning stove in the center of the room. The only light came from small windows, the only exit the front door. Here Mother tried with might and main to impress the mysteries of the Three Rs upon the minds of bewildered country children. I suspect she succeeded too because Mother didn't allow the word "can't" in her classroom.

Discipline posed no problem in these makeshift schools because Mother's firm, compact presence commanded authority. Still I was amazed at the orderliness of the children. Like docile little lambs they quietly took their seats and awaited my mother's instructions, their faces filled with a mixture of awe and anxiety, with a profound confusion shadowing their eyes. And how poorly dressed they were! The boys wore faded overalls, often patched at the knees and seat and denim jumpers and brogan shoes or rubber boots; the girls homemade gingham dresses and ragged ill-fitting coats. But they weren't lacking in pride and vanity. Every day they marched into school with faces glistening with vaseline, their hair plaited in neat squares of braids.

Actually, the patches on my pants were probably more numerous than those of my schoolmates. But somehow I didn't attribute mine to poverty. I had already cultivated enough middle-class conceit to rationalize my predicament—to suppress any reality that evoked either despair or embarrassment. I soon adjusted to the robust, homey freshness of my newfound friends, their vast knowledge of the mysteries of farm-life quickly deflating my "city-fied" self-importance. Yet I didn't really envy them for I found country life boring. For me it lacked the quick excitement one found lurking in the underbrush of groups of people living in dangerous proximity to one another.

In the country people shared the scrapings of a bare subsistence in neighborly cooperation. While in town human character was acutely scrutinized. Daily. Hourly. Tongues wagged, the gossip mill rolled, tempers flared and sometimes blows were struck, by next door neighbors or members of the same church! I longed to be back home. I missed my friends, school, the Saturday "cowboy" movies and serials. I missed the weekend jaunts in the cedar hills. There we fought noisy Indian wars, great gun battles, destroyed armadas of invading ships; we explored the mighty seas along the winding vein of shallow creek, discovering buried treasures and fighting off legions of pirates with Captain Blood derring-do.

Besides, Mother was a much tougher teacher than those in town. She demanded more, especially from her two sons who had no opportunity to invent lies for not completing our homework. Unlike our friends we lived under siege, with no hope of escape. Thus, for me school provided a kind of sanctuary, a few hours respite from a very devout mother. And oddly enough, I liked school. I excelled in my studies and in mischief and I was rarely caught, not because of my cleverness. Most of my teachers simply weren't alert enough.

Lacking adequate teaching skills, they were unable to channel our energy and imagination into creative activity. This contributed to classroom discipline problems. Only two of my teachers could hold their charges at bay—Mrs Lu Goodwin and Mrs Ophelia Lewis. And the latter alone was able to take us on intellectual outings beyond the rough grounds of rudimentary learning skills. Ophelia Lewis was a living monument to the teaching profession. To her it was a mission, a life-long assignment which she carried out with genius and immense dedication.

She tolerated no nonsense in her classroom. She accepted no academic performance below her expectations, the opaque glare of her thick lens glasses masking a deepfelt concern for the well being of all her students. She was intimidating. Weak students thought her heartless, the way she drilled us in our studies, unrelenting in her determination to ignite the creative vigor of our young minds. Considering our needs, she had set a modest goal—to mold each one of us into intelligent, productive, assertive men and women.

Experience had taught her the treachery of white supremacy. Ophelia Lewis knew that all roads to progress were mined with its terrors and she wanted us to be well prepared for its abuses. She wanted to fortify us against life's many disappointments. Education would liberate us from the thrall of ignorance, unleash the vitality of our dreams and free us from ever having to lick the boots of white supremacy. I am personally indebted to her for helping me discover my individuality, for helping me grasp more fiercely a sense of being a somebody.

She sharpened my awareness of a society pledged against my well being, against my enjoying human dignity and freedom. *Plessy vs Ferguson* had sanctioned Jim Crow as a Constitutional right! Destitution and despair marked the lives of generations of blacks victimized by a "separate-but-equal" school system. Yet in school we too sang the National Anthem, we too saluted and pledged allegiance to the flag. But in my heart and mind I knew the pledge was a lie—there was no "liberty and justice for all." Even then I suspected the American Democracy so gallantly depicted in my history books was a pageant of myths, tall-stories told by men contaminated with white supremacy.

I didn't trust the mural these historians painted so unblemished with the harsher details of reality. I didn't trust the rugged individualism their legendary pioneers portrayed in such broad strokes of romanticism. Didn't that vaunted individualism tilt heavily towards greed and national chauvinism? Whole Indian nations perished in the wake of the new settlers' cross-continent drive, a rapine enshrined by historians as the "conquest of the wilderness!" Hollywood further glorified this orgy of genocidal bloodletting. But unwittingly Hollywood also proved more accurate than my history texts in portraying the real state of the Union, past and present.

Cinema images vividly mirror the society portrayed. Thus, prior to the '50s Hollywood never placed a black person (except as a janitor or a delivery "boy") in an office building, a school or a Busby Berkeley chorus line. And those old Andy Hardy movies stated clearly that a "typical American" neighborhood was blindingly lily-white. Non-whites were not neglected, however. Willingly obeying a national mandate to ridicule their humanity, Hollywood enjoyed portraying non-whites as simpletons, buffoons or shiftless rogues. Stepin Fetchit in the movies and *Black Sambo* in my school books portrayed the essential qualities the dominant society attributed to the "Negro race."

White supremacy, Hollywood enlightened me, did not terminate at the Mason and Dixon Line—it swept across the moral wasteland of the entire nation. National sentiment still licensed the view that black citizens "had no rights whites were bound to respect." In this "democratic" atmosphere I grew up, desperate to strike manhood and set my course for an active and productive life. Brimming with youthful innocence, I still wanted to believe that America was larger than Mississippi, that fine ideals guided her destiny. I yearned to live in a place where they were practiced.

Sometimes I would stare with longing at the distant hills and dream of the exciting world beyond. One of my earliest ambitions was to "escape" from Macon, Mississippi, to go North and live in a great city—St. Louis or Chicago or New York. I hated being treated as a "nigger" or a negro or a colored boy, as something less than a pulsating human being. I demanded what Dr. W.E.B. Du Bois had articulated earlier: "every jot and title of (my) full manhood rights."

The North quickly stripped me of my illusions. The world beyond the Mississippi hills turned out to be a grimy, poverty-ridden St. Louis slum. But I sensed something different in its teeming streets. There was a vitality in the people, a bustling flow of humanity moving in long, steady strides. Their eyes shone, there was purpose in their expressions, an inner glow in their cheeks. Disdaining the grim surroundings, they seemed in communion with something grand ahead.

I thought of passengers waiting between trains at Union Station. These slum-dwellers too seemed somehow in spiritual transit, awaiting a train to a freer, happier life. They seemed certain of the schedule. I fell in step with this vibrant flow of humanity and caught a glimpse of my own destination. I too would board that train to find my place in the sun. For most of those waiting, however, the "train" never came. I realized then that mine would be a long and lonely journey.

To Praise Our Bridges

Fannie Lou Hamer

I was born October sixth, nineteen and seventeen in Montgomery County, Mississippi. My parents moved to Sunflower County when I was two years old, to a plantation about four and a half miles from here, Mr. E. W. Brandon's plantation. I've been here now almost 47 years in Sunflower County. My parents were sharecroppers and they had a big family. Twenty children. Fourteen boys and six girls. I'm the twentieth child. All of us worked in the fields, of course, but we never did get anything out of sharecropping. We'd make fifty and sixty bales and end up with nothing.

I was about six years old when I first went to the fields to pick cotton. I can remember very well the landowner telling me one day that if I would pick thirty pounds he would give me something out of the commissary: some Cracker-Jacks, Daddy Wide-Legs, and some sardines. These were things that he knew I loved and never had a chance to have. So I picked thirty pounds that day. Well, the next week I had to pick sixty and by the time I was thirteen I was picking two and three hundred pounds.

We'd make fifty and sixty bales and wouldn't clear enough money to live on in the winter months. My father kept sharecropping until one year on this plantation he cleared some money. It must have been quite a little bit because he bought some wagons and cultivators, plow tools and mules in the hope that he could rent the next year. We were doing pretty well. He even started to fix up the house real nice and had bought a car.

Then one night this white man went to our lot and went to the trough where the mules had to eat and stirred up a gallon of Paris Green into the mules' food. It killed everything we had. When we got there, one mule was already dead. The other two mules and the cow had their stomachs all swelled up. It was too late to save them. That poisoning knocked us right back down flat. We never did get back up again. That white man did it just because we were getting somewhere. White people never like to see Negroes get a little success. All of this stuff is no secret in the state of Mississippi.

Just recently there was this white man going around selling watermelons off of his truck, you know. This white lady saw him comin' down the road and she stopped him. When she asked to look at his watermelons he started acting sort of funny, like he didn't want to show them to her. She kept on asking him and finally he told her that couldn't sell her a watermelon because he had poisoned them and was going to sell them to colored people. Sixty watermelons! And he had poisoned all of them. Well, she went in the house and called the police and they arrested the man. Sure enough all of the watermelons had a deadly poison inside. So I'm telling people not to buy anything off these trucks and wagons that go 'round selling to colored people. Don't even buy from somebody you know. You can't trust these crackers down here.

Now a cracker like that is just too mean to live. I would have made him eat just a little bit out of each one of those watermelons. Not the whole melon, just a slice from all sixty. I'd a-killed him so dead every cracker in Mississippi would've known better than to try a low-down trick like that again.

People think that Negroes just take whatever the white man puts out and likes it. Well, I know different. I remember one time when I was a little girl. There was this man who lived on a plantation out from Drew. His name was Joe Pullum and he had worked on this man's plantation for quite a little while, but the man never would pay any money. So one day this white man wanted to send Mr. Pullum to the hill country to bring some families down to work on his plantation. Mr. Pullum said he would go and the man gave him a hundred and fifty dollars.

Mr. Pullum didn't go to the hills to get the people. He just figured that since the man had never paid him, he would use this money to fix up his house and do different things he needed to do. So after a while, the white man noticed that Mr. Pullum hadn't gone to get the people. He drove up to Mr. Pullum's house one day in his horse and buggy with another white man. He went up to the house carrying his gun with him and asked the Negro about it. Mr. Pullum told him what he'd done with the money and that he considered it his money 'cause the man had robbed him out of more than that anyway. The white man got mad and shot Mr. Pullum in the arm.

Mr. Pullum ducked in the house and got his Winchester and killed that white man dead. Well, the white man that was sitting out in the buggy saw this and he lit out for town, which was Drew. The Negro knew what this meant. As soon as that man got to town he'd be coming back with a lynch mob and they would hang him. So he got all the ammunition he had and went on out to Powers Bayou and hid in the hollow of a tree.

The lynch mob came. I ain't ever heard of no one white man going to get a Negro. They're the most cowardly people I ever heard of. The mob came to get Mr. Pullum but he was waiting for them and every time a white man would peep out, he busted him. Before they finally got him, he'd killed thirteen and wounded twenty-six, and it was awhile in Mississippi before the whites tried something like that again.

The way they finally got him was to pour gasoline on the water of the bayou and set it afire. When it burned up to the hollowed-out stump, he crawled out. When they found him, he was unconscious and was lying with his head on his gun. They dragged him by his heels on the back of a car and paraded about with that man for all the Negroes to see. They cut his ear off and for the longest time it was kept in a jar of alcohol in a showcase in a store window at Drew. I was about eight years old when that happened.

Well, after the white man killed off our mules, my parents never did get a chance to get up again. We went back to sharecropping, halving, it's called. You split the cotton half and half with the plantation owner. But the seed, fertilizer, cost of hired hands, everything is paid out of the cropper's half. My parents tried so hard to do what they could to keep us in school, but school didn't last but four months out of the year and most of the time we didn't have clothes to wear. I dropped out of school and cut corn stalks to help the family.

My parents were getting up in age and weren't young when I was born. I used to watch my mother try and keep her family going after we didn't get enough money out of the cotton crop. To feed us during the winter months mama would go 'round from plantation to plantation and would ask the landowners if she could have the cotton that had been left, which was called scrappin' cotton. When they would tell her that we could have that cotton, we would walk for miles and miles and miles in the run of a week. We wouldn't have on shoes or anything because we didn't have them. She would always tie our feet up with rags because the ground would be froze real hard. We would walk from field to field until we had scrapped a bale of cotton. Then she'd take that bale of cotton and sell it and that would give us some of the food that we would need.

Then she would go from house to house and she would help kill hogs. They would give her the intestines and sometimes the feet and the head and things like that and that would help to keep us going. So many times for dinner we would have greens with no seasoning and flour gravy. My mother would mix flour with a little grease and try to make gravy out of it. Sometimes there'd be nothing but bread and onions.

My mother was a great woman. She went through a lot of suffering to bring the twenty of us up, but still she taught us to be decent and to respect ourselves, and that is one of the things that has kept me going.

In 1930 when she was out working, cleaning up the new ground (or we used to call it deadening) for a quarter, when something flew up and hit her in the eye. When she died she was totally blind because we weren't able to carry her to a good eye specialist. She was about 90 years old when she died with me in 1961.

My life has been almost like my mother's was, because I married a man who sharecropped. We didn't have it easy and the only way we could ever make it through the winter was because Pap had a little juke joint and we made liquor. That was the only way we made it. I married in 1944 and stayed on the plantation until 1962 when I went down to the courthouse in Indianola to register to vote. That happened because I went to a mass meeting one night.

Until then I'd never heard of no mass meeting and I didn't know that a Negro could register and vote. Bob Moses, Reggie Robinson, Jim Bevel and James Forman were some of the SNCC workers who ran that meeting. When they asked for those to raise their hands who'd go down to the courthouse the next day, I raised mine. Had it up high as I could get it. I guess if I'd had any sense I'd a-been a little scared, but what was the point of being scared. The only thing they could do to me was kill me and it seemed like they'd been trying to do that a little bit at a time ever since I could remember.

But I've found out some things since I've been trying to organize in Sunflower County. People ask me, "Mrs. Hamer, why haven't they tried to dynamite your house or tried to shoot you?" I'll tell you why. I keep a shotgun in every corner of my bedroom and the first cracker even look like he wants to throw some dynamite on my porch won't write his mama again. One night somebody come calling up, "We're coming by tonight." I told him, "Come on. I'll be waiting for you." Guess you know that cracker ain't showed up yet. White folks may act like they's crazy, but they ain't that crazy. Ain't no man going to bother you if he know you going to kill him.

Well, there was eighteen of us who went down to the courthouse that day and all of us were arrested. Police said the bus was painted the wrong color—said it was too yellow. After I got bailed out I went back to the plantation where Pap and I had lived for eighteen years. My oldest girl met me and told me that Mr. Marlow, the plantation owner, was mad and raising sand. He had heard that I had tried to register. That night he called on us and said, "We're not going to have this in Mississippi and you will have to withdraw. I am looking for your answer, yea or nay?" I just looked. He said "I will give you until tomorrow morning. And if you don't withdraw you will have to leave. If you do go withdraw, it's only how I feel, you might still have to leave." So I left that same night. Pap had to stay on till work on the plantation was through. Ten days later they fired into Mrs. Tucker's house where I was staying. They also shot two girls at Mr. Sissel's.

That was a rough winter. I hadn't had a chance to do any canning before I got kicked off, so didn't have hardly anything. I always can more than my family can use 'cause there's always people who don't have enough. That winter was bad, though. Pap couldn't get a job nowhere 'cause everybody knew he was my husband. We made it on through, though, and since then I just been trying to work and get our people organized.

I reckon the most horrible experience I've had was in June of 1963. I was arrested along with several others in Winona, Mississippi. That's in Montgomery County, the county where I was born. I was carried to a cell and locked up with Euvester Simpson. I began to hear the sound of licks, and I could hear people screaming. I don't know how long it lasted before I saw Annell Ponder pass the cell with both her hands up. Her eyes looked like blood, and her mouth was swollen. Her clothes was torn. It was horrifying.

After then, the State Highway patrolmen came and carried me out of the cell into another cell where there were two Negro prisoners. The patrolman gave the first Negro a long blackjack that was heavy. It was loaded with something and they had me to lay down on the bunk with my face down, and I was beat. I was beat by the first Negro till he gave out. Then the patrolman ordered the other man to take the blackjack and he began to beat. That's when I started screaming and working my feet 'cause I couldn't help it. The patrolman told the first Negro that had beat me to sit on my feet. I had to hug around the mattress to keep the sound from coming out. Finally they carried me back to my cell.

Over in the night I heard screaming. I said, "Oh Lord, somebody else is getting it too." It was later that we heard that Lawrence Guyot was there. He was a SNCC worker who'd come up from Greenwood when he heard that we'd been arrested. I got to see him. I could walk as far as the cell door and I asked them please leave that door open so I could get a breath of fresh air every once in a while. That's how I got to see Guyot. He looked in pretty bad shape. That was the first time I had seen him and not smiling. After I got out of jail, half dead, I found out that Medgar Evers had been shot down in his own yard.

If them crackers in Winona thought they'd discouraged me from fighting, I guess they found out different. I'm going to stay in Mississippi and if they shoot me down, I'll be buried here. I don't want equal rights with the white man; if I did, I'd be a thief and a murderer.

What I really feel is necessary is that the black people in this country will have to upset this applecart. We can no longer ignore the fact that America is NOT the ". . . land of the free and the home of the brave." I used to question this for years—what did our kids actually fight for? They would go in the service and go through all of that and come right out to be drowned in the river in Mississippi.

There is so much hypocrisy in America. The land of the free and the home of the brave is all on paper. It doesn't mean anything to us. The only way we can make this thing a reality in America is to do all we can to destroy this system and bring this thing out to the light that has been under the cover all these years. The scriptures have said, "The things that have been done in the dark will be known on the house tops."

I've worked on voter registration here ever since I went to that first mass meeting. In 1964 we registered 63,000 black people from Mississippi into the Freedom Democratic Party. We formed our own party because the whites wouldn't even let us register. We decided to challenge the white Mississippi Democratic Party at the National Convention. We followed all the laws that the white people themselves made. We tried to attend the precinct meetings and they locked the doors on us or moved the meetings and that's against the laws they made for their ownselves. So we were the ones that held the real precinct meetings. At all these meetings across the state we elected our representatives to go to the National Democratic Convention in Atlantic City. But we learned the hard way that even though we had all the law and all the righteousness on our side—that white man is not going to give up his power to us.

We have to build our own power. We have to win every single political office we can, where we have a majority of black people. Some folks now are talking about sharing some of these offices with the whites who have been holding them down for the past hundred years. Just because this cracker is starting to show us a few teeth and talk nice doesn't mean he'll move over and let us have some of that power. Some of our people say, "Well let's start slow, this is new to us, we ain't qualified and all that." We know if we think about it that the way the white man qualified to be sheriff was if he talked the loudest about beating us up side our heads. A lot of us know that when some of these deputies or constables go to give traffic tickets—you got to help him spell because he's illiterate. If we ain't qualified for these jobs, then no one is.

The question for black people is not, when is the white man going to give us our rights, or when is he going to give us good education for our children, or when is he going to give us jobs—if the white man gives you anything—just remember when he gets ready he will take it right back. We have to take for ourselves.

So many of our people, though, seem like they don't want to be anything but white. They're these middle-class Negroes, the ones that never had it as hard as the grass roots people in Mississippi. They'll sell their parents for a few dollars. Sometimes I get so disgusted I feel like getting my gun after some of these school teachers and chicken eatin' preachers. I know these Baptist ministers, 'cause my father was one. I'm not anti-church and I'm not anti-religious, but if you go down Highway 49 all the way into Jackson, going through Drew, Ruleville, Blaine, Indianola, Moorhead, all over, you'll see just how many churches are selling out to the white power structure.

The only thing we've had in Mississippi that we could really call our own is the church. Now, the ministers, to get a little money, are selling their church to the white folks so the CAP program can run Headstart. These white teachers and white niggers can't teach black children to be proud of themselves and to learn all about the true history of our race. All I learned about my race when I was growing up was Little Black Sambo who was a simple, ignorant boy. I guess that's all they ever wanted us to know about ourselves. We have gone through too much blood and grief in this movement to let our children be educated to still thinking black is inferior.

We are 91 percent of the poor here in Sunflower County and we are going to control 91 percent of all the poverty money that comes through here. They have stolen from us for too long. That's why these crackers got involved in the poverty program—just another way to steal from black folks.

At the beginning of my young life I wanted to be white. The reason was that we worked every day, hard work, and we never did have food. The people that wasn't working, which was the white folks, they had food and they had clothes and everything. So I wanted to be white. I asked my mother one time why I wasn't white, so that we could have some food. She told me, "Don't ever ever say that again. Don't feel like that. We are not bad because we're black people." So when I hear the word now, Black Power, I think of how long people have used the word black. The white folks used it too, because they called us black this and a black that. But as soon as we identify ourselves as being black, they get scared.

It's nothing but fear that makes this white man scared, because he's had white power for the past three hundred years. I don't think nobody's simple enough to want black supremacy, but I think every man has a right to identify with their own people. Like they have St. Patrick's Day and all like that. Every race on earth, they have a day except us. I think its time for people to know that we have to identify with our own selves.

My grandmother used to talk a lot about how they separated them when they were selling them. She was a slave and she used to tell us how she was first a Gober and then a Bramlett. I didn't know what to make of it when I was a child, but since I've been grown I realized that it was the name that the white people give her. So I never will know what my name really was, because the white people took it from my grandmother when she came over from Africa.

And "Negro." That's another name they give to us. That's why I appreciate the word "black"—black America, because Negro is the name the white people give us just like they give us these other artificial names. You were sold to Mr. Jones and you were called Jones. Sold to somebody else and your name was changed again. What we got to be ashamed of to be called black.

I went to Africa in 1964 and I learned that I sure didn't have anything to be ashamed of from being black. Being from the South we never was taught much about our African heritage. The way everybody talked to us, everybody in Africa was savages and really stupid people. But I've seen more savage white folks here in America than I seen in Africa. I saw black men flying the airplanes, driving buses, sitting behind the big desks in the bank and just doing everything that I was used to seeing white people do. I saw, for the first time in my life, a black stewardess walking through the plane and that was quite an inspiration for me.

I wasn't in Guinea more than a couple of hours before President Toure came to see us. And I just compared my feelings. I've tried so hard so many times to see the president in this country and I wasn't given that chance. But the president over there cared enough to visit us. He invited us to his palace and that was the first time I'd ever had a chance to go in a palace. I just thought it was great to see African people so kind. It was so vice-versa what I'd heard that I couldn't hardly believe it.

One thing I looked at so much was the African women. They were so graceful and so poised. I thought about my mother and my grandmother, two people in particular and how they would carry things. It was so similar to my own family because it's very seldom that anybody see me without something tied on my head. Most of the African people wear their heads tied up. My mother would do the same thing. She could put something on her head, like could have two pails in her hand and a pail on her head and could go for miles and wouldn't drop them. I saw the same thing in Africa; tall women that were just like my grandmother. It got to me. I cried over there. If I'm living here, I just might have some people there. I probably got relatives right now in Africa, but we'll never know each other because we've been so separated that I'll never know them and they'll never know me.

I felt a closeness in Africa. I couldn't speak the French language and a lot of them couldn't speak English, but the comparison between my family and them was unbelievable. Two peoples that far apart and have so many things the same way.

A lot of the things they do over there I've done as a child. Little common things, like they boil peanuts with salt when they're real green. We used to do that so much when I was a child. It just looked like my life coming over again to me. Like some of the songs. I couldn't translate their language, but it was the tune of some old songs I used to hear my grandmother sing. It was just so close to my family that I cried.

I was treated much better in Africa than I was treated in America. I often get letters that say, "Go back to Africa." Now I have just as much if not more right to stay in America as whoever wrote those letters.

The black people have contributed more to America than any other race; our mothers and fathers were bought and sold here for a price; we built this country on our bent back and made it rich by the sweat of our brow; our kids have fought and died for what was called, "Democracy".

So when they say, "Go back to Africa," I say, "When you send the Polish back to Poland, the Italians back to Italy, the Irish back to Ireland and you get on that Mayflower from whence you came and give the Indians their land back."

It is our right to stay here and we stay and fight for what belongs to us.

Fire Over the Town

Barry Hannah

Down in deep deep Mississippi I played "Taps" a number of years for the United Daughters of the Confederacy at their ceremony for the Confederate dead. On my old Conn trumpet I mourned away with sweetness of tone. I felt for the soldiers, so dead, you know.

I had an uncle still missing from World War II, a handsome flyer called "Bootsy" who had disappeared over the South American jungles. Bootsy looked like Buster Crabbe, and for a long time I waited for him to appear on our front porch, having hacked out an incredible journey through the Amazon, say "I'm all right, kid," and take away all my dear mother's grief. Then, neighbors, I'd play my trumpet. You thought you'd heard trumpet playing. Bootsy would tear the ennui of this Sunday School town apart. His plane would come rolling over the cedars and magnolias, permanently on fire but surviving, and shock the old maid librarian with her head full of Tennyson and Hardy.

I'd bring Bootsy into the principal's office, my uncle merry, movie handsome, and a bit dangerous in his leather air jacket.

"Okay, mister, here's my unc. What're you going to say *now?*"

"Tell you what, Solly. This is my neph, a swell kid, lot of jazz. A trumpet man, ya know. I want him" (merry, menacing wink) "to have *free play,* eh? Got it?"

Then we would walk away and I would play some trumpet.

The last time I played for the Confederate dead, around age fifteen, I was calling them directly, *please,* to come out of their graves, lean, mean, hungry, in gamey gray rags, and level the better homes and gardens around me, the very gardens and lawns I had tended out of necessity—raked, mowed, dug, planted. My teenage years were being slain by irises and St. Augustine grass. I knew some jazz by then, and my messages were desperate, personal, ardent. The 82nd Airborne convoy had come through Clinton during the Korean war, and I had been paralyzed with awe, watching men in green, tanks, howitzer after howitzer. Fire at will,

I prayed, sparing my father, a decent guy who once made battleships for you guys down in Pascagoula.

These are not nice things, these dream cinemas of the id. But I am not alone.

Lucky I found a place in the marching band, where John Philip Sousa caressed and tamed my iniquitous soul. I played Sousa on the march for the inaugural of Dwight D. Eisenhower, 1957. I was a tiny bandsman in red wool Napoleonic rig, Sam Brown belts. I was too earnest, straight ahead, in a curious horde of practicing adults and near infants, to ever get a look at Dwight. The band was enormous, everybody was in it, all of us itching in wool, and we were probably very loud and bad. But I knew *my* part to "Washington Post." Sousa had me. There is a robust, muscular, airy wildness in the work of Sousa that engages heart, head, and the odd things remaining. It takes one over entirely. It speaks of higher grace. You are so far beyond tiny torpid grinding towns that revenge becomes irrelevant. It puts the heart in a happy uniform, gets you on a strut straight to blue spangling heaven, and you can feel amazing poetry written on the wind. A good marching band can make the street drop out from under you, and with Sousa it can make the air solid.

I made it to the Tomb of the Unknown Soldier, and there, in 1957 with the Marines standing bully watch, I finally knew where Bootsy was. It was all right. It was good to know, and especially it was fine they had a noble place for him.

Back in Clinton, Mr. Camp, the benign largehearted director with ulcers, brought me out front of the band in the concert auditorium, where I played the trio of "Washington Post" solo with the envious band muted behind. It was not that I was so good, more that I was just so tiny and improbable. But Sousa had me.

Then the great Prenshaw came to direct the band, and my high school years had a hero, an actual living adult that one would follow into flames. He was hip, educated at Northwestern, bebop to Mahler and back. He owned the first Volkswagen in town. His ear was perfect, and he would not dwell with imprecision on the march or in concert. But Prenshaw was no despot. We were not one of those bands of doomed youth paraded out by the village tyrant, honking for their life. It is more that imprecision made Prenshaw sad. He would lower his head and fix his glasses, looking a little wounded with his big eyes behind the thick glasses. You did not want to wound Prenshaw playing out of tune or squawking on a reed. You loved the man and did not want to distress him. You wanted to make him comfortable. You loved to see the slight smile when the tune was *there*, right. Also, he never said, "Ah gosh, I love you kids." Thank God. For, citizens, we were into Ideal Forms. We were making time and space sing. He did not care what you ate. Thank God. We were chomping on the high Olympian wind. Ah ennuied, renegade youth. You do "Eroica" right just once, and you will never be the same again.

The band took all the awards. The band had to apologize to nobody. One day the football coach caught me on the band room steps. I'd dropped football—yes, sports was losing me, and he was into it very solemnly. The implication was I was not a man. But I was. I had a new Reynolds Contempora trumpet and I had a good grip on it. I and the band had conquered Enid, Oklahoma, at the national contest, and I was on my way to conquering New York in the Lions Allstate Band that summer. Furthermore, I did not want to burn the coach's house down anymore. He was so small I could not find him.

I was a man because on the band trip back from Enid, I kissed a girl so long and desperately she disappeared. I was a regarded knight in the army of music. The head majorette loved me, and I had heroic indifference about the matter, a Gawain.

And in the band under Prenshaw. Well, it was the last time in my life I ever blended with anything. I went over the edge with wild Olympian hope, doing a solo mission of some agony with an occasional jolt from the gassy mountaintop, where I sit with Bootsy, Sousa, Prenshaw, and the old lads and lasses of the Clinton High band, drinking bowls of pure sweet form.

So, citizens, always give a cheer when you see a young band of merit come heaving into sight. They are burning the air instead of the town. They are playing for their great dead uncles and are paying you no mind.

Memories of Fawn Grove

PHYLLIS HARPER

I

MY GRANDFATHER WAS A Sacred Harp singer, and the annual Second Sunday Singing each May was a special time in our lives when I was a child. The whole family left early Sunday morning to drive to Oak Grove for the all-day affair with dinner on the ground.

Old Harp singing just about went out with Grandy's generation. It seems sad that it's an almost lost art because it's beautiful and strikingly different from any modern music form. It's also difficult. One didn't become a Harp singer overnight. An ability to read music (though I've heard stories of oldtimers who knew many songs by heart) and years of practice went into the making of a good Harp singer.

Sacred Harp is sung *a cappello,* probably because it developed when many churches didn't even have pianos or organs. The harmony is close and sometimes imperfect. Many songs are written in a minor key and the result is often plaintive and haunting, but lovely. Singers first go through a song singing the names of the notes, which are recognized by the shape. In Harp music only four notes are used—fa, sol, la, and mi. The music is usually written on a four-part brace and the tenor is the leading part, the others being bass, alto, and treble. The treble line is usually high—I can still hear Aunt Nancy Thornberry ring out that top line. Grandy sang bass, except when it was time for him to lead, and I loved his mellow voice that I could recognize even in a group.

Mostly men, but a few ladies, took turns leading songs. They announced the number and often gave a brief sermon as an introduction. Another part of the ritual was "sounding the chord" (on a piano or organ if one was available); then everyone hummed the first notes together to be sure they were on key. The leader held the big heavy songbook out in front of him in his left hand and marked time with his right. As the hand started to chop vigorously through the air, the voices burst into "la sol fa la sol sol la. . . ."

The sermons in song often dealt with the trials and hardships of this life, the rewards awaiting in heaven and the punishment of hell. There were numerous hymns of praise. Many of the songs, some of which have been in writing since the mid-fifteenth century, appear in slightly different form in modern Protestant hymnals. Dedicated singers sang all day, or until their voices gave out. Listeners came and went, spending a lot of time walking through the cemetery and church grounds visiting. Then everyone gathered in groups at noon to spread picnic dinners under the big shade trees.

Grandy was dedicated. I can still see him sitting in his chair by the fireplace at home, glasses down on his nose, practicing to get ready for a singing. He started early teaching me how to sing Old Harp, and I finally learned No. 79—"The Old Ship of Zion"—well enough to lead it, but the truth is that I was never a very good Harp singer. We went to a lot of singings though; many were held back then at county courthouses—inside or on the lawn depending on the weather. And years later, anytime I came home to visit for a few days, he always got out the Old Harp songbook so we could practice a little.

II

Fall was a happy time on the farm at Fawn Grove. Even in memory, there's something about gathering time that is indescribably satisfying and good. Perhaps the old work ethic had something to do with it. Farm folks lived by the maxim that "those who work eat and those who won't starve." All those who were able worked. There was pride in a job well done and in the knowledge that plenty of food for family and animals had been stored for the coming winter. So, satisfaction came naturally as crops were harvested in reward for the past summer's labor.

Watching corn cribs, cotton house, barn loft, storm cellar and smokehouse fill with the bounty made our whole world seem secure. The feeling that accompanied this reaping, especially after a good crop year, was jubilant.

But molasses-making time was the best of all; at least it was for children. I can still smell the sorghum cooking. After Grandy set up our sorghum mill, the project lasted about two weeks until all our cane, then that of some neighbors was cooked off, cooled and stored. The nature of this project brought a lot of hands together and the work went along better because folks could visit and talk while their hands were busy. From early morning till dusky dark, the assembly line from field to mill continued.

The mill was set up in the lane below the house, where wood had already been stacked to keep the fire going, and there were plenty of shade trees. Even if the mornings were chilly, the sun combined with the heat from the furnace under the 5×10-foot cooking pan soon had things warmed up.

Sorghum was stripped in the field, where wooden paddles swung by hand took off the leaves. Two people worked together to cut the stalks. One held a stalk upright while the other slashed near the ground. The cane was put in small piles where the heads were cut off, then into bigger piles to await the wagon. Sorghum was piled on clean grass near the mill after hauling, to be fed by hand into the turning mill where all the sweet raw juice was ground from the pulpy cane. Cane was then thrown across the nearby fence into the pasture for the cows to eat. We called the shredded cane "pummings," though Webster's says the word is "pomace or pumace."

A team of mules patiently walked their prescribed circle turning the mill, their tails flickering at buzzing insects. And there were plenty of these unwelcome guests. They knew a feast when they smelled one, and they must have smelled it from miles away. One person stood over the pan, swishing a long willow switch to keep them from doing kamikaze dives into the boiling syrup. Flies were pesky, but yellowjackets and bees were worse. There was always a danger of bare feet stepping on one. They must have become so syrup-logged they couldn't fly.

Skimming hoes were made from tin lids punched with nail holes and fastened on the end of long poles. The skimmings were discarded, but there was a little edible foam left after each pan of molasses had been drained from the funnel at the end of the pan and poured into storage containers—much to the delight of children who were allowed to taste it.

We made 400 to 500 gallons of molasses in a good year. Some of it went into wooden barrels for family use, and the rest into molasses buckets to be sold. We had plenty of molasses for pouring on hot buttered biscuits to warm up a cold morning, and more molasses for baking gingerbread and tea cakes that made children head for the kitchen after a long walk home from school on a wintry day.

III

Hog-killing came two or three times each winter on the farm at Fawn Grove—the first slaughtering as soon as temperatures dropped low enough. It was a cold job. Cold weather was necessary for the meat to cure without spoiling. Cured and smoked, meat from the last killing in January or February would keep well into spring. Pork was our main meat supply and plenty was cured and smoked, some even canned for use the following summer. Two or three hogs were butchered in a day.

I normally liked any activity that brought neighbors in to spend the day, but hog-killing was not my favorite time. I just didn't like the killing part. Though hunting and fishing, killing chickens and even yearling calves, were a necessary part of life that I accepted, I still dreaded that moment of truth when the shots rang out to kill the farm animals. Only the working animals—milk cows, horses, and mules—were given names. To my inquiry about naming a new litter of baby pigs, my grandfather's terse reply was, "Pigs don't have names." Pigs were penned at the back of the barn where one saw them two or three times a day at feedings, so some feeling for them developed anyway.

From an early age I was normally two steps behind Grandy, helping with any and all farm chores. By mutual agreement, however, I made myself scarce until hog-killing activities were well under way. In fact, I stayed busy in the house and tried not to hear the shots that killed the hogs.

Action started at sunup. By the time the neighbors arrived, equipment was ready and water was boiling in two big black pots that sat side by side near a big oak tree between the barn and the house. The slain hogs were dragged to the scalding place. Boiling water was dipped by buckets full from the pots and poured into a tilted rain barrel that had been carefully secured in position so it wouldn't tilt further and scald the workers. The hogs were dipped in the scalding water, then laid out on boards where several hands went to work with knives scraping off the bristly hair. More buckets of scalding water were poured over stubborn spots and scraping continued until the hides were clean. Cuts were made in both hind legs and a singletree inserted between the tendons. (A singletree, also called a whiffletree, is a wood bar with metal fittings, fashioned so it pivots or swings, and normally used to fasten the traces of a horse's harness to plow or wagon.) A heavy rope tied to the singletree went into a pulley attached to a limb of the oak tree and the hog was raised so it swung free. The head was cut off, the intestines removed, and the inside of the carcass cleaned. Then it was taken down and cut into parts. Hams, shoulders, and middlin' (country bacon) were cooled, then layered with salt in huge wooden boxes in the smokehouse.

At our house, the smokehouse was attached to the north porch, which afforded easy access in bad weather. The front half of it was floored, ceiled, and partitioned off for general storage; the back half had a sand floor. Periodically while the meat was curing, red pepper was sprinkled on a smouldering fire in the back of the smokehouse to discourage insects. When the meat was cured and ready to smoke, it was hung from rafters and a fire of hickory chips was kept smoking for two or three days, turning the meat dark brown.

Lard, sausage, pork chops, backbones, and spareribs had to be taken care of on butchering day. All fat was trimmed off the meat, cut into small pieces, and cooked in the black pots until only brown chunks were left swimming in the hot grease, which was then strained and stored in four-or five-gallon lard buckets. The brown bits of fat were saved for making cracklin' bread. Scraps of meat went through the meat grinder, and were then mixed with spices and pepper for sausage. Some of the sausage was sacked to be smoked later; the rest was canned. Pork chops, tenderloin, and spareribs were also canned.

Some meat was divided for the neighbors to take home with them. But before they left well after dark, there was a supper for everybody with fresh meat and gravy and plenty of my Aunt Ola's hot biscuits.

Growing Up Among the Soon-to-Be Rich and Famous

KENNETH HOLDITCH

THE TUPELO, MISSISSIPPI, of my childhood had a Confederate soldier's statue, which had once been located in the middle of the town's main intersection. But when the traffic passing through, going east to Alabama, northwest toward Memphis, or due west toward whatever lay beyond the Mississippi River, increased in volume with the appearance of more and more automobiles in the 1930s, the town fathers wisely had the monument removed to a corner of the courthouse lawn—not, however, before several local members and officers of high station in the United Daughters of the Confederacy had chained themselves to the base of the memorial to protest the desecration. Finally, the removal had to be accomplished in the dead of night, since the patriotic matrons' determination was limited to the daylight hours. Despite this dramatic episode, however, there was nothing particularly romantic in the old Southern sense of that word in the town in which I grew to maturity.

We had, like any southern town, our share of churches: Presbyterian and Methodist and Baptist—several Baptist churches, since they seemed always to be splintering off from First into Second and Third and Calvary and Bethany and other dissident congregations. We had a few Christian Scientists, an ever growing number of Pentecostals, and several "jakeleg" preachers, one of whom, nicknamed "Blackie," had a weekly radio program which he occasionally missed due to "alcoholic episodes" which often ended in his spending a couple of days in the local jail. We had service stations, grocery and dry goods and hardware and jewelry stores; three ladies' "ready to wear" shops, two men's clothiers, two movie theaters—the Lyric and the Strand—and two pool halls, both located on back streets, both the frequent objects of censure from occupants of the myriad pulpits in town. We had a few good restaurants serving fried chicken, fried pork chops, fried ham, chicken fried steak, fried fish, fried potatoes, redeye gravy, fried okra and vegetables seasoned with hog fat and stewed generally into an unidentifiable mass, because that was the way we liked them; we had as well an abundance of hamburger joints and Kiwanis, Civitan, and Lions and other "knife and fork" clubs as an old friend of my family referred to them. We had, in their day, two Civilian Conservation Corps camps, and a country club, a ladies' Fortnightly Musicale, a U.D.C., of course, and D.A.R. and W.C.T.U., and some women's organization called the Sorosis, which I for several of my teenaged years confused with a disease.

We had Community Concerts, annual visits from the Virginia Barter Theater, and from the Blue Mountain College operetta society, in whose productions all the parts, male and female, were played by undergraduate women. We had the glamorous (for those of us who were young) Mississippi-Alabama Fair and Dairy Show, which was within a few years to gain by one of those odd accidents of fate a place for itself in American musical history and finally to achieve in the 1980s the distinction—of debatable value no doubt—of being part of a question in the game called Trivial Pursuit, which was based on false information, by the way.

We had a population made up for the most part of Anglo-Saxons and blacks, although a scattering of Jewish and Italian and Greek residents, with one Belgian and one Creole from New Orleans, added spice to the mixture. We had our village atheist and a couple of village drug addicts—"dope fiends" as we rather inelegantly and perhaps a bit melodramatically referred to them in those days before euphemism became a national pastime—one of them the scion of a pioneer family of the area, whose particular devotion was, I recall, to paregoric. We also had our village Republican, just one, the father of a classmate and friend of mine, who cast Tupelo's sole vote for Thomas Dewey in the 1948 election, thereby aligning himself, for all those who knew his identity, with the camp of the dope fiends and the atheist. We had our fair share of eccentrics—men and women—those non-conformists who contribute to a town, if nothing else, an endless source of conversation, or, if you will, gossip. There was a man who claimed to have created fried bananas as a dish; a woman who insisted that she had drunk no water for twenty years, having survived exclusively on Coca Cola; another woman who professed to know government secrets and to be, as a result, the target of Communist agents. We had piano teachers,

Avon ladies, Fuller brush men, insurance salesmen, wife beaters, a couple of kleptomaniacs, one flasher, one woman who had tried out for the part of Scarlett O'Hara, a score of inveterate liars; four bootleggers, one of them a woman, and several fortune tellers, who worked out of their homes.

We had clean air and pure water!

We had a public library, two railroad lines, a federal fish hatchery, a meat packing plant famous for its country sausage made by a *secret recipe*, two garment manufacturing companies ("shirt factories" in the local parlance), a hospital, any number of doctors, several dentists, three chiropractors, and too many lawyers. We had several barbers and beauticians, two optometrists, numerous postmen and firemen and policemen; a sheriff, a mayor, a city council, and one mediocre newspaper whose Sunday comics were printed without color on pink paper. We had three hotels, one named not after Robert E. Lee but after Jefferson Davis, three drug stores, three banks, one of which had the distinction of having been robbed by Machine Gun Kelly, a reasonably good high school football team named, for God knows what reason, the Golden Wave, and three funeral parlors, two white and one black. We had, on the outskirts of town, two battlefields; one, Ackia, site of a decisive engagement during the French and Indian wars; the other associated with the history of the famous cavalry general Nathan Bedford Forrest. We had a military academy for many years until it closed and the buildings were taken over by a Pentecostal Bible college. We had an occasional murder and subsequent trial; a marital scandal now and then; a suicide every few years, and two couples who drove off in a T-Model Ford to the World's Fair in New York and were "never heard of again." We had dogs, cats, canaries, goldfish. We had a German shepherd who had served in the war and was given a military funeral with a twelve-gun salute.

We had, in short, everything a community needs to make it a reputable town, everything even to make it a recognizably Southern town, except for one crucial ingredient. Those rich (as they seemed to most of us at least) businessmen from Chicago and Detroit and those affluent wheat farmers from Iowa and Minnesota in their Cadillacs and Imperials passing through Tupelo on their way to spend winters in Florida must have thought, perhaps even said to their wives dreaming of suntans and sandcastles and perhaps even supple bronzed beachboys that awaited, "Can anything good come out of a burg like this?" Indeed, judged by appearances the town, which lies in a shallow valley scooped out of the hills sixty miles south of Tennessee, thirty miles west of Alabama, was unprepossessing then, is even more so now that industry and shopping centers and franchises for every kind of fast food ever dreamed of by man in his most voracious state line the new four-lane highways that encircle and bypass the self-proclaimed first T.V.A. city even as they seem to squeeze the life out of it. And there is that one crucial ingredient that is lacking, that one blot on the escutcheon—Tupelo was built *after* the War Between the States, which to a deep southern town is tantamount to being born out of wedlock, and although the Chamber of Commerce through the decades has latched onto various claims to fame, some dubious, some valid, there is no escaping that one awful void in the make-up of the community. Without antebellum homes—you will perhaps have noted their absence in the list above—including bedrooms where some rebel general or other slept, twenty-four place settings of silver with the family crest, holes in the library walls where yankee cannon balls came near to killing Granny or Great Uncle or Aunt, how could an overgrown village, centrally located at the intersection of two federal highways and one state road, hope to compete with those sister communities, Columbus and Oxford and Holly Springs, adorned with accoutrements of history like Southern belles laden down with the ancestral jewels? Not even the 1935 visit of President Franklin Delano Roosevelt and the locally detested Eleanor to dedicate a homestead community of some thirty-five houses north of town could raise it to any kind of legitimate status, could authenticate for it that sense of place that is vitally necessary for the Southern town.

That valley was in a paradoxical way to prove both a curse and a key to fame for that poor little bastard town, sprung up like a mushroom out of the rubble of war and Reconstruction. In 1937 a tornado ducked briefly down into the declivity and, departing, left behind unbelievable devastation of property, more than three hundred dead, and countless injured. For the next two decades, this was to be Tupelo's only claim to any kind of fame—or perhaps notoriety is a better word—"First T.V.A. City" notwithstanding, and old-timers (though in those days any native of Oxford or Holly Springs would have snickered at applying that label to any resident of such an upstart village) judged you not by your forebears alone but by whether you were B.T. or A.T., Before or After Tornado. If you had moved there too late to experience the big wind, you were as much an outlander as those transient Yankees in their expensive cars.

Before the middle of the twentieth century, Tupelo had produced only two famous citizens. Oh, there were plenty who ached to be sublime or fed on their descent, to use Edwin Arlington Robinson's phrase, and several who probably even thought that they had made the grade, but only two had achieved any degree of national recognition beyond that valley in which the town existed. One was a mere politician, flamboyant and interesting it must be admitted, an orator of the old school it cannot be denied, but his primary claim to posterity's attention involved his having hurled an inkwell at a fellow representative in the halls of Congress and having hurled racial epithets at a few other Congressmen, who had the bad judgment and taste to have been born Yankees and, of course, not Anglo-Saxons and had crossed his ideological path. The other, however, had achieved for himself an admirable place, still acknowledged periodically even today in various histories or compendiums of humor, as—though it seems like an anachronism in that day—a stand-up comedian.

Private John Allen was a Civil War veteran who acquired his unique honorific during a political campaign following the war. After his opponent, General "Bulldog" Tucker, who had lost an arm in conflict, had delivered his glory- and rhetoric-laden speech, Allen rose to commend his opponent for his achievements in the war and to urge all those in the audience who had been generals to vote for Tucker and all those who had been privates to vote for him. He won the election by a landslide and from that day forward was known as "Private." Among the famous and humorous speeches he delivered in the Congress of the United States is one in support of the establishment of a fish hatchery in Tupelo. President Lincoln, according to Allen, when told that the Southern states were threatening to secede from the Union, had replied in alarm that it must not be allowed to happen, that the nation could not afford to lose Tupelo (which, in reality, had not even been founded or dreamed of at the time). Millions of fish yet unborn would, according to Private John Allen, walk across land from all over the country for the privilege of being born in Tupelo. The fish hatchery was approved by an overwhelming majority of the Congressmen.

This then was Tupelo until the 1950s, a quiet, unassuming, not particularly Southern town which was, despite its anonymity and

Bethlehemesque quality, a good place to live, a good place to grow up. And then, in that middle decade of the twentieth century, another kind of tornado put Tupelo on the map of the world in a way that the old timers were not then and have not since been willing to acknowledge. Like the little old ladies who, or so the apocryphal stories go, left movie theaters in droves during screenings of *Gone with the Wind* at the first mention of General William Sherman's name, the town fathers and the dowagers of Tupelo could be counted on through the two decades after he gave their town a place of sorts in history to blush and turn away or scoff or snort at the mention of the name of Elvis Presley.

Despite their scorn and disavowals, however, Elvis would not disappear; his reputation grew and grew and after a while people all over the world knew about a little country town with a strange Indian name. Three years ago a teen-aged Japanese girl, visiting the United States for the first time with her professor father, asked me where I was from, and when I replied in typical Mississippi fashion, forgetting the places in which I had lived for two decades since leaving my hometown, "Tupelo," her face lit up and she squealed, in what I supposed to be an Oriental manner, "Oh, Elvis!"

He was born in East Tupelo, a low-lying part of the town subject in those days to periodic spring floods, a collection of jerry-built shacks that could have been used for a movie set of an Eastern mill town. It was 1935, and Mississippi was still in the grips of the Depression. Yes, we knew about F.D.R. (after all he had visited us) and N.R.A. and had the C.C.C. and the W.P.A., but it took World War II to bring any degree of prosperity to a region not yet even fully recovered from Reconstruction. A sad and dismal and wholly unlikely spot for the beginning of one of the strangest phenomena in musical history.

He would grow up there, attending Lawhon Jr. High School until the eighth grade when he would transfer with others of his age to Tupelo High. We who were already in the school were not kind to them, I suppose, being no kinder by nature than most young people. They were outsiders, and such is the nature of the human beast, especially at thirteen and fourteen and fifteen, that an outsider is a convenient target of whatever animosities may have developed or are developing.

I remember the first time I ever saw Elvis Presley, though I did not know his name then and was not to know it as a matter of fact until a decade later when almost everyone everywhere knew it. A sad, shy, not especially attractive boy, a bit clumsy, he stood on the stage of the Emma Edmonds Auditorium playing that cheap guitar about which much has since been written, as participant in a talent contest. I did not predict fame. And I did not help him with his math, as many of my contemporaries from Tupelo recall having done; he must have had the best math grades in Miss Essie Patterson's teaching career, with all that assistance.

Then he was gone, leaving almost no mark on the town or on the memory of its residents, except for his many relatives and few friends. The rest of us went on, finished high school, perhaps went to college or the Korean War or a variety of jobs, some of us achieving such laurels as are dear to the hearts of small town boys and girls—or at least to their parents—while Elvis just sort of . . . well, *fell* into immortality.

What can one say about him that has not been said already so often that it has become trite? That he never forgot what he had come from: he returned to Tupelo often, twice in concert at that Mississippi-Alabama Fair and Dairy Show, year after year to visit aunts and uncles and cousins and friends and a favorite school teacher from the old East Tupelo days, and donated a small fortune to build a park for young people in that deprived part of town. That he had a sense of humor: to one of the wealthy citizens of the town, whose two sons had had money and their own cars in the days when Tupelo High didn't even need a parking lot for its teachers, let alone for students, Elvis remarked, "Aren't you sorry you didn't buy those boys a guitar 'stead of a Cadillac?" That his long journey from such a lowly beginning to such immeasurable and incomprehensible (for most of us) fame and fortune was so fantastic that Horatio Alger would hardly have dared to write about it.

Adversely, one can say and should say that his life style exhibited some of the worst aspects of the American dream gone wrong: materialism, conspicuous consumption with a vengeance, abuses of body and consciousness. But given the background, the years of deprivation, of being an outsider, surely even the moralistic critics of our society can forgive that.

After the life he lived, the fame he achieved, never again would Tupelo be that forgettable town, born too late, unknown, unsung, unhonored. America's first T.V.A. city, sprung up belatedly where the highways and the railroad lines crossed, had been acknowledged and blessed; the Spirit of Place had descended upon it.

The Afternoon of a Young Poet

M. CARL HOLMAN

IN THE LATE WINTER of my senior year in high school I entered a poem in an annual literary competition sponsored by the Arts Club of St. Louis. Because I was almost pathologically shy, and because I was not sure I actually intended to go through with it until I was picking my way back up the icy street from the corner mailbox, I told no one what I had done. Until that night I had submitted poems to Negro newspapers and magazines and had won one or two small prizes, but I had never before ventured to enter a "white" contest.

I had found the announcement of the Arts Club competition in the section of one of the white dailies where I read avidly about plays, concerts and ballets which might just as well have been taking place on the moon. During that period of my life I was strongly influenced by three or four university-trained teachers on our high school faculty who were still caught up in the afterglow of the Negro Renaissance. Mr. Watts, Miss Armstrong, Mr. Blanton and Miss Lewis taught us from the "lilywhite" textbooks prescribed by the St. Louis school system, but they also mounted on their bulletin boards the works and pictures of Langston Hughes, James Weldon Johnson, Claude McKay, Sterling Brown, Countee Cullen and Jean Toomer.

Entering the contest, however secretly, represented unusual daring for me, though it would have been as easy as breathing for Miss Armstrong, a vibrantly energetic mahogany-skinned woman whose voiced flayed our budding manhood with contempt when she read McKay's poem "If We Must Die." (Her voice accused and disturbed me, conjuring up two confusing memories from my childhood downtown on Carroll Street—the first, that day in the depths of the Depression when half the fathers on the block straggled back from their protest march on City Hall, their heads broken and bleeding. Some of them weeping, but only one of them laughing. The potbellied little man next door who came stumbling up the alley apart from the others, tittering like a drunken woman, one eye puffed shut, his bloody rag of a shirt dragging in the dust. Giggling and whispering, *"Don't hit me no mo, Cap'n. You the boss. You sho God is the boss. . . ."* And less than five years later, Big Crew, standing in the middle of the yard, his lips drawn back from his blue gums in a wolfish grin, smashing his black fist like a hammer into the rent man's face, picking the man up like a sack of flour and knocking him down again. All the time talking to him as quietly as one friend to another: *"Git up and fight, you peckerwood sonuvabitch. Git up and fight for your country."*)

I yearned during those high school years to write something as defiantly bitter as McKay's "If We Must Die" or Sterling Brown's "Strong Men." My temper was capable of flaring up and consuming me so utterly that during a period of a few months I found myself in wildly hopeless fights with the older boys. Deep in hostile north St. Louis I had placed my life and those of two boys with me in jeopardy when, without thinking, I spat in the face of a young white boy seated on the stoop surrounded by at least seven members of his beefy family, because he called me a "skinny black nigger" as my friends and I were passing. My mother's long campaign to curb my temper had only taught me at last to swallow my feelings, hiding them so deep that I could not have dredged up my rages and despairs and found words for them even if I had wanted to. The long poem I finally mailed to the Arts Club was called "Nocturne on a Hill." Though it was probably honest enough in its way, it echoed more of the white writers I had been reading and told more about my reactions to the shapes and sounds of the city than it did about the people I loved and hated, or the things which delighted, hurt or confused me most.

We had moved from Carroll Street downtown three years earlier and we were living that year on Driscoll Avenue in midtown, halfway between the river on the east and that section of West End the whites had ceded to the Negro doctors, schoolteachers and postal workers. For a long time after the move to Driscoll Avenue I had continued to go back to the old neighborhood. In part this was because the customers to whom I sold Negro weekly newspapers lived there (ranging from an ancient self-ordained bishop, whose wife was never permitted to expose anything more than a slender wax-yellow hand and a black-clad sleeve as I handed the paper through the double-chained door, to the heavily powdered ladies in the big house on Seymour Street who had bought a dozen papers from me every Friday for a month before I learned how they made their living). But even on days when I had no papers to sell, Carroll Street for a long time continued to have the same love-fear magnetism for me it had exercised when I lived there; racked by sweaty nightmares on nights when the patrol wagons and ambulances pounded past our house, listening by the hour to the Italians singing from the backyards where they had strung light bulbs for the parties that left the alley littered with snail shells and the discarded bottles the winos fought over the next morning. On Carroll Street we had lived closely, though not intimately, with whites: the Italians on Bouie Avenue to the rear, the Jewish storekeepers, the Germans who worked in the bakery and the bank, the Irish truck drivers and policemen (and one saloon keeper who reconverted his storefront when Prohibition ended, returning to its old place in the window the faded, flyspecked sign whose legend we chanted up and down the street: "Coolidge Blew the Whistle, Mellon Rang the Bell, Hoover Pulled the Throttle and the Country Went to Hell").

Driscoll Avenue was a less impoverished and more self-contained world than Carroll Street. Except for the merchants and bill collectors, it was possible to walk through midtown for blocks without seeing a white face. We lived on the first floor of a three-story brick house set on a concrete terrace from which three stone steps led down to the street. My chores during that long winter included keeping the steps salted down and making sure the heavy hall door was kept tightly shut.

My mother was ill for a long time that winter, and the grown-ups came to visit her, stamped into the house wrapped like mummies with only their eyes showing, bringing pots of stew, pickled preserves and the latest tale of some drunk who had been found frozen stiff in an alley or a neighbor who had been taken to "Old Number Two" with double pneumonia. Number Two was the nearest city hospital, and the neighborhood saying was that they did more killing there than Mr. Swift did over at his packing house. Old people in the neighborhood sometimes clung stubbornly to their beds at home, hiding the seriousness of their ailments, for fear they would be sent to Number Two to die. My mother was not old, but I lay awake many nights that winter, listening to her rasping breathing and praying that she would not have to be taken to Number Two. Sometimes, after her breathing had smoothed out and she had fallen asleep, I would get out of bed and go over to the window, raising the shade enough to let in the white winter moonlight. Fumbling for a pencil and piece of paper, I would write lines and fragments which I could not see, then fold the paper and stuff it into my hiding place back of the piano which nobody in the house played.

My mother's conviction that both her children were going to finish high school and college and "amount to something" had persisted in the face of the bleakest realities her native Mississippi and a half-flat near the tracks in south St. Louis could marshal against her. Even in her illness, hollow-eyed and feverish, she wanted to know what we had done in school daily, what the teachers had said, whether our homework was done. A gifted seamstress and a careful manager of small change for most of her life, she never doubted she would one day find the proper use for the patterns, scraps of cloth, Eagle stamps, buttons and pins she scrupulously put aside, each in its proper place. She cooked huge pots of soup, with opulent aromas suggesting magnitudes of power and promise out of all proportion to the amount of meat in the pot. She felt she had ample reason to sing "He Leadeth Me," and when we had amazed ourselves and our teachers by prodigies of nerve-straining effort she only said mildly, "Didn't He promise He would make a way out of no way for those who believed in Him?"

Lacking her faith, I was so beset with premonitions and terrors during those months of her illness that I lost all recollection of the poem I had mailed to the Arts Club. The cousin I loved most had died in childbirth just two years before, at the age of nineteen, and I had been tormented ever since by the fragility of the web separating life and death. Though she met the slightest ache or pain visited on her children as if it were an outrider of the Devil's legions fully armed, my mother regarded her own illnesses as nuisances to be gotten through with as little fuss as possible. By the time the snow had melted in the gutters she was on her feet again, halfway through her spring cleaning and fretting to have the last frost gone so that she could start planting the narrow rectangle of earth out front she called her garden.

I came home from school one afternoon in early May to find a letter from the Arts Club in our mailbox. I was afraid to open it until I had first made sure it was not bulky enough to contain the rejected poem. There was only a single sheet inside, a note typed on the most elegant stationery I had ever seen, congratulating me on the selection of my poem as one of the five best works submitted in that year's contest and inviting me to meet the other winners at the club two weeks later.

The first surge of surprise and pleasure was followed almost at once by a seizure of blind panic. How could I go out there to Westmoreland Place, a street I had never seen, to meet a group of strangers, most if not all of them white—when I stammered or fell silent whenever I had to talk to one of my teachers without the supporting presence of the rest of the class? Reading the note again I saw that the meeting had been scheduled for midafternoon of a school day. For most of that next week I debated whether I should accept the club's invitation or prepare to be sick on that day. Finally, just forty-eight hours before the date set in the letter, I went down to the principal and secured permission to be excused from my afternoon classes to attend the Arts Club meeting.

That same afternoon I showed my mother the letter. She knew me well enough to play down the pride she felt, complaining instead about people who would miss Heaven one day because they always waited until the last minute. She consulted with a friend who worked in the section where the club was located and wrote down the directions for me, dryly reminding me to have the conductor give me a transfer when I boarded the trolley outside the school. I had once had to walk home a distance of some six miles away because I forgot to ask for a transfer. Actually, I was less concerned about the transfer than about the possibility that on the way out to the club I might develop motion sickness. This often happened when I rode the trolleys. Usually I got off the car as soon as the first queasy stirrings began in the pit of my stomach, and walked the rest of the way. But this time I would be in a part of town that I did not know at all. I resolved to ride standing up all the way, trusting that my mother's God would not let me be sick.

I left school on a hazily bright afternoon alive with the tarry tang of smoke and the green smell of growing things which I associate still with spring in St. Louis. It was good to be a privileged truant with the whole block in front of the school to myself, the typewriters clicking behind me in the principal's office and the unheeded voices of the teachers floating out of the classroom windows overhead. The first trolley was a long time coming. When I got on I remembered to ask for the transfer, and though over half the seats were empty on both trolleys, I stood up all the way. But when I got off the second car I found that I had managed to lose the directions my mother had given me. I could not remember whether I was to go north or south from the trolley stop. My palms promptly began sweating and I took out the letter from the Arts Club, reading the address again as if that would give me a clue. In my neighborhood most of the houses were row houses, or were separated from each other by nothing more than a narrow passageway. Even houses like the one we lived in, though not flush with the pavement, were close enough so that the addresses could be easily read from the sidewalk. But out here the houses were set back from wide lawns under shade trees and there was no way of making out the addresses without going up a long walk to the front door. No small children were playing outside, there were no stores into which a stranger might go and ask directions, and the whole neighborhood was wrapped in a fragrant but forbidding stillness. Remembering that my mother had said the club was only two blocks away from the trolley stop, I started walking south, deciding that if it turned out I was going the wrong way I could always come back and go two blocks in the other direction. I walked three blocks for good measure without finding Westmoreland Place, then turned and started back.

A red-faced old man with bushy military whiskers that reminded me of pictures I had seen of the Kaiser came down one of the walks with a bulldog on a leash. I braced myself to ask him where Westmoreland Place was, but before I could speak, his china blue eyes suddenly glared at me with such venomous hatred that I had the feeling he was about to set the dog on me. I averted my eyes and walked on, trembling suddenly with an answering hatred as senseless as his. Not noticing where I was going, I was about to cross into the next block when I looked up at the street sign and found that I was on Westmoreland Place. It was a street of thick hedges and houses which, if anything, were more inaccessible than those I had already passed. I walked up the street in one direction, then crossed and reversed my course. By now the letter was wilting in my hand. The trolley ride had taken longer than I had estimated and I was sure I was already late. One of the last things my mother had said to me that morning was, "Now try to be sure not to get out there on Colored People's Time." My mind groped for a plausible lie that would let me give up the whole business and go home. I thought of saying that the meeting had been called off, that the place was closed when I got there, that I had caught the wrong car and gone too far out of the way to get back in time. At one point, I almost convinced myself that I should go back to the trolley stop and catch a car that would take me downtown to my old refuge, the main public library. I could stay there reading for an hour or two, then claim I had actually attended the tea. But my spirit quailed at the prospect of inventing answers to all the questions that would follow. And what if in the meantime someone from the club had already called my home or the school? I hated myself for entering the competition and felt sick with envy when I thought of my schoolmates who by now were idling down the halls on free period or dreaming their way through the last classes before the liberating bell.

I was plodding down the same block for the second time when around the corner of a big stone house across the street came an unmistakably colored man in work clothes, uncoiling a garden hose. We might have been the only two living souls on a desert island. Almost faint with relief I angled across the street toward him. But the handyman, his high shiny forehead furrowed in elaborate concentration, adjusted the nozzle and began playing rainbow jets of spray across the grass. I halted at the edge of the lawn and waited for him to take note of my presence. In due time he worked himself close enough so that I was able to ask him if he knew where the Arts Club was. I held out the letter as I asked him, but he merely turned his rusty deepset eyes on me with a look that plainly said, *I hope to God you ain't come out here to make trouble for the rest of us*. In later years I have seen that look in the eyes of Negro businessmen, schoolteachers, college presidents, reverend ministers—and a trio of cooks and dishwashers peering through the swinging doors of a restaurant kitchen at the dark-skinned students sitting at counters where no one of their color ever presumed to sit before.

But I was of another generation, another temperament and state of mind from those students. So when the handyman flicked one hand in the direction from which I had just come and said, "There 'tis, over there," I thanked him—rather thanked his back, which was already turned to me.

I would never have taken the two-story brick building at the end of the flagstone walk to be anything other than the residence of a comfortably well-off family. Just before I pushed the button beside the broad door it occurred to me that the handyman might be playing his notion of a joke on me. Then I looked down at the thick mat on which I was standing and saw the letters "A-C." I pressed the button, waited and was about to press it again when the door swung open. The rake-thin white maid standing there had composed for her plain freckled face a smile of deferential welcome. The smile faded and her body stiffened in the neat gray uniform. For an instant I thought she would close the door in my face, but she braked it so that it was barely ajar and said, "Yes?" I mumbled something and held out the letter. She squinted at the envelope and said, "You wait here." The door closed and I stood there with my face burning, wanting to turn and go away but unwilling to confront the expression of sour satisfaction I expected to see on the face of the handyman across the street. After what seemed fifteen full minutes a gray-haired woman in a blue uniform with starched cuffs came to the door. "All right, what is it now?" she said, sounding like a very busy woman. I held out the letter and she took it, measured me up and down with her shrewd eyes and said to the younger woman hovering behind her, "I'll be right back." The freckle-faced thin one looked miles above my head toward the street but we shared the unspoken understanding that I was not to move from where I stood and that she was to watch me.

I stood rooted there, calling myself every kind of black fool for coming in the first place, my undershirt cleaving to my damp skin. It had become clear to me that I had received the invitation by mistake. And now that I had surrendered the letter, the only proof that I had been invited, my sole excuse for being there at all was gone. I pictured them huddled inside, talking in whispers, waiting for me to have the good sense to leave. Then I heard voices coming toward the door. My keeper faded back into the gloom of the hallway and an attractive woman in her forties held the door open and smiled at me. Everything about her, her fine-textured skin, the soft-colored dress and the necklace she was wearing, her candid gaze, defined an order of relationships which did away with any need for me to deal further with the other two women. "Hello," she said. "So you're the boy who came over to tell us Mr. Holman couldn't come?"

I stared dumbly at her, wondering how I could have been fooled into thinking she was one of those white women my mother would have described approvingly as "a real lady, as nice as they come."

"Please tell him we hope he'll be feeling better soon," the woman said. "We had so hoped to meet him."

"I'm—I got the letter saying to come out here," I blurted. We stood there for a minute staring at one another and then her pink skin flushed red. "Oh, you mean you—oh, I *am* so sorry," she said. "Please do come in. I didn't know." She glanced back at the maids. "I mean, we thought—"

It was finally clear to all of us what she had thought. That the white boy who wrote the poem had been unable to come so his family had thoughtfully sent their colored boy to tender his regrets.

"You come right on in," the woman said. "I'm your hostess. All the others are already here and we've been waiting for you." She drew me inside the cool, dim hallway and guided me up the stairs like an invalid. I could not remember ever walking on such thick carpets. I had a hazy impression of cut flowers in vases, and paintings hanging along the walls like those I had seen in the Art Museum in the park. As she went up she kept on talking, but I made very little of what she was saying because now I could hear the murmur of other voices and laughter coming from the floor above us. I had the feeling that an intimate and very pleasant family party was in progress which we were about to ruin and I wanted to ask my hostess if I might not be excused after all. Instead I let myself be piloted into a sunny high-ceilinged room which at one and the same time seemed as spacious as a playing field and so intimate that no one could move without touching the person beside him. A blur of white faces turned toward us, some of them young, some middle-aged, some older, but all of them clearly belonging to a different world from that of the uniformed women downstairs. A different world from mine. For a flickering moment there was a drop in energy like that sudden dimming of lights during a summer storm and then I was being introduced in a flurry of smiles, bobbing heads and a refrain seeming to consist of variations on "Delightful . . . delighted . . . so good you could come . . . a pleasure."

Whenever I have tried to recollect that afternoon since, the faces in that upstairs room elude me like objects seen through sunlit water. I remember that one of the girls was blonde and turned eagerly from one speaker to another as if anxious not to miss one word, that there was a boy there from a school out in the country who talked and moved with the casual, almost insulting assurance which for a long time afterward I automatically associated with private schools. All of the other students there who had won prizes or honorable mentions in the area-wide competition were either from private schools or from white high schools whose very names were new to me. One of the girls was from a Catholic school and one of the sisters from the faculty had come along with her. I discovered that other winners were accompanied by their teacher and I mentally kicked myself for not realizing that I might have been buttressed by the presence of Miss Armstrong or Mr. Blanton. Certainly they would have been much more at home in this company than I was. Gradually, as cookies, tea and punch were passed and the talk again swirled back and forth, I began to relax somewhat, content to be on the periphery of that closed circle. I kept stealing glances around the room, taking in the wide fireplace and the portrait above the mantel of some famous man whose identity kept eluding me, the rows of books in the recessed shelves along the wall, and the magazines scattered tantalizingly just out of reach on the long oaken table in the center of the room.

In school, except to recite, I had rarely ever talked even to my English teachers about poems, books and writers. But this group, comfortably seated or standing about the pleasant room with the haze of spring sunlight sifting through the windows, shared a community of language and interests which enabled them largely to ignore differences of age and individual preference and to move from one idea or work to another as effortlessly as fish in a pond. They talked of Shakespeare and Keats, Milton and Shelley, but there were other writers whose lines I had spoken aloud, sometimes in puzzlement, when I was alone. Now they were being argued over, attacked, defended, ridiculed: Eliot, Frost, Sandburg, Millay, Vachel Lindsay, Amy Lowell, Yeats. There were moments when someone touched on something I had read and I was tempted to speak out in agreement or disagreement. At other times I was overcome by the gloomy conviction that I could never in the years that were left to me read all the works some of them seemed to know by heart. I felt particularly lost as the talk shifted to novels only recently written, to concerts they had attended and plays seen at the American Theatre downtown or "on our last trip to

New York." (I had been drunk for days on the free concert given for Negro high school students by the St. Louis Symphony the year before, shutting myself off in my room with an umbrella spoke for a baton, trying to be all the voices of the orchestra and graceful Mr. Golschmann conducting the *New World Symphony.* Later I was to go to the American as often as I could to see the road companies in performance and, during intermissions, to devour the posters advertising the plays I would not be able to see. Often my companion and I were among less than a dozen Negores present. (Years afterward, on a trip back to St. Louis I was triumphantly informed that Negroes were no longer segregated in the second-balcony seats at the American. Second-balcony seats being all we could afford, my friend and I had never asked for anything else, a neat dovetailing of covert discrimination and economic necessity.)

Toward the end of the long afternoon, it was proposed that the young writers read their poems. Once again I was plunged into sweaty-palmed agony. My torment only increased as the first two readers read their poems like seasoned professionals, or so it seemed to me. When my turn came I tried to beg off, but the additional attention this focused upon me only increased my discomfort and I plunged in, at first reading too fast and almost inaudibly but finally recollecting some of the admonitions my teachers had dinned into my head in preparation for "recitations" before Negro school and church audiences as far back as the second grade. I had not realized how long a poem it was when I was writing it and I was squirmingly conscious of certain flaws and failures which had never before loomed so large. The applause and praise that followed when I finished, if anything, exceeded that given the others; a situation which, even then, aroused the fleeting suspicion that the dancing bear was being given higher marks than a man might get for the same performance. One of the older women murmured something about Paul Laurence Dunbar. Someone else asked me if I liked Pushkin. I could only look blank, since at that time I knew almost nothing about the great Russian's poetry and even less about his Negro lineage. Inevitably, there was a flattering and irrelevant comparison to Langston Hughes. A wavy-haired gentleman took his pipe out of his mouth to ask if I didn't think "The Negro Speaks of Rivers" was a marvelous poem. I said I certainly did. (But stopped short of trying to explain why the Mississippi always made me think not of Lincoln at New Orleans but of the playmate on Carroll Street drowned during an Easter baptism, the cold, feral grin of the garfish skeleton which two of us stumbled on as we moped along the riverfront toward the pickle factory and the high platform beyond where the city garbage trucks dumped their loads into the frothing stream, and the dimly remembered "high waters" sucking at the edge of the roadbed as the train brought my father and me back to St. Louis from our grandfather's funeral.)

Gradually, as the light faded outside the window, people began looking at their watches and saying good-by. One of the club members thanked all of us for coming and said she could not remember when the Arts Club had had such a fine and talented group. The blonde girl clapped her hands for attention, her eyes shining with the enthusiasm of the born organizer. Why, she wanted to know, did this year's group really have to scatter? It seemed to her that we should not let our companionship, our new friendships die. Some of us were going away for the summer, but there were still several weeks left yet before school would be out. Some might be going off to college in the fall, but others would not, and probably some of those who would be entering college would be going no farther away than the University of Missouri at Columbia, or St. Louis, Washington, or one of the other schools in the St. Louis area. I was silent as the others chimed in, suggesting that we meet at the various high schools or rotate meetings from one home to another before and after summer vacations. Such a point was made of including me in and I felt already so much the witch at the wedding party that I was not inclined to remind them that I would have a much harder time getting into a meeting at the schools they attended or the colleges in the area than I had had getting into the Arts Club that afternoon. To say nothing of what their parents and friends and mine would make of those meetings in the homes. I tried to picture those well-dressed and half-assured young white poets strolling past the cleaning and pressing shop to a meeting at my house. Nevertheless, my Driscoll Avenue cynicism began crumbling under the effervescent pressures of their youth and mine. We made our way down the thick-carpeted stairs, true poets and comrades, a verbal skyscraper of plans and projects rising as we descended. We would exchange our favorite original poems by phone and by mail. We would do a volume of poems together and a famous novelist who was a good friend of our hostess would get the book published for us. The Arts Club would serve as secretariat and haven, keeping track of addresses and phone numbers and providing a place where we could meet, read and write.

Good will, mutual admiration, flowering ambition united us as we parted in the gathering spring dusk. The air was scented with the watermelony smell of freshly cut grass. The lights were on in the stone house across the street, but the handyman was gone.

I did not hear from the young men and women I met that afternoon at the Arts Club the next week, the next month, or ever. But I had a great many more serious disappointments than that, along with a decent amount of good fortune, in the two remaining years I spent in my home town. Like many other young men similarly situated I was involved during those prewar years in a quiet but no less desperate scramble simply to hold on to life and not go under. By the end of that period of twenty-odd months I had run an elevator, worked as a machine operator, delivered parcels, patrolled a lake stocked with fish nobody ever tried to steal, and stood in half a hundred job lines with white and black men who showed up every morning less out of hope than the need to put off as long as possible that time of day when they must once again face their families. For me and a good many others my age it was not a question really of having something to eat and a place to sleep. The battle was, rather, to find ways of withstanding the daily erosion, through tedium, through humiliation, through various short-term pleasures, of the sense of your own possibilities. Necessary, too, was some sensitivity to possibilities outside yourself. Here I do not exclude chance, the lucky break. For me it came with the opportunity to become a part-time student at a college I might have attended full time two years earlier.

On the night before I left for college my mother gave a party for me, inviting a dozen of my friends. Some of them brought gifts. As I was walking past the Catholic church on Garth Avenue, shortly after midnight, going home to the flat I shared with my father, a squad car pulled up and two officers jumped out. Night sticks at the ready, they flashed a light in my face and wanted to know where I was coming from and where I had picked up all that stuff. They pawed through the presents I was carrying until they came across an anthology of poetry autographed for me that night by my friends. The first officer grunted and snapped off his light. The second seemed tempted to take a swipe at me anyhow for wasting their time. They got back in the car and drove off, leaving me to walk the two blocks remaining between the church and home.

The next morning, on a cold, sooty, old-style St. Louis day, I left home. I got on a bus and headed for Jefferson City, Missouri. That trip away from home has been a much longer journey than I had anticipated and a very much different one. On certain occasions, as when my poetry was published or while lecturing at Atlanta University, I have remembered that afternoon. And I have thought that perhaps when I next visited St. Louis, I would try once again to find my way to the Arts Club. I never have and it is probably just as well. It may be that I got as much as could reasonably be expected on that first visit.

The Best Advice I Ever Had

LAURENCE C. JONES

I MUST HAVE BEEN quite young when I first heard it, for the quaint, old-fashioned phrase runs through all my childhood memories with the persistence of a familiar tune: "Willful waste makes woeful want, and you may live to see the day when you will say, 'Oh, how I wish I had the bread that once I threw away.'"

I hear the words spoken in my mother's soft voice as she worked in her quick, industrious fashion around the neat little house in St. Joseph, Mo., where my sisters and I were born. Far from being the practical realist that those words suggest, my fragile, poetry-loving mother was a dreamer. But she knew that within that phrase lay the chance for her dreams, and mine, to come true.

At first the words meant literally the piece of bread and jam in my hand which I might have tossed aside uneaten. Later they meant money, for from the age of six I always had a job of some sort, and learned to save the pennies, dimes and quarters toward the dream of a college education.

At the University of Iowa, where I tended furnace and waited table to pay my way, waste came to mean time. Since I had only a few hours each day for study, I had to make up in extra concentration what I lacked in time. Consequently my lessons burned into my memory, and they did much to shape the course of my life.

When I finished college, waste suddenly took on a new important meaning: the possible waste of opportunity.

In 1907, the year of my graduation, comparatively few Negroes had a similar chance at formal education. Although I had tempting job offers which ranged from the insurance business to a subsidized career in musical comedy, it seemed to me that if I used my education for selfish profit, that too would be a form of "willful waste."

I decided to share my advantages with the neediest people of my race in the Black Belt of Mississippi. There was the most shocking waste of all: the waste of the human mind and soul. Men, women and children exhausted their bodies in the fields, making their living as farmers but having no knowledge of farming beyond the drudgery of chopping and picking cotton. Unable to read, write or figure, they had no way of knowing if what they were charged at the store was correct, or if their wages were paid in full. Winter diets were corn meal and dried peas, because the women had never learned how to can or preserve the summer yield from their gardens or the wild berries that grew at their doors.

My mother's phrase came sharply to mind. My job would be to begin at the bottom and teach them, first of all, how to save what pitiful little they had. I set up a school of practical education, to teach good work habits, sanitation, diversified farming, how to cook, can and sew. The dream that lay ahead of this practical saving was better living conditions, adequate schools and churches, and ultimately instruction in trades and professions.

Then, after almost 20 years of work, as Piney Woods began to take shape as a real school, with the beginnings of an adequate plant, a steady enrollment and nearly enough teachers, my wife died, leaving a void not only in my life but in the operation of the school in which she had played a vital role. The temptation to give way to personal grief was strong. But once again my mother's words echoed in my ears. Grief, too, was a luxury, a "willful waste," when 500 children were depending on me for their education, their chance to become useful citizens.

What is education, or civilization itself for that matter, but a form of saving? We harvest and keep the best of the world's ideas and inventions so that we may pass them along to the generations that follow.

My job in life has been to try to save human beings from the willful waste of ignorance and despair, and to help them take their places as competent citizens in tomorrow's world. It is a task that I would choose again, if I were young. It was motivated by these words which I share with you. I can vouch for the rewards they will bring.

FROM

A Slaveholder's Daughter

BELLE KEARNEY

WHEN I WAS sixteen years old an invitation was received from some relatives in Oxford, Mississippi, to attend the Commencement exercises at the State University. This was my first entrance into society as a young lady. My wardrobe consisted of inexpensive Swiss and organdie dresses trimmed with some old laces that mother had rescued from the wreck of time. My appearance was that of a woman and long since the decision had been made, to "put away childish things." My girlhood griefs were buried out of sight.

The desire of my heart had been to lead the life of a thoroughly independent creature; but I soon found that it seemed absurd to differ from other persons. Now there was nothing to do but drift with the tide. I laughed and talked and acted like the women about me; but there was a sting in it all to which the world was not blind. My society chat had a current of sarcasm, my merriment a tinge of bitterness. A knowledge of card-playing had been gained while attending school in Canton, and my first lesson in dancing was taken in such extreme youth that it is impossible to recall it. During Christmas holidays there were always several parties given in the neighborhood of Vernon, and in summer there were numerous out-of-door festivities. I attended them all and often danced through a winter night and a long, hot summer day when not over ten years old. Dancing was a part of a Southern girl's education. It was as natural as eating or laughing. After a young lady had made her debut, she would soon become "a wall-flower" in society if she did not dance. On going to Oxford it was an easy thing for me to fall in with the trend of custom. The days were divided between playing croquet with the University students and returning fashionable calls; the nights were given to games of euchre and attending entertainments.

The last and greatest social function of the season was the Commencement ball. Mother had unearthed an old ante-bellum blue silk and put it in my trunk for an emergency. This was now brought forth and laboriously transformed into an evening costume. The stains of years were covered up with the inevitable lace or hidden by sprays of flowers. My escort called at ten o'clock in a carriage with another youthful couple and we went to the ballroom. The dignified custom of chaperonage was then nearly obsolete. My program was filled out and I danced straight through it until the last strain of music ended with the advent of the sun next morning. With me nothing has ever been done by halves. Whatever has been undertaken at all has been undertaken with intensity.

The summer at Oxford was the beginning of gaieties that continued, almost without interruption, for three years. The winters were spent at my uncle's home in Canton and in Jackson with very dear cousins. Another visit was made to New Orleans under happier circumstances. In summer my friends visited me at the plantation. While in the country we rode on horse-back, had buggy drives and out-door games; went on fishing and camping excursions; attended picnics and barbecues; gave dinners and teas, and exchanged visits with two delightful families who had guests with them throughout the warm months. These families and ours had only recently become acquainted as they lived miles away from us; but distances are small considerations when "life is new" and pleasure the one pursuit in existence.

My stays at home were comparatively brief during these three years; but while there my reading was continued and mother and I managed to do a great deal of sewing for the negroes. My oldest brother had one year at the University and immediately after secured a position in a mercantile establishment in the northern part of the state. During my visits to the towns there was a ceaseless round of balls, theatres, receptions and card parties, nearly every one of which I attended; from the Governor's inaugural entertainment at the Mansion to an impromptu dance in a private home.

Those were fateful months. The foundations of ill-health were laid which haunted me for fifteen years. Often in freezing weather my thick shoes and heavy clothing were put aside for thin slippers and gauze dresses and bare neck and arms. After dancing till heat or fatigue became unbearable a rush would be made into the deadly night air, with only a filmy lace shawl thrown over my shoulders for protection.

There were few days in those three years in which I did not have a desperate fight with my soul. Conscious of not living up to my high conceptions of life, I hated myself and abhorred the way my time was spent. The truth forced itself upon me that theatres were rarely elevating, that the trail of the serpent was over every card, that round-dancing was demoralizing and that many of the young men who danced with me were not worthy of my friendship. Night after night on returning from an entertainment, I have sat before the fire pouring out my contempt for myself and all *my* world in scathing denunciation, always ending with the moan that had been in my heart since childhood, "What *is* there for me to do? Life is so empty, so unsatisfying! I wish I had never been born!" The girls who kept the vigils with me would greet my torrent of grief and rebellion with peals of laughter. Bessie Fearn, my cousin and constant companion, a most brilliant and fascinating young woman, would say, "It is impossible for me to understand you. How *can* you see any harm in cards or dancing or theatres? I am as untouched in spirit to-night as a child could be!" In later years, when a personal knowledge of Christ came to her, these things in which she once saw no "harm" palled upon her and in renunciation of them her life became a glad song of consecration until the time came of "entering into rest" where her eyes beheld "the King in his beauty" in "the land that is very far off."

After the last fierce struggle with the finer elements of my being, a definite determination was made to *abandon* the shallow, aimless life that had been entered upon;—and it was *done,*—suddenly and forever. It was concluded further that I must go to work, that an occupation uplifting and strengthening must be secured if every family tradition was shattered and if my life were forfeited in the attempt.

Father and I had always been congenial except along certain lines. In the light of after experiences we both became wise enough to avoid all splitting issues. Up to this time, however, the depths of his convictions concerning work for women had never been sounded. Mother believed in me utterly. She was my devoted, changeless, unquestioning ally. Father, on the contrary, with all his gentleness and affability, was a severe critic and, at times, a most sarcastic opponent. Consequently, whenever an embryo scheme was on hand, he was invariably sought in order to get an expression of opinion, regardless that his views might be totally different from mine. When a child rest never came to me until every important occurrence of my daily life had been related to him, heedless of the consequences of the confidence.

He had been terribly grieved over my indulgence in round-dancing. At the country festivities, I had been allowed to attend in childhood, only the dignified quadrilles of earlier times were in vogue. It had not occurred to him that my inclinations might reach out tendrils towards the customs of my own day. He had often tried to dissuade me from round-dancing, but was unable to extract a promise that it would be given up. However, when my decision was reached to dance no more I went at once to him and announced it. "Well, my daughter," he remarked, surveying me calmly, "you do not deserve a particle of credit, for you do not stop because it is right, but because you are disgusted." This diagnosis of the case was accepted, but with a tremendously offended ego.

Soon after this encounter, father was again interviewed. Broaching the subject abruptly I said: "Life has grown very tiresome to me and some change *must* be effected. It is my intention to work at some employment that will make it possible for me to support myself." Father looked at me a little dazed, and answered: "Work?" with a high-tide inflection on the word. "*Work?*" with renewed emphasis—"and may I ask of what nature your work will be?"

"Certainly," was my quick reply, "I intend to teach school."

"*In*deed!" said father, with a peculiar drawl of the prefix which would have sent terror to my soul when a child.

"Yes, sir!" came my answer with decision, "I am going to teach school."

"But you forget," he exclaimed, making a desperate effort to control the quaver in his voice and to hide the tremor of his eyelids that revealed the storm in his heart, "you *forget* that I am able to give you a support. You forget that you are my only daughter. Do you mean to tell me that you are going to teaching? I will *never* consent to it!"—and he walked off with an air which told too plainly that the conference was ended.

Without being in the least dismayed, and saying not a word to any one, I put on my sunbonnet and gloves and started forth determined to settle the school question. There were few children in the immediate neighborhood and the majority of these were very poor; but wherever there was a shadow of a chance for success, their homes were visited and a request made for pupils. An upstairs bedroom in our dwelling was transformed into a schoolroom, and the following Monday morning I entered upon my career as teacher. Father did not say one word. His courtesy was never at fault; besides, he had discovered in me a certain will-force, inherited from both "sides of the house," and an indomitable energy which he began to respect. At the end of the term he said to me: "Allow me, daughter, to congratulate you upon your fine success." Mother was radiant with delight from the beginning, for she understood my longings. Everything was made to bend to my wishes. The children were permitted to eat their lunches on the long front gallery upstairs, and to romp in the yard under the closely matted branches of the great cedars and among the trailing periwinkle vines whose green leaves carpeted almost every foot of ground. There were only seven pupils in my school and their tuition fees amounted to but $12 a month; but those twelve dollars were as large as twelve full moons in my eyes and as precious as blood-drops. Among the seven children there was only one at all well advanced; while teaching him I had a good chance to review text-books and to again get into the habit of study. While managing the others an excellent opportunity was afforded for the cultivation of the grace of patience, which was sorely needed, and of gaining some practical knowledge of the methods of teaching.

I was nineteen years old at the beginning of my little private school.

By Love Possessed

DON LEE KEITH

WHO WAS THAT LADY?

IT HAS TAKEN three and a half months and a determined search through seven attics and six junk shops, but at last I've got that page from the March 1950 issue of *Life* for my very own. It's tacked right up here on the wall by my desk, just where it belongs. I figure that's the least I can do for the girl in the picture. After all, it was because of her that L. J. Franks and I made it through the summer of 1950.

Some folks got the grins, and others shook their heads when they heard the news, but nobody in Wheeler, Mississippi, could very well ignore it when the daughter of the Hardshell Baptist preacher left town and the next thing they knew, turned up half nekkid and riding a pink elephant in *Life* magazine. Some thought she ought to be pitied. A few thought she ought to be crucified. L. J. and I thought she ought to be crowned Queen of the World.

It was that summer, that endless summer, when we were so bedeviled by boredom. We were nine—too old for teddy bears and too young for pool halls. Party-line prophets had warned that polio was lurking behind every gatepost and hawthorn bush, so no one got to go swimming. Next, dodge ball was forbidden, then red rover, then *anything strenuous*, and by the last of June, L. J. and I feared we'd go blind from looking at so many View Master reels. We took an oath on the blades of our Scout knives that somehow, *somehow*, we would find our way through the dreary maze that Dog Days had set before us. He tried to join the church three Sundays in a row, and I fairly begged to be circumcized. (I'd already had my tonsils out.) But mostly we just hung around the yard, sorting our arrowheads and seeing who could belch the loudest, and occasionally slipping off to watch the Castoria-colored spit run down the chins of the wizened gentlemen in front of Oakley's Store as they chewed tobacco and whittled on cedar sticks and took bets on how much longer the drought would last.

The oldest farmers in the county kept saying that it would get worse before it got better, so most folks fanned a lot and tried to be patient. But after a while, when push came to shove, as they say, somebody had to do something. So, everybody got together in the school lunchroom and had a prayer meeting, and right in the middle of it, L. J. and I got tickled and laughed out loud because a wasp stung Eloise Greenhaw on the elbow. Eloise could name the books of the Bible backwards and that's all she ever went around doing.

Sure enough, two days later it started raining. It was a Sunday, and afterwards, somebody said that when the first clap of thunder had sounded, the people over at the Holiness Church had all at once got the Holy Ghost and started shouting in the unknown tongue. It just made me sick as a dog to think I'd missed that.

Only problem was: once the rain commenced, it didn't stop. Every day from sunup to sundown, it rained for more than two solid weeks, with only an occasional, unannounced slack. My grandfather said that dadgummit, they'd prayed either too long or too loud. Everything—even the dinner napkins—began to reek of mildew. Birds refused to fly, and dogs lay silent on porches, stretching and yawning and watching twigs and Milky Way wrappers floating past in the swollen ditches. Tyce Keeton's chicken coop ended up in his minnow pond with a Dominecker rooster dead inside.

Nobody talked about anything except the weather. Aunt Jessie sat down and wrote a letter to the Farmer's Almanac demanding to know how come they'd not foreseen the mess we were in.

L. J. and I were the only ones who paid it no mind. Our thoughts were elsewhere, for on the same day that the wet spell had arrived, we had discovered a new magic between the covers of a four-month-old magazine. The girl astride the elephant now possessed our souls. The picture's caption identified her with the name we already knew—Ann Gardner—and L. J.'s mother said that if she heard us mention Ann Gardner one more time they'd have to cart her off to the asylum at Whitfield. But my mother said no, they ought to be glad we had that silly girl to think about, since otherwise we'd have gone loping off to the creek and drowned for sure.

We spent our mornings in the attic writing poems dedicated to

Ann Gardner. We created a new sandwich called the Ann Gardner Special (pimiento and cheese on a Ritz cracker with a criss-cross of bologna strips) and had them for lunch every day. Afterwards, we'd go out and swing in the front porch swing while we read our poems and argued about whether "caress" rhymed with "best." We threatened to put a snake on my little brother, Butch, if he didn't sit still and pay attention. One day Aunt Jessie finally agreed to listen, but she had a hot flash and had to go inside to the electric fan.

When the mail truck had come and gone and I was sure there was no long-awaited word from June Allyson, we'd go back to the attic. Again we would count our Blue Horse notebook coupons and consider what to order from the gift catalogue. We finally settled on a flashlight with a whistle on the end. L. J. said Ann Gardner would like that better than the pencil trimmer shaped like a skull.

We took an old frame and replaced its picture with the page from *Life*. We hung it on a nail and called the place sacred.

It took us two whole afternoons on that beat-up Remington to hunt-and-peck out a note to *Life*, saying why didn't they have more pictures of the lady on the elephant since everybody in the United States of America admired her beauty and poise.

We composed the lyrics of a song, "Sweet Ann Gardner," sung to the tune of "Mona Lisa." We planned and replanned the party we would give when she came back to Wheeler, which, we were so sure, would be real soon. We finally decided that we'd put the piano stool out in the grape arbor and screw the seat up high so she could be seen by everybody. We'd have L. J.'s cousin Mary Ann wear her cowgirl outfit and sing "Sioux City Sue," which she was so good at, and I'd play the Kleenex and comb. L. J. would do a routine with his hand puppets. He made a new puppet stage out of a big Kotex carton we'd saved from the trash behind Oakley's store.

Then one day—it was a Friday—right after we'd written our poems and finished our lunch of Ann Gardner Specials, we carried slices of yellow-meated watermelons out to the porch and walked into a world we had forgotten. From back inside the house, somebody hollered something about not slamming the screened door, but L. J. and I scarcely heard it; we stood motionless, gazing toward the front yard.

It had stopped raining.

A pair of Bun Grissom's bird dogs trotted down the middle of the road, taking turns sniffing each other. On each side of them, puddles the color of Ovaltine were now peaceful, no longer peppered by the steady drizzle we'd become so accustomed to. Several neighbors were huddled on their doorsteps, staring up at the clearing sky. My grandfather came out and looked around and told my grandmother that whatever she did, she'd best not start praying again.

L. J. and I planted two watermelon seeds in the iris bed as a tribute to Ann Gardner.

Later that afternoon, we pulled on our galoshes and tromped off through the back pasture and climbed up in my tree house to find that all that rain hadn't done a dab of damage to the venetian blinds we'd nailed in place last spring. From up there, you could see in every direction, but it was the view toward the south we noticed. That whole end of the pasture was now a lake, covering saltlicks and fenceposts and stretching clear to the foot of the little hill we called Choctaw Mountain. L. J. said it looked just like the Great Flood. I said that Hollywood ought to send some people real quick and make a picture show about Noah. L. J. said that they might not let him play the leading role, or, for that matter, might even pick somebody other than Mary Ann as Mrs. Noah, and I said I'd always thought Mary Ann was more Queen Esther, actually. He allowed as how she could be Queen Esther *and* Mrs. Noah if we had all the say-so, and I said that Noah's wasn't the only story that ought to be thought about, since my cousin Nicky was David made over, knew eight verses from Psalms by heart and was always hitting bluejays with his slingshot.

L. J. located a pencil in the rusty coffee can we kept in the tree house, but there wasn't a scrap of dry paper to be had. We'd have to hurry to the house so we could jot down every single idea. No detail can be overlooked when you're out to make the Old Testament into a picture show.

Late the next spring, Aunt Jessie found a watermelon vine growing in the iris bed. None of us could figure out how it got there.

Knee-Pants and Parasols

DON LEE KEITH

THE SUMMER OF OUR DISCONTENT

L. J. FRANKS came to New Orleans to see me last week, four hours and 22 minutes late on the Panama Limited. He wore a strand of Navajo beads and a T-shirt that said, "I Am A Follies Star," and he stayed to argue about prices at the Flea Market, and he spent an entire afternoon traipsing up and down Royal Street looking for some huaraches, which is something he can't very well get in Winona, Mississippi, where he and his wife and family live.

On Saturday he paid $15 for a sackload of old sheet music in a junque shoppe on Magazine Street, and he told one rather chunky woman in a black voile dress that the Lord would get her for overpricing chipped cameos. "And you, in mourning," said L. J.

Two hours after that, which was three days, 11 hours and 38 minutes after he had arrived, L. J. got back on the train and went home. It was the first time he had visited me since we were little boys, and it sure was good to have had him around again. It reminded me just how special he is. After all, he was the only little boy I ever knew who made a skirt out of an umbrella. Nine years old. Cut that thing up and stitched on a grosgrain ribbon for a waistband and had poor Martha Nell Glover wear it the livelong day. Told her she looked just like a movie star. Martha Nell wasn't all there, as they say.

That was back when we had our hearts set on making our own picture show out of the Old Testament. It was all settled. I'd write the script and he'd do the directing and get the costumes. Our first choice had been the tale of Noah, but that meant an ark, so we went on to Samson. Martha Nell was cast as Delilah. For costumes, L. J. started with the easiest, the closest at hand, which just happened to be a polka-dotted umbrella which just happened to belong to his grandmother, Miss Eller, which just happened to be why L. J. was forbidden to come over and play for two whole weeks.

By then, of course, we were ready to move on to other dreams.

Besides, about that time we found out that MGM had beat us to Samson, and Martha Nell had lost out to Hedy Lamarr.

The first thing L. J. did when he got here last week was to pull out a picture of his two little girls. And I must say they're beauties, which is something I would never have said (never would say) about L. J., who always was (and still is) more than a little on the scrawny side. So much, in fact, that the time we all got pogo sticks, when he jumped on his, nothing happened. The new pogo sticks all had rubber tops shaped like horses heads, so L. J. promptly took his off and made a hand puppet out of it, which was really a lot better than the pogo sticks anyway. At least he thought so. And I did, too.

Nobody got around to telling us, and we never figured it out for ourselves, but he and I were the only pre-pubescent eccentrics in Wheeler, with its 217 people spread over a seven-mile radius. We were separated by the Hardshell Baptist Church and three bridges over three creeks, but we were bound together by boredom. We were bored with collecting baseball cards, bored with Vacation Bible School, bored with bicycle chains that chewed up your pants legs, bored with chunking rocks through culverts, knocking down wasp nests, putting pennies on railroad tracks, bored.

For the entire month of June, I wrote a penny postcard every day to June Allyson, telling her she'd changed my whole life. I threatened to throw myself under the milk truck if she didn't answer. She didn't and I didn't.

Meanwhile, L. J., who swore he'd never love anyone else but Kathryn Grayson and could name every movie she'd ever made even if you didn't ask him to, wrote to Kathryn Grayson only once and after nothing but that single post card she sent him a picture of her in a fur bathing suit. I nearly bit clean through my bottom lip when it came. It was signed, "Cordially yours," and after that, L. J. signed everything, "Cordially yours."

Later that summer I found four little kittens in Lige Turner's storm house and L. J. found a silver spoon with a G in the creek that had gone dry. And he went around telling everybody that Miss Grayson had sent it to him all the way from Hollywood.

"Wouldn't you just know it?" shrieked my grandmother when she up-ended each of the kittens. "Every blamed one of them girls!" But L. J. cut the middle snowflake out of some old crocheted doilies we found in the sideboard, which were perfect for the kittens. So, we started planning a new version of "Little Women."

All I remember now is that Jo and Beth were both yellow, and the brindled Meg fell in the well late one afternoon and somebody tried to lower a bucket but it slipped and fell and they took me that very night to spend the rest of the time till school started with Aunt Susie, who had a whole porch full of wisteria with bumble bees as mean as snakes. L. J. wrote me a card and said he had decided to marry Mary Ann, his cousin, and they were going to become foreign missionaries because she could sing so well and he could put on shows. Cordially yours, L. J. Franks. I kept that card for years. It had a P.S. "I have sent off for a real magic kit. Do they have white doves in China or do you know?"

Last Saturday, just as L. J. was getting on the train to go home, he turned and hollered back to me, "Oh yeah, I meant to tell you that I saw June Allyson in some commercial not long ago, page boy and all. Hasn't changed one iota. I kept wondering if she knows exactly who was president and vice-president and everything else including the single, solitary member of the Prentiss County June Allyson Fan Club. Listen, you did a lot for June Allyson!"

"Listen, L. J.," I hollered back. "You did a lot for umbrellas."

Growing Up in Mississippi in a Time of Change

EDWIN KING

I

THE CRY FOR BLOOD was the strongest response from white Mississippi to the first news that spring day of 1954 that the U.S. Supreme Court had ruled against public school segregation. The *Jackson Daily News* carried a front page editorial in bold print condemning the Court and blaming it for the violence and racial conflict the longtime editor, Fred Sullens, said was inevitable. The title carried the theme: "Blood on the Marble Steps."

The reaction in Jackson was more surprising to me than the news from Washington. I was a senior at Carr Central High School in Vicksburg at the time. Many of my classmates talked of the Supreme Court ruling with a degree of approval. A smaller group was critical. Most students were just confused. But no one, students nor teachers, spoke in the angry, emotional tones of the Jackson editor. Most of my close friends were active in church youth groups such as the Methodist Youth Fellowship where there had been some discussion of race relations, changes, and Christian attitudes for several years. Through the Methodist Church in Mississippi I, myself, had learned that the Supreme Court would issue some kind of ruling that spring—and I had come to hope the Court would rule against segregation. But the church had not prepared me for the level of white resistance in Mississippi or the rest of the South.

The students in my school talked openly about the matter. We did not fear each other. Our high school teachers had not tried to indoctrinate us or control our thoughts and words. Perhaps this degree of freedom was possible because the segregation patterns of Mississippi had not been directly attacked and any change may have been inconceivable. At that point no demand for a totally unified white community response-resistance had been made. Only one teacher criticized the Supreme Court. This lady said that she would never teach colored children and would retire immediately; students joked about it since we thought she was already past seventy. Teachers and students both assumed that the federal government would soon enforce the Court's decision—and that loyal citizens of Mississippi would, as Americans, of course, obey. A civics teacher told her class that the law of the land was the law of the land, whether any of us liked it or not.

It soon became clear that change would not come quickly, quietly, or easily. The students who came back to that high school the next fall did not have open discussions about the Supreme Court or controversial issues. Those who still thought the Court was right did not dare speak their minds. The teachers were even more cautious. In the churches the atmosphere remained a little more tolerant but conformity soon came to rule even there. The "closed society," so well described by Jim Silver, was closing in.

All Mississippians were taught the racial facts of life early. I was no exception. The patterns of segregation were so absolute and so assumed that there was no need for explicit teaching. This knowledge (plus the awareness of one's own place, top or bottom) was absorbed by a child as part of growing up in the world. (It may have been more necessary for black parents to carefully instruct their children—for their own safety—in racial customs.) My wife, Jeannette, and I have talked to many white Mississippians of our generation and our training was similar. My parents, Ralph and Julia King, taught me and my younger brother, Mack, the same lessons—to respect myself and other people, to respect family, church, society, state, and nation. No teachings were overtly racist. White superiority was taken for granted. Middle class children were taught a few specific things—such as not to use the word "nigger" and not to hate. From our families, neighbors, churches, and schools we learned good manners, courtesy, the "Golden Rule," Bible stories, and traditional American beliefs about democracy, justice, and equality. Such teachings did not make us question racial patterns—but the possibility for a conflict in values and customs was always present. All white Americans, especially Mississippians, have some racism and, yet, are never totally immune to some form of conscience and the American dilemma.

At public school we learned of Jamestown and Plymouth Rock. Our racial learning had been almost completed long before the first grade started. Our childhood games and nursery rhymes reflected both a British background of "London Bridge" and a Deep South setting in a counting game like "Eeny, meeny, miney, moe." This is known in most of the South, perhaps most of the nation. A Movement friend, Joan Bowman, has written of the version used when she was a child in Georgia:

> Eeny, meeny, miney, moe.
> Catch a nigger by the toe.
> If he hollers let him go
> Eeny, meeny, miney moe.

The contemporary version we learned in Mississippi was not so moderate and revealed far more truth about the nature of segregation and the corruption of justice in the land:

> Eeny, meeny, miney, moe.
> Catch a nigger by the toe.
> If he hollers, *make him pay*
> Fifteen dollars every day.

In Mississippi blacks not only had to know their place and stay there but had better not even complain. (Later I met other Americans who knew the same counting rhyme but had never heard the racial references; they chanted about catching a monkey.)

Mississippi children learn of other minorities and their basic characteristics as well. The children I knew never used the word "nigger" as an epithet—but "Indian Giver" was one of the worst things a child could be called. (The connotation was untrustworthy, a child who takes back all he gives, one who cannot keep a bargain—a rather fantastic reversal of white and Indian roles when you think about it, perhaps even a transference of guilt.) But the white man had destroyed or isolated the red man long ago, so that was no issue and the child learned little special about it. Everywhere the child had to learn of black/white matters. The racial reality was present in something so simple, so innocent, as the names of flowers. "Black-eyed Susans" were know in my town as "niggertoes" to me and my friends—and in this context we were allowed to use the word. (A collegiate joke of 1955 said the NAACP wanted to change this to "Negro-toes." A variation of the joke would have "chiggers," changed to "Chegroes," as the proper word for a nasty, biting insect.)

Mississippi white children took the presence of blacks for granted. Some of my friends' families had black maids and yard men. Most Mississippians of all races were poor and having servant help of some sort was no sign of wealth. At my Grandmother Tucker's home, Percy Joyce helped her and my aunts—Nell, Marie, and Dorothy—raise several of my cousins, and she was and is a part of our family. Helping with the yard work was Mose, who, to me, always seemed old and whose full name I never knew. Blacks in other than familiar roles were never seen in my Vicksburg world of the thirties, forties, or early fifties. White children were not afraid of blacks—even the men on the chain gangs (although that was a situation that must have prompted questions until even that was taken for granted). Blacks were interesting, even fascinating, for white children. In Vicksburg the black people always lived close by—but in their own neighborhoods, if only one block away (and, in Vicksburg, in places with names like Marcus Bottom or areas sometimes still called Smith's Quarters or the name of some other of the white families which once had its slave quarters there). Blacks came into white neighborhoods daily, often selling vegetables from mule drawn wagons. The white children loved this sight—and were sometimes given rides on the wagons. I also enjoyed seeing the black laundry women with huge loads of clothes wrapped in a sheet or even a brightly colored bedspread balanced on their heads as they walked from the white home back to their own home to do the washing for the white woman.

The poverty of the blacks was not questioned. In Vicksburg whites lived on the hilltops; blacks in the bottoms. On Thomas Street, my one block-long home base, there was only a dirt trail down the hill to the black houses with their exotic yards full of pigs, chickens, children, black iron pots for heating water, and outhouses. Even the U.S. postman did not go that far. White homes had mail delivered to the door; black mail was placed in a row of boxes at the start of the path. No whites questioned this arrangement; no blacks dared.

In summer the trees almost blocked all view of the black houses, but in winter they could be seen easily. The music of church services and the smell of wood fires rose to the whites on the hilltops. Sometimes the wood fires could not be controlled in the inadequate fireplaces and a house burst into flames. That happened at least once every winter—in my own neighborhood. It must have happened all over the town. Whites always were generous with old clothing and left-over food. Helping poor blacks in wintertime was the proper role of a white Christian. In Mississippi with all roles there are certain duties. White children, parents, and grandparents saw no need for change—or even questioning.

As a child in Vicksburg I was especially conscious of the War Between the States. The town is surrounded by the battlefield. Children play among the cannons and in the trenches where thousands died. After spring rains I could find minnie balls, old bullets, by scratching in the earth around my Grandmother Tucker's home on South Washington Street. The Confederate legend is strong in all of Mississippi, but even stronger in Vicksburg. There was no Fourth of July celebration in my childhood, not till the end of the Second World War in the city—because this date marked the entry of Grant and the Union troops in 1863 after the terrible siege and struggle. Lincoln's birthday was unknown but we did observe holidays for the birthdays of Robert E. Lee of Virginia and our Warren County citizen Jefferson Davis. The late May Memorial Day was celebrated only by blacks; it was to honor the Union soldiers—and, perhaps, the only way blacks showed any defiance the only survival from the Reconstruction. Stories were told that blacks even had some sort of parade downtown. These were the only parades I ever missed as a child, the only parades my great uncle, J. Mack Moore, did not take me to, as he had taken my mother to civic and circus parades years before—but white children just did not go near black ceremonies of that sort. Whites did observe a legal holiday in April as Confederate Memorial Day.

With my elementary and junior high school friends I hated Yankees and all they stood for. My favorite uncle complained frequently when radio announcers would refer to the American troops in World War II as "Yanks." He thought that was insulting to the Southern boys—and my older cousins in service. This same uncle loved baseball and was a loyal fan of the Brooklyn Dodgers (as was I), perhaps because their arch enemy was the "Yankees." I remember the terrible day when the first black player, Jackie Robinson, was signed and my uncle swore he would never listen to Brooklyn games again. The war did bring some kind of nationalistic feelings of unity. In war games with my friends we never tried to separate northern and southern American troops while fighting imaginary Japanese and Germans. However the Southern loyalty was always close to the surface. After the atom bombs were used on Japan we heard of the American labs at Oak Ridge. At first I, a fourth grader not too sure of geography, thought this was the community of the same name in rural Warren County, twenty five miles from Vicksburg where "Bear Creek," the Tucker family plantation, with home and cemetery was and where lived my great aunt Em (a real Daughter of the Confederacy) and uncle Emmett, was. I was disappointed when I discovered the "atomic" Oak Ridge was not in Mississippi, but at least neighboring Tennessee was still a Southern state and some of us school boys gleefully talked of a new Southern Secession, sure to win this time with the bomb on our side.

The white southern church was responsible for my first questioning of the morality of segregation. (The same is true for Jeannette and most of my Millsaps college friends, of several denominations, but particularly the Methodist and the Episcopal churches.) New ideas reached us especially through the church youth programs. I was proud of the national connections of the Methodist Church in Mississippi, something I began to understand when in high school. I soon became aware of strong liberal statements of the national church favoring integration (and the contradictions of the actual practice of segregation in the church). I was one of many Mississippi youth who subscribed to the national Methodist youth magazine, *Concern*, which contained frequent helpful articles on segregation. (In Vicksburg some of the most conservative church members decided this magazine was "Communist" and tried to have it banned along with much other Methodist Sunday School literature. The wife of the pastor of the Crawford Street Church, Marjorey Granberry, was advisor to the youth program and she courageously insisted that the national church literature be available for Mississippi youth. The influence of Seth Granberry and Tom Prewitt had been a major factor in my decision to become a minister. I came along at a relatively easy time; by the late fifties many churches had purged such dangerous literature—and dangerous ideas—and dangerous persons.)

Perhaps the most important things that such church activities did for young teenagers in Mississippi other than initially raising questions was to provide the atmosphere where gradual change in our own thought patterns was possible. Through the church we knew we were not alone. Our questions were shared by others; our problems with our families were the same as those of many other young Mississippians we met through statewide church contacts.

One particular experience in 1953, in my senior year of high school, helped me resolve some of my confusion about the race issue and decide that something truly was wrong with segregation. A tornado struck Vicksburg, causing massive property damage and killing many people—including some school friends. Some weeks earlier one of my closest friends, Kenneth Little, had been killed in an accident. In the aftermath of the Christmas tornado many of my friends were ready for serious thoughts about many things. Most of us worked with the Red Cross and other volunteer groups distributing food and clothing to storm victims. For the first time we saw the terrible poverty and living conditions of many black residents of Vicksburg. The storm had done its worst damage in black neighborhoods. Once I stood in the hilltop yard of a friend and looked down on what had once been a black neighborhood in the valley below Fort Hill. The streets were not paved and firetrucks and ambulances had been unable to drive in the mud after the storm. Injured people had to be carried to the hilltop. Several blocks of houses had been completely burned out. I was not the only student to realize this was partially the result of segregation, that there was no such thing as separate but equal. Before this I had been blind. Now the questions and answers I had heard for several years at church youth meetings began to make sense. I was ready for the school decision of the U.S. Supreme Court five months later.

II

In the winter of 1962–1963 the Jackson Movement, led by Medgar Evers, Doris Allison, Pearlena Lewis, and John Salter, mounted a major Gandhian boycott and direct action campaign against segregation. Everything intensified in May 1963. Within weeks almost 1,000 people, mostly children and college students, had been jailed in nonviolent demonstrations and held in newly prepared "concentration camp-like" facilities in the animal pens and exhibit buildings of the Mississippi State Fairgrounds. A few whites protested the racism and the violence. Dr. W. B. Selah, pastor of Galloway Methodist Church, resigned his pulpit once blacks brought to the Sunday morning worship by Medgar Evers were denied admission. Two days later Evers was assasinated. Four days later, after his funeral, over 5,000 black people from all parts of

Mississippi walked behind his casket through the streets of Jackson in a protest funeral march. The last mourners in the long line began singing hymns and freedom songs in civil disobedience of the police order for silence. Soon there was confrontation between the young demonstrators and the nervous, confused, and angry white police. Officers beat and arrested many mourners in the streets and, even, entered a Farish Street building to rush to the second floor to strike and seize John Salter and myself. We were taken to the Fairgrounds prison.

John Salter and I began to understand what was happening on the Jackson streets as other prisoners were put into our police truck. Two more of them had bloody heads from police beatings. Finally, we were taken to the Fairgrounds prison. The ride was punctuated with deliberate stops and jerks by the driver which threw us around the vehicle for further battering. We were among the first adults in this new jail which had already held over five hundred students and children. [The children's stories were true; the children's nightmares were true.] It was like a concentration camp and the police, no doubt frightened and shaken by the near riot after the funeral of Medgar Evers, were now ready to punish, even torture, those of us in their hands.

When we arrived at the compound, the back doors of the truck were opened. We could see the famous prison. We had passed through a series of gates and were now inside the wire enclosed area. An officer looked into the truck and asked if King and Salter were there. He then instructed the guard, "Close the doors, and let them sweat awhile." We trembled as we thought of Anne Moody's report earlier that week of the horrors of this sweat box, so like Nazi railway cars crammed with victims, when Jackson children had been so near suffocation some had passed out. John Salter had been held this way only two days earlier while still bleeding from the police assault on the demonstrators on Rose Street, and he, too, had almost fainted that day. We were kept in this hot, closed truck about ten more minutes, taken out, and booked.

Soon, we were sent to join a line of prisoners, and forced to lean against a wall with our hands outstretched above our heads, braced against the wall at an almost straight angle. We had to stay in this position of terrible tension and severe pain for about twenty minutes. There were other prisoners present who had been there already more than half an hour. Whenever any one of us would groan or cry, and begin to drop our arms, or shift the position of our bodies, the armed guards would walk up, curse us, and sometimes poke people with their guns or clubs—an act almost as painful as being struck with force.

"Hey, you bastard," an officer would say, "what do you think this is? Straighten out your damn arms. Reach higher, higher on that wall." Although I wanted to scream and drop to the ground, to twist and curl my body to relieve the agony and pain of the position, I would respond to the order and stiffen my body again. I never saw any other prisoner dare to drop out of the position, although I didn't know how those who had been there longer could stand the pain without fainting. Since I was already bruised from being dragged down the stairs when captured, I felt the intended pain of this "magnolia torture" quickly. There was absolutely no reason for being forced to stand like this. We were inside the compound, surrounded by wire—and dogs—and heavily outnumbered by the police. And, of course, we, had no weapons.

The man standing next to me, about six feet away, was a stranger—a white person. I wondered how someone I did not even recognize could be in this place—and in his bloody condition. I whispered to him, and he told me his name was Peter Nemene. He had come down from New York to be interviewed for a math teaching job at Tougaloo College, and had stayed an extra day to attend the funeral. He had been badly beaten by the police. On the back of his head was an ugly patch of blood, almost black. His shirt collar showed bright red blood stains and the back of his coat had deep maroon stains. Flecks of bright, fresh blood oozed out of the head wound. Big horseflies were buzzing around, crawling on his bloody, sweaty coat. Some flies even crawled in his hair and in the wound on his scalp. The police had ordered me to keep face forward, towards the wall, but I had noticed this man's injuries when they brought me from the truck to stand next to him. I found what little courage I still had, and slowly turned my head in his direction as we whispered, hoping the police would not notice. Soon I turned far enough so I could clearly see the filthy, bloody wound on his head—then I saw the flies crawling in it. I was sick; I no longer cared about the police. I dropped my arms, pulled a handkerchief from my pocket, and stepped over to the wounded man. An officer shouted and ran up to us. "Hey, King, what the hell you doing out of line?"

What I was doing was obvious, but I tried to reason with the officer. Although my clothes were torn, I still wore part of my clerical collar, and looked like some sort of ragged priest. "I want to wipe off his wound, and chase the flies out of the blood, away from his head."

The police looked at me. He raised his rifle in the air, holding the butt end ready. "You nigger-loving son of a bitch. What the hell you think this is, a damn hospital? I know you ain't no damn doctor. Shit, you ain't no preacher either. You touch his head, and you get one just like it."

I hesitated. In the moment of silence a fly made a filthy buzzing noise. I moved one step closer towards the injured man. "My god," shouted the policeman, "You don't think I'll do it, do you? I'll beat the hell out of you. It's time somebody did!"

I stared at the rifle butt, and then at the man's eyes. I knew he wanted to kill me. I was afraid. Afraid—not so much of death, but just afraid of pain. I did not want that rifle butt crashing into my skull—and the blood—and the dirt—and the flies, those damned flies—and, mostly, the pain. My head had never stopped aching for the past hour since the police had bounced my head on the stairs and sidewalk when they had captured me and dragged me feet first. My whole body ached from stretching against the wall. Now this man was ready to club me, to beat me, perhaps to shoot me. I was afraid I could stand no more pain. . . .

Slowly, I turned away from the wounded man. I turned away from the sweat and the filth, from the flies and the blood. I turned towards the policeman. I saw only the danger to myself; I heard only the threat to me, to me. . . . If the injured man at my side had screamed, I would not let myself hear. If the man was dying at my feet, I would not look down. There was no courage, no goodness, no decency left, only fear. I spoke to the policeman, "I understand you. I know what you can do."

He lowered the gun, grabbed me by one arm, and jerked me away. He led me to the opposite end of the line of prisoners, and forced me to resume the same position. I felt some shame about my own weakness, but also I had become so conscious of my own pain, my thoughts were so centered on my own body. I was also quite aware that it had been helpful to walk that short distance and move my limbs. I would have stumbled and fallen to the ground several times had the policeman not held my arm; but it was a chance to move most of my bones and muscles. Now the pain was not as bad. . . . I never once looked back at the bloody man with the flies.

But after a few minutes in the tense position again, the pain returned. Making the pain even worse was the terrible thirst. The temperature was 103°. The police never allowed the prisoners a taste of water. But the officers enjoyed making jokes about the heat; they made a point of stirring the ice in a water cooler nearby so vigorously that we could hear the splash of water and clink of ice. They talked to each other about how good the cool water was.

I lost track of time. Eventually, John Salter and I and a few others were ordered away from the wall, and told we were being taken out of the prison compound and up to the city jail. This time we were told to stand in a new position. We had to place our hands flat atop our heads, elbows painfully extended to the sides. Again there was no reason for this except punishment. We waited like this perhaps ten minutes to be loaded into another truck for another battering ride to the city jail.

I looked at the policemen, and I knew that if they did this work more than one day they could invent torture worthy of the Huns. And I knew these ordinary folk could administer death camps and ovens as easily as any Nazis in time if the Movement did not change things. And I thought that if I was ever in an American death camp, I might be so afraid, so broken down in spirit, that I might be a docile prisoner tool of the guards. I had always wondered why the prisoners of the Germans did not organize themselves and revolt. Now I knew. Any of us could be good Mississippians, good Germans, good Americans.

These were the thoughts I had part of the time as I stood in the line. Most of the thoughts just centered on my own pain. Sometimes I moved from thoughts of self and pain to intense hatred for the white guards.

"Hey, King. Rev. King," a voice whispered. I was startled because this was not the voice of either prisoner next to me. It was a policeman, a hated white policeman. I was afraid. Even the jokes about water now hurt. I did not want any more pain. I thought I might suddenly begin crying. I could not take anything else. I pretended I did not hear the voice.

The policeman, one of the guards standing on the outside of the wire enclosure, came closer to the fence and looked at me. Then he whispered again—and I understood the words. "I hope you win," he said, "Some of us think the niggers oughta get a better break. We know things ain't right like it is in Miss'ssippi. Don't you give up now."

Before I could whisper a reply, had I dared, he was gone. Rifle on his shoulder, he marched on down the fence, looking like a proper concentration camp guard. A moment ago, I had wanted to kill all these Nazis. I hated every white policeman that existed. And now I couldn't even be sure whom to hate—or kill. . . . This was just too much to think about. I was almost glad to shift my attention back to my physical pain.

A White Girl Remembers

BEVERLY LOWRY

IN THE SAME WAY that we take a long time paying tribute to the ways in which our parents have helped shape our lives, it has taken me a while to reconcile myself to acknowledging the influence of the town of Greenville, Mississippi, on my life and writing, and to own up to the part William Alexander Percy, whom I never met, played. Denying one's background is common enough, wherever a person comes from, but white Southerners do seem to rage against their past with particular vehemence and I have been no exception.

I hear these stories, what it was like when Will Percy was alive and how that was the beginning of it all, when Greenville became a literary-minded town. Will Percy—poet, scholar, plantation owner, patriarch of the town—had this kind of informal salon, I hear, to which came cultured people of the time, writers and those who would be, sitting on his porch, talking poetry. Shelley, Byron, Keats. Reminiscing, listening to music. Mozart? Brahams? I had no way of knowing. I just got around to Mozart this year.

I hear Greenville was like that at one much-remembered time—not mine—for a small group of white people of a certain generation. Now the town is different. Sociological flipflops have taken place. Greenville has lost its place in the state as a literary center. But the spirit is still there. And so new kinds of stories are being told. I don't live there anymore, but I go back. And by going back, I have come to understand that I belong to a middled generation in the history of the town, halfway between Will Percy's time and today. Kids may not hear so much about William Alexander Percy anymore. But for my generation, he was like a mythical grandfather whose exploits children ask for stories about before going to sleep. I felt his existence constantly, not as a real person but as a beneficent shadow cast long and large over the town. A shadow no one had any desire to step out from under. A shadow which also had its very solid and substantial Other, in the shape of living writers who proved out the myth, and a mysterious bronze knight.

I never wanted to write about Greenville, or the South. I, in fact, considered the idea and decided against it. Too many Southern books had already been written. And the literary legacy of Will Percy—drilled into our heads from first grade to twelfth—had become burdensome. By the time I began writing a novel, I'd moved to new ground. I thought I was a different person. A city person, a Texas person. Who needed Greenville? Yet my first novel proceeded, not on its own exactly but willfully, gathering place and characters the way candy in a pocket collects lint. First there was a twirler marching down a street, tossing her silver baton in the sky to reflect against the setting sun, then there was the street itself—wasn't it Washington Avenue in downtown Greenville, wasn't the furniture store she passed actually Senoj Furniture, the owner having decided his name spelled backwards was more exotic than the other way around?—and little by little the town: with or without decisions, I was back in Greenville. In book jacket and publicity copy, my publisher kept claiming the book was set in Mississippi, although in no place in the book is the name of the state mentioned. There is a big river but it too is left unnamed. My one small victory.

My particular story, then, is of a white girl who grew up in Will Percy's town in the fifties. It was still his town, though at the time about which my memory is keenest, he was no longer alive. My basic cultural rhythms however, the drumbeats my heart kept time to, were not those of Keats and Mozart but mostly of black men—the Coasters, the Platters, Sam Cooke, Nat King Cole—plus local groups—the Re-Bops, Red Tops—and—they couldn't all be black—for variety, that one new white boy from Memphis. My culture was pop culture. Which felt like culture enough. "Hearts Made of Stone" made my own heart turn like a flopping fish; Elvis's young high voice singing "That's All Right, Mama" still takes me back to a summer night in Memphis, 1952. What more could a girl want? Underneath, however, something else was going on. Teachers were telling me things I didn't know I was listening to. Like whispers in the night, the town itself, its literary myth and mystery, were taking root. Repetition has its effect. When teachers got a certain evangelical look in their eyes, we knew what was coming, in the same way a practiced churchgoer can predict the onset of prayer. They were either going to bring up the name William Alexander Percy or the title of his book, *Lanterns on the Levee.* That such a ghost might provoke a lasting response should come as no surprise. Not many people in this country can lay claim to having grown up in a town which has for a patron saint, of all things, a poet.

I left Greenville soon after graduating from high school and for one reason and another did not go back for fifteen years. After college, I moved to Manhattan, where I lived from 1960 to 1965. During that time, I wrote my first fiction, some of which I have kept, buried deep in a drawer that is seldom opened. I look at that work now and recognize nothing. Not the voice or the strangely unfocused language. Not even the stories themselves. Is that me? I think. Where did this plot come from? The stories sound not as if they were told by somebody else, but as if they'd been written by nobody, so disconnected is the language from the life of the writer. This refusal to own up to one's heritage—the only past any of us will ever have—is nothing new. If Quentin Compson had to move North and hate the South, so also did many of the rest of us—particularly those who left home when I did. In New York in 1960, moving among fancy new actor friends, a girl did not exactly cast herself as God's own by admitting she grew up white in Mississippi. (Not that times change too much. It was only a couple of years ago that an old friend from New York tried to take me to a soul food restaurant in the East Village. When I told my friend I had grown up on mustard greens and cornbread and that, while I still liked greens and loved cornbread, I would as soon have linguine with white clam sauce, he refused to believe that I knew what I knew and that white and black people in Mississippi ate the same food.) Back in those days, I was going for the impossible: to write as if I had no past. Could I convince people I was a New Yorker, sharp and snappy with no discernible accent? I thought I'd try.

I had to leave New York to get over that. Texas was far enough; White Plains might have sufficed. The first writing I did in Texas has a more honest sound to it than any I did in New York. So, things work out. I learned other lessons in New York.

But what of the ghost, whose descendents still slip into my dreams? I studied no writing in college, yet I am a writer now. Where did the impulse originate? If William Alexander Percy played a part, what is it? I have thought about this a fair amount and have, in time, figured out a scheme: four different aspects of the man, which, like Marley, came at us from alternate directions and settled deep in our subconscious, like smoke. The four are simple enough. They are the work, the word, the flesh. And mystery itself.

The work, of course, is Percy's book, *Lanterns on the Levee*, about the 1927 flood, when the Mississippi River all but swallowed Greenville whole. The book was pressed time and again into my hands by awestruck teachers. You must read this, they said; it will tell you who you are and where you come from. And they got that look. The book looked so . . . poetic. Being a healthy adolescent, I did not read it. (Did not read Faulkner or Eudora Welty either until I was married and had a child, when *The Hamlet* and "Why I Live at the P.O." were pressed on me with the same urgency, by an actor friend born and raised in Brooklyn.) About ten years ago, a bookseller in Houston who knew I was from somewhere in Mississippi—Greenwood? Greenville?—approached me with a book in his hand. "Have you read this?" he said. He had the same glazed look in his eyes. I scanned the title. *Lanterns on the Levee* was out to get me.

Finally, I was old enough not to need to resist it. I'd already published my own novel. I had a new last name. I belonged to an organization of Texas writers. I had no family in Mississippi anymore. And so I took Will Percy's book home and read it, cover to cover that night. I was not prepared to have so much pure fun reading *Lanterns on the Levee*. It's a wonderfully lyrical and evocative piece of work, not to mention the fact that anything halfway decent written about a person's hometown can manage to give a girl a thrill. The teachers were right all along, but so was I. It is a special pleasure to come upon a book labeled classic and find the joy of it on your own, without assignment or need for virtue. I believe I discovered Jane Austen that same year, blessedly late. I remember one long family vacation when, to the disgruntlement of the others in my group, I spent the entire trip blissed-out in the backseat, immune to the children's bickering, as absorbed in Jane Austen if lost again in the adventures of Nancy Drew.

The word came from teachers. Not only must we read Will Percy's book; one of us had to do what he did. Someone had to be a writer. Literature was our legacy; the making of writers what set Greenville apart from, say, Greenwood. Let other towns boast of star fullbacks; we watched for prose. ("The town," of course, was us: white people, less than half the population of Greenville. That I received special treatment at the expense of all those others still nags at me: more guilt, as prickly as familial. But the town is less rigid than most. Now that the racial flipflop has taken place, the search is doubtless on for anyone of any color . . . unless with the inevitable fading of the ghost's presence, Greenville has become a different town altogether.)

I went back to Greenville three years ago to participate in a festival celebrating the town's proud history of producing not just writers, but artists in all fields. The festival was a big success. The literary events were the first I have been to in which the majority of the people attending were neither writers nor teachers. Neighbors of mine came; friends of my parents; towboat people, bankers, lawyers, farmers. The town, in short, turned out; no one expected it not to. In my time, art was as everyday as Elvis, or a toaster. We were encouraged to think of literature not only as something honorable to have done—for Shakespeare, for instance, to have done—but as a noble practice of the present, as possible a career as law or engineering. (Money wasn't much mentioned. Money is the dirty subject in the Delta . . . maybe a reason there's never enough.)

And who were the ones who had done it? The live writers who'd helped fulfill the legacy? The ones who came before me—Shelby Foote, Ellen Douglas, Will Percy's kin, Walker—those who sat on the porch discussing Keats, speak casually of the man Will Percy. In this piece, I too have called him by his familiar name, but uncomfortably and with an embarrassing brashness. I know no Will Percy. For me, the man is forever William Alexander Percy, a name on a book jacket. And if the word was to have any lasting effect, it had to have flesh and blood validification, which it did.

Shelby Foote lived on Washington Avenue down from my house, in a California-style bungalow located in a funky, but questionable neighborhood near downtown. I used to look for him when we passed his house. What, I wondered, was he doing in there? He was known to be strange. And reclusive: woe to the salesman who knocked at his door. When his novel, *Love in a Dry Season,* came out, I eavesdropped on my mother's bridge club as, between bids, the women gossipped. They were so excited! Assuming characters in a novel were only stand-ins for real people, they picked the book apart, attaching real names and faces to the ones in the book. I hoped someone I knew would be in the novel, that the novel would tell me what people I knew were really like. I listened hard to the women. The man Shelby Foote had been part of Will Percy's world and now he was part of mine. The myth had become flesh. All this is keenly knotted into the sensory memories of my adolescence, when every piece of news seemed sexually charged. And part of the larger mystery: *what were they doing in there?*

When I think about the geography of Greenville, I automatically place at its center its great bronze knight. Myth provokes the imagination by means of mystery. In Greenville, mystery has its concrete expression. In the middle of the town cemetery, there is a statue marking the grave of Will Percy's father. The statue is huge, a gloomy bronze knight in chain mail, his head down, eyes lowered, sword point between his feet. An enormous marble slab flanks the knight. Engraved in the marble atop the knight's head is the name PERCY. We used to go to the cemetery to visit the melancholy knight, to scare ourselves and touch him, to look up and wonder at his presence. Sometimes we'd turn down the wrong road and miss him and then come upon him by surprise, which scared us even more. The first time I saw the knight, I was no taller than his sword. One of Will Percy's descendents, Billy, was in school with me, a year younger than I. I used to look at Billy and try to imagine what it would be like, to be a PERCY and have your name engraved on such a thing.

Influence is quirky. Mystery sticks. The Percy statue has appeared in two of my books. I can see it as clearly this minute as if I were back there in the graveyard. Not too long ago I dreamed about the knight. More recently, I dreamed about Billy. During the arts festival, my brother and I went to the graveyard. Everything looked the same. The trees were bigger, the moss and mildew thicker. But we knew our way around. Children spend a lot of time in cemeteries when they're located in the heart of a town. We drove to the knight, parked and got out. Some damage had been done to the marble, scratches and nicks made by people wanting to attach themselves to the legend in a different way; initials gouged into the stone. My brother and I didn't say much. We looked at the knight a while, then left, he with his memories and me with mine.

Things work out. Nothing lasts forever. The tale-swapping about the salon on Will Percy's porch will fade. Barring major catastrophe, the books of the writers of his time and since will remain. New writers will come along to debunk the heritage of Percy and tell the story of the new Greenville. All this is proper. But a girl has to set her priorities. Myself, I hope the knight in the graveyard stands forever. A white girl could do worse than have its shadow to go back and stand in, now and then.

FROM

Reminiscences of an Active Life

JOHN ROY LYNCH

THE WAR CAME

BOTH MR. AND MRS. DAVIS had the reputation of being kind to their slaves. For slave owners, they were reasonable, fair, and considerate. Their house servants were very much attached to them. I was a particular favorite of both Mr. and Mrs. Davis. Mrs. Davis was a devout member of the Protestant Episcopal church. It was under her tutelage and influence that I became attached to that church. I was one of a class that was to be confirmed and baptized by Bishop [William Mercer] Green on the occasion of his next visit to Natchez, which was to be made the latter part of 1861. But the war broke out in the meantime, the blockade preventing the bishop from reaching Natchez. During and for a long time after the war, I seldom attended services at an Episcopal church, but attended services quite regularly at the colored churches, which were Methodist and Baptist, there being no colored Episcopal church at Natchez.

Since slavery had been abolished and I had reached a more mature age, I did not take kindly to the idea of occupying a prescribed seat in a white church. Hence I did not become connected with the church of my youth and choice until late in life. But the seed that was planted by Mrs. Davis had taken deep root and could never be eradicated or destroyed. She also organized a Sunday School class composed exclusively of colored boys. I was a member of the class and was usually at its head. No member of the class was suspected of being able to read. She gave us lessons from the catechism of the church which we were required to study, commit, and recite the following Sunday from memory. She also read interesting passages from the Bible and short stories from the lives of persons whose names figure in Bible history. One of the questions in the catechism and the answer to the same did not impress me favorably. It occurred to me that neither the question nor the answer had any business being in that book. The question was in these words: "What is the duty of a servant to his mistress and master?" The answer was, "To serve them heartily, with a good will and not with eye service." The teacher took particular pains to explain what those words meant. "An eye servant" she said, "is one that will shirk his duty every chance he can get and will not work unless an eye is kept on him. A good servant is one that will render honest and faithful service without being watched. This is what is meant by the words 'not with eye service.'" Of course we accepted the explanation with apparent satisfaction.

She also taught us to sing a number of hymns. A verse in one of them was in these words: "To serve the present age, my calling to fulfill. Oh may it all my powers engage to do my master's will." The impression the teacher endeavored to make upon our youthful minds was that the master referred to was our earthly master, in the person of her husband, Mr. Davis. Usually when this hymn was being sung, Davis would put in an appearance and join in the singing, his purpose being, of course, to illustrate in a practical way the fact of the explanation which had just been given by his wife, the teacher. While we took, of course, an entirely different view of the matter, we did not deem it safe or advisable to give expression to our opinions about it. While I was an especial favorite of both Mr. and Mrs. Davis, this seemed to be particularly true of Mrs. Davis. She would seldom, if ever, go shopping or visiting without having me occupy a seat on the carriage by the side of the driver to open and close gates on the road, and open and close the carriage door for her to get in and out. She would often have me come to her bed chamber during the day, especially when the weather was warm, and sit for hours at a time by her side and fan her and hand her ice water when thirsty. She was very fond of me and would speak of me in terms of commendation and praise when talking with friends and servants. And yet, in a way that was both harmless and innocent on my part, I incurred her ill will and displeasure and thus turned a good and true friend into a strong and bitter enemy, which came near to costing me my life.

It was my duty, among others, to brush the flies from the table during meal hours. Davis, who was of a mirthful nature, would frequently bring me into the conversation at the dinner table, for the reason, no doubt, that he enjoyed what he considered my cute and intelligent answers to his questions. On one occasion Mrs. Davis stated that some of the servants had complained of not getting enough to eat. She remarked that she knew of her own personal knowledge that there was no justifiable grounds for such complaints because she gave out the food herself and therefore knew that what was thus given out was ample. Davis gave me a wink of the eye and asked: "Roy, how is it with you, do you get enough to eat?" My prompt reply was in these words: "I get a plenty, such as it is, but I could eat as much more of anything that is better." Davis enjoyed this very much and laughed heartily, but his wife was very much incensed. She rebuked me sharply for what she called my insolence and threatened to get even with me in some way.

I took advantage of the first opportunity that presented itself shortly after dinner to approach her and begged her not to be displeased with me on account of the unfortunate remark that I made at the dinner table. I assured her that I was sorry I made it; that no insolence or disrespect was intended and that I would endeavor to be on my guard in the future and would not allow myself to make any remark to which she could take any exception. She relented without hesitation and as a result thereof we were as good friends thereafter as we had been in the past. But a few months later Davis again made the mistake of bringing me into the conversation at the dinner table. On this occasion the topic of conversation was "lying." Mrs. Davis remarked that she could never have any respect for a liar. No one, in her opinion, was ever justified or excused for telling a lie. In this connection she took pleasure in referring to a recent conversation she had with her sister. Mrs. Shields, who was not only a woman who was considerably advanced in years, but was the mother of a large family, some of whom were grown. In that conversation referred to, Mrs. Shields had informed her that she had never told a lie in her life.

Davis, who evidently accepted this statement with some grain of allowance, decided to bring me into the conversation. Looking me squarely in the face he quickly asked: "Roy, what do you think of that statement?" Without giving the matter serious thought I replied, "I think she told one when she said that." Of course, Davis enjoyed that very much and laughed heartily, but Mrs. Davis was so enraged and so indignant that she ordered me to leave the room immediately, remarking that she never wanted to see me or have me come about her again. But Davis, who was responsible for what had taken place, made an objection and, in consequence thereof, I was allowed to remain in the dining room until dinner was over.

Shortly after dinner I made an effort to approach her, as on the other occasion, to explain and apologize for what I had said, but the effort this time was fruitless. She not only repulsed me, but said she did not care to see me or hear anything I had to say. She therefore ordered me to leave her presence and never approach her again. She then gave positive orders that I be sent immediately to Tacony plantation and be subjected to hard plantation labor, but Davis interfered and revoked the order. Consequently I remained at Dunleith until the time came for Davis to go to the front as captain of a company of Confederate soldiers which he had raised. But the only condition upon which I could remain was that I could no longer be present in the dining room during meal hours, or have anything to do with, or say to, Mrs. Davis, one way or the other. In other words, I was to keep out of her sight and away from her presence.

After Davis's company had been ordered to join the Confederate forces then operating in Virginia, Mrs. Davis decided to go with her husband. It thus became necessary for nearly all of the servants to be sent to the plantation, it being necessary for only a few to remain to take care of the property. Davis insisted that my mother and her children should be among those to remain, but Mrs. Davis drew the line on me. She insisted that I be among those to be sent to the plantation. She claimed that I was bad, mischievous, and dangerous and that, notwithstanding my youth, if I were allowed to remain I might get bad notions and ideas in the heads of the other servants. She was so persistent and insistent that Davis at the last moment reluctantly consented and for the first time in my life I was separated from my mother and subjected to the hard and cruel fate of a plantation laborer. This was in 1862. There had just been a disastrous overflow in that part of Louisiana in consequence of which that section was very unhealthy. Shortly after I was put to work I was taken with a severe attack of the swamp fever, which very nearly resulted in death, and from the effects of which I did not fully recover for more than a year.

Davis, however, did not remain very long at the front. After an absence of a few months, he and his wife returned to Dunleith. I was not among those that went back from the plantation, but remained there until the occupation of Natchez by the Union forces in July 1863. The return of Davis after such a short absence was a great surprise and disappointment to many of his friends and neighbors. But that service, brief as it was, had no doubt given him all the experience he wanted in that line. He had resigned his commission and the resignation had been accepted. He could not be forced into the service, because the Confederate Congress had passed a law exempting from military service all slave owners who owned over twenty slaves. It was said by some of his friends that his resignation was due to friction and unpleasant relations with some of his superior officers. Whether or not there was any foundation for this report the public was never informed.

After the occupation of Natchez by the Union forces I decided to make an effort to get to my mother. But getting across the Mississippi River was the serious problem that was before me. I had, of course, no money, but I had made an effort to raise some chickens. In that line I had not been very successful, for when I got ready to leave the plantation, I could claim ownership of but one chicken and that one was almost too young to command a fair price. But I took my chance and made a start for Vidalia, the little town situated on the west side of the Mississippi River opposite Natchez. When I reached Vidalia I saw for the first time a live Yankee soldier. I approached him and inquired if he wanted to buy a chicken. "What is it worth?" he asked. "Whatever you choose to give," I replied. "Very well," he said, "I will give you a dime for it." The bargain was closed and I was immediately possessed of my first piece of Yankee money, which was a ten-cent paper bill, of which, however, I had possession only a short while, for I was not long in finding the owner of a small boat, to whom I gave the ten cents to take me across the river.

When I landed on the Mississippi side of the river I was a happy lad once more. I walked to Dunleith with the expectation of meeting my mother there, but in this I was disappointed. I soon found out that she and all the other servants had left. My heart almost melted when I saw Mrs. Davis in the kitchen endeavoring to prepare something for herself, husband, and children to eat. I said nothing to her but the meeting between Davis and myself was both cordial and friendly. He said he was glad to see me and have an opportunity to talk with me because he wanted to say to me that he never regretted anything more in his life than when he yielded to his wife and her determination to have inflicted upon me what he knew was a gross wrong and a grave injustice. He referred with much feeling to the promise he had made to my mother and stated that this cruel and unjust treatment to which I had been subjected was the only instance in which he felt that he had allowed that promise to be violated. And, what made him feel it more keenly, was a knowledge of the fact that he himself was the innocent instrument through whom the injustice had been done. He said he believed my mother appreciated his kindness towards her and her children and, but for this one act in my case, he believed she would have remained with him for a while at least, during the period of his sadness, sorrow, distress, and financial disaster.

As he thus spoke, I could see that he was not only deeply affected, but his emotions were an unmistakable indication of the deep mental strain under which he was laboring, while the visible moisture of the eyes revealed the sadness and sorrow of a broken heart. A few days prior to that time he was not only in opulent circumstances, with money, property, and many slaves at his service, but he was a strong and fortunate factor politically and otherwise in the community in which he lived. His word was law and his personal presence commanded attention, reverence, and respect. Now he found himself without power, without prestige, without slaves, and almost without means. It was a sad and pitiful picture. Even my own presence brought forcibly to his mind the humiliation to which he was then subjected, for I was no longer obliged to address him or refer to him as "master," but merely as Captain or Mr. Davis. Still, my heart went out with some degree of sympathy for him.

Before we separated he requested me to say to my mother that he still had and would continue to have a friendly interest in her and that he desired very much to have her come and see him. Then, with a cordial shake of the hand and an expression of good wishes on the part of each for the other, we separated. I then went to Natchez, and after spending several hours in search of my mother, I finally succeeded in locating her. When we met the union was, of course, cordial and affectionate. I informed her of my interview with Davis and delivered the message he sent her. She said she regretted very much that she could not see her way clear to remain at Dunleith, because she was much attached to Davis, who had always treated her kindly, but that she could never forgive his wife for her cruel and inhuman treatment of me. That, she said, was the reason she had left, as soon as it was possible for her to get away. All of the other servants, it appears, had left for substantially the same reason—dislike of Mrs. Davis. Hence Davis was the unfortunate victim of the unpopularity of his wife with their former house servants.

FROM

Witness in Philadelphia

FLORENCE MARS

PREFACE

ON JUNE 21, 1964, three young men, civil rights workers, disappeared from the Neshoba County jail in Philadelphia, Mississippi. Their decomposed bodies were eventually dug out of a twenty-foot earthen dam. Three and a half years later, eighteen men, most of whom were either known or assumed to be members of the White Knights of the Ku Klux Klan of Mississippi, went on trial for conspiracy to deprive these three men of their federal rights to life, liberty, and the pursuit of happiness. The eighteen defendants included the sheriff, deputy sheriff, former sheriff (and sheriff-elect) of Neshoba County, a Philadelphia city policeman, and the imperial wizard of the White Knights. . . .

It was not my intention to become involved. But I wanted the community to see that it should oppose murder no matter who committed it. Less than twenty-four hours after I testified before a grand jury investigating those murders (and the church burning that had preceded them), the Klan initiated a campaign to "ruin" me, a "WASP lady" with eight great grandparents buried in Neshoba County.

The Klan was successful in its boycott of my business; the community began to regard me as a "Communist agitator"; and, finally, Klan propaganda succeeded in separating me from the fellowship of First Methodist Church. Afterwards, I moved into the roll of spectator, in order to write this book and try to understand what had happened here. I learned, for one thing, how Nazi Germany is possible in a "law-abiding Christian society." And I learned, too, that society will act against its own best interest to protect itself from the truth. . . .

I

In Neshoba County, Mississippi, the basement of the past is not very deep. All mysteries of the present seem to be entangled in the total history of the county, a history that began in 1830. In that year the Choctaw Indians, bowing to the pressure of the young and expanding United States, ceded in the Treaty of Dancing Rabbit Creek the last of their lands east of the Mississippi River and were removed to Oklahoma. After this, white settlers from the Carolinas and Georgia moved into the timbered red clay hills of Neshoba County to scratch out a living in cotton. They settled in small farm communities built around churches—communities with names like Cushtusa, Hope, Muckalusha, and Waldo. Because most people made their livings in subsistence farming, there were relatively few slaves, and the Negro population at the time of the Civil War comprised about a quarter of the total population of eight thousand. There was virtually no migration into the county after the Civil War except for a back-and-forth movement with neighboring counties. The population was a homogeneous group, almost all white Anglo-Saxon Protestants, and proud of it. (There were a very few Irish Catholics in the county, descended from three pioneering brothers named Rush, the relatively low percentage of Negroes, and a population of Choctaws that did not hit a thousand until 1950.)

At the turn of the century Philadelphia was a sleepy village of less than a hundred inhabitants, though it had been the county seat since 1838. Only a few frame buildings stood on the courthouse square. The southern side of the square was a cornfield; goats ran through the dirt halls of the courthouse, and men played checkers under a mulberry tree in front. The town had no running water, telegraph, electric lights, or year-round roads. There was one telephone.

Everything changed when the railroad came through in 1905. Men of ambition moved to town and there was a period of rapid growth. In 1909, three years after the town was chartered, the editor of the county newspaper, the *Neshoba Democrat,* wrote, "At one time Neshoba County (and that was not too long ago) was classed as one of the most under-developed and backwoods counties in the state. This impression went out over the country not on account of the barrenness of the soil or the ignorance of the citizenship but on account of the fact that we were without telegraph and railroad communication with the outside world."

Cotton began to seriously deplete the soil around the turn of the century, and the farm economy was further depressed by the widespread appearance of the boll weevil in 1911. This caused many to leave the county in the teens, but those who remained felt a strong sense of community and an intense loyalty to the county. Besides the communal activities of church and summer revivals, there was an annual campground fair, and local entertainment such as womanless weddings and minstrel shows. Every fall the circus came to town and every winter the Great Swain Show came, presenting a variety of entertainment and such melodramas as "East Lynn," "Peck's Bad Boy," "Father and Mother in Society," "Orange Blossoms," and "Helen's Experience in the World of Today."

And there was progress. By the mid-1920s of my childhood some of the streets of Philadelphia were paved, and the square was filled with one- and two-story brick buildings with flat wood awnings that covered the sidewalks in front. There were several department stores and drugstores, hardware shops, feed and seed outlets, barbershops, a five-and-ten, two banks, and a post office. There were no liquor stores or saloons.

On Saturdays people came to town to shop for everything from plowstock to the latest in ladies' millinery. Crowds of Philadelphians—white farmers, Negroes, and Choctaw Indians—filled the lawn of the old red brick courthouse and the sidewalks of the stores around the square. Most of the country people dressed differently than we did in town—the men in overalls, khakis and flannel, the women in homemade cotton dresses. The Negroes dressed more colorfully, the women often wearing aprons and bandanas. The Choctaw Indians lined up against the buildings, hardly saying a word. The Choctaw men wore white shirts, black pants, and hats; the women wore colorful, ankle-length dresses with ruffles on the bottom. Almost all adults, except the Choctaw women, wore large-brimmed soft straw hats to protect themselves from the sun; some women wore their Sunday hats. Mules and wagons moved slowly through the streets and were left in vacant lots a block or two off the square. Men in overalls sat on the curbs and courthouse steps, whittling small sticks and spitting tobacco.

Evangelical groups came to the square to preach, either under the magnolia tree on the courthouse lawn or on the steps of the courthouse. Every week Miss Nannie Ogletree from the Linwood community preached on the east courthouse steps, across the street from Mars Brothers' Department Store. Wearing a straw hat and a long-sleeved, loose-fitting gingham dress that came to her ankles, she swayed back and forth with her eyes closed and chanted in a sing-song voice about sinners saving themselves from the fires of hell. Then she broke into the unknown tongue. Although most went on with their shopping and visiting, a few men in overalls and women with long hair braided or balled against their heads gathered around, listening and waiting for the collection plate to be passed.

Miss Nannie Ogletree was a Pentecostal. The most well-to-do families in the county tended to belong to the regular denominations—Baptist, Methodist, and Presbyterian; the tenants and some of the poorer farmers congregated in the Pentecostal and primitive sects, sometimes moving up to regular denominations as their circumstances improved. There was a tendency among the membership of the first churches of the regular denominations to look down socially on the noisier sects. In Philadelphia, we uptown Methodists even considered the uptown Baptists more backwoodsy and harder against the sins of the flesh like drinking, dancing, and card-playing. The Baptists did seem to be more successful in keeping their children from slipping around to participate in these activities, and the Baptist ladies were not as likely to belong to one of the several afternoon bridge clubs. There was an oft-repeated saying that a "Methodist is a Baptist who has learned to read; a Presbyterian is a Methodist who has moved to town; and an Episcopalian is a Presbyterian who has gotten rich." There were no Episcopalians in Neshoba County, and, literate or not, there were far more Baptists than members of all other denominations combined.

The few Catholics in the county had very different attitudes toward drinking. Roman Catholic priests did not preach about the evils of alcohol and even drank a little whiskey themselves. If nothing else, this difference set the Catholics apart from the Protestants. There was often anguish when a Catholic married into a fine old Protestant family.

There was not much difference between the Protestant denominations in the county. Once saved through immersion the Baptists were always saved; Methodists could fall from grace; and Presbyterians were born into salvation. But we all interpreted the Bible literally and subscribed to the hellfire-and-brimstone preaching of fundamentalism.

The preachers of my childhood taught that unless one had faith, "believed on" the Lord Jesus Christ as a personal savior who had been born of a virgin and who was resurrected from the dead, he was condemned to hell. They painted hell in vivid and terrifying images: a lake of fire and brimstone where the soul would be tormented day and night forever and ever. They said there was no earthly suffering comparable to the indescribable pain suffered in hell.

Fundamentalist preachers emphasized the sins of the flesh as the greatest stumbling block to salvation. These sins included smoking, drinking, gambling, dancing, and fornication outside of marriage. Some preachers, many of whom had very little formal education and no seminary training, bore down on the new "round" dancing in which men and women who weren't married danced close together. The Pentecostal and Holiness sects believed it was an abomination to the Lord for women to cut their hair. And some still preached about breaking the Sabbath.

During my childhood the sin that received the most attention from the pulpit was the use of alcohol. Though abstinence was only recommended in the Methodist church, especially for church officers, in practice total abstinence was regarded as necessary for salvation. Biblical verses were quoted, such as, "Wine is a mocker, strong drink is raging, and whoever is deceived thereby is not wise." Drinking whiskey was a sure sign that the devil was at work in an individual.

Born in sin, endowed with a sinful nature, it was faith and faith alone that led men to salvation. The road to salvation began when one joined the church and made a public profession of faith in God and a confession and repentance of sins. This profession of faith was supposed to be a deeply emotional experience, when the Holy Ghost entered into the soul. Congregations were told that there was nothing so horrible to look upon as a dying person whose soul was doomed to hell. At the close of regular church services the preachers always opened the doors of the church and pleaded in anguished tones for the sinners in their congregations to come to the altar and make peace with God, lest their lives be snuffed out in the next instant without time for a deathbed conversion. Although some were converted at the close of church services, most souls were saved at the week-long summer revivals and camp meetings. During the summer months, evangelical groups set up tents on the edge of town and preachers like Railroad Spinks and Howard Williams (who was converted by Billy Sunday) preached. In addition, every church in the county had its own revival. Besides bringing souls to Christ for the first time, preachers at revivals emphasized the "rededication" of lives to Christ. They issued numerous altar calls, and the success of a revival was determined by the number of souls saved and rededicated.

Once men put themselves in the hands of God they lived in a state of grace. Through faith and daily prayer and meditation they gained the strength to do God's will and overcome temptation. There were no problems that could not be endured or overcome, and it was quoted that "all things work for good for them that love the Lord." This was interpreted to mean that whatever happened, good or bad, was the Lord's will.

Since Methodists taught that it was possible to fall from grace, we were called backsliding Methodists. We did believe that through a perfect love of God it was possible to arrive at a permanent state of grace, called sanctification, but that very few attained it.

Once saved, it was one's responsibility to bring others to Christ. As long as there was life, there was a possibility of salvation, even through deathbed conversion. Though the Bible said,

> Wide is the gate
> narrow the path
> and very few shall enter therein,

the prospects of hell were so horrible that an inordinate number of people in Neshoba County considered themselves to be saved. My grandfather, Poppaw, whose name was William Henry Harrison Mars, was reared in the strictest Methodism. He was born in 1867 in the Cushtusa community in Neshoba County, the seventh of eleven children. Down home, as Poppaw put it, the day started before breakfast with his father reading the Bible while the family knelt in chairs turned backwards at the table. At night the family gathered for evening prayers, just before the children went to bed. Poppaw's father helped found the Mars Hill Methodist Church at Cushtusa, and every summer after the crop was laid by, the family attended a Methodist camp meeting for a week. They camped out in rough cabins built around a pavilion and heard visiting preachers morning, noon, and night. Poppaw said his mother so strongly felt the spirit of the Holy Ghost that sometimes when she had just walked into the church she shouted praises to the Lord. Poppaw thought his parents lived the finest Christian lives of anyone he had ever known. In fact, he was mighty proud of the whole Mars family and said our stock was the salt of the earth. . . .

II

As I was growing up I learned how the South saw itself; the image was one I never fully accepted: southerners were white; Negroes were Negroes. The white civilization of the South was one of the greatest in the history of the world. Negro culture was primitive and greatly inferior. Negroes as a rule were a smiling, carefree people who accepted their place of inferiority in society and were satisfied with their lot.

Segregation of the races was a fundamental cornerstone in the southern way of life—something that was never discussed or questioned. Without segregation it was thought the races would mix and the great white southern civilization would be ended. As it was, the society was said to be harmonious; southerners had been good to Negroes and taught them all they knew.

Neshoba County prided itself on its good race relations, and white citizens boasted that they had friends among the Negro race that they would "do anything in the world for." Neshoba County also prided itself on its "good Negroes," those who worked hard but knew their place. Any Negro who wasn't appreciative was considered a troublemaker.

I first heard about the Civil War from Great Granny Latimer. One of my earliest memories is standing at her knee while she did her tatting and talked about the War Between the States. Granny Latimer was a strong, gentle, good-humored woman. Once, when our grocery bill came to nine dollars for the month, Poppaw complained to Mother and Granny that "Hon [Grandmother Florence] never had a bill such as that." Granny said, "We'll fix him," and she and Mother served cornbread and turnip greens every day for a month. Poppaw didn't say a word.

Granny Latimer had been a Carter from South Carolina, and both the Carters and the Latimers had owned a few slaves. Granny's husband, Montgomery Latimer, had been a captain in the Confederate Army, and Granny told me awesome stories about the days when the men were away and Yankee soldiers roamed the area. When Granny told me about the Yankees stealing, burning, and looting through here I figured she was talking about Sherman, but I later learned that Granny was referring to Grierson's Raiders.

In grammar school I learned more about the War Between the States, some of it from textbooks:

Before the Civil War, the South had been a cultured and wealthy society. Mississippi had been the fifth-richest state in the Union. (We were aware that Mississippi didn't have any "real" cities and understood that we were supposed to have had Memphis and Mobile, but the surveyors got drunk.) Before the war the South had slaves that were brought uncivilized from Africa by Yankee traders and sold to the South to work cotton. Southerners taught them the ways of civilization, especially Christianity, and the life of the slave was much better than the Negro's life in Africa, because his master felt responsible for him and protected and looked after him. I was taught that the war was fought because the North was trying to impose its will on the South. The South wanted to be a separate country and live its own life without federal power over it, but the North would not allow the South to secede from the Union. The issue in the war had not been slavery as Yankees said, but states' rights. The South would eventually have freed the slaves anyway. Yankees, who were no match on the battlefield for southern gentlemen, were able to defeat the Confederacy only because of overwhelming odds and barbaric tactics.

After the war some in the North wanted to treat southerners as brothers, but those who wanted vengeance won out. Had Lincoln lived it might have been different. Yankee carpetbaggers came down and promised the Negroes forty acres and a mule. In some places where there were Negro majorities, Negroes and scalawags were elected to office and were under the influence of the carpetbaggers who cared nothing for the well-being of the South. The government during Reconstruction was very corrupt. During this period Negroes were uppity and disrespectful. Although the Yankees built up the Negroes' expectations, they didn't deliver.

The Ku Klux Klan was organized after the war to control bad Negroes. The Klan was not nice, but it was necessary. After Reconstruction, without the Yankees to prod and push, Negroes settled back into their old ways. They quit voting, which they really hadn't cared about, and generally returned to their former masters. They found out that it was the southerner who helped them survive and was their best friend. Whereas southerners truly liked Negroes and vice versa, northerners did not.

Even after the South took over its own government, the national government continued to discriminate with unfair freight rates and tariffs. Yankees still had it in for the South and should be viewed with suspicion. (This supicion was easily come by, as I only knew three or four people in Neshoba County who were born north of the Mason-Dixon Line.)

The schoolroom story of the Civil War never seemed completely right to me. I believed that the Yankees had done what they were said to have done, but I was not sure that the South had really treated the slaves so well. And though the textbook told us that the Klan was a patriotic group, I was taught at home that the Klan was never any good. (I didn't know it then but during my childhood in the 1920s there was a resurgence of the Klan. Several leading citizens strongly opposed it; they ridiculed it, wrote letters to the editor of the paper, and forced the Klan to move out of the Masonic Temple. Poppaw told me that a few men who should have known better belonged to it. He and my parents had only disdain for the Klan.)

I also early questioned the belief that the Negro was so happy with his lot. When I was very young I remember feeling sorry for the domestic workers and being glad I was not a Negro. Poppaw had a servant house in one corner of the garden where our domestic help lived. The singing that came from this house or out over the washtub in the yard was depressing to me. The women sang in mournful tones about suffering and called on the Lord to have mercy on them and help them bear their troubles. This was puzzling to me at first, since I thought Negroes were supposed to be happy. I soon realized they had every reason not to be.

Other domestics walked to work at least six days a week, arriving by 7:00 A.M. and leaving between midafternoon and supper. They then walked home to take care of their own families. I wondered how they made ends meet. I knew that the custom of allowing the kitchen help to take leftovers from the table must have helped, as did the custom of letting them take some flour, meal, and sugar. Most white women were able to afford servants, because Negro women worked for practically nothing and seemed grateful for the job.

After finishing up in the white kitchens, maids carried the dirty clothes home with them to be boiled in iron wash pots, scrubbed on washboards in the zinc tubs out in their yards, and then pressed with flat irons heated on wood stoves or in front of the fireplace. Although most white families in town had electricity, none of the Negroes in town owned their houses and none of them had electricity. Once I asked Poppaw about this depressing situation. He lowered his head, leaned forward, and said, "They've been treated mighty bad." He didn't elaborate and didn't need to.

I also knew fairly early that the races were not so separate and distinct as they were supposed to be. I once asked the grandmother of a friend about a Negro woman I saw carrying what appeared to be a white baby. The woman hardly batted an eye before she explained to me that all Negro babies were born white, like the palms of Negroes' hands, and turned dark later when their skin was exposed to sunlight. I didn't believe that very long. Poppaw told me that certain colored families were related to white families, and often as not he told me the connection. He greatly disapproved of white men "carrying on" with Negro women. The opposite was virtually unheard of.

My other grandfather, Oscar Johnson, whom I called Pappy, told me that after the Civil War it was customary for former slaveholders to build a house in the backyard and retain one of the better-looking Negro women. He said his own grandfather Johnson had retained a woman and that his father Raz had a mulatto half-brother. I asked Pappy how white women felt about the relationship between white men and Negro women. Pappy chuckled and said, "Well, it was just sort of convenient."

There are other early memories. One night I heard Essie, who had cooked my dinner that day, moaning and screaming from her house in the backyard. The next morning I found out she was dead. I heard the grownups talking and learned that during the night Poppaw had been called to the back door by a friend of Essie's and asked for something to ease Essie's stomach pains. He said he didn't have anything and told Essie's friend to give her an aspirin. I was horrified that Essie had died, and I thought Poppaw should have gone out to see her.

I also remember once when Daddy paced the floor all night because a Negro client of his was going to be hanged the next day. I didn't know what the man had done, but I had the feeling he was being hanged because he was a Negro. I knew that white men didn't get hanged in Neshoba County. In fact, white men very often killed each other without being punished. Under the "unwritten law" used in Neshoba County courtrooms, a white man had the right to kill anyone he suspected of threatening his home, which usually meant being "too friendly" with his wife. "Self-defense" was also widely used. When I was a child a Tingle killed an Arledge on the square and a few years later a Powell killed a Cumberland in front of Mars Brothers' Department Store. Neshoba County juries rarely convicted a white man of murder and white men almost never went to the penitentiary for murder. We had a saying that "if you want to kill somebody, Neshoba County is the place to do it." (Precedent was broken in the early 1940s when a Catholic bootlegger named Grady White shot a popular vending-machine operator, Sam McCune. White was convicted and for the first time the electric chair was used on a white man. The electric chair, a then-recent replacement for hanging, was brought in from Jackson and a crowd gathered late at night on the courthouse square with chairs, crackers, and children—waiting for the current to be turned on and the street lights to dim.)

Besides not believing that the lot of the Negro was as just as it was said to be, I saw other discrepancies between what was supposed to be and what in fact was. Though the county was supposed to be dry and good Christians were not supposed to drink, it seemed to me that the denunciation and illegality of alcohol had no effect on the amount consumed. During the national Prohibition of my childhood, two drugstores on the square sold wood alcohol in milkshakes. During the same period the young men about town were said to keep bourbon in five-gallon barrels at the Hotel Rush, located on a corner of the square. Some of the men in town began to walk a little like Charlie Chaplin, one leg swinging out in a goose step. They were said to have the Jake Leg or Country Jake, a "temporary" nervous disorder caused from the shipment of bad Jamaica rum. The manufacture of moonshine whiskey, sometimes called white lightning, has always been one of Neshoba County's leading home industries. Anyone with a little corn and sugar and a pot to boil it in could brew moonshine. Some made it for the use of family and friends; others made large quantities that they wholesaled to bootleggers. It was made in all sections of the county, but one hilly and isolated section called Four Corners was noted for its number of stills. During Prohibition moonshine became increasingly sought, and increasingly raw. No amount of raiding by local sheriffs could begin to dry up this source.

For a brief period after Prohibition was repealed in 1933, one could buy 3.2 beer all over the state. The jails of Neshoba County filled to overflowing every weekend and as soon as state election machinery was set up, beer was voted out. Neshoba County remained one of the wettest dry counties in the dry state of Mississippi. Although some sheriffs raided stills and retailers more vigorously than others, never was there a time when a half-pint couldn't easily be bought in Neshoba County and even delivered to the door by taxi.

For a few, there was also the problem of morphine addiction. For years morphine was widely available in patent medicines. Some men in Poppaw's generation were addicted, and it was said there were a number of ladies who "took to their beds" because of addiction. Once addicted there was no trouble being supplied, as morphine was legally and freely prescribed until the 1914 Harrison Drug Act. For a number of years after that, the drug was not difficult to obtain. In the 1920s a small group of prominent young men became addicted, and this, plus the reputation for frontier violence and widespread bootlegging, gave the county an unenviable reputation; Philadelphia, especially, was referred to as a city of sin and was held up as an example of a present-day Sodom in revivals held in neighboring counties. Needless to say, the reputation was deeply resented in Philadelphia.

Morphine addiction deeply affected the world I lived in. As early as I can remember I knew that both Daddy and my uncle William took medicine they were not supposed to take. William was arrested several times for breaking into drugstores, and when I was five he was convicted for one incident and sentenced to two years in Parchman Penitentiary, a sentence he never served. Though William's bad habits were openly discussed in the house, it was from other children that I first heard William called a "dope fiend." I immediately knew that Daddy must be called that too. At about the same time I noticed that the preachers spoke not only of drunkards but also of dope fiends to illustrate what was most evil in all the world. . . .

III

As I was growing up I knew a world entirely different from Poppaw's house in Philadelphia. Mother's parents, Lou and Oscar Johnson, lived out in the country in the Coldwater community, eight miles west of town, where they ran a large country store. I often visited them on weekends with Mother, and every summer I spent a few weeks with them by myself. Mammy and Pappy were unassuming people who did not tell others what was right and wrong. Pappy was tall and trim, with only a fringe of red hair around his head. He had a quiet sense of humor and none of Poppaw's puritanical attitudes. Born in 1868 on Lonsa Laka Creek, three miles west of Philadelphia, Pappy was the second oldest of five children. His boyhood dream had been to be a merchant prince, and he loved to recall how as a small boy he went with his father to Meridian to sell the cotton and buy goods for the family. They sometimes brought back extra goods to sell as an accommodation. Usually a few of the neighbors banded together to make the trip by ox wagon. It took about a week to travel the forty-five miles to Meridian and back. Sometimes they would camp out with wagon trains, leaving Meridian with barrels of whiskey. Pappy and the other young boys straddled the barrels, stuck straws through the bung holes, and sucked whiskey.

By boarding in Philadelphia and then out of the county, Pappy got the equivalent of a high school education. His older brother Neil went to business school in Jackson but contracted typhoid fever and died. In 1893 he married Lou Sikes from nearby Waldo community; she had been engaged to Neil. Down the road from his father's house Pappy built a store with a long gallery across the front. In back of the store he built a log house with one big room plus a stove room with a dirt floor. Pappy and Mammy lived there until he and his neighbors finished a large house further down the road.

Mammy was an energetic, no-nonsense woman who reared seven children, ran the household, and spent almost as much time in the store as Pappy. Mammy reared the first five children as Baptists, which was Pappy's church, and the last two in her own Methodist church. Pappy always took Mammy and the children to church, but sometimes he sat around outside during services with some of the other men.

Mammy and Pappy were not as concerned about sins of the flesh as Poppaw. When the children were growing up Pappy kept a little whiskey in his house, as his father had before him. In his closet he kept a bottle, which he called his "medicine," and he also had a little trunk out in the hall where he kept a small supply of good liquor that merchants from New Orleans sent him during Prohibition. On the dining room table he kept a bottle of Peruna, a patent medicine, and took a spoonful before every meal. It was at least 80 percent alcohol. Mammy didn't care for alcoholic beverages herself, but for years she made a little blackberry wine, which was stronger than she realized. Once when Pappy drank too much, she poured out a whole churn and never made any more. The children got their appreciation of music from Pappy, who loved to play hoedowns on the fiddle, especially "Leather Britches."

When I went to the country in the summer Pappy, Mammy, and I went to the store in the morning and stayed all day, except for dinner. Pappy had a few peddlers who went through the countryside with goods from the store to trade for hides, furs, corn, chickens, eggs, and beeswax. When Pappy hit his peak in the late teens he had had about fifteen peddlers going out with horses and wagons every day. A wholesale merchant from New Orleans, Frank de la Tour, came to visit Pappy once; he said he wanted to meet the man who shipped him more chickens and eggs than anyone else. Pappy enjoyed another distinction of sorts: he ordered stuff by the freightcar load. A well-known brand, Garrett's, advertised that Neshoba used more snuff than any other county in the world. It was common for a customer to walk in with a struggling chicken under his arm or a basket of eggs or a towsack of corn to trade for merchandise. The most interesting customers were the Choctaw Indians.

The Choctaw legend I learned as a child was that they came to settle here from the West, following the direction of a stick they put in the ground each night. When they got to the land at Nanih Waiya, a Choctaw sacred mound located just north of the Neshoba County line, the stick stood straight, and they knew this was where the spirits wanted them to settle. After most of the Indians moved to Oklahoma, oil was struck out there. We had a joke that we should have taken the land in Oklahoma and let them keep Neshoba County. In the Treaty of Dancing Rabbit Creek it was agreed that those who did not want to go to Oklahoma could remain here, and Neshoba County was designated the capital of the Choctaw Nation. Every head of household was to get 640 acres of land, and others were to get land in other amounts. I heard that when the white settlers first began to come here the Indians who had remained chose to live off in the woods and wouldn't have anything to do with white people. I knew that the terms of the treaty hadn't been carried out and that one man here made his living collecting money from the Indians to finance alleged efforts to get the money due them.

A lot of Choctaws lived in the same part of the county as Mammy and Pappy, and they had a good rapport with the Indians. Pappy grew up with Choctaw tenants on his father's farm. Many of the Choctaw men who walked into the store spoke a little English. The women, in their ankle-length dresses, sometimes with a baby on their backs, were shy and rarely spoke. If no man was along, they would point and grin, their heads tucked. Choctaws never addressed anyone by a title; they used only first names. Even the children, if they spoke at all, called Mammy and Pappy Lou and Oscar; everyone else said Miss Lou and Mr. Oscar.

The Choctaws had a curious way of trading. They bought only one item at a time, and as a result it took an hour or two to get everything. My grandparents understood this and just stood and waited. After receiving change from one item, the Choctaw would pick another, then another, each time paying and receiving change before selecting the next item. They never overspent.

Pappy had a grist mill across from the store, and on grinding days the newly ground corn meal ran out of the bin with a fresh fine smell, feeling like warm sand. While the meal poured out, Pappy filled cloth sacks that had his name printed on them. When a number of sacks had been filled, Pappy would grab one end of an open bag, wind thread around the cloth under his fist, forming a nub that looked like a cow's teat. He would then rhythmically sew across the top of the other end and form another nub.

In the evenings Mammy and Pappy played cards games like rook and set-back. They had a homemade checkerboard and would sit and play, with the board between them on top of a barrel. They used soda pop tops for checkers. They also had old records that I listened to in the front room. I especially liked one in Negro dialect about two black crows. It had jokes such as one black crow saying to the other, "I'll meet you on the corner. If you get there first, draw a line. If I get there first I'll rub it out." There was also band music and the latest jazz records brought home from New Orleans by Mother's sister Ellen. If the night was hot, we'd sit on the porch with our feet on the banisters until it cooled off. We listened to the whippoorwills and watched the sky, and sometimes we'd see the reflection of car lights from faraway hills. Often there were shooting stars, and Pappy and Mammy would tell me about seeing Halley's comet.

The most wonderful event in my life every year was the Neshoba County Fair, held in late summer. I looked forward to it from one year to the next and saved money all summer for it. My great grandfather Raz Johnson was one of the founders of the fair. In 1888 he took Pappy's younger brother Norman to the Lake Patron's Union, a campground fair in neighboring Scott County. Others from the Coldwater community had visited the fair, and the next year the patrons of the Coldwater community school got together for one day in the pine grove behind the school building. The women stretched rope between the trees and hung quilts to mark off areas for each family. They brought their handiwork and some special cooking. The men brought farm products and animals to compare.

The activities began with prayers, followed by a sacred harp song—"Holy Manna"—sung by the children in the community singing school. A pony-riding contest for the boys was held in the afternoon. Cool lemonade was made possible by a block of ice hauled forty miles from Newton in an ox wagon. Keeping the ice covered with sawdust made it last all day.

The next year there was a three-day get-together in a twenty-acre pine thicket across the road from the school. It was during that three-day meet in 1890, while camping out around the covered wagons, that the patrons elected a board of directors and organized the Neshoba County Stock and Agricultural Fair. Horse-racing was part of the very first fairs. The boys raced bareback around the pine grove. That proved too dangerous; so a half-mile track was built on the edge of the fairgrounds. The men began to build the fairgrounds when they could spare the time from their farming. They cleared some of the pines out of the thicket and cut them into weatherboarding for a few buildings. The first building was a lemonade stand, then an exhibit hall, and finally the most important, a pavilion. The pavilion had a stage at one end and wooden benches that seated several hundred people. It was covered with a wood-shingle roof held up by hand-hewn poles. This building stood in the middle of the clearing in the pine grove, and families began to build cabins around the pavilion, forming a square. It soon became necessary to build a thirty-room, woodframe hotel to house visitors and politicians. From the earliest days the fair was a political forum for the governor, senators, and all aspirants to political office, including local constables. Anselm L. McLaurin, whose term ran from 1896 to 1900, was the first governor to speak at the fair. He rode the train from Jackson to Newton and came the last forty miles from Newton to the fairgrounds by two-horse buggy. Almost every governor since McLaurin has spoken at the fair. Both James K. Vardaman and Theodore G. Bilbo spoke while making their political careers and after attaining office.

The early fair was lighted with burning pine knots placed on wood platforms covered with sand. Dress at the fair was formal. Women wore hats and gloves and their best dresses. They carefully chose their Tuesday and Wednesday dresses, but the Thursday dress highlighted the three-day wardrobe. The earliest activities included—besides political speakings—horse-racing, farm and handiwork exhibits, school plays and recitations, and tent shows. The first tent show featured a petrified man with one arm. Great Grandfather Raz was so fascinated by this specimen that he wrote a letter to a county in Texas inquiring about its authenticity.

Mammy and Pappy attended the fair from the earliest days. Mammy especially loved the fair, as it was her only chance all year to be away from home. At first Mammy and Pappy stayed in the Johnson family's double-box cabin with Pappy's parents and his aunt's family. When the boys in the cabin kept borrowing Mammy's water to cool their beer, the arrangement got to be too much for her, so Pappy built his family a separate house. Mammy "cooked up" the week before and canned everything in jars, including chickens, sausages, and vegetables. Sometimes she took live chickens and cooked them at the fair. The family loaded mattresses on a wagon and moved the two miles to the fairgrounds until 1916 when Pappy bought the first commercial truck in the county, a studebaker. After getting Mammy settled, he went back home to mind the store. On Thursday he closed it and spent the day at the fair.

Even in the beginning there were individuals outside the Coldwater community interested in the fair and gradually other communities actively joined in. By 1911 the *Neshoba Democrat* referred to it as Neshoba's World Fair.

I always went out to Mammy and Pappy's house a day or two before the fair and moved out to the fair with them. Even though some people had recently started moving out on Monday, Mammy continued to move on Tuesday, as she always had. We stayed in the house Pappy built, and Mother and Daddy joined us, as did the rest of Mother's family. Poppaw came out for Thursday dinner.

At the fair I felt as if I had been transported to another world. In the morning I lay in my bed and listened to Mammy getting breakfast ready. The air was cool and fresh, and light streamed in through holes in the roof. Then I got up with my cousins Hugh and Oscar and we ate a breakfast of ham and eggs, biscuits and molasses. While our parents still slept, Mammy took us to the woman's privy back in a grove where, in the morning, women lingered and talked. The privies had two rows of back to back seats, called tenholers. I never liked this arrangement. After we came back to the cabin, Mammy did the early preparations for noon dinner, changed her dress, put on her hat, and went out to the pavilion for the morning program. There was always a crowd milling around on the square and sitting on the benches built around the large oak trees—white and Choctaw fairgoers, and a number of Negroes looking for jobs.

The exhibit hall was built under the grandstand, and each community in the county had its own exhibit. Small cash prizes were given in categories for cooking, sewing, and farm produce. Some of the prize categories were pies, cakes, fresh and canned fruits and vegetables; quilts, dresses, needlepoint, crochet; tallest stalk of corn, cotton stalk with the most bolls, biggest watermelon, and best bunch of peanuts. There was fierce competition for the prize given to the community for the best over-all exhibit. The exhibits were judged on the first day, and the women especially discussed the results with great interest. Mammy entered in the Coldwater community and I always went through the exhibit hall with her at least once. There was always a little grumbling among the ladies that too much money was being spent on the races and not enough attention being paid to the exhibits.

Next to the exhibit hall was the midway where the carnival was located. It was the single most exciting place on the grounds. The carnival had eight or ten rides, including a merry-go-round, bumper cars, and a ferris wheel. There was a hall of mirrors; there were midgets, a fat lady, and two-headed babies. Games like dice and bingo were played; and candy apples, cotton candy, snow balls, and lemonade could be purchased.

Every year a visiting brass band came and played in the pavilion as the first activity of each morning and right after dinner. Then the band moved down to the race track to play before the harness-racing began. The grandstand was a large, wooden building, with a roof supported by large poles that covered all the seats. The box seats, in the front of the grandstand, were right next to the red-clay track, which was circled by thick woods. After a warming-up period, the races went on all afternoon.

In the evenings Mammy washed us down before putting us to bed. I was almost always asleep before the electric generator for the entire fair went off at midnight. I knew my parents and their friends stayed up long after that.

IV

I learned about the whole population of the county on the almost-daily rides I took with Poppaw to see about his tenants. Poppaw first began to buy land by taking a mule as payment for medical services, and then swapping the mule for his first forty acres. He started to buy large amounts of land in the teens and by the Depression days of the late 1920s and 1930s he owned more land than any other individual in the county. For a while I was most interested in how we were going to make the journey and get back home the same day. Except for a sprinkling of native gravel in the hillier sections of the county, and an occasional sandy spot, the roads were pure red clay, which, when they were wet, we either slid over or bogged down in. The roads weren't made for automobiles in those days, though not many people had them anyway.

During the long winter rains, oak sapling poles were laid side by side across the swamps to make what we called a corduroy road. Terrifying holes washed out in the middles and stayed filled with water until spring. There were no holes Poppaw wouldn't attempt to cross. If we got a running start, and the car didn't stall as the wheels started to spin, we could usually make it across, provided the hole wasn't too deep. But we could never tell how deep it was until we hit it.

When we stalled, there were several possibilities. Sometimes a little backing up and going forward would do it. Sometimes prying up the back end with a pole or cutting a pine top from the side of the road and placing it in front of the back wheels to create traction would work. If we spun the wheels too much and bogged down axle deep there was nothing to do but send or walk to the nearest house for a team of mules. People were very accommodating about this. It wasn't considered neighborly to take pay, though Poppaw customarily asked how much he owed.

Poppaw always carried a shotgun beside him on our drives and sometimes he killed a rabbit crossing the road. He kept the double-barreled shotgun between us with the barrel resting on the floor board. I never understood how he was able to get the gun out of the window and fire so fast. When we came back from a ride with a dead rabbit, nobody in the house wanted to clean the rabbit, much less eat it. But someone always cleaned it, and we always ate it.

As we rode along Poppaw talked incessantly, pointing out the houses of prominent pioneer settlers. These houses were mostly of the settlement type, with an open hall down the middle, a porch across the front, and chimneys at each end. Then Poppaw would give me a biographical sketch of the family, when and where they came from before they settled in Neshoba County, which of the children had married whom, where they had moved to, and particular family traits that accounted for any success or misfortune the family might have had. If I asked Poppaw a question about the family's conduct, I sometimes wearied when he gave me more family history instead of a straight answer. Eventually I learned that *was* the answer.

Besides the pioneer settlers whom Poppaw considered leading citizens in the county, there was a much larger group of yeoman farmers. They were farmers who might have come to the county as early as the leading citizens, but who had had less acreage and hadn't gotten ahead. It was difficult to pinpoint why some fared better than others. The difference between those who became the leading citizens of each community and those who just got by seemed to lie in different attitudes and temperaments.

When we drove out into the county we never appeared to be going anywhere in particular, except occasionally when Poppaw would say he had heard someone was stealing timber or a mule. Generally we stopped and visited his tenants to see how the crops were getting along. It was a never-ending process, year in and year out.

Poppaw had several different arrangements with his tenants. If the tenant had his own mules and plowstock, he would rent from

Poppaw on thirds and fourths. This meant that for the use of the land and a place to live, the tenant paid Poppaw one-third of his corn crop and one-quarter of his cotton crop. Almost always the tenant would not have enough cash left from the preceding year's crop to buy staples like flour, coffee, and sugar for the winter, or to pay for fertilizer and seed. Poppaw sold these supplies—a "furnish," they were called—to his tenants from Mars Brothers' store. In addition to paying thirds and fourths for rent, the tenant paid Poppaw for the furnish at the standard 8 percent interest rate.

If the tenant had no mules, or wagon, or plowstock, he was said to be working on shares, or halves. This meant that he paid Poppaw half his crop for the use of the land, a place to live, and the use of mules and plowstock. In addition, Poppaw provided half the fertilizer and seed free and the tenant paid Poppaw for the balance of the furnish of feed, seed, and food at the standard interest rate out of the profit from the rest of his crop. If a tenant worked hard and had good luck it was possible to save enough to buy stock and mules and move to an arrangement of thirds and fourths. But whatever the arrangement, it was almost impossible to get much ahead; often tenants were lucky just to break even.

Poppaw had still another arrangement with tenants. To take advantage of the 160-acre homestead exemption *ad valorem* tax that went into effect in the early 1930s, Poppaw often contracted with his tenants to buy the land. Even though there was little hope that they could pay the loan out, they made small mortgage payments and saved Poppaw some tax money. Poppaw would deed land to any of his tenants, Negro or white, without a down payment and at the same time would contract to sell them mules and plowstock. The tenant was in effect renting his land for the cost of the mortgage payment. Poppaw again furnished him with seed, fertilizer, and food, and at the end of the year the tenant paid out his furnish and made payment on the land, plowstock, and mule. If there was a bad crop for several years, the tenant might deed the land back and try someplace else.

A number of Poppaw's white tenants belonged to a group that he referred to as "the great unwashed crowd," though he sometimes called them "poor white trash," "rednecks," "peckerwoods," or "sons of bitches." Poppaw said he had the sorriest tenants in the county, people who came to him when they couldn't get money anywhere else. Poppaw was careful to make me understand that the difference between the great unwashed crowd and other people was not just that they were poor, but that they came from a sorry class of people. What distinguished the poor white trash was their manner of living. They were transient, had no community ties and usually no church affiliation. They didn't live like decent white folks were expected to. They went dirty and did not change their clothes when they came to town. In fact they didn't change at all. The great unwashed crowd made unreliable tenants. They might move off before the crop was gathered, and take the mule with them. Some were too sorry to plant a garden. They were sullen and standoffish, and some spent what little money they could get hold of on whiskey. As a rule they didn't send their children to school, saying "I don't reckon it'll hurt 'em. I didn't go myself and it didn't seem to hurt me none." They were quick to anger if they thought they had been insulted, and they settled their differences with fists or firearms. They were especially mean to Negroes.

Others of Poppaw's white tenants were not members of the great unwashed crowd. They were poor, but their word was their bond. They were dependable, clean, and could not be picked out on the streets like the unwashed crowd. They just happened to be tenants but were the same kind of people as the yeoman farmers, many of whom also required a furnish.

Although we stopped and exchanged pleasantries with these hardworking tenants, who often sent us on our way with a watermelon or a mess of greens, I early developed a preference for our stops with the Negro tenants. Poppaw looked forward to these stops too and was kindlier to Negroes than most were, greeting them the same way he greeted whites, with a "howdy, honey." The Negroes seemed to be the only people who knew how to relax and enjoy life; they were kind and gracious and always made us feel welcome. One place I especially liked to stop was at Poppaw's old home place in Cushtusa where the Rosses lived. They were "old family Negroes"; Aunt Liza Ross's parents had been owned by a prominent Neshoba County family named Ross. Aunt Liza was always glad to see us; she would often cook up something for us even if it wasn't dinner time. Sometimes Poppaw would stop out at the Mt. Zion community and visit the homes of Negroes who were more well-to-do than most—families like the Coles, Calloways, and Seales. Their homes were neater, cleaner, and they dressed better not only than most Negroes, but than most of Poppaw's white tenants. They owned their land, like some of their fathers before them, and Poppaw told me they sent their children to college. These few Negro families were better off than the white tenant and some white small landowners. They were treated with a respect not ordinarily afforded Negroes or even some whites; they could borrow money on their names and reputations.

Though some people were known to go out of their way to be mean to Negroes, they were mostly people in the great unwashed crowd. The leading citizens were protective of Negroes and tried to help them with their churches and education. These citizens were not intimidated by the attitudes of those who were mean. When I was a child our neighbors down the street, the Lukes, had a chauffeur and houseboy named Toy. One summer the Lukes's grandson Billy took a special liking to Toy and followed him wherever he went. Toy often took him up to the Busy Bee Cafe where Billy ate hamburgers at the counter with Toy and his friends. One day as Mrs. Luke and Billy were sitting on the front porch three strange men walked up and told her Billy had been "messing around with them niggers uptown. And we don't allow things like that around here."

Mrs. Luke replied that if they had any sense she would try to explain how a young boy feels about an old Negro man who is kind to him. "But you don't have any sense and if you don't get off this porch in two minutes, I've got a shotgun and I'll blow the heads off every one of you."

In general the community did not approve of violence toward Negroes, so long as the Negroes stayed in their place. However, it was understood by everyone that Negroes had to be disciplined if they stepped out of line by disputing a white man's word or by looking at a white woman.

As I was growing up, I saw a world I lived in as a very well ordered and generally uncomplicated place. It was controlled by the leading citizens—doctors, lawyers, merchants, large landowners, and the directors in the two banks. Everyone seemed to know who belonged to this group and who didn't. Most of the men were members of prominent families and lived in town. Each outlying community contained its own leading families, who differed from the county leaders only in that they hadn't moved to town when the railroad came through and for the most part weren't quite as well-to-do.

Neshoba County was made up of the leading families in town and in the country, the yeoman farmers, the hardworking tenant class, the poor white trash, the Negroes, and a few Choctaw Indians. The leading families controlled the purse strings in the county. Though it was not clear to me why some had prospered and some had not, it seemed that those who had gotten ahead were the ones with the most ability and ambition.

FROM

Three Years in Mississippi

JAMES MEREDITH

RETURN TO MISSISSIPPI: AUGUST 1960

IT WAS A HOT, sultry, sunshiny day—a perfect day to return to my home state of Mississippi. I had left this land—God's country claimed by the white Mississippian as his "heaven on earth"—in August 1950, spent one year at a Florida high school, and served nine years in the United States Air Force. I am a soldier at heart, and I suppose I always will be. If there is anything that I ever wanted to be, I guess it would have been a general. But let's begin our drive into Mississippi.

Buy Gasoline in Memphis

Highway 51 is a code word for the millions of Negroes who have driven north to south and south to north for the past twenty-five years. This was the route taken by us—my wife and six-months-old son and me—into Mississippi. We were completing the last leg of the long drive from California, where we had landed after a three-year tour of duty in Japan at Tachikawa Air Force Base. I had traveled this road many times and knew practically every hill and curve, or at least I thought I did. It had long been my practice to fill up the gas tank in Memphis, so I would not have to face the "peckerwoods" at a station in Mississippi. One tank of gas would take you to Kosciusko or Jackson where you could go to a Negro-operated station. This time it was more pressing than ever to get gas because I had my wife and son with me, and God only knew what I would do if an incident occurred while I was with my family. I pulled into a station that I had used for quite a few years on this route, because they did not have segregated toilets for "White Ladies," "White Men," and "Colored." Thinking that the practice would be the same as before, I didn't go through the customary ritual used when a Negro pulls into a gas station in the South and is not sure about the discrimination practices. Since some of the white folks there are a little more human, or just plain smarter, than the crackers and rednecks, they mark their facilities for whites as just "Ladies" and "Men" and put the Negro toilet in the back where you cannot see it. The Negro will ask the attendant, "Do you have a bathroom?" (although he is looking right at the big signs that read "Ladies" and "Men"). If the attendant says, "Yes, right there," then the Negro says, "Fill it up, and check everything." If the answer is, "Yeah, go round the back," then the Negro drives away and looks for another station. I pulled up, spoke to the man, and told him to "fill it up." Then my wife left to go to the bathroom. When she reached the toilet, the sign read "White Ladies ONLY." Upon asking the attendant about the restrooms, we were told that the "Colored" was in the back. By this time the tank was already full and it was useless to tell him to stop pumping the gas. We went around to the back and found one cubbyhole for all Negroes to use—men and women and children. It was filthy, nasty, and stinking. The toilet wouldn't flush and there was no toilet paper or water to wash one's hands. It has always been said that Memphis was the northern capital of Mississippi. Now I was convinced that it was true. This was the much talked-about progress that I had been making since the 1954 Supreme Court decision that said "separate but equal" was no longer the law of the land, but left the new law of the land to the discretion of the White Supremacists.

Welcome to Mississippi

The first thing that you see when you head south on old U.S. 51 from Memphis and Shelby County, Tennessee—the home of the Cotton Queens and the famous, or infamous, "Crump political machine" and the place where the Negro blues originated—is a big flashy sign: WELCOME TO MISSISSIPPI. This sign arouses mixed emotions in the thousands of Negroes who pass it. For many it is a joke; for others it recalls the days gone by, their work in the cotton fields in Mississippi, their migration to the North, their jobs in the warplants during the forties and in the factories of today.

For me, it is indeed a sign of frustration. Always, without fail, regardless of the number of times I enter Mississippi, it creates within me feelings that are felt at no other time. There is the feeling of joy. Joy because I have once again lived to enter the land of my fathers, the land of my birth, the only land in which I feel at home. It also inspires a feeling of hope because where there is life there is also a hope, a chance. At the same time, there is a feeling of sadness. Sadness because I am immediately aware of the special subhuman role that I must play, because I am a Negro, or die. Sadness because it is the home of the greatest number of Negroes outside of Africa, yet my people suffer from want of everything in a rich land of plenty, and, most of all, they must endure the inconvenience of indignity.

Then, there is the feeling of love. Love of the land. To me, Mississippi is the most beautiful country in the world, during all seasons. In the spring, all is green and fresh, the air is clean and sweet, and everything is healthy. As a boy I knew that any running stream of water was fit to drink. I feel love because I have always felt that Mississippi belonged to me and one must love what is his.

In the summer there is maturity. The grass begins to level off and seed. A feeling of repose overcomes you. You have the urge to pull alongside the road and take a cowpath up into the bushes and lie down under a big tree. The effect of the heat shows everywhere. Blackberries begin to ripen; muscadine vines begin to hang from the burden of a good crop; and a black snake is likely to cross the road at any moment. Since the crops are nearly all laid by, the whole state takes on a relaxed and idle atmosphere. Summer is also the most suitable season for a lynching.

The fall of the year is perhaps the most colorful. Nature begins to fade away. The grass dries up and draws closer to the earth. Trees and bushes start to color and a slow deterioration asserts itself. All remaining fruits and nuts come to full maturity. A great feeling of urgency is generated by such abundance. You feel that time is squeezing you and harvest you must. The temptation to gather the falling nuts—acorns, hickory nuts, scaly barks, pecans, chincky berries, and all kinds in abundance—pulls you to them.

Finally, the "Welcome to Mississippi" sign reminds me of winter in my home state. Winter is my favorite season for looking at the land. Everything, except for the cedar trees and a few other evergreens, is bare. You can see for miles.

Shortly after passing the sign, I have often stopped by the side of the road and just looked at the land. The most dominant thought was, "if only I had my fair share in the running and managing of the state of Mississippi, what a wonderful land this could be." And I always ended the meditation with an assurance to myself, from myself, that I would have that share in my land or die trying to get it.

Mississippi Country Towns

As you drive along U.S. 51 from Memphis into Mississippi, you are immediately aware of the many towns and communities—incorporated and unincorporated. The most troublesome aspect of the drive is the slow speed limit, often as low as 20 mph on what appears to be a completely open road. Of course, it is well known to the traveler, especially to the Negro, that there is likely to be a deputy sheriff or a town constable behind every house or thicket. For many a law enforcement officer in Mississippi traffic violations are a source of revenue second only to his profit from bootleg whiskey.

However, for one with an eye for discovering the road of the future through a look into the past, these towns are bursting with hints toward understanding Mississippi. Let's just take their locations: Hernando, Coldwater, Senatobia, Como, Sardis, Batesville, Pope, Oakland, Tillatoba, Grenada, Duck Hill, Winona, Vaiden, West, Durant, McAdams, Kosciusko—all are approximately ten miles apart. Mississippi, although today the most southern state, was the last area settled in the Old South. Most Mississippi farms were not established as self-sufficient units and provisions had to be obtained from the country store, which was located so that the farmer could walk to the store, buy his weekly provisions, and return home on the same day. This distance happened to be about five miles. The towns grew around the stores, and this development led to an important aspect of the Negro-white relationship in Mississippi. Provision day became a social day and the daddy of the "Satiday Night," which is still observed by Mississippians at home and away in spirit, if not in practice. On the large plantations and self-sufficient farms, the Negroes and whites were separated physically and the two groups came in contact with one another only under well-defined circumstances. At first, however, there were no clear rules in the towns: there was one store, one street, one bench, etc. Since this was the only place where the masses of Negroes came into direct contact with the masses of whites, a substitute for the organized placement and separation of the plantation had to be found for the town. Segregation in public and private establishments and facilities was the outcome. Segregation led to many of the evil practices that became a part of southern life.

The town was also the chief place of contact between the poor white men and the Negro women. The rich or well-to-do whites had more convenient means by which to satisfy their desires for a black woman. The white woman has long been considered the main object of conflict between the whites and the Negroes. I can assure you that the greatest point of friction between the races has not been the white woman; rather, it has been and still is the colored woman.

The Last Nineteen Miles

The last nineteen miles to Kosciusko has always been a drive that appeared to me ten times as far as it really is, probably because the trip from Durant is the same trip in my mind as it was when I was a boy. Durant is the place where everyone in the surrounding area catches the train going north. I suppose by now every Negro in Attala County above the age of seven has been to Durant to catch the Illinois Central north or, better still, "The City of New Orleans" to Chicago. In addition, Durant is where the Negroes had to go to get a legal bottle of beer. Everyone knows that Mississippi is the only dry state in the Union, but my home county went even further and forbade the sale of beer. It was six of one and a half dozen of the other for the Negro in Attala County. If he stayed in the county and took a drink of "white-lightning" or "moonshine," he was arrested for buying illegal alcohol. If he bought whiskey in Durant, which was just across the county line, he was stopped by the Attala County police as soon as he crossed the river and arrested for having "whiskey on his breath." The only advantage in going to Durant was that he could have a good time in the two or three big joints there.

At Durant we turned left off U.S. 51 onto Mississippi Highway 12 at the sign that reads—Kosciusko 19 miles. When we came to the multi-track Illinois Central Railroad line, the highway was blocked by the train just arriving from the North. We went into the train station to freshen up, get a bottle of soda pop, and see if anyone we knew had got off the train. Someone is always either going or coming that you know. The unboarding of a train in Durant is something like the docking of a large ship. There is an atmosphere of excitement, gladness, and sorrow. Whenever a Negro comes home from the North—"home" because a Negro returning to Mississippi, even though he may have been away for forty years, always thinks of himself as coming home, and the one leaving is never going home, but is always going to Chicago, St. Louis, or Detroit—the major reunion is at the station because the whole family usually meets the passenger there. The station at Durant seems to belong to the Negro since you seldom see a white passenger.

The train pulled out after unloading in Durant, and we were off to my home town. We crossed the long, frighteningly narrow bridge that spans the Big Black River and the surrounding lowlands, which are flooded as often as not. We passed the familiar farms, houses, clay hills, and newly planted tree farms, which had sprung up on the vacant land once worked by the very people whom we had seen at the station coming from and going to the North. In my county alone more than 10,000 Negroes had migrated North during the past ten years.

We drove for ten miles and passed through the only community along the nineteen-mile stretch—unincorporated McAdams. It is the same as most of the others we had passed, except for one peculiar trait that I have never understood. I have never heard of a motorist being arrested in McAdams, not even a Negro. The speed limit is reduced only to 45 mph. I guess the man for whom the community was named must have owned everything, been the chief official, and his sons must have been his deputies, and they all must have been too busy or too rich to bother with the passersby.

From McAdams we went over four large hills and around three curves, including the big curve, which many Kosciuskans have failed to make after a trip to a "Satiday Night" in Durant. On the left, just before you get to the radio tower, is a motel, the final landmark, because around the next curve is Kosciusko, Mississippi, my home town.

A Drive through Kosciusko

The Square. Every time, without fail, when I return home after being away, I go first to the town square and drive around it at least once, and often more times, before taking "Beale Street" home. Kosciusko's town square is typical of town squares in Mississippi county seats. The courthouse is in the center with the major stores and offices surrounding it. With its population of 6,000, Kosciusko is one of the major towns in Mississippi. On the square, there are two banks, two or three large supermarkets, a couple of dime stores, about three drugstores, several ladies' and men's shops, some cafes and restaurants for whites only, a movie house for whites only, and a number of doctors', lawyers', and other professional offices. People always loiter around the square and gossip, trade, and socialize. Of course, the big day is Saturday when every place is crowded with the country folks. Just one trip around the square on any day, however, and fifteen minutes later everyone in town knows you are home. The fact that I was driving a big blue air-conditioned Cadillac and wearing a suit and tie when the temperature was 98° and the sun was burning down did not lessen the local interest. In addition, I had a Japanese license plate on my car. Any out-of-state tag arouses the curiosity of the people of Kosciusko, because the town is not located on a major highway and the strangers are few, but a northern license plate provokes their anger—that is, of the whites. In this instance, however, I think it was just plain confusing to see an out-of-country license.

The Police Station. Located in the most strategic spot on the square is the police station, the most important place in town for the Negro. It is at the southeast corner of the square overlooking the entrance to South Natchez Street, the Negro street of Kosciusko, and better known as "Beale Street." No one can enter this street without being seen by a policeman. I always drive very slowly past the police station in order to make sure that all the policemen get a chance to take a good look at me. This may seem strange, but it is perhaps the main reason why I was seldom trailed or bothered by the police during my many visits home while I was in the Air Force. It is a fact that within a very short time after one arrives in town practically everyone knows it, including the police, and if there is anything that a Mississippi cop hates, it is for someone to know something about a Negro that he doesn't know first. By giving the police the first look, the Negro relieves them of the necessity of finding the "nigger" and "getting the goods on him." When a Mississippi policeman has to suffer the embarrassment of looking for a "nigger," he is likely to make the trip worth his while. I always took great care not to give a "peckerwood" a chance to put his hands on me. No white man in Mississippi had ever put his hands on me, and God alone knows what would have happened had the event occurred.

Beale Street. A Negro hasn't been to town if he hasn't been to Beale Street. Actually it is just one long block extending from the southeastern corner of the square to Wesley Chapel Methodist Church, the biggest Negro church in town. About ninety per cent of the buildings on the street are owned by white landlords and rented to the Negroes. The first store is a strange combination of general store and cafe—probably the only one of its kind remaining in Mississippi. It sells everything from pencils to overalls and from groceries to farming tools, but from a very limited stock, however. The most amazing thing about this establishment is the selling of hamburgers. All day on Saturdays a Negro cook stands in the middle of the store at a grill with a counter on two sides and cooks nothing but hamburgers. They are sold from the same grill, prepared by the same Negro cook, to the Negroes for ten cents and to the whites for fifteen cents. Naturally they are served over separate counters.

Bell's Cafe. The first Negro-operated business is a small cafe, about twenty-five feet by fifty feet, but it is the largest eating and socializing place for Negroes in Kosciusko. This is the cafe of the Attala County elite. I would venture to say that not one of the Negroes who patronizes the general store has ever set foot in Bell's Cafe, although it is only three doors away. It is operated by a family—the manager is the wife and the chief employees are all related—that moved to Kosciusko from a rural community about twenty-five miles away. There are at least eight or nine children, all of whom were educated through college from the profits from this small cafe. There had been very little social life for me in Kosciusko, but whatever public socializing that I did as a boy was done here. To the best of my recollection, I don't remember ever buying even a hamburger at any other cafe on Beale Street. This was the place where you went with a quarter on Saturday and sat all day long. In the course of the day you were certain to see everyone in town and, in addition, anyone in the county who was visiting back home from the North. There is a jukebox and the latest records, but you would never find the soul blues or the lowdown boogie-woogie. You had to go to the lower end of Beale Street to find this type of music.

Funeral Home. Across the street is one of the three funeral homes on the block. The funeral business, or I should say, the Negro funeral business, is the only enterprise in which the Negro has a monopoly. With few, if any, exceptions, the most prosperous Negro in any town in Mississippi is the funeral director. Consequently, he is always an important man in the community. This particular funeral home is located on the first floor of the old Negro Masonic Temple. I understand that the lodge had been very active during the twenties and thirties, and I have heard it said that two or three of the "big" Negroes in town had worked successfully to disband the lodge, because some of the white folks didn't think Negroes should have meetings and gatherings. The owner-operator of the funeral home is always in his office, unless he is out picking up a dead body, collecting insurance, or occasionally making an emergency call. Three or four part-time helpers are always around to aid the funeral director, and on Saturday a girl helps with the insurance collections from the people living in the county. In front of the building are two or three benches, or Coca-Cola bottle cases, for loiterers to sit on and talk and "lollygag," as they call it.

Murray's Cleaning Shop. A couple of doors down from the funeral home is the only Negro-owned and operated dry cleaning business in town. It is a one-man business with the man's wife as the chief assistant. With almost no formal schooling, the owner had started on a wish after the war, and with a strong will, hard work, and good "horse sense," he is now a prosperous businessman. Besides his cleaning shop, he owns a development of rental houses, a number of other profitable interests, and a beautiful new brick home for himself on the outskirts of town. He also owns the new office located next door to his shop. The sign above the office window reads, "Dr. So-and-So-Dentist." He had built this office three or four years ago in the hope of attracting a Negro doctor or dentist to the town. So far, there has been none. A Negro dentist in the Delta about a hundred miles away had promised to visit Kosciusko once every two weeks, but he had only come twice in three years. The owner will not rent the space for any other purpose. This is an excellent example of the feeling that Mississippi Negroes have for one another. The day will come, and I hope soon, when his long-felt wish for a doctor will be fulfilled.

The Barber Shop. The barbering profession, as the barbers like to call it, has been well established and respected for a long time in

Mississippi. The barber is in the Negro middle-income group, even though haircuts are still fifty cents in some of the best barber shops. The barber shop is a sort of sanctuary for the Negro in Mississippi. The local police use all the other Negro establishments to make their presence felt, as a regular and unannounced practice; this tactic is one of the chief weapons used to enforce the doctrines and conditions of "White Supremacy" in the South. But they stay out of the barber shops for one reason or another. As a result, the conversation in the shops is the most relaxed and least guarded of any you are likely to hear in public places.

There are four or five barber shops on the block, but I have always gone to the same shop and the same barber since I started getting barber shop haircuts. We were money-poor, and my father had a pair of Sears, Roebuck clippers with which he used to give us "clean head" haircuts when we were children. The barber is a distant cousin who started a shop when he came home after the war. His barber shop is, I believe, the only establishment on Beale Street that has not made any significant physical changes during the past several years. There are four chairs but only two are operated daily; the others go into full swing on Saturday when the country people come to town. There is also a shoeshine parlor in the shop, although it is not likely to be in operation except on Saturdays. In the back is a beauty shop operated by the owner's wife. I did not know this until 1960, and it made me realize how hard it is to know what is going on in the Negro world in Mississippi. Out of curiosity I had asked the barber what was in the back and he said, "My wife's beauty shop," as if I should have known. He went on to say that his wife had been there for at least fifteen years. Evidently the women used a side or back entrance, because in the fifteen-odd years that I had frequented his shop, not only had I not known that the beauty shop was in the rear, but I had never even seen his wife.

The Pool Hall. At the lower end of Beale Street, where a decent woman would not be caught slowing her walking pace, is the pool hall—a Negro-owned and operated business. The building belongs to a Negro contractor and the business and concession stands are owned by a young bricklayer as a part-time venture. Boys and young men congregate around in the usual pool-hall fashion. They play the games, talk loudly, brag about their skill with the "stick" (pool-hall stick), boast about their conquests of women, and play a little "nine ball" (a game on which they bet small sums) every now and then. Kosciusko's Beale Street is not typical of Negro drags in most Mississippi towns, since there is very little open vice. Several of the regulars who hang around the pool hall are known police informers and stooges who have, as far as I know, done nothing else.

The operator of the hamburger stand in the pool hall is one of my cousins. He is best known for whipping Negroes who get colored women for white men, and he has been run out of Mississippi dozens of times for this "crime." In the late fifties he was beaten by a mob of whites, left for dead, and had to remain in the hospital for over a year. This happened in another town about thirty-five miles away when he worked as a porter for the Illinois Central Railroad. His conflict with these "peckerwoods" began when a Negro approached him at the station, I suppose because he was a porter, and asked if he knew where to get some women. When my cousin found out that he wanted the Negro women for white men, he whipped the Negro pimp. The pimp told the white men, who then proceeded to put the "nigger in his place."

Dean's Cafe. Down on the "low end of Beale," there are two or three honkytonk cafes. Dean's Cafe is directly across the street from the pool hall. Even at the age of twenty-seven, when I returned to Mississippi after nine years in the Air Force, I had never been inside. I could not positively identify more than two or three people whom I had seen going in or coming out. It will be difficult, if not impossible, for anyone not growing up in Mississippi to understand the deep separation that exists, not only by race but also by class structure within the races. The side aspects of a society segregated by force are tremendously important and very essential to the social system. Although the oppressed group may never accept the permanency of their oppressed status, the fact that they choose temporarily to accept this position rather than to chance death acknowledges that at the least they recognize the dominance of their oppressors and for the bare minimum of just being alive the oppressed must accept the major tenets of their oppressors' doctrines.

The Only Residence. While it may seem odd that the only dwelling on Beale Street is occupied by whites, it is not unusual in Mississippi. The big two-story house sits back off the street twenty or twenty-five feet, and, of course, the doors to all the businesses open onto the sidewalk. It is located next to the pool-hall building and is the last structure on the street. I am not sure that I can explain my relationship to this house, but an empathic insight is absolutely essential to understand most of what I have to say about Mississippi and the Negro, the white and myself. I remember nothing about this house. Although I passed it on my way to school at least two times a day, five days a week for eleven years, and the church I attended was directly across the street, I could in good faith swear that I had never seen anyone in or around this house. It would be difficult for me to determine whether I saw and didn't see or whether I never saw at all what was before my eyes.

It is interesting to me to look back over what I have written about my home town and to note that I have said almost nothing about the white part of town. Except in a general way, I find that I know very little about that part of Kosciusko. Frankly, I never saw any of it that was not an absolute necessity for living. I can very easily recall the names of every business and businessman in town that have been there for more than twenty years, because I have heard their names mentioned so often, but I could tell you practically nothing about their business, and I couldn't identify more than two of the men by sight. I can think immediately of several well-known places, such as Vic's Cafe, Bell's Grocery, and the movie house, and realize that in all the thousands of times that I passed these places, I never once looked at them and saw them. Separation dominated my childhood completely.

Wesley Chapel. At the end of Beale Street is a three-way junction and on the opposite side of this junction is located the largest Negro church in town, the Wesley Memorial Chapel. It belongs to the Methodist Episcopal division of the Methodist churches and is the only Negro church still in the white conference. To know that this is the largest church in town tells quite a lot about Kosciusko. Mississippi is overwhelmingly Baptist and the largest church in most towns is Baptist. I would imagine that perhaps three fourths of the leading Negroes in Kosciusko are members of Wesley Memorial. This is the church in which I was baptized when I was twelve years old and where I received my religious training. The Negro city-style Methodist Church has a very rigid method of conducting its services. There are no physical outbursts from the congregation like those so prevalent among the Baptists. No one gets "happy" and shouts, and an odd "Amen" is considered very much out of place. The singing is very formal and not lively and free as in the Baptist churches. That this type of religious influence is dominant in Kosciusko is of great importance to the basic character of its Negroes.

The Schoolhouse. Driving along the pavement—it was paved because whites lived on the right-hand side of the street—for about two blocks and then turning left, one approaches the heart of the Negro community. This road is unpaved. In Mississippi the practice is to pave the roads in the white areas and leave them unpaved in the Negro areas. This was the same road that as a boy I had walked thousands of times going the four miles each way back and forth to school. Perhaps the major difference between then and now in the road and houses and surroundings was in me. For three quarters of a mile we drove the distance of a very long hill and another half of a hill to the schoolhouse. Just before you get to the school is the Second Baptist Church. Most of the other leading Negroes in Kosciusko belong to this church. It is a very "high-class" Baptist Church, for the services are toned down and are conducted more like the Methodist. "Second Baptist," what's in this name? You never hear of a white Second Baptist Church. The First Baptist Church in most Mississippi towns is known to be the white church. If you recall the basic premise of "White Supremacy," you will see why many Negro communities have a Second Baptist Church and no white community ever has a "second" church.

Across the street from the church is Kosciusko's Negro school with grades running from first through twelfth. Next to the Negro church, the Negro school ranks as the most important established institution. Often the Negro high school principal is the number-one Negro in a Mississippi community. In the South education has almost become a religion since the days of Booker T. Washington. The Mississippi Negro will almost concede anything and sacrifice everything to get an education. Like everyone else, the school along with the home and family had the greatest impact on my early life. When I left this school in 1950 I had never been able to use a toilet because there was none, and I had never had a teacher with a college degree. This is no reflection on the teachers or on their dedication, however. They taught what they knew in the winter for thirty of forty dollars a month, saved most of it, and went away in the summer to learn something to teach the next winter, that is, if they found a school in the state to attend.

We had now come to the last minutes of our long journey from the airstrip in Japan to the dirt roads of my home in Mississippi. In one sense I was not really returning home at this moment, rather, I was returning to a house in Kosciusko where my folks were now living. When I made that last turn off East South Street onto the yet unnamed street of my father's house, the cloud of dust trailing the wheels of my car caused me to face the hard, cold fact that the price of freedom for myself and my people is indeed high.

Return Home

The New House. I wondered what the new house would be like. I was deeply involved in this venture and my future was indirectly, if not directly, affected by it. Early in 1960, as I was finishing the last months of my military career, I received the second letter ever written me by my father in his own handwriting. As fate would have it both letters were written at a time of family tragedy. The letters are filed in my permanent records under the label, "Important Accomplishments." This one-page letter, only eight lines long, stated in effect, "I am dying and I want to build a house in town for your mama before I die." My family home was a small eighty-four-acre farm four miles from town. My mother worked in the school cafeteria, my youngest brother was graduating from high school that spring, and my youngest sister walked to school alone, since there was no "colored" school bus. In order to pay for the new house, my father was going to sell his farm, and he wanted to give me first chance to buy it. But more than that, he wanted me to buy it.

Since this was the first piece of land ever owned by a member of my family, there was really nothing to consider. Certainly if God provided air to breathe, as far as I was concerned no white man would ever buy that piece of land. For a long time my wife and I had been saving for our return to Mississippi, and I immediately bought our old home place. In spite of the fact that every lending institution in Kosciusko was willing to lend my father the money to build the house, he was dead set on paying for everything; he did not want to leave his family under any possible threat from the whites. This was the kind of protective shielding that my family and I had been receiving all our lives from my father.

The last three houses on the street were new, but it was not difficult to determine which one belonged to Moses "Cap"

Meredith. Even though my family had moved in only two weeks before, there was a freshly cut lawn with transplanted flowers and bushes. The street was dirt, like all Negro streets, but a concrete drive led up to the open carport. And there was the old "gallery swing," newly painted white, in the front yard. The dying man had not died. I guess it was the will to advance that had kept him alive.

The Old Farm. As I pulled into the driveway of this new house, I noticed a shellacked cedar post holding up the carport roof; I was certain that it was one of the old cedars which grew in the cow pasture behind the barn at our farm. I could not help but think of the old home place, now legally mine, but which would always remain, as long as he lived, my father's house. I could vividly remember all the other thousands of times that I had returned home. Instead of turning right off Highway 12, I would have turned left on the Old Natchez Trace Road, the oldest and most famous road in Mississippi, and possibly in the Deep South. I know every inch of this road. For the first half mile the houses are mostly small "shot-gun" houses (a long narrow one-unit affair shaped like a railroad boxcar, with two partitions dividing it into three rooms with a small kitchen in the middle). You can almost always assume that a "shot-gun" house belongs to a white landlord, because a Negro would never build, and very seldom buy, one. The few big frame houses scattered about usually belong to Negro school-teachers.

Just past the "shot-guns" is the only brick house on the road. It belongs to the owner of the Negro dry cleaning shop. Across the road, a short distance away, is the house of the high school principal, probably the biggest house in town owned by a Negro. Across from the principal's house is another row of "shot-gun" houses and at the end of this row is the Kosciusko city limits sign. A little farther on, at the top of the hill, is a vacant one-room store—the only business that had existed between my old home and town. It ceased operation when the lady operator died. It is at the corner of the only Negro-owned farm on the main road. The old house on this farm sits an unusually long distance back from the road. For many years it was customary for Negroes not to build their homes on the main road in rural areas; even if they owned the land, they had to build their homes on the side roads. My father had often expressed his displeasure with this practice to me when I was a boy. At the corner of this farm is the Negro graveyard.

Across the road from the cemetery is Shine's house. Shine was a well-known dealer in bootleg whiskey; I don't know if his name derives from his trade in moonshine or from the common custom of calling Negroes "Shine." Down from his house is the only white house, and I don't mean the color of the house, between my old farm home and town. All the other houses are occupied, if not owned, by Negroes. The fact that only one white-occupied house was between my old home and town was very important to me as a child, because it made possible an environment in which I never had to come into direct contact with whites and therefore was never forced to conduct myself in a consciously inferior manner.

Up the hill from the white house is the main barn of the richest man and by far the largest landowner in the county. He owned every acre on the left side of the road all the way to my old home and ninety-nine per cent on the right side. He was in every type of operation: timber, cattle, and farming of all sorts, except cotton, which was most unusual in Mississippi. All his farm help were paid by the day and not on the traditional sharecrop basis. The workers always knew that they would have at least some money at settlement time. He held his workers in a position that was hardly better than the sharecroppers, however. All of them had to call him "Cap'n Sam." He often amused himself by hitting his "niggers" with the heavy walking cane he always carried or by throwing nickels and pennies into the air and watching the Negroes fight over them. Beyond the big barn there are few dwellings, since the land is kept cleared for farming or for cattle.

Finally we come to the "mailbox." In rural Mississippi it is often possible to know the economic, social, and racial circumstances of the owner of a particular mailbox. Ours was middle size. I remember the many steps into the bigger box era. During the latter part of World War II our last mailbox status change was the result of an allotment check from a brother in the Army, money sent home from a brother and two sisters working in war plants in Detroit, and the biggest cotton harvest on record for our farm and the highest price ever paid for cotton. I recall that a trip to Jackson was made to buy the new mailbox. By that time there was an addition—a nameplate, "Moses Meredith, Route 2, Box 10." My father retained his box number, although there were hundreds of new numbers between our farm and town by 1960.

At the mailbox you turn off the main road and drive three quarters of a mile of narrow, winding road to the house. You go through a swamp-like hollow, where the undergrowth is thick and tall, known as "hant hollow" to us (ten children). My oldest brother swears that hants dwell in it. For years a big sweet gum tree (two trees grown together) stood in the middle of the road. I can remember that I used to tease one of my older sisters by splitting the tree (when two or more persons are walking together and they do not pass the tree on the same side). She believed to the end that it was bad luck to split a tree. My father's first wife, the mother of my older brothers and sisters, had died when the youngest half-sister was still a baby. Their mother had been extremely superstitious, while my mother was not superstitious at all.

I come from the hill section of Mississippi. For nearly a half mile the last stretch of the road runs up a long hill. About two hundred yards up the next hill in the southeast corner of our eighty-four-acre farm is located the old house—the place where I was born. This is the end of the road. Anytime someone came down this road, you knew he coming to Cap Meredith's house. This farm was called "my own place" by some of the descendants of the scattered children of African origin mixed with European and American Indian blood, identified by the ethnic name of Negro, incorporating within its meaning a past condition of slavery, and by the acquired name of "Meredith." My father was the first member of his family ever to own a piece of land. In his house I learned the true meaning of life. Here I learned that death was to be preferred to indignity.

The greatest intangible that the house had to offer was pride. The second was order. If these are taken away, only poverty is left. At the time my family moved into the new house in town—years after the atomic bomb, in the era of jet airplanes and rockets orbiting the earth—my old family home had no toilet, no bath, no running water, and the wind still blew freely through the unblocked cracks in the walls of half the rooms. The beds which had been acquired during the days when my father was a sharecropper, some forty-odd years earlier, were still in use. But there was pride and there was order.

My father kept his boundary line fences always in good repair. Although the neighboring landowners, all white, wanted to go together on the boundary fences to split the cost and work, my father insisted on pulling his fences back two feet from the actual line and maintaining them on his own. He did not want a white man ever to have an excuse to invade his privacy. If anyone was a king in his own domain, it was Cap. It was as if our eighty-four acres constituted a sovereign state and we neither recognized nor had any diplomatic relations with our neighboring states. The house of a white family was within one hundred yards of the back side of our place, and yet I never saw it. Because of his desire to shield us, my father forbade us even to go to that area of our farm. Some Negro families lived on the white man's farm and their children were our best friends. Since we were not allowed to visit them, they had to come over to our side of the fence to play with us.

When I left Mississippi in 1950 I had never seen the inside of a white person's house, chiefly because a Negro had to enter by the back door. I was taught to believe that the most dishonorable thing that a Meredith could do was to work in a white woman's kitchen and take care of a white man's child. I know that I would starve to death rather than do either. I am sure that the Negroes with the greatest sense of pride come from the farms, because working in the fields never carried the disgraceful connotations that working in the white folks' kitchens did.

Perhaps I should approach the old home place from another point of view: the estimate of our peers. To the average Mississippi Negro we were indeed well off. We had a very big house with eleven rooms, and for as long as I can remember there was paint of some quality on the outside. There was some kind of furniture in every room; the living room, main bedroom, and guest room were always presentable, so that my folks were never embarrassed by their home—as most Negroes have been from time to time. I can recall listening to the first Joe Louis championship fight over the radio at home, and I cannot remember a single day that my father did not listen to the evening news. We had a radio when few whites and very few Negroes had one in Mississippi. I have sopped bread and molasses for breakfast, dinner, and supper for many weeks at a time, but never did I go without food. Windowpanes were usually in the windows and the screens were sufficient to keep away most of the mosquitoes. While I have been conscious of our home's shortcomings when it is compared with the typical white American's, at the same time I have been aware of our fortunate circumstances compared with the average Mississippi Negro. As I remembered my old home, I was certain that I was returning to Mississippi by choice.

FROM

Coming of Age in Mississippi

ANNE MOODY

CHILDHOOD

THAT WHITE LADY Mama was working for worked her so hard that she always came home griping about backaches. Every night she'd have to put a red rubber bottle filled with hot water under her back. It got so bad that she finally quit. The white lady was so mad she couldn't get Mama to stay that the next day she told Mama to leave to make room for the new maid.

This time we moved two miles up the same road. Mama had another domestic job. Now she worked from breakfast to supper and still made five dollars a week. But these people didn't work Mama too hard and she wasn't as tired as before when she came home. The people she worked for were nice to us. Mrs. Johnson was a schoolteacher. Mr. Johnson was a rancher who bought and sold cattle. Mr. Johnson's mother, an old lady named Miss Ola, lived with them.

Our house, which was separated from the Johnsons' by a field of clover, was the best two-room house we had been in yet. It was made out of big new planks and it even had a new toilet. We were also once again on paved streets. We just did make those paved streets, though. A few yards past the Johnsons' house was the beginning of the old rock road we had just moved off.

We were the only Negroes in that section, which seemed like some sort of honor. All the whites living around there were well-to-do. They ranged from schoolteachers to doctors and prosperous businessmen. The white family living across the street from us owned a funeral home and the only furniture store in Centreville. They had two children, a boy and a girl. There was another white family living about a quarter of a mile in back of the Johnsons who also had a boy and a girl. The two white girls were about my age and the boys a bit younger. They often rode their bikes or skated down the little hill just in front of our house. Adline, Junior and I would sit and watch them. How we wished Mama could buy us a bike or even a pair of skates to share.

There was a wide trench running from the street alongside our house. It separated our house and the Johnsons' place from a big two-story house up on the hill. A big pecan tree grew on our side of the trench, and we made our playhouse under it so we could sit in the trench and watch those white children without their knowing we were actually out there staring at them. Our playhouse consisted of two apple crates and a tin can that we sat on.

One day when the white children were riding up and down the street on their bikes, we were sitting on the apple crates making Indian noises and beating the tin can with sticks. We sounded so much like Indians that they came over to ask if that was what we were. This was the beginning of our friendship. We taught them how to make sounds and dance like Indians and they showed us how to ride their bikes and skate. Actually, I was the only one who learned. Adline and Junior were too small and too scared, although they got a kick out of watching us. I was seven, Adline five, and Junior three, and this was the first time we had ever had other children to play with. Sometimes, they would take us over to their playhouse. Katie and Bill, the children of the whites that owned the furniture store, had a model playhouse at the side of their parents' house. That little house was just like the big house, painted snow white on the outside, with real furniture in it. I envied their playhouse more than I did their bikes and skates. Here they were playing in a house that was nicer than any house I could have dreamed of living in. They had all this to offer me and I had nothing to offer them but the field of clover in summer and the apple crates under the pecan tree.

The Christmas after we moved there, I thought sure Mama would get us some skates. But she didn't. We didn't get anything but a couple of apples and oranges. I cried a week for those skates, I remember.

Every Saturday evening Mama would take us to the movies. The Negroes sat upstairs in the balcony and the whites sat downstairs. One Saturday we arrived at the movies at the same time as the white children. When we saw each other, we ran and met. Katie walked straight into the downstairs lobby and Adline, Junior, and I followed. Mama was talking to one of the white women and didn't notice that we had walked into the white lobby. I think she thought we were at the side entrance we had always used which led to the balcony. We were standing in the white lobby with our friends, when Mama came in and saw us. "C'mon! C'mon!" she yelled, pushing Adline face on into the door. "Essie Mae, um gonna try my best to kill you when I get you home. I told you 'bout running up in these stores and things like you own 'em!" she shouted, dragging me through the door. When we got outside, we stood there crying, and we could hear the white children crying inside the white lobby. After that, Mama didn't even let us stay at the movies. She carried us right home.

All the way back to our house, Mama kept telling us that we couldn't sit downstairs, we couldn't do this or that with white children. Up until that time I had never really thought about it. After all, we were playing together. I knew that we were going to separate schools and all, but I never knew why.

After the movie incident, the white children stopped playing in front of our house. For about two weeks we didn't see them at all. Then one day they were there again and we started playing. But things were not the same. I had never really thought of them as white before. Now all of a sudden they were white, and their whiteness made them better than me. I now realized that not only were they better than me because they were white, but everything they owned and everything connected with them was better than what was available to me. I hadn't realized before that downstairs in the movies was any better than upstairs. But now I saw that it was. Their whiteness provided them with a pass to downstairs in that nice section and my blackness sent me to the balcony.

Now that I was thinking about it, their schools, homes, and streets were better than mine. They had a large red brick school with nice sidewalks connecting the buildings. Their homes were large and beautiful with indoor toilets and every other convenience that I knew of at the time. Every house I had ever lived in was a one- or two-room shack with an outdoor toilet. It really bothered me that they had all these nice things and we had nothing. "There is a secret to it besides being white," I thought. Then my mind got all wrapped up in trying to uncover that secret.

One day when we were all playing in our playhouse in the ditch under the pecan tree, I got a crazy idea. I thought the secret was their "privates." I had seen everything they had but their privates and it wasn't any different than mine. So I made up a game called

"The Doctor." I had never been to a doctor myself. However, Mama had told us that a doctor was the only person that could look at children's naked bodies besides their parents. Then I remembered the time my Grandma Winnie was sick. When I asked her what the doctor had done to her she said, "He examined me." Then I asked her about "examined" and she told me he looked at her teeth, in her ears, checked her heart, blood and privates. Now I was going to be the doctor. I had all of them, Katie, Bill, Sandra, and Paul plus Adline and Junior take off their clothes and stand in line as I sat on one of the apple crates and examined them. I looked in their mouths and ears, put my ear to their hearts to listen for their heartbeats. Then I had them lie down on the leaves and I looked at their privates. I examined each of them about three times, but I didn't see any differences. I still hadn't found that secret.

That night when I was taking my bath, soaping myself all over, I thought about it again. I remembered the day I had seen my two uncles Sam and Walter. They were just as white as Katie them. But Grandma Winnie was darker than Mama, so how could Sam and Walter be white? I must have been thinking about it for a long time because Mama finally called out, "Essie Mae! Stop using up all that soap! And hurry up so Adline and Junior can bathe 'fore that water gits cold."

"Mama," I said, "why ain't Sam and Walter white?"

" 'Cause they mama ain't white," she answered.

"But you say a long time ago they daddy is white."

"If the daddy is white and the mama is colored, then that don't make the children white."

"But they got the same hair and color like Bill and Katie them got," I said.

"That still don't make them white! Now git out of that tub!" she snapped.

Every time I tried to talk to Mama about white people she got mad. Now I was more confused than before. If it wasn't the straight hair and the white skin that made you white, then what was it?

HIGH SCHOOL

About two weeks after school opened, all my plans were in operation. I was busy for a total of eighteen hours a day. Each day I spent the last two periods of school on the band or on basketball. Then I would go straight to work. I was never home until eight or nine at night and as soon as I entered the house, I'd begin helping Adline them with their lessons so I wouldn't even have to talk to Mama or Raymond. On Wednesday and Friday nights I took piano lessons. On Sundays I taught Sunday school and B.T.U.

I was so busy now that I could work for Mrs. Burke and not think of her or her guild meetings. I would fall asleep at night without dreaming old, embedded, recurring dreams. I had to keep a lot of things in the back of my mind until I finished high school.

When our mid-semester grades were released, I discovered I had made A's in all my subjects. Everything seemed so easy now. Sometimes I got scared because things were moving along too smoothly. Things had always seemed hard before. But now I was doing three times as much and I felt as if I could take on the whole world and not be tired by it. I was even better in basketball than I had ever been. In fact, I was the number one girl on the team.

Mr. Hicks, our new coach, was a nut for physical fitness—especially for girls. He hated women who were dumb about sports and he used to practice us until we were panting like overplowed mules. Sometimes he'd even take us out to play touch football with the boys so that we could learn that game. All the girls who didn't go along with his physical fitness program or who were fat and lazy he dismissed immediately. He was determined to have a winning team and was interested only in tall, slim girls who were light and fast on their feet. I think I worked harder than almost anyone else.

Shortly after mid-semester, Mr. Hicks organized a gymnastic and tumbling team. All the basketball players were required to participate. Running and heaving a ball on that open basketball court wasn't so bad, but falling on it when we did somersaults, handsprings, and rolls was like falling on steel.

Mr. Hicks was the most merciless person I had ever met. The first few weeks some of the girls could hardly walk, but he made them practice anyhow. "The only way to overcome that soreness and stiffness is to work it out," he would say. We all learned to like Mr. Hicks, in spite of his cruelty because in the end he was always right. After three weeks our stiffness was completely gone and we all felt good. Now I took in all the activities without even getting shortwinded. And I finished the semester with straight A's.

One Wednesday, I was ironing in Mrs. Burke's dining room as usual when she came to me looking very serious.

"Essie, I am so tired and disgusted with Wayne," she said, sitting down in one of the dining room chairs. "He almost flunked out of school last semester. At this rate he won't finish high school. I don't know what to do. He's in algebra now and he just can't manage it. I've tried to find someone to tutor him in math, but I haven't been able to. How is *your* math teacher?" she asked me.

"Oh, he is very good, but he hardly ever teaches our class. Most of the time he lets me take over," I said.

"Are you that good in algebra?" she asked.

"Yes, I make all A's in algebra, and he thinks I am one of his best students."

She looked at me for a moment as if she didn't believe me. Then she left the dining room.

"Look, Essie," she said, coming back with a book. "These are the problems Wayne is having trouble with. Can you work them?"

"Yes, we've passed these in my book. I can do them all," I said.

"See if you can work these two," Mrs. Burke said to me. "I'll press a couple of these shirts for you meanwhile."

I sat down at the dining room table and began working the two problems. I finished them before she finished the first shirt.

When I gave her the paper, she looked at me again like she didn't believe me. But after she had studied it and checked my answers against the ones given in the back of the book, she asked me if I would tutor Wayne a few evenings a week. "I'll pay you extra," she said. "And I can also help you with your piano lessons sometimes."

Within a week I was helping Wayne and a group of his white friends with their algebra every Monday, Tuesday, and Thursday night. While Mrs. Burke watched television in the living room, we would all sit around the dining room table—Wayne, Billy, Ray, Sue, Judy and me. They were all my age and also in the tenth grade. I don't think Mrs. Burke was so pleased with the even proportion of boys to girls in the group. Neither did she like the open friendship that was developing between Wayne and me. She especially didn't like that Wayne was looking up to me now as his "teacher." However, she accepted it for a while. Often Wayne would drive me home after we had finished the problems for the night.

Then, one Tuesday, she came through the dining room just as Wayne was asking me a question. "Look Essie," he said, "how do we do this one?" He asked this as he leaned over me with his arms resting on the back of my chair, his cheek next to mine.

"*Wayne!*" Mrs. Burke called to him almost shouting. Wayne and I didn't move, but the others turned and stared at her. "Listen to what Essie is saying," she said, trying to get back her normal tone of voice.

"Mother, we *were* listening," Wayne said very indignantly, still cheek to cheek with me.

The room was extremely quiet now. I felt as if I should have said something. But I couldn't think of anything to say. I knew Wayne was purposely trying to annoy his mother so I just sat there, trying to keep from brushing my cheek against his, feeling his warm breath on my face. He stared at her until she looked away and went hurriedly into the kitchen.

Wayne straightened up for a moment and looked at each of his friends as they looked to him for an explanation. His face was completely expressionless. Then he leaned over me again and asked the same question he had asked before. At that point, Mrs. Burke came back through the dining room.

"Wayne, you can take Billy them home, now," she said.

"We haven't done this problem, Mother. If you would stop interrupting maybe we could finish."

"Finish the problem then and take Billy them home, but drop Essie off first," Mrs. Burke said and left the room.

I explained the problem. But I was just talking to the paper. Everyone had lost interest now.

When we left the house Mrs. Burke watched us get into the car and drive off. Didn't anyone say a word until Wayne stopped in front of my house. Then Billy said, "See you Thursday, Essie," as cheerfully as he could. "O.K.," I said, and Wayne drove away.

The following evening when I went to work, Mrs. Burke wasn't home and neither was Wayne. Mrs. Burke had left word with Mrs. Crosby that I was to do the ironing and she had put out so many clothes for me to do that by the time I finished I was late for my piano lesson. I ran out of the house and down the front walk with my music books in my hand just as Mrs. Burke and Wayne were pulling into the driveway.

"Did you finish the ironing already, Essie?" Mrs. Burke asked me, as she got out of the car.

"I just finished," I said.

"Where are you going in such a hurry?" Wayne asked.

"I'm late for my piano lesson."

"Let me drive you then," he said.

"I'm going to use the car shortly, Wayne," Mrs. Burke snapped.

"It's not far from here. I can walk," I said, rushing down the sidewalk.

The next evening Sue and Judy didn't show up. Only the boys came. Mrs. Burke kept passing through the dining room every few minutes or so. The moment we finished doing the problems, she came in and said, "Essie, I gotta stop in and see Mrs. Fisher tonight. I'll drop you off."

I had begun to get tired of her nagging and hinting, but I didn't know what to do about it. In a way I enjoyed helping Wayne and his friends. I was learning a lot from them, just as they were from me. And I appreciated the extra money. Mrs. Burke paid me two dollars a week for helping Wayne and Wayne's friends paid me a dollar each. I was now making twelve dollars a week, and depositing eight dollars in my savings account. I decided not to do anything about Mrs. Burke. "She will soon see that I won't mess with Wayne," I thought.

The Saturday afternoon I was out in the backyard hanging clothes on the line while Wayne was practicing golf.

"Essie, you want to play me a round of golf?" he asked as I finished and headed for the back door.

"I don't know how to play," I said.

"It's easy. I'll teach you," he said. "Come, let me show you something."

He gave me the golf club and tried to show me how to stand, putting his arms around me and fixing my hands on the club.

"Essie, the washing machine stopped long ago!" Mrs. Burke suddenly yelled out of the house.

"I'll show you when you finish the wash," Wayne said as I walked away. I didn't even look back at him. Walking into the house, I felt like crying. I could feel what was happening inside Wayne. I knew that he was extremely fond of me and he wanted to do something for me because I was helping him and his friends with their algebra. But the way he wanted to do it put me up tight. By trying to keep him from doing it, Mrs. Burke only made him want to do it more. I knew Wayne respected me and wouldn't have gotten out of his place if I'd remained distant and cool. Now I wanted to tell him that he didn't have to do anything for me—but I didn't know how.

Wayne, Billy, and Ray received B's on the mid-semester exams. They were so happy about their marks they brought their test papers over for me to see. I shall never forget that night. The four of us sat around the table after we had corrected the mistakes on their papers.

"Gee, Essie, we love you," Billy said. "And just think, Wayne, we could have gotten A's, and if we make an A on the final exam we will get a B for a final grade." Wayne didn't say anything for a while. He just looked at Billy, then at me. When he looked at me he didn't have to speak.

"Boy, let's call Sue and Judy and see what they got," he finally said. He ran to the phone in the hall, followed by Billy and Ray.

When they left me sitting there, I began to wonder how it was that Wayne and his friends were so nice and their parents so nasty and distasteful.

Sue and Judy came back to me for help because they almost flunked the exam. Mrs. Burke seemed more relaxed once the girls were back. However, they were not relaxed at all. They felt guilty for leaving in the first place. For a week or so they brought me little gifts and it made me nervous. But after that we were again one little happy family.

The dining room in Mrs. Burke's house had come to mean many things to me. It symbolized hatred, love, and fear in many variations. The hatred and the love caused me much anxiety and fear. But courage was growing in me too. Little by little it was getting harder and harder for me not to speak out. Then one Wednesday night it happened.

Mrs. Burke seemed to discuss her most intimate concerns with me whenever I was ironing. This time she came in, sat down, and asked me, "Essie, what do you think of all this talk about integrating the schools in the South?"

At first I looked at her stunned with my mouth wide open. Then Mama's words ran through my head: "Just do your work like you don't know nothin'." I changed my expression to one of stupidity.

"Haven't you heard about the Supreme Court decision, and all this talk about integrating the schools?" she asked.

I shook my head no. But I lied.

"Well, we have a lot of talk about it here and people seemingly just don't know what to do. But I am not in favor of integrating schools. We'll move to Liberty first. I am sure that they won't stand for it there. You see, Essie, I wouldn't mind Wayne going to school with *you*. But all Negroes aren't like you and your family. You wouldn't like to go to school with Wayne, would you?" She said all this with so much honesty and concern, I felt compelled to be truthful.

"I don't know, Mrs. Burke. I think we could learn a lot from each other. I like Wayne and his friends. I don't see the difference in me helping Wayne and his friends at home and setting in a classroom with them. I've learned a lot from Judy them. Just like all Negroes ain't like me, all white children I know ain't like Wayne and Judy them. I was going to the post office the other day and a group of white girls tried to force me off the sidewalk. And I have seen Judy with one of them. But I know Judy ain't like that. She wouldn't push me or any other Negro off the street."

"What I asked you, Essie, is if you wanted to go to school with Wayne," Mrs. Burke said stiffly. "I am not interested in what Judy's friends did to you. So you are telling me you want to go to school with Wayne!" She stormed out of the dining room, her face burning with anger.

After she left I stood at the ironing board waiting—waiting for her to return with my money and tell me she didn't need me any more. But she didn't. She didn't confront me at all before I left that evening. And I went home shaking with fear.

The next evening when I came to work I found a note from Mrs. Burke stating she was at a guild meeting and telling me what to do. That made things even worse. As I read the note my hand shook. My eyes lingered on "the Guild." Then when Wayne and his friends didn't show up for their little session with me, I knew something was wrong. I didn't know what to do. I waited for an hour for Wayne and Judy them to come. When they didn't, I went to Mrs. Crosby's room and knocked.

When Mrs. Crosby didn't answer my heart stopped completely. I knew she was in there. She had been very ill and hadn't been out in a month. In fact, I hadn't even seen her because Mrs. Burke had asked me not to go to her room. At last I put my hand on the knob of her door and slowly turned it. "She can't be dead, she can't be dead," I thought. I opened the door slowly.

"Mrs. Crosby," I called. She was sitting up in bed as white as a ghost. I saw that she must have been sleeping. Her long, long hair was not braided as usual. It was all over the pillow everywhere.

"How do you feel, Mrs. Crosby?" I asked, standing at the foot of her bed. She beckoned for me to come closer. Then she motioned for me to sit on her bed. As I sat on the bed, she took my hands and held them affectionately.

"How do you feel?" I repeated.

"Weak but better," she said in a very faint voice.

"I was suppose to help Wayne them with their algebra this evening, but they didn't come," I said.

"I know," she said. "I heard Wayne and his mother fighting last night. Wayne is a nice boy, Essie. He and his friends like you very much. However, his mother is a very impatient woman. You study hard in school, Essie. When you finish I am going to help you to go to college. You will be a great math teacher one day. Now you go home. Wayne and his friends aren't coming tonight." She squeezed my hands.

The way she talked scared me stiff. When it was time to go home and I walked out on the porch, it was dark. I stood there afraid to move. "I can't go through the project now," I thought. "Mrs. Burke them might have someone out there to kill me or beat me up like they beat up Jerry. Why did I have to talk to Mrs. Burke like that yesterday?" I took the long way home that went along the lighted streets. But I trembled with fear every time a car drove past. I just knew that out of any car five or six men could jump and grab me.

The following day, I didn't go to work. I didn't even go to school. I told Mama I had a terrible headache and I stayed in bed all day.

"Essie Mae, it's four o'clock. You better git up from there and go to work," Mama called.

"My head's still hurting. I ain't going to work with my head hurting this bad," I whined.

"Why is you havin' so many headaches? You been lazin' in bed all day. Miss Burke gonna fire you. Junior, go up there and tell Miss Burke Essie Mae is sick."

I lay in bed thinking I had to find some other ache because

Mama was getting wise to my headaches. If I could only tell her about Mrs. Burke, I wouldn't have to lie to her all the time. I really missed Mrs. Rice. Mrs. Rice would have told me what to do. I couldn't talk to any of the other teachers. "What can I do?" I thought. "I can't just quit, because she'll fix it so I can't get another job."

When Junior came back, I called him into my room.

"What did Mrs. Burke say?" I asked him.

"She ain't said nothing but for you to come to work tomorrow, 'cause the house need a good cleanin'. She want me to come with you to mow the yard."

I felt a little better after Junior told me that. But I couldn't understand Mrs. Burke's actions. It worried me that she was still going to keep me on. What if she was doing that just to try and frame me with something? "I'll see how she acts tomorrow," I finally decided.

At seven o'clock on Saturday morning Junior and I headed through the project for Mrs. Burke's house. Usually I took advantage of my walk through the project to think about things and compose myself before I got to work, but today I didn't have a single thought in my head. I guess I had thought too much the day before. When I walked up on her porch and saw her standing in the hall smiling it didn't even register. I was just there. I realized at that point I was plain tired of Mrs. Burke.

I went about the housecleaning like a robot until I got to the dining room. Then I started thinking. I stood there for some time thinking about Mrs. Burke, Wayne, and his friends. It was there I realized that when I thought of Wayne my thoughts were colored by emotions. I liked him more than a friend. I stood softly looking down at the table and the chair where Wayne sat when I helped him with his lessons.

When I looked up Mrs. Burke was standing in the doorway staring at me. I saw the hatred in her eyes.

"Essie," she said, "did you see my change purse when you cleaned my room?"

"No," I answered, "I didn't see it."

"Maybe I dropped it outside in the yard when I was showing Junior what to do," she said.

"So, that's how she's trying to hurt me," I thought, following her to the back door. "She better not dare." I stood in the back door and watched her walk across the big backyard toward Junior. First she stood talking to him for a minute, then they walked over to a corner of the yard and poked around in the grass as though she was looking for her purse. After they had finished doing that, she was still talking to Junior and he stood there trembling with fear, a horrified look on his face. She shook him down and turned his pockets inside out. I opened the door and ran down the steps. I didn't realize what I was about to do until I was only a few paces away from them.

"Did you find it out here, Mrs. Burke?" I asked her very coldly, indicating that I had seen her shake Junior down.

"No, I haven't found it," she answered. She looked at Junior as if she still believed he had it."

"Did you see Mrs. Burke's purse, Junior?" I asked him.

"No, I ain't saw it." He shook his head and never took his eyes off Mrs. Burke.

"Junior hasn't seen it, Mrs. Burke. Maybe we overlooked it in the house."

"You cleaned my bedroom, Essie, and you said you didn't see it," Mrs. Burke said, but she started back to the house, and I followed her.

When we got inside, she went in the bedroom to look for her purse and I went back to housecleaning. About thirty minutes later she interrupted me again.

"I found it, Essie," she said, showing me the change purse in her hand.

"Where was it?" I asked.

"I had forgotten. Wayne and I watched TV in his room last night." She gave me a guilty smile.

"I am glad you found it." I picked up the broom and continued sweeping.

"I'll just find me another job," I thought to myself. "This is my last day working for this bitch. School will be out soon and I'll go back to Baton Rouge and get a job. Ain't no sense in me staying on here. Sooner or later something might really happen. Then I'll wish I had quit."

"Essie, I don't have enough money to pay you today," Mrs.

Burke said, sitting at the big desk in the hallway. She was looking through her wallet. "I'll pay you on Monday. I'll cash a check then."

"You can give me a check, now, Mrs. Burke. I won't be back on Monday."

"Do you go to piano lessons on Monday now?" she asked.

"I am not coming back, Mrs. Burke," I said it slowly and deliberately, so she didn't misunderstand this time.

She looked at me for a while, and then said "Why?"

"I saw what you did to Junior. Junior don't steal. And I have worked for white people since I was nine. I have worked for you almost two years, and I have never stole anything from you or anybody else. We work, Mrs. Burke, so we won't have to steal."

"O.K., Essie, I'll give you a check," Mrs. Burke said angrily. She hurriedly wrote one out and gave it to me.

"Is Junior still here?" I asked.

"No, I paid him and he's gone already. Why?" she asked.

I didn't answer. I just slowly walked to the front door. When I got there, I turned around and looked down the long hallway for the last time. Mrs. Burke stood at the desk staring at me curiously as I came back toward her again.

"Did you forget something?" She asked as I passed her.

"I forgot to tell Mrs. Crosby I am leaving," I said, still walking.

"Mama doesn't pay you. I do! I do!" she called to me, as I knocked gently and opened Mrs. Crosby's door.

Mrs. Crosby was propped up on pillows in bed as usual. But she looked much better than she had the last time I was in her room.

"How are you feeling, Mrs. Crosby?" I asked, standing by the side of her bed.

"Much better, Essie," she answered. She motioned for me to sit down.

"I just came to tell you this is my last day working for Mrs. Burke, Mrs. Crosby."

"What happened? Did she fire you, Essie?" she asked.

"She didn't fire me. I just decided to leave."

"I understand, Essie," she said. "And you take care of yourself. And remember when you are ready for college let me know, and I'll help you." She squeezed my hand.

"I gotta go, Mrs. Crosby," I said. "I hope you'll be up soon."

"Thanks, Essie, and please take care of yourself," she said.

"I will, Mrs. Crosby. 'Bye."

"'Bye, Essie," she said. She squeezed my hand again and then I left her room.

When I walked out of Mrs. Crosby's room, Mrs. Burke was still standing in the hallway by the desk.

"Maybe you would like to come back tonight and say good-bye to Wayne, too," she said sarcastically.

I didn't say anything to her. I walked past her and out of that house for good. And I hoped that as time passed I could put not only Mrs. Burke but all her kind out of my life for good.

THE MOVEMENT

During my senior year at Tougaloo, my family hadn't sent me one penny. I had only the small amount of money I had earned at Maple Hill. I couldn't afford to eat at school or live in the dorms, so I had gotten permission to move off campus. I had to prove that I could finish school, even if I had to go hungry every day. I knew Raymond and Miss Pearl were just waiting to see me drop out. But something happened to me as I got more and more involved in the Movement. It no longer seemed important to prove anything. I had found something outside myself that gave meaning to my life.

I had become very friendly with my social science professor, John Salter, who was in charge of NAACP activities on campus. All during the year, while the NAACP conducted a boycott of the downtown stores in Jackson, I had been one of Salter's most faithful canvassers and church speakers. During the last week of school, he told me that sit-in demonstrations were about to start in Jackson and that he wanted me to be the spokesman for a team that would sit-in at Woolworth's lunch counter. The two other demonstrators would be classmates of mine, Memphis and Pearlena. Pearlena was a dedicated NAACP worker, but Memphis had not been very involved in the Movement on campus. It seemed that the organization had had a rough time finding students who were in a position to go to jail. I had nothing to lose one way or the other. Around ten o'clock the morning of the demonstrations, NAACP headquarters alerted the news services. As a result, the police department was also informed, but neither the policemen nor the newsmen knew exactly where or when the demonstrations would start. They stationed themselves along Capitol Street and waited.

To divert attention from the sit-in at Woolworth's, the picketing started at J. C. Penney's a good fifteen minutes before. The pickets were allowed to walk up and down in front of the store three or four times before they were arrested. At exactly 11 A.M., Pearlena, Memphis, and I entered Woolworth's from the rear entrance. We separated as soon as we stepped into the store, and made small purchases from various counters. Pearlena had given Memphis her watch. He was to let us know when it was 11:14. At 11:14 we were to join him near the lunch counter and at exactly 11:15 we were to take seats at it.

Seconds before 11:15 we were occupying three seats at the previously segregated Woolworth's lunch counter. In the beginning the waitresses seemed to ignore us, as if they really didn't know what was going on. Our waitress walked past us a couple of times before she noticed we had started to write our own orders down and realized we wanted service. She asked us what we wanted. We began to read to her from our order slips. She told us that we would be served at the back counter, which was for Negroes.

"We would like to be served here," I said.

The waitress started to repeat what she had said, then stopped in the middle of the sentence. She turned the lights out behind the counter, and she and the other waitresses almost ran to the back of the store, deserting all their white customers. I guess they thought that violence would start immediately after the whites at the counter realized what was going on. There were five or six other people at the counter. A couple of them just got up and walked away. A girl sitting next to me finished her banana split before leaving. A middle-aged white woman who had not yet been served rose from her seat and came over to us. "I'd like to stay here with you," she said, "but my husband is waiting."

The newsmen came in just as she was leaving. They must have discovered what was going on shortly after some of the people began to leave the store. One of the newsmen ran behind the woman who spoke to us and asked her to identify herself. She refused to give her name, but said she was a native of Vicksburg and a former resident of California. When asked why she had said what she had said to us, she replied, "I am in sympathy with the Negro movement." By this time a crowd of cameramen and reporters had gathered around us taking pictures and asking questions, such as Where were we from? Why did we sit-in? What organization sponsored it? Were we students? From what school? How were we classified?

I told them that we were all students at Tougaloo College, that we were represented by no particular organization, and that we planned to stay there even after the store closed. "All we want is service," was my reply to one of them. After they had finished probing for about twenty minutes, they were almost ready to leave.

At noon, students from a nearby white high school started pouring in to Woolworth's. When they first saw us they were sort of surprised. They didn't know how to react. A few started to heckle and the newsmen became interested again. Then the white students started chanting all kinds of anti-Negro slogans. We were called a little bit of everything. The rest of the seats except the three we were occupying had been roped off to prevent others from sitting down. A couple of the boys took one end of the rope and made it into a hangman's noose. Several attempts were made to put it around our necks. The crowds grew as more students and adults came in for lunch.

We kept our eyes straight forward and did not look at the crowd except for occasional glances to see what was going on. All of a sudden I saw a face I remembered—the drunkard from the bus station sit-in. My eyes lingered on him just long enough for us to recognize each other. Today he was drunk too, so I don't think he remembered where he had seen me before. He took out a knife, opened it, put it in his pocket, and then began to pace the floor. At this point, I told Memphis and Pearlena what was going on. Memphis suggested that we pray. We bowed our heads, and all hell broke loose. A man rushed forward, threw Memphis from his seat, and slapped my face. Then another man who worked in the store threw me against an adjoining counter.

Down on my knees on the floor, I saw Memphis lying near the lunch counter with blood running out of the corners of his mouth. As he tried to protect his face, the man who'd thrown him down kept kicking him against the head. If he had worn hard-soled shoes instead of sneakers, the first kick probably would have killed Memphis. Finally a man dressed in plain clothes identified himself as a police officer and arrested Memphis and his attacker.

Pearlena had been thrown to the floor. She and I got back on our stools after Memphis was arrested. There were some white Tougaloo teachers in the crowd. They asked Pearlena and me if we wanted to leave. They said that things were getting too rough. We didn't know what to do. While we were trying to make up our minds, we were joined by Joan Trumpauer. Now there were three of us and we were integrated. The crowd began to chant, "Communists, Communists, Communists." Some old man in the crowd ordered the students to take us off the stools.

"Which one should I get first?" a big husky boy said.

"That white nigger," the one man said.

The boy lifted Joan from the counter by her waist and carried her out of the store. Simultaneously, I was snatched from my stool by two high school students. I was dragged about thirty feet toward the door by my hair when someone made them turn me loose. As I was getting up off the floor, I saw Joan coming back inside. We started back to the center of the counter to join Pearlena. Lois Chaffee, a white Tougaloo faculty member, was now sitting next to her. So Joan and I just climbed across the rope at the front end of the counter and sat down. There were now four of us, two whites and two Negroes, all women. The mob started smearing us with ketchup, mustard, sugar, pies, and everything on the counter. Soon Joan and I were joined by John Salter, but the moment he sat down he was hit on the jaw with what appeared to be brass knuckles. Blood gushed from his face and someone threw salt into the open wound. Ed King, Tougaloo's chaplain, rushed to him.

At the other end of the counter, Lois and Pearlena were joined by George Raymond, a CORE field worker and a student from Jackson State College. Then a Negro high school boy sat down next to me. The mob took spray paint from the counter and sprayed it on the new demonstrators. The high school student had on a white shirt; the word "nigger" was written on his back with red spray paint.

We sat there for three hours taking a beating when the manager decided to close the store because the mob had begun to go wild with stuff from the other counters. He begged and begged everyone to leave. But even after fifteen minutes of begging, no one budged. They would not leave until we did. Then Dr. Beittel, the president of Tougaloo College, came running in. He said he had just heard what was happening.

About ninety policemen were standing outside the store; they had been watching the whole thing through the windows, but had not come in to stop the mob or do anything. President Beittel went outside and asked Captain Ray to come and escort us out. The captain refused, stating the manager had to invite him in before he could enter the premises, so Dr. Beittel himself brought us out. He had told the police that they had better protect us after we were outside the store. When we got outside, the policemen formed a single line that blocked the mob from us. However, they were allowed to throw at us everything they had collected. Within ten minutes, we were picked up by Reverend King in his station wagon and taken to the NAACP headquarters on Lynch Street.

After the sit-in, all I could think of was how sick Mississippi whites were. They believed so much in the segregated Southern way of life, they would kill to preserve it. I sat there in the NAACP office and thought of how many times they had killed when this way of life was threatened. I knew that the killing had just begun. "Many more will die before it is over with," I thought. Before the sit-in, I had always hated the whites in Mississippi. Now I knew it was impossible for me to hate sickness. The whites had a disease, an incurable disease in its final stage. What were our chances against such a disease? I thought of the students, the young Negroes who had just begun to protest, as young interns. When these young interns got older, I thought, they would be the best doctors in the world for social problems.

FROM

North Toward Home

WILLIE MORRIS

LIKE MARK TWAIN and his comrades growing up a century before in another village on the other side of the Mississippi, my friends and I had but one sustaining ambition in the 1940s. Theirs in Hannibal was to be steamboatmen, ours in Yazoo was to be major-league baseball players. In the summers, we thought and talked of little else. We memorized batting averages, fielding averages, slugging averages, we knew the roster of the Cardinals and the Red Sox better than their own managers must have known them, and to hear the broadcasts from all the big-city ballparks with their memorable names—the Polo Grounds, Wrigley Field, Fenway Park, the Yankee Stadium—was to set our imagination churning for the glory and riches those faraway places would one day bring us. One of our friends went to St. Louis on his vacation to see the Cards, and when he returned with the autographs of Stan Musial, Red Schoendienst, Country Slaughter, Marty Marion, Joe Garagiola, and a dozen others, we could hardly keep down our envy. I hated that boy for a month, and secretly wished him dead, not only because he took on new airs but because I wanted those scraps of paper with their magic characters. I wished also that my own family were wealthy enough to take me to a big-league town for two weeks, but to a bigger place even than St. Louis: Chicago, maybe, with not one but two teams, or best of all to New York, with three. I had bought a baseball cap in Jackson, a real one from the Brooklyn Dodgers, and a Jackie Robinson Louisville Slugger, and one day when I could not even locate any of the others for catch or for baseball talk, I sat on a curb on Grand Avenue with the most dreadful feelings of being caught forever by time—trapped there always in my scrawny and helpless condition. *I'm ready, I'm ready,* I kept thinking to myself, but that remote future when I would wear a cap like that and be a hero for a grandstand full of people seemed so far away I knew it would never come. I must have been the most dejected-looking child you ever saw, sitting hunched up on the curb and dreaming of glory in the mythical cities of the North. I felt worse when a carload of high school boys halted right in front of where I sat, and they started reciting what they always did when they saw me alone and day-dreaming: *Wee Willie Winkie walks through the town, upstairs and downstairs in his nightgown.* Then one of them said, "Winkie, you *gettin'* much?" "You bastards!" I shouted, and they drove off laughing like wild men.

Almost every afternoon when the heat was not unbearable my father and I would go out to the old baseball field behind the armory to hit flies. I would stand far out in center field, and he would station himself with a fungo at home plate, hitting me one high fly, or Texas Leaguer, or line drive after another, sometimes for an hour or more without stopping. My dog would get out there in the outfield with me, and retrieve the inconsequential dribblers or the ones that went too far. I was light and speedy, and could make the most fantastic catches, turning completely around and forgetting the ball sometimes to head for the spot where it would descend, or tumbling head-on for a diving catch. The smell of that new-cut grass was the finest of all smells, and I could run forever and never get tired. It was a dreamy, suspended state, those late afternoons, thinking of nothing but outfield flies as the world drifted lazily by on Jackson Avenue. I learned to judge what a ball would do by instinct, heading the way it went as if I owned it, and I knew in my heart I could make the big time. Then, after all that exertion, my father would shout, "I'm whupped!" and we would quit for the day.

When I was twelve I became a part-time sportswriter for the *Yazoo Herald,* whose courtly proprietors allowed me unusual independence. I wrote up an occasional high school or Legion game in a florid prose, filled with phrases like "two-ply blow" and "circuit-ringer." My mentor was the sports editor of the *Memphis Commercial Appeal,* whose name was Walter Stewart, a man who could invest the most humdrum athletic contest with the elements of Shakespearean tragedy. I learned whole paragraphs of his by heart, and used some of his expressions for my reports on games between Yazoo and Satartia, or the other teams. That summer when I was twelve, having never seen a baseball game higher than the Jackson Senators of Class B, my father finally relented and took me to Memphis to see the Chicks, who were Double-A. It was the farthest I had ever been from home, and the largest city I had ever seen; I walked around in a state of joyousness, admiring the crowds and the big park high above the River, and best of all, the grand old lobby of the Chisca Hotel.

Staying with us at the Chisca were the Nashville Vols, who were there for a big series with the Chicks. I stayed close to the lobby to get a glimpse of them; when I discovered they spent all day, up until the very moment they left for the ballpark, playing the pinball machine, I stationed myself there too. Their names were Tookie Gilbert, Smokey Burgess, Chuck Workman, and Bobo Hollomon, the latter being the one who got as far as the St. Louis Browns, pitched a no-hitter in his first major league game, and failed to win another before being shipped down forever to obscurity; one afternoon my father and I ran into them outside the hotel on the way to the game and gave them a ride in our taxi. I could have been fit for tying, especially when Smokey Burgess tousled my hair and asked me if I batted right or left, but when I listened to them as they grumbled about having to get out to the ballpark so early, and complained about the season having two more damned months to go and about how ramshackle their team bus was, I was too disillusioned even to tell my friends when I got home.

Because back home, even among the adults, baseball was all-meaning; it was the link with the outside. A place known around town simply as The Store, down near the train depot, was the principal center of this ferment. The Store had sawdust on the floor and long shreds of flypaper hanging from the ceiling. Its most familiar staples were Rexall supplies, oysters on the half shell, legal beer, and illegal whiskey, the latter served up, Mississippi bootlegger style, by the bottle from a hidden shelf and costing not merely the price of the whiskey but the investment in gas required to go to Louisiana to fetch it. There was a long counter in the back. On one side of it, the white workingmen congregated after hours every afternoon to compare the day's scores and talk batting averages, and on the other side, also talking baseball, were the Negroes, juxtaposed in a face-to-face arrangement with the whites. The scores were chalked up on a blackboard hanging on a red and purple wall, and the conversations were carried on in fast, galloping shouts from one end of the room to the other. An intelligent white boy of twelve was even permitted, in that atmosphere of heady freedom before anyone knew the name of Justice Warren or had heard much of the United States Supreme Court, a quasi-public position favoring the Dodgers, who had Jackie Robinson, Roy Campanella, and Don Newcombe—not to mention, so it was rumored, God knows how many Chinese and mulattoes being groomed in the minor leagues. I remember my father turned to some friends at The Store one day and observed, "Well, you can say what you want to about that nigger Robinson, but he's got *guts,*" and to a man the others nodded, a little reluctantly, but in agreement nonetheless. And one of them said he had read somewhere that Pee Wee Reese, a white Southern boy, was the best friend Robinson had on the team, which proved they had chosen the right one to watch after him.

There were two firehouses in town, and on hot afternoons the firemen at both establishments sat outdoors in their shirtsleeves, with the baseball broadcast turned up as loud as it would go. On his day off work my father, who had left Cities Service and was now a bookkeeper for the wholesale grocery, usually started with Firehouse No. 1 for the first few innings and then hit Number Two before ending up at The Store for the post-game conversations.

I decided not to try out for the American Legion Junior Baseball team that summer. Legion baseball was an important thing for country boys in those parts, but I was too young and skinny, and I had heard that the coach, a dirt farmer known as Gentleman Joe, made his protégés lie flat in the infield while he walked on their stomachs; he also forced them to take three-mile runs through the streets of town, talked them into going to church, and persuaded them to give up Coca-Colas. A couple of summers later, when I did go out for the team, I found out that Gentleman Joe did in fact insist on these soul-strengthening rituals; because of them, we won the Mississippi State Championship and the merchants in town took up a collection and sent us all the way to St. Louis to see the Cards play the Phillies. My main concern that earlier summer, however, lay in the more academic aspects of the game. I knew more about baseball, its technology and its ethos, than all the firemen and Store experts put together. Having read most of its literature, I could give a sizable lecture on the infield-fly rule alone, which only a thin minority of the townspeople knew existed. Gentleman Joe was held in some esteem for his strategical sense, yet he was the only man I ever knew who could call for a sacrifice bunt with two men out and not have a bad conscience about it. I remember one dismaying moment that came to me while I was watching a country semi-pro game. The home team had runners on first and third with one out, when the batter hit a ground ball to the first baseman, who stepped on first and then threw to second. The shortstop, covering second, stepped on the base but made no attempt to tag the runner. The man on third had crossed the plate, of course, but the umpire, who was not very familiar with the subtleties of the rules, signaled a double play. Sitting in the grandstand, I knew that it was not a double play at all and that the run had scored, but when I went down, out of my Christian duty, to tell the manager of the local team that he had just been done out of a run, he told me I was crazy. This was the kind of brainpower I was up against.

That summer the local radio station, the one where we broadcast our Methodist programs, started a baseball quiz program. A razor blade company offered free blades and the station chipped in a dollar, all of which went to the first listener to telephone with the right answer to the day's baseball question. If there was no winner, the next day's pot would go up a dollar. At the end of the month they had to close down the program because I was winning all the money. It got so easy, in fact, that I stopped phoning in the answers some afternoons so that the pot could build up and make my winnings more spectacular. I netted about $25 and a ten-year supply of double-edged, smooth-contact razor blades before they gave up. One day, when the jackpot was a mere two dollars, the announcer tried to confuse me. "Babe Ruth," he said, "hit sixty home runs in 1927 to set the major-league record. What man had the next-highest total?" I telephoned and said, "George Herman Ruth. He hit fifty-nine in another season." My adversary, who had developed an acute dislike of me, said that was not the correct answer. He said it should have been *Babe* Ruth. This incident angered me, and I won for the next four days, just for the hell of it.

On Sunday afternoons we sometimes drove out of town and along hot, dusty roads to baseball fields that were little more than parched red clearings, the outfield sloping out of the woods and ending in some tortuous gully full of yellowed paper, old socks, and vintage cow shit. One of the backwoods teams had a fastball pitcher named Eckert, who didn't have any teeth, and a fifty-year-old left-handed catcher named Smith. Since there were no catcher's mitts made for left-handers, Smith had to wear a mitt on his throwing hand. In his simian posture he would catch the ball and toss it lightly into the air and then whip his mitt off and catch the ball in his bare left hand before throwing it back. It was a wonderfully lazy way to spend those Sunday afternoons—my father and my friends and I sitting in the grass behind the chicken-wire backstop with eight or ten dozen farmers, watching the wrong-handed catcher go through his contorted gyrations, and listening at the same time to our portable radio, which brought us the rising inflections of a baseball announcer called the Old Scotchman. The sounds of the two games, our own and the one being broadcast from Brooklyn or Chicago, merged and rolled across the bumpy outfield and the gully into the woods; it was a combination that seemed perfectly natural to everyone there.

I can see the town now on some hot, still weekday afternoon in mid-summer: ten thousand souls and nothing doing. Even the red water truck was a diversion, coming slowly up Grand Avenue with its sprinklers on full force, the water making sizzling steam-clouds on the pavement while half-naked Negro children followed the truck up the street and played in the torrent until they got soaking wet. Over on Broadway, where the old men sat drowsily in straw chairs on the pavement near the Bon-Ton Café, whittling to make the time pass, you could laze around on the sidewalks—barefoot, if your feet were tough enough to stand the scalding concrete—watching the big cars with out-of-state plates whip by, the driver hardly knowing and certainly not caring what place this was. Way up that fantastic hill, Broadway seemed to end in a seething mist—little heat mirages that shimmered off the asphalt; on the main street itself there would be only a handful of cars parked here and there, and the merchants and the lawyers sat in the shade under their broad awnings, talking slowly, aimlessly, in the cryptic summer way. The one o'clock whistle at the sawmill would send out its loud bellow, reverberating up the streets to the bend in the Yazoo River, hardly making a ripple in the heavy somnolence.

But by two o'clock almost every radio in town was tuned in to the Old Scotchman. His rhetoric dominated the place. It hovered in the branches of the trees, bounced off the hills, and came out of the darkened stores; the merchants and the old men cocked their ears to him, and even from the big cars that sped by, their tires making lapping sounds in the softened highway, you could hear his voice, being carried past you out into the delta.

The Old Scotchman's real name was Gordon McLendon, and he described the big-league games for the Liberty Broadcasting System, which had outlets mainly in the South and the Southwest. He had a deep, rich voice, and I think he was the best rhetorician, outside of Bilbo and Nye Bevan, I have ever heard. Under his handling a baseball game took on a life of its own. As in the prose of the *Commercial Appeal*'s Walter Stewart, his games were rare and remarkable entities; casual pop flies had the flow of history behind them, double plays resembled the stark clashes of old armies, and home runs deserved acknowledgment on earthen urns. Later, when I came across Thomas Wolfe, I felt I had heard him before, from Shibe Park, Crosley Field, or the Yankee Stadium.

One afternoon I was sitting around my house listening to the Old Scotchman, admiring the vivacity of a man who said he was a contemporary of Connie Mack. (I learned later that he was twenty-nine.) That day he was doing the Dodgers and the Giants from the Polo Grounds. The game, as I recall, was in the fourth inning, and the Giants were ahead by about 4 to 1. It was a boring game, however, and I began experimenting with my father's short-wave radio, an impressive mechanism a couple of feet wide, which had an aerial that almost touched the ceiling and the name of every major city in the world on its dial. It was by far the best radio I had ever seen; there was not another one like it in town. I switched the dial to short-wave and began picking up African drum music, French jazz, Australian weather reports, and a lecture from the British Broadcasting Company on the people who wrote poems for Queen Elizabeth. Then a curious thing happened. I came across a baseball game—the Giants and the Dodgers, from the Polo Grounds. After a couple of minutes I discovered that the game was in the eighth inning. I turned back to the local station, but here the Giants and Dodgers were still in the fourth. I turned again to the short-wave broadcast and listened to the last inning, a humdrum affair that ended with Carl Furillo popping out to shortstop, Gil Hodges grounding out second to first, and Roy Campanella lining out to center. Then I went back to the Old Scotchman and listened to the rest of the game. In the top of the ninth, an hour or so later, a ghostly thing occurred; to my astonishment and titillation, the game ended with Furillo popping out to short, Hodges grounding out second to first, and Campanella lining out to center.

I kept this unusual discovery to myself, and the next day, an hour before the Old Scotchman began his play-by-play of the second game of the series, I dialed the short-wave frequency, and, sure enough, they were doing the Giants and the Dodgers again. I learned that I was listening to the Armed Forces Radio Service, which broadcast games played in New York. As the game progressed I began jotting down notes on the action. When the first four innings were over I turned to the local station just in time to get the Old Scotchman for the first batter. The Old Scotchman's account of the game matched the short-wave's almost perfectly. The Scotchman's, in fact, struck me as being considerably more poetic than the one I had heard first. But I did not doubt him, since I could hear the roar of the crowd, the crack of the bat, and the Scotchman's precise description of foul balls that fell into the crowd, the gestures of the base coaches, and the expression on the face of a small boy who was eating a lemon popsicle in a box seat behind first base. I decided that the broadcast was being delayed somewhere along the line, maybe because we were so far from New York.

That was my first thought, but after a close comparison of the two broadcasts for the rest of the game, I sensed that something more sinister was taking place. For one thing, the Old Scotchman's description of the count on a batter, though it jibed 90 percent of the time, did not always match. For another, the Scotchman's crowd, compared with the other, kept up an ungodly noise. When Robinson stole second on short-wave, he did it without drawing a throw and without sliding, while for Mississippians the feat was performed in a cloud of angry, petulant dust. A foul ball that went over the grandstand and out of the park for short-wave listeners in Alaska, France, and the Argentine produced for the firemen, bootleggers, farmers, and myself a primitive scramble that ended with a feeble old lady catching the ball on the first bounce to the roar of an assembly that would have outnumbered Grant's at Old Cold Harbor. But the most revealing development came after the Scotchman's game was over. After the usual summaries, he mentioned that the game had been "recreated." I had never taken notice of that particular word before, because I lost interest once a game was over. I went to the dictionary, and under "recreate" I found, "To invest with fresh vigor and strength; to refresh, invigorate (nature, strength, a person or thing)." The Old Scotchman most assuredly invested a game with fresh vigor and strength, but this told me nothing. My deepest suspicions were confirmed, however, when I found the second definition of the word—"To create anew."

So there it was. I was happy to have fathomed the mystery, as perhaps no one else in the whole town had done. The Old Scotchman, for all his wondrous expressions, was not only several innings behind every game he described but was no doubt sitting in some air-conditioned studio in the hinterland, where he got the happenings of the game by news ticker; sound effects accounted for the crack of the bat and the crowd noises. Instead of being disappointed in the Scotchman, I was all the more pleased by his genius, for he made pristine facts more actual than actuality, a valuable lesson when the day finally came that I started reading literature. I must add, however, that this appreciation did not obscure the realization that I had at my disposal a weapon of unimaginable dimensions.

Next day I was at the short-wave again, but I learned with much dissappointment that the game being broadcast on short-wave was not the one the Scotchman had chosen to describe. I tried every afternoon after that and discovered that I would have to wait until the Old Scotchman decided to do a game out of New York before I could match his game with the one described live on short-wave. Sometimes, I learned later, these coincidences did not occur for days; during an important Dodger or Yankee series, however, his game and that of the Armed Forces Radio Service often coincided for two or three days running. I was happy, therefore, to find, on an afternoon a few days later, that both the short-wave and the Scotchman were carrying the Yankees and the Indians.

I settled myself at the short-wave with notebook and pencil and took down every pitch. This I did for four full innings, and then I turned back to the town station, where the Old Scotchman was just beginning the first inning. I checked the first batter to make sure the accounts jibed. Then, armed with my notebook, I ran down the street to the corner grocery, a minor outpost of baseball intellection, presided over by my young Negro friend Bozo, a knowledgeable student of the game, the same one who kept my dog in bologna. I found Bozo behind the meat counter, with the Scotchman's account going full blast. I arrived at the interim between the top and bottom of the first inning.

"Who's pitchin' for the Yankees, Bozo?" I asked.

"They're pitchin' Allie Reynolds," Bozo said. "Old Scotchman says Reynolds really got the stuff today. He just set 'em down one, two, three."

The Scotchman, meanwhile, was describing the way the pennants were flapping in the breeze. Phil Rizzuto, he reported, was stepping to the plate.

"Bo," I said, trying to sound cut-and-dried, "you know what I think? I think Rizzuto's gonna take a couple of fast called strikes, then foul one down the left-field line, and then line out straight to Boudreau at short."

"Yeah?" Bozo said. He scratched his head and leaned lazily across the counter.

I went up front to buy something and then came back. The count worked to nothing and two on Rizzuto—a couple of fast called strikes and a foul down the left side. "This one," I said to Bozo, "he lines straight to Boudreau at short."

The Old Scotchman, pausing dramatically between words as was his custom, said, "Here's the windup on nothing and two. Here's the pitch on its way—There's a hard line drive! But Lou Boudreau's there at shortstop and he's got it. Phil hit that one on the noze, but Boudreau was right there."

Bozo looked over at me, his eyes bigger than they were. "How'd you know that?" he asked.

Ignoring this query, I made my second prediction. "Bozo," I said, "Tommy Henrich's gonna hit the first pitch up against the right-field wall and slide in with a double."

"How come you think so?"

"Because I can predict anything that's gonna happen in baseball in the next ten years," I said. "I can tell you anything."

The Old Scotchman was describing Henrich at the plate. "Here comes the first pitch. Henrich swings, there's a hard smash into right field! . . . This one may be out of here! It's going, going—*No!* It's off the wall in right center Henrich's rounding first, on his way to second. Here's the relay from Doby . . . Henrich slides in safely with a double!" The Yankee crowd sent up an awesome roar in the background.

"Say, how'd you know that?" Bozo asked. "How'd you know he was gonna wind up at second?"

"I just can tell. I got extra-vision," I said. On the radio, far in the background, the public-address system announced Yogi Berra. "Like Berra right now. You know what? He's gonna hit a one-one pitch down the right-field line—"

"How come you know?" Bozo said. He was getting mad.

"Just a second," I said. "I'm gettin' static." I stood dead still, put my hands up against my temples and opened my eyes wide. "Now it's comin' through clear. Yeah, Yogi's gonna hit a one-one pitch down the right-field line, and it's gonna be fair by about three or four feet—I can't say exactly—and Henrich's gonna score from second, but the throw is gonna get Yogi at second by a mile."

This time Bozo was silent, listening to the Scotchman, who described the ball and the strike, then said: "Henrich takes the lead off second. Benton looks over, stretches, delivers. Yogi swings." (There was the bat crack). "There's a line drive down the right side! It's barely inside the foul line. It may go for extra bases! Henrich's rounding third and coming in with a run. Berra's moving toward second. Here comes the throw! . . . And they *get* him! They get Yogi easily on the slide at second!"

Before Bozo could say anything else, I reached in my pocket for my notes. "I've just written down here what I think's gonna happen in the first four innings," I said. "Like DiMag. See, he's gonna pop up to Mickey Vernon at first on a one-nothing pitch in just a minute. But don't you worry. He's gonna hit a 380-foot homer in the fourth with nobody on base on a full count. You just follow these notes and you'll see I can predict anything that's gonna happen in the next ten years." I handed him the paper, turned around, and left the store just as DiMaggio, on a one-nothing pitch, popped up to Vernon at first.

Then I went back home and took more notes from the shortwave. The Yanks clobbered the Indians in the late innings and won easily. On the local station, however, the Old Scotchman was in the top of the fifth inning. At this juncture I went to the telephone and called Firehouse No. 1.

"Hello," a voice answered. It was the fire chief.

"Hello, Chief, can you tell me the score?" I said. Calling the firehouse for baseball information was a common practice.

"The Yanks are ahead, 5–2."

"This is the Phantom you're talkin' with," I said.

"Who?"

"The Phantom. Listen carefully, Chief. Reynolds is gonna open this next inning with a popup to Doby. Then Rizutto will single to left on a one-one count. Henrich's gonna force him at second on a two-and-one pitch but make it to first. Berra's gonna double to right on a nothing-and-one pitch, and Henrich's goin' to third. DiMaggio's gonna foul a couple off and then double down the left-field line, and both Henrich and Yogi are gonna score. Brown's gonna pop out to third to end the inning."

"Aw, go to hell," the chief said, and hung up.

This was precisely what happened, of course. I phoned No. 1 again after the inning.

"Hello."

"Hi. This is the Phantom again."

"Say, how'd you know that?"

"Stick with me," I said ominously, "and I'll feed you predictions. I can predict anything that's gonna happen anywhere in the next ten years." After a pause I added, "Beware of fire real soon," for good measure, and hung up.

I left my house and hurried back to the corner grocery. When I got there, the entire meat counter was surrounded by friends of Bozo's, about a dozen of them. They were gathered around my notes, talking passionately and shouting. Bozo saw me standing by the bread counter. "There he is! That's the one!" he declared. His colleagues turned and stared at me in undisguised awe. They parted respectfully as I strolled over to the meat counter and ordered a dime's worth of bologna for my dog.

A couple of questions were directed at me from the group, but I replied, "I'm sorry for what happened in the fourth. I predicted DiMag was gonna hit a full-count pitch for that homer. It came out he hit it on two-and-two. There was too much static in the air between here and New York."

"Too much *static?*" one of them asked.

"Yeah. Sometimes the static confuses my extra-vision. But I'll be back tomorrow if everything's okay, and I'll try not to make any more big mistakes."

"Big mistakes!" one of them shouted, and the crowd laughed

admiringly, parting once more as I turned and left the store. I wouldn't have been at all surprised if they had tried to touch the hem of my shirt.

That day was only the beginning of my brief season of triumph. A schoolmate of mine offered me five dollars, for instance, to tell him how I had known that Johnny Mize was going to hit a two-run homer to break up one particularly close game for the Giants. One afternoon, on the basis of a lopsided first four innings, I had an older friend sneak into The Store and place a bet, which netted me $14.50. I felt so bad about it I tithed $1.45 in church the following Sunday. At Bozo's grocery store I was a full-scale oracle. To the firemen I remained the Phantom, and firefighting reached a peak of efficiency that month, simply because the firemen knew what was going to happen in the late innings and did not need to tarry when an alarm came.

One afternoon my father was at home listening to the Old Scotchman with a couple of out-of-town salesmen from Greenwood. They were sitting in the front room, and I had already managed to get the first three or four innings of the Cardinals and the Giants on paper before they arrived. The Old Scotchman was in the top of the first when I walked in and said hello. The men were talking business and listening to the game at the same time.

"I'm gonna make a prediction," I said. They stopped talking and looked at me. "I predict Musial's gonna take a ball and a strike and then hit a double to right field, scoring Schoendienst from second, but Marty Marion's gonna get tagged out at the plate."

"You're mighty smart," one of the men said. He suddenly sat up straight when the Old Scotchman reported, "Here's the windup and the pitch coming in. . . . Musial *swings!*" (Bat crack, crowd roar.) "He drives one into right field! This one's going up against the boards! . . . . Schoendienst rounds third. He's coming on in to score! Marion dashes around third, legs churning. His cap falls off, but here he *comes!* Here's the toss to the plate. He's nabbed at home. He is *out* at the plate! Musial holds at second with a run-producing double."

Before I could parry the inevitable questions, my father caught me by the elbow and hustled me into a back room. "How'd you know that?" he asked.

"I was just guessin'," I said. "It was nothin' but luck."

He stopped for a moment, and then a new expression showed on his face. "Have *you* been callin' the firehouse?" he asked.

"Yeah, I guess a few times."

"Now, you tell me how you found out about all that. I mean it."

When I told him about the short-wave, I was afraid he might be mad, but on the contrary he laughed uproariously. "Do you remember these next few innings?" he asked.

"I got it all written down," I said, and reached in my pocket for the notes. He took the notes and told me to go away. From the yard, a few minutes later, I heard him predicting the next inning to the salesmen.

A couple of days later, I phoned No. 1 again. "This is the Phantom," I said. "With two out, Branca's gonna hit Stinky Stanky with a fast ball, and then Alvin Dark's gonna send him home with a triple."

"Yeah, we know it," the fireman said in a bored voice. "We're listenin' to a short-wave too. You think you're somethin', don't you? You're Ray Morris' boy."

I knew everything was up. The next day, as a sort of final gesture, I took some more notes to the corner grocery in the third or fourth inning. Some of the old crowd was there, but the atmosphere was grim. They looked at me coldly. "Oh, man," Bozo said, "*we* know the Old Scotchman ain't at that game. He's four or five innings behind. He's makin' all that stuff up." The others grumbled and turned away. I slipped quietly out the door.

My period as a seer was over, but I went on listening to the short-wave broadcasts out of New York a few days more. Then, a little to my surprise, I went back to the Old Scotchman, and in time I found that the firemen, the bootleggers, and the few dirt farmers who had short-wave sets all did the same. From then on, accurate, up-to-the-minute baseball news was in disrepute there. I believe we all went back to the Scotchman not merely out of loyalty but because, in our great isolation, he touched our need for a great and unmitigated eloquence.

One day that spring, two months before I was to graduate from high school, my father gave me some unexpected advice. He was reading the *Commercial Appeal* in our front room, and he turned to me and told me, quite simply, to get the hell out of Mississippi. I do not quite know why. Perhaps he knew something about doom, though his argument, he said, was based on a lack of *opportunity.*

At first I ignored this advice. I was obsessed with Belle Prairie and the blond belle who graced its gullies, swamps, and tenant shacks. I had my heart set, at the age of seventeen, on entering Mississippi's educated landed gentry—by taking a degree at Ole Miss, as all my friends planned to do, and by returning to that plantation with my majorette, to preside there on the banks of the Yazoo over boll weevils big enough to wear dog tags, pre-Earl Warren darkies, and the young squirearchy from the plantations abutting on Carter, Eden, Holly Bluff, Sidon and Tchula.

I saw no reason to leave. I was athlete, sports announcer, valedictorian, and, my greatest pride, editor of the *Flashlight.* I knew Mississippi and I loved what I saw. I had just been voted most likely to succeed. In Yazoo I knew every house and every tree in the white section of town. Each street and hill was like a map on my consciousness; I loved the contours of its land, and the slow changing of its seasons. I was full of the regional graces and was known as a perfect young gentleman. I was pleasant, enthusiastic, and happy. On any question pertaining to God or man I would have cast my morals on the results of a common plebiscite of the white voters of Yazoo County. "One shudders at the thought of the meaninglessness of life," I read years later in *Winesburg, Ohio,* in a moment when I was trying to remember these years, "while at the same instant, and if the people of the town are his people, one loves life so intensely that tears come into the eyes."

Yet more than being desperately in love, I was sorrowfully ignorant—ignorant of myself, ignorant of the world of moving objects I was about to enter. One hundred miles to the north of Yazoo, Faulkner was writing his great tales of violence and the destruction of honor. In the spring of my senior year, when I was at Oxford for a convention, I watched as they filmed the jail scenes for the movie *Intruder in the Dust,* yet this did not inspire me much one way or the other. Had I known that great books were for one's own private soul rather than mere instrumentalities for achieving those useless trinkets on which all American high schools, including small ones in Mississippi, base their existence, perhaps I would have found in Faulkner some dark chord, some suggestion of how this land had shaped me, how its isolation and its guilt-ridden past had already settled so deeply into my bones. Unfortunately this was to come later. Then I joined easily and thoughtlessly in the Mississippi middle-class consensus that Faulkner, the chronicler and moralist, was out for the Yankee dollar.

My first seventeen years had been lived rich in experience—in sensual textures, in unusual confrontations. I had moved easily among many kinds of people, I had seen something of cruelty and madness, and I had survived fundamentalist religion. My father had taught me the woods; from everyone I had had love. The town in which I had grown up had yet to be touched by the great television culture, or by the hardening emotions and the defensive hostilities unloosed by the Supreme Court in 1954. Something was left, if but an oblique recollection: a Southern driftlessness, a closeness to the earth, a sense of time standing still, a lingering isolation from America's relentless currents of change and homogeneity. Something else also remained, some innocent and exposed quality that made possible, in the heart of a young and vulnerable boy, an allegiance and a love for a small, inconsequential place. Only retrospect would tell me I was to take something of these things with me forever, through my maturing into my manhood. But then I could not connect them, because I had yet to go beyond the most fundamental awareness of myself.

What was it, then, that led me to leave, to go to a place where I did not know a soul, and eventually to make such a sharp break with my own past that I still suffer from the pain of that alienation? Was there some small grain of sand there, something abrasive and unrecognized in my perception of things, some hidden ambition and independence that finally led me away from everything I knew and honored? Was there something in me that needed some stark removal from my deepest loyalties?

In trying to recapture a turning point in one's life at such an age, it is almost impossible to ascribe tangible motives to some great change in one's direction, to isolate a thought, or a decision. But there are a handful of things that stand out so clearly that they become, after many years, almost symbol. They embody in retrospect the very substance of one's existence at a given moment. They may be fleeting recollections, chance encounters, the thread of an old thought, but they are revealing in themselves, and they become more than memory.

My father took out one day for Austin, Texas, to see the campus of what we had sometimes heard was the best and certainly the biggest state university in the South. Four or five days later, my friend Bubba Barrier and I, quite by chance, ran into him in the lobby of the Edwards House in Jackson. He had just returned. "That's one hell of a place they got out there," he said. They had a main building 30 stories high, a baseball field dug right out of stone, artificial moonlight for street lamps, the biggest state capitol in the Republic, and the goddamndest student newspaper you ever saw. "I think you ought to go to school out there," he said. "Can't nuthin' in *this* state match it."

I would wander off by myself to that place of my childhood, the town cemetery. Here I would walk among all those graves I knew that had given me such a sense of the town when I was a boy—of the reprobates and early settlers, the departed gospelists and bootleggers, and all the boys we had buried with the American Legionnaires. I cannot remember what my thoughts were on these excursions, except that I had the most dramatic conception of imminent departure. Something different was stirring around in my future, and I would brood over the place where I was and some place where I would end up, and for days I carried a map of the University of Texas in my shirt pocket. I was bathing in self-drama; perhaps it was my *imagination*, which had never failed me even as a child, that sought some unknown awakening.

I had been commissioned to write the prophecy of the Class of 1952 of Yazoo High School, and I delivered it on class day that spring in the school auditorium. Afterward one of the senior class teachers cornered me and said it was the most disgusting thing she had ever heard, that only the day before she had recommended me to two FBI agents as promising material for that agency, but that she was going to write a letter telling them I was unfit for their service. These were unusual words for me, the favorite of every teacher in school and the winner of the American Legion Citizenship Award, but on rereading this curious statement I saw what had aroused her. I had consigned each member of the fifty-two-member graduating class to destruction. Honest Ed Upton, the salutatorian, was to die an agonizing death in quicksand in a Mississippi swamp. Billy Bonner would be shot down by Italians in the streets of Brooklyn. All the others were to go the way of violence, treachery, corruption, and oblivion, except myself, their chronicler, who did not figure in the predictions. "You just as well get out of here to Texas," that teacher said, "because it's pretty clear you don't appreciate the people around you." On graduation night in the school gymnasium, on a wet spring night in June, my comrades who were doomed to destruction and I stood finally on the podium and sang the last lines of our alma mater: "*Yazoo, Yazoo, in closing let us say . . . that forever and a day . . . we'll be thinking of you, Yazoo . . . Yazoo.*"

And one cold, dark morning in the early fall, sick with leaving for the first time the place where I grew up, and the blond majorette whom I had said goodbye to for the first and as it proved the last time in my old DeSoto car near the railroad tracks the night before, I caught a Southern Trailways bus in Vicksburg for Austin. My mother, as the story always goes, cried, and my father looked thin as death as the bus pulled out to cross the great bridge into Louisiana. I turned on the red portable radio the local radio station had given me as a farewell present, and I remember the song that came on over in Louisiana, a popular song of that time:

> Fly the ocean in a silver plane,
> See the jungle when it's wet with rain,
> Just remember 'til you're home again
> You belong to me.

FROM

The Courting of Marcus Dupree

WILLIE MORRIS

MORE THAN FOOTBALL ITSELF

ON THIS HOT September night, Number 22 walked through the door of the gymnasium with his fifty or so teammates. He stood there beyond the end zone and waited with them to run onto the field. They were a small-town Mississippi football team.

The stadium behind the old brick high school was crowded with four thousand people. There was a pale quarter-moon on the horizon. A train whistle from the Illinois Central echoed across from Independence Quarters, and crickets chirped from a nearby hollow. The grass was moist from yesterday's rains.

He was big. He was carrying his helmet, which he put on now over a copious Afro haircut kept in place by a red hairnet. He was seventeen years old and he was wearing glasses.

A group of children had gathered near him, and a few dogs. "Get 'em, Marcus!" a little white boy shouted. He acknowledged this injunction with a slight wave of his hand. Under the helmet his glasses reflected the lights of the stadium.

From the grandstands the home band burst into an off-key fight song. The team sprinted onto the field through a large papier-mâché sign with the words "Go Tornadoes!" The crowd stood to cheer.

There was more behind his entrance on this night than football itself.

I had heard about him for many months, ever since I came back from the North to live in Mississippi. Going into his senior year, he was the most sought-after and acclaimed high school football player in America, a swift and powerful running back whom many were already comparing with the legendary Herschel Walker of Georgia. The town of his past and his people—Philadelphia, Mississippi, in Neshoba County—as in the Biblical sense certain places sometimes are, was suffused with its remembrance of self-destruction. Its history evoked for me as a Southerner those lines of Yeats:

> *Mere anarchy is loosed upon the world,*
> *The blood-dimmed tide is loosed, and everywhere*
> *The ceremony of innocence is drowned;*
> *The best lack all conviction, while the worst*
> *Are full of passionate intensity.*

His great-great-grandparents had been slaves, and he was born one month less a day before three young men, two New York Jews and a Mississippi black, were murdered seven miles from his birthplace and buried fifteen feet under an earthen dam. The two young whites had been shot once each in the heart with .38s, and the black had been shot three times. Their names were Michael Schwerner, Andrew Goodman, and James Earl Chaney. Their disappearance, along with the harassments, beatings, burnings, and mob cruelties—not only in that haunted summer of 1964 but in the months which followed—attracted the attention of the nation and the world and became a symbol of the entire civil rights movement and of the recalcitrance which greeted it. The names Lawrence Rainey and Cecil Price, the sheriff and deputy sheriff, would become inscribed on the national consciousness, just as in those days the names Bull Connor and Jim Clark had been, and Emmett Till, Rosa Parks, Medgar Evers, Ross Barnett. The town remained for a long time in the grip, as James Silver described them, of "anxious, fearful, marginal white men." The FBI inspector who led the investigations subsequently called the Neshoba Klavern of the White Knights of the Ku Klux Klan "one of the strongest Klan units ever gathered and one of the best disciplined groups." Neshoba County, he later observed, did not need a Klan, for the people were the most conspiratorial he had ever encountered, and Assistant United States Attorney General John Doar said that the town and the county had, for all practical purposes, closed ranks after the murders. Two years later, on the anniversary of the killings, Martin Luther King came to Philadelphia to give a sermon and to lead a memorial march. "This is a terrible town, the worst I've seen," he said. "There is a complete reign of terror here." Not long before his death, he said his visit to Philadelphia was one of only two times that he ever feared for his life.

An observer writing in 1964 would say that among all of Neshoba County's twenty thousand human beings, perhaps not many more than a hundred were capable of the planned murders of three unarmed young men, and of the officially organized domination of the town which these deliberate murders symbolized. But Reinhold Niebuhr, speaking for much of the American sentiment of the day, as Lyndon Johnson's Civil Rights Act was being passed and before the great riots in the Northern cities, would indict a place in which "the instruments of justice are tools of *in*justice" and where "there are no limits to inhumanity, cruelty, and sheer caprice once social and communal restraints are no longer in force. Mississippi's standards can sink so low that only the legal and moral pressure of the larger community can redeem them—just as only the pressure of the British Commonwealth can save Northern Rhodesia from becoming another South Africa." And Hodding Carter III, along with his father a principal voice of racial moderation in the Deep South of that time, would write: "The FBI's records indicate that, on the whole, Mississippi is one of the most crime-free states in the nation. The brutality, the bombings, the terror, and the murders can be accurately attributed to the silence of good men, bound by a system which in the name of self-preservation dictated public toleration of the excesses of the vicious and the ignorant."

No moderate white leadership came forward in those hard days in Philadelphia and Neshoba. The dissenters were largely a handful of "ladies," in the Southern essence of that word, much like Miss Habersham in Faulkner's *Intruder in the Dust,* who out of her tenacious and indomitable Southern womanhood felt so strongly for justice that she would help a white and a black child rob graves at night to absolve a black man of murder. There were a few other dissident voices. The risks may have been high, but one is not sure *how* high. Few in the town seemed to have read or appreciated the dreadful nuances of our history—of slavery, the Civil War, Reconstruction, the Klan in the 1920s—and sensed the cadences of doom. It is not difficult, of course, to be brave from such a horrific remove, in time as well as geography, just as it is facile to misjudge the genuine anxieties of a local population over the organized integrationists, many of them outsiders, of the 1960s. Yet unlike Oxford, Mississippi, two years before, which was a university town and had its James Silvers and Duncan Grays in the wake of the James Meredith Riots, in Philadelphia there seemed to be no men of courage, but especially of *wisdom,* who would stand up for the larger community in the name of civilized values, indeed of civilization itself. Where were the Sartorises?

In the town's most agonized times, there were the few notable exceptions, particularly a forty-year-old woman named Florence Mars, descendant of one of the old and distinguished families of the town. She had attended Millsaps in Jackson, which Hodding Carter had called "the most courageous little college in America" because of its stands in the 1960s. After having lived elsewhere, she had come home to stay in 1962. She began raising Hereford cattle and owned the Neshoba County stockyards. She became active in the First Methodist Church, where she sang in the choir and taught a women's Sunday School class. "The church," she remembered, "offered the best hope as a moderating influence." In its moments of crisis she spoke out against what was happening to the town. The community began to regard her as a "Communist agitator," and the White Knights of the Klan succeeded in a boycott of her business. Later the LSU Press would publish her memoir, *Witness in Philadelphia.* "I learned . . . how Nazi Germany is possible in a 'law-abiding Christian society.' And I learned, too, that society will act against its own best interests to protect itself from the truth."

Turner Catledge, who was born and raised in Philadelphia, took his first newspaper job with *The Neshoba Democrat,* and later became managing editor of *The New York Times,* would write of his home:

> Our reporters told me that my friends and my relatives, although greeting them politely, would rarely discuss the murders with them. They closed ranks against outsiders. Worse, within the community few voices were raised to condemn the murders. The "good people" of the community were intimidated. They feared both physical violence and economic retaliation if they denounced the murders or the Klan, which was responsible for the murders. A friend in Philadelphia wrote me a long troubled letter several months after the murders, describing the atmosphere there. The local attitude, she said, was to cry "hoax" when the three civil-rights workers were said to be missing. And then "they asked for it," after their bodies were found. As newsmen flocked to the town, it came to see itself (not the dead men) as the "victim" of the affair, and to blame the news media for once again lying about the South. I was told that some of my old friends thought I had let the town down because of *The Times'*

extensive coverage of the murders. But I felt the town had let me down. Or perhaps I had just expected too much.

Nearly three and a half years after the civil rights workers disappeared, eighteen men went on trial in federal court for conspiracy. They included the sheriff, the deputy sheriff, the former sheriff and sheriff-elect, a city policeman, and the Imperial Wizard of the White Knights of the Ku Klux Klan.

Gradually, almost imperceptibly in the years which followed, something would begin to stir in the soul of the town. A brooding introspection, a stricken pride, a complicated and nearly indefinable self-irony, all but unacknowledged at first, would emerge from its dreadful wounds. A long journey lay ahead, marked always by new aggrievements and retreats, yet this mysterious pilgrimage of the spirit would suggest much of the South and the America of our generation.

When Marcus Dupree was a child in the Independence Quarters section of the town, he began attending the Baptist church down the street from his house. It was called Mount Nebo. When he was eleven years old, a memorial was erected in front of his church to Schwerner, Goodman, and Chaney. Later, in 1982, as throughout Mississippi and the Deep South, his high school graduating class would be the first in which young whites and blacks had gone through all twelve grades together.

Notes from a Voluntary Exile

LINDA PEAVY

THOUGH I SPENT the first twenty-three years of my life in Mississippi, never once did I hear the name of Ida B. Wells. Once I left the state, another decade would pass before I stumbled upon her story while researching possible subjects for *Women Who Changed Things*, a collective biography featuring turn-of-the-century women of achievement. Here was a Mississippian who had changed history. How could I have grown up with no knowledge of her accomplishments? Why had I never heard her name in a Mississippi history course? I know why. It's the why that answers all such questions. Ida B. Wells was black. And I am white.

Furthermore, Ida B. Wells refused to accept some of the basic assumptions upon which the stability of status-quo life in the South depended, and until the last quarter of this century, no person who questioned those assumptions made it into any Mississippi history book. Her life was a monument to that forbidden questioning.

Well-sheltered from all such bothersome questions, I grew up accepting as a given the lines drawn between blacks and whites. My grandparents lived on a large farm owned by their grandparents before them, and the black women who cooked and cleaned for us were the children and grandchildren of slaves who had worked on that farm. My mother and her siblings had grown up playing with the black children who grew up to be their servants. But my own childhood was spent in town, where segregated housing divided us carefully enough to ensure that no black children would be tempting playmates.

My brother and I loved the black women who worked for us, loved them for their songs, their laughter, the fierce sense of protection they showed for us. We loved them, yet we knew, almost from infancy, the limits within which we could show that love. At Christmas we wrapped packages for Missie, the cook, and for O.D., the cleaning woman. But those packages always contained partly used bottles of perfume or boxes of dusting powder—never anything new. And since Missie and O.D. were as much a part of the system as we were, they tittered and squealed and hugged as happily as if we'd given them something new. Under such circumstances, it never occurred to us to question what writer Lillian Smith has well labeled "love without dignity."

When we rode out to the country to bring the women to work, we knew where to sit—in front with the grownup who was driving. And the women knew where to sit—in back. Alone. On those infrequent occasions when we were allowed to go inside one of the rough-board, tin-roofed houses in which these women lived, we stared in awe at the yellowed newspapers and rows of colored ribbon serving as wallpaper—understanding at last the use to which they had put all those stacks of old papers we'd saved for them. We looked, too, at other more personal cast-offs—a saucepan with a burned handle. A pair of run-down slippers. A dangerously worn string of Christmas tree lights. And never once did we think to question whether or not these women ever grew tired of second-hand goods or second-class living.

We did not think to question because we never heard anyone else question. And because life was good to us all. The bills got paid (though I overheard many a conversation that seemed to say they would not). We went to and from school on a big yellow bus filled with white faces—with no real thought as to where the black children we saw about town on Saturdays went to school. And, most comforting of all, we went to church, heard sermons on the Good Samaritan, and joined in rousing choruses of "Love Lifted Me," "The Old Rugged Cross," and "Amazing Grace."

We were loyal churchgoers, attending Sunday school and church on Sunday morning, Training Union and preaching on Sunday night, and prayer meeting on Wednesday evening. As pre-schoolers we climbed the magnolia trees or wandered in the cemetery during long afternoon meetings of the Woman's Missionary Union. As grade schoolers we all sang "Jesus Wants Me for a Sunbeam," then graduated to Girls' Auxiliary while the boys went on to become Royal Ambassadors.

It was there in that little church, having heard sermon after sermon on how the world out there needed the message of God's love, that I dedicated my life to Christian service. I would be a missionary nurse, healing the bodies and souls of the little children of Africa. The decision was met with great rejoicing on the part of the church members at large and with restrained joy on the part of my parents, they being wiser than I in matters of hardship and self-sacrifice. I was ten. They were over forty. There were those in the congregation who were nearing ninety. None of us thought to question the irony of going abroad to take the story of God's love to black people.

That was, of course, primarily because the black folks around us had heard the gospel story from their own preachers. Those who had, like the women who worked for us, "accepted Jesus Christ as their personal savior," lived quiet, God-fearing lives. They attended church and Sunday school and prayer meetings just as we did. It was unfortunate, of course, that they didn't always choose to obtain legal sanction for their marriages, but that was just further evidence of their natural inferiority to those people who did. Blacks who didn't go to church but drank beer in neighboring Pike County's honkytonks were beyond the gospel anyway. Our mission clearly lay elsewhere.

My determination to fulfill that mission never waned. I worked hard to prepare myself to follow my calling, and despite the fact that my academic record might have given me a fair shot at a scholarship to Vassar or Radcliffe, neither I nor my parents nor any of my teachers ever thought to question my decision to attend Mississippi College, the state's largest Baptist institution. After all, why would I want to go away to college—especially to a Yankee college?

Then, in 1960, I was chosen one of six Mississippi youth delegates to the White House Conference on Children and Youth. We were an exemplary group. Our eldest member was a Mississippi College senior, daughter of the editor of the *Baptist Record*. Blond, blue-eyed, immaculately groomed, she was the epitome of genteel Southern womanhood. Her name I recall. The names of the others I have forgotten. The adult delegates were all unknowns as well, though I assumed they must be people I should respect—judges, lawyers, well-dressed clubwomen—the state's best citizens. None of them were black, of course. I wasn't surprised. It simply never occurred to me that any of the delegates should be black.

But in Washington there were surprises. After the first banquet, I stood on the edge of the polished floor of a hotel ballroom, astonished to see blacks and whites dancing together. Later, jammed in a crowded convention hall, I listened to a heated debate concerning the absence of black delegates from the Southern states. The question apparently *had* occurred to others. I heard a college student from Louisiana, a young man whose oratory was in the tradition of Huey P. Long, decry the Little Rock decision, forecast much upheaval and violence if integration came "too soon," and plead, "We know it's coming, but for God's sake, don't cram it down our throats." I left that meeting feeling proud of his passionate plea, for, after all, only a Southerner knew how things at home really were.

There were more surprises in store. Back in my room I was met by our unofficial leader, the ivory-complected M.C. senior. She wore a sorrowing look. It seemed that one of our trusted six, a highschooler from Meridian, had disgraced us all by double-dating with a mixed couple. Worse yet, she'd been dumb enough to let herself be photographed standing next to the black man.

Back home, when I tried to talk about what I had seen and heard, I was quickly reassured by my parents and teachers that I was not to worry over such matters. I was almost afraid to ask how folks at home had reacted to the scandalous newspaper photo and greatly relieved to learn that the photo had not been run in the state papers. The full implication of such censorship was lost to me. Protecting the innocent from life's unpleasantries was a way of life. And I am sure the speech I gave to a hometown audience did not touch on any of those things we were not to question.

I completed my high school days in an event-filled senior year touched only once by political or social issues. Vice-President Richard M. Nixon came to Jackson on a campaign tour and I, being the good Protestant conservative that I was, went up to see him—and even shook his hand. I wasn't really "for" Nixon. But I was firmly against that monied Irish Catholic who wanted to let the Pope run our business.

My freshman year, passed under the bell jar of my chosen Baptist college, was not greatly disturbed by news of the first Woolworth sit-in in North Carolina, though I found news of a sit-in in Jackson—just thirty miles away—a bit harder to dismiss. Even though I was shocked by a *Life* magazine photo showing a Jackson policeman kicking one of the demonstrators in the stomach, it never occurred to me to take up the cause of equal rights. All M.C. students had been duly warned against going near a demonstration, and we were regularly assured by trustworthy sources—state newspapers, state radio and television newscasters, and even the pastors of our churches—that all those involved were "outside agitators."

I kept my distance from all such disturbances, and it was years later before I learned that an M.C. coed had been one of the whites who braved ketchup, mustard, and billy sticks to join blacks at the Woolworth counter.

My sophomore year brought the wars and rumors of wars closer to hand as James Meredith's admission to Ole Miss shook the state to its core and set off rioting that no newspaper or television coverups could deny. I recall not knowing whether to laugh or be outraged at rumors that all-night shifts of volunteers were bouncing basketballs on the floor above Meredith's dorm room. Probably I smiled politely and pushed the matter aside. After all, I was about to be married and had other things on my mind.

Then, in June of 1963, Medgar Evers was shot down in his driveway, and national television news showed the grief of his wife and children. In September, TV brought into our living room the weeping parents of the four little girls who died in the Birmingham church bombing. In November, while student teaching in a rural school, I heard shouts of glee mingled with gasps of horror as the principal announced the assassination of President John F. Kennedy. The following summer in nearby Neshoba County, Schwerner, Goodman, and Chaney were murdered by men who claimed to have the support of their entire community. The world had gone mad in the name of protecting the status quo.

In fall of 1964, I accepted a contract from Jackson's Central High, an inner-city school that also served vo-tech and business students from across the city—all of them white, of course, and most of them lower to lower-middle class. Then, in my second year at Central, faced with a court order to integrate, the principal asked me to take a black girl into my senior English class. Though I was the youngest and least experienced member of the faculty, he said he felt I was more open to this situation than were some of my colleagues. He was right. I was finally learning. The mission field had come home.

A year later I found myself in a similar situation during the integration of Glen Oaks Senior High in Baton Rouge, Louisiana. The school was perched on the very line between an all-white subdivision whose look-alike homes represented the fulfilled dreams of the blue-collar workers who manned the nearby oil refineries, and Scotlandville, home to the thousands of blacks who represented the greatest threat to the jobs of those white refinery workers. And though white supremacy was an integral part of the self-concept of that neighborhood, Glen Oaks opened its doors to blacks with a minimum amount of disturbance.

Still blinded by my old assumptions that all was well that seemed well, I am sure I never fully understood just how difficult it was for those young blacks to give up positions of leadership and respect in Scotlandville High in order to become the butt of jokes and sneers at Glen Oaks. But there were some things I could and did understand. I cried with the black students over news of the assassination of Dr. Martin Luther King, pled for their readmission without penalty after they'd skipped classes to participate in a march on the day of his funeral, visited in their homes and talked with their parents, and learned to see and love them as people.

I left Louisiana for graduate school in Chapel Hill, North Carolina, then entered upon four years of teaching at Oklahoma Baptist University, a school that featured blacks on a winning basketball team and allowed them into a federally supported nursing program. Yet it was with great difficulty that I was able to help my black friend Mary find housing in an all-white neighborhood, and I well remember the stir caused by the announcement that she would be teaching in the city's public schools. And though Mary was welcome in the university church I normally attended, it was in her church in Southtown that I found once more an intensity of feeling that I thought I'd lost forever. For as I walked down to the altar with my black friends, singing "The Lord Is Blessing Me, Right Now," I knew the truth of those words.

But those feelings came in Oklahoma, at a safe distance from the disapproving eyes of the folks back home. And while a 1974 move to Montana increased that distance still further, it also robbed me of the opportunity to enjoy experiences such as those I shared with Mary. For blacks are a small minority in Bozeman, Montana. Fortunately, life in a university town such as this one affords frequent opportunities for interaction and friendship with people of many lands, many races, many heritages, and my children accept such opportunities as a given. That's how life is in this place. And this place is home for them.

It is home for me. Except in springtime. For in spring when these mountains are deep in snow, I cannot stop the call of the South, cannot resist the profusion of new beauty and new life. So it is that I have come to make spring pilgrimages, journeys that are almost pilgrimages in a sacred sense, journeys on which I dare to confront again the scenes I think I am free of, the me that I have been.

Sometimes, surprises await me. During one visit home, I spoke to an integrated journalism class in my old high school, spoke to them and marveled at the differences I saw, spoke to them and knew that, for many reasons, I should be there on the home front, teaching them day in and day out, letting my children grow up in the wonderful, still to me almost otherworldly, atmosphere of a thoroughly integrated Mississippi.

But that same week, when I took my children to the church of my childhood and heard once more the impassioned call to salvation and service, a call still being issued to an unblemished sea of white faces, I was no longer so certain of where I belonged. As the familiar strains of "Just As I Am" rose about me, I was momentarily swept by all the old stirrings. But only momentarily, for the words of the old hymn had taken on a new meaning. More surely than ever, I was truly "tossed about/With many a conflict, many a doubt." Having dared to ask forbidden questions, I could no longer find peace in the easy answers promised in that place.

The conflicts and doubts were mine again on a February night in 1979. Having been drawn home by my mother's illness I stayed at her bedside though I knew that I should be down at a meeting in Beartown where blacks and a few whites were crowded into a church discussing the fate of a twelve-year-old black boy who had been convicted of holding up a white woman at a fireworks stand and sentenced to serve time in the state penitentiary at Parchman. I knew I should be down at that church, doing what I could to help that boy, yet I knew with equal conviction that I had come home to support my mother, not to destroy her. And so I stayed at home that night. But I did not sleep, for now that I had begun to ask the forbidden questions, I could no longer pretend that my mission lay elsewhere. It was here at hand . . . and I was still making excuses.

I am still making excuses. For I really don't want to leave Montana and move South again. I really don't want to be where the humidity stifles and the heavy memories of the manners and mores of my past reach out like tendrils of kudzu, threatening to entangle and ensnare me once more in a world that allows no questions. I know that there have been changes. I marvel in them, rejoice in them. But I am not beguiled.

I remain in voluntary exile, preferring to bring up my children in an atmosphere in which an almost daily questioning of all human relationships is not only allowed, but expected.

When my conscience tells me that I've run away from the issues back home, I reply that my integrity as a person and as a writer demands this distancing. Even at such great distance, I am never far from my beginnings. Much of my fiction and poetry reflects a telling and retelling of the stories of my past, a past seen now in the stark light of all the questions I never then thought to ask.

Once in a while I find past, present, and future falling mysteriously together, find all the threads that have been so separate weaving together in unforeseeable ways. That happened in June of 1983 when, stranded by car trouble in a Wyoming wilderness campground, my family and I were helped by two black men from Chicago. As one drove my husband for assistance, the children and I enjoyed a visit with the other, a visit that began with our introducing him to birdwatching and ended in my sharing with him the joy I'd known in discovering, researching, and writing the story of Ida B. Wells. A smile played over the face of my listener.

He knew all about Ida B. Wells, for he too had grown up in Mississippi. Having attended school only a few miles from her native Holly Springs, he had heard her story many times over from a teacher who'd known Ida Wells in person, back in the days when hers was the only voice raised in protest of the lynchings that made a mockery of all the Christian and democratic laws we Southerners earnestly believed we were upholding.

That day in the Wyoming campground, that man and I both knew that though we had left Mississippi, the tangle of kudzu had followed us all the way, stretching its long, green arm into our lives forever. And that day we rejoiced in the tie that bound us to each other and to the woman whose story I had written so that his children and mine would never forget that love without dignity is no love at all.

INTRODUCTION TO *Lanterns on the Levee*

WALKER PERCY

I REMEMBER THE first time I saw him. I was thirteen and he had come to visit my mother and me and my brothers in Athens, Georgia, where we were living with my grandmother after my father's death.

We had heard of him, of course. He was the fabled relative, the one you liked to speculate about. His father was a United States senator and he had been a decorated infantry officer in World War I. Besides that, he was a poet. The fact that he was also a lawyer and a planter didn't cut much ice—after all, the South was full of lawyer-planters. But how many people did you know who were war heroes and wrote books of poetry? One had heard of Rupert Brooke and Joyce Kilmer, but they were dead.

The curious fact is that my recollection of him even now, after meeting him, after living in his house for twelve years, and now thirty years after his death, is no less fabled than my earliest imaginings. The image of him that takes form in my mind still owes more to Rupert Brooke and those photographs of young English officers killed in Flanders than to a flesh-and-blood cousin from Greenville, Mississippi.

I can only suppose that he must have been, for me at least, a personage, a presence, radiating that mysterious quality we call charm, for lack of a better word, in such high degree that what comes to mind is not that usual assemblage of features and habits which make up our memories of people but rather a quality, a temper, a set of mouth, a look through the eyes.

For his eyes were most memorable, a piercing gray-blue and strangely light in my memory, as changeable as shadows over water, capable of passing in an instant, we were soon to learn, from merriment—he told the funniest stories we'd ever heard—to a level gray gaze cold with reproof. They were beautiful and terrible eyes, eyes to be careful around. Yet now, when I try to remember them, I cannot see them otherwise than as shadowed by sadness.

What we saw at any rate that sunny morning in Georgia in 1930, and what I still vividly remember, was a strikingly handsome man, slight of build and quick as a youth. He was forty-five then, an advanced age, one would suppose, to a thirteen-year-old, and gray-haired besides, yet the abiding impression was of a youthfulness—and an exoticness. He had in fact just returned from the South Seas—this was before the jet age and I'd never heard of anybody going there but Gauguin and Captain Bligh—where he had lived on the beach at Bora Bora.

He had come to invite us to live with him in Mississippi. We did, and upon my mother's death not long after, he adopted me and my two brothers. At the time what he did did not seem remarkable. What with youth's way of taking life as it comes—how else can you take it when you have no other life to compare it with?—and what with youth's incapacity for astonishment or gratitude, it did not seem in the least extraordinary to find oneself orphaned at fifteen and adopted by a bachelor-poet-lawyer-planter and living in an all-male household visited regularly by other poets, politicians, psychiatrists, sociologists, black preachers, folk singers, itinerant harmonica players. One friend came to seek advice on a book he wanted to write and stayed a year to write it. It was, his house, a standard stopover for all manner of people who were trying to "understand the South," that perennial American avocation, and whether or not they succeeded, it was as valuable to me to try to understand them as to be understood. The observers in this case were at least as curious a phenomenon as the observed.

Now belatedly I can better assess what he did for us and I even have an inkling what he gave up to do it. For him, to whom the world was open and who felt more at home in Taormina than in Jackson—for though he loved his home country, he had to leave it often to keep loving it—and who in fact could have stayed on at Bora Bora and chucked it all like Gauguin (he told me once he was tempted), for him to have taken on three boys, age fourteen, thirteen, and nine, and raised them, amounted to giving up the freedom of bachelorhood and taking on the burden of parenthood without the consolations of marriage. Gauguin chucked it all, quit, cut out and went to the islands for the sake of art and became a great painter if not a great human being. Will Percy not only did not chuck anything; he shouldered somebody else's burden. Fortunately for us, he did not subscribe to Faulkner's precept that a good poem is worth any number of old ladies—for if grandmothers are dispensable, why not second cousins? I don't say we did him in (he would laugh at that), but he didn't write much poetry afterwards and he died young. At any rate, whatever he lost or gained in the transaction, I know what I gained: a vocation and in a real sense a second self, that is, the work and the self which, for better or worse, would not otherwise have been open to me.

For to have lived in Will Percy's house, with "Uncle Will" as we called him, as a raw youth from age fourteen to twenty-six, a youth whose only talent was a knack for looking and listening, for tuning in and soaking up, was nothing less than to be informed in the deepest sense of the word. What was to be listened to, dwelled on, pondered over for the next thirty years was of course the man himself, the unique human being, and when I say unique I mean it in its most literal sense: he was one of a kind: I never met anyone remotely like him. It was to encounter a complete, articulated view of the world as tragic as it was noble. It was to be introduced to Shakespeare, to Keats, to Brahms, to Beethoven—and unsuccessfully, it turned out, to Wagner whom I never liked, though I was dragged every year to hear Flagstadt sing Isolde—as one seldom if ever meets them in school.

"Now listen to this part," he would say as Gluck's *Orfeo* played—the old 78s not merely dropped from a stack by the monstrous Capehart, as big as a sideboard, but then picked up and turned over by an astounding hooplike arm—and you'd make the altogether unexpected discovery that music, of all things, can convey the deepest and most unnameable human feelings and give great pleasure in doing so.

Or: "Read this," and I'd read or, better still, he'd read aloud, say, Viola's speech to Olivia in *Twelfth Night:*

> Make me a willow cabin at your gate,
> And call upon my soul within the house;
> . . . .
> And make the babbling gossip of the air
> Cry out "Olivia!"

You see? he'd as good as say, and what I'd begin to see, catch on to, was the great happy reach and play of the poet at the top of his form.

For most of us, the communication of beauty takes two, the teacher and the hearer, the pointer and the looker. The rare soul, the Wolfe or Faulkner, can assault the entire body of literature single-handedly. I couldn't or wouldn't. I had a great teacher. The teacher points out and says *Look;* the response is *Yes, I see.*

But he was more than a teacher. What he was to me was a fixed point in a confusing world. This is not to say I always took him for my true north and set my course accordingly. I did not. Indeed my final assessment of *Lanterns on the Levee* must register reservations as well as admiration. The views on race relations, for example, diverge from my own and have not been helpful, having, in my experience, played into the hands of those whose own interest in these matters is deeply suspect. But even when I did not follow him, it was usually in *relation* to him, whether with him or against him, that I defined myself and my own direction. Perhaps he would not have had it differently. Surely it is the highest tribute to the best people we know to use them as best we can, to become, not their disciples, but ourselves.

It is the good fortune of those who did not know him that his singular charm, the unique flavor of the man, transmits with high fidelity in *Lanterns on the Levee.* His gift for communicating, communicating himself, an enthusiasm, a sense of beauty, moral outrage, carries over faithfully to the cold printed page, although for those who did not know him the words cannot evoke—or can they?—the mannerisms, the quirk of mouth, the shadowed look, the quick Gallic shrug, the inspired flight of eyebrows at an absurdity, the cold Anglo-Saxon gaze. (For he was this protean: one time I was reading *Ivanhoe,* the part about the fight between Richard and Saladin, and knowing Richard was one of Uncle Will's heroes, I identified one with the other. But wait: wasn't he actually more like Saladin, not the sir-knight defender of the Christian West but rather the subtle easterner, noble in his own right? I didn't ask him, but if I had, he'd have probably shrugged: both, neither . . .)

There is not much doubt about the literary quality of *Lanterns on the Levee,* which delivers to the reader not only a noble and tragic view of life but the man himself. But other, nonliterary questions might be raised here. How, for example, do the diagnostic and prophetic dimensions of the book hold up after thirty years? Here, I think, hindsight must be used with the utmost circumspection. On the one hand, it is surely justifiable to test the prophetic moments of a book against history itself; on the other hand, it is hardly proper to judge a man's views of the issues of his day by the ideological fashions of another age. Perhaps in this connection it would not be presumptuous to venture a modest hope. It is that *Lanterns on the Levee* will survive both its friends and its enemies, that is, certain more clamorous varieties of each.

One is all too familiar with both.

The first, the passionate advocate: the lady, not necessarily Southern, who comes bearing down at full charge, waving *Lanterns on the Levee* like a battle flag. "He is right! The Old South was right!" What she means all too often, it turns out, is not that she prefers agrarian values to technological but that she is enraged at having to pay her cook more than ten dollars a week; that she prefers not merely segregation to integration, but slavery to either.

The second, the liberal enemy: the ideologue, white or black, who polishes off *Lanterns on the Levee* with the standard epithets: racist, white supremacist, reactionary, paternalist, Bourbon, etc., etc. (they always remind me of the old Stalinist imprecations: fascist, cosmopolitan, imperialist running dog).

Lanterns on the Levee deserves better and of course has better readers. Its author can be defended against the more extreme reader, but I wonder if it is worth the effort. Abraham Lincoln was a segregationist. What of it? Will Percy was regarded in the Mississippi of his day as a flaming liberal and nigger-lover and reviled by the sheriff's office for his charges of police brutality. What of that? Nothing much is proved except that current categories and names, liberal and conservative, are weary past all thinking of it. Ideological words have a way of wearing thin and then, having lost their meanings, being used like switchblades against the enemy of the moment. Take the words *paternalism, noblesse oblige,* dirty words these days. But is it a bad thing for a man to believe that his position in society entails a certain responsibility toward others? Or is it a bad thing for a man to care like a father for his servants, spend himself on the poor, the sick, the miserable, the mad who come his way? It is surely better than watching a neighbor get murdered and closing the blinds to keep from "getting involved." It might even beat welfare.

Rather than measure *Lanterns on the Levee* against one or another ideological yardstick, it might be more useful to test the major themes of the book against the spectacular events of the thirty years since its publication. Certainly the overall pessimism of *Lanterns on the Levee*, its gloomy assessment of the spiritual health of Western civilization, is hard to fault these days. It seems especially prescient when one considers that the book was mostly written in the between-wars age of optimism when Americans still believed that the right kind of war would set things right once and for all. If its author were alive today, would he consider his forebodings borne out? Or has the decline accelerated even past his imaginings? Would he see glimmerings of hope? Something of all three, no doubt, but mainly, I think, he'd look grim, unsurprised, and glad enough to have made his exit.

Certainly nothing would surprise him about the collapse of the old moralities, for example, the so-called sexual revolution which he would more likely define in less polite language as alley-cat morality. I can hear him now: "Fornicating like white trash is one thing, but leave it to this age to call it the new morality." Nor would he be shocked by the cynicism and corruption, the stealing, lying, rascality ascendant in business and politics—though even he might be dismayed by the complacency with which they are received: "There have always been crooks, but we've not generally made a practice of re-electing them, let alone inviting them to dinner." All this to say nothing of the collapse of civil order and the new jungle law which rules the American city.

Nothing new here then for him: if the horrors of the Nazi holocaust would have dismayed him and the moral bankruptcy of the postwar world saddened him, they would have done so only by sheer dimension. He had already adumbrated the Götterdämmerung of Western values.

But can the matter be disposed of so simply: decline and fall predicted, decline and fall taking place? While granting the prescience of much of *Lanterns on the Levee*'s pessimism, we must, I think, guard against a certain seductiveness which always attends the heralding of apocalypse, and we must not overlook some far less dramatic but perhaps equally significant counterforces. Yes, Will Percy's indictment of modern life has seemed to be confirmed by the holocaust of the 1940s and by American political and social morality in the 1970s. But what would he make of some very homely, yet surely unprecedented social gains which have come to pass during these same terrible times? To give the plainest examples: that for the first time in history a poor boy, black or white, has a chance to get an education, become what he wants to become, doctor, lawyer, even read *Lanterns on the Levee* and write poetry of his own, and that not a few young men, black and white, have done just that? Also: that for the first time in history a working man earns a living wage and can support his family in dignity. How do these solid social gains square with pronouncements of decline and fall? I ask the question and, not knowing the answer, can only wonder how Will Percy would see it now. As collapse? Or as contest? For it appears that what is upon us is not a twilight of the gods but a very real race between the powers of light and darkness, that time is short and the issue very much in doubt. So I'd love to ask him, as I used to ask him after the seven o'clock news (Ed Murrow: *This*—is London): "Well? What do you think?"

The one change that would astonish him, I think, is the spectacular emergence of the South from its traditional role of loser and scapegoat. If anyone had told him in 1940 that in thirty years the "North" (i.e., New York, Detroit, California) would be in the deepest kind of trouble with race, violence, and social decay while the South had become, by contrast, relatively hopeful and even prosperous, he would not have believed it. This is not to say that he would find himself at home in the new Dallas or Atlanta. But much of *Lanterns on the Levee*—for example, the chapter on sharecropping—was written from the ancient posture of Southern apologetics. If his defense of sharecropping against the old enemy, the "Northern liberal," seems quaint now, it is not because there was not something to be said for sharecropping—there was a good deal to be said—and it is not because he wasn't naive about the tender regard of the plantation manager for the helpless sharecropper—he was naive, even about his own managers. It is rather because the entire issue and its disputants have simply been bypassed by history. The massive social and technological upheavals in the interval have left the old quarrel academic and changed the odds in the new one. It is hard, for example, to imagine a serious Southern writer nowadays firing off his heaviest ammunition at "Northern liberals." Not the least irony of recent history is that the "Northern liberal" has been beleaguered and the "Southern planter" rescued by the same forces. The latter has been dispensed by technology from the ancient problem, sharecroppers replaced by Farmall and Allis-Chalmers, while the former has fallen out with his old wards, the blacks. The displaced sharecroppers moved to the Northern cities and the liberals moved out. The South in a peculiar sense, a sense Will Percy would not necessarily have approved (though he could hardly have repressed a certain satisfaction), may have won after all.

So Will Percy's strong feelings about the shift of power from the virtuous few would hardly be diminished today, but he might recast his villains and redress the battle lines. Old-style demagogue, for example, might give way to new-style image manipulator and smooth amoral churchgoing huckster. When he spoke of the "bottom rail on top," he had in mind roughly the same folks as Faulkner's Snopeses, a lower-class, itchy-palmed breed who had dispossessed the gentry who had in turn been the true friends of the old-style "good" Negro. The upshot: an unholy hegemony of peckerwood politicans, a white hoi polloi keeping them in office, and a new breed of unmannerly Negroes misbehaving in the streets. But if he—or Faulkner for that matter—were alive today, he would find the battleground confused. He would find most members of his own "class" not exactly embattled in a heroic Götterdämmerung, not exactly fighting the good fight as he called it, but having simply left, taken off for the exurbs where, barricaded in patrolled subdivisions and country clubs and private academies, they worry about their kids and drugs. Who can blame them, but is this the "good life" Will Percy spoke of? And when some of these good folk keep *Lanterns on the Levee* on the bed table, its author, were he alive today, might be a little uneasy. For meanwhile, doing the dirty work of the Republic in the towns and cities of the South, in the schools, the school boards, the city councils, the factories, the restaurants, the stores, are to be found, of all people, the sons and daughters of the poor whites of the 1930s and some of those same uppity Negroes who went to school and ran for office, and who together are not doing so badly and in some cases very well indeed.

So it is not unreasonable to suppose that Will Percy might well revise his view of the South and the personae of his drama, particularly in favor of the lower-class whites for whom he had so little use. In this connection I cannot help but think of another book about the South, W. J. Cash's *The Mind of the South,* published oddly enough the same year by the same publisher as *Lanterns on the Levee.* Cash's book links Southern aristocrat and poor white much closer than the former ordinarily would have it. Both books are classics in their own right, yet they couldn't be more different; their separate validities surely testify to the diversity and complexity of this mysterious region. Yet in this case, I would suppose that Will Percy would today find himself closer to Cash in sorting out his heroes and villains, that far from setting aristocrat against poor white and both against the new Negro, he might well choose his present-day heroes—and villains—from the ranks of all three. He'd surely have as little use for black lawlessness as for white copping out. I may be wrong but I can't see him happy as the patron saint of Hilton Head or Paradise Estates-around-the-Country Club.

For it should be noted, finally, that despite conventional assessments of *Lanterns on the Levee* as an expression of the "aristocratic" point of view of the Old South, Will Percy had no more use than Cash for genealogical games, the old Southern itch for coats of arms and tracing back connections to the English squirearchy. Indeed if I know anything at all about Will Percy, I judge that in so far as there might be a connection between him and the Northumberland Percys, they, not he, would have to claim kin. He made fun of his ancestor Don Carlos, and if he claimed Harry Hotspur, it was a kinship of spirit. His own aristocracy was a meritocracy of character, talent, performance, courage, and quality of life.

It is just that, a person and a life, which comes across in *Lanterns on the Levee.* And about him I will say no more than that he was the most extraordinary man I have ever known and that I owe him a debt which cannot be paid.

FROM

Lanterns on the Levee

William Alexander Percy

THE RETURN OF THE NATIVE

PROBABLY THERE IS NO nostalgia so long-lived and hopeless as that of the college graduate returning to his native town. He is a stranger though he is home. He is sick for a communal life that was and can never be again, a life merry with youth and unshadowed by responsibilities. He is hungry for the easy intimacies which competitive anxious living does not provide. He is unproved when proof is demanded on every side. In this alien environment, the only one he may now call his own, he is unknown, even to himself.

My case was no different from most, I suppose, and I hated it: eight years of training for life, and here I was in the midst of it—and my very soul whimpered. I had been pushed into the arena and didn't even know the animals' names. Besides, I labored under individual disabilities: I had been to Europe; I had been to Harvard; my accent, though not Northern, was—well, tainted; I had had it easy; I probably considered myself *it.* For crowning handicap, I was blessed with no endearing vices: drunkenness made me sick, gambling bored me, rutting per se, unadorned, I considered overrated and degrading. In charitable mood one might call me an idealist, but, more normally, a sissy.

It must have been difficult for Father too. Enjoying good liquor, loving to gamble, his hardy vices merely under control, he sympathized quizzically and said nothing. But his heart must often have called piteously for the little brother I had lost, all boy, all sturdy, obstreperous charm. Fortunately I wasn't meek and I wasn't afraid. When put upon, I discovered that a truculent tongue did more to save than a battalion of virtues. But it wasn't fun. I had attacks of nausea, but not of tears.

Yet these handicaps on my debut were a minor worry. My real concern was what the show was all about and what role I should or could play in it, queries which, since the curtain was up and I on the stage, seemed fairly belated.

For eight years—in fact, for twenty-three—a great number of people had been pouring out money, skill, time, devotion, prayers to create something out of me that wouldn't look as if the Lord had slapped it together absent-mindedly. Not Alexander the Great nor Catherine II had been tended by a more noble corps of teachers. It humbles me to call their roster, but calling it is no penance: Nain and Mur, Mère and Père, Sister Evangelist and Judge Griffin, Father Koestenbrock and Mr. Bass, Dr. Henneman and Professor Williston, the Roman Catholic Church and Browning, the sea and the sun, Beethoven and Wagner, Michelangelo and Andrea del Sarto, loneliness and friendship, Sinkler and Harold, Mother and Father. They made a longer procession than the Magi and the shepherds combined, and the gifts they brought were more precious. Obviously I was cast to justify the ways of man to God, as it were. But how? What does one do with a life, or at any rate intend to do? It was time to inventory my ambitions and, having selected one as paramount, to pursue it whole-heartedly. For months (maybe for years, maybe until now) I hunted about for a good ambition. Money? No, positively—not because my financial future was assured or my financial present anything more than adequate to supply my simple needs, but it wasn't interesting and it wasn't worthy. Nothing to debate here. Fame as a lawyer? I had been a B man at the law school, which is eminently respectable but not brilliant as Harold and George had been. I suspected that if I should give everything I had to the law I might realize such an ambition, but I had no notion of doing any such thing. I wanted to do whatever piece of work fell to my care as well as I could, but beyond that I wasn't concerned over what opinion my brethren of the bar held of me. Power? I knew nothing about it and it certainly wasn't my métier. Civic usefulness? Perhaps; that was getting warmer, but I had no desire to hold office and I knew no way of dedicating one's unendowed life to usefulness. Other things, I did not know what, except that they were things inside, seemed realities, while money, fame, power, civic virtue seemed things which required an audience to become real. So with my ruminations I reached nowhere, a lonesome sort of spot. Now that the show is nearly over, I'm only just beginning to see what one may truthfully call the good life, but of the plot I still know so little that

I can't swear whether it's been tragedy or comedy, though I have an inkling. Perhaps, after all, stumbling through life by ear, though slower, makes more exciting traveling, and if you have a good ear you're just as apt to arrive as if you'd dipped about in the wake of one of those twitchy compasses.

I didn't exactly plunge into life, rather I tipped in, trepidly. In spite of doubts and misgivings, there was living to be done and I set about it. Our town wasn't a thing of beauty in those days. The residences looked like illegitimate children of a French wedding cake. Besides all the icing they usually sported a turret or cupola to which Sister Ann couldn't have climbed if she *knew* somebody was coming, for it never had stairs. The brick stores, most of them still in situ, as we lawyers say, managed to look stark without looking simple. Curbs, gutters, and open ditches, while satisfactory to such stalwart conservatives as crawfish and mosquitoes, still abided hopefully the coming of the W.P.A. Sidewalks were often the two-board sort that grow splinters for barefoot boys, and the roads, summer or winter, were hazards. There were lovely trees and crape myrtles but where they grew was their business. There were flowers, but no gardens. Just a usual Southern town of that period, and its name was Greenville. There must be something in that name attractive to towns because every state in the Union has one. It's a name without charm for me. I prefer Alligator or Rolling Fork or Nitta Yuma or Rosedale, our neighbors—at least they have individuality, of one sort or another. But, aside from all that, in 1909 I retook Greenville for my home (and kept it) and could boast that I was a full-fledged practicing attorney-at-law.

While not what you might call indispensable in the office, I looked up authorities for Father with great interest and once or twice stumbled on an original legal theory, the discovery of which pleased him even more than myself. I was terrified at the thought of arguing a case, particularly before a jury, but somehow I steeled myself to do it and with some passion, though never brilliantly and never to this day without a spasm of nerves before and after. But the law was the least of my troubles. Making a rut, for comfort, was a grimmer endeavor, one that required years of effort—probably it is one of those lifetime jobs, and just when you are beginning to feel snug you are routed out permanently.

In those days the center of social life for the young people was the Elysian Club. The oldsters played poker at the Mississippi

Club and the middling mature indulged their usual bacchanalian bent, unassisted by pards and maenads, at the Elks'. No doubt about it, our town was plumb social. Although it cherished a "reading-room" and a poolroom, our club's raison d'être was its dance floor. It was a fine floor, but it was housed in a room replete with unsynchronized angles and curves which it must have taken the local builder months to conceive and no time to execute. Beyond question it was the ugliest room in the world, but thoroughly entrancing when Handy appeared and the dancing started. Delta girls are born dancing and never stop, which is as it should be, for surely it is the finest form of human amusement except tennis and talking. The club's dances were famous from Hushpuckna to Yazoo City, and they were the right sort of affairs, with rows of broad-bosomed lares and penates against the wall and so many good-looking animated girls drawling darkest Southernese and doing intricate steps by instinct or inspiration that no one could think of going home before daylight. Drinking was not permitted in the clubhouse and there were no parked cars for intermissions. An intoxicated youth was a crying scandal and an intoxicated female would certainly have caused harakiri or apoplexy among the penates. There are dances now in the Delta, a never ending round, but I am told they are more stimulated and less stimulating.

Now and then Father and Mother appeared at our functions and remained an hour or two because they loved young people. Father himself would occasionally indulge in a whirl on the dance floor, but, being practically tonedeaf, he was an awful dancer and knew it, though fairly unabashed and invariably amused. Mother never understood or forgave in me a certain lack of enthusiasm for things social. People, whole throngs of them, delighted her, and her delight was infectious. Everyone became a little more charming than he was meant by God to be when she was around. I liked people, too, but individually and separately, not in throngs. I soon learned, when surrounded, not to go bounding off like a flushed fawn, but crowds were not then and are not now my natural habitat, and even individuals, no matter how fascinating, I find more exhausting than hard work or boredom. Mother regarded my antisocial tendencies as pure mulishness, but Father, although disappointed no doubt, never showed it except by a far-away expression and a little smile.

I often took to the levee in sheer lonesomeness and confusion of soul. Our woods are not made for walking because the vines and bushes are too rampant and the rattlesnakes too much at home. But the high levee is perfect for a stroll, which you can extend, if so minded, a hundred miles in either direction. Across the river you see Arkansas, a state almost as unfamiliar to us as Montana, but we know it has one great virtue—it grows willows and cottonwoods right down to the water line. In spring they are done by Puvis de Chavannes in pastel green, in summer they are banked in impenetrable tiers of lushness, in fall they have a week of pale flying gold, and in winter they are at their best with their wands rose- and copper-colored and their aisles full of blue smoke. There wasn't a time of year I didn't walk there and watch them across the vari-colored river, which, though it seems home, seems too the most remote and secret stretch of all God's universe. It is most itself and to my liking when with the first crystal rush of winter the ducks and geese and water-turkeys, in wedges, follow its pale protecting sandbars south. At first I walked there alone, but later I discovered three familiar spirits who also enjoyed walking and talking. Will Francis and Lyne Starling and George Roth certainly tided me over a bad passage and are with me still.

It was on these levee walks that I began to think of poetry and to jot down lines. At Sewanee I had tried my hand at lyrics and unfortunately, as I was editor of the college magazine, some of them found their way, anonymously, into print. I reread them a few years ago and I cannot imagine an experience more embarrassing. In Paris I had written a feeble sonnet on Chatterton and at Harvard I improved slightly with two winter songs, one of which, to my amazement and delight, *McClure's* published, still anonymously. All these were secret indulgences and only Miss Carrie knew of them.

This is not an account of my poetry nor of me as a poet. But since much of my life has gone into the making of verse which I hope is poetry, I may as well state now and as briefly as I can how and why I wrote.

What I wrote seemed to me more essentially myself than anything I did or said. It often gushed up almost involuntarily like automatic writing, and the difficulty lay in keeping the hot gush continuous and unselfconscious while at the same time directing it with cold intellect into form. I could never write in cold blood. The results were intensely personal, whatever their other defects. But by some quirk I was always aware in the act of putting words to paper that what I was feeling and thinking had been felt and thought by thousands in every generation. Only that conviction would have permitted me to publish without feeling guilty of indecent exposure.

I judge there's nothing at all unusual about such mental processes, or about these:

When you feel something intensely, you want to write it down—if anguish, to stanch the bleeding; if delight, to prolong the moment. When after years of pondering you feel you have discovered a new truth or an old one which suddenly for you has the excitement of a new one, you write a longish poem. To keep it free from irrelevant photographic details you set it in some long-ago time, one, of course, you love and perhaps once lived in.

That is how I wrote and why I wrote. As to technique I tried to make it sound as beautiful and as fitting as I could. Old patterns helped, but if rhyme seemed out of place, the choruses of *Samson Agonistes,* some of Matthew Arnold's unrhymed cadences, and Shakespeare's later run-on pentameters suggested freer and less accepted modes of communication. As far as I can make out, the towering bulk of English poetry influenced me tremendously, but not any one poet, though I hope I learned as much as I think I owe to Browning's monologues and to Gilbert Murray's translations of Euripides.

Thinking of these lonely trial years would be impossible for me without thinking of Caroline Stern. Everybody in town called her Miss Carrie. The first time I saw her I was far gladder than she realized. One of the convent boys, a fattish one who loomed huge to my apprehensive vision, had announced to me as we dawdled on the corner that I would have to fight him then and there. As in so many conflicts, the casus belli was obscure and immediately forgotten. I accepted the challenge with the least possible enthusiasm and began taking off my coat very deliberately, to give the Lord time to take a hand. At this moment Miss Carrie appeared, surveyed the scene, and paused. The conflict petered out before a blow was struck. Evidently my guardian angel had taken the form of Miss Carrie. It was an unusual guise. She was as tiny as Sister Evangelist, but birdlike. She must have weighed eighty pounds. She had a sensitive face, pale, with a large Jewish nose and enormous brown eyes, lustrous and kind. Her hair, which curled pleasantly, was just darker than wasp red. But I found later there was nothing else waspish about her, though she was a gallant fighter. She never thought anything was worth fighting for except moral issues, and it sickened her when an individual or a nation refused to fight for them. On this occasion she stopped and viewed our bellicose stance, meaning no doubt to whirl in if developments required. Then as always she looked tidy but a tiny bit disheveled, as if a not very rough breeze had just deposited her unexpectedly. She had the air of a volunteer as we gardeners use the term, and that air always kept Mother from appreciating her, because Mother by instinct and training was chic.

Miss Carrie—she must have been in her twenties then, though of course she seemed to me far gone in overblown maturity—had mistaken my unwilling preparations for battle for simon-pure heroism and, since she admired nothing more than knightly prowess, I found myself a few days later a visitor in her little house. It was a bare little place with an improvised look and hardly enough furniture for convenience. Her dwarf of a father, an Alsatian Jew, lived with her, a querulous old fellow who had failed as a country merchant and, now idle, lived by her scanty earnings as a teacher. She tended and scolded him as if he were a child. Her passionate adoration had been for her mother, whose death a few years before had left her the bread-winner and spiritually in solitary confinement. It would have been mortally lonely for her had she not known Judge Griffin, who gave her the nourishment she needed, his deep patriarchal love.

Miss Carrie's passion for painting was beyond bounds, consuming. While still in her teens, by impossible denials and scrapings, she had managed to save enough money to study in New York for a year. I think she must have lived in a state of ecstasy that whole year—she needed to, for I am sure she went hungry half the time. She would tell me about the classes, about copying the head of Bastien-Lepage's *Joan of Arc,* about her friend Annie Goldthwaite, who became famous, about all the young doings of the League. She loved to remember it and longed to go back. But hardly had she returned home to her school work than she developed lead poisoning. Her doctor forbade her to paint again. Against orders she was trying it when I met her. While sketching me, she would say with shy pride: "At the League they said I had a real sense of color. Someone once mistook one of my oils for a Henner," and she laughed softly at the delightful recollection. But in a year or two the blood-poison returned and she had to give up painting again, this time forever. It was her whole life and that meant she had lost her life and must find another. If this had been different and that had not happened, she might have become a great painter. Instead she became a great soul.

She was a teacher born. Mr. Bass recognized her gift and soon had her teaching anything, everything—painting, history, English, whatever classes happened to be without a teacher at the moment. She was always exhausted, generally undernourished, and always eager. The children adored her. She read me my first poetry (Milton and Shakespeare didn't count, they were just Milton and Shakespeare) and I resisted it mightily. This resistant attitude of mine lasted for years—in fact, until I read *Dover Beach* at Sewanee. Perhaps it was due to Father's having read me when I was a little fellow Tennyson's *I'm to be Queen of the May, Mother,* which I had found so unbearably pathetic I had burst into tears. Or perhaps I did actually detest poetry's inversions and circumlocutions as much as I thought I did. But poetry fascinated me, like a fearful sin, and Miss Carrie kept on reading it to me. Mother disapproved of these goings-on and observed, accurately enough, that there was no telling what kind of impractical notions Carrie was putting into my head, and my visits to her must stop. Father wondered if they did any harm anyway. But I announced I was going to see her when I wanted to. Mother closed the discussion, not weakly but impotently, by remarking that for an obedient child I was the most hard-headed she had ever encountered.

I kept on seeing Miss Carrie until I could see her no more. Many of the young people, mostly her former students, felt similarly drawn to her, and those who had moved from town were eager to visit her on their return trips. We came to her as to a clean upland spot smelling of pine. There was a childish gaiety about her, and her great wisdom was completely innocent. Apparently she made no effort to be right, she just was right. She gave you the fine feeling you were shielding her when in fact you were drawing from her your strength.

While I was at college she joined the Episcopal Church. That must have been a cruel decision for her to feel she must make, for it meant, and she knew it meant, breaking with her own people and with the faith of her fathers. The Jews at home never forgave her for it. After a few years she stopped attending church, and that too must have meant a grievous struggle. So she went her way alone and built her own lonely altar. She must have been a very Jacob for wrestling with God, but when I knew her best, after her youth, she didn't wrestle any more, she merely walked with Him and leaned on Him when she was tired. It's a good thing He was there because she was often tired and she had no one else to lean on.

Beginning with my return home from Harvard, every scrap I ever wrote I showed Miss Carrie or mailed to her, coming by her house Sundays for her criticism. Though a partial critic in my case, she was a sensitive and a fearless one. We fought over words and cadences and sometimes I was worsted. She knew far better than I when I was growing didactic, and vehemently opposed the tendency. One week I sent her three or four short pieces and when I arrived I was pleased and astonished to hear her say ardently: "At last you have written a perfect poem!" I didn't know to which one she was referring, but it was *Overtones*, the one poem of mine which critics and anthologists, almost without dissent, have liked. At the very time she was giving me so much, she was making a selection of her own poems and saving every nickel to have them published. For years she had been writing poetry and a good many of her lyrics had appeared in the more distinguished magazines. At last she named her collection and found a publisher, one of those who advertise little and charge much. Denied an outlet in painting, she had turned to poetry, and now her very own book—*At the Edge of the World*, by Caroline Stern—in a pretty yellow binding was to appear in the kindly world. She was so excited and hopeful, she often wore a cherry-red ribbon at her throat, but though it was not her color, none of us would tell her so because that ribbon made her feel reckless and mischievous. Although there was plenty of Joan of Arc and St. Theresa in her, she was fundamentally a little girl. Her book appeared, and that was all. The critics ignored it, there were no sales, after a year the publisher wrote no copies were available. It did not deserve such treatment. Though she had more fancy than imagination, more feeling than art, and though she was not endowed with the sense of the magic word, they were good poems, charming, and so like her. She was hurt inside, but she did not complain and she never grew accusatory or bitter. When she read favorable reviews of my volume, a little later, she was thrilled, and when the reviews were unfriendly she was furious. All the while she continued to teach with undiminished enthusiasm hundreds of children and to give cheer or comfort to her numerous young friends in their happiness or troubles.

After her father's death she had built herself a small home with two extra rooms which she rented as an apartment. Between paying by the month for it and paying for the publication of her poems she had little enough left to fill her birdlike needs. When I think of the stark little living-room where I found so much peace and encouragement and of the scanty meals she referred to vaguely and when I remember I never gave her a present worth having or thought of helping out in any one of a hundred possible ways, I am appalled at the self-centered egotism of youth and its incapacity for real understanding or pity.

Once in a while you would find she had visited the doctor or was not feeling so well, but none of us was disturbed or really interested—people were always getting sick and Miss Carrie was naturally frail. She was alone most of the time and bought a Ouija board for company. It did astounding things for her—wrote hours on end faster than anyone except her could read, leaped into the air, went into frenzies, or moodily refused to budge. It amused us enormously. But I found after a while it wasn't so amusing to her. Her mother would speak to her, and God, and Matthew Arnold would send me long messages. She was puzzled and incredulous, but Ouija became almost alive, almost a person to her. She had no one else to live with except God, and He isn't enough by Himself. One night when Ouija had announced God was speaking and she was listening intently to the strange poetic moralizing, the wretched three-legged thing suddenly bounded into the air and spelled out violently: "Carrie, you are a damn fool. This isn't God. Good night," and could not be coaxed into further comment. The incident distressed her more than she would confess.

Once as I was leaving she told me quietly she was going to the hospital next day—an operation, she didn't know what for; she'd be out in two weeks. She was out in a few days, although they had operated. Then she began to waste away before our eyes. Soon she was taken to the hospital again, and this time for good. Although she didn't complain she asked everyone what was the matter with her. At last they took Ouija away from her. One afternoon when I came in she smiled and said: "I know the truth now. I asked the nurse and as she was leaving without answering I picked up a pencil and said: 'Ouija, tell me,' and it wrote: 'Cancer'" The last time I saw her she had drawn a heavy white veil across her face and her body weighed no more than a bird's.

Miss Carrie was not "my favorite Jew." I have had dozens of favorites. To no people am I under deeper spiritual obligation. But I am not unaware of the qualities in them (absent in her) which have recurrently irritated or enraged other people since the Babylonian captivity. Touch a hair of a Jewish head and I am ready to fight, but I have experienced moments of exasperation when I could willingly have led a pogrom. No, Miss Carrie was not my favorite Jew. She was my favorite friend. She never failed me, but looking back I am not certain I did not fail her despicably—I suspect I was patronizing. She was so different, so unworldly, so fundamentally innocent, and her friendship was so unwithheld and shameless. I don't often trouble to be ashamed, but if I was patronizing, Miss Carrie and her God would have to forgive me. I never could.

Miss Carrie had failed in everything—in painting, in poetry, in making money, in winning love, in dying easy. Yet she was one of the few successes I ever knew. I think I learned more from her of what the good life is and of how it may be lived than from almost anyone else.

FROM

Black Rituals

STERLING D. PLUMPP

I REMEMBER very vividly the night I got 'ligion and jined church. It was in 1951, and the Mississippi July was hot and humid as ever; the sun was up sparkling down its beams before six when I got up, and was flowing gently behind formidable woods after seven in the evening. All the crops had been laid by, the horse and cattle pastured, and everywhere Mother Nature gave evidence of her role as nurturer: lima and butter beans were twirled round poles as if in some fierce amorous embrace, potato vines covered the head of the ground, and watermelons could be seen resting quietly amid a tribe of grass. It was the time of year when people go fishing, visit friends, or wade in the serenity of shade trees. I was happy and spent much time swimming in the ponds and lakes within a ten mile radius of my house. I had been told about God, Christ, and getting saved all my life but now that I was eleven, just one year before I would become responsible for my own soul at the age of twelve, I was prime target for those holy ad-men of the Lord whose sole function was to get the lost to come to Revival Meetings. Momma had been trying to get us to go to Sunday School for some time and we had made personal contact with a Sunday School teacher by cutting her grass, pruning her peach trees, and doing general handy work for her.

The immediate impetus to my getting converted was not the Black Church but a Revival sponsored by a Reverend Younger, a white Evangelist. Every year he had black children remember verbatim a chapter from the New Testament as the key for their admittance into Summer Camp. In 1951 it was First and Second Thessalonians. I had trouble remembering every word and I didn't have any clothing suitable enough to wear to the occasion. Fortunately, a black friend of the family was also a friend of the reigning Revivalist and interceded for me, and I went to his house and was given all the clothing that would fit. The occasion marked the first time in my life that I had entered the front door of Mister Charlie's house. And it was also the first time that I had ever really had any Sunday clothes. I got several pairs of shoes, two suits, ties, shirts, and, of course, a Bible. The son of the minister, Bobby, sealed the deal by being very friendly. In fact, when the Minister brought me home, he and I sat on the front seat and his two little daughters sat on the back one.

Revival wasn't my first introduction to Black Religion; it was merely my first lesson on the rhetoric of Black Rituals, for I had been bathed in Black Religion since the day I opened my eyes. I knew that there was an omnipotent God who made the rains fall, an omniscient God who knew what was best, and that there was an all-forgiving God who would forgive all who bowed to their knees in submission to His Being. My grandfather and grandmother went to church every Sunday, read the Bible to us, talked about how good God was, and prayed aloud to Him at night before they went to bed. They even taught us a prayer:

Now I lay me down to sleep
I pray the Lord my soul to keep.
If I should die before I wake
I pray the Lord
My soul to take. AMEN.

In fact, our whole home was run like a sort of mundane Heaven; Poppa was the all-powerful and all-knowing God, and Momma an angel supporting him. We, the children, were angels when we were good and did something that pleased Poppa, and devils when we dabbled in mischief and displeased him. Our punishment was our banishment from the heaven of his praises to the lowest depths of hell where his razor strap was the final arbiter.

Revival Time was a time of intense spiritual duress for me. I had always thought whatever I did was natural but when I found out that doing what one wants to do conflicts with the Savior's Plan, I became despondent and sought ways to defend what my life had been. The architects of the Revival had an airtight case against me as a sinner; I would have to admit my sins, accept the Christ and be baptized into a new way of life. It wasn't easy. To sort of catch me off guard, the Revivalists held spontaneous watermelon contests where we black children were lined up and given slices of watermelons; at the word "go" we began eating as fast as we could until only one diner remained. Our pictures were taken. The results were bellyaches, soiled clothing, and much laughter. Often the watermelon eating contest was followed by impromptu prayers or songs.

In the evening before we left our barracks and made our way to the meeting place, supper was served; we had as much as we wanted. Normally, we went over in groups; the boys together and the girls together.

But naturally, there was mating among us. The ones most experienced at attending Revival Meetings had learned the trick of slipping off into the solitude of the woods. The sinners sat in the front rows of the auditorium and the Evangelist and his cast manned the stage of what was our assembly room during school days. A memorable feature of the Revival was the Williams Singers. I can only remember Miss Josie Pearl Williams who played the piano and was the lead singer. It was her screaming voice, leaping up through the ceiling, dancing out the doors, calling, beckoning the lost, that made me feel my deep need to be saved. Every night Sister Josie Pearl ended the meeting with "Oh, If We Never Meet Again," crooning, "I know God will be with us/if we never meet again." Somehow, I wanted to meet again, and one night after many testimonies, yes Lords, and songs, I followed the line of those who had accepted the Lamb. I was perspiring madly and could barely keep from screaming out in jubilation, but I merely walked up to the Reverend and knelt with him as he prayed and thanked the Lord. My grandmother was out there among the happy faces and she gave me spending money after the event. The night I accepted the Lord is a night I still never forget for I felt a relationship with everything. I could start all over and walk the steps of righteousness. I looked forward to the day I would be baptized and jine church.

My conversion was my first step in accepting the formal Black Church because after summer camp, Holy Ghost Baptist Church held its Revival and I went regularly to the meetings. One night my cousin and I went up to the preacher when the "Sheaves" were being brought in and told him that we had been saved during summer camp and wished to be baptized and jine his church. I lived in grave anticipation awaiting my baptism. I was as light as a feather and Momma and Poppa asked me if I knowed what I was doing and I told them yes'um. They told me I could be baptized but that I would have to go to church and Sunday School every Sunday. They said that they would give me money to pay my dues. My life took on a very structured manner, getting up early, shining my shoes, and walking down the dusty roads to the church for Sunday School and Church Service later.

Baptism was on a late Saturday evening in Lake Kickapoo. I wore a gown made of a corn meal sack. I trembled in fear for I had heard of embarrassing incidences where the elect on their maiden immersion into the rite of holy initiation had nearly strangled from the dive. I didn't want to cause a scene. I walked slowly to the edge of the water to a cadre of baptismal ushers who comforted neophytes before leading us out into the cool water about waist deep. After the Reverend had raised his right into the sky to beckon down the Holy Spirit, he placed his hand over my eyes and bent me backwards into the waters and brought me back up very abruptly. My weak frame shook and my wet gown stuck to my body like the wrappings of a mummy. I was ashamed and cold as I was led away to a nearby shelter to dry myself and dress. The entire evening after my baptism, I felt relieved, cleaned, chosen. I was very conscious of my words, walks, and ways. I carefully laid out my attire for the following day, shined my shoes, and went to bed early, for on Sunday I would be receiving the Right Hand of Fellowship and the Lord's Supper.

I was sharp as a tack as I sat in Sunday School the next day. All of us new converts suddenly found ourselves the equals of the veteran Christians. We were very enthusiastic during the class and everybody was quick to congratulate us with a smile, a handshake, or a pat on the shoulder. After Sunday School we meandered from group to group receiving the praises of the grown folks who were scattered on the lawn of the church during the interlude between Sunday School and Church Service. Older people wandered in by ones, twos, and threes—older people who didn't go to Sunday School anymore but always managed to make Service. In fact, Poppa and Momma, members of Mount Hood Baptist Church, made it to the various sessions of talkers before church service began.

Gradually the grown folks and then the chilluns drift into the church and take seats. The chilluns sit up in the front and the grown folks in the back except for the Sisters, who have special places for them set aside up front on either side of the pulpit. The choir is seated up front. In the pulpit, there was a rostrum with a huge family Bible on it. Sitting around in circles like the Knights of the Round Table are the pastor in the center, his son and various other pastors close to him, and the many, many jackleg preachers sitting farthest away, on the outer perimeter.

The service begins with a prayer by one of the jackleg preachers who does his thing for about ten minutes. Then immediately following, the whole church, along with the choir, sings "Every Time I Feel the Spirit." After this, the "Welcoming" is given by one of the select Sisters, the Scriptures read by one of the visiting pastors, and another song is sung—probably "Some Glad Morning When This Life Is Over." The pastor then rises and reminisces about his childhood and when he was saved: he jokes with the circle of preachers and congratulates the deacons and sisters for their service to the church; he tells the new converts how fortunate they are that they have had the chance to seek, see, and accept the Light. Then he thanks the Lord for everybody in church for fifteen minutes.

The pastor then breaks in with his favorite, "Give Me That Old Time Religion," and the ushers parole the aisle with collection baskets. A few Sisters let out shouts of happiness but the song ends before the spirit really comes over anybody. The son of the pastor soon rises and tells about how understanding his father has been, forgiving him his trespasses, and leading him down the road to the Servanthood of the Lord. He then reads a text from the Old Testament; then he repeats it, then he asks the congregation a question which he answers. As the preacher leads the congregation to the very stairs of the Last Judgment, his voice is no longer the voice of a speaker, but the voice of a chanter; his words come very fast, yet they come in a very rhythmic manner.

Suddenly, when happiness makes him close the Bible and leave the pulpit, hopping from side to side in the outer perimeter of it, he chants his sermon and the deacons and brothers begin chants of "AMEN," but the other preachers merely sit with their legs crossed nodding their heads. Soon the sisters begin to chant with him, parts from songs are interjected into his sermon, and soon one sister jumps up crying, "Oh Lord" and stands with her body quivering, but her lips are still. The female ushers dressed in white saunter around her, and to the tune of "It's okay, sister," they waltz her toward the door for some fresh air. The pastor and the sisters preach for forty minutes and the sermon is followed by a song, "This Little Light of Mine." After this, the main collection is taken. The loaded ushers walk toward the treasurer and he announces that only three dollars are needed to make one hundred dollars; then he announces that only three cents are needed to make one hundred and ten dollars; then he announces that only fifty cents are needed to make one hundred and fifty dollars.

The formal initiation into Black Religion is the "Right Hand of Fellowship" ceremony; all the new converts stand in a circle and all the members of the church go around them shaking their hands. The whole thing takes about thirty minutes and your hands are sore after the many, many hand-squeezes and sincere admonishments.

I felt honored during my initiation because all the big shots talked with me, even the pastor clad in a black suit, white shirt, black tie, black shoes, and cleanly-shaven head; his teeth were sparse with the two front ones being covered with gold. When the pastor laughed it came from the depth of his being like cool waters coming up from a deep well; he told me that he and my grandfather had been boys together and that he knew both my mother and my father and that he had been to my house and had eaten on many occasions. I was very happy and knew I would feel at home when I went to church instead of feeling like an accused killer waiting for some dreadful verdict. Later, after my initiation was over, I got my first taste of the Lord's body and the Lord's blood; it was really yeast bread and grape juice.

Conversion changed my life greatly because my actions were controlled by guidelines which I was responsible for. Before I jined church I wasn't twelve and therefore was not responsible for the fate of my soul. I found that I felt guilty whenever I broke one of the Lord's Commandments, and I really thought my soul would be hellbound if I deliberately defied holy laws. I gradually learned to fear the Lord and never to mock holy things or be disrespectful to old people. It was hard for me, and much of the carefree, natural joy I had known earlier left me. I began to worry more about the state of my soul than about the state of my body. I gradually learned to say "if the Lord is willing" whenever I stated that I intended to do something in the future. I was always told that tomorrow wasn't promised to me and I walked with cautious steps. But the newness of conversion wears off after six months and you begin to feel that playing ball all day long, shooting marbles, hunting birds, or going off into the woods on Sundays are more important than going to church and Sunday School. In fact, only the "young men of promise" kept their appointments at the Lord's Temple; we others went sporadically, and found ourselves in frequent consultations with our parents and with the spiritual overseers of the community.

The longer I was a Christian the more my interest fluctuated with the rhythms of the seasons; I looked forward to fall because I always had new clothes to wear and I could also see the new converts sitting on the mourners' bench, being baptized, and finally being initiated into the Lord's Temple; winters always found me ready to go to church because it gave me an opportunity to see classmates that I saw five days a week at school, and it also gave me something to talk about at school the next week; in spring I was interested in church until my shoes lost their soles; and, summers were always boring because it was hot and the pleasure of Nature was too much competition. Even when I did not go to church on Sundays I felt something was going to happen to me for not doing so; if I fished I thought I would catch something that would swallow me whole; if I swam I thought I would surely drown; if I climbed trees I thought I would fall; and if I walked down the railroad tracks I thought some fast train would run me down without warning. I could never get away from the law of the Church. Finally, my irregularity at attending and my laxity in paying my dues forced my name from the roll call. I was slipping from the King's Highway and didn't know how to get back on the right trail. But every night before I went to bed I got on my knees and asked the Lord to forgive me for my sins; I didn't want to die in a state of unforgiveness.

As the years went by and I entered my teens, the Lord's message continued to come to me through the words and ways of my parents; they always paid tribute to the Lord and had faith that He would stand by them no matter how great a trial they had to go through; and finally when the boat of life had wandered long enough over rough and tempestuous seas, the Lord would take the ship home and there would be much rejoicing. I have never wanted to die, yet I rejoiced when my parents rejoiced because I saw the same happy, near ecstatic, yet serene expression on their faces when they talked about the Goodness of the Lord and being with Him that I had witnessed in them when they were genuinely gay, laughing, eating watermelon, or watching tall, green corn, with its tassle and ribbons flowing to a cool afternoon breeze. I walked under the shadow of the Cross during all my younger years and no matter how far I strayed from the road of righteousness, I always knew how to fall upon my knees and thus avoid eternal damnation. I never wanted to challenge Nature, though I wanted to be a part of it. I never doubted the validity of Black Religion as long as I was a part of it; I just knew that the laws of the Church were the right ones to live by. All through my life old people had died, young ones were killed, and babies born all because it was the Lord's Will. I had no notion of statistics and could not analyze the births, deaths, etc. . . . on a statistical basis. I was conditioned to bear hardships when they came and to rejoice when good times came. I grew up aware that I didn't have absolute control over my life and I knew that if I wanted to be happy and live to be an old man, then there were certain rituals that I had to perform, and they all had their origin in the Black Church. The whole Black Church's spirituality became so much a part of me that I could never quite free myself of it. I will always believe in a spiritual dimension of life because so much of what I know was experienced at the spiritual level. I learned by sensing before I was taught that I could conceptualize the world, operationally defining it in material terms. My earliest reality was cloaked in a very, very profound mythology.

I never knew how ingrained Black Religion had been instilled into the marrow of my being until I became a convert to Catholicism at the age of fifteen. I was lured into the Catholic Church because guardian angels, Holy Eucharist, Confession, and purgatory led to a foolproof way of gaining eternal life. But long before I had finished my instructional and probationary period, I genuinely missed the preaching, singing, and shouting of the Black Baptist Church. Somehow I always felt that the Catholic Church was too rational, too proper, and I never felt anything in it; I always went through their rituals and hoped for the best, but when I went to Black religious services, I knew that the Lord had been present and had touched me. There was always a rhythm in the Black Church paced by handclaps, footstomps, yes Lords, Amens, nods, and shouts, that made me know that religion was something experienced, and not something learned logically; you felt religion. My shift from Black Rituals to White Rationalism also created other problems for me. As long as I was under the guidance of Black Rituals, I never questioned the circumstances of my birth and I could've become a preacher if the Lord called me. But within the Catholic Church the Lord didn't call young men, they decided that they wanted to enter a seminary; however, bastards needed a special diocesan dispensation to enter, and I was a bastard. I wanted to become a priest because I thought the Lord told all young men "to go and sell what thou hast . . . and come and follow me." I didn't have anything to sell but I wanted to follow Him.

My sojourn in the Catholic Church was a five-year disappointment because I was always doing something which didn't go to the essences of me; I wasn't faking but I was never moved. I was outside of my culture and consequently a stranger, and didn't know how to deal with the fact. I became a picture Catholic, an altar boy; Mass and Communion daily, rosary daily, and Confession weekly, but I never had the same feeling of salvation that I had felt when Sister Josie Pearl sang "Oh, If We Never Meet Again." I never thought Catholic priests preached, merely that they read and talked. I never got used to the organ, and the kyries, christes and agnus deis never replaced "Every Time I Feel the Spirit" and "Swing Low, Sweet Chariot." Deep within my heart I felt that I had betrayed my people as long as I was a Catholic—not that I really found the answers to my life in the Black Church and Black Rituals—but I definitely wouldn't find them in the Catholic Church; besides, my parents weren't Catholic and I didn't make my First Communion at six but at fifteen.

When I graduated from high school and entered college at the age of twenty, I began my comeback trail to Black Rituals. I had the fortune and misfortune to win a scholarship to St. Benedict's College in Atchison, Kansas. The experience a black man undergoes in a predominantely white college with only ten or so Negroes there is enough to drive a rock insane. The only thing that could save me at St. Benedict's was Black Rituals and all I could get was the blues. I bought several Lps by Ray Charles and I again got the religious feeling I had known as a child. Through them I found strength enough to remain at St. Benedict's for two years. Those two years of college and priests who drank as much as Dean Martin made me doubt the validity of Catholic teaching. I began a serious reading of everything written by black writers after my sophomore year. I left

Kansas and came to Chicago to the Main Post Office where I witnessed more life than I had read about in all of those books. W. E. B. DuBois, James Baldwin, Richard Wright, and Ralph Ellison made me know that something was special about the experience of a black man born in America; he had a special vision and could see what others couldn't. DuBois, Baldwin, and Wright made me seriously doubt the necessity of religion, even doubt that God existed. What I thought was a rebellion against Black Rituals and the Catholic Church was merely a reaction against what I had been taught; I had never defined for myself what religion is, what or who God is, and who I was, and it was this process of the birth of my mind that made me call myself an atheist. I had no other label to place upon myself, but I was no atheist for I was desperately trying to find answers about God; if I had been an atheist, then I would have had the answers—God didn't exist and that was it.

Quite another change came over me when I spent two years in the Army from 1964–1966 because I had grown older and had read more about other religions, particularly, Buddhism and Hinduism. I also read Sartre, Camus, Kirkegaard, Henry Miller, and Arthur Miller and the thing I found out about religion, reality, truth, and life was that everything depended on how well the individual evaluated his own experiences. Thus I ceased calling myself anything and started to play music that really moved me—jazz, rock-and-roll, gospels, spirituals, blues, and sermons. I re-discovered in the Army just how religious I was at my base and I accepted the fact. I no longer equated Black Religion with the confines of a church building and I knew it was a source of power within me. When I started to write, it was the spring of my experiences with the Black Church that gave energy and direction to my efforts. I'm religious and Black Rituals are as much a part of me as my hair, my eyes, my ears, my soul, but I've been taught various rational ways to conceptualize my experiences and I can verbalize what I feel. When I left the Catholic Church, and after that the silly belief that I was an atheist, and returned to an acceptance of Black Religion on my own terms, it was the dawn of my mind, the awakening in me of an unnoticed sea.

Notes from the Laughing Factory

SAMUEL PRESTRIDGE

I

THE CROWD MOVED towards the Klan, taking directional cues from police cars and people ahead of them. I found a student of mine, and we walked together, stopping to talk, stopping to watch others. It was like a carnival.

The Klan, appearing in the distance, was in ranks of marching, spotless white. They looked like militant laundry and were too far away for photographs, so my student played with his camera, and we walked on. Closer, we saw faces. Some were masked, some smoked. All were calm enough, except for a furtiveness around their eyes. They expected trouble—someone to throw something; someone to charge their ranks. All were silent. From the sides of the street came boos, jeers, occasional signs of support, all met with a silence greater than any response. They carried Rebel flags, which was, after all, the point. I thought of the magnificent pointlessness of lemmings.

I justified my going to the parade by calling myself "a witness to a historical stupidity." That way, I felt justified, if only marginally. I had asked friends if they were going. The response, usually emphatic, was *No, I don't want to show them any sign of support*—which says neither, *I don't want to get involved*, nor, *I can't take them seriously*. My own feelings were a mesh of the latter two sentiments.

Mostly, I just wanted to see what would happen.

It was the first time I'd seen the Klan. I was thirty and from Mississippi. My student was eighteen and from Wisconsin. We talked about the Klan, and I suspected that he thought that, as a Southerner, I'd attended Klan rallies *at least* as often as I'd boiled chitterlings. He asked questions, and I answered them. I felt knowledgeable about the whole affair, proprietorial, like a tour guide through a wax museum of the grotesque. This was, after all, my home, my heritage, and it followed, my Klan.

We watched as they turned the corner, marched down a block, and turned left, headed for the Square. I felt a sense of recognition as they marched. Not identification, and certainly not sympathy, but a sense of the tradition, the history that was mine just because I was Southern.

We walked toward the Square. I lost my student to something scenic, so I read the placards. The more direct ones (THE KLAN SUCKS) were being shepherded off the street by a black policeman. The Klan's opposition, disorganized, was on the wrong street, so there was a general milling toward the Square. I walked and looked for faces I'd seen earlier.

I recognized an older man now wandering along the sidewalk. He'd marched part of the way with the Klan, then broken off from the parade and headed toward a fat woman who was waiting for him in a parking lot. He still carried a Rebel flag about the size of a pack of Camels, and as he walked through the crowd, he met everyone with a slight feint with the flag in greeting or polite defiance as he interpreted your sympathies.

I moved away from him and took a place in the crowd.

II

It went like this:

John Hawkins was the first black cheerleader at Ole Miss. He refused to carry a Rebel flag because he said that, to him, it was a symbol of slavery. People got mad.

Then James Meredith came to campus to speak at the commemoration of the twentieth year of desegregation at Ole Miss. During the speech he announced that he was filing suit to have "Dixie" removed as the Ole Miss fight song and Colonel Rebel removed as the school mascot. There were to be no more Rebel flags at football games. Some students walked out during the lecture and chanted "Hoddy Toddy" outside the auditorium. People got mad.

Later a spokesperson for the students claimed that they, the Hoddiers, were simply on their way to a mixer and were just loosening up. People felt a little better, but in general people were still mad.

There were interviews, comments, retorts. For the first time in the school's history, a cheerleader was a controversial figure. Hawkins called a press conference and talked about being controversial. People got mad.

Finally the Klan announced a march to be held in Oxford in support of the Rebel flag. It was scheduled for Saturday, October 23. In an interview in the student newspaper, *The Daily Mississippian*, Gordon Galle, Grand Dragon of Mississippi's KKK, outlined the Klan's reasoning: "If we do away with the [Confederate] flag, pretty soon they'll be putting a hammer and sickle on the American flag. They [the students] haven't bothered to defend it, and I will. They're going to sit on their backsides, and let the blacks do what they want, but I'm not willing to do that. I want to let the young people know that if they need any help protesting, we'll give it to them."

There *is* a man for every hour.

III

I was teaching at Ole Miss when Hawkins made his pronouncements. I don't like football and probably never will be able to take seriously anything any cheerleader does or doesn't carry, so Hawkins's claim that, to him, the flag represented slavery seemed regressive, like the tradition his actions were meant to oppose.

There are issues, as there are people, that are simply not worth responding to. There are absurdities that cannot be addressed, but can only be lived with. Somehow, this got to be one of the rules. To violate this rule is inelegant, because your response on these occasions only cheapens the impulse behind your intentions and makes you look as absurd as the issue that, ignoring all warnings from your sense of humor, you address. Your relationship to the inviolable absurdity becomes roughly that of Brer Rabbit to the tar baby. That the Rebel flag has been retained as a school symbol for all these years is sad; that it became an issue at all is sad. That Hawkins chose to address the issue made him seem to many incredulous. It's just hard to be taken seriously when, to many watching, you're only tilting windmills.

But Hawkins's success was this: he, along with Meredith, brought to the forefront a series of emotionally charged images, areas of sensitivity that show how little progress we've made in freeing ourselves—black and white—from the power of those symbols of that part of our heritage that time, morality, and legislation have condemned. An antique flag, a cartoon mascot, a minstrel song cannot be taken seriously as issues themselves, and the insistence on the removal of the flag seemed as ridiculous as the adamancy of the response to the proposals. Or maybe the division created by the suggestion simply showed that Hawkins and Meredith were right to want the removal of the Confederate flag, a symbol that embodies a heritage that names them as inferior.

I think both possibilities are accurate, though antithetical.

If Frost had been a Southerner, he would not have said in 1962, "This land was ours before we were the land's." A Southerner might have expressed it, "We considered ourselves a land before the land, for a time, acquiesced to the notion." That is, the South was a separate entity before it was a sovereign state. This notion of separateness can be claimed by other regions, but there is a difference.

The South had the idea of its separateness confirmed—first by a political fact, then by a war, and finally by a military occupation. The notion of separateness, of sovereignty, was instilled and endorsed long after the fact of sovereignty was a pile of rubble. The notion raised itself, or was raised, to a folk mythology that continues to be more of a threat than a heritage.

And even before the political *fact*, before the South became a sovereign state, its people considered itself a sovereignty, not because of any homogeneity of its people, but by an odd melding of regional concerns that were reinforced by counterpointing northern ones: they are industrial—we are agrarian; they are urban—we are rural; they are federalists—we uphold the sovereignty of the state; they are abolitionists—we are slaveholders; and ultimately, but throughout implicitly, they are wrong—we are right; they are North—we are South.

Finally, even when the South was a short-lived political fact, it had little else besides the notion of sovereignty, of community to give it definition; little besides its antipathy to what it perceived as Northern, as foreign to give it even a geographic shape. It was a nation bordered by water on the south and east, unassimilated lands to the west, and an abstract border on the north that separated it from what it separated itself from—a nation that gave it definition by providing counterpointing standards that it, the South, was to be antithetical to, and thereby extant from, as a separate but theoretically confederate entity.

IV

Mercy.

Admittedly, the paragraphs above lean heavily on Faulkner. Any discussion of a Southerner's notion of heritage, that mixed sense of pride, sorrow, and profound waste, is most readily discussed in Faulknerian syntax, rhythms, and tones. It's just the easiest way to deal with it all. It's like finding yourself in a strange city and attaching yourself to someone who, though a total stranger, has an accent from your region. The notion of community becomes a convenient projection, and the physical characteristics expressing that notion are wholly stance.

Stance isn't necessarily bad. It's a way of blending in, of being at home. It becomes an issue when one loses sight of the fact that stance is an expression of community, not an evidence. When the expression is accepted as a proof of community, of solidarity, the individual or group for whom the stance is a common coinage becomes indistinguishable from the stance. And the individual divorcing himself from the accepted stance, from its adherents, often can only adopt a counter-stance, which only states that the old ways still have a strong claim on him: you don't fight what doesn't threaten you. The position of counter-stance is not one of individual expression, but one of simple, almost visceral, reaction to the established mean. Which is not necessarily bad. It just shouldn't be confused with freedom.

The two sides of the problem can be illustrated.

I was in junior high school when desegregation began to make some changes. On the first day of school, I looked around for black students, as I believe everyone did, in an informal census to determine what kind of "danger" we were in. There were seven black students, mostly girls, and there were about a thousand whites in the school. I felt we were still "safe."

At home after school, a neighbor was visiting my mother. "Well," she said, "how many of 'em ya'll got?"

Affecting the nasal yell of my northern Alabama relatives, simply the most adult, the hippest tone I could then imagine, I said, "Seb'n lil' niggers!"

Both my mother and her guest toned me down with frantic waves. Our maid was in the next room. When I walked through, she was crying. I felt bad about it, but I thought of myself as neither unkind, nor racist. Just adult.

In aligning oneself with that kind of heritage, one aligns oneself with a notion of community that is a myth. The gap between this myth and fact can be bridged only by assent to a code of behavior. To a system of rank, regalia, and regimen. On the ability to recognize someone as "one of us" and, further, to know exactly what that means.

I remember walking along a road near my grandmother's home in northern Alabama. A car would pass. If a man was driving, he'd wave, and I'd wave back. They hadn't done that a year ago. *I was suddenly a man!* I began to wave at everyone. Twenty years later, the same waving began to anger me. It became not a greeting, but an assumption: *We're neighbors! You're more than one of us—you're just like us!*

Even now, I feel clumsy waving and ridiculous if I refuse to. Either way, I assent to the power my heritage has over me.

I remembered how that felt when I heard about John Hawkins; how the issue was stance, but it wasn't the problem.

The problem comes in choosing a stance, and having chosen, coming to believe in its singular virtue above all other possibilities; in losing touch with responsible, realistic alternatives. One solution is the personal vision and courage to say "no" to stance; to reject it for what it is—narrow, simplistic, and false—and through this denial, which is a larger act of faith and assent, to recognize and assume one's place in the larger community of the world and the human spirit. Further, the history of our state in this century documents that such vision, such an act of faith, is a response to an external set of circumstances, a response to the times. Florence Mars, Medgar Evers, Hodding Carter, Fannie Lou Hamer, William Faulkner are all twentieth-century Mississippians who, through a human act of faith and denial of the inevitability of cultural and personal paralysis, have transcended their "place" and their time, and have affected change and progress in the political, cultural, and artistic consciousness of our state and our nation.

If the response to the times is an act of vision, courage, and imagination, then a lack, a paucity of those three characteristics indicates the nature of the time—a time without qualities, a time listless and without redeeming features. In such a time, the most absurd issue can become the focal point for emotional energies with no other outlet and no better mode of expression. In such a time, the listless look for a cause, a reason. Someone to stir their lethargy into a muck. A rallying point.

A cheerleader . . .

I stood on the corner and watched the Klan entering the Square. People were yelling. People were waving placards. The Klan had flags to wave and so paid no attention to the placards, or to anyone. Suddenly, I felt we were all punched out of cardboard. I felt mechanical and emotionally hollow. I thought of a poem by Robert Hass describing his experiences in the South. One line stuck and stayed:

Everything is easy, but wrong . . .

V

At Shiloh Battlefield Park there's a ditch in which men are buried. Several ditches, actually. Once, I stood on the edge of one. A film at the tourist information center said the men in this ditch were put there by Grant after the battle. So many people had been killed, and he didn't have time to bury them all. He was afraid of contagion and counterattack. He was in Tennessee with an army of men who'd just received a baptism of fire at Shiloh. He had a lot of wounded people, and he was in confused control of an area vital to the South. Dead people were not something he could spend much time worrying with. He buried them in mass graves, and if he couldn't trouble with ceremony, he couldn't trouble with distinction. He just shoveled them in regardless of rank or the color of the uniform.

When the battlefield became a park the dead in these ditches were exhumed and sorted. What identification that was possible was made, and the Union dead were transported to the national cemetery established on the park grounds. The Confederate dead were put back into the ditch. With what ceremony, I don't know.

The ditch I stood on the lip of was bordered by cannon balls freshly painted a shiny black. It was off the main track, but there was a marker saying where it was. I thought about the men in this ditch. If given a choice, would they want to be left here instead of the national cemetery? I'm sure they don't qualify to be put there. I'm sure there's a law somewhere that says they can't be, but I wondered about it. They died as a part of the stupidity that was the Civil War, and though they died on the wrong side, they are a part of what this nation did to itself during that period. And they're buried in a ditch.

And again, I thought about it and thought that maybe they'd have preferred to be in the ditch rather than the national cemetery . . . a last act of defiance. Which only goes to prove that anything can be romanticized if you're Southern.

I tried to imagine what I'd want if I was dead and in the ditch. I decided that I probably would have opted just to be alive. Beyond that, I doubt I would have cared about the uniform.

Finally, I realized that it wasn't a question of what they wanted, but of what had been done. We recognize our obligation to the dead by covering them up and getting on with being alive. If they do anything at all, they probably envy us, but for all that, they're probably most content when not being dragged about.

I tried to explain the people in the ditch to a friend. She said, "I never realized that you were so *Southern!*" I hadn't thought of it as any particular regionalism, certainly not in terms of *We got to git our boys outten that ditch!* But on the other hand, I didn't feel moved about the Indians at the Little Big Horn or wonder about the Mexican dead at San Jacinto.

The question suddenly enlarged. Was I that Southern? What did *that* mean? I did a quick inventory and found that I lacked most southern accouterments, but I also knew that I'd probably never live outside the South.

My friend and I talked about it some and never came to any conclusions . . . this dead versus that dead, this heritage implying these preconceptions. We finally opted for beer and the late show. We turned on the television just in time to find out what we missed. It was *Rebel Without a Cause*.

Irony is inherent in a southern point of view.

VI

As I hurried up the street toward the Square where the rally was to be held, I passed a group of black students who told me they'd come from Jackson for the rally. They were holding placards. A woman with them asked me politely, cautiously, which side I was on. I told her that I just came to see what would happen. She seemed satisfied.

When I reached the Square, the Klan was marching across the other side. The crowd was thick around them, so I cut across the Square to the courthouse and waited. On the far side of the Square, under a large oak tree on the edge of the courthouse lawn, the Klan stopped and began to arrange themselves in something of a line facing the assembling crowd. Several of them, all larger men, faced the courthouse. These men wore mirrored shades.

The crowd assembled around this nucleus.

From somewhere, a bull-horn was produced and started up. Much static, and a sound quality like a can opener cutting through galvanized tin. The first speaker was a plump, pale man whose hair touched his eyebrows. He was to introduce Gordon Galle. He addressed us, smiling slightly. "We are the Imperial Knights of the Ku Klux Klan. We want to thank you for turning out—whether or not you support us—because at least you'll hear what we have to say."

I thought of my friends, at home and spared.

The first speaker droned on. The reaction, which he ignored, was a varied patina of taunts and jeers. He did, however, secure some applause with one thing he said: *We're here to support the Rebel flag*.

Eventually, he introduced Gordon Galle, the principal speaker. Galle looked like a car salesman who'd stumbled into costume, into Oxford, and into the parade. His speech was a disconnected series of emphatics, a jumble, owing as much to the range of his obsessions as to the fact that the issues he addressed were negligible. I knelt in the crowd and took notes, preserving intact some of his speech:

> We're here to defend the Rebel flag! Don't sit down and let these people destroy the most sacred symbol of the South!
>
> We stand against the perverts, the dope pushers, the homosexuals.
>
> This is a race war!
>
> The only thing that will satisfy blacks is when you're six feet under or out in the cotton patch!
>
> We're laying our lives on the line! We're out here with our women. Any one of you people could pull out a machine gun and kill us all!

After speaking, Galle and his followers regrouped to march to the parking lot of the Old Miss School of Law. The crowd pressed close around them as they marched away. A car spangled with Rebel flags crawled slowly behind the column of Klansmen. Inside the car was a woman and a sleeping child. The woman rolled down the window just enough to speak through and was providing a running commentary on the crowd, the march, the Klan, and the *future*. People got mad.

I went in the opposite direction with a handful of notes and into a restaurant to sort them out to get something to eat. A writer for *The Daily Mississippian* joined me. She told me how, back at the parking lot, she'd been in on an informal instructional on the hierarchy of the Klan by Galle. They, the reporters, were introduced to the Klan Kleagle. The Kleagle explained the responsibilities of the job and asked if there were any questions. One reporter asked him if he could spell the unfamiliar title.

He paused for a moment and then said, "No ma'am, I can't."

I started to laugh. Harshly, automatically, it cranked itself out.

FROM

Christmas Gif'

CHARLEMAE ROLLINS

FOREWORD

THE NAME OF this anthology represents much to me—the pleasure of giving, and recollections of a happy tradition that had its origins in the days of slavery. The custom of "Christmas Gif'" has been a part of the holiday celebration in my family for as long as I can remember.

As a child I spent much time with my grandmother, who had been a slave. From her I learned that "Christmas Gif'" was a surprise game played by the slaves on Christmas Day. Two people, meeting for the first time that day, would compete to be the first to call out, "Christmas Gif'!" The loser happily paid a forfeit of a simple present—maybe a Christmas tea cake or a handful of nuts. Truly, there was more pleasure in being "caught," and having to give a present—the giving, though comically protested, was heartwarming to a people who had so little they could with dignity share with others.

The practice of "Christmas Gif'" spread from the slave cabins to the "Big House," and soon became a traditional part of the celebration of Christmas, a joyful time felt and shared even by an enslaved people.

Over the years, in my experience as a librarian, I have been asked by teachers and parents and children for Christmas stories and poems specifically related to Negroes. I have found such material in old magazines, in collections of the works of Negro writers, but never have I found one single book about the Negro and Christmas. I felt there was a place for such a book, and that is how *Christmas Gif'* began. It is a book for people of all ages, for families to read together, for everyone to enjoy. . . .

It is my earnest hope that this book may help every reader to appreciate the Negro's contribution to the love and reverence, the joy and brotherhood, that is the universal spirit of Christmas.

Christmas Recipes from the "Big House" and the Cabin

The slave cooks were famous for their rich and varied foods. The most renowned were the female slaves who cooked solely for "Ol' Massa" and his family in the "Big House." The slave owner took pride as the fame of his table spread throughout the immediate area. The slave cook was valued highly, and she was justifiably proud of her work. It was not at all unusual to find a rather autocratic slave cook, who held sway over the kitchen helpers, enjoyed a status higher than that of the field hand, and was given special liberties by her owner. Pride in her work, and the subsequent pleasing of her master, insured a continuation of the slave cook's favorable status. She further utilized this freedom by using a lavish hand when working with choice cuts of meat, thick cream, spices, and other ingredients.

Not so lucky was the slave who cooked for her own family. To her went the lest desirable of foodstuffs—the head, feet, and tail of the pig, while the choice hams and cuts of meat suitable for roasting went to the "Big House." The slave family cook, however, used imagination, and with the ingredients at hand, created dishes to provide a welcome variety to the monotony of a diet composed of the inexpensive, bulky foodstuffs allocated by her owner. Both cooks used ingredients native to the region: unrefined sugar, molasses, cornmeal, nutmeats—some plentiful, some available only in limited quantities, but all used with ingenuity. Regardless of the location of the kitchen, the slave cook passed on recipes by word of mouth. Few recipes ever were written down.

The recipes that I have included here represent some from the "Big House," and some from the cabin. Most of the recipes came to me from my grandmother; others are family recipes given to me by friends. The recipes only recently were written down; formerly they were verbal instructions, and contained such picturesque directions as, "Use a piece of butter the size of your fist"; "Throw a handful of rice in the pot"; "Use a smidgin of sage"; "Punch holes in the top of biscuit dough with a five-tine' fork." The recipes have been slightly adapted to conform with modern cookery, but I have attempted to retain their unique character.

Most of these recipes were used only for Christmas week, a time for the most lavish cooking of the year. Nuts, gathered in the fall of the year, were saved especially for this time. My grandmother and her contemporaries started their cooking the week before Christmas; then, freed from the labor of the fields, time would be spent more happily in the cookshed. Working hard, no good cook would ever let Christmas "catch" her with less than six cakes, and a dozen assorted pies, prepared and waiting in the "safe" for Christmas guests. The "safe" was a fly-proof cupboard with shelves, the top doors of which were made of tin, punctured in a perforated design. The perforations served as vents to let in cool air to preserve the food. Into the "safe" at Christmas week, went also tea cakes, baked chicken, roast wild turkey, duck and goose.

At Christmas time, tea cakes were made in abundance. These simple nutmeg-flavored sugar cookies were standard equipment in any "safe." They were useful for passing out on the call of "Christmas Gif'!" Other times of the year, tea cakes were made sparingly as a simple dessert, for my grandmother recalled that no long journey was ever made without taking along "a flour sack half-full of tea cakes."

TEA CAKES

(approximately 24 small cakes)

3½ cups sifted flour
1 teaspoon baking soda
½ teaspoon salt
½ cup butter
1 cup sugar
2 beaten eggs
1 teaspoon vanilla
½ teaspoon nutmeg
½ cup thick sour cream

Sift together flour, baking soda, and salt. Cream butter and sugar. Add beaten eggs, vanilla, and nutmeg. Alternately add flour mixture and sour cream. Beat until smooth. Roll out on floured board to ¼-inch thickness. Sprinkle lightly with sugar. Place on well-greased baking sheet, and bake at 450°F. about 12 minutes, until golden brown. When cool, using cooky cutter or knife, cut into sections suitable for serving.

SPOON BREAD

(4 servings)

1 pint milk
1 cup cornmeal
2 tablespoons butter
4 eggs
1 teaspoon baking powder

Place milk in top of double boiler and heat to scalding. Slowly add cornmeal and whip with beater until smooth. Add butter and cook for 20 minutes. Separate eggs; add beaten yolks and 1 teaspoon baking powder to mixture. Beat egg whites until they peak; fold in. Pour into well-greased baking dish and bake at 350°F. for 45 minutes.

Serve hot with sausages for Christmas breakfast.

"HOG'S-HEAD" CHEESE

(12–14 servings)

1 pig's head
4 pig's feet
2 pig's ears
2 medium-size onions, whole
1 bunch celery, including leafy tops
2 bay leaves
¼ teaspoon cayenne pepper
1 teaspoon black pepper
2 tablespoons salt
1 cup vinegar

Place pig's head, feet, and ears in large, deep pot, and add water to cover. Add all seasonings except vinegar; cover pot and boil over low flame 2–3 hours until meat leaves bone. Mince meat coarsely; arrange in mold or pan. Add vinegar to juice remaining in pot. Pour this liquid over meat in mold; refrigerate until mold has set, or congealed. When cold, slice and serve.

FROM

Mississippi: The Closed Society

JAMES W. SILVER

FROM THE WHITE HOUSE at eight o'clock on the night of September 30, 1962, John F. Kennedy began to plead eloquently with Mississippi students to understand that they must not interfere with the court-ordered admission of Negro James Howard Meredith to their University. Unknown to the President, at almost exactly the moment his sober face appeared on television screens across the nation, tear gas was being fired by United States marshals into an unruly crowd in front of the Lyceum Building on the Ole Miss campus. Choking and gasping, the spectators fell back across the Circle toward the Confederate monument, pursued by the marshals as far as the flag pole.

Within ten minutes, five or six green army sedans, each carrying six white-helmeted marshals, came over the Illinois Central bridge, which spans Hilgard Cut between the campus and the town of Oxford, and moved toward the Lyceum. As they made the slow turn to the right at the Confederate monument, they were assaulted with a hail of bricks thrown at close range. Windshields and car windows were smashed. My wife and I could see the men inside huddling to protect themselves from the splintering glass. The pounding of the bricks on the cars and the screams—"The sons of bitches have killed a coed." "We'll kill the bastards." "We'll get the God-damned marshals!"—these, plus shrill cries of filth and obscenity, proved that eighteen- and nineteen-year-old students had suddenly been turned into wild animals.

My wife and I suspected then that we were in for a night of terror. Earlier in the afternoon, warned by our nine-year-old daughter Gail, who had heard the news over the radio, we had driven out to the airport to watch the arrival of the marshals and Justice Department officials, little dreaming of the agony in store for us. As our University-owned home is only a half mile from the administration building (Lyceum), which had been requisitioned for federal headquarters, we could not have avoided the excitement had we wished to do so. In front of that majestic ante-bellum structure, both of us did what little we could to help maintain the calm that prevailed until after six o'clock, partly by carrying to those assembled the Chancellor's message that the marshals and the Mississippi Highway Patrol were acting in concert to keep order. Governor Ross Barnett had finally capitulated to federal authority; had, in fact, selected Sunday for the admission of Meredith—that was the word.

The hour before eight was filled with apprehension and foreboding as demonstrations and violence increased, and once the tear gas was fired we moved slowly back, comfortably out of range, past the flag pole to the old Science Building. When the army cars came by, we were sitting on the edge of the Cardinal Club memorial; I was nursing a couple of cracked-open knees, having been accidentally tripped and knocked to the concrete crosswalk by a large Confederate flagstaff carried by a young man in more of a hurry than we. Already the students were yelling about regrouping to attack and about keeping up the attack on the marshals until their ammunition ran out.

It is not my purpose to recount the frightening events of that unbelievable night of passion and fury. Separated more often than not, my wife and I were once more together between two and three o'clock in the morning of October first, at the side of the Chancellor's house, facing the Grove. Two contingents of federal troops, about a hundred men in each, newly arrived from the airport, marched by in full battle dress. As they turned the Circle, away from the pre-Civil War "Y" building and toward the Fine Arts Center, these American soldiers were assailed with fire bombs. We saw two sheets of flame about the size of our small house fall among the troops. They hardly got out of step. Only a miracle kept any number from catching on fire. Their colonel later said that if a single man had been seriously burned, both squads would have wheeled and turned their guns on the rioters in the smoke-filled Circle. By this time the student insurrectionists were far outnumbered by other Mississippians, to whom had been added a few unsavory out-of-state volunteers.

There were other occasions that night when a tragic event lacked only a hair of expanding into a holocaust—when, for instance, the marshals' supply of tear gas was twice almost miraculously saved from exhaustion by a daring truck driver who ran gauntlets of stones and gasoline-fueled fire. Disciplined as they proved themselves to be, the marshals would not have submitted to savage personal beatings without resorting to their firearms.

As it was, the manly bearing of the hastily gathered marshals fighting for their lives and the exemplary conduct of the Mississippi National Guardsmen and the regular soldiers are matters for great American pride. Like many observers, I was alternately enraged and heartsick that my fellow Mississippians, particularly the students, felt called upon to engage in a mad insurrection against their own government. To me it was and still is nothing less than incredible. Later, when the state of Mississippi was being flooded from within by malignant propaganda about what had happened at Ole Miss that fateful night, I felt a growing compulsion to try to tell the truth, to relate in plain fashion what had taken place, and then to put it all in historical perspective. For more than a year and a half this has been in my mind and in my heart—my wife says that I am obsessed with the subject. The result of my thought and study and research is in this book.

I have tried to approach an intensely emotional subject without sentimentality. I am no longer angry with anyone. I have found it necessary to criticize the conduct of certain individuals, some of whom have been my friends. While names have been kept to a minimum and language has been restrained, and while nothing has been put down in malice, I am quite sure that the feelings of some will be hurt by these pages. I will be deeply sorry for such an outcome, but the need for telling the story is greater than the importance of protecting personal feelings, whether those of fellow Mississippians or my own.

It has been suggested to me by well-meaning people that we ought to forget the recent nightmare, to put it in the past where bad dreams belong. And go on from there. The sad truth is that within minutes of the start of the insurrection such a course became impossible for me. For what was happening was distorted with passionate and deliberate speed and was made into the inspiration for some future insanity, an insanity just as inevitable as the bloodshed at Ole Miss. The point is that when people are told from every public rostrum in the state on every day of their lives—and such is the case with the undergraduates who assaulted the marshals—that no authority on earth can legally or morally require any change in the traditional terms of Mississippi social life, this very process generates conditions that will explode into riot and insurrection.

Less than a week after the murder of four Negro children in a Birmingham church, the Mississippi State Sovereignty Commission, that curious arm of the state legislature, unanimously endorsed the behavior of Alabama's Governor George C. Wallace in "standing in the schoolhouse door" to oppose the admission of two qualified Negroes to the University of Alabama, a masquerade of resistance to the will of the nation as expressed by the federal courts. In the summer of 1963 both the Sovereignty Commission and the State Building Commission were willing to risk the accreditation of every state college and university by holding up the diploma of James Meredith. Such actions not only indicate that Mississippi has officially learned nothing; they may well be considered to foreshadow future disaster. Some day Mississippians are going to have to grow up, to accept the judgments of civilization. Else we are doomed to many September 30ths to come.

I am reminded, perhaps presumptuously, of Lucius Quintus Cincinnatus Lamar. In another time of stress that distinguished Mississippian, a man who knew how to serve first his state and then his state and nation in the reunited republic, said: "Upon the youth of my state it has been my privilege to assist in education I have always endeavored to impress the belief that truth was better than falsehood, honesty better than policy, courage better than cowardice."

In more than a quarter of a century at the University, it has been my good fortune to know some truly remarkable native Mississippians, among them David L. Cohn, Robert J. Farley, James P. Coleman, James Howard Meredith, Aaron Henry, and William Faulkner. These six men, beyond all others, have influenced my thought and action.

After several months' pleading on my part, Bill Faulkner agreed to participate in what turned out to be the most exciting meeting in the history of the Southern Historical Association: a discussion of the Supreme Court's 1954 segregation decisions with Benjamin Mays, president of Morehouse College, and Cecil Sims, an eminent Nashville lawyer. The occasion was an integrated dinner in the Peabody Hotel in Memphis, in early November, 1955, at the very time that white supremacists were congratulating themselves on the outcome of the trial of two white men accused of kidnaping and murdering Emmett Till. In a way this session revealed, as Bell Wiley has pointed out in his introduction to the published transcript of the proceedings, "the existence of another and a liberal South—soft-spoken and restrained, but articulate and powerful—that is earnestly pledged to moderation and reason."

My purpose in bringing up the Memphis meeting is not to recall Sims' calm and judicial analysis of the legal implications of the segregation decision, or Mays' impassioned commentary on the immorality of segregation, or even Faulkner's admonition that "To live anywhere in the world of A.D. 1955 and be against equality because of race or color, is like living in Alaska and being against snow." It is to remind myself that less than ten years ago, when it was decided to publish *Three Views of the Segregation Decisions,* my friends and I were in agreement that if my connection with the pamphlet were known my job as chairman of the department of history at the University of Mississippi would be jeopardized. This was at a time when the Citizens Council was in the "town meeting" stage of its infancy! A *Clarion-Ledger* columnist from the state capital in Jackson made his customary assault on the publication when it came out, though he apparently never learned of my connection with it. A year or so later an indignant alumnus formally protested to the Board of Trustees that I had presided over the "Faulkner" meeting, which, of course, I could deny, inasmuch as the chairman and toastmaster had been well-known Mississippi expatriates, one the head of the history department at the University of Kentucky, and the other the president of the University of Louisville.

In a more lasting if less amusing way, this meeting profoundly influenced my own thinking and subsequent conduct. Emphasizing his hope that the speeches would be printed and distributed by "southern amateurs," Faulkner readily consented to the use of his own talk. On December 1, 1955, on my request for a short statement that might be added to the introduction to the pamphlet, Faulkner slipped a rather soiled sheet of yellow scrap paper into his battered old typewriter and, as if he had been musing over the matter all morning, quickly tapped out these words:

> The question is no longer of white against black. It is no longer whether or not white blood shall remain pure, it is whether or not white people shall remain free.
>
> We accept contumely and the risk of violence because we will not sit quietly by and see our native land, the South, not just Mississippi but all the South, wreck and ruin itself twice in less than a hundred years, over the Negro question.
>
> We speak now against the day when our Southern people who will resist to the last these inevitable changes in social relations, will, when they have been forced to accept what they at one time might have accepted with dignity and goodwill, will say, "Why didn't someone tell us this before? Tell us this in time."

This message from William Faulkner is one of my most prized possessions. Add to it a few words from *Intruder in the Dust* and one has a firm basis for "standing up to be counted" when the proper time arises: "Some things you must always be unable to bear. Some things you must never stop refusing to bear. Injustice and outrage and dishonor and shame. No matter how young you are or how old you have got. Not for kudos and not for cash; your picture in the paper nor money in the bank either. Just refuse to bear them."

In spite of a few statements to the contrary, sometimes by people who should have known better, and in spite of a general confusion in the mind of the public, there never has been any real uncertainty about Faulkner's long view on the question of Negro equality. He was sure, as he said in his speech to the Southern Historical Association, that the Negro "knows there is no such thing as equality *per se*, but only equality *to:* equal right and opportunity to make the best one can of one's life within one's capability, without fear of injustice or oppression or threat of violence."

William Faulkner assisted in a minor way in the publication, in 1956, of the only issue of the *Southern Reposure*, a modest satire on white supremacy which never once mentioned the colored man. Thousands of copies were mailed out in Mississippi but the "southern amateurs" involved were unable to pool their resources for another number. In his own home that fall, Faulkner met three or four times with a handful of Oxonians, including a minister, a bank president, an editor, a prominent businessman, and a couple of professors, to talk over the prospect of setting up a "moderate" organization to counter the Citizens Council. He was greatly perturbed over the growing strength and arrogance of the radical right. I remember with clarity one evening in particular in which he sat on a straight chair to the right of the glowing fireplace in his library. He never was one for extended conversation, but he said over and over, as if to himself, "We are sitting on top of a powder keg." After a slight survey of sentiment among the men doing business on the Oxford Square, it was concluded that the local Citizens Council would never get off the ground if it were ignored. In general this has been the case, for the Council chapter in Lafayette County has neither gained respectability nor attracted intelligent leadership. Whether the little band of moderates gathered in the Faulkner home could have helped forestall the amazing Council development in the rest of Mississippi is now anyone's guess.

Never an activist, and in his last years spending more and more time in Virginia, William Faulkner made few further pronouncements on the race question. Neither did he change his mind, as some have indicated. The last time I talked with him about the Mississippi situation—or anything else—was on the day he voted enthusiastically for the moderate, Frank Smith, for Congress, on June 5, 1962. A month later he was dead.

FROM

God's Step Chilluns

Ann Odene Smith

Moonlight poured through the large cracks of the wall, making senseless and strange patterns on the floor. Stars in the sky winked cheerily at me. The soft mattress was uncomfortable, and the brightness of the night came through the shadeless window and reflected off the newspaper covered walls. Maybe I could have slept had it not been for the stink of a big, grunting hog which lived under the floor of my room. Each time it coughed, my room shook. It must have been ill. Only the warped floorboards separated the huge hog from me. We were almost sharing the same room.

I wasn't complaining. The choice had been mine. I was a rural school teacher in the most needed location. Happily, that was the last thought I remember. I must have slept.

A soft knock and someone calling. Several moments passed before the reality of my situation became clear. Fumbling in the morning darkness, I got into my robe. Opening the door, I found my landlady, a hot kettle of water in one hand and the brand new tin washpan in the other.

"Good mawning!" she beamed. "Hate ter be so early, but hits time to git up! Here's your water and your breakfast is ready."

I thanked her and took the water and the shiny new pan.

"Mrs. Chase, I can't see a thing in here. May I have a light, please?"

After my abbreviated bath, I went into the kitchen and sat at a crudely, but strongly built wooden table. The seat was a heavy slab of timber nailed to two thick wooden blocks. The wood stove had no oven door and smoke and sparks could be seen through the rusted-out holes.

I sat down to breakfast.

The hot, heavy biscuits, the crispy fatback and the thick, black sorghum on the table were welcome, but my appetite was not for food. I was hungry to see my first classroom and my first students.

Excitement was unconcealable. MY FIRST DAY AS A RURAL SCHOOL TEACHER! I wanted to run to that little one-roomed building in the middle of the pasture. The two Chase grandchildren ran before Mr. Chase and me. Of course, I could have kept up with them easily, but the old man would not have been able to. I walked as fast as I dared to. My heart was saying run, but my maturity said, "Take it easy!"

Mr. Chase looked up at me and smiled, showing his one long, tobacco-stained tooth. "Miss Smif, you know you is the purtiest teechur us is evvr had. I been truste for 'bout thurty years. If I wuz a young man, I'd shore come courtin' you."

I smiled at his effort to make me feel welcome to the strange and new community.

Rounding a bend in the road, I got a glimpse of the unpainted building. A small group of children stood in nervous anticipation on the bare, clay yard. Two mules, several horses and a small herd of cattle grazed lazily in the morning sun. My heart beat furiously as I tried to compose myself and rid myself of the impulse to run.

"Thar she is!" Mr. Chase grinned. "Thas our church too!" He beamed proudly. The next few yards were like trying to push the entire world with a broomstraw. My urge to investigate, to get acquainted, to begin was so strong! Yet, finally, I reached Marks Chapel.

Mr. Chase, whom I later learned to call Uncle Ben, introduced me to the trustees and parents. My eyes were on the children. Never had I seen nor had I expected to see such a forsaken looking bunch of children.

The school's morning devotion would have put to shame an old fashion revival meeting, and through it all I observed each child. Their voices were melodious and strong as they sang the old hymns. Deacon Green prayed a long, soul-saving, fire-and-damnation prayer, and Trustee Sims stumbled through one of the Psalms. Another short hymn, and devotion was over.

Now, each trustee made me publicly welcome and each promised to be at my beck and call. Uncle Ben murmured the benediction and I began to register the children.

Jessie Mae Brown was the first to register her child. Little Bertha Lee was a tiny child of seven years old. Timidly, she stood before me with her little, skinny finger in her mouth. Her big, pretty brown eyes shown in her black, smooth face. Her uncombed hair was decorated with a few cockle burrs and a great deal of cotton lint. Her feet were as bare and as dusty as they could be. Only her clean, flour-sack dress showed any signs of cleanliness. Her mother was also barefoot and very, very overweight. Her gingham, unironed dress was much too short and too small. It was the light of love on her face, the concern for her little girl that brought a lump to my throat. In that first registration, in that little child, and in her mother, I understood my being a teacher. I understood my position and placement.

The impact and realization of the needs and of the condition of these people was greater than I had dreamed. Silently, I prayed to God for his help and for guidance for a fruitful term at this place.

By noon, I had registered fifty-four distinctly different, and very needy personalities. Some had been registered by older children. Ages ranged from five to nineteen years old and grades ranged from pre-primer to eighth grade.

Flora Jones called me aside to tell me that her children could not attend until the cotton was all picked. Willie Mae Dibbs and others had the same excuse.

Watching the children and parents who had to leave brought tears to my eyes. I wanted to draw them back to the school, and my love for them reached out vainly and silently. Away they went down the dusty road as if in haste to return to the fields and get the cotton picked as quickly as possible.

I felt sad and a little disappointed to find myself almost alone. Only sixteen children were left with me. The remaining adult, Mr. Sims, suggested it would be best to dismiss and get myself together for the next day.

Walking home with me, Mr. Sims told me of the poverty, the inhumane treatment of some of the share hands. Mr. Sims was one of the few blacks who owned land here. He told me about his little farm and the fact that he worked by the day for some of the white landowners. He confided that he was called a "crazy nigger" by some because he refused to be shortchanged. If he worked, he worked an eight hour day and expected, and received, his correct wages. He was not a man to argue with. Looking at his muscles, I felt that no one would want to fight him. His tar black, smooth and handsome face showed both emotional and spiritual strength of character.

Little Bill and Celeste were waiting to show me my lunch when I reached home. Their neatly starched and ironed clothes had been exchanged for clean and patched work clothes. After showing me my food, they skipped away to the cotton field.

The loneliness was soothing. As far as my eyes could see, there were large fields of cotton that stretched out like giant, white sheets. A great patch of yellow and brown corn covered part of the landscape. In the distance, and surrounding the fields were dense, green forests. Evergreen trees of pine and cedar sat solidly against the brown-oranges, yellows, and reds of autumn. The land was rolling and very rich. The cotton close to the house had been picked.

I walked through the field, meditating. Looking back on the old house, I shuddered at having slept there the night before. The kitchen sat on the ground, and bricks from a long unused fireplace lay scattered about the yard. Long logs lay on pieces of brick to protect the wood from burning. I still don't understand why they didn't burn. The rest of the house sat on log blocks and old shingles covered the roof, reinforced by pieces of rusty tin and pieces of roofing. Around the sides of the house, the boards were rotted and falling apart. In places, pieces of tin had been used to keep out the cold. However, there were still cracks in the room in which I had slept. A big hog-pen was built against the side of the house.

I wondered if the hogs would come into the house if the floor got any weaker.

The sound of an approaching wagon drew my attention. The Chases were returning from the fields, tired and dusty. I realized that I'd had the luxury of spending an entire afternoon with my thoughts.

I watched as poor Uncle Ben lowered his tired, aged body to the ground and opened the cotton house door. The cotton house was the only decent building here. Little Bill drove the wagon to the door and with the help of little Celeste emptied the big sacks of cotton into it. Mrs. Chase and Uncle Ben began throwing armfuls from the wagon as the two children stomped it down, packing it tightly. For a moment, bitter thoughts came to me. Here, in this age and time, these two old people, along with their grand-children, slaved and were underpaid for their hard labor. Their struggle only made the rich richer. Mrs. Chase, overweight from eating too much flour bread, fatback, and sorghum molasses, suffered with serious hypertension. Uncle Ben was skinny and puny and old. It was a page from past history. Bill and Celeste knew no other way of life. Too bad their mother had not taken them with her when she ran away from home. Too bad she hadn't taken the whole family.

Little Bill washed his hands and went to milk the old Jersey cow. Celeste fed the hogs.

I soon discovered that offering my help to Mrs. Chase to prepare supper was an insult: "No mam, Miss Smif, nobody want the teacher to help cook. No mam! You ain't got to do no wek here!"

Supper was extra special. Croquettes of Eat Well Mackerel, fried salt pork, piping hot biscuits, collard greens, and Kool Aid were served. This was an unusual menu for me. Nevertheless, it was quite delicious.

Shortly after supper, elated, exhausted and full, I said a prayer and crawled into my very soft feather bed. As the hogs grunted and coughed, I slept soundly.

I was up extra early the next morning, raring to go to my little school house in the pasture.

Marks Chapel was a one-roomed, one-story, square building. Once upon a time, the rough, weather-beaten boards had been stained in red barn paint. Inside, there were no sealed walls, nor sealed lofts. A big, rough-lumber door graced the front of the building. A smaller, heavy, rough door was at the rear of the building. The well-scrubbed floor had almost turned white. The front of the building was graced with a raised platform on which sat a homemade pulpit. Several straw-bottomed chairs sat around the little platform. A lovely, antique chair sat close to the pulpit. I was glad to see there was a piano. On the north end of the building was a very worn desk and its chair. A dozen rough, worn, homemade benches sat in two neat rows of six each. Three lights hung on long cords from the high "V" shaped ceiling. Around the wall, kerosene lamps with blackened shades hung. A wide board nailed to the wall at the rear of the building served as a cabinet to hold the tin cans and mayonnaise jars which were used for drinking glasses. A large, galvanized pail sat along with them. Glancing upward to the ceiling, I saw the lovely art work of countless spiders, hornets, wasps, and dirt daubers. Opening the back door I saw a large, short log to serve in the place of steps.

The view from the back door was beautiful. A large pasture was behind the building. The land was rolling and specked with autumn flowers, trees, a few cattle, blue morning sky and bright sunshine above.

After getting acquainted with the physical layout of the school, I wondered about the water supply. There was no cistern nor well in sight. I was also worried about the books. When I went to separate and make inventory of them, several frightening mice jumped from the big musky boxes in which the books had been stored. The foul odor of rat infestation and rotting paper stung my nostrils. I found roaches and a nest of little baby rats in the boxes before I emptied them. I cleaned and stacked the books and placed the damaged ones in a box for burning.

Little Bertha Lee was the first to arrive. The only difference in her appearance from the day before was that she was much filthier, and she smelled strongly of urine.

Overwhelmed with love and pity for the little child, I embraced her. To my surprise, she put her little arms about my neck and kissed my cheek. From my bag, I took my comb and brush and carefully combed and brushed her hair. I braided it as neatly as possible. There was no water to wash the dirt and grime from her face.

By 8:40 all sixteen of my regular students had arrived. Some had walked ten miles "as the snake crawls." A few had come on mule back. However the mode of transportation, I was thankful they were there.

The family from across the creek in the other county explained the importance of having to leave early. The ten miles each way was a long walk for the smaller kids. Whenever it looked like rain, they would leave for home immediately, because if the creek rose it would be impossible to get home at all. These students from across the creek were big and strong. Big Eddie, the oldest, was eighteen and at least six feet four inches tall. I should have been afraid of him, but I wasn't. He would sit and stare at me in adoration. I wondered what I could or would do if he became angry.

The Burns family was one of the few fortunate black families who owned a few acres of land. The Burns were able to attend school on a regular basis.

After the noon break, I was pleasantly surprised to have another family arrive. Mr. Haney was as black as a man can possibly be, and so were the neatly dressed children that he brought with him. The twin boys were dressed in brand new overalls and shiny brown brogan shoes. The little girl was dressed in a pretty gingham dress and a pair of black, high-topped shoes. The little girl was eight and the twins were twelve. There were other children in the family who would be attending later.

I learned many things about the Mr. Reverend Haney. Mr. Haney was a "jack-leg preacher" and a very stern man. He was a Negro without any mixture. He was a proud, independent, black man made in the image of the Creator God. He was not a loud mouthed braggart. He was mild-mannered and modest, a God-fearing man. I knew from my interview with him that he had brought up his children in the fear and in the love of God. He owed nothing to no man that he would not pay. Yet, for all his mild manneredness, I never saw him smile. He left after having registered his five children.

With grades ranging from Big Primer to eighth, coupled with the vast differences in age, I felt that I had an impossible job to do. But I also felt that I was just the teacher to accomplish the impossible. God was going to answer my prayers for the strength, wisdom, and guidance to accomplish what I purposed to do.

This was only the beginning of the school term, yet some of the children began asking about school programs. They informed me that the usual practice here was to present frequent entertainment for the community. It seemed that the progress of the school depended on "school programs." In addition to the programs which the teachers and pupils presented, there were frequent quartet contests. The yearly event of summer revivals was third in importance.

From the reports of these children, I learned that too much precious time had been used in the past for rehearsals. There had been too little time spent in actually learning. The children, most of them, showed disappointment in my attitude and expectations. They were here to learn, and I was here to teach reading, writing, arithmetic, English, history, and the purpose of the process of education. I was not surprised that the learning process and the idea of education had not been instilled into their minds. My committment and concerns were made as clear and as simple as possible. My expectations were emphasized. After all of this, my students and I made one another a promise: If satisfactory progress was made in the few months before the end of the year, their program would be allowed—but never once a month as they were accustomed to.

Working diligently and earnestly with the students, definite progress was made. This had been accomplished with a sincere love, patience, and understanding. The interest in education itself had caught on.

Because of my stand on physical punishment, a rumor started in the neighborhood. It was rumored that Miss Smith was afraid to whip the children. Physical punishment was simply not my way of doing things. The older children were usually very cooperative. If there were minor problems, an older sister or brother corrected the little sister or brother. The teenaged children respected me even though I was only slightly older and definitely smaller than most of them. They were learning what school was all about.

After Thanksgiving, most of the cotton had been picked and the corn had been pulled. The classroom began to fill. With the late pupils came new problems. The teenaged girls, having heard that there were no whippings, decided to try "the new teacher."

Fights began between the late-comers and the ones who had attended from the first of the session. Keeping students after school brought results. The trustees paid me a visit, and informed me that it was customary to "put a rattan on their backs." I disagreed. I informed the trustees that I was there to teach and not to whip, and if ever there were serious problems, the guilty student would be expelled.

The fighting continued. Convinced that the children expected to be whipped, and were, in a way, daring me to whip them, I had to make a stand.

Everyone was quiet when Big Eddie arrived with a bunch of rattans over six feet long. For some, it was the rule of the rod! Before the day was over, I had firmly convinced several that Miss Smith was not afraid of any of them.

For one half an hour, I talked to the children trying to convince them that it was better to sit quietly, listen, and learn than to start confusion, and to get along on the playground without the fights. I asked the reasons for their fighting and disturbances. Sadly, it seemed that that was a way of life with a few. It seemed to give them something to do.

After having been there for three months, I decided that it was time to begin attending church services. My first was the second Sunday in December.

The deacons opened the church service with the singing of hymns. The scripture was read and a long prayer was made. The services were the same as the first day of school.

The tall, freckled, yellow man sitting in the preacher's seat stood up and said, "Let everybody say Amen!" Taking his text from somewhere in the Bible, he began to preach. His voice got louder and louder! He began moaning and groaning and gasping for breath. Women began to moan. The louder they moaned, the more fervent the sermon. He yelled about the hard times, hard trials and tribulations. He screamed about meeting his mother and his father in heaven. The deacons were saying "Amen" and cheering him on. Women began shouting; hats and wigs were flying through the air. Pocket books flew across the benches and women were jumping up and down. Some fainted and had to be carried from the building. I did not fully understand the actions nor the reasons for them.

After more than an hour of this very lively service, the pastor, all wet with sweat, sat down. It was time for the "surcument." As the grape juice and soda crackers were passed around, the congregation sang, "Dark Was the Night and Cold the Ground on Which My Lawd Was Laid." It was a very touching hymn. After this, the doors of the church were opened. No one joined.

After this emotional experience, the pastor came back to the little pulpit. He announced his need for a raise in salary. The congregation gave him a wave of big "Amens!" Through all of this, I wondered just how this would be accomplished. The people could hardly live now.

The people lingered long after the services as this was their only time for visiting. Many had brought food for the younger children to eat. I was offered baked potatoes, jelly cake, and crackling bread. The pastor was having dinner at the Chase home.

I mingled with the congregation, and became acquainted with people I had not met, and talked with those whom I had met.

Sunday dinner at the Chase home was unusually sumptuous.

Chicken was always prepared for preachers. Maybe that's why they are so often called "chicken eaters." On the table were fried chicken, chicken and dumplings, potatoes, rice and gravy, jelly cake, okra, a pot of peas, hot cornbread, and biscuits.

I had decided on a Christmas program for the students. We began work on it a week before it was to be presented. I knew the capabilities of each child. They could do it with the few days left before I would be leaving for the two-week Christmas vacation.

Cold winds knifed through the cracks in the thin walls of the old building. The big, roaring fire in the heater could not drive the cold entirely out. Benches were all pulled closely together. The children huddled together to keep warm. There was nothing that could be done about the cold. Overnight, the weather had changed drastically: it was cold. Looking at them huddled together, squirming, trying to get comfortable was heartbreaking. But they were here. All of them! They had braved the zero weather. The trustees had come early and fixed as many cracks as possible. They made a good fire and brought enough coal and wood inside to last the week.

The weather was cold but I felt so warm and good inside, so happy that I had decided to have a program for this community. The announcement concerning plans for a program was welcomed. The pupils forgot the cold weather and the discomfort.

Teaching them the real Christmas and the pagan ideas of Christianity concerning this season was very important to me. Not one child knew why December 25th was called Christmas day. All they knew about the season was that a "Sanny Clauf" or something was supposed to bring toys to good children and that Jesus was born. Or something. Eating and drinking excessively, having a good time . . . that was all they knew. And they were exactly right. It had all started like that. For the present, there was too much to teach them and too little time in which to do it. I decided to stick with the basic Christian traditions.

The motif for the program would be very simple and very educational. They would know the basic Christmas tradition which engulfed the Christian world, and enough of the pagan beginnings to give a brief outline for future belief.

Players were chosen for the parts. Carols were learned quickly. So proud were they of the program! The rest of the week was spent in rehearsing for the best entertainment ever at Marks Chapel.

Friday, each child knew his part. Every word of the carols had been learned. They were naturals when it came to having programs. We had a full dress rehearsal which shocked even me!

Staying over that Saturday, we went to the forest for more greenery and evergreens for the final decoration: red balls, holly berries, blueberries, wild nuts, leaves—even a few wildflowers. There was mistletoe—everything that could be used was brought into the building. The ancient pagan traditions were made as evident as possible. I did not expect the children to grasp everything at once, but the seeds of truth were sown in many areas.

The stage was set, the tree was decorated, a star was in the center of the stage and a manger with cardboard animals was waiting. We were ready for our presentation. My expectations were sky high and my joy was without measure.

The final night. Everything was ready. The building was dark and the sheet curtains were closed. Two candles were burning in their holders on top of the piano. Parents entered first, followed by the rest of the congregation. When everyone was seated, I began to play the old piano. On this cue, the curtains were opened and the lights were turned on. Excitement was not what I felt. It was indescribable—a mixture of joy and love, a feeling of accomplishment. I wanted to cry and I wanted to laugh. The scene was so much lovelier than I had imagined. The tree was decked with hundreds of tiny, colorful bulbs and a blue star, shining from the ceiling. As I played "Go Tell It on the Mountain," the children in gay crepe paper costumes marched in singing with lighted candles. My heart rejoiced as the children sang in perfect harmony. They stood in order in front of the pulpit with lighted candles and sang two traditional carols. Needless to say, the crowd went wild! There were cheers and applause that echoed for miles. On cue, the Christmas tree lights were unplugged and their candles blown out. Only the star was visible. In soft harmony, they sang, "Behold the Star." As I softly played the much loved "Silent Night," Celeste recited her memorized essay on the origin of the Christmas holiday. While Celeste was reciting, the children placed the tree behind the manger scene. All was ready.

The Christmas tree was a radiant gem against the velvety blackness of the stage. On the left, the three wise men in colorful robes carried candles, as shepherds knelt in the light of the tree in adoration of the mother and baby. Joseph stood with hands raised towards the heavens. The wise men stood in reverence as my best reading student read from the New Testament. The pageant was lovely, though I was a bit afraid that the candle might possibly ignite the hay on which Mary and the baby sat.

The program being ended, it was time for comments from the parents. The lights came on. There was an ovation. I think the whole congregation went wild.

Deacon Green, with tears running down his wrinkled face, was the first to speak. Choking back the tears, he said, "Folks, this is th' best progrum we's evver had. Ah ain't nevver seed th' laks uv nothin' lak us seed here ternight. Folks, us is had a good time. You know, I feels the speerit. Feels lak I been in church." He continued, "Folks, we's gotta be with us teechur. We gon stan with her in all thangs. Us teechur made dat ole peeanna talk, didn' she folks?" Everyone gave a big Amen." "Us chilluns shore made me proud ternight! But the teechur is 'sponsibal fer it all." With a few more words he sat down.

One parent remarked, "I ain never known whut Christmas meant till ternight. Now, I kin really understan' better."

Fighting tears of gratitude and of joy, I was hugged by happy parents and friends. I heard someone say, "That tree wuz purtier than the white foks."

Very early the next morning, I was awakened with the sound of a wagon. It was too early for the truck that was taking me to my hometown. What was the commotion? Hearing more voices than I had expected, I peeked out of the paneless window to see what was happening. Seeing more people than I expected, I put on my robe and went outside. To my surprise, there was a small farewell party waiting.

"We brung yer some Christmus." One spoke as they started bringing boxes and bags to the rickety old porch. Speechless, I stood with a heart that was bursting with love. As the peas, peanuts, sweet potatoes, pumpkins, and chickens were placed around my feet, my tears could no longer be held. Some were surprised by my gratitude, but as they were learning, Miss Smith was just as human and as black as anybody there.

FROM

Congressman from Mississippi

FRANK E. SMITH

AN AFTERNOON IN JULY

JULY AFTERNOONS IN THE Mississippi Delta are always hot. In the days before air conditioning, however, summer heat was the norm and left little impression. My recollections as an eight-year-old on a July day in 1926 are not of heat, but of the abrupt destruction of the pattern of life. I was playing with a neighbor boy when my mother called me home to say that she had to go to the hospital. My father had been shot.

"He was shot in the arm," Mama told me. The hospital must have told her that to soften the shock of the news. Daddy had been shot in the arm but also twice in the body, a bullet entering from each side. A neighbor lady came to take my younger brother and baby sister to her house, and my playmate and I speculated as to which arm of my father had been shot, as we went to tell his mother the news. Half an hour later I was the only one at home when a carload of men turned into Crockett Street and pulled up before our house.

"Where are Frank's guns?" two of the men shouted as they came to the porch. "We're going out to help get the nigger that shot your daddy, and we haven't got a gun for everybody in the car."

I led the two men, father and son, whom I vaguely knew as distant cousins, into the house to claim my father's shotguns. A deputy sheriff might have little money, but there was always available to him a wide choice of confiscated weapons.

All through the rest of the afternoon I knew little more. My little brother Fred and I stayed with one neighbor, and another cared for our six-month-old sister, while Mama was at my father's bedside. In the early morning of the second day, Daddy's best friend, a fellow deputy, came to tell me that he had died during the night. I learned the full story as the days and the years went by.

Frank Smith was the chief deputy in the Leflore County sheriff's office. On that July day he came home to dinner (then, as it often still is, the word for the midday meal in Mississippi) and afterwards played with his baby Sadie for a few minutes in the shade of the screen porch. Then he drove off in his Ford touring car to serve a jury summons in the northern part of the county.

As he drove along the gravel road toward the town of Money, just north of the Tallahatchie river, Daddy came on a Negro carrying a suitcase, walking in the same direction as he was driving. Daddy stopped to pick the man up, as he automatically did for all he passed on the road in a day before hitchhiking had become customary.

The Negro came to the right side of the car, and then stooped to pick up his suitcase and swing it into the car. His face seemed vaguely familiar to Daddy, who said, "Wait a minute!" and reached to his shirt pocket for the packet of postcard pictures of escapees from the state prison which he always carried while out on the job. (There was an automatic fifty dollar reward for any prisoner returned to Parchman.)

When Daddy looked up again, the Negro (whose name turned out to be Sylvester Mackey) had a revolver in his hand. Mackey fired, and the bullet entered Daddy's right side. Daddy desperately grabbed for his own gun, which he never wore in the car but always placed down beside the driver's seat on his left side. Weakened and stunned, he could not pull the gun from its holster with his left hand, so he opened the car door and sprawled to the ground at the car's side. He tried to crawl away across the road. This moment of respite had come only because Mackey's gun had jammed after one shot. The assailant now ran behind the car and came around to the driver's side, where he picked up Daddy's gun and shot him a second time through his left side.

At this moment another car rounded the curve, carrying a Negro farmer and his wife. Panic struck Mackey, and he ran away across the nearby cotton field. The farmer and his wife picked up Daddy and drove him to Greenwood and the hospital.

Daddy was still conscious, being prepared for surgery that the doctors hoped would save him, when Mama arrived at the hospital. He told her what had happened, and then asked her to tell Sheriff Ed Crippen to do everything he could to make sure there was no lynching.

"I've been a deputy trying to enforce the law too long for us not to try to enforce it now," he said.

Ed Crippen had sent another deputy to the hospital to check about Frank before he joined the groups searching for the assailant. Mama gave him Daddy's message and added her own appeal to his.

The Leflore County peace officers honored the request, in a day and era when lynchings were still commonplace. The sheriff arrived at the scene of the shooting with Paul White, the assistant police chief in Greenwood. The leaderless group, gathered largely from Greenwood, had had no great trouble in cornering Sylvester Mackey. Plantation Negroes had spotted the fugitive running across the fields and then taking refuge in a sharecropper's cabin that stood alone in the midst of a field of knee-high cotton. The posse, in that moment of indecision between remaining a crowd or becoming a mob, milled around the cabin. Sylvester Mackey was inside with a gun, and no one wanted to move in after him immediately. There was talk of burning him out, but decisions for action were slow.

The one quick, sure way to avert a lynching was to arrest the cornered assailant and to get him safely to the county jail in Greenwood. After a few minutes of discussion, Paul White volunteered to go in and take the man. When the policeman entered the one main room of the cabin, it was obvious that the gunman must be hiding under the bed. White plunged under after him, and Mackey fired at the officer. He missed, but the pistol was so close that powder burns singed White's face. In another moment he grabbed Mackey and pulled him out. The posse made no attempt to take the prisoner or change its course when Sheriff Crippen told them that it was Frank Smith who wanted the law enforced. The Greenwood *Commonwealth* made the same plea editorially, again in the name of the wounded deputy. Even after Daddy died, no more talk of mob vengeance came out into the open.

Sylvester Mackey was tried within a few weeks and hanged for the murder. His only statement about the crime was "I didn't know he was an officer," and no real motive was ever discovered for the senseless killing. He was from the southern part of the state and had never lived in the Delta. As far as the Leflore County authorities ever learned, he was not being sought by police anywhere else in the country. Sylvester Mackey, like Frank Smith, was a victim of the nameless terror, the fear and suspicion between white and black that always has walked in the shadows with the people of Mississippi.

My father had died, and I had had my first serious encounter with the race problem. But learning to live with the relationship between white man and black man was and is part of the experience of growing up in Mississippi. It leaves its imprint on us all, white and black, rich and poor.

GREENWOOD

In the winter of 1923 we moved to Greenwood, from the village to the town. Greenwood had started—a little before Sidon, but in much the same manner—as a steamboat landing on the Yazoo to serve the hill country to the east. The town was named for Greenwood Leflore, the former Choctaw chief who was the largest landholder in neighboring Carroll County as well as one of the most romantic and colorful figures in early Mississippi history.

As a county seat, Greenwood eclipsed all rivals as a river trading center. In 1924 the town had a population of about 10,000, and its growth had been steady for fifty years. It was a city of shaded streets. Houses came lot by lot, with room to leave the old trees and rich soil for new ones to grow. The exception was in the Negro sections. Gritney and Baptist Town were made up of shotgun houses so close together that there was rarely room to leave the old trees, let alone room for new ones.

We moved into a quiet part of North Greenwood, across the Yazoo from the business district. In the post-World War II buildup, North Greenwood was to be the part of town where most of the residential expansion took place, but in the time of my childhood it was small enough to be served by a four-room schoolhouse with six grades. Everybody walked to school, except for a lucky few who had bicycles.

While I was in the second grade, the North Greenwood teachers decided it would be best for me to skip half a grade, and that meant that the rest of my grammar school days were spent with the uneven graders across the river in Jefferson Davis School, which served the main part of town. A few of my classmates were skipgraders like me, but most of them were boys and girls who had been set back one or more times. Consequently, most of them were two, three, or four years older than I. None of my classmates lived in my part of North Greenwood, and I lost out on most of the classic schoolmates-growing-up-together sagas of childhood, but I also came firsthand to a side of Greenwood life from which the children of North Greenwood were sheltered. Perhaps all of this contributed to an introverted shyness that has been with me all my life.

When Daddy died, he left $1,000 in insurance and a very small equity in the farm below Sidon. Mama rented the farm on shares during the next few years but was never able to meet all the payments. She lost the whole investment in 1932, the year before a federal farm program came into being and ended the torrent of farm bankruptcies. Mama's school teaching of ten years before had been done without the preparation of a college degree, so returning to that as a means of providing for her family was not possible. She invested her capital in a business college course.

Daddy had been the universal favorite to win the sheriff's election of 1927. After his death, most of the candidates who now came into the race made giving Mama a job as office deputy part of their platform. She went to work for $100 a month, and after long years, the pay finally became $150. There was no margin for luxuries raising a family on this income, but neither was there the suffering that the depression brought to many others. Because the job was subject to change with a new sheriff every four years, however, Mama never felt any real sense of security in it. My father's brother Harry was twice sheriff during the period, but even his political opponents kept Mama on their staff. She worked too hard and was too popular with the voters for them to consider any other course.

After Daddy was killed, the people of Leflore County had raised money by public subscription, carried on through the columns of the local paper, for us to buy a house. It was a generous spontaneous reaction to the way of his passing. Mama chose a house in North Greenwood two blocks from where we had been living, this time on Claiborne Street, on the river front. Along Claiborne, west toward the bridge and downtown, there were houses. To the east a cotton farm began that surrounded us, even to the extent of a vacant lot on the west. The actual river channel was a quarter of a mile in front of our house, and we could see the river only in times of high water. A strip of that stretch was high enough to be farmed most of the time, but much of the area was wooded wasteland, an ideal place for boys to play.

The road past our house led on to a large plantation, the property of Congressman Will M. Whittington. As boys, my brother and I came to know all of the regular tenants. We either picked cotton for them in the fall at a penny a pound, caught rides with them on their cotton wagons headed for the Whittington gin across town, or played with their children in the pastures along the river bank. Our house, inhabited by three children, my mother and her mother, stood a few feet from a road over which hundreds of Negroes passed regularly, and through all hours on Saturday night, but I don't think our peace was ever disturbed. We never thought of locking the door at night.

The 1927 flood which broke the main Mississippi levee damaged a good part of the west Delta, but very little of its overflow bothered people in the Greenwood area. This flood awakened the country to the necessity of having the federal government take responsibility for flood protection of the Mississippi, a policy written into law in 1928. The Flood Control Act of 1936 extended the responsibility throughout the country. The Delta's ever-recurrent battle with the water first came home to me in 1932, when the Yazoo flooded and water covered nearly all of North Greenwood. We stayed in our Claiborne Street house until the water was just a foot below the floors, and then moved out with the help of an ice wagon that rode high above most of the water. Our place of refuge was the judge's chambers in the top story of the courthouse. One year later the first major public works project in our area was an earth levee around North Greenwood. From that time forward our view was the levee, not the stretch of land to the river.

When I was eleven years old, I got the only job I ever had as a schoolboy—the only one that was available in town and the one I kept until the summer after I was graduated from high school. The *Greenwood Commonwealth* paid its carriers a flat sum, not a commission on each subscriber, and it never gave a pay raise. My pay was $1.50 a week for five years. It was a magnificent sum for a boy my age in Greenwood at that time, but it grew much smaller as I advanced into high school. But it was all there was, and its actuality made a boyhood in Greenwood far more meaningful. Through the years most of it went into books and magazines and a growing concept of the world outside.

Reading was something that began with the legend on oatmeal boxes, before even starting to school at Sidon. When we first moved to Greenwood, Grandfather Ellis had come to live with us for the year or so before he died. He helped me read the newspaper headlines, and talked to me about them. I remember asking him, "Who was William Jennings Bryan?" when the headlines in the *Commercial Appeal* told of the death of the Great Commoner at Dayton. "He was a man too good to be President," Daddy Ellis replied.

One of the advantages of going to Davis School uptown was that the Greenwood Public Library was along the way to school. Thanks to the generosity of the Carnegie Fund, Greenwood had a library that looked big and inspiring to a small boy. Before I had finished high school, it had begun to seem small, for I had read practically all the volumes of history and biography, and a large part of the fiction. In the depression days the library budget for new books was limited to the income from "overdue" fines, although there may have been some grants from the WPA in return for assistance to the WPA community libraries. Regardless of its limitations, the Greenwood library was good for Frank Smith. There was a basement reading room, wonderfully cool in the summer, where the magazines were kept, together with most of the personal library of the late Senator J. Z. George, whose daughter lived next door. The library introduced me to many of the current magazines, but the discovery of *The New Republic* and *The Nation* probably made the strongest impression. Here were two magazines which devoted most of their space to politics and public affairs. They were something to revel in and eventually to subscribe to in order to be sure I had them every Monday.

The library, of course, did not satisfy all my reading needs. In my high-school days, with my income of $1.50 per week, for a couple of years I belonged to both the Book-of-the-Month Club and the Literary Guild, in addition to subscribing to *The New Republic* and *The Nation*, patronizing a lending library that two young women had opened in a drugstore downtown, and buying magazines such as *Story* and other odd items that reached the newsstands in the local drugstores.

The first magic of the newsstand for me as an eleven-year-old was the *Open Road for Boys*. The stories seemed more vivid than those in *Youth's Companion* and *American Boy*. The pulp magazines were all exciting, but for a few years during this period the only one that got my fifteen cents every week was Street and Smith's *Wild West*

Weekly. The comic books have destroyed both the boy's magazines and the pulps, and I think they have taken something out of the lives of our sons thereby. It was from the advertisements in the *Open Road* that I was introduced to the world of boys' amateur journalism. Papers put out by teen-age editors were being published in every corner of the country, printed by companies who would produce 100 copies of your paper on a 2 × 4 folder for a couple of dollars and half the space for their own ads. The productions of these schoolboy editors varied from the near professional to the rankest amateur, but they also published each other's pieces and were the source of most of the mail circulation of each other's papers. My own efforts found print in some of these brother publications, but the big production was my own paper, printed through the services of the G. Blake Printing Company of Burlington, Iowa. I'm sure that none of the editors who worked over the G. Blake imprint ever paid their expenses—I've often wondered since then whether the G. Blake Company itself, which sounded so professional to me, paid its way either.

The only copy of the *Boy's Friend* that has survived the years is Volume I, Number 4, for February 1930. We had graduated from G. Blake to twelve pages (still 2 × 4) prepared by another printer who must have been Hubert Motsinger of Route 3, Marion, Illinois, because he had a full-page ad for printing. The subscription price of the *Boy's Friend* was a bargain—six months for 20 cents or 35 cents for a full year. By the time that I had developed enough talent to produce a semiprofessional-looking edition, I had outgrown their appeal, but that must have been the normal cycle for the boy publishers.

The Greenwood school system for white children was probably well above the average in Mississippi. What it was for Negro children I had no way of knowing, and there was not much chance of the average white adult's finding out anything about it either. On the plantation to our east the children attended a one-room country school, probably as good or better than schools on the other plantations of the county, but not likely to encourage even an ambitious student to struggle with the difficulties of traveling every day to the other side of Greenwood to go to high school. There were no school buses for Negroes—Mississippi had not yet been driven to embracing the "equal" part of the "separate but equal" doctrine. Richard Wright has written an eloquent account of a talented Negro boy's growing up in Mississippi in the years just ahead of me in his book *Black Boy.*

Any member of Sadie Smith's family was an active member and participant in the affairs of the First Methodist Church. Both the church and the Sunday school were a major part of my life. The people in the church were the people I knew first in town, except for our few immediate neighbors in North Greenwood, until the years of delivering papers made all the *Commonwealth's* subscribers part of my daily circle. For several years the boys in my age group had a rich old retired farmer and businessman as Sunday school teacher. He liked us because we afforded him a captive audience, and we liked him because every Sunday he would award two or three nickels to the boys who had memorized the Scripture best or who could give the best answers to the series of questions in the Sunday school lesson book. One Saturday morning there was a fairly large crowd on the courthouse lawn, and the big topic of conversation was the capture of two Negroes, accused of a recent murder, who were in the county jail in the courthouse annex. Old Mr. Jones was in the crowd, and I listened on the edge of his circle to what he had to say:

"They have no business locking those black sonsfabitches up and keeping 'em out of our hands. Stringing them up right now would be the cheapest and easiest way to handle this."

I don't know whether I was shocked more by the profanity of the Sunday school teacher or by his advocacy of lynching. Lynching, I had learned from my father and from the other members of my family who had become peace officers, was wrong. We had had no lessons or sermons in the church on Christian race relations, but the whole concept of Christianity to which I was constantly exposed was a contradiction of the racial pattern in which I was growing up. In the process of my intellectual development there is nothing I can put my finger on as having made my views on race different from those of my friends and neighbors. It was a gradual accumulation of influences, and having been raised in the sheriff's office and regularly attending Sunday school were two of the significant ones. There were many other people who felt the same influences and wound up with different attitudes. I think in most cases they recognized the influences but did not have enough inherent independence to respond to them in the face of the ingrained community pressures.

Growing up in the Delta involved a constant awareness of race. The Delta had been opened up to cotton, and the original plantation system survived here longer than anywhere else. Two-thirds of the people were Negroes, and from the days of Reconstruction the white population had unquestioningly accepted the doctrine that their economic and social order could not survive unless the Negroes were rigidly controlled by being excluded from any voice in the political system and rigidly segregrated in their participation in all other forms of community life.

Outsiders who looked at the Delta were universally impressed by the white and colored caste system, and what they saw was a white society so stratified by class consciousness that its rigid bounds scarred those at every level, leaving no man or woman free to function in a manner of their own choosing. The class system was actually far more flexible than it appeared—most of the Delta was only two or three generations old, and large land-ownership before the New Deal was never stable enough to develop the traditional landed aristocracy of a rural society. Plantation ownership was the mark of the Delta's upper class, but there were few cases of inherited opulence for more than one generation in the 1920's and 1930's. At every hand there were examples of "planters" who had started as sharecroppers, and quite often there were paupers who had been planters. This flexibility did not breach support of the caste system, however, which all whites accepted as an inviolate part of the social order. To express the simplest accurate explanation, the Negro was regarded as an inferior being, beyond the pale of religious and political doctrines of brotherhood and equality.

In the Greenwood of my youth, cotton completely dominated the economy. Poor prices for cotton could sometimes be offset by seasons of good yield, but when both yield and price were poor, everyone felt the result. The size rather than the price of the crop influenced the demand for cotton choppers and pickers among the town's Negro population. In good crop years, anywhere from 1,500 to 2,000 Greenwood Negroes would be hauled to fields each day to pick cotton. This total included probably 90 percent of the town's maids, cooks, and children's nurses. The cotton economy of the times demanded a surplus of Negro population available for seasonal farm work.

Greenwood was the narrow world in which I first learned politics. Through the years my family was always in local politics and consequently never took an active role in state elections (Mississippi elects all its county and state officials, from constable to governor, every four years, and local candidates just don't have the time to get involved in state campaigns, not to mention their disinclination to risk alienating their own voters by supporting a possibly unpopular state candidate). But political activity at any level begets an interest in the whole spectrum. I lived part of the excitement of all of it—in the state candidates' rallies, in the columns of the Memphis *Commercial Appeal*, the Jackson *Daily News* and the *Commonwealth*, and in the overheard conversations of my elders.

Greenwood was a traditional Delta town as far as most politics went, which meant that it seldom offered a candidate the big audiences for speeches typical of the hill country where politics was the sport of all the people. The town and county vote was big enough, however, for all the candidates to have to speak in Greenwood, and sometimes twice. I still remember a remark I heard from one listener as we filed out after hearing my first Bilbo speech in 1927—"That man can make you believe him even when you know he's lying." There wasn't a political rally in town, from 1927 until I went to college in 1934, without me as part of the audience. I listened to all the state politicians and their local supporters who showed up for their appearances, but I don't think I ever was forward enough to go up and shake the hand of one of the candidates until I was a local candidate speaking on the program myself.

In many of the hill counties there are organized speaking tours for county candidates that cover each major voting precinct in the county. Leflore County candidates didn't follow this, but there were occasional barbecues and Brunswick stews built around the campaign—sometimes strictly community affairs and sometimes special efforts to promote state or district candidates. Perhaps there is no relationship, but Brunswick stew has always been my favorite among distinctively Southern dishes.

Leflore County didn't have a political machine in the traditional sense. There were sometimes factions built around one man or one family, but they were transitory. Candidates won elections by having a reputation that was respected by the people who knew them and building from this by energetically getting to know the individual voters. The man with special influence was the one paying large blocs of poll taxes for voters who otherwise would not have gotten around to it. As the years went by, "getting to know the people" came to be virtually a house-to-house canvass of the white residents of the county, but knowing the people was actually much more than this for the really successful politician. It required knowing something about a man's family, the background of his people before they came to the Delta, the history of his farm, the bank and the merchants with whom he traded. More activity was expected in election years, of course, but the successful politician had to know his people and be sure they knew he knew them, all the time; he lived his campaign, more or less without letup, year in and year out.

The sheriff's office changed every four years (by law, the sheriff cannot succeed himself in Mississippi), but other county offices rarely changed hands. This could have led to a machine-type "courthouse ring," but it didn't, at least not in Leflore County. There were natural friendships that developed through long association, but the officeholders were too concerned about their own welfare to risk alienating voters for someone else's sake.

My mother took a plunge into politics on her own in 1935 and ran against the circuit court clerk, who had held his office for more than twenty years. She ran into hundreds of voters whose marriage licenses had been supplied with a waiver of the fee by the clerk, and another large group who thought a lady that had a steady job in the sheriff's office didn't need the job as badly as her opponent did—a combination which resulted in her losing by a heartbreaking couple of hundred votes. The immediate bitterness of the defeat didn't last, though, and eight years later Mama went to work for the man she had tried to oust from office.

That defeat was much harder for me to take than my own 27 years later. If she had won, I would have been able to go on to senior college—I had already made plans to study journalism at Emory University. But more than that, I simply could not understand how the voters could turn her down. What in the world did they want for that office?

There was a Senate campaign in 1928 that failed to register any lasting imprint. I remember that Congressman T. Webber Wilson made a speech everyone called impressive, but it failed to dislodge Senator Hubert Stephens, and I probably wouldn't remember that much of it were it not for the fact that Wilson spent the night with the Johnstons next door. A man from up in the north Delta ran against Congressman Whittington on a platform calling for legal beer, but he couldn't get over the levees that Mr. Whittington was making his trade-mark.

The state campaign I remember best was in 1934, when Senator Stephens was turned out of office for not being a wholehearted New Dealer. Ex-Governor Theodore G. Bilbo was the one who turned him out, but I was heart and soul for the man who ran third, Congressman Ross Collins of Meridian. For several years Collins had been engaged in a seesaw battle with the War Department over what he considered its wasteful weapons system and its failure to build up air strength. Collins' stand, based on the normally politically sound assertion that he opposed military waste, attracted the attention of the national press and brought applause from people such as Oswald Garrison Villard in *The Nation*. It was the first favorable comment I had ever seen in *The Nation* or *The New Republic* about a Mississippian, and it immediately put me in the Collins camp. Unadulterated vanity is the hallmark of the young, and I was no exception. I promptly wrote a letter to Mr. Villard, praising his support of Collins' position and vowing that I would be a candidate for the legislature when I reached 21. What a relief it must have been to Villard thus to be assured that his opinions were sound and that the state of Mississippi stood but five short years removed from political salvation! At sixteen, my conceit must have been exceeded only by my optimism—it seems unlikely, however, that Mr. Villard suffered unduly through the eight extra years it took me to get to the legislature.

Emerging as a Writer in Faulkner's Mississippi

ELIZABETH SPENCER

COMING BACK TO Mississppi after not so long away in terms of visiting, but a long time away in terms of living—though in another sense a real Mississippian is never really away—means the arousing of many memories, some of the most pleasant, in my case, being associated with the years I taught here in the '40s and '50s. Even if I hadn't ever taught here, it would be impossible to think of Oxford without thinking of her most famous citizen, William Faulkner.*

When I was growing up in Carrollton, sixty miles west of here, where I was born, Oxford was mainly associated with the University, "Ole Miss," its various well-known professors, its law school, its football team, and several families, like the Somervilles and the Hemingways, with whom we—the Spencers, the McCains, the Youngs—were somehow "connected." Two of my uncles went here—one was to become the Admiral, John Sidney McCain, for whom the building on campus here has been named; and my brother came here also, and every one of them was Phi Delta Theta.

It was a long, twisting drive over narrow, gravel roads to get over here in the old days, but once here one immediately felt something distinguished about both town and campus, as though the cultural roots were firm and strong and secure. On the campus, the Lyceum, the observatory, and the grove seemed to have been created to impart a sense of the past, of classical studies, of tradition. Some campuses have this meditative quality and one need know no one ever connected with them to feel it. Others, I believe, never acquire it at all. Ole Miss had it, and Oxford itself had a serene, golden quality all its own. I would be many long years, however, in associating Oxford and Ole Miss with William Faulkner. There was, in fact, during the '30s when I was growing

*From paper presented at the 1981 Faulkner and Yoknapatawpha Conference at the University of Mississippi

up, almost no importance attached to Faulkner at all. Why was this? Didn't we read books? Yes, we not only read, but some of us read extensively and intelligently. There were those, it is true, who did not read much of anything but the *Commercial Appeal* and the *Farmer's Almanac* and the *Christian Observer,* but many were very attached to books. My mother's family had a pretty large library—they would have just said that "we had a lot of books"—and most of them loved talking about their reading, comparing thoughts and impressions and judgments. The emergence of a writer of real potential in their area should have been of great interest to them, and his work should have sustained that interest. But the truth is I never remember people at home talking about Faulkner very much though it was known he was a writer who had begun to publish. One book was mentioned, *Sanctuary.* It was usually said that he had written it to make money, but the implication was that the writer and the book both were flashy, and without substance. If more was said, it was that this writer and others like him (Erskine Caldwell comes to mind) were trying to paint the South in false colors, to drag our culture through the dirt, to degrade and make fun of our ideals. To go a little further with remembering, I think I recall someone saying, "No book of his will ever be in my house." I also have a vague recollection of one of my aunts, glancing about to see that no children or men were present, whispering the name of Temple Drake, but I failed to get the rest of it, and of my mother saying, "Oh, awful, just awful. How could anybody write such a thing?"

But mainly nobody spoke of Faulkner at all. When I say we had a life which made ready reference to books and literature, I feel I must back this up, as too many have fallen into the way of praising the South for its "oral tradition," letting this so-called "oral tradition" account for all we have enjoyed in the way of a literary flourishing. To me this is to simplify what our culture was like. It was no interruption in small town social life, or family life or church-going or hunting or fishing, to have your mother read to you every night out of Greek and Roman myths, the story of the Bible, Robin Hood, Arthurian legend, Uncle Remus, Hawthorne, Aesop, Grimm, Robert Louis Stevenson, George MacDonald, Louisa May Alcott, and all those others, who followed naturally after Mother Goose and Peter Rabbit. Later there were Dickens, Thackeray, Jane Austen, George Eliot, Victor Hugo, all of the fine Victorians.

The characters in these books were often discussed as though they were live people we had all known. My uncle had a fondness for *Les Miserables* and pressed me to read it when I was about ten; too young, I got lost in all the history, French geography, manners, and characters with unpronounceable names. A cousin of mine from up the street who often used to play with the rest of us at my house in the summer, used to quote Swinburne by the yard, and even before that, my brother, whose bent was certainly not "literary," would recite long stanzas from Macaulay along with Robert W. Service. His favorite book was *Moby Dick;* he had several copies around the house. My aunt taught Latin and relished reading fiction. Long scraps of original poems were to be found in the notebooks of some of the family members. All this was to be considered, I think, as a kind of liveliness. It made life more enjoyable, expanded it, to have feelings for somebody in New England, or France or England, or for never-never characters out of myths.

I should like here to say a word about my home town of Carrollton. They have a pilgrimage there now, for people to visit its old homes and gardens. However, Carrollton never grew very much. I guess maybe it has shrunk. I recently saw it listed in a study published in one of the Mississippi quarterlies as a "dying town." My mother always said that while nobody much was left in Carrollton, half the Delta was *from* Carrollton. Carrollton is a hill town, older than both Oxford and Holly Springs. It was close enough to the Delta to be a refuge place during floods and yellow fever epidemics. There was once a "female academy" there; it was the birthplace of two U. S. Senators; it was considered the ideal setting for Faulkner's *The Reivers* when this book was photographed as a movie. (Oxford itself had got too modern and no longer looked like "Jefferson," or so it was judged.) Carroll County is adjacent to Leflore County, Leflore being named for Greenwood Leflore, the last of the Choctaw chiefs, part French-Canadian, whose plantation was largely in Carroll County, as was his splendid plantation home, Malmaison. My own family's plantation was neighbor to his, being called Teoc, after the Choctaw name, Teoc Tillila, meaning Tall Pines.

Carrollton was a sleepy town in the '20s and '30s, when I was growing up. It was really two towns, separated by Big Sand Creek. When this creek got up and roared after a big rain, it was always threatening to wash the bridge out. The town on the other side of the creek was called North Carrollton. North Carrollton got mad at Carrollton once, back in the mists of time, or Carrollton got mad at North Carrollton, I forget which. At any rate, we had, between us, never more than 1,000 souls, but two separate 12-year high schools, two separate post offices, two mayors and boards of aldermen, and any number of separate reasons to feel different and superior, each to the other. I think, though, that since Carrollton had the courthouse and the county records, we quite possibly were more successful snobs, if this is any distinction. There were no paved roads in the state then, except maybe one or two down around Jackson, or up near Greenville. There was one half-paved road, I remember, that is, paved on one side only. It was up near Greenville and was done so the milk wouldn't get churned on the way to town. It was difficult to go any distance by car without getting covered in dust. We usually counted on one or two flat tires on the way to Jackson, a hundred miles away. A teacher who came from elsewhere to our town school in the '30s was astonished that we had no school library. Since everybody I knew had books at home, I never thought a library was necessary in the schoolhouse, yet we were glad at the signs of progress when she raised some money to order books, stuck reference cards in a shoe box, and entered fines in a nickel notebook. Before that, a teacher I had in the fourth grade, whose home was there, had thought the textbook prescribed by the state was boring and had got us to buy copies of a book called *One Hundred and One Best Poems*. She loved reading aloud, and I can see her yet, completely wrapped up in the words and rhythm, chanting Poe's "The Bells" or "The Raven," or Bryant's "Thanatopsis," or something of Robert Browning's or Tennyson's, shaking her head until the hairpins fell out and peppered the floor. She was a grand reader named Miss Willie Keenan, really Mrs. Keenan (everybody was "Miss" something), and really a Money, one of the Senator's family. Before Miss Willie, though, there had been Miss Jennie Nelson McBride in grades one, two, and three, one of which I was let to skip, I forget which. But for two years, along with arithmetic, spelling, reading, and penmanship, I was taught the alphabet by Bible verses, committed to memory and recited daily. I remember to this day: A—A good name is rather to be chosen than great riches and loving favor rather than silver and gold. B—Be ye kind one to another, tenderhearted, forgiving one another.

C—Create in me a clean heart, O God, and renew a right spirit within me.

After Miss Jennie and Miss Willie, we had a teacher from Agnes Scott, who happened into our town by accident of marriage to one of the local boys and who wanted to work. She got us into Latin about grade seven, instead of waiting for grade nine; so beating ahead toward Virgil, we were reading Caesar's Gallic Wars in the eighth grade and Ovid (probably expurgated) in the ninth. A friend of hers came to Carrollton in need of work, this one being quite fond of Shakespeare. We read the plays aloud, sitting around an iron stove with our knees toasting and our backs cold and hunks of plaster threatening to fall down on our heads, taking parts in *Romeo and Juliet, The Merchant of Venice,* or *As You Like It,* building up to grade 12, when she moved full-scale into *Macbeth.* She had studied it in Nashville under Walter Clyde Curry, and it was her favorite play. "Life's but a walking shadow . . . a tale told by an idiot, Full of sound and fury, signifying nothing." All this was great in itself, but we studied a lot of other writers too, even though my summertime attentions had gone to pot as far as literature was concerned. The boys and the cousins who played tennis at our house were hooked on Edgar Rice Burroughs and other adventure stories, so I read those, and the girls I ran around with had discovered picture shows and *Photoplay* magazine.

A mixed education, but it was much richer than statistics would lead anybody to believe. Down here we were all supposed, in little societies like mine, to have no culture at all, except possibly this famous "oral tradition." It does seem to me that every place has, in one way or another, an oral tradition. Ours, it may be, was extraordinary—varied and expansive. Our talkers were great talkers; but people do talk most everywhere. And a Southerner can be as big a bore as anybody. Evenings of swapping local stories lead to wonderful laughter and a good night's sleep, but not necessarily to literature. It was the church-going crowd who got the most out of the sermons, and the politically-involved sat drinking in every word at the "speakings." So I do believe that making books springs from a love of books, and that many cultural forces, some of a literary nature, were at work around those small, dusty, obviously "backward," apparently asleep, possibly dead, little old Southern towns.

We had books by Southerners back then, too, though I have not yet mentioned any. Thomas Nelson Page was pointed out to me as a good writer; his *Red Rock* was on our shelves. There was also Stark Young, a distant cousin, whose *So Red the Rose* met with general approval as being true to the South, as so it was. It was true to what this society thought of itself. Mr. Stark had no reason even to change the names of some of his families in that novel, as he was painting them just in the way they believed themselves to be. I think quite possibly they really were this way. I see no reason to believe that Hugh McGehee and Sallie Bedford weren't as good as Stark Young makes them out to be. There were people that noble and that fine in the society then; they never hesitated one minute to be as good as humanly possible. I was fortunate enough to be born when some of that generation was still around, plus any number of people who had known them, and I don't think he exaggerated. And I think *So Red the Rose* is a fine book. *Gone with the Wind* appeared and was immediately read and widely discussed. I remember long arguments. Scarlett O'Hara was not "representative of Southern womanhood." Melanie Wilkes was "representative of Southern womanhood." But just about everybody who read at all, read it, and thought it was a great story and true to "what our people had endured." This was often said.

I began to get the reasoning little at a time. Southern writers were supposed to be "loyal to the South." It was as if we were still in a war and if you weren't loyal to the South you were a traitor, a turncoat, and should be scorned and regarded as a pariah, if not actually shot. This was a sensitive society. Proud, it had been humiliated by defeat and Reconstruction. This humiliation, it seemed to me, the more I heard people talk about it, had been the worst part of the Civil War experience. Now here was somebody, one of us, right over here at Oxford, shocking us and exposing us to people elsewhere with story after story, drawn from the South's own private skeleton closet . . . the hushed-up family secret, the nice girl who wound up in the Memphis whorehouse, the suicides, the idiot brother kept at home, the miserable poverty and ignorance of the poor whites—(Now, the truth is I never heard the term "poor white," just as I never heard the term "Deep South," until I got out of the South. But anyway, he wrote about whites who were poor)—the revenge shootings, the occasional lynchings, the real life of the blacks. What was this man trying to do? Humiliate us again? Tell on his own people in order to make money? Few people wanted to try to sort it out. Those few who did, agreed, I think, that here was a great talent. Talent should be recognized and encouraged, but how were you to "encourage" William Faulkner? (He did, as we know, find encouragement with friends like Phil Stone, Ben Wasson, and perhaps others.)

I wish to say that I think the question of what Mississippi was to think about William Faulkner really was a difficult one. Now, many years later, we come to his books after a world of critical work at the very highest levels has been accomplished. We can look back on critics, not confined to the South, who misjudged, underrated, and misunderstood his amazing vision and the variety of his efforts in fiction to make it all plain. Even today if you come to Faulkner by way of only one fragment, say, one story or one novel (I have an opportunity to do this because I live in Montreal and I teach students who have not been as widely exposed to Faulkner as we here have)—if you come to Faulkner by way of only one work, you are apt to be confused, not as to the brilliance or even value of this particular piece, if you have chosen a good one, but as to the motive for it, the writer's focus. Faulkner, of course, we know now, had read widely in modern literature from the first; there was not much he didn't know about the French writers, and a study of modern literature makes us know that the modern writer's attempt is to hide within the work. Faulkner had as much right to this method as did Flaubert, whose precise focus is also not discoverable. Looking horizontally, regarding the literary scene of his moment, which is the only moment the artist ever knows, he had every aesthetic right to mask himself. The question that arose with many Southerners was not of aesthetic but of moral right. Did Faulkner have a right to make use of his own society (that is to say by extension, his own family, as the South or Mississippi was, in those days, something like a vast family connection), to create a shocking literature?

I was sent to a small Presbyterian school in Jackson, Mississippi, Belhaven by name. There was something that met each spring around among those colleges. I guess it still meets, at Millsaps, Ole Miss, Southwestern, Mississippi State, Blue Mountain, Mississippi Southern, MSCW. It was known as the Southern Literary Festival. If I'm not mistaken Robert Penn Warren founded this.* Warren taught for a time at Southwestern, and as happened everywhere he

*Warren spoke at the first Southern Literary Festival. Its founder was Charles D. Johnson of Blue Mountain College.

went, something positive and creative resulted. He thought that if the students in this area could get together once a year, students interested in writing, that is, and talk about what was going on in the world of writing, perhaps have writers or literary critics as speakers, then good things might happen. He was right. One thing that happened was that it came the turn of Belhaven College to have this festival and several literary people, writers and critics, were about to show up and students from the whole area were about to attend. It was then discovered that here in 1939 not a single book by the man who had become Mississippi's best-known writer was in the college library, any more than any book of his was in the Carrollton High School library, or in the Spencer residence. Yet an exhibit of Mississippi writing was being set up. A quandary. The college president, Dr. Guy Gillespie, was a very fine and learned and highly religious man. If people sometimes seem to act or think narrowly out of convictions, we have to recall the overwhelming numbers of people who have no convictions to act out of. Anyway, Dr. Gillespie had his troubles with literature. At times, he speculated that Shakespeare probably should not be taught to his girls in college, because he personally could not tell what Shakespeare's theology was. (As a matter of fact, I can't either.) Milton was all right, but he had more trouble yet with the romantic poets—Wordsworth was probably a pantheist, Coleridge undoubtedly took dope, Shelley was a declared atheist, Byron a libertine, and Keats was a pagan. Dr. Gillespie taught the required course in philosophy himself, lest something go wrong. Now here were the college librarian and the English department wishing to acquire one or two books by the notorious William Faulkner. Fortunately, Faulkner himself had innocently furnished Dr. Gillespie with a solution, as some up-to-date person on the committee realized. He had just published *The Unvanquished,* his most gentle and loving book about the trials of the Sartoris family in War and Reconstruction times. I remember seeing this book on the display table in the library at the time of the festival and thinking I would certainly check it out and read it when the meeting was over. I did so and encountered disappointment. I was looking for sex and violence, but found little of either. I put Faulkner aside indefinitely.

I confess with shame that it wasn't until I was in my early twenties and in graduate school at Vanderbilt that I realized I must find out more about Faulkner. I had still read very little of him, maybe an anthologized story or two. Nevertheless in the Modern British and American Novel course under Donald Davidson, I dauntlessly picked out a book by Faulkner on which to base one of my required papers. The book was *Sartoris*. I admitted in the paper to never having read widely in the writer's work. I took it, however, from this book that Faulkner was trying to present a decadent picture of the South, especially Mississippi—a deteriorated society. Mr. Davidson did not agree with the paper or its thesis, but was intrigued by it enough to read it aloud to the class and tear it to shreds. Faulkner was not pointing the finger at a terrible place called Mississippi. He was not out to reform anybody. The secrets of his writing lay deeper than that. Davidson did not try to give them all to us at once, but he pointed the way by indicating criticism that was already beginning to outline the Sartoris-Snopes poles of character, that was probing the mystery of Quentin Compson, and suggesting how Faulkner really regarded, and meant the reader to regard, the outrageous Bundrens. Much more serious after my scolding, I began a long commitment to try to understand slowly and as thoroughly as possible the literary genius of my own locale. I had hoped to find a quick way out of doing this, but finally I was so challenged I had to go on with it, and I then read a great deal of Faulkner, all the books up through *The Hamlet*, *Go Down, Moses*, some as they were appearing, and finally *The Collected Stories*. And then I thought I understood enough, as much as I ever would, and being not so interested in the later ones, I called it as much as I could do.

But by that time I was thoroughly converted and baptized. More than baptized, I was saturated. More than converted, I was almost fanatical. If anybody said anything about Faulkner that wasn't thoroughly positive and to my mind correct, I would undertake to lecture them. I thought everyone should be enlightened about his work, read it, see it as I had come to. To discover Faulkner was a great experience, of the sort which few writers can offer a reader. In our time, Proust can offer it, as can Joyce. Who else? Perhaps others. I can think of none. The work is there, complex and difficult, but finally understandable; we read it as though we visited a new country—I should say, being from Mississippi, another county. We can read its history, meet its people, see its sights, learn its language. The characters become like people personally known, part of our acquaintance who crop up from time to time.

I saw, of course, the perils all this was letting me in for, as a young woman who had wanted to write since childhood and who, worse luck, came from what was rapidly getting to be known as "Faulkner country." Once you were in it, especially as a writer, how in the world did you get out of it? (That was the 1940s.)

I think now that writers, would-be writers, beginning writers, writers already publishing, all over the South (for the South did, as we know, experience a real flowering of literature, call it what you will) were facing the same question as I. Faulkner was a lion in the path, menacing further advance—or a bear in everybody's private wilderness, if you prefer. Maybe some of us gave up. But a lot of us didn't. Few got by without a claw mark or two. I thought my work was original, all my own, but critics inevitably compared me to Faulkner. Some of them must have been simply aware of superficial resemblances in the landscape or the architecture or the characters or the speech. I knew little about any world other than the North Mississippi world where I had been born and my parents and their parents before them. But some of the critics must have been right; perhaps resemblances are really there between my work and Faulkner's and also the work of many other Southern writers and Faulkner's. For one thing, the Faulkner style, once it gets into your thinking, tends to want to get out on paper. Faulkner found a way of expanding the English sentence from within, elongating its rhythms so that line after line of subordinate matter could be introduced without losing or damaging the presiding thought it was intended to qualify. He knew how to lay clause after clause in long, richly worded sentences, not like equal stones along a flat path, but builder's units, raising some complex image before us, involving it along the way with his story's history, feeling and character all together. All this he managed to tune into the idiom that was native to him, in all its range. Should this great gain in stylistic method then be lost to other writers because none are strong enough to use it without becoming imitative? Many writers have learned from Joyce, even though few would even covet his enormous interest in linquistics, and perhaps none, even if they wished, would have the learning to bring it into full play. Many have found in Proust the courage to let memory create symphonic fiction out of past event. Well, a good many writers have found a way to borrow from this extraordinary style of Faulkner's without sounding too much like the one who invented it. We can, of course, immediately mention

William Styron and Robert Penn Warren. But every so often, these rhythms crop up in some New Englander's novel, or in a Midwestern Jewish family saga, or are heard in Canada from some lonely dreamer on some of the prairies of Saskatchewan. Any day now I expect to find the Aurora Borealis—the Northern Lights—described in rolling Faulknerian rhetoric. When we run across these things, we have to wonder if new writers are catching hold, putting the style to good use, or if it has come sneaking up out of the swamps and bayous and caught them. The first way would be the right one, the second is a kind of cop-out. The question, as it says in *Alice*, is who's to be master.

I can remark on all this now, but twenty or thirty years ago for me, it was a stiff problem. I personally managed to work out the threat of the Faulkner style, by reading certain other writers I lavishly admired, who served as counter-influences, neutralizers. (It's a bit like chemistry, where the solution turns from pink to blue.) One writer I read was the Russian, Turgenev. I read him, of course, in translation, yet his style got through to me as flexible, apparently simple, certainly lucid, and capable of both subtlety and feeling. There was the strong direct appeal of Chekhov, also his lyrical vein; for someone writing a bit this way in English you could read Katherine Mansfield. There was also, right in our own Southern literature, the crystalline style of Katherine Anne Porter, while Willa Cather bore a creditable resemblance to Turgenev; and Hemingway's strict economies of language, though almost ballet-like in their stylization, were always a good antidote to Faulkner's baroque flamboyance. There were many ways, then, to hack your way out of the jungle, praying not to get snake bit. Another way I found to escape from the Faulkner overdose was to go back to what I knew before I ever encountered his work. The discipline of Latin phrasing, the patient diagramming of English sentences, the rhythms of the King James Bible, the plain admonitions of country teachers, to say nothing of one's parents, aunts, uncles, and grandfathers: "Say what you mean! Mean what you say!" There is no better advice for anybody, and for a writer you can't beat it.

Newbery Award Acceptance Speech

MILDRED D. TAYLOR

AS A SMALL CHILD I loved the South. I used to look forward with eager anticipation to the yearly trips we took there when my father would pack the car and my mother would fry chicken, bake a cake and sweet-potato pies, stir up jugs of ice water and lemonade, and set them all in a basket on the back seat of the car between my sister and me. In my early years the trip was a marvelous adventure, a twenty-hour picnic that took us into another time, another world; down dusty red roads and across creaky wooden bridges into the rich farm country of Mississippi, where I was born.*

And life was good then. Running barefoot in the heat of the summer sun, my skin darkening to a soft, umber hue; chasing butterflies in the day, fireflies at night; riding an old mule named Jack and a beautiful mare named Lady; even picking a puff of cotton or two—there seemed no better world. And at night when neighboring relatives would gather to sit on the moonlit porch or by the heat of the fire, depending on the season, talk would turn to the old people, to friends and relatives who then seemed to have lived so long ago. As the storytellers spoke in animated voices and enlivened their stories with movements of great gusto, I used to sit transfixed, listening, totally engrossed. It was a magical time.

Yet even magical times must end.

I do not remember how old I was when the stories became more than tales of faraway people, but rather, reality. I do not remember when the twenty-hour picnic no longer was a picnic, the adventure no longer an adventure. I only remember that one summer I suddenly felt a climbing nausea as we crossed the Ohio River into Kentucky and was again admonished by my parents that my sister and I were now in the South and must remain quiet when we pulled into the gas stations, that we must not ask to use the restrooms, that they would do all the talking.

*Address delivered in acceptance of the Newbery award for *Roll of Thunder, Hear My Cry*.

That summer and the summers to come I grew to realize that the lovely baskets of food my mother always packed for the trips, she prepared because we could not eat in the restaurants; that the long overnight ride was because we could not sleep in the motels; that the jugs of water and lemonade were because we could not drink at the water fountains—at least not the fountains marked "White Only," which were usually newer and cleaner. I was to learn the fear of the police siren. I was to learn to hate the patrolmen who frisked my father and made him spread-eagle—all because of thirty-five miles an hour. I was to learn the terror of the back road and the long, long wait for morning while my father, exhausted from the drive, tried to sleep as my mother watched guard.

These were hard things for a child to learn. But I was blessed with a special father, a man who had unyielding faith in himself and his abilities, and who, knowing himself to be inferior to no one, tempered my learning with his wisdom. In the foreword to *Roll of Thunder, Hear My Cry* I described my father as a master storyteller; he was much more than that. A highly principled, complex man who did not have an excellent education or a white-collar job, he had instead strong moral fiber and a great wealth of what he always said was simply plain common sense. Throughout my childhood he impressed upon my sister and me that we were somebody, that we were important and could do or be anything we set our minds to do or be. He was not the kind of father who demanded A's on report cards, although he was pleased when we got them, or ranted and raved if there was a D or two. He was more concerned about how we carried ourselves, how we respected ourselves and others, and how we pursued the principles upon which he hoped we would build our lives.

There was never a moment when he was too busy or too tired to share my problems or to give guidance to my sister and me. Through him my growing awareness of a discriminatory society was accompanied by a wisdom that taught me that anger in itself was futile, that to fight discrimination I needed a stronger weapon. When my family was refused seating in a Wyoming restaurant, he taught me that I must gain the skill to destroy such bigotry; when "For Sale" signs forested the previously all-white neighborhood into which we had moved, he taught me pride in our new home as well as in myself by reminding me that how I saw myself was more important than how others saw me; and when I came home from school one day versed in propaganda against the Soviet Union, he softly reminded me that Black people in the United States of the fifties had no more rights than I had been told the citizens of the Soviet Union had. From that I learned to question, to reason.

The effects of those teachings upon me are evident to anyone reading *Roll of Thunder, Hear My Cry.* Also evident are the strong family ties. Through David Logan have come the words of my father, and through the Logan family the love of my own family. If people are touched by the warmth of the Logans, it is because I had the warmth of my own youthful years from which to draw. If the Logans seem real, it is because I had my own family upon which to base characterizations. And if people believe the book to be biographical, it is because I have tried to distill the essence of Black life, so familiar to most Black families, to make the Logans an embodiment of that spiritual heritage; for, contrary to what the media relate to us, all Black families are not fatherless or disintegrating. Certainly my family was not.

During my childhood a family that offered aunts and uncles who were second parents, and cousins who were like brothers and sisters, was as natural to me as a mother and father are to most children. Even today the family remains a tight, extensive group, as Phyllis Fogelman, editor-in-chief of Dial, found out in early February when we were both in Washington celebrating the announcement of the Newbery-Caldecott awards with the Dillons and the rest of the Dial family. As Phyllis continued to glow from the yet unbelievable reality of the Dial sweep, I innocently asked her how many invitations I could have for the American Library Association banquet in June. Phyllis, unsuspecting, said that of course my mother and sister would be invited to the banquet as Dial's guests.

My heart quickened. Only two? To Phyllis, I said, "But I'll need more than two."

Phyllis, now becoming aware of what I was leading up to, looked a bit apprehensive, but asked pleasantly, "How many will you need, Mildred?"

I began to make a silent count, coming up with a number that I didn't have the heart to hit Phyllis with on her great day. "I'll let you know," I said.

A few days later when I was settled back in the comfort of my own home with the typewriter in front of me, I brazenly typed the number I had not had the courage to speak: thirty. I could picture Phyllis falling out of her chair when she saw the letter but consoled myself with the fact that I had trimmed the list as much as I could. After all, no one could expect me to exclude these essential people, people who have supported me not only in the writing of my books but throughout my life. Phyllis, upon receiving the letter, must have sensed this, for after recovering from her initial shock she began to make arrangements for the seating of the clan. And tonight to my great delight there sits before you and me the core of the Taylor-Davis family.

It is good to see them there, for their gathering now is exemplary of the many gatherings we had when I was a child. At those gatherings there was always time for talk, and when we children had finished all the games we could think to play, we would join the adults, soon becoming enraptured by their talk, for it would often turn to a history which we heard only at home, a history of Black people told through stories.

Those stories about the small and often dangerous triumphs of Black people, those stories about human pride and survival in a cruelly racist society were like nothing I read in the history books or the books I devoured at the local library. There were no Black heroes or heroines in those books; no beautiful Black ladies, no handsome Black men; no people filled with pride, strength, or endurance. There was, of course, always mention of Booker T. Washington and George Washington Carver; Marian Anderson and occasionally even Dr. Ralph Bunche. But that hardly compensated for the lackluster history of Black people painted by those books, a history of a docile, subservient people happy with their fate who did little or nothing to shatter the chains that bound them, both before and after slavery. There was obviously a terrible contradiction between what the books said and what I had learned from my family, and at no time did I feel the contradiction more than when I had to sit in a class which, without me, would have been all white, and relive that prideless history year after year.

As I grew, and the writers of books and their publishers grew, I noticed a brave attempt to portray Black people with a white sense of dignity and pride. But even those books disturbed me, for the Black people shown were still subservient. Most often the Black characters were housekeepers and, though a source of love and strength to the white child whose story it was, they remained one-dimensional because the view of them was a white one. Books about Black families by white writers also left me feeling empty, not because a white person had attempted to write about a Black family, but because the writer had not, in my opinion, captured the warmth or love of the Black world and had failed to understand the principles upon which Black parents brought up their children and taught them survival. It was not that these writers intentionally omitted such essential elements; it was simply that not having lived the Black experience, they did not know it.

But I did know it. And by the time I entered high school, I had a driving compulsion to paint a truer picture of Black people. I wanted to show the endurance of the Black world, with strong fathers and concerned mothers; I wanted to show happy, loved children about whom other children, both Black and white, could say: "Hey, I really like them! I feel what they feel." I wanted to show a Black family united in love and pride, of which the reader would like to be a part.

I never doubted that one day I would grasp that bright spark of life in words for others to see, for hadn't my father always said I could do anything I set my mind to do? But as the years passed and what I wrote continued to lack the vitality of the world I knew, there began to grow within a very youthful me an overwhelming impatience, and the question: *when?*

Well, the *when* was not to come until almost four years ago, after I had seen much of the world, returned to school for graduate study, and become a Black student activist. It was then that on a well-remembered day in late September a little girl named Cassie Logan suddenly appeared in my life. Cassie was a spunky eight-year-old, innocent, untouched by discrimination, full of pride, and greatly loved, and through her I discovered I now could tell one of the stories I had heard so often as a child. From that meeting came *Song of the Trees.*

If you have met Cassie and her brothers—Stacey, the staunch, thoughtful leader; Christopher-John, the happy, sensitive mediator; and Little Man, the shiny clean, prideful, manly six-year-old—then perhaps you can understand why, when I sent that final manuscript off to Dial, I did not want to give them up. Those four children make me laugh; they also make me cry, and I had to find a way of keeping them from fading into oblivion. In August, 1974, came the answer: I would write another book about the

Logans, one in which I could detail the teachings of my own childhood as well as incorporate many of the stories I had heard about my family and others. Through artistic prerogative I could weave into those stories factual incidents about which I had read or heard, as well as my own childhood feelings to produce a significant tapestry which would portray rural Black southern life in the 1930s. I would write *Roll of Thunder, Hear My Cry.*

Writing is a very lonely business. It is also a very terrifying one emotionally if a writer knows and cares about the people of her novel as well as I know and care about the Logans. Cassie's fears were my fears and what she feared from the night men, so did I. More than once my dreams were fraught with burnings and destruction, with faceless men coming in the night, with a boy being beaten, with a boy about to die. In September 1975, the month I had promised Phyllis and Regina Hayes, my editors, the first draft of the book, I found I could not write the final chapters, all of which dealt with explicit violence. I wanted to forget about the book. I began to wish that I had never gotten into it, that I had never signed a contract which obligated me to finish it, for I hate violence and I dreaded writing about it. But with October on its way, I knew I had to force myself to write those chapters. Feeling the pressure of my own deadline, I worked and worked with the final pages trying to make them catch fire and burn with passions of fear and anger and hate—but they still had no life.

Finally one Saturday afternoon after I had retyped the manuscript to send to Phyllis and Regina, I looked once more at those chapters. Frustrated and angry with myself because my words were too limited, my power too weak to convey what I knew the Logans felt, because I had failed where I could not fail, my mind seemed to snap. Rage welled within me, and I sent all two-hundred-plus sheets of the manuscript spinning into the air. Then I began to let fly everything I could lay my hands on. It was not until I had broken a precious irreplaceable treasure, a brightly painted ostrich egg brought from Africa, that my rage passed and was replaced by an aching sorrow. Holding the pieces of that broken egg I cried for the loss of it, and for my inability to write what was inside me.

Sleep has always been a great healer for me, and I slept almost the entire weekend. Late Sunday evening I awoke perfectly calm, renewed, and with a tugging thought that I knew *why* what I had written was wrong. I had attempted to make Cassie play too big a part in the climax. I had wanted her to be with David when his leg was broken, to be with him when the fire started, to fight the fire. After all, it was she who had to tell the story and how could she if she wasn't there? But the character of David Logan wouldn't let me put her into the center of the action. I thought of my own father and what he would have done. He, like David, would never have taken his young daughter on such dangerous missions. It was clear to me now. All I had to do was allow my characters to remain true to themselves; that was the key.

I believe that that key served me well in the writing of *Roll of Thunder, Hear My Cry,* and I hope that it will continue to guide me through the next two books about the Logans, which will chronicle the growth of the Logan children into adolescence and adulthood. Winning this distinguished award makes me shiver more than a little as I realize how difficult it will be to live up to readers' expectations as well as my own. Yet I will continue the Logans' story with the same life guides that have always been mine, for it is my hope that these four books, one of the first chronicles to mirror a Black child's hopes and fears from childhood innocence to awareness to bitterness and disillusionment, will one day be instrumental in teaching children of all colors the tremendous influence that Cassie's generation—my father's generation—had in bringing about the great Civil Rights movement of the fifties and sixties. Without understanding that generation and what it and the generations before it endured, children of today and of the future cannot understand or cherish the precious rights of equality which they now possess, both in the North and in the South. If they can identify with the Logans, who are representative not only of my family but of the many Black families who faced adversity and survived, and understand the principles by which they lived, then perhaps they can better understand and respect themselves and others.

As we all know, Cassie's South of the thirties is no more. The changes have come hard but sure, and even at this moment continue. Those changes have been heralded by Black people everywhere, but most of all I think, by the thousands like my father who left the South during and after World War II. Now many of those same thousands speak with longing of returning to that land of their childhood.

My father, too, had wanted to return.

He believed that as the North in the years following the War had held opportunities for Blacks, now the opportunities were in the South and he had, even in his last days, the dream of "going back home." He had never forgotten the feel of the soft red earth. He had never forgotten the goodness of walking on acres of his own land, of knowing that land had a history that stretched back over many generations. There, next to the house which my great-grandfather had built, he hoped to build his own house, surrounding it with flowers and fruit trees, with horses and cows, tending his land with the love he had felt for it as a boy.

Yet even as he dreamed, he knew it would not be so. Once as he lay in his hospital bed, he confided to me that he would never see the land again. I protested, for I never believed that he would die, not when he was only fifty-six, not he who was so strong, the rock upon which so many of us who loved him leaned for strength and guidance. But he was wiser than I, and speaking in that voice which I had heard too often of late, a voice which held confidence and sadness but not fear, which echoed of good-bye, he said: "You know, I've always tried to be a good father. Sometimes I was hard on you and your sister, but I did what I thought was right." He paused and then spoke slowly words which I shall always remember: "You and your sister," he said, "I'm so proud of y'all."

There is a great loneliness tonight in accepting this award, for my father, the person who would have rejoiced most at my receiving it, is not here to share the moment of triumph. He once told me that I had been given a great gift by knowing how to write. He also told my uncle that I had a special mission to fulfill. I don't think he ever realized how much he contributed to either that gift or to that mission, if that mission is to open to boys and girls, men and women, another dimension of the Black experience. While he lived, there were no banquets in his honor, no awards for his achievements. Instead, his awards and his honors have come through me and I feel loving pride that I can offer them to his memory.

There are others to thank for my receiving this award—Phyllis Fogelman and Regina Hayes, editors who have been more than editors, but rather trusted friends, whose insight into what I have attempted to portray and whose faith in me has been paramount in making reality believable; my dear mother, who has always urged perseverance; my sister, grandparents, aunts, and uncles, all the family. But it is my father to whom I owe most, for without his teachings, without his words, my words would not have been. Therefore, it is now with greatest gratitude that I accept in the name of my father, Mr. Wilbert Lee Taylor, the Newbery Medal from the American Library Association for *Roll of Thunder, Hear My Cry,* one of four books drawn from his legacy.

FROM

Smile Please

Mildred Spurrier Topp

NEW WORLDS TO CONQUER

GRANDPA SENT MOTHER the two thousand dollars she had written for, and when the photo gallery was nearly finished, she sent for us, so that we could start to school in Greenwood in September. There was a big yellow-fever scare, and people were not allowed to travel from one state to the other without a certificate saying they had not been exposed. We had a certificate, and a big yellow badge, which was a yellow-fever pass, and also a tag saying, "In case I get lost or have an accident, please notify Mrs. Lillian Spurrier, Greenwood, Mississippi, or V. M. White, Murfreesboro, Tennessee." As we wore all of these documents pinned to the front of our dresses, there was not much room left to spill things on.

Mother had written Cousin Ollie in Memphis, asking him to help us change trains there. He met us, and since his wife was out of town, he took us to a restaurant for supper. We had spaghetti, but I thought it was white worms, and it turned my stomach so I could eat only two helpings of everything.

Since the Photo Gallery was not quite ready to move into, the big event of our first few weeks in Greenwood was the opening of school. Mother had sent to Montgomery Ward for some red shoes and stockings for us, and, as they were the first ever worn in Greenwood, they created a sensation when we wore them to school and all the little boys liked us right away, "because we had such pretty legs."

I had met some nice boys and girls in the fourth grade, and I thought I would like to be in the fourth grade too. But before we got in line that first day, I looked the fourth-grade teacher over. She had dirty yellow hair, and teeth with green moss on them, and she bit her fingernails; so I decided not to be in the fourth grade. The third-grade teacher was old and rickety, with a saggy black dress and a stiff knee, and she had blackheads in the end of her nose; so I decided not to be in the third grade either. The fifth-grade teacher was the pick of the lot. She had on a clean, starched shirtwaist and a neat black bombazine skirt, and she looked as if she had enough sense to teach long division. So I decided to be in the fifth grade.

But when we had marched into the schoolroom that first day and I had found a single desk, a big boy named Benny Dent, who had been in the fifth grade two years already, plumped himself down in the seat beside me and tried to hug me. It had been raining that day, and I had brought my red umbrella. When I jumped up and started beating him over the head with it, he grabbed the umbrella and broke the handle. Then I bit him as hard as I could. I almost bit his thumb off.

He yelped, and Miss Ginny pulled me off him. She sent him to his seat and made him say he was sorry. Then she said to me, "Aren't you sorry, too, to get into a fight the first day of school?" I said, "I'm sorry he broke my umbrella, and he's going to be sorry too, if he doesn't bring me a new one. I'm going to bite him every day until he does." The next day, when he did not bring the new umbrella, I leaned over while passing his desk and took a piece out of the back of his neck. He let out a horrible howl, and Miss Ginny stood me in the corner for half an hour. "If you bite Benny again," she threatened, "I'm going to have to send you to the office."

The office was the lair of " 'Fessor," the presiding ogre of the school. When he walked into a schoolroom a hush fell over everything, and children and teacher alike were taut until he moved on. The thought of being sent to the office made my blood run cold, so all day, whenever I could think of it, I prayed, "God, you've just got to make Benny bring me a new umbrella tomorrow so I won't have to bite him again." But the next day found Benny empty-handed as usual. He leered at me whenever he could catch my eye, and finally wrote me a note, "I duble-dog dare you to bight me now fradycat."

I thought, "I'll wait 'til recess and bite him in the yard. Maybe that won't count as bad as if I bit him in Arithmetic." When recess came, I scouted the playground until I spotted him playing marbles. He was squatting on his haunches, so it was not hard for me to take off the top of his ear, as I swooped by.

When the bawling Benny showed Miss Ginny his bleeding cartilage, after recess, she called me to her desk sternly. "Take this note to Mr. Selbridge," she ordered, "in the office."

As soon as my wobbly legs had propelled me down the hall a safe distance, I opened the note and read it. It said, "The bearer bites."

When I entered the office, Mr. Selbridge was sitting at his desk with two seventh-grade boys quaking before him. "If you don't stop that infernal fighting on the school grounds," he was saying, "I'm going to tan your hides so you'll look like a pair of half-soles."

Then his baleful glance fell upon me. "What do you want?" he inquired belligerently.

Without a word, I handed him the note. He glanced at it, then looked me up and down. "So you bite, do you? Well, there's just one thing to do about that. Here, Jack, you and Brower go down to the boiler room and bring me the tool chest. It's under the steps." And the two recent culprits sprinted out of the room.

When they lugged the heavy box in, Mr. Selbridge said, "Put it there on my desk." Then he opened it, and began laying out tools. "Here's the pliers and the Stillson wrench; we'll need them. And here's the hammer for knocking the hard ones out after we've loosened them up with this crowbar. Now come here."

But I stood rooted in terror. "What are you going to do?" I quavered.

"Pull your teeth out," he said heartily. "That's the best way in the world to break a body from biting. Come here and open your mouth."

But instead, I backed into a corner, and locked my jaws in a vise.

"We'll hold her for you, 'Fessor, while you prize her mouth open," volunteered Brower.

Mr. Selbridge picked up the pliers and took a step toward me. "How's your mother going to feel when you come home without any teeth this afternoon?" he asked.

"She's going to be mad—at you," I answered. "She's been buying milk at twenty-five cents a gallon so we'll have good teeth."

At that moment Velma passed the office door on the way to the basement to be excused. When she saw me in the office, she paused, transfixed with horror. I beckoned to her frantically. She glimmered in the doorway, and 'Fessor roared, "Well, either come in or go out! What do you want?"

"Nothing," she murmured faintly. "I'm her sister."

"And do you bite, too?"

"No, sir," she replied modestly. "My teeth are not as big and sharp as hers, so I never have did much biting. I carry a knife instead." And she fingered a small pearl-handled knife that was suspended from her neck by a red ribbon.

"Holy smoke!" bellowed Mr. Selbridge. "What is this—a vendetta? Give me that knife before you get into trouble with it."

"Don't do it!" I cried. "He's trying to pull my teeth out, and you may have to cut him!" Then I turned on Mr. Selbridge. "She never has cut anybody up to now, and if you make her cut you, it will start her on the downward path, and she'll prob'ly turn out to be a proselyte or something."

This gave Mr. Selbridge pause. "I'll tell you what," said he, "I'll put away my tools and won't pull your teeth if you'll promise never to bite anybody again."

"I'm sorry I can't promise," I said miserably. "I've got to keep on biting Benny until he brings me a new umbrella for the one of mine he broke. I said I was going to do it, in front of Miss Ginny and the whole class, so I've got to."

"Well, what on earth am I to do with you!" he cried.

"Mother has tried tying my mouth shut, and once she made me wear the birdcage over my head all morning, but that didn't stop me. You see, I've got to bite when I'm fighting, because that's the only way I can win. When I hit or kick anybody, they just laugh. But they don't laugh when I bite them."

Mr. Selbridge was eyeing me with a look of profound distaste.

"Why don't you give me a real good whipping with a club or strap or something, then make Benny bring me one of those new umbrellas out of his papa's store?" I suggested.

"I don't whip little girls," he snorted.

"You mean you would pull out all of my teeth and make me a hopeless cripple for life, and yet you wouldn't whip me?"

"If Benny brings you a new umbrella, will you promise never to bite anybody else?" he asked wearily.

"I promise never to bite anybody else *at school,*" I agreed. "I'll wait and catch them somewhere else. It's not really true, is it, that you try to run the whole town?"

"So that's the lie they're circulating on me now, is it!" he shouted. "You can go! Get out! And tell Benny I want him!"

The next day when I came to school, there on my desk was a new umbrella. It was red, just like the one that Benny broke.

As soon as school got under way, Miss Ginny began talking to us about increasing our vocabularies. "Our language has thousands of beautiful, expressive words in it, and it's a shame for us never to make use of them," she said. "For us to keep on using the same common, worn-out words over and over again is being trite. It's just like going into a fine café, where you could order a delicacy like cream puffs or chocolate éclairs, and ordering old corn bread and pot licker."

For our language lesson once a week, we were to bring in sentences using at least five new words. Such assignments were manna from heaven to me. I attacked my dictionary with zeal, producing results that were sometimes clinical as well as alliterative. One of my early offerings was, "The vivacious vixen had vertigo, vermin, and virginity." The week that I contributed "The reprehensible plenipotentiary had hallucinations, hystericals, and hemorrhoids," was the last of our vocabulary-building. After that we switched to nouns and pronouns.

Mawmaw and Pawpaw

GLENNRAY TUTOR

I. Winter

A BED THAT WAS so cold no one could sleep in it was in the backroom of her house where there was also the wringer washer and the canning closet. The door to the room was usually closed because she didn't want any grandkids playing with the washer and getting their fingers caught. But sometimes she would let us feed the clothes in when she was there with us to watch, and the dresses and slacks and shirts and underwear would go in limp and dripping and come out falling in stiff motion like frozen waterfalls.

Instead of a door the canning closet had two drapes, dark purple with lighter flower designs, and inside there was a single lightbulb hanging on a long cord. With it on, and you standing under it, the drapes together, it was like being in a kind of jar yourself, surrounded with the peaches and tomatoes and pickles and beets and jelly and all the others looking at you with their swollen faces through their dusty glass masks, wondering which part of you they'd like to open and eat for supper tonight. And you couldn't remain in there like that for long. You tore through the drapes fighting for a breath of air.

Along with a couple of my cousins who weren't old enough to start to school yet either, until I was six years old I spent the weekdays at that house which belonged to my mom's parents, who we called Mawmaw and Pawpaw. My house was on the highway about five miles from town and Mawmaw and Pawpaw's was about ten miles farther out. Mom had to be at work at 7:30, so she'd have to leave early enough to give herself time to drop me at Mawmaw's and then drive back into town to her job. In the winter it would be dark when we left, Dad's pickup gone from the driveway an hour already, the air cold, everything still, even the highway quiet at that time of morning. On the way, I'd look at the dark ground rushing past near me and flowing more slowly farther off. Behind the dark trees at the other end of the black fields, the sky would turn orange and purple, dropping sparks of itself down the frozen fieldrows and ditches, and the day would lighten until you could see that you were riding in a car with your mom breathing quietly, driving, on a gray highway cutting between gray field. And standing on the seat, leaning against her, you'd start to wake up enough to remember where you were going for another day.

Mawmaw loved to talk. She'd talk to us all day, except for the hour or so she made us take naps in the afternoon. By the time I was six I knew all she could tell me about her life, the lives of people she'd known, and of course, too, the lives of those people she invented, in that natural, honest way she had of inventing. As she flavored our heads with them she didn't say this one is true and this one isn't. As far as my cousins and I knew *all* her stories were based on authentic events and, no matter how horrifying or fantastic, we believed them.

There was a woman who stayed in the backroom. This was one of Mawmaw's favorites. The woman was ugly, at least as old as Mawmaw, and crazy. Lizzie Mae. We heard her moan sometimes. Mawmaw warned us that if we didn't behave just right, Lizzie Mae would come out and carry us back with her. Lord knows to where. Maybe behind the shelves of canned goods in the walls, or through a hatch in the floor down to the spiderwebs and cat bones. To some place awful, though, for certain. Sometimes just for meaness Mawmaw pleaded with her to come out and get us even when we'd been doing our best to mind her. Maybe Mawmaw's purpose wasn't all mean; she might have just liked to feel us hugging and clutching her, begging her to stop, and then seeing our relief and happiness when she finally did.

About Lizzie Mae I thought this: the woman was to be feared, but also pitied. She had no home. She'd lost it, by all indications, through some person's cruelness a long time before. Mawmaw had taken her in, but the displacement had driven her mad. She didn't want anything else to do with people. She'd quit the world of social interaction. She lurked in the backroom and when anybody was in that part of the house she hid in the canning closet and when you went in there she slipped behind the rows of jars or scuttled down through the floor. You couldn't get her to show herself. But she would obey Mawmaw. She'd come out if Mawmaw wanted her to bad enough, because Mawmaw was the only thing which remained that she could still recognize. Everything else that meant anything to her was in a distant place of thicker woods and less roads, where she could never get back to. Mawmaw gave her understanding and protection. She'd do what Mawmaw wanted her to. Mawmaw was the only house she had now. I knew this and my cousins knew this and when Lizzie Mae's name started coming up we made sure we were acting our best.

At night Mawmaw and Pawpaw would go to bed by 8:00 and anyone staying with them had to turn in then too. There was only the stove in the kitchen and the one in the livingroom and neither of them were maintained after you went to bed so it really didn't matter in the winter where you slept; the whole house was eventually going to get cold. You just had to use a lot of quilts and draw yourself up tight and hope you stayed asleep until the morning. However, the bed in the backroom was too cold to sleep in no matter what you did and everybody knew it. Not even grown people such as Mawmaw and Pawpaw's brothers and sisters could sleep in it, Mawmaw said, when they came to visit in cold weather. But every time I spent the night with Mawmaw and Pawpaw she'd put me in that bed.

There was always a cousin or two spending the night when I did, and we'd lie in the bed awhile listening to Mawmaw tell one last story, then she'd make sure we were well covered, turn out the light, and go back through the house, humming to herself, then faraway talking to Pawpaw, their bed squeaking as they got fixed, and finally there was the strange quiet of the house at night, fifteen miles from the nearest town.

You were under the quilts in the bed, your legs drawn up away from the cold foot of it, close against your cousins, the room dark except for the moon-bleached window that tinkled occasionally as winter pressed against it. You would look at the closet and see the blackness of it there, stirring like an uncomfortable shadow wanting to pry itself off the pale wall. Your teeth were chattering it was so cold, and it was getting colder. You could see your cousins' eyes glinting, blinking next to you. You'd try to make yourself go to sleep simply to get out of the coldness and whatever might at any time come out of the closet. But it was too cold to go to sleep. Maybe fifteen minutes would go by, maybe an hour. Finally all of you would get out of bed and go through the house to Mawmaw and Pawpaw's bed and crawl up and huddle down between them. They were big and soft and warm and it was like a good dream you were having of being comfortable and safe and resting.

Then it was morning.

Pawpaw rattling some kindling and tumbling a log or two down into the stove, waking you up, with no television on like there would have been at home, but with Mawmaw up and already talking, presenting programs so much more vivid and historical and fantastic that you didn't care if you ever watched television again.

Still in her flannel gown she stood in the kitchen in front of her handed-down, half-century old cookstove, hair yellow-gray, brushed back, frying eggs and ham and baking biscuits, and if she paused a minute from talking, then she hummed some song she had learned from her mother or grandmother. And sitting at the table waiting for breakfast, listening, I remember thinking it was like Mawmaw had found a special kind of pie her mother had cooked and left for her in the old stove, and she had brought it out and sliced it open and the fragrant smell had drifted through the window-frosted room, something you knew was there but couldn't touch, as she hummed the tune from somewhere far away.

II. Summer

Pawpaw's name was Wilson Lindsay. His father had died when Pawpaw was ten and his mother when he was seventeen. As soon as he was old enough to find a job he'd gone to work to help support the rest of his family. He had two sisters still living and one sister and one brother who lived to be in their thirties and then had died within a year of each other, both from cancer. All this information had come to me through Mawmaw. It was rare that Pawpaw spoke about his past, or about anything for that matter. He preferred listening to talking. He'd spent his life working at jobs where it was best not to talk, just do; years and years of farm work mostly, occasionally a dollar a day job like loading cross-ties or cutting lumber those years when the crops had been poor. In his mid-sixties he'd had two heart attacks and his kids had convinced him it was time to quit working so hard. He had turned the farm over to his son Lowell, and still helped him half-days sometimes, but usually he spent his time now around the house, gardening, repairing things, or walking across the fields to some ditch to go fishing.

In all the time I was around him, the most I ever remember him saying at one time, even to Mawmaw or his own children, was one day when it was almost time for my mom and my cousins' mom to get off work and drive out and pick us up. Mawmaw was in the swing holding my cousin Jane who was two years old, talking and sometimes singing to her. Mike and Murlin, who were both my age, were in the yard playing under the poplars which lined both sides of the long driveway. I was sitting on the porch next to Pawpaw listening to Mawmaw, the swing squeaking as she went back and forth, and the trees rattling in the late summer afternoon wind.

Far off on the highway a car roared by with its window down and someone's hair blowing and a hand slung the day's paper. Pawpaw carefully got out his glasses and put them on as Mike ran the paper up to the house. Pawpaw rolled the rubberband off one end and let the paper come undone. I always liked the funnies and the page of movie ads. Pawpaw located these and separated them from the rest of the paper and gave them to me. I struggled with the giant sheets of paper, trying to look at the cartoons and the ads of monsters and screaming women and lovemaking and violence, and it was like fighting a pterodactyl, its wings frantic in the hot wind. Finally I laid the pages flat on the porch and held them with my knees.

"Look here," he said, after watching me a minute. "I'll show you how to fold a newspaper."

I watched as he spread the paper out with his hands, holding it in front of us.

"First hold it like this . . . and let half of it fall over . . . like that. Then take your fingers and run them down the edge, giving it a good crease. Then fold it another time in the middle like this . . ." He was demonstrating as he went along, slowly, making sure I understood. ". . . Then you can relax and just enjoy it." He looked at me. "Think you can do it?"

"I don't know."

"Try it." He unfolded what he had just folded and gave it back to me. "Find the page you want and then fold the rest of the paper around it, just like I showed you."

I worked with it for a while and didn't do a very good job. Pawpaw grinned and said I'd get better with practice—at least I knew the proper procedure now for doing it.

There was the sound of tires over gravel then and Mom was

coming up the driveway, here to pick me up and take me home, and I forgot about the newspaper and Pawpaw and ran out to meet her.

But I tried it again that night with our paper. Except for the funnies and the movie ads I really didn't care that much for newspapers. To me they were mostly just endless amounts of words that I didn't know how to decipher. But Pawpaw had made it seem like such an important thing, opening to a page, stroking every inch with his eyes as though his eyes were hands and the black and white paper a cherished pet, then tenderly folding to another section, so I kept practicing what he'd shown me until I could do it fairly well I thought.

One morning I showed him what I'd learned. He stood over me watching, then put his big hand on my shoulder. He went out to the barn and in a little while came back with a can of worms and two cane poles. Mawmaw was putting breakfast on the table. "Looks like somebody's goin' fishin'," she said.

Pawpaw came in and sat down. He opened a couple of biscuits, inhaled the smoke, then spooned gravy on them and started to eat.

"Gonna be hot today, W.D.," she said, bringing the ham in a platter and setting it between us. "You be sure to wear your straw hat, and find a place under a shade tree to fish." She fixed a jar of ice water while we finished breakfast and put it in a flour sack with some ham and biscuits wrapped in wax paper. "The day's gonna be a hot one," she said, tying a knot in the sack and giving it to Pawpaw.

After breakfast, before any of my cousins had arrived, we headed straight into the cottonfields in the early sun. Dew was still on the leaves, shimmering around us. We kept a steady pace crossing the field, but once Pawpaw stopped so suddenly I ran into him, and he showed me a garden spider we'd almost walked into, waiting in his sun-glistening web between the green rows. When we came to the end of the field we turned and went along a fencerow with the trees thick and making noise in the breeze. It was like we were walking on a long narrow peninsula and the fields around us were lakes of sunlight, bright and wide and sparkling.

Pawpaw would stop periodically and wipe his face with his handkerchief, and when he did this he'd always show me something—the way the bark flaked on certain trees, a bird perched on a high branch watching us, the winding mound of a mole's tunnel, the way the sap leaked out of a sweetgum tree, drooping vines that were strong enough for human nests if you wanted to climb on them, caravans of ants leaving the ground in quest of some magical sustenance up the tree trunks in the green and blue flashing foliage—all kinds of things, never commenting at all, just pointing them out.

We entered a dense clump of woods and inside was the water, green-topped and full of fallen trees and still. Only the birds and insects and snakes were moving.

We crawled out on a big log and Pawpaw showed me how to fix the bait on our poles. We sat and watched our floaters. The sun fell through the trees in patches. It was mid-July but surprisingly cool where we were, with the shadows moving, the sunlight sparkling, and the water green and as still as the ground. Then, right under us, the water kind of swelled and my floater bounced, and disappeared. I was so startled I made Pawpaw take my pole and he pulled out a flapping, shimmering catfish. Then his floater went under and he handed me my pole and yanked his pole up and brought out another one.

"Fishing's always best on two kinds of days, Glennray," he said, putting our two fish on the stringer. "The hottest days of the year, and the coldest." He put the stringer in the water and baited us up again.

I wanted to stay until we got hungry, so we could get out the ham and biscuits Mawmaw had sent along, and drink out of the jar of water with the ice cubes chiming around in it, then fish some more. But before long the mosquitoes got bad. They weren't bothering us at first, for maybe an hour, then it was as if a scout had discovered us and reported to the rest and there were suddenly so many making such a loud humming, cloaking attack on us that we had to stand up and move around. Pawpaw held his hand up in front of me, giving the mosquitoes undisturbed access to it, and it looked as if he had on a squirming black glove. We were about to go down under them. We grabbed our gear and headed home.

It was getting close to noon and it was hot.

At first we were keeping as good a pace as we had on our way out, but then something started happening to Pawpaw, and we'd have to stop every few minutes for him to rest and wipe the sweat off his face. Because of this the way back seemed much longer than the way out. The first few times we stopped, just as he'd done that morning, Pawpaw found things to show me—a terrapin's back curving up out of the leaves, a hole in a hollow tree swarming with bees, a double-winged dragonfly caught by a lizard and being eaten, an ant struggling at the loose sides of an ant lion's pit and the sand shifting, lifting with the movement of something at the bottom. But then we'd stop and Pawpaw would just stand there, wiping his face and neck, his eyes seeming not to be seeing out as much as somehow looking back into himself, hard, as though something had been misplaced and there was a frantic search going on in there for it.

I started getting scared. I began to think that maybe we were lost and would never get back.

We stopped again and he opened the jar of water and raised it up. His hands were shaking and some of the water ran out the sides of his mouth and fell in wet splotches on his shirt. He gave it to me and helped me hold the cold sweating jar jangling with a few last ice cubes, and the water was cold and good.

We had walked another short distance and paused again and were sitting on the fallen, vine-shrouded fence wire in the small shade under the trees. Pawpaw was wiping his face and staring into the hot field and I was watching him.

He smiled.

I followed his look and there in the middle of the hot green ocean was the house, bobbing the way our floaters had when a fish was under them, sending out ripples of light that spread across the shimmering expanse toward us.

Leaning against Pawpaw, feeling his wet shirt, glad, looking at the far spot of house, I thought I could hear Mawmaw's voice coming across as light and delicate as the ripples, and Pawpaw took a deep breath, got up, and led me into the glaring day, back toward where we'd come so long ago that morning.

Growing Out of Shadow

MARGARET WALKER

WHEN I WAS FIVE, I was busy discovering my world, and it was a place of happiness and delight. Then, one day, a white child shouted in my ears "nigger" as if he were saying "cur," and I was startled. I had never heard the word before, and I went home and asked what it meant, and my parents looked apprehensively at each other as if to say, "It's come." Clumsily, without adding hurt to the smart I was already suffering, they sought to explain but they were unable to destroy my pain. I could not understand my overwhelming sense of shame, as if I had been guilty of some unknown crime. I did not know why I was suffering, what brought this vague unease, this clutching for understanding.

When I went to school, I read the history books that glorify the white race and describe the Negro as a clown and a fool or a beast capable of very hard work in excessive heat. I discovered the background of chattel slavery behind this madness of race prejudice. Once we were slaves and now we are not, and the South remains angry. But when I went home to the good books and the wonderful music and the gentle, intelligent parents, I could see no reason for prejudice on the basis of a previous condition of servitude.

I went to church and I wondered why God let this thing continue. Why were there segregated churches and segregated hospitals and cemeteries and schools? Why must I ride behind a Jim-Crow sign? Why did a full-grown colored man sit meekly behind a Jim-Crow sign and do nothing about it? What could he do? Then I decided perhaps God was on the side of the white people because after all God was white. The world was white, and I was black.

Then I began to daydream: it will not always be this way. Some day, just as chattel slavery ended, this injustice will also end; this internal suffering will cease; this ache inside for understanding will exist no longer. Some day, I said, when I am fully grown, I will understand, and I will be able to do something about it. I will write books that will prove the history texts were distorted. I will write books about colored people who have colored faces, books that will not make me ashamed when I read them.

But always I was seeking for the real answer, not the daydream. Always I wanted to know. I lay awake at night pondering in my heart, "Why? Why? Why?"

I heard Roland Hayes and Marian Anderson sing, and James Weldon Johnson and Langston Hughes read poetry. In the audiences were well-dressed, well-behaved colored people. They were intelligent, yet they were not allowed to sit beside white people at concerts and recitals. Why? Every night Negro cooks and maids and chauffeurs and nursemaids returned home from the white people's houses where their employers were not afraid to sit beside them.

I learned of race pride and consciousness and the contribution of the Negro to American culture. Still I was bewildered. America was a place of strange contradictions. The white grocery man at the corner who was so friendly when I was in his store thought it a crime for a white and colored boxer to fight in the ring together. But he did not think it a crime for a Negro to be drafted to fight for America.

I decided vaguely the white man must think these things because of fear; because he felt insecure. Perhaps he was a little afraid of what would happen in a free America.

How did I first discover the color of my skin? I had only to look in my mirror every morning to know. I must say it appeared to me a good healthy color. But there is a difference in knowing you are black and in understanding what it means to be black in America. Before I was ten I knew what it was to step off the sidewalk to let a white man pass; otherwise he might knock me off. I had had a sound thrashing by white boys while Negro men looked on helplessly. I was accustomed to riding in the Jim-Crow street cars with the Negro section marked off by iron bars that could not be moved. For a year and a half I went to school in a one-room wooden shack. One year when my father's school work took him out of town constantly, my mother lived in fear of our lives because there was no man in the house to protect us against the possibility of some attack. Once we climbed the fire escape to see a movie because there was no Negro entrance, and after that we saw no movies. Another time my mother stood for hours upstairs in a darkened theatre to hear a recital by Rachmaninoff because there were no seats for colored. My father was chased home one night at the point of a gun by a drunken policeman who resented a fountain pen in a "nigger's pocket." My grandmother told the story of a woman tarred and feathered in the neighborhood. A mob came and took her from her home because it was rumored that a white man was visiting her. Although they took her deep into the woods, her screams were heard by relatives and neighbors. My grandmother heard them, too. Next day the woman's family went to the woods and brought her home. She was still alive, so they removed the tar and feathers with turpentine. She was horribly burned and scarred.

And always the answer and the question in a child's mind to each of these was "Why? Why do they do these things?"

Negroes congregating on a city block to argue and talk about the race question imitated what they heard from the pulpits or what the white folks told them: The trouble with the Negro problem in America is just we needs to git together . . . we don't co-operate . . . we always kicking one another . . . this is a white man's country and black man ain't got no place in it . . . we just cursed by God, sons of Ham, hewers of wood and drawers of water . . . our leaders are crooked and they betray us . . . we need to get a little money and make ourselves independent of the white man . . . if it wasn't for the white man we'd be way back in the jungles of Africa somewhere . . . we oughta thank the white man for bringing us to this country and making us civilized . . . trouble is we scared to fight, scared to stick up for our rights . . . we'll fight for the white man but we won't fight for ourselves . . . all the progress we've made we owe to the white man . . . I hates a white man worsener I hates poison, left to me I'd kill up every paleface in the world . . . don't let 'em fool you when they grinning in your face, they want something . . . only God can help us . . . it takes time, that's all, to solve the Negro problem . . . all we got to do is humble ourselves and do right and we'll win out . . . colored man hurts hisself most of the time . . . all we got to do is do like the children of Israel and the slaves done way back yonder, pray . . . colored people oughta get out of the notion that they are Negroes . . . that word Negroes is what hurts us. . . ."

But all of it was no real answer to the anxious questioning of a child burdened constantly with the wonder of what race prejudice is.

When I went away to college in my teens, I left the South with mingled emotions. I had been told that Negroes in the North were better off than Negroes down South; they had more sense and more opportunities; they could go any place, enjoy recreational facilities such as parks and movies, eat in restaurants without discrimination; there were no Jim-Crow transportation restrictions, and if Negroes were subjected to any indignity they could sue the person or company involved; there was no such thing as lynching. Best of all Negroes could vote.

I was, nevertheless, shy and afraid over the prospect of going to a white school; I might prove backward as a result of my southern training. I had also perforce become somewhat anti-white myself and I feared coming into close contact with white people. Yet I anticipated a new kind of freedom once I crossed the Mason-Dixon line.

Imagine my great hurt to discover that few of the wonderful promises came true. I was refused service in restaurants in Evanston and Chicago time and again. In the South I had suffered no similar embarrassment because there I had known what to expect. I discovered that most of the Negroes in the northern colleges and universities were from the South, for the majority of Negroes in the Middle West had no money with which to take advantage of higher education.

What was most amazing was my discovery of my own prejudices and my first realization of the economic problem.

Because of the nature of segregated life in America many Negroes have misconceptions of white life. I was no exception. As servants, Negroes know certain elements of white life and we characterize the whole in this way. My first step toward understanding what it means to be black in America was understanding the economic set-up in America.

In the South I had always thought that, naturally, white people had more money than colored people. Poor white trash signified for me the lazy scum of the marginal fringe of society with no excuse for poverty. Now I discovered there are poor white working people exploited by rich white people. I learned that all Jews are not rich. I discovered that all Negroes are not even in the same economic class. While there are no Negro multi-millionaires, there are many wealthy Negroes who have made money by exploiting poor Negroes, who have some of the same attitudes toward them that rich whites have toward poor whites and that prejudiced whites have toward all Negroes. Imagine my amazement to hear a white girl tell me she was forced to leave Northwestern because she had no money. But I, a poor Negro girl, had stayed even when I had no money. They never threatened me with expulsion. Yet I did not find a white school in the Middle West free of prejudice. All around me was prejudice. To understand the issues out of which it grew had become my life's preoccupation.

A year out of college found me working with poor whites—Jew and Gentile—and poor Negroes, too. In Chicago for the first time I began to see that Negroes, as almost entirely a working-class people, belong with organized labor. My background was so thoroughly petty-bourgeois with parents who belonged to a professional small-salaried class, that I had not understood that people who worked with their brains were also workers. I knew we were poor and decent, and that was all I knew. In the South many, if not most, petty-bourgeois Negroes are anti-union, anti-strike, and anti-white. This, of course, is not strange when one considers the history of Negroes in unions in the South, their forced role as scabs, the brutal treatment they received as such, prior to CIO, the general nature of Negro life in the South, threatened always by sinister undertones of white violence.

Thus there began for me in Chicago a period in which I was given an analysis of the whole strata of class-society in America. As soon as I began working in close contact with whites, I discovered startling things peculiar to both racial groups, all adding up to one main conclusion: that whites suffer psychologically from the problem of race prejudice as much as Negroes. I began to see race prejudice as a definite tool to keep people divided and economically helpless: Negroes hating whites and whites hating blacks, with conditions of both groups pitiful, both economically and psychologically. I saw, too, that it was not beyond the ability of both groups to reach understanding and to live peaceably side by side, that labor organization of Negroes and whites was certainly one step forward toward that end.

The second step toward understanding what it means to be black in America came in understanding the political problem. By 1932 and 1936, the Negro had, out of the dire necessity of destitution, become politically conscious even in the Deep South where he has no real voice in politics. In the North, the East, and particularly the Middle West, his vote assumed significant proportions and in many instances proved a balance of power.

In 1936 I cast my first vote in Chicago in a Presidential election. It was a great time to come of age. There had been four years of the New Deal, and many of the ills and evils of our society, as they immediately touched Negroes and all poor people, had been somewhat alleviated. We had benefited from the WPA, the NYA, the Federal Housing and Federal Farm Administration, Social Security, the adult education program; we had benefited in many instances where there had previously been evil practices of discrimination. I began to dig into the historical background of politics in America, to read the record where Negroes were concerned. I began to see parallels. When the thirteen colonies revolted, they revolted on the premise that taxation without representation is tyranny. Yet that is precisely what the Negro suffers in the South today. Moreover, poor white people as well have no voice in their government. If the truth could be nationally known and understood, the small number of votes cast in electing southern Representatives and Senators to Congress, as compared with the population, would not merely appear ridiculous but alarming. Not that these citizens of America are too indifferent to vote; they are disfranchised under the pretense of a poll-tax not paid or a grandfather clause. The old saying that a voteless people is a helpless people became a basic fact in my understanding of the Negro problem.

A third step came from a growing world perspective. As a child, reading the history books in the South, I was humiliated by some unhappy picture or reference to a Negro. They made me burn all over. It was as if we were cut off from humanity, without sensitivity. I could make no connection between my life as a Negro child in the South and the life of Chinese children or Indian children or children in South Africa. I grew up and became self-supporting, yet I had not connected myself with working women all over the world, with poor peasant women who are white as well as black. Now I began to reach out. I saw it was eternally to the credit of Negroes in America that we were represented in Spain on the side of the Loyalists with men, nurses, volunteer workers, our humble gift of an ambulance, our moral support. We can be proud that Ethiopia found a willing ear for help from us. While white America is far too prone to appreciate the struggle of people in distant lands and forget the problems on its own doorstep, its disadvantaged groups are often too obsessed with their own problems to see further than the bridge of their nose. I realized it was essential for Negroes to be identified with every heroic struggle of an oppressed people, with the brave Chinese, the Indians, the South Africans, the Negroes in the West Indies who fight for liberty. Now that we are engaged in a global war, it is even more essential that all peoples of the earth gain a world perspective and become conscious of our common humanity and man's struggle to be free.

Yet I am sure that economic, political, and social understanding is not all. There is need for a new type of spiritual understanding, and I use the word not in its narrow religious meaning. I am concerned with something far more meaningful in the lives of individual men and women, of greater practical value and far better potentialities for personal and social growth. Once the human spirit is washed clean of prejudices, once the basic needs of men are considered and not the pocketbooks of the few nor the power of a handful, once institutionalized religion is liberated into religious meaning, of necessity there must begin to bloom upon the earth something spiritually more durable than any of the mystic conceptions of religion that mankind has thus far brought forth. Then no man will look at another with fear, patronage, condescension, hatred, or disparagement, under pain of his own spiritual death.

Mississippi and the Nation in the 1980s

MARGARET WALKER

MISSISSIPPI STANDS ON THE threshold of a decade of destiny. Her potential is great and her future is indeed brighter than usual. As we compare our state here in the Sunbelt with other states in and beyond this region, we have reason to take courage today and hope for a bigger and better Mississippi. Of course, when we look at the past and the future, we must take into consideration the outlook for the nation and a global look at the world in general in order to see Mississippi in perspective.*

This state has never been the typical sample of the United States because we have here a unique and peculiar position. History declares that we have been among the last of the states formed along the Mississippi River when that river was the western frontier of colonial North America. When she was admitted to the Union in the early nineteenth century, 1817 to be exact, and as late as the post-Civil War period or Reconstruction, Mississippi was still largely wilderness with hundreds of acres of virgin forest and soil. A rural state with an agricultural economy, Mississippi remained almost virtually untouched by the Industrial Revolution for a hundred years from the middle of the nineteenth century until the middle of the twentieth century. Then suddenly like an explosion of time this state felt the weight of both the Industrial Revolution and the Einsteinian or Electronic Revolution almost simultaneously. The result of that explosion has been nearly a quarter century of phenomenal growth, an attempt to balance diversified and light industry with agriculture and the establishing of three major economic assets: The Space Center NASA, the expansion of Ingalls Shipyard at Pascagoula, and the great Tombigbee Waterway. Mushrooming manufacturing centers, with major plants and industries from the northeast establishing branches in the Sunbelt here in Mississippi, cause a healthy economy to assume a

*Address given at the inauguration of Mississippi's Governor William F. Winter, 1980.

brave new look, and all this in the face of mounting unemployment and inflation all over the nation.

Mississippi may not be typical of the national economy; we are however, typical in that we are here a part of the great pluralistic fabric of this nation. Historically, Mississippi has been home to four races in the family of mankind: the red men were here first—the Chickasaw and Choctaw, the Creeks and the Natchez. The white men from Europe imported black Africans to build their cotton plantations, and the Delta has for more than a century been home to a group of Oriental Americans. They came when the railroads were crossing this land. Mississippi is therefore multi-racial as well as multi-cultural. William Faulkner has written this history in prize-winning fiction, and Richard Wright, a "Native Son," began his search for a common ground of humanity here in his native Mississippi. It is along these multi-racial and multi-cultural lines that I wish to look as we think about the challenges of the decade of the 1980s as these challenges face Mississippi and our American nation.

The economic, political, and social factors are only the necessary background for more specific indicators of a good life in Mississippi and what we can hope and expect in the 1980s. As a black woman, I am particularly interested in what the opportunities for minorities will be in the decade of the eighties. I am especially interested in education, family and community life, health, recreation, and the cultural life of Mississippi as major concerns for the state as well as the nation in the 1980s. If the world is at war, then we are at war. If inflation persists and unemployment rises while the problems of energy and world hunger remain unsolved, we in Mississippi cannot help but be affected in every area of our lives.

Perhaps an even greater challenge lies in what may seem intangibles and abstractions, but which are of utmost importance if we as a state and a nation are to develop the indomitable will and the stamina we need to meet the challenges of a new decade and a world already in social upheaval. These intangibles and abstractions are no less than the spiritual values, the moral, ethical, and even religious standards which form the bedrock of our American culture and which our nation has from its inception considered fundamental. Today the super powers of the world are locked in a deadly ideological conflict. As we begin the eighth decade of this century we look back on seven decades of war and revolution. Europe, Asia, Africa, and the islands in the Caribbean and the South Pacific have one by one been drenched in a bloodbath of war and revolution. Although the United States in this century has escaped this bloodbath on its own soil, that is not to say we have not been involved. Mississippi has given her sons in every war of the century, and her finest youth have bled and died in foreign wars. Foreign policy involves us and is as relevant as any national or global issue. Whether that foreign policy is one of isolationism or globalism, the necessity for intervention in foreign affairs must continue to place us on the horns of a dilemma. But foreign war is only one of the specters and phenomena of the century. In the short space of our lifetime the world has witnessed the horrible specter of famine and hunger in at least five countries: China, India, Bangladesh, Biafra, and now Cambodia. These are all non-white and non-European but this segment of suffering humanity must not and cannot be ignored. World hunger or famine and the problem of raising enough food to feed the world is a number one challenge to a state that is largely rural and agricultural as well as a challenge to the nation as a whole. This is a challenge that must be met in the 1980s. Obviously the problems of energy which touch all our lives whether at the gas pump or the utility bill must be seen as inextricably bound to the problems of unemployment and inflation as well as oil and our foreign policy.

When this century began, the price of a loaf of bread in the world marketplace was determined by the price of grain, whether wheat, corn, oats, millet, rice, or barley. Now it is determined by the price of a barrel of oil. We have within the past decade witnessed a shift in the economic order of the world. We must meet the challenge that shift demands and we have an urgent need to meet this in the eighties.

Today Mississippi is beginning a new gubernatorial administration, and the challenge to that administration is to meet the crisis in leadership that we are witnessing all over the world. We have been promised positive and competent leadership from our newly elected governor. Nothing short of this will suffice. This is a herculean task and I am sure he recognizes that leadership for tomorrow must come from our youth of today. Therefore we must re-examine our educational system in Mississippi and America in order to develop the creative thinking of our young people and prepare them for creative leadership if they are to meet the challenge of a decade of destiny. All over America we are still basing our educational system on Newtonian physics together with a fundamentalist religious faith and a narrow, almost bigoted, belief about people who look and think differently from us. At the beginning of this century the Einsteinian Revolution gave us a new concept of the Universe, and although our post-World War II world has seen an electronic revolution in space, atomic energy, cybernation, and automation, we have still not witnessed an intellectual change in basic ideas about education, religion, race, and culture.

We need to stretch our minds and stretch our faith in order to accommodate our thinking to the problems of our systemic crises so that we can meet the challenges of the 1980s. We need to understand the Einsteinian principles of unity in diversity—racial and cultural diversity as well as an illimitable universe with a space-time continuum. Then we can better understand our pluralistic universe. We need to develop international understanding and peace on the basis of such unity in cultural and racial diversity. We need to develop religious tolerance so that we respect all religious faiths and know that God is truly the Father/Mother of all mankind and every man is our brother, every woman is our sister, every child has the light of God, and all human personality is holy and divine.

My family has been involved in education for black people in Mississippi for over one hundred years. In 1878 my great uncle, James A. Ware (the Jim of *Jubilee*), and my grandfather, the Reverend Edward Lane Dozier, a Baptist minister (who married Minna in my story) came to the Mississippi Delta and established a school for black children in the oldest black Baptist Church in Greenville. Uncle Jim died there in 1932. During the school year 1920–1921 my mother and father taught school at old Haven Institute in Meridian and there I went to school for the first time.

In the 1940s my sister came to Prentiss Institute for her first teaching experience and I have been in Mississippi since 1949 at Jackson State University where I retired in May. When I came, it was with the full intention of staying and making Jackson my home, a home for my family, my husband and then three children, a fourth was born several years later, and now my grandchildren. Why have I remained here so long and now that I am retired why don't I leave?

I believe that despite the terrible racist image Mississippi has had in the past, despite her historic reputation for political demagoguery, despite racial violence and especially lynching, despite all the statistics about being on the bottom, Mississippi, and especially urban Mississippi, offers a better life for most black people than any other state in which I have lived or visited. I have lived in the Middle West, the Northeast, the border South, and the deep South and I have travelled through thirty-five of these United States, particularly the eastern half and this side of the Rocky Mountains. I observed on first coming to Mississippi in the 1940s that most black people in Mississippi are thrifty, proud, and generally intelligent despite substandard and dual systems of education. In Jackson the average black family struggles to own a home, pridefully keep it, send their children to college, and participate in their community as law-abiding and voting citizens. There are more elected black public officials in Mississippi today than in any other state. Proud black Mississippians have this year sent seventeen black members to the State Legislature.

Our martyred dead, Medgar Evers and Fannie Lou Hamer, as well as Martin Luther King, have not died in vain. Not only is Mississippi noted for beautiful women (both Miss America and Miss Black America are this year from Mississippi) and great athletes, but it is also a proven climate for genius for William Faulkner, Tennessee Williams, Richard Wright, and Eudora Welty. The folk-culture of Mississippi is part of my heritage; therefore it is home.

Superficially, Mississippi has an ideal climate, a mild winter and a long growing season. She also has a growing economy, better housing for all her people, and widening recreational opportunities. The problems with welfare and public programs are the problems of the nation as a whole. But health costs, hospitals, doctors, and pharmaceuticals cost less than in the Middle West and the Northeast. Even high taxes are comparatively lower. If school integration has worked well anywhere in the nation, which is doubtful, it has worked better in Mississippi than in most other places. There is documentary proof of this. Life is not idyllic in Mississippi for black or white. The same hard realistic facts of American life prevail here as elsewhere, but the racial climate is certainly no worse here. The Civil Rights Movement liberated both black and white. A more liberal racial climate has helped business and politics, and therefore the society is more open and generally better. Today there is hope for a change and a better tomorrow. Mississippi was the determining factor in the presidential election of 1976. She may well be again in 1980 or 1984 or even 1988.

All of us must be prepared for the drastic changes of the 1980s if for no other reason than that we are already living in another age, and the life of the twenty-first century is already upon us. Somewhere in the past two decades of the sixties and seventies we passed the watershed of the twentieth century and we can never go back. Mississippi, like all the rest of this nation, must be prepared to meet the challenges and cope in every respect with the changes of a new decade, a decade of destiny in the 1980s.

We must be prepared to deal with world revolution and sinister war threats, to cope with ideological conflict and cultural shock, to deal with a shifting economic order and not least of all with multi-racial, multi-cultural diversity. We must test our spiritual endurance and our religious faith if we are to survive, not only as a state and a nation, but as a people, as humanity on the planet earth.

A Christmas Remembered

Dean Faulkner Wells

When I was a little girl, at Christmas I always went to Rowan Oak, Pappy's fine white house not far from where my mother and I lived with Nanie, my grandmother.

One of the first Christmases I remember was a warm, sultry day, much too hot for the long-sleeved, green velvet dress I proudly wore. I rode to Pappy's in the rumble seat of Nanie's yellow Buick roadster. I could not see over the sides of the car, so I spent most of the short ride admiring my long white stockings and shiny new black patent-leather Mary Janes.

But as soon as the small car bounced and lurched into the first pothole, I knew we had turned into Pappy's driveway. It was dark for a moment. Then, through thick branches, the sunlight made yellow patterns dance on my hands and dress. I looked up into the tall cedars, closed my eyes and knew just from their smell that we were almost there. At the end of the driveway, the house loomed—bigger than a courthouse and twice as grand to my child's eyes.

Pappy stood on the gallery alone, arms folded across his chest, staring down the driveway. We chugged past him, Nanie tooted the horn, and I waved exuberantly. I was still waving when we stopped by the steps.

He did not look at us. My fat little arm wilted into my lap, and as the moments passed, I began to fidget in my seat. Pappy continued to stand motionless, his gaze riveted to the driveway. I sat back there in the rumble seat for what seemed an eternity, feeling increasingly exposed and vulnerable as the austere figure within 6 feet of me held his pose. Finally, he turned toward us. He seemed to see the car for the first time, and with characteristically precise movements, he rebuttoned his tweed jacket, tugged its corners straight, and walked toward the car.

I sank lower and lower in the leather seat. I could hear Nanie and my mother chatting amicably. I knew they were busily pulling on their gloves and gathering up their handbags, totally unaware of his approach and of my impulse to bolt.

Then he was at the side of the car. I looked up into his tired, familiar face, at the fine lines etched around his eyes, the great hawk nose, the mustache which always hid his mouth and never let anyone see whether or not he was smiling. I wanted to reach out and touch him. He bent slightly to help my mother out of the car, and the moment he spoke to her, even though I could not make out the words, I knew everything was all right. The sound of his voice was warm and gentle. We were where we belonged.

He opened my mother's door with all the courtliness of an 18th-century gallant, and when he took her hand, she stepped out of the car as if she were walking on air or, at the very least, on somebody's coat. He came around the car and helped Nanie out with the same care and formality. He pulled her gently to him; then they joined my mother. They made a stately procession as they mounted the steps, one lady on each of his arms.

Alone and seemingly ignored, I was about to howl when Pappy said in a stage voice, much louder than his usual tone: "Oh, have we forgotten somebody?" He turned back to the car, chuckling.

I scrambled over the side into his arms. He stopped me on the steps to straighten my dress and whispered: "I like pretty girls in pretty dresses." Hand in hand, we joined my mother and Nanie. He took their arms again, and I brought up the rear, attempting a swaybacked stance in imitation of Pappy's distinctive walk, bent slightly backwards from the waist.

The front door was open to the balmy afternoon, and the smells of roasting turkey drifted out to the gallery. Aunt Estelle and members of the family, big and little, greeted us in the hall. Amid all the to-do, I scurried into the front parlor.

The tree was as big as I knew it would be, a cedar which touched the ceiling and smelled almost as good as the ones outside. My eyes caught on the presents piled beneath it.

This was the first Christmas I remember hearing Pappy say, "Don't buy me anything, just make me something." And the first thing I looked for under the tree was my present for him. The white tissue paper was smudged and torn at the corners, and its red ribbon, one of my tired hair ribbons—Nanie did not believe in buying fancy wrappings—had come undone. But there it was, atop the other presents with my labored Christmas message in full view: "I luve Papi."

In years to come, the same edict would hold, and Pappy's daughter Jill, his granddaughter Vicki and I would begin work on Christmas presents for Pappy right after Thanksgiving. Over the years, he received countless drawings of horses, several bad poems and, when Nanie decided I was old enough to learn the ladylike art of needlework, even more scandalous failures. The first year he got 16 rows of a navy wool scarf with the knitting needles and unused skeins of yarn wrapped up in a shoe box; the next, one-half of one argyle sock. Finally, when I was much older, I gave him a hand-hooked, red wool rug—all finished, I might add. He kept it by his bed until he died.

But this gift in tattered tissue was my first homemade present, and when he opened it and smiled at what was in all likelihood the single most hideous rendering in oils of an Indian tepee at dawn, I almost burst with pride. I had painted for weeks at Nanie's side in her dining room, with my own small easel and pallet, until I forced my squat fingers to make some sort of pattern on a cardboard square. It was signed with a big "DF," and I thought it was wonderful. I knew he thought so too.

Then it was Nanie's turn. The box from Pappy was enormous, shiny and splendid. Obviously store-bought and store-wrapped, I thought to myself with the condescension of an original-present-maker. She took her time opening it, as we all crowded around to see. Inside the gold cardboard box lay a beaded, blue chiffon evening gown. She didn't touch it for a moment, then shook it out with a precise gesture, letting the tail end trail across the floor. It was the most gorgeous thing I'd ever seen. Nanie muttered, "It's probably too big," and let it drop back into the box. She gave Pappy a funny look and said, "Thank you, Billy." I wondered if he knew, too, that she was going to take it back.

Then it was my turn. The box was almost as big as Nanie's. I tore the fancy wrappings away in short order. Inside was a beautiful, long-sleeved yellow sweater. But it was the plaid skirt, all red and green and with a tiny yellow stripe, that took my breath away. I felt very grown-up just looking at it.

I could hardly wait to rush upstairs and try it on, but Pappy held my squirming body still, long enough to convince me that I might miss dinner entirely if I left right then. When I was quieted, he told me about the skirt. The plaid was the Murry tartan, handed down from the Murrys and the MacAlpines from a long time ago in Scotland. It belonged to our family. "This skirt is part of your heritage," Pappy said, "and you must wear it with pride."

Next day, when I tried it on, I found that it swallowed me—but I wore it anyway. It was too big for the next two years; two years after that, it was too small. I put it on whenever I was sad or scared, or whenever I needed to be strong or brave. I seem to have it on in every snapshot taken of me for the next four years. I cried when I couldn't wear it anymore.

As Pappy finished his story about our past, Jack, the houseboy, came in and announced dinner. The adults moved in a formal procession to the dining room.

I scooted ahead of my elders to catch the first glimpse of the long table—elegant as always, with fine linens heavily starched, shining crystal, silver water goblets, and bread and butter plates that reflected the lights of many candles as well as one's own wonderfully distorted image. I circled the table, trying to decide which was the best spot for me.

I had just made my choice, right next to Pappy, when I felt his hand on my shoulder, gently but firmly guiding me away from the long table—that was for the grown-ups—to a smaller one for us children, set up in the east corner of the room. It was laid in equally fine style, with china and crystal and silver.

I sat down eagerly with a ravenous appetite that would no longer be denied. After all, Christmas or not, it was 2 o'clock, far past my dinner hour. I unfolded the heavy, linen napkin, plunked it in my lap, swung my legs impatiently, and waited for Pappy to get on with the carving and serving and passing of plates.

Then Jack appeared at the pantry door bearing a perfect, golden-brown turkey. Instead of placing it before Pappy, however, he promenaded around the room and offered just a glimpse to everyone there. Finally, he placed the bird in front of Pappy.

I reared back in my seat, anticipating every mouthful that was to come. At the head of the table, Pappy rose and in his most solemn voice began: "A toast, ladies and gentlemen." Then the adults stood, their chairs pushed far back from the table, their wine glasses raised, their faces serious and intent, their eyes on Pappy. Then the children stood. Everyone in the dining room was on his feet, except me. Blissfully unaware, I kept my seat.

Pappy left his place and made his way to my table. I felt his hand touch the top of my head softly, as he bent close and whispered. "We all stand when toasts are given."

"Me, too?"

"Everybody."

My toes searched for the floor.

I felt the blood rush to my face. My chair moved slowly backward beneath me. I looked around anxiously, just as I felt Pappy's hand on my arm. I took it gratefully, found my footing, and hefted my bottom off the chair.

"You get to sit down and eat soon as this is done," he whispered. Then he walked back to his place, raised his glass and, with only a slight nod toward my table, began: "A toast. . ." The watered wine nearly gagged me.

Jack and Pappy's cook Narcissus outdid themselves. Each course was perfect, and for the first time I managed to serve myself, thanks to Jack's steadying hand at my elbow. I made my way through turkey and dressing, Aunt Estelle's homemade jellies, three vegetables, rolls, the finger bowls, and flaming plum pudding.

We sat impatiently until the grown-ups finished; and finally it was time to go outside and play. As we headed out the front door, the ladies went into the front parlor for coffee, and the gentlemen, with one exception, moved to the library for after-dinner drinks. Pappy came outside with us.

What a fine, raucous afternoon we had. After sitting fairly still for nearly two hours, listening to soft conversations that we could not understand, concentrating on not spilling and on sitting up straight, we were as worn out with the adult world as we were with turkey and dressing. The giggles started before we left the table and picked up volume as we tore through the front hall. A perfunctory "don't run in the house" was lost in the banging of the heavy screen door as we scampered down the front steps to freedom.

The shadows were already long as Pappy organized the first of many games, and we played with uninhibited fury, as if we knew that soon this perfect day would be over. We had relay races and endless contests: who-can-jump-the-farthest, and who-can-stand-on-her-head-longest.

We ended with a series of disastrous cartwheels and our favorite, "Sling the Statue." Pappy was judge. The older children grabbed the younger ones by the hands and began turning faster and faster in place until our feet flew out behind us. The whole world was upended. The cedars and the house were upside down. Even

Pappy, with pipe in hand, seemed to be standing on his head. Then they let us go. We sprawled onto the soft grass, holding our positions until Pappy passed slowly by, judging the shapes that the "statues" took, offering comments such as, "This one might be a mule. . ." He chuckled often, and occasionally his face would redden, he would make a funny snorting sound through his nose, and all of us would laugh until our bodies crumpled into the wet grass.

Then it was over. My mother and Nanie came down the brick walk and talked quietly to Pappy. Other mamas gathered up their grass-stained, muddy-kneed, bedraggled offspring. It was almost dark, and the night was cool against my face.

Pappy walked us to the car. He carefully handed my mother and Nanie into the front seat and deposited me in the rumble seat. I snuggled down against the leather, my energies spent, a tired, happy little girl. As we headed out the driveway, I looked up over the back seat. Pappy stood alone on the gallery.

"Merry Christmas," I called. He raised his hand in a stiff, formal salute. I faced forward again and watched the beams from the Buick's headlights bounce off the tall cedars.

Suddenly I wanted one last look at the big white house, and I scrambled to my knees, riding backwards in the car. Lights from the downstairs windows shone softly onto the yard. Somebody turned on the gallery light behind Pappy, and I couldn't see his face anymore. He was just a small, dark figure silhouetted against the house.

"Oh, Pappy," I called again, as we rounded the bend in the driveway and the house grew smaller and smaller, and he was farther and farther away from me. "Thank you."

I hope he heard me.

FROM

Crusade for Justice

IDA B. WELLS

I

A YOUNG WOMAN recently asked me to tell her of my connection with the lynching agitation which was started in 1892. She said she was at a YWCA vesper service when the subject for discussion was Joan of Arc, and each person was asked to tell of someone they knew who had traits of character resembling this French heroine and martyr. She was the only colored girl present, and not wishing to lag behind the others, she named me. She was then asked to tell why she thought I deserved such mention. She said, "Mrs. Barnett, I couldn't tell why I thought so. I have heard you mentioned so often by that name, so I gave it. I was dreadfully embarrassed. Won't you please tell me what it was you did, so the next time I am asked such a question I can give an intelligent answer?"

When she told me she was twenty-five years old, I realized that one reason she did not know was because the happenings about which she inquired took place before she was born. Another was that there was no record from which she could inform herself. I then promised to set it down in writing so those of her generation could know how the agitation against the lynching evil began, and the debt of gratitude we owe to the English people for their splendid help in that movement.

It is therefore for the young people who have so little of our race's history recorded that I am for the first time in my life writing about myself. I am all the more constrained to do this because there is such a lack of authentic race history of Reconstruction times written by the Negro himself.

We have Frederick Douglass's history of slavery as he knew and experienced it. But of the time of storm and stress immediately after the Civil War, of the Ku Klux Klan, of ballot-box stuffing, wholesale murders of Negroes who tried to exercise their new-found rights as free men and citizens, the carpetbag invasion about which the white South has published so much that is false, and the Negroes' political life of that era—our race has little of its own that is definite or authentic.

The gallant fight and marvelous bravery of the black men of the South fighting and dying to exercise and maintain their newborn rights as free men and citizens, with little protection from the government which gave them these rights and with no previous training in citizenship or politics, is a story which would fire the race pride of all our young people if it had only been written down.

It is a heritage of which they would be proud—to know how their fathers and grandfathers handled their brief day of power during the Reconstruction period. There were Lieutenant Governor Pinchback of Louisiana, who served for a time as governor of that great state. Senators Revels and Bruce of Mississippi, who sat in the United States Senate, and the eloquent and scholarly Robert Browne Elliott of South Carolina, who represented his state in the House of Representatives. All of these and many others there were who could say with Julius Caesar, "All of which I saw and part of which I was." Yet we have only John R. Lynch's *Facts of Reconstruction*.

The history of this entire period which reflected glory on the race should be known. Yet most of it is buried in oblivion and only the southern white man's misrepresentations are in the public libraries and college textbooks of the land. The black men who made the history of that day were too modest to write of it, or did not realize the importance of the written word to their posterity.

And so, because our youth are entitled to the facts of race history which only the participants can give, I am thus led to set forth the facts contained in this volume which I dedicate to them.

II

I was born in Holly Springs, Mississippi, before the close of the Civil War [16 July 1862]. My parents, who had been slaves and married as such, were married again after freedom came. My father had been taught the carpenter's trade, and my mother was a famous cook. As the erstwhile slaves had performed most of the labor of the South, they had no trouble in finding plenty of work to do.

My father [called Jim] was the son of his master, who owned a plantation in Tippah County, Mississippi, and one of his slave women, Peggy. Mr. Wells had no children by his wife, "Miss Polly," and my father grew up on the plantation, the companion and comfort of his old age. He was never whipped or put on the auction block, and he knew little of the cruelties of slavery. When young Jim was eighteen years old, his father took him to Holly Springs and apprenticed him to learn the carpenter's trade, which he expected him to use on the plantation.

My mother was cook to old man Bolling, the contractor and builder to whom my father was apprenticed. She was born in Virginia and was one of ten children. She and two sisters were sold to slave traders when young, and were taken to Mississippi and sold again. She often told her children that her father was half Indian, his father being a full blood. She often wrote back to somewhere in Virginia trying to get track of her people, but she was never successful. We were too young to realize the importance of her efforts, and I have never remembered the name of the county or people to whom they "belonged."

After the war was over Mr. Bolling urged his able young apprentice to remain with him. He did so until election time. Mr. Bolling wanted him to vote the Democratic ticket, which he refused to do. When he returned from voting he found the shop locked. Jim Wells said nothing to anyone, but went downtown, bought a new set of tools, and went across the street and rented another house. When Mr. Bolling returned he found he had lost a workman and a tenant, for already Wells had moved his family off the Bolling place.

I do not remember when or where I started school. My earliest recollections are of reading the newspaper to my father and an admiring group of his friends. He was interested in politics and I heard the words Ku Klux Klan long before I knew what they meant. I knew dimly that it meant something fearful, by the anxious way my mother walked the floor at night when my father was out to a political meeting. Yet so far as I can remember there were no riots in Holly Springs, although there were plenty in other parts of the state.

Our job was to go to school and learn all we could. The Freedmen's Aid had established [in 1866] one of its schools in our town—it was called Shaw University then, but is now Rust College. My father was one of the trustees and my mother went along to school with us until she learned to read the Bible. After that she visited the school regularly to see how we were getting along. A deeply religious woman, she won the prize for regular attendance at Sunday school, taking the whole brood of six to nine o'clock Sunday school the year before she died. She taught us how to do the work of the home—each had a regular task besides schoolwork, and I often compare her work in training her children to that of other women who had not her handicaps. She was not forty when she died, but she had borne eight children and brought us up with a strict discipline that many mothers who have had educational advantages have not exceeded. She used to tell us how she had been beaten by slave owners and the hard times she had as a slave.

The only thing I remember about my father's reference to slave days was when his mother came to town on one of her annual visits [after slavery]. She and her husband owned and tilled many acres of land and every fall brought their cotton and corn to market. She also brought us many souvenirs from hog-killing time. On one such occasion she told about "Miss Polly," her former mistress, and said, "Jim, Miss Polly wants you to come and bring the children. She wants to see them."

"Mother," said he, "I never want to see that old woman as long as I live. I'll never forget how she had you stripped and whipped the day after the old man died, and I am never going to see her. I guess it is all right for you to take care of her and forgive her for what she did to you, but she could have starved to death if I'd had my say-so. She certainly would have, if it hadn't been for you."

I was burning to ask what he meant, but children were seen and not heard in those days. They didn't dare break into old folks' conversation. But I have never forgotten those words. Since I have grown old enough to understand I cannot help but feel what an insight to slavery they give.

I was visiting this grandmother down on the farm when life became a reality to me. Word came after I left home that yellow fever was raging in Memphis, Tennessee, fifty miles away, as it had done before, and that the mayor of our town refused to quarantine against Memphis. Our little burg opened its doors to any who wanted to come in. That summer the fever took root in Holly Springs. When we heard that the fever was there, we were sure my father would take the family out in the country; and because the mail was so irregular we didn't expect letters.

One day after a hard chill I was sweating off the resulting fever common to that malarial district when a hail at the gate brought me to the door. Three horsemen were there, and came in. My grandmother, aunt, and uncle were picking the first fall cotton out in the field. The men were all known to me as friends of my father and mother. They were refugees from Holly Springs whom I thought had come to make a social call. After they were seated I asked if they had any news from home. The answer was yes, and one of them handed me a letter that had just been received by one of the refugees in their party. As they were next-door neighbors of ours, I was glad to have first-hand information as to conditions there. I never dreamed there would be anything of personal interest in it. We were so sure that our family was in the country with my aunt Belle.

I read the first page of this letter through, telling the progress of the fever, and these words leaped out at me, "Jim and Lizzie Wells have both died of the fever. They died within twenty-fours hours of each other. The children are all at home and the Howard Association has put a woman there to take care of them. Send word to Ida." That is as far as I read. The next thing I knew grandmother, aunt, and uncle were all in the house and ours indeed became a house of mourning. I wanted to go home at once, but not until three days later, on the receipt of a letter from the doctor in charge, who said I ought to come home, were they willing to let me go.

When my uncle and I got to the next railroad town, from which I was to take the train to Holly Springs, all the people in that station urged me not to go. They were sure that coming from the country I would fall victim at once, and that it was better for me to stay away until the epidemic was over, so that I could take care of the children, if any were left. They assured me no home doctor would have advised me to come into the district; that it was one of the stranger doctors who had been sent there and who would be gone soon and have no responsibility about those left. I consented to stay there and write home. But when I thought of my crippled sister, of the smaller children all down to the nine-month-old baby brother, the conviction grew within me that I ought to be with them. I went back to the station and the train that should have carried my letter took me home.

It was a freight train. No passenger trains were running or needed. And the caboose in which I rode was draped in black for two previous conductors who had fallen victims to the dreaded disease. The conductor who told me this was sure I had made a mistake to go home. I asked him why he was running the train when he knew he was likely to get the fever as had those others for whom the car was draped. He shrugged his shoulders and said that somebody had to do it. "That's exactly why I am going home. I am the oldest of seven living children. There's nobody but me to look after them now. Don't you think I should do my duty, too?" He said nothing more but bade me good-bye as though he never expected to see me again.

When I got home I found two of the children in bed with the fever—all had had slight attacks of it save Eugenia, my older sister, who was paralytic and seemingly immune. The baby, Stanley, had died.

Everybody asked why I had come home. The family physician scolded; also my sister, who could not walk a step; yet she seemed to be greatly relieved to have me there. She told me how our father went about his work nursing the sick, making coffins for the dead; that he would come to the gate bringing food and finding out how all were getting along. She said our mother was taken first and a young Irish woman had been sent to nurse her. The first thing the nurse did was to take the nine-month-old baby from the breast, which increased our mother's fever. The milk clotted in her breast, and when she knew she was going to die asked what would become of her children. Our father came home then to help nurse her but was stricken himself and died a day before she did.

Having seen his nurse going through her father's pockets, she asked the doctor who came every day to see them to take the money our father had with him when he came home and lock it in the safe downtown. This he did and gave her a receipt for three hundred dollars. It was this doctor who had written me to come home—getting the address from my sister.

As the fever was abating, the imported nurses and doctors of the Howard Association were leaving town every day, and my sister was anxious for me to get this money before they were all gone. I had a chill the day after getting home. I will always believe it was one of the usual malarial kind I had been having, but the old nurse in the house who had taken care of the children would take no chances. She put me to bed and sweated me four days and nights on hot lemonade.

Dr. Gray had not been to the house during this time and my

sister gave me the receipt and a note to him as soon as I was able to go downtown. It was commissary day and a large crowd was waiting its turn to be served with groceries, clothing, shoes, etc., as no stores of any kind were open. Seeing persons I knew in the crowd, I asked them to point out Dr. Gray to me. When I handed him the note he said, "So you are Genie's big sister. Tell her the treasurer has the key to the safe and he is out in the country to see his family. He will be back this evening and I will bring her the money tonight, as I am leaving tomorrow."

He came and brought it that evening and told me that we had a wonderful father—one of the best aids in helping to nurse, since he was cheerful and always inspired confidence. He said, "Your father would be passing through the court house, which was used as a hospital, on his way to the shop, carrying some lumber to help make a coffin. If he passed a patient who was out of his head, he would stop to quiet him. If he were dying, he would kneel down and pray with him, then pick up his tools and go on with the rest of the day's work. Everyone liked him and missed him when he was gone."

After Dr. Gray had gone, the old nurse, who was from New Orleans said, "That Dr. Gray sure loved your pa. He came over where we nurses stayed and after looking us all over he said he was going to send me on a case where nobody was sick; that he just wanted me to stay with the children whose father and mother had died until something could be done for them. He said that he'd see that I got my pay same as if I was on a case—and I have, too. Dr. Gray sure is one good white man."

I never met Dr. Gray before nor saw him again, but in all these years I have shared and echoed that nurse's opinion every time I think of his humane and sympathetic watch over Jim Wells's family when they needed it.

My sister, Eugenia, who was next to me in age, had been an active, healthy child until two years before, when her spinal column began to bend outward. It started from a knot the size of one's knuckle in the middle of her backbone. That knot grew until the spinal cord was paralyzed and she was bent nearly double. She became paralyzed in the lower part of her body and was not able to walk. Then came two brothers, James and George. Another brother, Eddie, had died of spinal meningitis years before. Last were two sisters:

Annie, five years old, and Lily, two. The nine-month-old baby, Stanley, had also died before I got home. Thus there were six of us left, and I, the oldest, was only fourteen years old [1876]. After being a happy, light-hearted schoolgirl I suddenly found myself at the head of a family.

When the fever epidemic was over, there was a gathering of Masons at our house to decide what to do with us. Since my father had been a master Mason, the Masonic brothers were our natural protectors. After a long discussion among them that Sunday afternoon the children had all been provided for except Eugenia and myself. Each of two brother Masons' wives wanted a little girl, and the Masonic brothers decided that they could have my two little sisters. A home was thus waiting for them. Two men wanted to apprentice the boys to learn their father's trade. One of those was a white man who knew James Wells's work and thought that his boys had inherited some of their father's ability. Genie was to go to the poorhouse because she was helpless and no one offered her a home. The unanimous decision among the Masonic brothers was that I was old enough to fend for myself.

When all this had been arranged to their satisfaction, I, who said nothing before and had not even been consulted, calmly announced that they were not going to put any of the children anywhere; I said that it would make my father and mother turn over in their graves to know their children had been scattered like that and that we owned the house and if the Masons would help me find work, I would take care of them. Of course they scoffed at the idea of a butterfly fourteen-year-old schoolgirl who had never had to care for herself trying to do what it had taken the combined effort of father and mother to do.

But I held firmly to my position and they seemed rather relieved that they no longer had to worry over the problem. Two of them, Bob Miller and James Hall, had been appointed by the Masons as our guardians and they advised me to apply for a country school. I took the examination for a country schoolteacher and had my dresses lengthened, and I got a school six miles out in the country. I was to be paid the munificent sum of twenty-five dollars a month. While I waited at home for the opening of school we lived on the money that my father had left.

Of course as a young, inexperienced girl who had never had a beau, too young to have been out in company except at children's parties, I knew nothing whatever of the world's ways of looking at things and never dreamed that the community would not understand why I didn't want our children separated. But someone said that I had been downtown inquiring for Dr. Gray shortly after I had come from the country. They heard him tell me to tell my sister he would get the money, meaning my father's money, and bring it to us that night. It was easy for that type of mind to deduce and spread the rumor that already, as young as I was, I had been heard asking white men for money and that was the reason I wanted to live there by myself with the children.

I am quite sure that never in all my life have I suffered such a shock as I did when I heard this misconstruction that had been placed upon my determination to keep my brothers and sisters together. As I look back at it now I can perhaps understand the type of mind which drew such conclusions. And no one suggested that I was laying myself open to gossiping tongues.

My grandmother came from her country home to stay with us after that, and although she must have been seventy years old she tried to help out by doing work by the day. One evening after a hard day's work she got up to cross the room and fell with a paralytic stroke. My aunt, who was her only daughter, came and took her back to the country, where she lived until her death a few years later.

I then found a woman who had been an old friend of my mother's to stay at the house with the children while I went out to my country school to teach. I came home every Friday afternoon, riding the six miles on the back of a big mule. I spent Saturday and Sunday washing and ironing and cooking for the children and went back to my country school on Sunday afternoon. The country folks were kind and sympathetic, and almost every week they gave me eggs and butter to take home to the children.

After one term, I went to Memphis on the invitation of an aunt who lived there. She had been widowed by the same yellow fever epidemic which took my parents, and she had three small children of her own to care for. My aunt Belle, my mother's sister, said she would take care of Eugenia. My two brothers were put to work on their farm and I took the two little girls with me to Memphis.

I secured a school in Shelby County, Tennessee, which paid a better salary and began studying for the examination for city schoolteacher, which meant an even larger increase in salary. One day while riding back to my school I took a seat in the ladies' coach of the train as usual. There were no jim crow cars then. But ever since the repeal of the Civil Rights Bill by the United States Supreme Court in 1877* there had been efforts all over the South to draw the color line on the railroads.

When the train started and the conductor came along to collect tickets, he took my ticket, then handed it back to me and told me that he couldn't take my ticket there. I thought that if he didn't want the ticket I wouldn't bother about it so went on reading. In a little while when he finished taking tickets, he came back and told me I would have to go in the other car. I refused, saying that the forward car was a smoker, and as I was in the ladies' car I proposed to stay. He tried to drag me out of the seat, but the moment he caught hold of my arm I fastened my teeth in the back of his hand.

I had braced my feet against the seat in front and was holding to the back, and as he had already been badly bitten he didn't try it again by himself. He went forward and got the baggageman and another man to help him and of course they succeeded in dragging me out. They were encouraged to do this by the attitude of the white ladies and gentlemen in the car; some of them even stood on the seats so that they could get a good view and continued applauding the conductor for his brave stand.

By this time the train had stopped at the first station. When I saw that they were determined to drag me into the smoker, which was already filled with colored people and those who were smoking, I said I would get off the train rather than go in—which I did. Strangely, I held on to my ticket all this time, and although the sleeves of my linen duster had been torn out and I had been pretty roughly handled, I had not been hurt physically.

I went back to Memphis and engaged a colored lawyer to bring suit against the railroad for me. After months of delay I found he had been bought off by the road, and as he was the only colored lawyer in town I had to get a white one. This man, Judge Greer, kept his pledge with me and the case was finally brought to trial in the circuit court. Judge Pierce, who was an ex-union soldier from Minnesota, awarded me damages of five hundred dollars. I can see to this day the headlines in the *Memphis Appeal* announcing DARKY DAMSEL GETS DAMAGES.

The railroad appealed the case to the state's supreme court,

*Wells is in error about the date. The Civil Rights Act was held unconstitutional by the U.S. Supreme Court in 1883.

which reversed the findings of the lower court, and I had to pay the costs. Before this was done, the railroad's lawyer had tried every means in his power to get me to compromise the case, but I indignantly refused. Had I done so, I would have been a few hundred dollars to the good instead of having to pay out over two hundred dollars in court costs.

It was twelve years afterward before I knew why the case had attracted so much attention and was fought so bitterly by the Chesapeake and Ohio Railroad. It was the first case in which a colored plaintiff in the South had appealed to a state court since the repeal of the Civil Rights Bill by the United States Supreme Court. The gist of that decision was that Negroes were not wards of the nation but citizens of the individual states, and should therefore appeal to the state courts for justice instead of to the federal court. The success of my case would have set a precedent which others would doubtless have followed. In this, as in so many other matters, the South wanted the Civil Rights Bill repealed but did not want or intend to give justice to the Negro after robbing him of all sources from which to secure it.

The supreme court of the nation had told us to go to the state courts for redress of grievances; when I did so I was given the brand of justice Charles Sumner knew Negroes would get when he fathered the Civil Rights Bill during the Reconstruction period.

I had already secured my appointment as a teacher in Memphis before the railroad case was finally settled; so I had my salary to fall back on to help pay the costs against me. None of my people had ever seemed to feel that it was a race matter and that they should help me with the fight. So I trod the winepress alone. I had always been a voracious reader. I had read all the fiction in the Sunday school library and in Rust College. In the country schools where I had taught many times there was no oil for lamps and there were no candles to spare. My only diversion was reading and I could forget my troubles in no other way. I used to sit before the blazing wood fire with a book in my lap during the long winter evenings and read by firelight. I had formed my ideals on the best of Dickens's stories. Louisa May Alcott's, Mrs. A. D. T. Whitney's, and Charlotte Brontë's books, and Oliver Optic's stories for boys. I had read the Bible and Shakespeare through, but I had never read a Negro book or anything about Negroes.

In Memphis I first heard of the A.M.E. church and saw a Negro bishop—Bishop Turner. I worshiped in the first big, fine church I had ever seen and watched the crowds, and I wondered why the preachers did not give the people practical talks. I had already found out in the country that the people needed guidance in everyday life and that the leaders, the preachers, were not giving them this help. They would come to me with their problems because I, as their teacher, should have been their leader. But I knew nothing of life except what I had read.

The bishops I had known were scholarly, saintly men in the Methodist Episcopal church and most of the pastors we had were the same. All my teachers had been the consecrated white men and women from the North who came into the South to teach immediately after the end of the war. It was they who brought us the light of knowledge and their splendid example of Christian courage.

As a green girl in my teens, I was no help to the people outside of my schoolroom, and at first, I fear, I was very little aid in it, since I had had no normal training. The only work I did outside of my schoolroom, besides hard study to keep up with the work, was to teach in Sunday school. I had read the Bible through before I left Holly Springs. Indeed, I could read nothing else on Sunday afternoons at home, because my parents would not permit it.

In Memphis, after becoming a teacher, I joined a lyceum composed mainly of teachers of the public schools. We met every Friday afternoon in the Vance Street Christian Church. The literary exercises consisted of recitations, essays, and debates interspersed with music. It was a breath of life to me, for this program was like the Friday afternoon oratoricals in school. The exercises always closed with the reading of the *Evening Star*—a spicy journal prepared and read by the editor. There were news items, literary notes, criticisms of previous offerings on the program, a "They Say" column of pleasant personalities—and always some choice poetry.

The editor, who had held a position in the city of Washington for a number of years, was a brilliant man. In the course of time, he got his job back and returned to Washington, leaving the *Evening Star* without an editor. To my great surprise, I was elected to fill the vacancy. I tried to make my offering as acceptable as his had been, and before long I found that I liked the work. The lyceum attendance was increased by people who said they came to hear the

Evening Star read. Among them one Friday evening was Rev. R. N. Countee, pastor of one of the leading Baptist churches, who also published a weekly called the *Living Way*. He gave us a very nice notice in his paper the next week, copying some of my matter, and invited me to do some writing for his paper.

All of this, although gratifying, surprised me very much, for I had had no training except what the work on the *Evening Star* had given me, and no literary gifts and graces. But I had observed and thought much about conditions as I had seen them in the country schools and churches. I had an instinctive feeling that the people who had little or no school training should have something coming into their homes weekly which dealt with their problems in a simple, helpful way. So in weekly letters to the *Living Way*, I wrote in a plain, common-sense way on the things which concerned our people. Knowing that their education was limited, I never used a word of two syllables where one would serve the purpose. I signed these articles "Iola."

It was not long before these articles were copied and commented on by other Negro newspapers in the country, and I received letters from other editors inviting me to write for them.

A Sweet Devouring

Eudora Welty

When I used to ask my mother which we were, rich or poor, she refused to tell me. I was then nine years old and of course what I was dying to hear was that we were poor. I was reading a book called *Five Little Peppers* and my heart was set on baking a cake for my mother in a stove with a hole in it. Some version of rich, crusty old Mr. King—up till that time not living on our street—was sure to come down the hill in his wheelchair and rescue me if anything went wrong. But before I could start a cake at all I had to find out if we were poor, and poor *enough;* and my mother wouldn't tell me, she said she was too busy. I couldn't wait too long; I had to go on reading and soon Polly Pepper got into more trouble, some that was a little harder on her and easier on me.

Trouble, the backbone of literature, was still to me the original property of the fairy tale, and as long as there was plenty of trouble for everybody and the rewards for it were falling in the right spots, reading was all smooth sailing. At that age a child reads with higher appetite and gratification, and with those two stars sailing closer together, than ever again in his growing up. The home shelves had been providing me all along with the usual books, and I read them with love—but snap, I finished them. I read everything just alike—snap. I even came to the *Tales from Maria Edgeworth* and went right ahead, without feeling the bump—then. It *was* noticeable that when her characters suffered she punished them for it, instead of rewarding them as a reader had rather been led to hope. In her stories, the children had to make their choice between being unhappy and good about it and being unhappy and bad about it, and then she helped them to choose wrong. In *The Purple Jar,* it will be remembered, there was the little girl being taken through the shops by her mother and her downfall coming when she chooses to buy something beautiful instead of something necessary. The purple jar, when the shop sends it out, proves to have been purple only so long as it was filled with purple water, and her mother knew it all the time. They don't deliver the water. That's only the cue for stones to start coming through the hole in the victim's worn-out shoe. She bravely agrees she must keep walking on stones until such time as she is offered another choice between the beautiful and the useful. Her father tells her as far as he is concerned she can stay in the house. If I had been at all easy to disappoint, that story would have disappointed me. Of course, I did feel, what is the good of walking on rocks if they are going to let the water out of the jar too? And it seemed to me that even the illustrator fell down on the characters in that book, not alone Maria Edgeworth, for when a rich, crusty old gentleman gave Simple Susan a guinea for some kind deed she'd done him, there was a picture of the transaction and where was the guinea? I couldn't make out a feather. But I liked *reading* the book all right—except that I finished it.

My mother took me to the Public Library and introduced me: "Let her have any book she wants, except *Elsie Dinsmore.*" I looked for the book I couldn't have and it was a row. That was how I learned about the Series Books. The *Five Little Peppers* belonged, so did *The Wizard of Oz,* so did *The Little Colonel,* so did *The Green Fairy Book.* There were many of everything, generations of everybody, instead of one. I wasn't coming to the end of reading, after all—I was saved.

Our library in those days was a big rotunda lined with shelves. A copy of *V.V.'s Eyes* seemed to follow you wherever you went, even after you'd read it. I didn't know what I liked, I just knew what there was a lot of. After *Randy's Spring* there came *Randy's Summer, Randy's Fall* and *Randy's Winter.* True, I didn't care very much myself for her spring, but it didn't occur to me that I might not care for her summer, and then her summer didn't prejudice me against her fall, and I still had hopes as I moved on to her winter. I was disappointed in her whole year, as it turned out, but a thing like that didn't keep me from wanting to read every word of it. The pleasures of reading itself—who doesn't remember?—were like those of a Christmas cake, a sweet devouring. The "Randy Books" failed chiefly in being so soon over. Four seasons doesn't make a series.

All that summer I used to put on a second petticoat (our librarian wouldn't let you past the front door if she could see through you), ride my bicycle up the hill and "through the Capitol" (shortcut) to the library with my two read books in the basket (two was the limit you could take out at one time when you were a child and also as long as you lived), and tiptoe in ("Silence") and exchange them for two more in two minutes. Selection was no object. I coasted the two new books home, jumped out of my petticoat, read (I suppose I ate and bathed and answered questions put to me), then in all hope put my petticoat back on and rode those two books back to the library to get my next two.

The librarian was the lady in town who wanted to be it. She called me by my full name and said, "Does your mother know where you are? You know good and well the fixed rule of this library: *Nobody is going to come running back here with any book on the same day they took it out.* Get both those things out of here and don't come back till tomorrow. And I can practically see through you."

My great-aunt in Virginia, who understood better about needing more to read than you *could* read, sent me a book so big it had to be read on the floor—a bound volume of six or eight issues of *St. Nicholas* from a previous year. In the very first pages a serial began: *The Lucky Stone* by Abbie Farwell Brown. The illustrations were right down my alley: a heroine so poor she was ragged, a witch with an extremely pointed hat, a rich, crusty old gentleman in—better than a wheelchair—a runaway carriage; and I set to. I gobbled up installment after installment through the whole luxurious book, through the last one, and then came the words, turning me to *un*lucky stone: "To be concluded." The book had come to an end and *The Lucky Stone* wasn't finished! The witch had it! I couldn't believe this infidelity from my aunt. I still had my secret childhood feeling that if you hunted long enough in a book's pages, you could find what you were looking for, and long after I knew books better than that, I used to hunt again for the end of *The Lucky Stone.* It never occurred to me that the story had an existence anywhere else outside the pages of that single green-bound book. The last chapter was just something I would have to do without. Polly Pepper could do it. And then suddenly I tried something—I read it again, as much as I had of it. I was in love with books at least partly for what they looked like; I loved the printed page.

In my little circle books were almost never given for Christmas, they cost too much. But the year before, I'd been given a book and got a shock. It was from the same classmate who had told me there was no Santa Claus. She gave me a book, all right—*Poems by*

Another Little Girl. It looked like a real book, was printed like a real book—but it was *by her. Homemade* poems? Illusion-dispelling was her favorite game. She was in such a hurry, she had such a pile to get rid of—her mother's electric runabout was stacked to the bud vases with copies—that she hadn't even time to say, "Merry Christmas!" With only the same raucous laugh with which she had told me, "Been filling my own stocking for years!" she shot me her book, received my Japanese pencil box with a moonlight scene on the lid and a sharpened pencil inside, jumped back into the car and was sped away by her mother. I stood right where they had left me, on the curb in my Little Nurse's uniform, and read that book, and I had no better way to prove when I got through than I had when I started that this was not a real book. But of course it wasn't. The printed page is not absolutely everything.

Then this Christmas was coming, and my grandfather in Ohio sent along in his box of presents an envelope with money in it for me to buy myself the book I wanted.

I went to Kress's. Not everybody knew Kress's sold books, but children just before Christmas know everything Kress's ever sold or will sell. My father had showed us the mirror he was giving my mother to hang above her desk, and Kress's is where my brother and I went to reproduce that by buying a mirror together to give her ourselves, and where our little brother then made us take him and he bought her one his size for fifteen cents. Kress's had also its version of the Series Books, called, exactly like another series, "The Camp Fire Girls," beginning with *The Camp Fire Girls in the Woods.*

I believe they were ten cents each and I had a dollar. But they weren't all that easy to buy, because the series stuck, and to buy some of it was like breaking into a loaf of French bread. Then after you got home, each single book was as hard to open as a box stuck in its varnish, and when it gave way it popped like a firecracker. The covers once prized apart would never close; those books once open stayed open and lay on their backs helplessly fluttering their leaves like a turned-over June bug. They were as light as a matchbox. They were printed on yellowed paper with corners that crumbled, if you pinched on them too hard, like old graham crackers, and they smelled like attic trunks, caramelized glue, their own confinement with one another and, over all, the Kress's smell—bandannas, peanuts and sandalwood from the incense counter.

Even without reading them I loved them. It was hard, that year, that Christmas is a day you can't read.

What could have happened to those books?—but I can tell you about the leading character. His name was Mr. Holmes. He was not a Camp Fire Girl: he wanted to catch one. Through every book of the series he gave chase. He pursued Bessie and Zara—those were the Camp Fire Girls—and kept scooping them up in his touring car, while they just as regularly got away from him. Once Bessie escaped from the second floor of a strange inn by climbing down a gutter pipe. Once she escaped by driving away from Mr. Holmes in his own automobile, which she had learned to drive by watching him. What Mr. Holmes wanted with them—either Bessie or Zara would do—didn't give me pause; I was too young to be a Camp Fire Girl; I was just keeping up. I wasn't alarmed by Mr. Holmes—when I cared for a chill, I knew to go to Dr. Fu Manchu, who had his own series in the library. I wasn't fascinated either. There was one thing I wanted from those books, and that was for me to have ten to read at one blow.

Who in the world wrote those books? I knew all the time they were the false "Camp Fire Girls" and the ones in the library were the authorized. But book reviewers sometimes say of a book that if anyone else had written it, it might not have been this good, and I found it out as a child—their warning is justified. This was a proven case, although a case of the true not being as good as the false. In the true series the characters were either totally different or missing (Mr. Holmes was missing), and there was too much time given to teamwork. The Kress's Campers, besides getting into a more reliable kind of trouble than the Carnegie Campers, had adventures that even they themselves weren't aware of: the pages were in wrong. There were transposed pages, repeated pages, and whole sections in upside down. There was no way of telling if there was anything missing. But if you knew your way in the woods at all, you could enjoy yourself tracking it down. I read the library "Camp Fire Girls," since that's what they were there for, but though they could be read by poorer light they were not as good.

And yet, in a way, the false Campers were not better either. I wonder whether I felt some flaw at the heart of things or whether I was just tired of not having any taste; but it seemed to me when I had finished that the last nine of those books weren't as good as the first one. And the same went for all Series Books. As long as they are keeping a series going, I was afraid, nothing can really happen. The whole thing is one grand prevention. For my greed, I must have unwittingly dealt with myself in the way way Maria Edgeworth dealt with the one who put her all into the purple jar—I had received word it was just colored water.

And then I went again to the home shelves and my lucky hand reached and found Mark Twain—twenty-four volumes, not a series, and good all the way through.

The Little Store

EUDORA WELTY

TWO BLOCKS AWAY from the Mississippi State Capitol, and on the same street with it, where our house was when I was a child growing up in Jackson, it was possible to have a little pasture behind your backyard where you could keep a Jersey cow, which we did. My mother herself milked her. A thrifty homemaker, wife, mother of three, she also did all her own cooking. And as far as I can recall, she never set foot inside a grocery store. It wasn't necessary.

For her regular needs, she stood at the telephone in our front hall and consulted with Mr. Lemly, of Lemly's Market and Grocery downtown, who took her order and sent it out on his next delivery. And since Jackson at the heart of it was still within very near reach of the open country, the blackberry lady clanged on her bucket with a quart measure at your front door in June without fail, the watermelon man rolled up to your house exactly on time for the Fourth of July, and down through the summer, the quiet of the early-morning streets was pierced by the calls of farmers driving in with their plenty. One brought his with a song, so plaintive we would sing it with him:

> Milk, milk,
> Buttermilk,
> Snap beans—butterbeans—
> Tender okra—fresh greens . . .
> And buttermilk.

My mother considered herself pretty well prepared in her kitchen and pantry for any emergency that, in her words, might choose to present itself. But if she should, all of a sudden, need another lemon or find she was out of bread, all she had to do was call out, "Quick! Who'd like to run to the Little Store for me?"

I would.

She'd count out the change into my hand, and I was away. I'll bet the nickel that would be left over that all over the country, for those of my day, the neighborhood grocery played a similar part in our growing up.

Our store had its name—it was that of the grocer who owned it, whom I'll call Mr. Sessions—but "the Little Store" is what we called it at home. It was a block down our street toward the capitol and half a block further, around the corner, toward the cemetery. I knew even the sidewalk to it as well as I knew my own skin. I'd skipped my jumping-rope up and down it, hopped its length through mazes of hopscotch, played jacks in its islands of shade, serpentined along it on my Princess bicycle, skated it backward and forward. In the twilight I had dragged my steamboat by its string (this was homemade out of every new shoebox, with candle in the bottom lighted and shining through colored tissue paper pasted over windows scissored out in the shapes of the sun, moon and stars) across every crack of the walk without letting it bump or catch fire. I'd "played out" on that street after supper with my brothers and friends as long as "first-dark" lasted; I'd caught its lightning bugs. On the first Armistice Day (and this will set the time I'm speaking of) we made our own parade down that walk on a single velocipede—my brother pedaling, our little brother riding the handlebars, and myself standing on the back, all with arms wide, flying flags in each hand. (My father snapped that picture as we raced by. It came out blurred.)

As I set forth for the Little Store, a tune would float toward me from the house where there lived three sisters, girls in their teens, who ratted their hair over their ears, wore headbands like gladiators, and were considered to be very popular. They practiced for this in the daytime; they'd wind up the Victrola, leave the same record on they'd played before, and you'd see them bobbing past their dining-room windows while they danced with each other. Being three, they could go all day, cutting in:

> Everybody ought to know-oh
> How to do the Tickle-Toe
> (how to do the Tickle-Toe)—

they sang it and danced to it, and as I went by to the same song, I believed it.

A little further on, across the street, was the house where the principal of our grade school lived—lived on, even while we were having vacation. What if she would come out? She would halt me in my tracks—she had a very carrying and well-known voice in Jackson, where she'd taught almost everybody—saying "Eudora Alice Welty, spell OBLIGE." OBLIGE was the word that she of course knew had kept me from making 100 on my spelling exam. She'd make me miss it again now, by boring her eyes through me from across the street. This was my vacation fantasy, one good way to scare myself on the way to the store.

Down near the corner waited the house of a little boy named Lindsey. The sidewalk here was old brick, which the roots of a giant chinaberry tree had humped up and tilted this way and that. On skates, you took it fast, in a series of skittering hops, trying not to touch ground anywhere. If the chinaberries had fallen and rolled in the cracks, it was like skating through a whole shooting match of marbles. I crossed my fingers that Lindsey wouldn't be looking.

During the big flu epidemic he and I, as it happened, were being nursed through our sieges at the same time. I'd hear my father and mother murmuring to each other, at the end of a long day, "And I wonder how poor little *Lindsey* got along today?" Just as, down the street, he no doubt would have to hear his family saying, "And I wonder how is poor *Eudora* by now?" I got the idea that a choice was going to be made soon between poor little Lindsey and poor Eudora, and I came up with a funny poem. I wasn't prepared for it when my father told me it wasn't funny and my mother cried that if I couldn't be ashamed for myself, she'd have to be ashamed for me:

> There was a little boy and his name was Lindsey.
> He went to heaven with the influinzy.

He didn't, he survived it, poem and all, the same as I did. But his chinaberries could have brought me down in my skates in a flying act of contrition before his eyes, looking pretty funny myself, right in front of his house.

Setting out in this world, a child feels so indelible. He only comes to find out later that it's all the others along his way who are making themselves indelible to him.

Our Little Store rose right up from the sidewalk; standing in a street of family houses, it alone hadn't any yard in front, any tree or flowerbed. It was a plain frame building covered over with brick.

Above the door, a little railed porch ran across on an upstairs level and four windows with shades were looking out. But I didn't catch on to those.

Running in out of the sun, you met what seemed total obscurity inside. There were almost tangible smells—licorice recently sucked in a child's cheek, dill-pickle brine that had leaked through a paper sack in a fresh trail across the wooden floor, ammonia-loaded ice that had been hoisted from wet croker sacks and slammed into the icebox with its sweet butter at the door, and perhaps the smell of still-untrapped mice.

Then through the motes of cracker dust, cornmeal dust, the Gold Dust of the Gold Dust Twins that the floor had been swept with, the realities emerged. Shelves climbed to high reach all the way around, set out with not too much of any one thing but a lot of things—lard, molasses, vinegar, starch, matches, kerosene, Octagon soap (about a year's worth of octagon-shaped coupons cut out and saved brought a signet ring addressed to you in the mail. Furthermore, when the postman arrived at your door, he blew a whistle). It was up to you to remember what you came for, while your eye traveled from cans of sardines to ice cream salt to harmonicas to flypaper (over your head, batting around on a thread beneath the blades of the ceiling fan, stuck with its testimonial catch).

Its confusion may have been in the eye of its beholder. Enchantment is cast upon you by all those things you weren't supposed to have need for, it lures you close to wooden tops you'd outgrown, boy's marbles and agates in little net pouches, small rubber balls that wouldn't bounce straight, frazzly kitestring, clay bubble-pipes that would snap off in your teeth, the stiffest scissors. You could contemplate those long narrow boxes of sparklers gathering dust while you waited for it to be the Fourth of July or Christmas, and noisemakers in the shape of tin frogs for somebody's birthday party you hadn't been invited to yet, and see that they were all marvelous.

You might not have even looked for Mr. Sessions when he came around his store cheese (as big as a doll's house) and in front of the counter looking for you. When you'd finally asked him for, and received from him in its paper bag, whatever single thing it was that you had been sent for, the nickel that was left over was yours to spend.

Down at a child's eye level, inside those glass jars with mouths in their sides through which the grocer could run his scoop or a child's hand might be invited to reach for a choice, were wineballs, all-day suckers, gumdrops, peppermints. Making a row under the glass of a counter were the Tootsie Rolls, Hershey Bars, Goo-Goo Clusters, Baby Ruths. And whatever was the name of those pastilles that came stacked in a cardboard cylinder with a cardboard lid? They were thin and dry, about the size of tiddlywinks, and in the shape of twisted rosettes. A kind of chocolate dust came out with them when you shook them out in your hand. Were they chocolate? I'd say rather they were brown. They didn't taste of anything at all, unless it was wood. Their attraction was the number you got for a nickel.

Making up your mind, you circled the store around and around, around the pickle barrel, around the tower of Cracker Jack boxes; Mr. Sessions had built it for us himself on top of a packing case, like a house of cards.

If it seemed too hot for Cracker Jacks, I might get a cold drink. Mr. Sessions might have already stationed himself by the cold-drinks barrel, like a mind reader. Deep in ice water that looked black as ink, murky shapes that would come up as Coca-Colas, Orange Crushes, and various flavors of pop, were all swimming around together. When you gave the word, Mr. Sessions plunged his bare arm in to the elbow and fished out your choice, first try. I favored a locally bottled concoction called Lake's Celery. (What else could it be called? It was made by a Mr. Lake out of celery. It was a popular drink here for years but was not known universally, as I found out when I arrived in New York and ordered one in the Astor bar.) You drank on the premises, with feet set wide apart to miss the drip, and gave him back his bottle.

But he didn't hurry you off. A standing scales was by the door, with a stack of iron weights and a brass slide on the balance arm, that would weigh you up to three hundred pounds. Mr. Sessions, whose hands were gentle and smelled of carbolic, would lift you up and set your feet on the platform, hold your loaf of bread for you, and taking his time while you stood still for him, he would make certain of what you weighed today. He could even remember what you weighed the last time, so you could subtract and announce how much you'd gained. That was goodbye.

Is there always a hard way to go home? From the Little Store, you could go partway through the sewer. If your brothers had called you a scarecat, then across the next street beyond the Little Store, it was possible to enter this sewer by passing through a privet hedge, climbing down into the bed of a creek, and going into its mouth on your knees. The sewer—it might have been no more than a "storm sewer"—came out and emptied here, where Town Creek, a sandy, most often shallow little stream that ambled through Jackson on its way to the Pearl River, ran along the edge of the cemetery. You could go in darkness through this tunnel to where you next saw light (if you ever did) and climb out through the culvert at your own street corner.

I was a scarecat, all right, but I was a reader with my own refuge in storybooks. Making my way under the sidewalk, under the street and the streetcar track, under the Little Store, down there in the wet dark by myself, I could be Persephone entering into my six-month sojourn underground—though I didn't suppose Persephone had to crawl, hanging onto a loaf of bread, and come out through the teeth of an iron grating. Mother Ceres would indeed be wondering where she could find me, and mad when she knew. "Now am I going to have to start marching to the Little Store *for myself?*"

I couldn't picture it. Indeed, I'm unable today to picture the Little Store with a grown person in it, except for Mr. Sessions and the lady who helped him, who belonged there. We children thought it was ours. The happiness of errands was in part that of running for the moment away from home, a free spirit. I believed the Little Store to be a center of the outside world, and hence of happiness—as I believed what I found in the Cracker Jack box to be a genuine prize, which was as simply as I believed in the Golden Fleece.

But a day came when I ran to the store to discover, sitting on the front step, a grown person, after all—more than a grown person. It was the Monkey Man, together with his monkey. His grinding-organ was lowered to the step beside him. In my whole life so far, I must have laid eyes on the Monkey Man no more than five or six times. An itinerant of rare and wayward appearances, he was not punctual like the Gipsies, who every year with the first cool days of fall showed up in the aisles of Woolworth's. You never knew when the Monkey Man might decide to favor Jackson, or which way he'd go. Sometimes you heard him as close as the next street, and then he didn't come up yours.

But now I saw the Monkey Man at the Little Store, where I'd never seen him before. I'd never seen him sitting down. Low on that familiar doorstep, he was not the same any longer, and neither was his monkey. They looked just like an old man and an old friend of his that wore a fez, meeting quietly together, tired, and resting with their eyes fixed on some place far away, and not the same place. Yet their romance for me didn't have it in its power to waver. I wavered. I simply didn't know how to step around them, to proceed on into the Little Store for my mother's emergency as if nothing had happened. If I could have gone in there after it, whatever it was, I would have given it to them—putting it into the monkey's cool little fingers. I would have given them the Little Store itself.

In my memory they are still attached to the store—so are all the others. Everyone I saw on my way seemed to me then part of my errand, and in a way they were. As I myself, the free spirit, was part of it too.

All the years we lived in that house where we children were born, the same people lived in the other houses on our street too. People changed through the arithmetic of birth, marriage and death, but not by going away. So families just accrued stories, which through the fullness of time, in those times, their own lives made. And I grew up in those.

But I didn't know there'd ever been a story at the Little Store, one that was going on while I was there. Of course, all the time the Sessions family had been living right overhead there, in the upstairs rooms behind the little railed porch and the shaded windows; but I think we children never thought of that. Did I fail to see them as a family because they weren't living in an ordinary house? Because I so seldom saw them close together, or having anything to say to each other? She sat in the back of the store, her pencil over a ledger, while he stood and waited on children to make up their minds. They worked in twin black eyeshades, held on their gray heads by elastic bands. It may be harder to recognize kindness—or unkindness, either—in a face whose eyes are in shadow. His face underneath his shade was as round as the little wooden wheels in the Tinker Toy box. So was her face. I didn't know, perhaps didn't even wonder: were they husband and wife or brother and sister? Were they father and mother? There were a few other persons, of various ages, wandering singly in by the back door and out. But none of their relationships could I imagine, when I'd never seen them sitting down together around their own table.

The possibility that they had any other life at all, anything beyond what we could see within the four walls of the Little Store, occurred to me only when tragedy struck their family. There was some act of violence. The shock to the neighborhood traveled to the children, of course; but I couldn't find out from my parents what had happened. They held it back from me, as they'd already held back many things, "until the time comes for you to know."

You could find out some of these things by looking in the unabridged dictionary and the encyclopedia—kept to hand in our dining room—but you couldn't find out there what had happened to the family who for all the years of your life had lived upstairs over the Little Store, who had never been anything but patient and kind to you, who never once had sent you away. All I ever knew was its aftermath: they were the only people ever known to me who simply vanished. At the point where their life overlapped into ours, the story broke off.

We weren't being sent to the neighborhood grocery for facts of life, or death. But of course those are what we were on the track of, anyway. With the loaf of bread and the Cracker Jack prize, I was bringing home the intimations of pride and disgrace, and rumors and early news of people coming to hurt one another, while others practiced for joy—storing up a portion for myself of the human mystery.

FROM

This Is My Country Too

JOHN A. WILLIAMS

JACKSON, MISSISSIPPI. That name, on my mind when I awoke next morning, depressed me. When I came to New Orleans four days before and people asked where I was next headed, I said lightly, "Jackson." But, as the time for me to go approached, I muttered the name of the city, and people, sensing what I felt from the way I had said it, merely nodded and said nothing. Jackson. How much nicer to take a plane to Puerto Rico and forget about Jackson. Who was I kidding? Hell, I didn't want to go to Jackson. Then, turning over in M. L.'s bed, I remembered that I had already come through a part of Mississippi, driving along carefully, looking at the sea and palm trees. Yes, I said to myself, you've been to Mississippi. Besides, think of all those colored people who've always lived there. That's *their* problem, I thought in the shower.

Jackson is my mother's birthplace, and was her home for a time. I was born there. My parents were married and made their home in Syracuse, where I was conceived (I refuse to give all my heritage to Mississippi), but they returned to Jackson for the birth of their first child, according to the custom of that time. Thus, in my family, a line of "free" Negroes on my father's side, and one of former "slave" Negroes on my mother's side, were merged.

Some years ago, my boys asked me, "Dad, where do we come from?" Although years before I had started thinking what to tell them, I was startled. Quickly I mentioned Jackson, but I was in panic. A man *ought* to be able to tell his children where they come from. I envied those Italians who return to Italy to visit their homes, the Polish and Hungarian Jews who return to see their relatives, the Irish who make the hop to Shannon and go off in search of old homes and friends. But the boys and I, seeking our lineage before Mississippi, moved to the map of Africa on the wall. We looked at the West African coast, and with falling voices and embarrassed eyes concluded that we could have come from anywhere along the 3,000-mile coast and up to 1,500 miles inland.

Then to books with photographs of Africans. Did we resemble any of the people shown? Around the eyes? The cheekbones? The mouth? Which were our brothers? Another check: which peoples were brought to Mississippi? Ah, how can you tell, when they arrived in coffles from other states, already mixed with a hundred different peoples? Mandingo? No, most certainly not. Kru? What, then—Baule?

"Dad, where do we come from?" Up to great-grandfather, some trace; beyond him, fog. We came out of fog. We did not perish in it. We are here.

But Jackson lay north; that fact offered some consolation, for I had tired of watching my step, had tired of creeping along five or ten miles below the speed limit while white drivers tore along at twenty to thirty miles above it. I had tired of down-home Southern cooking, soul food. Let them sing about it; now I know the dark, greasy gravy, the greens cooked to a softness the consistency of wet tissue paper, the grits, the red-eye gravy, the thick, starchy rice. But I ate breakfast, one of soul food, and then I took a Dexedrine tablet. I drove out past Metairie to the Pontchartrain Causeway. The twenty-four-mile drive over the soft, blue waters was hypnotizing; it was as if the only fitting climax to the ride over that stretch of steel, concrete, and asphalt had to be a plunge into the lake. At first, up ahead, there was only the suggestion of land, a silvery haze rimmed in a darkness; only that and the causeway with one or two cars on it, going and coming. The land at the northern end of the lake became solid, took on color, green and brown. Then the lake lay behind me, clean, small, dancing morning waves simpering now for other drivers. All I could think was that I was now in "stomp-down cracker" land, and I had to start watching my step all over again. I began searching for pecan-stand signs. I had seen many en route to New Orleans, thinking that I would pick up a bag or two later and give them to Ola, my mother. "Here you go, baby, pecans from down home." Something like that. But there were no more pecan stands.

I stopped for gas and again the ritual of the South was trotted out; a Negro attendant came to take care of me. The white attendants, in the stations that can afford this silly double standard, take care of white customers. Before long I had threaded my way across the border and back into Mississippi and a couple of names assailed me: Emmett Till, whose murderers wrote an article, got paid for it, were acquitted, and live still; Medgar Evers, of course; and all the other nameless ones. The land along the way was flat. Although I watched the speedometer and the mirrors, sometimes the car seemed to have a mind of its own. It would leap forward like a new colt, and it would be seconds before I could get that big, fat motor to simmer down, behave itself, and keep me out of jail. "I'm gonna let you run, baby," I promised it. "Later."

My *Travelguide* had given me the name of a hotel in Jackson, and I came upon the city cautiously, looking for the street. From the south, the city sweeps from a plain to a modest hill, but the overall aspect is one of flatness and of rigidly dull buildings. The pace of the people was easy, one of assurance. I saw small groups of Negroes sitting together, as if for moral support. Used-car lots filled the street on the east and small hardware stores to the west. Driving up the sweep of the low hill, the stores improved in quality and in merchandise. Following directions, I drove off the main street, went two blocks, and suddenly the streets were filled with Negroes. I had arrived in the Negro section; it seemed boxed in. Almost at once I saw two colored cops; they were the result of summer demonstrations, and seemed, in their new uniforms, as proud as kids in new drum-corps suits.

The hotel was very much like the one in Montgomery, even to the key deposit. But why run a place like that simply because Negroes, having no other place to go, have to go there? Segregation has made many of us lazy but also has made many of us rich without trying. No competition; therefore, take it or leave it—and you have to take it. The slovenly restaurant keeper, the uncaring hotel man, the parasites of segregation have only to provide the superficial utensils of their business. I had coffee in the dingy little dining room and rushed out, overwhelmed by the place, which did not dismiss the code of Mississippi but enforced it to the hilt.

I fled to Jackson State College, where an old friend was teaching and coaching. He was in a class, but came into the hall and brought me before his class; I think he was teaching first aid. I say "I think" because I could not believe that whatever it was could be considered a course for a college.

"This is my old friend, Johnny Williams," he said, towering over me. "He's a writer. You basketball players—we played ball in the Navy. John was a guard. Good with the hands. Two-handed set." That dated the hell out of me. No one shoots with two hands anymore. "Say something, John." That was my introduction to Jackson State.

Somewhere this must end, I thought, walking around the campus later. Tennessee State, Alabama State, Jackson State, a pattern. High school-like buildings, surplus prefab buildings, some grass, some dirt. Here, you colored people, take this! But was I seeing these campuses through brainwashed eyes perhaps? I have seen many rolling among soft hills or edging up the sides of valleys, overhung with chestnut and maple and cedar. I have seen domes and columns, baroque and Gothic, cushioned lecture seats and marble walls inscribed with gold; I was spoiled.

I wrestled with these thoughts and finally knew them to be, however brainwashed I was, true. No great ideas of the past stalked these bricked halls or sandy stretches of walks. When the state legislatures of the South created the Southern Negro school, they thought they knew what they were doing. Books, and teachers, and space. Build what you will. But the white schools had grass, and baroque and Gothic structures, and great ideas sometimes trod those halls, unminded.

But out of the wastelands whites and Negroes together call colleges, there has come, for America at least, the rebirth of the greatest idea: that a man is a man, is free under sky and over earth. From brick buildings so new that they still sparkle red, from dingy prefabs with reused floors, from out of the desert, and despite many of their teachers—from here have come sit-ins, freedom walks, kneel-ins.

Since my friend was a coach, he was called "Coach." Since his friends on the faculty were also coaches, he called them "Coach." Thus it went at lunch. I was introduced to some people in the English Department and looked forward that afternoon to sitting down with them, but I never did. My friend said that maybe they didn't want the meeting because it would reveal their lacks. The magic words had been: New York and writer. Later I thought that they may not have liked my friend and therefore would not be bothered with me. People who dabble in intellect often have an abhorrence for athletes or former athletes. Oh, well, one if by land, two if by sea.

More than half the day was gone, and my friend showed a curious disinclination to talk about the obvious. I had honored his attitude at first, then felt that it would begin leaking out. But it didn't and I asked him why, like Bill Eure, being raised in the North, he could live in the South, in Mississippi, which is the worst of the South.

With a heavy sigh that indicated that he knew he would have to answer that question, he began. "After the war I went to Kentucky State. I've been in the South a long time now. We have this house. I have my doctorate. I make good money and I'm in a position to maneuver for more. I've got security, Johnny," and he reached over and pushed my knee. "Up there—you know how we lived in my town—we had nothing and couldn't *do* anything, couldn't go places. It was a big thing when we came to Syracuse to play you guys, and if we couldn't stay overnight, we'd bitch like hell. Here, I keep my nose clean. I don't look at white women. I have my contacts. Hell, everyone in this business has his contacts, better have 'em. I've our own doctors for the athletes. My wife works, not hard. She has an easy life and would rather work than stay home. She has her car, I have mine. Johnny, I ask you, what in hell would I have had up there?"

Security. You are damned if you have it, and *god*damned if you don't. Big house, two cars, a yard, television, a savings account. Good, good, but at what expense? Oh, this is not true only of my friend, it is true of most Americans who almost invariably confuse security with status. And they saddle themselves throughout brief lifetimes with jobs and bosses they don't like, associating with people they detest or even hate, just for security and/or status. My friend was looking at me for some kind of confirmation.

I nodded, too depressed to go on, too confused by the disastrophism of time. In the early life of my parents, it was the Southern Negro migrating to the North who gave that section life, but my friend was an example of the reverse: for a cloistered but secure kind of life, he had come South. I remembered once when we were playing ball, my friend had punched a white boy from Texas who was on our team. Duff was the boy's name. I remember him because every time he looked at the basket, he scored. My friend had hit the white boy because he had said "nigger," hit him so hard that Duff had dented a locker when he was slammed into it. Duff hadn't meant anything by it; it was just his way of talking, like Ralph McGill slipping into "nigra." "Remember Duff?" I asked.

"Yeah," he said, "I remembered Duff."

I suppose all the way down I had noticed that the elite among the Negroes, the academicians, the professionals, and the like, were as estranged from the masses of Negroes as the whites. If New Orleans is any example, the people I knew there were not of the campus, not of the professions, and they seemed totally without leadership. Where, they seemed to ask, do we turn for it? At least they talked about the movement. In Mississippi, few did.

What can instructors so far removed from life give their students?

"We give them a cycle of ignorance," a Jackson man said bitterly. "The college instructors have created a cycle of ignorance. Many instructors are ill prepared to teach, and the only reason they do is that in the South the legislatures don't care how well or little prepared they are as long as they make the shoddy mark set up for them. They in turn pass on a haphazard education to the students, many of whom become teachers themselves. From the 1962 class, for example, seventy-six students became teachers; only eight went on to graduate or professional schools; five went into service; two became secretaries; five are unemployed, etc. Seventy-six teachers. They will pass on to their students what their instructors passed on to them, and so down the line. Yes, they go to the big schools in the North for advanced degrees, but not because they're really interested in the courses. More money."

The man who was speaking was not a teacher. Strictly speaking, he was not even a professional. His occupation (mortician) has been a necessary one ever since people began to die. A part of his bitterness may have extended from the fact that he was not a part of the academic circle, that the title, preceded by a comma after his name, was a screaming joke. But like my friend, he too had pecan trees in his yard and two cars in the driveway, a station wagon and a Jaguar; I saw these through a great picture window.

It is never bad that one wants to make money. But there are those professions we believe to be ones of dedication rather than profit. Teaching is one. Yes, it is true that even though profit may be the first consideration, some of what the teacher learns during those hot summers in the North may filter down to his students. But if the motive isn't pure, can the method be?

I knew there were students in Jackson who were very much involved in the protest demonstrations and voter registrations, but they wore no badges, and no one pointed them out. I knew one co-ed by reputation, but was given very little help in locating her.

On the way to Tougaloo, where my mother, Ola, went to school, my friend said, "Johnny, I don't want you looking at these white girls. Even with those sunglasses on. Not even out of the corner of your eyes because, if the man stops us, I'm going to tell him you're a stranger, and I'm just giving you a lift." It was supposed to be funny, and I guess we did laugh out of a sense of embarrassment. He, embarrassed because he was telling me the truth, even though he was laughing, and I, because I was ashamed for him. Even as we were sifting through the dregs of our laughter and the reasons for it, we pulled into a gas station. It was a poor one, for a white man waited on us. When my friend handed over his credit card and signed, the attendant said, "You the first left-handed colored man I ever did see."

My friend said, laughing again, "See there, I brought you luck, didn't I?"

Infinitely more beautiful than Jackson State, Tougaloo Southern Christian College was set among grass-covered mounds, within touch of a half-timbered land, and a forest in the background. I tried to picture Ola walking through the iron grill-worked fence when she was a youngster. When she went, it was a domestic school where young Negro girls were taught that their mission was to serve white people, unless they could find something else, by accident, and the chances then were rare. Ola has spent better than half her life in other people's kitchens and bedrooms and bathrooms. Like the mythical Aunt Bessie, she knows more about white people than they can ever know about her. I hoped the campus had been as nice then as it was at the moment.

Although, at the moment, the place was buzzing quietly. White men had been riding past the campus at night and firing blindly into it. Co-eds had become unsettled, and male students now mounted night guard. My mother would call people like the raiders, "night riders," and every Negro who has ever lived in outlying sections knows precisely what it means. A woman or a girl caught alone at night was automatically subject to mass rape. A lone Negro male walking home, subject to a beating. It was for these reasons that my grandfather, who had five daughters to worry about, kept a loaded rifle slung above the door. He knew how to use it. The trouble with these male students at Tougaloo, however, was that they shot at everything that moved, including, sometimes, instructors returning from Jackson. Perhaps they knew what they were doing.

Tougaloo reminded me of a kibbutz in Israel, isolated from the cities, always within range of the enemy, and yet carrying on the daily routine as if the threat of sudden violence did not exist.

I met the Reverend Edwin King, chaplain of the college and civil-rights leader. A slight, pale, brown-haired man, he was rushing to Hattiesburg to bail out some of his campaign workers. King was running for Lieutenant Governor, on an independent ticket with Aaron Henry. This was the first mixed ticket in Mississippi since Reconstruction.

It was my final night in Jackson. An eerie kind of darkness was falling, partly because the weather was suddenly turning cold. I felt disassociated; I had not found the family roots there, no distant relatives, no one who remembered my grandfather, Joseph Jones, or his family. What had I expected? I remembered how, one by one, my relatives came North, the aunts and uncles, and how each one turned to help those remaining in Mississippi to get out. Over the years we heard of cousins who had moved up to Chicago or Washington or Pittsburgh. There was nothing there for me. Now our roots scrape along the concrete walks of cities, trying to get down into solid earth once more.

I went with my friend that night to a practice session of his basketball team. His players were all fast and lean, all on full scholarships. He put them through their paces, the lay-ups, the feeds, foul shots, two-on-ones, three-on-twos.

"How they lookin', Johnny?" he'd call out.

"Great," I'd reply.

I watched him. He was getting gray and fleshy in the face and full in the gut, and I knew that he would never have been head coach of a college basketball team in the North. Never, never. Then I realized that in the middle of a hate-filled land he had found what he wanted: the thud of swift feet on a hardwood floor, the acrid odor of sweat, the challenge of competition, and security for his family. I drove back to my hotel. When I checked out the next morning, the boarders in the dining room were talking about oil drilling going on and hoping some would be discovered on property they had. They would be rich because, as one said, guffawing into his coffee, "All the scared niggers done left Mississippi and ain't got no more claim on anything." More laughter, general this time, in time to my exit.

There are two reasons why Greenville, Mississippi, is unlike Jackson. One, it is on the river, and thus for decades has been vulnerable to ideas and people from outside the state. Two, the Hodding Carter family lives there and publishes the *Delta-Democrat Times,* a "liberal" newspaper. I had talked to Hodding Carter, Sr., in New Orleans, where he held a chair at Tulane. Failing eyesight had forced him to turn the paper over to his son, Hodding Carter, Jr. I had driven northwest, through and around the low hills, through Vicksburg. I thought, as I drove carefully through the neat, quiet streets of Greenville, This is a place where a man ought to be able to relax. But still I was very cautious when I asked for directions to the paper, and I usually got some vague reply and wave. "Down that way." I should have been more relaxed; I could have been, I think, for I had been in the South long enough to know that whites and blacks weren't continually at each other's throats; that their backyards touched and that they sometimes borrowed tools from each other and chatted across the back fences; that they shopped in the same places, depending upon neighborhood. I know, because in Atlanta, in Nashville, in Jackson, I heard cashiers say "Thank you" to Negro customers, had seen clerks waiting on Negroes go off to the storeroom for items that were not on the shelves. There was not the cleared space, the No Man's Land, the demilitarized zone. No, lives dovetailed.

I waited for Carter. He hadn't come in yet. I sat on a bench and stared at the police station across the street. Next to it was a high mound, covered with grass. A levee? ("Tote dat barge, lift dat bale.") Like the next scene in a film there appeared, in front of the bleak view of jail and levee, two young men. One held a briefcase. Carter I guessed. He kept turning to look at me as the conversation ran on briefly. The other young man passed out of view; the police station again was on camera. Then the other young man, swinging the briefcase, entered the office.

"Mr. Williams?" he said, pausing before me.

"Mr. Carter?"

"Yes."

"Yes."

He excused himself, then asked me to follow him into what

might be called the city room. It was rather small, but there were a great many desks and phones. Carter was handed a proof. "Excuse me." When he finished, there were orders to give, and then we went into his office, a dark, leathern kind of place, comfortable, with the kind of air that would make you unburden your deepest secrets with a glass or two of white lightning or Mississippi corn. It was a world away from the bright, battered, cream-colored city room; there was something solid here, I felt.

In the dimness—the office faced west—Carter seemed to have light hair. Strangers, like medieval knights challenging one another on a narrow path, must also have their preliminaries, the chance to study, to plumb, to prepare the reserves for loosing or retire them altogether. I knew something about the Carters—not much, to be sure, but something. I knew that even though he was away from home, someone was guarding his family with a loaded firearm. I knew that he had learned to live with threats on his life and on his family's with a minimum of nervousness. This was the price, not for crusading, but for holding and advocating a view unpopular in the city as well as the state—namely, that a law existed, a federal law, and should be obeyed. The Carters were not for Negroes but for law, and because they were, in the minds of the white masses they were "nigger-lovers."

Of all the newspaper people I had talked to, only Carter said, "It's going to get worse before it gets better."

The other newsmen must have been aware of the steady approach of widespread violence, but they avoided the problem as if to wish it away. Carter: "We almost had a breakthrough here last summer. The Negroes demonstrated, the police didn't hamper them. It wasn't like Jackson. Then it went; how or when or why, I don't know. It was washed away."

For Carter there was not even the hope that with the changing of the Old Guard the situation would be altered. The throb of violence was too near; only a miracle could avert it.

It had become almost a macabre game by now, asking questions and having them answered, or making comments and having them enlarged upon or whittled down. And I found myself trying to concentrate on what he was saying, to find some new nuance. No, civil rights had us as slaves on the waterwheel; we had to go around and around. The questions we asked, the answer we gave, bounded from one corner of a closed box to another, like Mexican jumping beans. I tried to conceal a sudden, billowing tiredness, but Carter saw it. "What's the matter?"

"Tired," I admitted, not at all surprised that I would admit it to this stranger, who, in a larger way, was not a stranger at all. "Tense," I said.

"I'll bet the hell you are," he said and grinned. "First time South?"

"Since nineteen-forty-six, but I was born in Hinds County."

His nod was an understanding one.

As we parted he gave me directions through a less troublesome part of the state to the border. But driving away, I knew I had to take the other route, the one where trouble lay, in order to live with myself and in order to overcome the shame I suddenly felt to confess my tiredness, my tension, to this white man. Drive the cliff edge.

The land was flat, the earth powdery. Trees rimmed the distance, so far from the fields that I could not tell what they were. Cotton fields, Negroes pulling long gunnysacks, and I thought of Ola and her sisters and brothers, and wondered what it had been like for them to pad between the bushes snatching off the cotton, dumping it into the bag in one motion, for speed meant money, money meant survival. There were fields filled with peas and corn. How even the land was, empty almost, as if even the great Mississippi had fled in terror, leaving no trace, not even an immediate valley through which it had once coursed.

Above, the sky held blue. It was colder now, but the drought continued. I edged through the dangerous towns, tired but somehow hyperalert, seeing what wasn't always there and hearing what was without sound. The twin pipes of the car stuttered out behind me. North. Cleveland. Clarksdale. Ah, there was a town Carter had warned me about, but I was through it and on the open road again. Tunica, Hollywood, and the land continued flat, but the timber was growing taller. Now the fields began to tilt upwards, the timber thickening, the brown, powdered earth gobbled up by grass. Eudora off to the right, and then, right on the Mississippi-Tennessee border, Walls! Coffee now, a ham sandwich, and a rest. The next town was Whitehaven, Tennessee.

Facts About Me

Tennessee Williams

I was born in the Episcopal rectory of Columbus, Miss., an old town on the Tombigbee River which was so dignified and reserved that there was a saying, only slightly exaggerated, that you had to live there a whole year before a neighbor would smile at you on the street. As my grandfather, with whom we lived, was the Episcopal clergyman, we were accepted without probation. My father, a man with the formidable name of Cornelius Coffin Williams, was a man of ancestry that came on one side, the Williams, from pioneer Tennessee stock and the other from early settlers of Nantucket Island in New England. My mother was descended from Quakers. Roughly there was a combination of Puritan and Cavalier strains in my blood which may be accountable for the conflicting impulses I often represent in the people I write about.

I was christened Thomas Lanier Williams. It is a nice enough name, perhaps a little too nice. It sounds like it might belong to the son of a writer who turns out sonnet sequences to Spring. As a matter of fact, my first literary award was $25.00 from a Woman's Club for doing exactly that, three sonnets dedicated to Spring. I hasten to add that I was still pretty young. Under that name I published a good deal of lyric poetry which was a bad imitation of Edna Millay. When I grew up I realized this poetry wasn't much good and I felt the name had been compromised so I changed it to Tennessee Williams, the justification being mainly that the Williamses had fought the Indians for Tennessee and I had already discovered that the life of a young writer was going to be something similar to the defense of a stockade against a band of savages.

When I was about twelve, my father, a travelling salesman, was appointed to an office position in St. Louis and so we left the rectory and moved north. It was a tragic move. Neither my sister nor I could adjust ourselves to life in a Midwestern city. The schoolchildren made fun of our Southern speech and manners. I remember gangs of kids following me home yelling "Sissy!" and home was not a very pleasant refuge. It was a perpetually dim little apartment in a wilderness of identical brick and concrete structures with no grass and no trees nearer than the park. In the South we had never been conscious of the fact that we were economically less fortunate than others. We lived as well as anyone else. But in St. Louis we suddenly discovered there were two kinds of people, the rich and the poor, and that we belonged more to the latter. If we walked far enough west we came into a region of fine residences set in beautiful lawns. But where we lived, to which we must always return, were ugly rows of apartment buildings the color of dried blood and mustard. If I had been born to this situation I might not have resented it deeply. But it was forced upon my consciousness at the most sensitive age of childhood. It produced a shock and a rebellion that has grown into an inherent part of my work. It was the beginning of the social consciousness which I think has marked most of my writing. I am glad that I received this bitter education for I don't think any writer has much purpose back of him unless he feels bitterly the inequities of the society he lives in. I have no acquaintance with political and social dialectics. If you ask what my politics are, I am a Humanitarian.

That is the social background of my life!

I entered college during the great American depression and after a couple of years I couldn't afford to continue but had to drop out and take a clerical job in the shoe company that employed my father. The two years I spent in that corporation were indescribable torment to me as an individual but of immense value to me as a writer for they gave me firsthand knowledge of what it means to be a small wage earner in a hopelessly routine job. I had been writing since childhood and I continued writing while I was employed by the shoe company. When I came home from work I would tank up on black coffee so I could remain awake most of the night, writing short stories which I could not sell. Gradually my health broke down. One day, coming home from work, I collapsed and was removed to the hospital. The doctor said I couldn't go back to the shoe company. Soon as that was settled I recovered and went back South to live with my grandparents in Memphis where they had moved since my grandfather's retirement from the ministry. Then I began to have a little success with my writing. I became self-sufficient. I put myself through two more years of college and got a B.A. degree at the University of Iowa in 1938. Before then and for a couple of years afterwards I did a good deal of travelling around and I held a great number of part-time jobs of great diversity. It is hard to put the story in correct chronology for the last ten years of my life are a dizzy kaleidoscope. I don't quite believe all that has happened to me, it seems it must have happened to five or ten other people.

My first real recognition came in 1940 when I received a Rockefeller fellowship and wrote *Battle of Angels* which was produced by the Theatre Guild at the end of that year with Miriam Hopkins in the leading role. It closed in Boston during the tryout run but I have rewritten it a couple of times since then and still have faith in it. My health was so impaired that I landed in 4F after a medical examination of about five minutes' duration. My jobs in this period included running an all-night elevator in a big apartment-hotel, waiting on tables and reciting verse in the Village, working as a teletype operator for the U.S. Engineers in Jacksonville, Florida, waiter and cashier for a small restaurant in New Orleans, ushering at the Strand Theatre on Broadway. All the while I kept on writing, writing, not with any hope of making a living at it but because I found no other means of expressing things that seemed to demand expression. There was never a moment when I did not find life to be immeasurably exciting to experience and to witness, however difficult it was to sustain.

From a $17.00 a week job as a movie usher I was suddenly shipped off to Hollywood where MGM paid me $250.00 a week. I saved enough money out of my six months there to keep me while I wrote *The Glass Menagerie.* I don't think the story from that point on requires any detailed consideration.

FROM

Black Boy

RICHARD WRIGHT

GRANNY WAS AN ardent member of the Seventh-Day Adventist Church and I was compelled to make a pretense of worshiping her God, which was her exaction for my keep. The elders of her church expounded a gospel clogged with images of vast lakes of eternal fire, of seas vanishing, of valleys of dry bones, of the sun burning to ashes, of the moon turning to blood, of stars falling to the earth, of a wooden staff being transformed into a serpent, of voices speaking out of clouds, of men walking upon water, of God riding whirlwinds, of water changing into wine, of the dead rising and living, of the blind seeing, of the lame walking; a salvation that teemed with fantastic beasts having multiple heads and horns and eyes and feet; sermons of statues possessing heads of gold, shoulders of silver, legs of brass, and feet of clay; a cosmic tale that began before time and ended with the clouds of the sky rolling away at the Second Coming of Christ; chronicles that concluded with the Armageddon; dramas thronged with all the billions of human beings who had ever lived or died as God judged the quick and the dead . . .

While listening to the vivid language of the sermons I was pulled toward emotional belief, but as soon as I went out of the church and saw the bright sunshine and felt the throbbing life of the people in the streets I knew that none of it was true and that nothing would happen.

Once again I knew hunger, biting hunger, hunger that made my body aimlessly restless, hunger that kept me on edge, that made my temper flare, hunger that made hate leap out of my heart like the dart of a serpent's tongue, hunger that created in me odd cravings. No food that I could dream of seemed half so utterly delicious as vanilla wafers. Every time I had a nickel I would run to the corner grocery store and buy a box of vanilla wafers and walk back home, slowly, so that I could eat them all up without having to share them with anyone. Then I would sit on the front steps and dream of eating another box; the craving would finally become so acute that I would force myself to be active in order to forget. I learned a method of drinking water that made me feel full temporarily whether I had a desire for water or not; I would put my mouth under a faucet and turn the water on full force and let the stream cascade into my stomach until it was tight. Sometimes my stomach ached, but I felt full for a moment.

No pork or veal was ever eaten at Granny's, and rarely was there meat of any kind. We seldom ate fish and then only those that had scales and spines. Baking powder was never used; it was alleged to contain a chemical harmful to the body. For breakfast I ate mush and gravy made from flour and lard and for hours afterwards I would belch it up into my mouth. We were constantly taking bicarbonate of soda for indigestion. At four o'clock in the afternoon I ate a plate of greens cooked with lard. Sometimes on Sundays we bought a dime's worth of beef which usually turned out to be uneatable. Granny's favorite dish was a peanut roast which she made to resemble meat, but which tasted like something else.

My position in the household was a delicate one; I was a minor, an uninvited dependent, a blood relative who professed no salvation and whose soul stood in mortal peril. Granny intimated boldly, basing her logic on God's justice, that one sinful person in a household could bring down the wrath of God upon the entire establishment, damning both the innocent and the guilty, and on more than one occasion she interpreted my mother's long illness as the result of my faithlessness. I became skilled in ignoring these cosmic threats and developed a callousness toward all metaphysical preachments.

But Granny won an ally in her efforts to persuade me to confess her God; Aunt Addie, her youngest child, had just finished the Seventh-Day Adventist religious school in Huntsville, Alabama, and came home to argue that if the family was compassionate enough to feed me, then the least I could do in return was to follow its guidance. She proposed that, when the fall school term started, I should be enrolled in the religious school rather than a secular one. If I refused, I was placing myself not only in the position of a horrible infidel but of a hardhearted ingrate. I raised arguments and objections, but my mother sided with Granny and Aunt Addie and I had to accept.

The religious school opened and I put in a sullen attendance. Twenty pupils, ranging in age from five to nineteen and in grades from primary to high school, were crowded into one room. Aunt Addie was the only teacher and from the first day an acute, bitter antagonism sprang up between us. This was the first time she had ever taught school and she was nervous, self-conscious because a blood relative of hers—a relative who would not confess her faith and who was not a member of her church—was in her classroom. She was determined that every student should know that I was a sinner of whom she did not approve, and that I was not to be granted consideration of any kind.

The pupils were a docile lot, lacking in that keen sense of rivalry which made the boys and girls who went to public school a crowd in which a boy was tested and weighed, in which he caught a glimpse of what the world was. These boys and girls were will-less, their speech flat, their gestures vague, their personalities devoid of anger, hope, laughter, enthusiasm, passion, or despair. I was able to see them with an objectivity that was inconceivable to them. They were claimed wholly by their environment and could imagine no other, whereas I had come from another plane of living, from the swinging doors of saloons, the railroad yard, the roundhouses, the street gangs, the river levees, an orphan home; had shifted from town to town and home to home; had mingled with grownups more than perhaps was good for me. I had to curb my habit of cursing, but not before I had shocked more than half of them and had embarrassed Aunt Addie to helplessness.

As the first week of school drew to a close, the conflict that smoldered between Aunt Addie and me flared openly. One afternoon she rose from her desk and walked down the aisle and stopped beside me.

"You know better than that," she said, tapping a ruler across my knuckles.

"Better than what?" I asked, amazed, nursing my hand.

"Just look at that floor," she said.

I looked and saw that there were many tiny bits of walnut meat scattered about; some of them had been smeared into grease spots on the clean, white pine boards. At once I knew that the boy in front of me had been eating them; my walnuts were in my pocket, uncracked.

"I don't know anything about that," I said.

"You know better than to eat in the classroom," she said.

"I haven't been eating," I said.

"Don't lie! This is not only a school, but God's holy ground," she said with angry indignation.

"Aunt Addie, my walnuts are here in my pocket . . ."

"I'm Miss Wilson!" she shouted.

I stared at her, speechless, at last comprehending what was really bothering her. She had warned me to call her Miss Wilson in the classroom, and for the most part I had done so. She was afraid that if I called her Aunt Addie I would undermine the morale of the students. Each pupil knew that she was my aunt and many of them had known her longer than I had.

"I'm sorry," I said, and turned from her and opened a book.

"Richard, get up!"

I did not move. The room was tense. My fingers gripped the book and I knew that every pupil in the room was watching. I had not eaten the nuts; I was sorry that I had called her Aunt Addie; but I did not want to be singled out for gratuitous punishment. And, too, I was expecting the boy who sat in front of me to devise some lie to save me, since it was really he who was guilty.

"I asked you to get up!" she shouted.

I still sat, not taking my eyes off my book. Suddenly she caught me by the back of my collar and yanked me from the seat. I stumbled across the room.

"I spoke to you!" she shouted hysterically.

I straightened and looked at her; there was hate in my eyes.

"Don't you look at me that way, boy!"

"I didn't put those walnuts on the floor!"

"Then who did?"

My street gang code was making it hard for me. I had never informed upon a boy in the public school, and I was waiting for the boy in front of me to come to my aid, lying, making up excuses, anything. In the past I had taken punishment that was not mine to protect the solidarity of the gang, and I had seen other boys do the same. But the religious boy, God helping him, did not speak.

"I don't know who did it," I said finally.

"Go to the front of the room," Aunt Addie said.

I walked slowly to her desk, expecting to be lectured; but my heart quickened when I saw her go to the corner and select a long, green, limber switch and come toward me. I lost control of my temper.

"I haven't done anything!" I yelled.

She struck me and I dodged.

"Stand still, boy!" she blazed, her face livid with fury, her body trembling.

I stood still, feeling more defeated by the righteous boy behind me than by Aunt Addie.

"Hold out your hand!"

I held out my hand, vowing that never again would this happen to me, no matter what the price. She stung my palm until it was red, then lashed me across my bare legs until welts rose. I clamped my teeth to keep from uttering a single whimper. When she finished I continued to hold out my hand, indicating to her that her blows could never really reach me, my eyes fixed and unblinking upon her face.

"Put down your hand and go to your seat," she said.

I dropped my hand and turned on my heels, my palm and legs on fire, my body taut. I walked in a fog of anger toward my desk.

"And I'm not through with you!" she called after me.

She had said one word too much; before I knew it, I had whirled and was staring at her with an open mouth and blazing eyes.

"Through with me?" I repeated. "But what have I done to you?"

"Sit down and shut up!" Aunt Addie bellowed.

I sat. I was sure of one thing: I would not be beaten by her again. I had often been painfully beaten, but almost always I had felt that the beatings were somehow right and sensible, that I was in the wrong. Now, for the first time, I felt the equal of an adult; I knew that I had been beaten for a reason that was not right. I sensed some emotional problem in Aunt Addie other than her concern about my eating in school. Did my presence make her feel so insecure that she felt she had to punish me in front of the pupils to impress them? All afternoon I brooded, wondering how I could quit the school.

The moment Aunt Addie came into the house—I reached home before she did—she called me into the kitchen. When I entered, I saw that she was holding another switch. My muscles tightened.

"You're not going to beat me again!" I told her.

"I'm going to teach you some manners!" she said.

I stood fighting, fighting as I had never fought in my life, fighting with myself. Perhaps my uneasy childhood, perhaps my shifting from town to town, perhaps the violence I had already seen and felt took hold of me, and I was trying to stifle the impulse to go to the drawer of the kitchen table and get a knife and defend myself. But this woman who stood before me was my aunt, my mother's sister, Granny's daughter; in her veins my own blood flowed; in many of her actions I could see some elusive part of my own self; and in her speech I could catch echoes of my own speech. I did not want to be violent with her, and yet I did not want to be beaten for a wrong I had not committed.

"You're just mad at me for something!" I said.

"Don't tell me I'm mad!"

"You're too mad to believe anything I say."

"Don't speak to me like that!"

"Then how can I talk to you? You beat me for throwing walnuts on the floor? But I didn't do it!"

"Then who did?"

Since I was alone now with her, and desperate, I cast my loyalties aside and told her the name of the guilty boy, feeling that he merited no consideration.

"Why didn't you tell me before?" she asked.

"I don't want to tell tales on other people."

"So you lied, hunh?"

I could not talk; I could not explain how much I valued my code of solidarity.

"Hold out your hand!"

"You're not going to beat me! I didn't do it!"

"I'm going to beat you for lying!"

"Don't, don't hit me! If you hit me I'll fight you!"

For a moment she hesitated, then she struck at me with the switch and I dodged and stumbled into a corner. She was upon me, lashing me across the face. I leaped, screaming, and ran past her and jerked open the kitchen drawer; it spilled to the floor with a thunderous sound. I grabbed up a knife and held it ready for her.

"Now, I told you to stop!" I screamed.

"You put down that knife!"

"Leave me alone or I'll cut you!"

She stood debating. Then she made up her mind and came at me. I lunged at her with the knife and she grasped my hand and tried to twist the knife loose. I threw my right leg about her legs and gave her a shove, tripping her; we crashed to the floor. She was stronger than I and I felt my strength ebbing; she was still fighting for my knife and I saw a look on her face that made me feel she was going to use it on me if she got possession of it. I bit her hand and we rolled, kicking, scratching, hitting, fighting as though we were strangers, deadly enemies, fighting for our lives.

"Leave me alone!" I screamed at the top of my voice.

"Give me that knife, you boy!"

"I'll kill you! I'll kill you if you don't leave me alone!"

Granny came running; she stood thunderstruck.

"Addie, what are you doing?"

"He's got a knife!" she gasped. "Make 'im put it down!"

"Richard, put down that knife!" Granny shouted.

My mother came limping to the door.

"Richard, stop it!" she shouted.

"I won't! I'm not going to let her beat me!"

"Addie, leave the boy alone," my mother said.

Aunt Addie rose slowly, her eyes on the knife, then she turned and walked out of the kitchen, kicking the door wide open before her as she went.

"Richard, give me that knife," my mother said.

"But, mama, she'll beat me, beat me for nothing," I said. "I'm not going to let her beat me; I don't care what happens!"

"Richard, you are bad, bad," Granny said, weeping.

I tried to explain what had happened, but neither of them would listen. Granny came toward me to take the knife, but I dodged her and ran into the back yard. I sat alone on the back steps, trembling, emotionally spent, crying to myself. Grandpa came down; Aunt Addie had told him what had happened.

"Gimme that knife, mister," he said.

"I've already put it back," I lied, hugging my arm to my side to conceal the knife.

"What's come over you?" he asked.

"I don't want her to beat me," I said.

"You're a child, a boy!" he said.

"But I don't want to be beaten!"

"What did you do?"

"Nothing."

"You can lie as fast as a dog can trot," Grandpa said. "And if it wasn't for my rheumatism, I'd take down your pants and tan your backside good and proper. The very idea of a little snot like you threatening somebody with a knife!"

"I'm not going to let her beat me," I said again.

"You're bad," he said, "You better watch your step, young man, or you'll end up on the gallows."

I had long ceased to fear Grandpa; he was a sick old man and he knew nothing of what was happening in the house. Now and then the womenfolk called on him to throw fear into someone, but I knew that he was feeble and was not frightened of him. Wrapped in the misty memories of his young manhood, he sat his days out in his room where his Civil War rifle stood loaded in a corner, where his blue uniform of the Union Army lay neatly folded.

Aunt Addie took her defeat hard, holding me in a cold and silent disdain. I was conscious that she had descended to my own emotional level in her effort to rule me, and my respect for her sank. Until she married, years later, we rarely spoke to each other, though we ate at the same table and slept under the same roof, though I was but a skinny, half-frightened boy and she was the secretary of the church and the church's day-school teacher. God blessed our home with the love that binds . . .

I continued at the church school, despite Aunt Addie's never calling upon me to recite or go to the blackboard. Consequently I stopped studying. I spent my time playing with the boys and found that the only games they knew were brutal ones. Baseball, marbles, boxing, running were tabooed recreations, the Devil's work; instead they played a wildcat game called popping-the-whip, a seemingly innocent diversion whose excitement came only in spurts, but spurts that could hurl one to the edge of death itself. Whenever we were discovered standing idle on the school grounds, Aunt Addie would suggest that we pop-the-whip. It would have been safer for our bodies and saner for our souls had she urged us to shoot craps.

One day at noon Aunt Addie ordered us to pop-the-whip. I had never played the game before and I fell in with good faith. We formed a long line, each boy taking hold of another boy's hand until we were stretched out like a long string of human beads. Although I did not know it, I was on the tip end of the human whip. The leading boy, the handle of the whip, started off at a trot, weaving to the left and to the right, increasing speed until the whip of flesh was curving at breakneck gallop. I clutched the hand of the boy next to me with all the strength I had, sensing that if I did not hold on I would be tossed off. The whip grew taut as human flesh and bone could bear and I felt that my arm was being torn from its socket. Suddenly my breath left me. I was swung in a small, sharp arc. The whip was now being popped and I could hold on no more; the momentum of the whip flung me off my feet into the air, like a bit of leather being flicked off a horsewhip, and I hurtled headlong through space and landed in a ditch. I rolled over, stunned, head bruised and bleeding. Aunt Addie was laughing, the first and only time I ever saw her laugh on God's holy ground.

In the home Granny maintained a hard religious regime. There were prayers at sunup and sundown, at the breakfast table and dinner table, followed by a Bible verse from each member of the family. And it was presumed that I prayed before I got into bed at night. I shirked as many of the weekday church services as possible, giving as my excuse that I had to study; of course, nobody believed me, but my lies were accepted because nobody wanted to risk a row. The daily prayers were a torment and my knees became sore from kneeling so long and often. Finally I devised a method of kneeling that was not really kneeling; I learned, through arduous repetition, how to balance myself on the toes of my shoes and rest my head against a wall in some convenient corner. Nobody, except God, was any the wiser, and I did not think that He cared.

Granny made it imperative, however, that I attend certain all-night ritualistic prayer meetings. She was the oldest member of her church and it would have been unseemly if the only grandchild in her home could not be brought to these important services; she felt that if I were completely remiss in religious conformity it would cast doubt upon the staunchness of her faith, her capacity to convince and persuade, or merely upon her ability to apply the rod to my backside.

Granny would prepare a lunch for the all-night praying session, and the three of us—Granny, Aunt Addie, and I—would be off, leaving my mother and Grandpa at home. During the passionate prayers and the chanted hymns I would sit squirming on a bench, longing to grow up so I could run away, listening indifferently to the theme of cosmic annihilation, loving the hymns for their sensual caress, but at last casting furtive glances at Granny and wondering when it would be safe for me to stretch out on the bench and go to sleep. At ten or eleven I would munch a sandwich and Granny would nod her permission for me to take a nap. I would awaken at intervals to hear snatches of hymns or prayers that would lull me to sleep again. Finally Granny would shake me and I would open my eyes and see the sun streaming through stained-glass windows.

Many of the religious symbols appealed to my sensibilities and I responded to the dramatic vision of life held by the church, feeling that to live day by day with death as one's sole thought was to be so compassionately sensitive toward all life as to view all men as slowly dying, and the trembling sense of fate that welled up, sweet and melancholy, from the hymns blended with the sense of fate that I had already caught from life. But full emotional and intellectual belief never came. Perhaps if I had caught my first sense of life from the church I would have been moved to complete acceptance, but the hymns and sermons of God came into my heart only long after my personality had been shaped and formed by uncharted conditions of life. I felt that I had in me a sense of living as deep as that which the church was trying to give me, and in the end I remained basically unaffected.

My body grew, even on mush and lard gravy, a miracle which the church certainly should have claimed credit for. I survived my twelfth year on a diet that would have stunted an average-sized dog, and my glands began to diffuse through my blood, like sap rising upward in trees in spring, those strange chemicals that made me look curiously at girls and women. The elder's wife sang in the choir and I fell in love with her as only a twelve-year-old can worship a distant and unattainable woman. During the services I would stare at her, wondering what it was like to be married to her, pondering over how passionate she was. I felt no qualms about my first lust for the flesh being born on holy ground; the contrast between budding carnal desires and the aching loneliness of the hymns never evoked any sense of guilt in me.

It was possible that the sweetly sonorous hymns stimulated me sexually, and it might have been that my fleshy fantasies, in turn, having as their foundation my already inflated sensibility, made me love the masochistic prayers. It was highly likely that the serpent of sin that nosed about the chambers of my heart was lashed to hunger by hymns as well as dreams, each reciprocally feeding the other. The church's spiritual life must have been polluted by my base yearnings, by the leaping hunger of my blood for the flesh, because I would gaze at the elder's wife for hours, attempting to draw her eyes to mine, trying to hypnotize her, seeking to communicate with her with my thoughts. If my desires had been converted into a concrete religious symbol, the symbol would have looked something like this: a black imp with two horns; a long, curving, forked tail; cloven hoofs, a scaly, naked body; wet, sticky fingers; moist, sensual lips; and lascivious eyes feasting upon the face of the elder's wife . . .

A religious revival was announced and Granny felt that it was her last chance to bring me to God before I entered the precincts of sin at the public school, for I had already given loud and final notice that I would no longer attend the church school. There was a discernible lessening in Aunt Addie's hostility; perhaps she had come to the conclusion that my lost soul was more valuable than petty pride. Even my mother's attitude was: "Richard, you ought to know God through *some* church."

The entire family became kind and forgiving, but I knew the motives that prompted their change and it drove me an even greater emotional distance from them. Some of my classmates—who had, on the advice of their parents, avoided me—now came to visit and I could tell in a split second that they had been instructed in what to say. One boy, who lived across the street, called on me one afternoon and his self-consciousness betrayed him; he spoke so naïvely and clumsily that I could see the bare bones of his holy plot and hear the creaking of the machinery of Granny's maneuvering.

"Richard, do you know we are all worried about you?" he asked.

"Worried about me? Who's worried about me?" I asked in feigned surprise.

"All of us," he said, his eyes avoiding mine.

"Why?" I asked.

"You're not saved," he said sadly.

"I'm all right," I said, laughing.

"Don't laugh, Richard. It's serious," he said.

"But I tell you that I'm all right."

"Say, Richard, I'd like to be a good friend of yours."

"I thought we were friends already," I said.

"I mean true brothers in Christ," he said.

"We know each other," I said in a soft voice tinged with irony.

"But not in Christ," he said.

"Friendship is friendship with me."

"But don't you want to save your soul?"

"I simply can't feel religion," I told him in lieu of telling him that I did not think I had the kind of soul he thought I had.

"Have you really tried to feel God?" he asked.

"No. But I know I can't feel anything like that."

"You simply can't let the question rest there, Richard."

"Why should I let it rest?"

"Don't mock God," he said.

"I'll never feel God, I tell you. It's no use."

"Would you let the fate of your soul hang upon pride and vanity?"

"I don't think I have any pride in matters like this."

"Richard, think of Christ's dying for you, shedding His blood, His precious blood on the cross."

"Other people have shed blood," I ventured.

"But it's not the same. You don't understand."

"I don't think I ever will."

"Oh, Richard, brother, you are lost in the darkness of the world. You must let the church help you."

"I tell you, I'm all right."

"Come into the house and let me pray for you."

"I don't want to hurt your feelings . . ."

"You can't. I'm talking for God."

"I don't want to hurt God's feelings either," I said, the words slipping irreverently from my lips before I was aware of their full meaning.

He was shocked. He wiped tears from his eyes. I was sorry.

"Don't say that. God may never forgive you," he whispered.

It would have been impossible for me to have told him how I felt about religion. I had not settled in my mind whether I believed in God or not; His existence or nonexistence never worried me. I reasoned that if there did exist an all-wise, all-powerful God who knew the beginning and the end, who meted out justice to all, who controlled the destiny of man, this God would surely know that I doubted His existence and He would laugh at my foolish denial of Him. And if there was no God at all, then why all the commotion? I could not imagine God pausing in His guidance of unimaginably vast worlds to bother with me.

Embedded in me was a notion of the suffering in life, but none of it seemed like the consequences of original sin to me; I simply could not feel weak and lost in a cosmic manner. Before I had been made to go to church, I had given God's existence a sort of tacit assent, but after having seen His creatures serve Him at first hand, I had had my doubts. My faith, such as it was, was welded to the common realities of life, anchored in the sensations of my body and in what my mind could grasp, and nothing could ever shake this faith, and surely not my fear of an invisible power.

"I'm not afraid of things like that," I told the boy.

"Aren't you afraid of God?" he asked.

"No. Why should I be? I've done nothing to Him."

"He's a jealous God," he warned me.

"I hope that He's a kind God," I told him.

"If *you* are kind to Him, He *is* a kind God," the boy said. "But God will not look at you if you don't look at Him."

During our talk I made a hypothetical statement that summed up my attitude toward God and the suffering in the world, a statement that stemmed from my knowledge of life as I had lived, seen, felt, and suffered it in terms of dread, fear, hunger, terror, and loneliness.

"If laying down my life could stop the suffering in the world, I'd do it. But I don't believe anything can stop it." I told him.

He heard me but he did not speak. I wanted to say more to him, but I knew that it would have been useless. Though older than I, he had neither known nor felt anything of life for himself; he had been carefully reared by his mother and father and he had always been told what to feel.

"Don't be angry," I told him.

Frightened and baffled, he left me. I felt sorry for him.

Immediately following the boy's visit, Granny began her phase at the campaign. The boy had no doubt conveyed to her my words of blasphemy, for she talked with me for hours, warning me that I would burn forever in the lake of fire. As the day of the revival grew near, the pressure upon me intensified. I would go into the dining room upon some petty errand and find Granny kneeling, her head resting on a chair, uttering my name in a tensely whispered prayer. God was suddenly everywhere in the home, even in Aunt Addie's scowling and brooding face. It began to weigh upon me. I longed for the time when I could leave. They begged me so continuously to come to God that it was impossible for me to ignore them without wounding them. Desperately I tried to think of some way to say no without making them hate me. I was determined to leave home before I would surrender.

Then I blundered and wounded Granny's soul. It was not my intention to hurt or humiliate her; the irony of it was that the plan I conceived had as its purpose the salving of Granny's frustrated feelings toward me. Instead, it brought her the greatest shame and humiliation of her entire religious life.

One evening during a sermon I heard the elder—I took my eyes off his wife long enough to listen, even though she slumbered in my senses all the while—describe how Jacob had seen an angel. Immediately I felt that I had found a way to tell Granny that I needed proof before I could believe, that I could not commit myself to something I could not feel or see. I would tell her that if I were to see an angel I would accept that as infallible evidence that there was a God and would serve Him unhesitatingly; she would surely understand an attitude of that sort. What gave me courage to voice this argument was the conviction that I would never see an angel; if I had ever seen one, I had enough common sense to have gone to a doctor at once. With my bright idea bubbling in my mind, wishing to allay Granny's fears for my soul, wanting to make her know that my heart was not all black and wrong, that I was actually giving serious thought to her passionate pleadings, I leaned to her and whispered:

"You see, granny, if I ever saw an angel like Jacob did, then I'd believe."

Granny stiffened and stared at me in amazement; then a glad smile lit up her old wrinkled white face and she nodded and gently patted my hand. That ought to hold her for a while, I thought. During the sermon Granny looked at me several times and smiled. Yes, she knows now that I'm not dismissing her pleas from my mind . . . Feeling that my plan was working, I resumed my worship of the elder's wife with a cleansed conscience, wondering what it would be like to kiss her, longing to feel some of the sensuous emotions of which my reading had made me conscious. The service ended and Granny rushed to the front of the church and began talking excitedly to the elder; I saw the elder looking at me in surprise. Oh, goddamn, she's telling him! I thought with anger. But I had not guessed one-thousandth of it.

The elder hurried toward me. Automatically I rose. He extended his hand and I shook it.

"Your grandmother told me," he said in awed tones.

I was speechless with anger.

"I didn't want her to tell you that," I said.

"She says that you have seen an angel." The words literally poured out of his mouth.

I was so overwhelmed that I gritted my teeth. Finally I could speak and I grabbed his arm.

"No . . . N-nooo, sir! No, sir!" I stammered. "I didn't say that. She misunderstood me."

The last thing on earth I wanted was a mess like this. The elder blinked his eyes in bewilderment.

"What did you tell her?" he asked.

"I told her that if I ever saw an angel, then I would believe," I said, feeling foolish, ashamed, hating and pitying my believing granny. The elder's face became bleak and stricken. He was stunned with disappointment.

"You . . . you didn't see an angel?" he asked.

"No, *sir!*" I said emphatically, shaking my head vigorously so that there could be no possible further misunderstanding.

"I see," he breathed in a sigh.

His eyes looked longingly into a corner of the church.

"With God, you know, anything is possible," he hinted hopefully.

"But I didn't see *anything*," I said. "I'm sorry about this."

"If you pray, then God will come to you," he said.

The church grew suddenly hot. I wanted to bolt out of it and never see it again. But the elder took hold of my arm and would not let me move.

"Elder, this is all a mistake. I didn't want anything like this to happen," I said.

"Listen, I'm older than you are, Richard," he said. "I think that you have in your heart the gift of God." I must have looked dubious, for he said: "Really, I do."

"Elder, please don't say anything to anybody about this," I begged.

Again his face lit with vague hope.

"Perhaps you don't want to tell me because you are bashful?" he suggested. "Look, this is serious. If you saw an angel, then tell me."

I could not deny it verbally any more; I could only shake my head at him. In the face of his hope, words seemed useless.

"Promise me you'll pray. If you pray, then God will answer," he said.

I turned my head away, ashamed for him, feeling that I had unwittingly committed an obscene act in rousing his hopes so wildly high, feeling sorry for his having such hopes. I wanted to get out of his presence. He finally let me go, whispering:

"I want to talk to you sometime."

The church members were staring at me. My fists doubled. Granny's wide and innocent smile was shining on me and I was filled with dismay. That she could make such a mistake meant that she lived in a daily atmosphere that urged her to expect something like this to happen. She had told the other members and everybody knew it, including the elder's wife! There they stood, the church members, with joyous astonishment written on their faces, whispering among themselves. Perhaps at that moment I could have mounted the pulpit and led them all; perhaps that was to be my greatest moment of triumph!

Granny rushed to me and hugged me violently, weeping tears of joy. Then I babbled, speaking with emotional reproof, censuring her for having misunderstood me; I must have spoken more loudly and harshly than was called for—the others had now gathered about me and Granny—for Granny drew away from me abruptly and went to a far corner of the church and stared at me with a cold, set face. I was crushed. I went to her and tried to tell her how it had happened.

"You shouldn't've spoken to me," she said in a breaking voice that revealed the depths of her disillusionment.

On our way home she would not utter a single word. I walked anxiously beside her, looking at her tired old white face, the wrinkles that lined her neck, the deep, waiting black eyes, and the frail body, and I knew more than she thought I knew about the meaning of religion, the hunger of the human heart for that which is not and can never be, the thirst of the human spirit to conquer and transcend the implacable limitations of human life.

Later, I convinced her that I had not wanted to hurt her and she immediately seized upon my concern for her feelings as an opportunity to have one more try at bringing me to God. She wept and pleaded with me to pray, really to pray, to pray hard, to pray until tears came . . .

"Granny, don't make me promise," I begged.

"But you must, for the sake of your soul," she said.

I promised; after all, I felt that I owed her something for inadvertently making her ridiculous before the members of her church.

Daily I went into my room upstairs, locked the door, knelt, and tried to pray, but everything I could think of saying seemed silly. Once it all seemed so absurd that I laughed out loud while on my knees. It was no use. I could not pray. I could never pray. But I kept my failures a secret. I was convinced that if I ever succeeded in praying, my words would bound noiselessly against the ceiling and rain back down upon me like feathers.

My attempts at praying became a nuisance, spoiling my days; and I regretted the promise I had given Granny. But I stumbled on a way to pass the time in my room, a way that made the hours fly with the speed of the wind. I took the Bible, pencil, paper, and a rhyming dictionary and tried to write verses for hymns. I justified this by telling myself that, if I wrote a really good hymn, Granny might forgive me. But I failed even in that; the Holy Ghost was simply nowhere near me . . .

One day while killing my hour of prayer, I remembered a series of volumes of Indian history I had read the year before. Yes, I knew what I would do; I would write a story about the Indians . . . But what about them? Well, an Indian girl . . . I wrote of an Indian maiden, beautiful and reserved, who sat alone upon the bank of a still stream, surrounded by eternal twilight and ancient trees, waiting . . . The girl was keeping some vow which I could not describe and, not knowing how to develop the story, I resolved that the girl had to die. She rose slowly and walked toward the dark stream, her face stately and cold; she entered the water and walked on until the water reached her shoulders, her chin; then it covered her. Not a murmur or a gasp came from her, even in dying.

"And at last the darkness of the night descended and softly kissed the surface of the watery grave and the only sound was the lonely rustle of the ancient trees," I wrote as I penned the final line.

I was excited; I read it over and saw that there was a yawning void in it. There was no plot, no action, nothing save atmosphere and longing and death. But I had never in my life done anything like it; I had made something, no matter how bad it was; and it was mine . . . Now, to whom could I show it? Not my relatives; they would think I had gone crazy. I decided to read it to a young woman who lived next door. I interrupted her as she was washing dishes and, swearing her to secrecy, I read the composition aloud. When I finished she smiled at me oddly, her eyes baffled and astonished.

"What's that for?" she asked.

"Nothing," I said.

"But why did you write it?"

"I just wanted to."

"Where did you get the idea?"

I wagged my head, pulled down the corners of my mouth, stuffed my manuscript into my pocket and looked at her in a cocky manner that said: Oh, it's nothing at all. I write stuff like this all the time. It's easy, if you know how. But I merely said in an humble, quiet voice:

"Oh, I don't know. I just thought it up."

"What're you going to do with it?"

"Nothing."

God only knows what she thought. My environment contained nothing more alien than writing or the desire to express one's self in writing. But I never forgot the look of astonishment and bewilderment on the young woman's face when I had finished reading and glanced at her. Her inability to grasp what I had done or was trying to do somehow gratified me. Afterwards whenever I thought of her reaction I smiled happily for some unaccountable reason.

FROM

Bodies & Soul

AL YOUNG

BLACK, BROWN AND BEIGE
DUKE ELLINGTON ORCHESTRA, 1947
(—or, Miz Chapman tells us the score)

"NOW SON, I know you can do better than that. You've *got* to do better. You know how come? Because you're black, that's why. Nothing's going to come easy in this world that's laying for you out there, so you might as well get used to having to be twice as good as white folks at whatever you do if you intend to ever make anything out of yourself."

The woman speaking wasn't my mother. It was Miz Chapman, my second-grade teacher at Kingston Primary School for Colored in Laurel, Mississippi, 1947. My mother, who later bombarded me with similar warnings, was still quite young then. Unable to look after and provide for all of her children, she had sent me and a much younger brother back from Detroit to our native state to spend a couple of years with her sister, my Aunt Doris, and her family. This practice wasn't unusual then, long before such notions as the Nuclear Family, the Civil Rights Struggle and Black Pride were widespread.

Zora Neale Hurston, the late and eminent novelist and folklorist, spoke of being "passed around the family like a bad penny." Perhaps because I was only seven at the time, I didn't feel as though I were being farmed out. Still, it felt peculiar to be separated from my true parents—that is until I landed in Miz Chapman's room in that big, dilapidated, gray wooden structure surrounded by mud.

She was indeed a remarkable woman, this scolder and molder of minds, this Miz Chapman. Dark-skinned, white-haired, scalding of eye and seemingly telepathic, she was often given to warm laughter. Moreover, she possessed an uncanny ability, common to the elderly in those days, of being able to train her laser-like sight on your very soul. With a look that variously melted or chilled, Miz Chapman was capable of reading everything there was to know about you—past, present or future—at a glance. And she was memorably tough on her secret favorites, pupils from whom she expected nothing short of excellence. Unfortunately, I happened to be one of those.

One chilly Friday morning in late autumn, while we were putting away our readers and bringing out arithmetic homework, Miz Chapman casually announced that anyone who wanted to stick around after school to "learn a little something about the history of the Negro race" was welcome to do so. "It's important that you all know about that," she added.

Given all the activities, sanctioned and unsanctioned, that went on after school in our sad little corner of that textile mill and cannery town, I was surprised to find myself remaining after class had let out just to learn what Miz Chapman had to teach us. Leontyne Price, a native of Laurel, might have been weaving her girlish, operatic dreams at that very moment. Since it was all entirely voluntary—and that went for our teacher's time as well—only a handful of us had been curious enough to take up the invitation.

Drawing a long face, the twinkle never leaving her eye, Miz Chapman gave us each a special look, then seated us in a semicircle around the rotund wood heater, now grown cold, that squatted in one corner of the rickety room. Chilly, we had to keep on our coats and jackets and sweaters. This arrangement, of course, was far more intimate than when she presided over us from her mean-looking desk up front by the blackboard.

"You poor things," she began, removing her glasses and pinching the bridge of her nose. "Poor babies. I wish there were more of you here because this here is something you really need to know about. We'll just have to start where we have to. Nothing makes a failure but a trial."

Those cryptic, prefatory remarks of Miz Chapman's were making me giddy with anticipation. I was innocently fascinated and yet, at the same time, slightly frightened. What on earth was she about to tell us that was so important that she found it necessary to lower her voice so mysteriously, so ominously?

"I reckon we'll have to begin with slavery," she said. "Now, you all know about slavery, don't you?"

Some of us knew vaguely about slavery and some of us didn't. It must be remembered that public school classrooms back then were often filled with pupils of varying ages. Not everyone was automatically passed on the way they are now, and certainly not in Miz Chapman's class. You simply had to master the material she was teaching before she would advance you to the next grade. There was no getting around it. In that second-grade class of hers, there were kids old enough to be third-graders, and several lanky, strapping ones of fourth, fifth or possible sixth grade age.

"Miz Chapman, ma'am," I raised my hand and asked, "would you please explain what slavery was?"

She folded her hands in her lap and leaned forward on her chair. "There was a time—and it wasn't all that long ago either—when colored people were in slavery. That was how we started out, in this country anyway, in these United States, this place we call America."

A stickler for correct speech and grammar, Miz Chapman, in her role as teacher, customarily spoke in gentle, cultivated Southern tones. Her voice was musical and proper when she wanted it to be. Naturally, she was also very much one of the people: a public servant who was on familiar terms with practically everybody in the community. She knew who your parents or guardians were and made a point of socializing with them as regularly as she could. In fact, chances were better than reasonable that she'd taught them when they were children. At the drop of a ruler, she could shift linguistic gears and become vigorously—if not wickedly—colloquial when the occasion called for it.

There was many a youngster, myself included, who knew what it was like to look up and blink just in time to duck an oncoming blackboard eraser hurled at top speed by Miz Chapman herself right at your unsuspecting head. "Next time I'll take better aim" she might shout down the aisle of desks at the offender. "Since you so doggone hardheaded, maybe that's the only way I can get through to you. Don't worry. I *will* get through!" Those old erasers weren't the soft felt kind in use today. They were chalky strips of heavy cloth glued to hard blocks of wood. Used accurately as missiles, they could cause severe concussions.

This afternoon, however, nobody was fooling around. We were all giving Miz Chapman our best attention. The message that she was warming up to was as clear and cold as ice water.

"Slavery," she continued, rising from her seat and pointing, "is when you—and by you I do mean *you, you and you*—are owned by somebody else, the same way somebody might own a dog or a cat or a mule or a cow. Now, the way the Creator meant for things to go, there wasn't supposed to be any such thing as slavery. People all over the world, all they are is brothers and sisters. But we don't always go by God's laws. We're like a world full of wayward children. We forget about the Lord and do things our way, and what that means is any old kinda way."

She paced around the heater momentarily, as though pulling her urgent thoughts together, "People out of Spain, England, France, Holland and different places, they hopped in their little boats and sailed over here to start them up a new country, so they say. Now, you all remember when we were studying about Christopher Columbus and the Pilgrims and all those folks? Remember how the Indians were already here when they stepped off the boat? Well, keep that in mind because that's important. We'll get back to that and talk about it some more because all that fits in with what I'm fixing to tell you."

Somewhere down inside my stomach, a little knot was beginning to tighten. I looked around at the other faces to see how my classmates were taking this old woman's words. Like the rest of this motley assemblage, I had seen my share of western movies, but had never stopped to consider why the Indians were always going on the warpath, or why Tom Mix, Bob Steele, Hopalong Cassidy and other cowboy heroes were forever shooting at them. Everybody sat engrossed, entranced and wide-eyed.

"You see," said Miz Chapman, peeping around furtively before sitting again, "you can go buy yourself a mule and hitch that mule up to pull your wagon or plow your land. You don't have to pay that mule a salary. All you have to do is give him feed and give him water, and maybe have a barn or a shed to put him in at night or when the weather gets rough. I mean, who ever heard of a mule or a cow or a chicken drawing a paycheck?"

When she broke out into a smile, we all knew that it was OK to follow her lead. We smiled back and a couple of us laughed nervously.

"Wellsir," she went on, "Back in those days, going way, way back—three four hundred years at least—you could buy yourself a person. That's right, a person, a human being, a man, a woman, a child—depending on what you needed 'em for—and you could train that person and put 'em to work just like you might any other poor beast of burden. And that's what was done with us. Slavetraders—men who made their living catching and selling slaves—traveled all up and down the coast of Africa, packing their slaveships with the strongest men and women and little bitty children they could round up and bringing 'em back over here to sell."

"But why'd they have to go all the way over there?" some girl wanted to know. "Couldn't they capture 'em some white folks and Indians right here?"

Miz Chapman shook her head and smiled again. "Whoa, now, that's a good question! Bless your heart! Shows me you got your thinking cap on. What you say! Fact of the matter is they did have a right sizeable few of their own kind in slavery all along. There used to be something called debtors prison. You owe so much money and can't pay off your debts and bills. Well, over yonder in England, say, they might slap you in prison and then you might could work out a deal where you'd get shipped over here to the Colonies and be put in slavery—indentured servitude, they called it—until you worked off what you owed. But, you see, white folks, it looked like, could always buy their way out of slavery somehow, but the Negro couldn't, not in most places anyway. You have to remember something, though—and if you don't remember this, then nothing else I'm trying to tell you today'll make much sense—so pay attention. White folks won't treat us the same way they treat other white folks. Listen at what I'm saying. White folks treat colored people different. They always have, and they still do!"

"And the Indians?" I asked.

"This Indian," she said, shaking her head. "Seems like they never could get him to work for them the way they could us. See, child, it's one thing when you pile in and take over somebody else's country, and another thing when you go yanking people from out their home and drag and carry 'em off someplace that's thousands of miles across the ocean, put 'em in chains, then dare 'em to run away or do anything about their condition. That's how they did us. They snatched us up the way you might go out in the woods and catch a rabbit or a possum or a squirrel, then they pent and cooped us up. They put us to planting cotton, chopping cotton, picking cotton, cooking, sewing, scrubbing, building, mending, riding shotgun on one another and every other kinda chore you can think of, even raising their little privileged children and—"

"But why?" It was the same girl's voice interrupting her. "I need to know why!"

"Girl, I already told you! It was cheaper to do it that way than it was to pay somebody, that's why. It's always cheaper to make somebody work for you for nothing than it is to pay 'em."

Miz Chapman's gaze turned suddenly toward the row of tall windows in back of us—kept sparkling clean by pupils forced to work off violations—where the late afternoon light had begun to fade.

"You know," she told us, getting to her feet, "for all that, we're still here. We are still here. We're still struggling, but we're still here. Y'all know that old spiritual we sing about 'I Been 'Buked and I Been Scorned'? Well, for all that, for all they have done to us and're trying to do to us, we are still here, right here, carrying on . . . still trying to make that journey home."

Her face softened wistfully. A tear slipped down one of her tall cheekbones. "Everything they could see to take away from us, they took. They took away our homeland, our families and the people we loved, our language, our customs, our music, our history. . . . But you know what? All we are is children of God, and the Almighty will take care of His own. No need for you to worry about *that.* Just like He parted the waters of the Red Sea and led the Israelites out of bondage in Egypt, the Lord is looking after all of His children.

"And for everything they took away, we came up with something new. We commenced to making a new religion. We sang us some new songs and danced us some new dances. We created new families, built us some new homes, and commenced to making some new history, too. See, you can put a hurting on the body, but you can't touch the soul. You know how come that is? It's because the soul of man, the same as God's love, is everlasting. The Good Book says, 'And I will dwell in the house of the Lord *forever*'!

"Now, it also says in the Good Book that God helps those who help themselves, and that's just what we've been doing and what we're bound to do more of. The way we go about doing that is first by learning *how* we can help ourselves. You young 'uns have opportunities we didn't have when I was coming along. You can go to school and study. You all are in a position to do a whole lot more than we could. But you're still dealing with the same situation. You don't have to be all that smart to look around at the way we're being treated and cheated to see that we aren't a free people yet. No, not yet.

"I feel like it's part of my job to tell you all what I know about what our people have been through before you got here, before you were born. I want you all to know about the Negro race and some of the people, *great* people, who didn't sit around and lay around waiting for somebody else to get busy. There were some who saw what had to be done, who went on ahead and did it, and what they did *stayed* done! I'm talking about folks like Phillis Wheatley, Harriet Tubman, Sojourner Truth, Frederick Douglass, Paul Laurence Dunbar, Booker T. Washington, W. E. B. DuBois, George Washington Carver, Mary McCleod Bethune, A. Philip Randolph, Langston Hughes, and plenty other Negro geniuses you aren't liable to find out too much about in history books these white folks put out."

One older boy seated next to me screwed up his face and raised his hand. "Miz Chapman," he asked, "how come white folks so doggone mean?"

"Now, that's something you've got to be careful about," she told him. "Not everybody's the same. Even with the white folks, some're different. You can't go putting good white folks, quality white folks, in the same category as crackers and peckerwoods. Y'all are old enough to know by now that there's a big difference between good and bad anything. If it wasn't for good-thinking white folks, then the Underground Railroad wouldn't have worked as well as it did."

"The Underground Railroad," I asked. "What was that?"

"I see we have a lot of catching up to do," said Miz Chapman. "That's why I want you all to listen and think about some of this stuff I'm telling you, then I want you to come back here with some questions. You know, there's such a thing as slavery of the mind too. You have to think. Next time we meet, we'll be talking about some of these Negro geniuses, like, now, you take Dr. George Washington Carver. By the way, who can tell me who he was?"

A girl raised her hand. "He invented the peanut, didn't he?"

Miz Chapman laughed. "No, child, he didn't exactly *invent* the peanut, but you're on the right track. George Washington Carver took the common little peanut, studied it real hard, then did things with it that people all over the world are still benefiting by. He was a botanist, one of our great scientists known the world over. Fact of business, he just died a few years ago over in Tuskegee. And when people would ask him how he got to know so much, Dr. Carver would explain how important it was to study *and* to have faith in the Lord. It was by listening to God that he was able to figure out so much and get to be so great.

"All of us are children of God, don't care what anybody else tells you—and before you turn grown, you'll be hearing a whole gang of explanations about how the world was created and how mankind got here. You just take your strength from the Almighty, trust in Him, use your own good sense and go on about your business. Anybody with any kind of sense knows good and well that man did *not* make this world and the stars and the planets and the seasons and all that comes with it. This earth is our home for *now,* that's all. We just pass through here on our way someplace else. But, see, that doesn't mean we won't have to fight for what we have a right to. There are going to be trials and there are going to be tribulations. Nobody's going to give you a durn thing! When they wrote the Constitution, white folks weren't thinking about us because Negroes were considered the same as property and livestock. 'Kill a mule and I'll hire another'n; kill a nigger and I'll buy another'n!' That's how the old saying went. But after the Civil War and President Abraham Lincoln signed the Emancipation Proclamation, that was a step in the right direction. Yet and still, nobody's going to just walk up and hand you nothing for free. You've got to work and struggle for it, and most times you've got to fight for it. 'Here, old So-and-So, we want you to have this here freedom on accounta you all right with us.' Hunh, what you say? That isn't how it works. You have got to earn it; but before you can earn, first you have to learn. Get something in your head and then—no matter what they do to you, no matter how lowdown the world becomes—they can't knock it out of you! But you can't operate on muscle and nerve and brains alone. You need heart; you need God. You need the Master to lean on and guide you."

Then rising and resting her hands in the pockets of her well-worn coat, Miz Chapman looked at the wall clock and said, "Now, who wants to lead us in reciting the 'Twenty-Third Psalm'?"

Looking back now from a vantage point of some thirty-odd years, it's easy to see how there must have been countless Miz Chapmans in Black classrooms all over the country who loved their calling devotedly, and who strove to give Black, Brown and Beige children charged to their care the skills, both practical and spiritual, that they would be needing to build halfway meaningful lives for themselves in a society that has traditionally spurned and rejected their kind. From that day on, I heeded such shibboleths as "What you get in your head, nobody can knock out." I heard them echoed so repeatedly, in fact, that they began to sound platitudinous. The vividness, however, of Miz Chapman's pronouncements at the first of those after-school study sessions has lasted.

I remember that it was growing dark as I made my way home from the schoolyard. Clutching my books wrapped in grocery bag paper, I hurried along the dirt roadways and partially asphalted paths, cutting across trash-strewn vacant lots and fields of weeds leaping over sluggish puddles and mud holes, some of them rumored to be mined with quicksand.

"Yea, though I walk through the valley of the shadow of death, I will fear no evil; for Thou art with me. . . ."

Finally I was sprinting past the broken-down fences and ramshackle houses of my own little block in that part of Laurel known as Kingston Bottom.

"Thou preparest a table before me in the presence of mine enemies. . ."

The smell of suppers cooking filled the air. I could see lights burning in the windows of our place, the last house on the road before you came to the creek. My Aunt Doris would be inside where it was warm, preparing a meal of neckbones and rice, turnip greens, cornbread, molasses, buttermilk. To top it all off, there'd be no school tomorrow!

I didn't know exactly yet who "mine enemies" were but, like the distant croaking of frogs hidden in darkness by the creek, I knew that they were out there somewhere, crouched, setting their traps, laying for me like wild game hunters. And I knew that I was either going to learn to be strong, clever and swift or forever play dead.

A surge of pure joy was bubbling inside me as I raced down the final stretch home.

LERONE BENNETT, JR., (1928) was born in Clarksdale, Mississippi. When he was young, his family moved to Jackson, Mississippi, where he received his education in the public schools. After high school, he went to Atlanta to attend Morehouse College, from which he was graduated in 1949. After further study at Atlanta University, Bennett became a journalist and worked for the *Atlanta Daily World* (1949–53), *Jet* magazine (1953), and *Ebony* magazine as an associate editor from 1954 to 1957. In 1958 he became the senior editor of *Ebony*, a position he holds today. Bennett is a historian, critic, poet, essayist, and writer of short stories. His *Before the Mayflower: A History of the Negro in America, 1619–1966* is considered by many the "bible of black history."

In an interview with Felicia Lee of *USA Today* Bennett says, "Black history studies saved my life. It's made it possible for me to have some sense of why black people are where they are; why black people are what they are. It's given me a sense of optimism." His love for black history was ignited, as he was growing up in Jackson, by the "extraordinary" teachers in the public schools, and grew stronger as he sought understanding of Jackson. "I developed the mad idea that if I mastered the written word I could figure out why Mississippi existed, why black people lived as they did. I *had* to know," he said. "It was a matter of life and death. It had nothing to do with academics, it had nothing to do with books. I had friends who were whipped, attacked. I was threatened. It was rare for a black person to reach adulthood without having that kind of an experience."

There were good times for Bennett too, of course—having his first newspaper editorial published when he was eleven; playing clarinet and saxophone in a jazz band; being the editor of his high school yearbook and newspaper; and editing the newspaper at Morehouse College.

Concluding the interview he said, "We have to go back to the beginning and create a common American history—one that takes into account that America is not a creation of white people alone. In too many presentations we pop up suddenly as slaves, and Lincoln 'frees' us. We came here before the Mayflower, and . . . we were essentially involved in creating the economic settlement of this country. It is my view that it's impossible for white people to understand themselves and this country without understanding black history."

In addition to *Before the Mayflower* (1962, revised 1969), Bennett is the author of *The Negro Mood and Other Essays* (1964), *What Manner of Man: A Biography of Martin Luther King, Jr.* (1964), *Confrontation: Black and White* (1965), *Black Power U.S.A.: The Human Side of Reconstruction, 1867–1877 (1967),* and *Pioneers of Protest* (1968).

JASON BERRY (1949) was born in New Orleans, Louisiana. In 1971 he was graduated cum laude from Georgetown University with a B.A. in English literature. Berry divides his time between investigative reporting and cultural reportage with writings appearing in the *New York Times, Nation, New Republic, Washington Post, Columbia Journalism Review,* and many regional publications. Forthcoming is his *Up from the Cradle of Jazz,* a history of post-World War II New Orleans music, which will be published in collaboration with Jonathan Foose and Tad Jones by the University of Georgia Press.

In 1973 his book *Amazing Grace: With Charles Evers in Mississippi,* a personal account of what it was like for a white southerner to work as press secretary in Evers's first campaign for governor, was published. Berry says, "It is the most candid assessment of my youth I have written." He wrote the book on his family's farm in Poplarville, Mississippi, which "remains," he says, "the best place I know to write."

Berry notes: "Anyone who reads an anthology about childhood and youth embarks upon a search—a journey through the memory of writers summoning the sounds and scenes of their impressionable years. This trail is lined with messages about the lives all of us lead today because history is finally an echo of generations. It lives in the social prophecy of Faulkner's fiction: we hear it in the great passion lyrics of B.B. King and Muddy Waters and the many blues poets before them, without whom there never would have been an Elvis. Between those two realities, the cultural memory of Africans and of Americans, lies the shared inheritance of late 20th century Mississippi and so much of the surrounding South.

"Mississippi will always be a beautiful, haunted zone of my imagination. The cruelty of racism and the eloquence of folk life, the strength of literature and the stirring oratory of black preachers and polemicists, the tender daily courtesies so absent in most cities—all exist in Mississippi in such outsized variations. It is where I learned first lessons about power and it is where I became a writer."

NASH K. BURGER (1908) was born in Jackson, Mississippi, and educated in Jackson public schools. After attending Millsaps College for two years he transferred to the University of the South where he received a B.A. in 1930. In 1935 he earned an M.A. from the University of Virginia. From 1932 to 1937 he was head of the department of English in the Jackson school system and later (1937–1939) taught English and French in Richmond, Virginia. Between 1939 and 1942 he was editor of the Historical Records Survey, sponsored by the Mississippi Department of Archives and History; during this time he also became the first historiographer of the Episcopal Diocese of Mississippi. In 1945 he became editor of the *New York Times Book Review*. In addition to reviews, newspaper articles, and magazine essays, Burger has written two books on the Confederacy. *South of Appomatox* (1959), co-authored with John K. Bettersworth, presents biographies of ten men who were influential during and after the Civil War. *Confederate Spy* (1967) is a biography of Rose O'Neale Greenhow.

Burger lives in Charlottesville, Virginia.

WILL D. CAMPBELL (1924) was born in Amite County, Mississippi, and educated at East Fork High School. After attending Louisiana College for one year he transferred to Wake Forest University where he received an A.B. in 1948. The Reverend Campbell earned a Bachelor of Divinity degree from Yale University in 1952. He served as pastor of the Baptist Church in Taylor, Louisiana, for two years and from 1954 to 1956 was Director of Religious Life at the University of Mississippi before becoming a consultant on race relations for the National Council of Churches from 1956 to 1963. During this period, Campbell wrote *Race and Renewal of the Church* (1962). In 1963 Campbell became affiliated with the Committee of Southern Churchmen and served in the position of preacher-at-large and for a time as director of the organization.

Most of Campbell's time is now spent writing, speaking, and lecturing. It has been reported that he is the model for the Reverend Will B. Dunn of the *Kudzu* newspaper comic strip.

Known to many during the civil rights movement as Brother Will and to those in his ministry as Preacher Will, Campbell describes himself as a "steeple dropout," a preacher without a pulpit whose parishioners come from all over America. He is the author of the award-winning *Brother to a Dragonfly* (1977), *Glad River* (1982), and numerous essays and religious works.

ROBERT CANZONERI (1925) was born in San Marcos, Texas, and grew up in Clinton, Mississippi, the son of a Sicilian turned Baptist minister. In 1943 he joined the United States Navy and upon discharge, attended Mississippi College, receiving a B.A. in 1948. An M.A. from the University of Mississippi followed in 1951. After teaching at several universities and colleges, Canzoneri received a Ph.D. from Stanford University. Since 1965 he has been at Ohio State University. His books include *"I Do So Politely": A Voice from the South* (1965), *Watch Us Pass* (1968), *Men with Little Hammers* (1969), *Barbed Wire and Other Stories* (1970), and *A Highly Ramified Tree* (1976), which won the Ohioana award for the best book of the year in the field of autobiography.

Canzoneri writes: "I was a Mississippi boy—my mother was a Barnett from Standing Pine—but my father had a funny accent and told stories about his boyhood in Sicily. The dual heritage affected me from the time that I can remember, but it was a visit with my father to Palazzo Adriano, where he was born, that gave impetus to the self-exploration embodied in

A Highly Ramified Tree. Because so much of it was painfully intimate (as well as for esthetic reasons) I wrote a number of chapters in the third person, as short stories; they are, nevertheless, in essence and in as many details as possible, factual."

Of *A Highly Ramified Tree* Malcolm Cowley says, "The writing is consistently good and the book is as charming as anything I have read for a long time."

CHARLOTTE CAPERS (1913) was born in Columbia, Tennessee, and grew up in Jackson, Mississippi, where "home" was an Episcopal rectory. She attended Millsaps College and received her B.A. from the University of Mississippi in 1934. Shortly after her graduation Capers took a temporary job at the Mississippi Department of Archives and History. She worked there forty-five years, serving as director from 1955 to 1969. During her tenure as director, the Old Capitol was restored, the State Historical Museum organized, and plans for the Archives and History Building completed. When she resigned as director in 1969, she became director of information and education, and in this capacity was editorial director of all Department publications. In 1972 she was appointed principal executive for the restoration of the Governor's Mansion, and upon her retirement in 1983 the Archives and History Building was named in her honor.

"One of the things that I'm proudest of," she said in a *Jackson Daily News* interview, "is the acquisition of the Eudora Welty papers. Her collection of manuscripts, correspondence, and first editions has drawn scholars from all over the world to Jackson."

Capers has reviewed books for the *New York Times Book Review* and has written historical articles for the *Encyclopedia Britannica* and the *Americana*. Editor of the *Journal of Mississippi History* from 1942 to 1969, she has been an officer of the Mississippi Historical Society since 1955, serving as its president in 1974–75.

Her book *The Capers Papers* is a collection of essays from her *Jackson Daily News* and Jackson *Star-Times* columns, and her "Good Life" pieces in *The Delta Review*. Of it, Eudora Welty writes: "These pieces vary in subject and mood and kind. But they convey in common a warmth of feeling you won't fail to recognize as Charlotte's own. In reading the Capers papers we hear the Capers voice. The beautifully written 'God and My Grandmother,' an essay given the full development it deserves, has the power to deeply stir us."

ANNE CARSLEY (1935) has spent most of her life in Jackson, Mississippi, where she was born. She received a B.A. from Millsaps College in 1957 and an M.A. from the University of Mississippi in 1959. For her essays she has received awards from Millsaps College, the Southern Literary Festival, the Mississippi Arts Festival, and the Mississippi Commission on the Arts. In 1970 she received third prize for a screenplay in a contest sponsored by the Mississippi Authority for Educational Television.

Since 1980 Carsley has published six romantic novels with historical settings—*This Ravished Rose* (1980), *The Winged Lion* (1981), *This Triumphant Fire* (1982), *Defiant Desire* (1983), *The Golden Savage* (1984), and *Tempest* (1985). Her interest in archaeology led her to set *The Winged Lion* in Sumer (now Iran) in 2350 B.C. and *The Golden Savage* in Crete in 1650 B.C. Her work in progress is *The Sword and the Rose*, a novel of the Civil War.

"All that I write and will ever write," Carsley says, "grows out of this enduring Mississippi land, the sight, sound, and smell of it, the people, their lives, and passions. The pattern was set in youth and touches all I write. It all comes together for me and produces the reality—the power of words and the finished tale, the communication."

HODDING CARTER (1907–1972), Pulitzer Prize-winning journalist, was born in Hammond, Louisiana. He attended public schools in Hammond and received a B.A. in 1927 from Bowdoin College in Maine. He studied at the Pulitzer School of Journalism at Columbia University (1927–28), taught freshman English at Tulane University (1928–29), and entered newspaper work in 1929 a member of the staff of the New Orleans *Item-Tribune*. Night manager of the New Orleans bureau of the United Press in 1930, Carter began working for the Associated Press bureau in Jackson, Mississippi, in 1931. The next year he was dismissed from the Associated Press for "insubordination" and was told he would "never make a newspaperman."

In 1932 in the midst of the Depression, Carter returned to his hometown and with his life savings of $367 started the Hammond *Daily Courier*. Four years later, he sold the newspaper which had assets of $16,000. From 1932 to 1936 one of Carter's chief targets was Louisiana political boss and United States Senator Huey Long. In 1936 Carter was persuaded by William Alexander Percy and David Cohn to move to Greenville, Mississippi, to start a paper to compete with the Greenville *Democrat-Times*. Soon afterward, the *Democrat-Times* sold out to Carter and his backers, and the *Delta Democrat-Times* was born.

For the rest of his life he was actively involved in community affairs. Although his political and social views were often different from many natives, Carter remained intensely loyal to Greenville, following Percy's injunction that "our mission is to live as men of good will in Greenville, Mississippi, because it is the sum total of all the Greenvilles in our country that will make the kind of nation that we want or don't want."

Throughout his journalistic career Carter was a major advocate of racial justice and a fierce opponent of the system of state-supported racial segregation in Mississippi and in the South. But before becoming a prophet honored in his own country, there were years when Carter was one of the most hated white men in Mississippi. The Mississippi Legislature resolved in 1955 by a vote of 89 to 19 that he was a traitor for criticizing the white Citizens Council. At that time he was chairman of the Rotary Club's Ladies Night, a counselor to the Boy Scouts, a Cub Scout den father, a director of the Chamber of Commerce, a member of the Board of Visitors of Tulane University, president of the Mississippi Historical Society and a vestryman at St. James Episcopal Church. He was a frequent speaker to school and civic groups and served as master of ceremonies for horse shows, high school newspaper conventions, and debutante balls.

Except for brief periods—1940 as a Nieman Fellow at Harvard, a few years with the United States Army during World War II, and some time in New Orleans as a writer-in-residence at Tulane—Carter spent the years 1936 to 1972 in Greenville. In 1946 he was awarded a Pulitzer Prize for editorials in the *Delta Democrat-Times*.

During his lifetime Carter published numerous books including *Lower Mississippi* (1942), *The Winds of Fear* (1944), *Flood Crest* (1947), *Southern Legacy* (1950), *Where Main Street Meets the River* (1953), *The Angry Scar: The Story of Reconstruction* (1959), *First Person Rural* (1963), and *So the Heffners Left McComb* (1965).

TURNER CATLEDGE (1901–1983) was born in New Prospect, Mississippi, a crossroad community six miles south of Ackerman. When he was three years old his family moved to Philadelphia, Mississippi. After completing high school he enrolled in Mississippi A&M College, now Mississippi State University, and earned a B.S. in 1922.

Catledge began his career in journalism under the tutelage of Clayton Rand, who offered him a job managing the Tunica (Mississippi) *Times*. From Tunica he moved to the job of managing editor of the Tupelo (Mississippi) *Journal*. In 1923 he joined the staff of the Memphis *Commercial Appeal* where he came to the attention of Herbert C. Hoover during his tour of areas affected by the Mississippi River flood of 1927. Hoover, then Secretary of Commerce under Calvin Coolidge, suggested to Adolph S. Ochs, publisher of the *New York Times*, that Catledge be hired as reporter. When two years later, this time as President of the United States, Hoover repeated his request, Catledge was hired by the *Times*. With the exception of a brief period at the *Chicago Sun* from 1941 to 1943, he remained with the *Times* for more than forty years.

In 1945 Catledge joined the editorial staff of the *Times*. Six years later, in March 1951, he was named executive managing editor and was responsible for coordinating the work of the day and night editors. Catledge became executive editor in 1964 and assumed authority over both the daily and Sunday papers. In 1968 he became *Times* company vice president and a member of the board. Retiring to New Orleans in 1970, he published his autobiography, *My Life and the Times*, in 1971.

Catledge expanded the coverage of foreign and national news in the *Times* and stressed the importance of writing, as he put it, "in terms of people and how they lived." Under Catledge, the paper also stepped up its reporting on religion and other specialized subjects, began devoting more space to biographical material about people in the news, and covered politics with the general reader in mind, rather than the political specialist.

After Catledge's death in New Orleans in 1983 Arthur Ochs Sulzberger, the publisher of the *Times*, said, "Turner Catledge made a vital contribution to American journalism. His was a unique talent with an unfailing sense of mission. He never lost sight of journalism's ultimate purpose—to inform the reader, to bring him each day a letter from home and never to permit the serving of special interests. His love of his craft and his deep affection for those who practiced it well have left an enduring imprint on the *Times*. He was loved and we will miss him."

Colleagues said it was a combination of gifts—intelligence, enterprise, and courage—that made Catledge an esteemed journalist.

SUNG GAY CHOW (1947) was born in China, but his family moved to Cleveland, Mississippi, when he was less than a year old. He received a B.A. and an M.A. in English from Mississippi State University and is currently in the English doctoral program at the University of Alabama.

Of his experience in growing up in Mississippi, he says, "Because I am from the Delta, I have long held an interest in the Chinese who live in the area. However, I never felt like writing about the Chinese community until I learned that although many people knew Chinese live in California, they never realized a relatively large Chinese population lives in the Delta. My desire to inform others, coupled with a need to examine my own heritage, impelled me to begin a long-range project—a book length study of the Mississippi Chinese. Every chance I get, I return to the Delta and interview Chinese of my generation as well as the previous one."

CRAIG CLAIBORNE (1920) was born in Sunflower, Mississippi. He attended Mississippi State College and received a degree from the University of Missouri in 1942. In both World War II and the Korean War, Claiborne served in the United States Navy.

From 1946 to 1949 Claiborne worked for the American Broadcasting Company in Chicago, after which he went to Lausanne, Switzerland, to study at the École Hôteliére, the professional school of the Swiss Hotel Keepers Association. Claiborne, upon his return to the United States, became an editor for *Gourmet* magazine. In 1957 he became food editor for the *New York Times* and held that position until 1972, only to return in 1974.

He is the author of more than twenty books including *The New York Times Cook Book* (1961), *An Herb and Spice Cook Book* (1963), an autobiography, *A Feast Made for Laughter* (1982), and, most recently *The New York Times Food Encyclopedia* (1985) and *Craig Claiborne's Memorable Meals* (1985).

THOMAS D. CLARK (1903) was born in Louisville, Mississippi. He attended the Mississippi Common Schools of Winston County and Choctaw

County Agricultural High School. In 1929 he received an A.B. from the University of Mississippi and that same year an M.A. from the University of Kentucky. After receiving his Ph.D. from Duke University in 1932 Clark secured a teaching position at the University of Kentucky where he served as Chairman of the Department of History from 1942 to 1965. In 1968 Clark left Kentucky to assume the position of Distinguished Professor of History at Indiana University. He has received honorary degrees from Indiana University, the University of Kentucky, University of Louisville, Washington and Lee University, Eastern Kentucky University, and Transylvania University as well as awards such as a Guggenheim Fellowship and has traveled to many universities in the United States and abroad as a visiting lecturer and scholar.

Additionally Clark served as president of the Southern Historical Association (1947), as editor of the *Journal of Southern History* (1948–1952), and as president of the Mississippi Valley Historical Association (1957), later known as the Organization of American Historians.

In *Lives of Mississippi Authors, 1817–1967*, Michael V. Namorato writes: "While Clark's teaching and professional activities have brought him deserved recognition, it is his research and writing for which he is most known. A prolific author, Clark's interests are wide-ranging but, paradoxically, highly concentrated. He has written on a variety of topics including the history of Kentucky, the evolving South, the American frontier, state and university libraries, the growth of American railroads, rural life, the history of Indiana University, and others. But, in all of these seemingly diffuse subjects, there is a thematic unity which stands out if one knows anything about Thomas Clark, the man. Few scholars have been able to apply and use their own life experiences, whether they be political, social, or cultural, to the study of the past as Clark has done."

David L. Cohn (1897–1960) was born in Greenville, Mississippi, the son of Jewish immigrants from Poland. He received an education in keeping with his affluent background and studied law at the University of Virginia and at Yale University, where he took classes under former United States President William H. Taft. After his university training Cohn moved to New Orleans where he began a career in business. By the age of thirty-two, he was President and General Manager of Feibleman-Sears Roebuck. However, he became dissatisfied with his career, resigned his position, and moved back to Greenville to begin writing. For two years he lived in the household of William Alexander Percy where he wrote *God Shakes Creation*, which was published in 1935. This book, a study of Delta life, was reissued in 1948 under the title *Where I Was Born and Raised*. Cohn called the book "an exercise in the re-discovery of the land where I was born."

Cohn, who wrote and spoke on international issues, published more than sixty articles in the *Atlantic Monthly*, and wrote political essays and speeches for William J. Fulbright, Estes Kefauver, Averell Harriman, Sam Rayburn, Stuart Symington, and Adlai Stevenson. Cohn's books include

Picking America's Pockets: The Story of the Costs and Consequences of Our Tariff Policy (1936), *The Good Old Days: A History of American Morals and Manners as Seen Through the Sears Roebuck Catalogs 1905 to the Present* (1940), *New Orleans and Its Living Past* (1941), *Love in America: An Informal Study of Manners and Morals in American Marriage* (1943), and *This Is the Story* (1947).

DANNY COLLUM (1954) was born in Greenwood, Mississippi. Upon graduation from Greenwood High School in 1972, he spent three years at Mississippi College with a major in political science. He wrote political commentary for the campus newspaper before moving to Washington, D.C., in 1977 to write for *Sojourners* magazine. In addition to being an author, editor, and peace activist, Collum plays guitar, sings, and writes songs for a rock and roll band called The Fugitives.

"The most important thing I absorbed from growing up in Mississippi," Collum has written, "was a deep reverence for tradition combined with an equally deep impulse toward rebellion. In some quarters that's known as schizophrenia, but I think it's probably the healthiest mental state one could have in America today. I could also mention that the longer I'm away from the place the more I feel that being from the same land as Robert Johnson, Jimmie Rodgers, and Fannie Lou Hamer in some way places a heavy obligation on my life that I still don't really understand."

PAUL CONKLIN (1929) was born in Louisville, Kentucky. He holds a degree in journalism from Wayne State University and an M.A. in history from Columbia University. Conklin has traveled throughout the world on photographic assignments. His pictures have appeared in numerous magazines, as well as in textbooks and encyclopedias. In addition to *Choctaw Boy* (1975), he is the author of *Cimarron Kid* which he photographed in New Mexico, and he collaborated with writer Seymour Reit in providing photographs for two other books. *Child of the Navajos* is set on the Navajo reservation in northern Arizona and *Rice Cakes and Paper Dragons* pictures New York's Chinatown.

WYATT COOPER (1927–1978) was born and grew up on a farm in Quitman, Mississippi. He attended school there and was graduated from high school in New Orleans before studying theatre arts at the University of California, both in Berkeley and in Los Angeles. He worked as a radio announcer in Meridian, Mississippi, as an actor on stage and in television, as a screenwriter, and as an editor. In 1963 he was married to the artist Gloria Vanderbilt and lived with her and their two sons, Carter and Anderson, in New York City until the time of his death.

Families: A Memoir and a Celebration (1975) came about because of an essay Cooper wrote on the meaning of the family for the Christmas 1973 issue of *Town and Country* magazine. In the foreword to *Families* Cooper writes: "In September, 1974, as I was about to end this book, I went with my wife and sons to Quitman, Mississippi, to visit the farm where I grew up. My nine-year-old son Carter had often asked to see the place where my life began. Seven-year-old Anderson was looking forward to catching some fish from the pond on the land that had nurtured my family for generations. . . .

"I was born there in 1927 and the land, then, provided our total living. We lived on it much as my grandparents had before us, with independence and self-reliance and pride, and our wants were modest. Our transportation was still the horse and buggy, and my first lessons were at the same one-room schoolhouse that my mother had attended. . . . The town itself had grown, but in essence it remained unchanged. The Confederate soldier, high on his monument in front of the Clarke County Courthouse, still gazed down Main Street. We walked along the street, my family and I, and went into the stores, where I found the familiar friends I had known. What had not survived elsewhere survived in the warmth of their welcomes and embraces. One woman, old now, but not old when I knew her, looked at my sons and said, 'Lord, Buddy, it's like seeing you starting all over again.'"

"Wyatt was the most extraordinary father," said Gloria Vanderbilt. "From the beginning he treated our children as persons. It was something I never had growing up."

L. C. DORSEY (1938) was born in Tribbett, Mississippi. Educated in Mississippi public schools, she attended Mary Holmes College and the State University of New York at Stony Brook, from which she received a Masters in Social Work in 1973. In addition, Dorsey studied for a year at the University of Mississippi Law School and at Workers' College in Tel Aviv, Israel. She has participated in two study tours of the Peoples Republic of China and is currently working on a doctorate in social work at Howard University.

A civil rights activist, Dorsey has participated in numerous economic development activities in Mississippi and was one of fifteen people selected by President Jimmy Carter to serve on the National Advisory Council on Economic Opportunity. She was formerly the Administrative Director of the Mississippi Prisoners' Defense Committee and also the Director of Social Services of Washington County Opportunities, Inc. Dorsey also served as director, coordinator, and organizer of an agricultural cooperative serving 800 families in Bolivar County. Before going to Washington, Dorsey was the associate director of the Delta Ministry, a human rights group of the National Council of Churches. She was also state director of the Southern Coalition on Jails and Prisons, a nine state human rights organization devoted to prison reform, abolition of the death penalty, and a moratorium on prison construction.

Her publications include articles and editorials about prison life for the *Jackson Advocate*, a weekly newspaper, and for the *Southern Coalition Reports*. She is also the author of a column called "If Bars Could Talk," numerous social work articles and poetry for various periodicals, and two books, *Freedom Came to Mississippi* (1977) and *Cold Steel* (1983). Her essay "Harder Times Than These" was first published in *Southern Exposure*. Her unpublished work includes a study of an alternative economic system for displaced sharecroppers, the effect of chemicals used in agriculture, and a report of her China visit called "Serving the People."

"I would encourage students," Dorsey writes, "to look first for the rainbow's pot of gold at home. The experiences I have had in Mississippi, while viewed by some as harsh and oppressive, have been like the blacksmith's fire on steel. I'm stronger for the experiences. Without romanticizing the plantation, I learned how to survive there, and the knowledge gained there prepared me to understand the Washington, D.C. plantation and the United States-Russian plantations in the world community. Students should prepare themselves to make Mississippi a better community and not rush to escape its customs, tradition, racism, and poverty. For all of these things exist everywhere; only not always are they as obvious, or honest, as is our state."

ELLEN DOUGLAS (1921) is the pen name of Josephine Ayres Haxton. Born in Natchez, Mississippi, she was graduated from the University of Mississippi in 1942. In her acceptance speech as the first recipient of the Mississippi Institute of Arts and Letters Literature Award in 1979, Douglas noted that "it came to me that the trees, the landscape—water and forest, fields, and pastures, river and Delta and the dissolving hills—are a gift, the gift of my state, not just to me, but to us all; the place that informs all my books, the place that we—all of us—hold in precarious trust and must jointly cherish and guard, threatened now more than ever before by a rootless and destructive world."

As a writer concerned with the human condition, Douglas has used the gift from her state well. She has repaid her debt admirably with *A Family's Affairs* (1962, winner of the Houghton Mifflin-Esquire Fellowship Award and named by the *New York Times* critic Orville Prescott as one of the five best novels of the year), *Black Cloud, White Cloud* (1963, her story, "On the Lake," which became a part of that book's novella, "Hold On," was first published in the *New Yorker* and won an O. Henry Prize Award), *Where the Dreams Cross* (1968), *Apostles of Light* (1973, nominated for the National Book Award), *The Rock Cried Out* (1979, a Book-of-the-Month Alternate Selection and the winner of the Mississippi Institute of Arts and Letters Literature Award), and *A Lifetime Burning* (1982, awarded the Mississippi Institute of Arts and Letters Literature Award).

Douglas has anchored her fiction in time and place. This firm rooting provides great strength against the universal stresses of human existence. "Place is the repository of history," Douglas says, "Place is the means by which you enter a story. I need the familiarity of my own surroundings to hear the voice."

In addition to her fiction, Douglas has written a short study of Walker Percy's novel, *The Last Gentleman*. She received a grant from the National Endowment for the Arts for work on *The Rock Cried Out* and is currently at work on a new novel with the help of a second NEA grant. She has participated in a number of literary festivals and writing workshops. She has been writer-in-residence at Northeast Louisiana University, the University of Virginia, and now teaches at the University of Mississippi.

CHARLES EAST (1924) was born in Shelby, Mississippi, and grew up in Cleveland, Mississippi, where his family moved when he was twelve. He received a B.A. from Louisiana State University in 1948. That same year he went to New York City to work for *Collier's* magazine and then to Baton Rouge where he worked for the *Morning Advocate* and the *State-Times*. In 1962 he joined the staff of Louisiana State University Press and from 1970–75 served as director. East has published in numerous literary magazines, including the *Virginia Quarterly Review*, the *Southern Review*, and the *Yale Review*. His collection of short stories, *Where the Music Was*, was published in 1965. He now works as a free-lance writer and editor.

In a 1971 interview with Gordon Weaver, East stated, "I was born in Mississippi and grew up there, and my material has come largely out of that experience. . . . It [Mississippi] is the place I unconsciously or subconsciously turn to when I sit down to write. . . . I grew up in a small town. I don't think that I would have written the same sort of thing, possibly may not have written at all, if I had grown up in a larger place. . . . I feel that coming out of this kind of world was important to me as a writer."

LEHMAN ENGEL (1910–1982), composer, conductor, teacher, and writer, was born in Jackson, Mississippi. He was educated in the public schools of Jackson, where he was graduated from Central High School at the age of sixteen. He attended the Cincinnati Conservatory of Music for two years and studied with Arthur Goldmark at the Julliard Graduate School before becoming a private pupil with Roger Sessions.

Three times a Tony winner, Engel conducted over a hundred and fifty musicals, including *Li'l Abner*, *Wonderful Town*, and *Call Me Mister*. He was requested on numerous occasions to conduct his own compositions, which include incidental music for plays such as *Hamlet*, *Macbeth*, and *Murder in the Cathedral* as well as operas, symphonies, and the music for seven ballets by Martha Graham. He recorded extensively for RCA-Victor, Columbia, Decca, Brunswick, and Atlantic. He also conducted over fifty recordings of musical shows and served as guest conductor of the Boston Symphony Orchestra and of the St. Louis Municipal Opera.

In April 1968 he combined talents with his lifelong friend Eudora Welty for a ballet based on her book *The Shoe Bird*. His composition to her story was performed at a world premiere dedication of the Municipal Auditorium in their hometown.

In his varied career of more than fifty years, Engel worked with Aaron Copland, Leonard Bernstein, John Gielgud, Lillian Gish, Rosalind Russell, Mary Martin, Robert Merrill, Bing Crosby, Jeanette McDonald, Nelson Eddy, Liza Minnelli, Barbara Streisand, Tennessee Williams,

Pearl Bailey, Ed Sullivan, George Cukor, Ernest Hemingway, Elliott Gould, Tommy Tune, and many more.

As a writer Engel addressed his profession in such books as *Planning and Producing the Musical Show* (1957), *The American Musical Theatre: A Consideration* (1967), *Words with Music* (1971), *Getting Started in the Theatre* (1973), *Their Words Are Music* (1975), *The Critics* (1976), and *The Making of the Musical* (1977). His 1974 autobiography, *This Bright Day,* is a record of his development in the musical profession.

CHARLES EVERS (1922) was born on his parents' farm near Decatur, Mississippi, and lived there until he finished high school. He joined the army in 1940 and served in Australia, New Guinea, and the Philippines. Honorably discharged in 1946, he enrolled at Alcorn A&M College where he majored in social science. He also engaged in various business ventures, among them providing a taxi service for the Alcorn community and, with the assistance of his brother, Medgar, selling peanuts and sandwiches to students who lived in the campus dormitories. After earning his degree in 1951, Evers moved to Philadelphia, Mississippi. He taught history and coached football at Noxapater High School, worked in his uncle's funeral home, sold insurance, operated a taxi business, opened a hotel and a cafe, and worked in voter registration campaigns throughout Mississippi. He also became the first black disc jockey in the state.

"I was on station WOKJ and had a very good listening response," Evers later wrote. "I would always say, 'Pay your poll tax. Register and vote.' I'd say this when I came on the air and when I'd go off the air. And I'd tell them, 'If you can't register to vote, pay your poll tax anyway.' The white racists and bigots didn't like that, so I was a problem."

At that time, however, white racists were still very much in control of life in Philadelphia, Mississippi. Charles Evers was fired from his teaching job and after a series of economic reprisals lost his businesses, home, and furniture. By 1956 he was so broke that he was forced to use money collected from friends to help him and his family leave town before his opponents could carry out their threats to have him killed. His wife and four daughters went to stay with her mother, and he set off for Chicago. There he worked at a packing house, was a washroom attendant at the Palmer House, and took other odd jobs until he obtained a teaching position with the Cook County school system and was able to send for his family. Eventually he made a great deal of money by gambling, bootlegging, and operating taverns and other businesses.

In 1963 Evers returned to Mississippi and took the place of his slain brother, Medgar, as field secretary of the NAACP. During the next few years he urged blacks to register to vote, organized and led demonstrations and boycotts, helped desegregate public accommodations, and worked to help blacks obtain jobs and win elections. Evers resigned as field secretary in 1969 when he ran for office in Fayette and became the first black mayor of a biracial southern town since Reconstruction. The year before, he had failed in his bid for a seat in the United States Congress.

About him the authors of *Mississippi Black History Makers* have written: "Charles Evers was a catalyst for change. He remained on the battlefront, chiding the establishment for additional political positions for blacks on the city, state, and federal levels. Because he was crafty and frugal, he accumulated wealth and represented the increasing number of black capitalists in Mississippi. . . . Many of the changes Evers sought did not conform to the will of the black community. In the 1980 presidential election Charles Evers supported Ronald Reagan and Reaganomics. The black voters demonstrated their disapproval in the 1981 mayoral election when they selected Kenneth Middleton mayor of Fayette, thereby ending Charles Evers's twelve year reign." In the 1983 gubernatorial election, he lost in his bid as an independent candidate against the Democratic nominee, Bill Allain. But, "in spite of the adversities and disappointments, Charles Evers has carved his place in Mississippi and American history."

MEDGAR EVERS (1925–1963) was born near Decatur, Mississippi, and attended school there until he was inducted into the army in 1943. After serving in Normandy, he entered Alcorn College where he majored in business administration and became a campus leader. In addition to being a member of the debate team, the college choir, and the football and track teams, he held several student offices and was editor of the campus newspaper for two years and the annual for one year. For his accomplishments at Alcorn he was listed in *Who's Who in American Colleges*.

After marrying Myrlie Beasley of Vicksburg and receiving his B.A. degree, Evers moved to Mound Bayou, Mississippi. He worked as an insurance agent and spent a great deal of time establishing local chapters of the NAACP throughout the Delta and organizing boycotts of gasoline stations that refused to allow blacks to use their restrooms. After the 1954 Supreme Court decision declaring school segregation unconstitutional, Evers applied for admission to the University of Mississippi Law School. He was denied admission, but his attempt to integrate the state's oldest public university attracted the attention of the national office of the NAACP and led to his appointment as that organization's first field secretary in Mississippi.

Moving to Jackson, Evers and his wife, whom he hired as his secretary, worked together to set up the NAACP office. He then began investigating violent crimes committed against blacks and sought ways to prevent them. About this work Myrlie Evers wrote in *For Us, the Living:* "He placed himself between the wounded, the beaten, the frightened, the threatened, the assaulted, and the white racist society that invariably had everything its own way. He investigated, filed complaints, issued angry denunciations, literally dragged reporters to the scenes of crimes, fought back with press releases, seeking always to spread the word beyond the state, involve the federal government, bring help from the outside." His boycott of Jackson merchants in the early sixties did attract national attention, and his efforts to have James Meredith admitted to the University of Mississippi in 1962 brought the federal help he had sought, but these activities also increased the hatred many people had for this civil rights advocate who constantly urged that "violence is not the way" and that "returning physical harm for physical harm will not solve the problem."

On June 12, 1963, as he was returning home, Medgar Evers was killed by an assassin's bullet. Black and white leaders from around the nation came to Jackson for his funeral and then gathered at Arlington National Cemetery for his interment. Many tributes have been paid to Medgar Evers over the years, but perhaps the greatest tribute to this man can be found in changes noted in *Mississippi Black History Makers:* "Ten years after Medgar's death the national office of the NAACP reported that Mississippi had 145 black elected officials and that blacks were enrolled in each of the state's public and private institutions of higher learning. . . . In 1970, according to statistics compiled by the Department of Health, Education, and Welfare, more than one-fourth or 26.4 percent of black pupils in Mississippi public schools attended integrated schools with at least a 50 percent white enrollment. When Medgar died in 1963, only 28,000 blacks were registered voters. By 1971, there were 250,000 and by 1982 over 500,000."

MYRLIE EVERS (1933), widow of civil rights leader Medgar Evers, was born in Vicksburg, Mississippi, where she was raised by her paternal grandmother and an aunt, both teachers. A good student and an accomplished musician, she planned to major in music in college. "Encouraged by two of my four piano teachers, spurred by years of applause at recitals, and driven by a deep love of music, it was a goal toward which my whole life had long been pointed," she wrote. Since Mississippi's white colleges would not admit the young black woman and neither of the state's black colleges—Alcorn and Jackson State—offered a major in music, she requested aid to study music at Fisk University in Nashville, Tennessee. When Mississippi officials denied her request, she was outraged but helpless. "School segregation was simply a fact of life," she stated. "I had never heard it seriously challenged by anyone. And as I slowly recovered from my rage, I swallowed my disappointment and chose, reluctantly, to go to Alcorn, where I would major in education and minor in music."

On her first day at college Myrlie met Medgar Evers, a twenty-four-year-old veteran who was a serious student, a campus leader, and a star athlete. The next year, on December 24, 1951, the couple married and returned to Alcorn for a semester during which she completed her sophomore year and he completed a bachelor's degree. Then they moved to Mound Bayou, Mississippi, where Medgar Evers worked as an insurance agent until 1954 when he accepted an appointment as Mississippi's first field secretary for the National Association for the Advancement of Colored People. During the next few years Myrlie supported her husband in his civil rights activities, even though she knew that those activities made life dangerous for them and their three children. How very dangerous became apparent on June 12, 1963, when Medgar Evers was assassinated outside their home in Jackson.

To protect herself and her children, Myrlie Evers moved to Claremont, California, where she wrote *For Us, the Living* (1967) and earned a B.A. degree at Pomona College. *For Us, the Living* gives an extraordinary portrait of the lives of Myrlie and Medgar Evers, their families, the society in which they lived, and the heroic efforts of civil rights workers during the 1960s. For her contributions to the civil rights movement and for her achievements as a writer, Myrlie Evers has received numerous awards, among them the Freedom House Award (1963), the Literary Award of Sigma Gamma Rho (1968), and the Humanitarian Award from the National Council of Christians and Jews (1969).

JOHN FAULKNER (1901–1963) was born in Ripley, Mississippi, but spent most of his life in Oxford, where he was educated in the public schools and at the University of Mississippi. He worked for the Mississippi Highway Department, the Memphis Flying Corps, and as manager of his brother William's farm.

Although he changed the spelling of his birth name by adding a "u" as had William, the styles of writing of the two men were very different. As E. O. Hawkins writes in *Lives of Mississippi Authors, 1817–1967:* "If John Faulkner resembles any other author, it is Erskine Caldwell, whose poverty-ridden Georgia crackers prefigure the hapless Taylors of *Men Working* and the incredible simpletons of *Cabin Road*. The prose of both men is simplistic to a fault; 'plain style' it is called, and both men are masters of the social levels of dialect which the native ear discerns. Finally, the two use comparable settings, remote areas almost untraveled by modernity and villages their residents occasionally journey to for supplies or entertainment."

Faulkner's first book, *Men Working* (1941), is a satirical comedy that exposes the bureaucracy of the "WP and A." *Dollar Cotton* (1942), his most respected book, chronicles the life of a Delta planter and the collapse of the cotton market in 1921. *Chooky*, published in 1950 after Faulkner had returned from the Navy in World War II, consists of entertaining sketches of an eleven-year-old boy who lives on a farm. His next book, *Cabin Road* (1951), is considered a fine example of what is called southwestern humor. In the 1969 reprint from Louisiana State University Press, Redding S. Sugg, Jr. writes "that in *Cabin Road* he hit upon the one [approach] which best suited him and which led to humorous fiction of a high order." Unlike his previous books, which were sold in hardback, *Cabin Road* was published as a twenty-five-cent paperback original with a sexy girl and a ramshackle cabin on the front. It established Faulkner as what is today called a "popular writer" and, according to his publisher, "over a million copies of the book were sold, chiefly it would seem from newsstands in drug stores, terminals, and other places of popular resort." Characters from *Cabin Road* continued to appear in Faulkner's next four books—*Uncle Good's Girls* (1952), *The Sin Shouter of Cabin Road* (1955),

Ain't Gonna Rain No More (1959), and *Uncle Good's Week-End Party* (1960). John Faulkner died shortly after completing *My Brother Bill*, which he subtitled "An Affectionate Reminiscence."

WILLIAM FAULKNER (1897–1962) was born in New Albany, Mississippi. When he was five years old his family moved to Oxford, where he lived most of his life except for brief periods spent in Hollywood and Charlottesville, Virginia. Faulkner's education was sporadic. Dropping out of high school in his senior year, he attended the University of Mississippi as a special student for only one year (1919–20). He was a voracious reader and, through his friend and earliest critic, Phil Stone, was introduced to modern writers, including the French Symbolist poets. Their influence, along with the influence of Hardy and Yeats, can be seen in Faulkner's first book, *The Marble Faun*.

Influenced by Sherwood Anderson, Faulkner wrote his first novel, *Soldiers' Pay*, which appeared in 1926. Its publication began an extraordinarily prolific career. The next decade produced eight novels, including many of the finest he would write: *The Sound and the Fury* (1929), *As I Lay Dying* (1930), *Light in August* (1932), and *Absalom, Absalom!* (1936). However, his creative output was not matched by financial returns, so, in 1932, Faulkner went to Hollywood as a screen writer, a position he kept, under financial duress, until 1948, when the commercial success of *Intruder in the Dust* and its subsequent sale to the movies enabled him to return to Mississippi. With the exception of tours for the State Department and time spent as a writer-in-residence at the University of Virginia, he remained in Oxford the rest of his life. Faulkner won numerous awards for his fiction, including the 1949 Nobel Prize and two Pulitzer Prizes, one for *A Fable* (1954) and another for *The Reivers* (1962). He is considered by many critics to be the finest writer America has produced and one of the finest writers in the English language.

Robert Penn Warren has said, "The study of Faulkner's writing is one of the most challenging tasks in our literature. It is also one of the most rewarding." Faulkner, who admitted that he had learned to write "from other writers," advised hopeful poets and novelists to "read all you can."

WILLIAM FERRIS (1942) was born and raised on a farm near Vicksburg, Mississippi. After attending a rural elementary school near his father's farm and going to junior high in Vicksburg, he completed high school at Brooks in Andover, Massachusetts, and received a B.A. in English from Davidson College, an M.A. in English from Northwestern University, and M.A. and Ph.D. degrees in folklore from the University of Pennsylvania. While teaching at Jackson State University from 1970 to 1972 and at Yale University from 1972 to 1978, he spent summer vacations working in Memphis, Tennessee, at the Center for Southern Folklore, a nonprofit media center he helped found. In 1979 he returned to his native state to be the first director of the Center for the Study of Southern Culture at the University of Mississippi.

As an undergraduate student Ferris began recording and photographing blues musicians and church services near his home in Vicksburg, and he studied Mississippi traditions and made films about them as part of his graduate work at the University of Pennsylvania. Since then he has produced many publications and films about southern life. He is the author of *Blues from the Delta* (1978; reprinted 1984), *Images of the South: Visits with Eudora Welty and Walker Evans* (1978), *Local Color: A Sense of Place in Folk Art* (1982), and numerous articles. In addition, he is editor of *Afro-American Folk Art and Crafts* (1983) and co-editor of *Folk Music and Modern Sound* (1982) and the *Encyclopedia of Southern Culture* (forthcoming). Among the films Ferris has produced are *Gravel Springs Fife and Drum, Ray Lum: Mule Trader, Fanny Bell Chapman: Gospel Singer, Give My Poor Heart Ease: Mississippi Delta Bluesmen, Two Black Churches, Four Women Artists*, and *Painting in the South: Artists and Regional Heritage*.

SHELBY FOOTE (1916) was born in Greenville, Mississippi, where he was educated in the public schools. He attended the University of North Carolina from 1935 to 1937 and served in Europe as a captain of field artillery during World War II. According to Foote, his parents were not literary. He writes, "My principal connection with a literary home was through my friendship with the Percys (William Alexander Percy, author of *Lanterns on the Levee,* and his three nephews, among them Walker Percy). There were literally thousands of books in the Percy house. It's probable that if those Percy boys hadn't moved to Greenville, I might never have become interested in literary things.

"I wrote five novels in five years in Greenville," Foote said, "I wrote all of them on Washington Avenue. But, that was the beginning of my writing life and sort of the first chapter of it." Twenty years elapsed after his first five novels, but in 1974 publication of his massive three-volume history, *The Civil War: A Narrative,* was completed. According to Polk and Scafidel (*An Anthology of Mississippi Writers,* 1979, University Press of Mississippi), Foote "brought to the writing of his heavily researched history not just the historian's reservoir of facts and dates but also the novelist's eye for meaningful detail and the capacity for understanding and depicting character. In addition, his history reflects the novelist's natural way with story-telling and a superb, clear, prose style." It was a unique achievement and won him a nomination for the Pulitzer Prize.

His first five novels were *Tournament* (1949), *Follow Me Down* (1950), *Love in a Dry Season* (1951), *Shiloh* (1952), and *Jordan County* (1954). Foote's sixth novel, *September, September,* was published in 1977. He now lives in Memphis, Tennessee, and is working on his seventh novel.

RICHARD FORD (1944) was born in Jackson, Mississippi, and lived in the state until his graduation from high school. He received a B.A. from Michigan State University and an M.F.A. from the University of California. Recently Ford bought a house near Coahoma, Mississippi, where he lives with his wife, Kristina.

Ford has published widely in periodicals such as *Esquire, Harpers,* and

Paris Review. His essay "The Three Kings: Hemingway, Faulkner, and Fitzgerald" appeared in the 50th Anniversary Edition (December 1983) of *Esquire*. *A Piece of My Heart* (1976), Ford's first novel, was published to critical acclaim. *Newsweek* noted "the beginning of a career that could turn out to be extraordinary." For his second novel, *The Ultimate Good Luck* (1981), Ford won fellowships from the Guggenheim Foundation and from the National Endowment for the Arts. His third novel, *The Sportswriter*, was published in 1986.

JAMES FORMAN (1928) was born in Chicago, but grew up with his maternal grandmother in Marshall County, Mississippi, seven miles from Moscow, Tennessee. "These are my recollections of the farm of my grandmother, where I was raised," Forman writes. "We lived in a rural section of Mississippi, in Marshall County, one mile from the Tennessee line. There were no white people and the only white man we saw was the mailman when he stopped at our house or drove past, delivering the mail. . . .

"My grandmother and two cousins had bought a plot of land which they divided into three farms. She had moved onto her farm from Benton County; it was 180 acres, but poor and hilly land, unlike the rich Mississippi Delta. Shortly after arriving there, my grandfather died. Left alone to raise nine children and pay off the debt from the farm, my grandmother survived by plowing the land and planting cotton, growing corn for the stock, and raising some crops for her own food. She was a subsistence farmer, using the only modern method of farming that she had—the plow and the mule. From the few bales of cotton that she would sell and the food she grew, she barely managed to keep her family alive.

"This poverty had driven my mother and the rest of the sons and daughters away from the farm and into the industrial cities. My mother went to Chicago. There she met my father and I was born on October 4, 1928, in Chicago. When I was eleven months old, my mother sent me back to live with my grandmother while she tried to eke out a living in the ghetto.

"I grew up in my grandmother's large, four-room house. It had no electricity, and was heated by two fireplaces and the wood stove in the kitchen. . . . Adjacent to my room stood the dining room, which did not have a fireplace and was unusable in the wintertime. Next to it was the kitchen. On the back porch stood the stand for the water which we carried in from a well; and it was also there that we used to churn. We never had a refrigerator and only later did we buy ice from town; that was to make ice cream for a Saturday treat. Our life on the farm was literally dirt poor; I can remember eating dirt on the side of the road. It was supposed to be good for you; some said it contained vitamins. Whether it did or not, dirt was a staple for us and we were hungry all the time, all the time."

Forman received a B.A. from Roosevelt University, an M.A. in African and Afro-American studies from Cornell University, and a Ph.D. from the Union of Experimenting Colleges and Universities in cooperation with the Institute for Policy Studies.

A political thinker, historian, and civil rights leader, Forman was executive secretary of the Student Nonviolent Coordinating Committee (SNCC) and proposed the Black Manifesto, which calls for reparation from the churches to black people of the United States. In addition to writing and speaking publicly on political issues, Forman is chairperson of the Unemployed and Poverty Action Council (UPAC) and holds an elected position in local politics in Washington.

The Making of Black Revolutionaries (1972) is Forman's autobiography and personal account of the civil rights movement. Stanford University historian and author of *In Struggle: SNCC and the Black Awakening of the 1960s*, Clayborne Carson, writes, "*The Making of Black Revolutionaries* was the most ambitious, politically astute, and emotionally engrossing memoir to emerge from the 1960s. Anyone interested in understanding the present state of black politics should read this outstanding example of engaged historical analysis."

Other books by Forman include *Liberation Viendra d'une Chose Noir* (1968), *Sammy Younge, Junior* (1968), *The Political Thought of James Forman* (1970), and *Self-Determination: An Examination of the Question and Its Application to the African-American People* (1984).

ELLEN GILCHRIST (1935) was born in Vicksburg, Mississippi. She received a B.A. in philosophy from Millsaps College and did graduate work at the University of Arkansas in creative writing. She has served as contributing editor of the *Courier* in New Orleans and was the recipient in 1979 of a Fellowship Grant in Fiction from the National Endowment for the Arts. Also in 1979 her book of poems, *The Land Surveyor's Daughter*, was published by Lost Roads Press.

Her first collection of short fiction, *In the Land of Dreamy Dreams*, received the 1981 Mississippi Institute of Arts and Letters Literature Award. Her first novel, *The Annunciation* (1983), and her second short story collection, *Victory Over Japan*, (1984) were published by Little, Brown and Company. *Victory Over Japan* won the 1984 American Book Award for Best Fiction and the 1984 Mississippi Institute of Arts and Letters Literature Award. She lives in Jackson, Mississippi, where she is a commentator for National Public Radio's "Morning Edition" and is completing a third collection of short stories.

Of the process of writing, Gilchrist says, "I no longer believe that I understand the creative process except for two or three things. I believe that it is some form of trusting yourself to know the truth and to be able to tell the truth past all the things which pass for facts. Truth is a beautiful and complex and very funny song. When I am lucky and trust myself I am able to sing it long enough to make a poem.

"The other thing that I believe is that a writer must be terribly healthy and very patient. It is hard work to be a writer. You have to make up the job as you go along. You have to keep on trying and believing in yourself when nothing seems to be happening and when what you are doing seems to be the most absurd activity in the world. But it is exciting work."

LOYLE HAIRSTON (1926) was born in Macon, Mississippi, and lived there for fourteen years, at which time his family moved to St. Louis. After graduation from high school, he enlisted in the United States Navy and served two years. Upon discharge, he moved to New York City and studied creative writing at New York University. He was one of the founders of the Harlem Writers Guild, a workshop that has been a major influence on the development of contemporary black writing. His first published short story was "The Winds of Change." Since then he has been widely published and is a frequent contributor to *Freedomways*. He still lives in New York City.

"I wanted to be a writer," Hairston writes, "an irrational idea that came to me after I became a voracious reader of black newsweeklies, *The Chicago Defender* and *The Pittsburgh Courier*. But it was really Jack London's autobiographical novel, *Martin Eden*, that sealed my doom. After that book the idea of being a writer grew to an obsession. St. Louis became stifling—too many people tried to make me come to my senses. Moreover, I didn't know a single writer or anyone vaguely interested in literature. Obviously, I needed 'breathing' room.

"In New York I enrolled in school as a GI Bill student, eventually studying for a while at New York University. But more importantly, I joined a writers' workshop and began my apprenticeship among such people as Alice Childress, Eugene Gordon, Julian Mayfield, John Henrik Clarke, John Hudson Jones, John O. Killens, Rosa Guy, Willard Moore, Paule Marshall, Lonnie Elder III. A few years later some of us broke away and founded a new writers group, the Harlem Writers Guild."

FANNIE LOU HAMER (1917–1977), civil rights activist, was the youngest of twenty children born in Montgomery County to a sharecropper family. When she was two years old her family moved to Sunflower County where she began to pick cotton at the age of six. Because of seasonal field work her school term lasted only four or five months a year, and at age twelve she attended school for the last time.

In 1962 while Hamer was working as a plantation timekeeper, she joined a voter registration group led by James Bevel of the Southern Christian Leadership Conference (SCLC) and James Forman from the Student Nonviolent Coordinating Committee (SNCC). In order to register, Hamer and the others were required to take the literacy test—to read, copy, and interpret an arcane section of the Mississippi Constitution to the satisfaction of the county examiner. It took her four months to gain the right to vote, and by then she had lost her job and had been evicted from her home. Because of this Hamer became an active SNCC worker, mostly registering voters and conducting literacy training. Under constant attack and harassment, she received the greatest threat to her life in June 1963. As Hamer explains it in John Egerton's *A Mind to Stay Here*, she and a group of SNCC and SCLC activists were returning by bus from a voter education workshop in Charleston, South Carolina. They stopped in

Winona, Mississippi. "Some members of the group got off the bus to go into the cafe and to the restroom. The local chief of police and a state highway patrolman, who were sitting in the cafe, told them to get out. They did, but one of the SCLC workers stopped outside to write down the license number of the patrol car; the two officers arrested them. Altogether, Hamer and five others—all but one of them women—were taken to the county jail." They were held for three days and brutally beaten. When James Bevel and Andrew Young of SCLC finally managed to get them out of jail, they had received no medical attention. Hamer suffered kidney damage and developed a blood clot in her left eye that permanently impaired her vision. Recalling that horror, Hamer said: "I just wonder how many more times is America gonna turn its head and pretend nothin' is happenin'. I used to think the Justice Department was just what it said—justice. I asked one of those men, 'Have y'all got a Justice Department or a *In*justice Department?' That's the way I feel now. They didn't investigate what *happened* to us—they investigated *us*. So I tell people I don't want no *equal* rights any more. I'm fightin' for *human* rights. I don't want to become equal to men like them that beats us. I don't want to become the kind of person that would kill you because of your color."

In 1964 Hamer spoke on national television for the Mississippi Freedom Democratic Party at the Democratic Convention held in Atlantic City. There the Freedom Democrats unsuccessfully challenged the seating of the all-white Mississippi delegation but won a ruling ending exclusive delegations in the future.

In addition to leading the way for voter registration in Sunflower County, Hamer helped to get the Head Start program into Mississippi and raised money for the construction of two hundred units of low-income housing in Ruleville, Mississippi. She organized the Freedom Farm Cooperative, a vegetable-and-livestock enterprise designed to raise the income of Sunflower County residents and to obtain land for workers who were left unemployed by farm mechanization. It eventually grew into six hundred and eighty acres. Hamer was invited to speak all over America and became one of the nation's most admired and beloved civil rights activists. On her headstone are marked the words which were her motto and rallying cry: "I am sick and tired of being sick and tired."

BARRY HANNAH (1942) was born in Meridian, Mississippi. His early home was near Forest, Mississippi, in Scott County. When he was young his family moved to Pascagoula and then to Clinton, where he grew up. Hannah received a B.A. from Mississippi College and an M.F.A. from the University of Arkansas. He has been writer-in-residence at Clemson University, Middlebury College, the University of Alabama, the University of Iowa, the University of Montana, Memphis State University, and currently the University of Mississippi.

His first novel, *Geronimo Rex* (1972), won a William Faulkner Prize. A second novel, *Nightwatchmen* (1973), was followed by *Airships* (1978), a collection of short stories, which won the Arnold Gingrich Short Fiction Award. Of the collection James Dickey wrote, "One reads Barry Hannah and is amazed! *Airships* places him in the very first rank of American literary artists, and leaves us breathless with the force of its feeling." Hannah's recent novels, *Ray* (1980) and *The Tennis Handsome* (1983), have achieved international acclaim. His fifth novel, *Captain Maximus,* was published in 1985. He has been honored by the American Academy of Arts and Letters and has received, among his many honors, a Guggenheim Fellowship.

Hannah lives in Oxford, Mississippi. To students interested in creative writing, he says, "Write more, talk less. Pretty soon you may have an *opus major.*"

PHYLLIS HARPER (1933) was born near Mooreville, Mississippi, and grew up on her grandfather's farm in the isolated rural community of Fawn Grove in Itawamba County. She attended three-room Fawn Grove School, Mooreville High School, Itawamba Junior College, and the University of Mississippi.

Harper left Mississippi in 1954 and lived in several other states before returning to her native hill country to rear her five children. She has worked for the *Northeast Mississippi Daily Journal* since 1969, first as a proofreader, then a news reporter, and later as copy editor and desk editor. Since 1977 she has been the *Journal*'s feature editor and also writes a column called "Seems to Me" three times a week.

KENNETH HOLDITCH (1933) was born in Ecru, Mississippi. He received a B.A. from Southwestern College at Memphis and an M.A. and the first Ph.D. in English from the University of Mississippi. Holditch is a professor of English at the University of New Orleans. He conducts literary tours of New Orleans; his book *In Old New Orleans* was published by the University Press of Mississippi in 1983. He has published numerous essays, poems, and short stories.

Holditch says of his Mississippi heritage: "I would simply say that most of the inspiration I have received to write fiction or poetry has come from my background, and that background is, of course, inextricably linked with Mississippi. It has been said so often that one does not need to say again that more writers have come from our state than from any other—more good writers. There is a reason for that. I don't know what that reason is. Part of it certainly involves the agrarian atmosphere which was so much a part of the state when I was growing up. I think of what Berry Morgan once said to me in describing the state from which both of us came and from which both of us have drawn great strength: Mississippi is 'a schizophrenic piece of heaven.' That says it better than I could say it in any other words."

M. CARL HOLMAN (1919) was born in Minter City, Mississippi. He holds an A.B. degree from Lincoln University, an M.A. from the University of

Chicago, and an M.B.A. from Yale University. A former English professor at Clark College in Atlanta, he has edited a weekly newspaper, the *Atlanta Inquirer.*

Holman has served as Information Officer of the United States Commission on Civil Rights and is currently president of the National Urban Coalition in Washington, D.C.

Holman's prose and poetry have appeared in such periodicals as *Verse* and *Phylon,* and in such collections as *Poetry of the Negro,* edited by Langston Hughes and Arna Bontemps, and *Soon, One Morning: New Writing by American Negroes.* Holman received, as a University of Chicago graduate student, the John Billings Fiske Poetry Prize and has been the recipient of a Rosenwald Fellowship.

LAURENCE C. JONES (1882–1975) was born in St. Joseph, Missouri. His father was a porter, and his mother a seamstress. Both parents emphasized the importance of education, and Jones's childhood was filled with books. As an adolescent, he left St. Joseph to live with relatives in Marshalltown, Iowa, where he was the first black to graduate from Marshalltown High School. He went on to the University of Iowa, where he received a bachelor of philosophy degree in 1907. As one of the few blacks of his time to have completed a formal education, he enjoyed several lucrative job offers, all of which he declined in order to take a position at the Utica Institute, now Utica Junior College, in Hinds County, Mississippi. In later life, Jones outlined his reasoning:

During my sophomore year, I heard our President, Dr. George E. MacLean, use the phrase, *noblesse oblige,* and one day in the botany class Professor Thomas H. MacBride explained to me its meaning. More than ever I realized that because of the superior advantages for schooling that had been mine, I was morally obligated to pass the opportunity on to those less fortunate than myself. I believe I had always had a subconscious desire to engage in the poultry business. One of my fondest dreams was to realize enough money from this business some day to cross the ocean and see the countries of the Old World. *Noblesse oblige,* however, taught me that my duty was down in the black belt among the less fortunate of my people.

During the Christmas of 1908 Jones visited Braxton, Mississippi, with a student. Seeing the poverty and ignorance of the black community there, Jones determined to establish a practical school in that area. In the summer of 1909 he arrived in Braxton with a Bible, several clean shirts, copies of agricultural manuals, his diploma from the University of Iowa, and $1.65. He spent the summer traveling over Rankin and Simpson Counties talking to both blacks and whites about the need for the establishment of a practical school. He met with little success.

While resting beneath a cedar tree one day, reading, Jones was approached by a black child who wanted to learn to read. When Jones agreed to teach him, the boy returned the next day with two friends. This was the beginning of the Piney Woods School. As the number of students increased, and as winter approached, Jones realized the need of a building. A northern educated former slave donated an abandoned cabin that had been serving as a sheep shed, forty acres, and fifty dollars. The deed was made to the trustees of the Piney Woods School. Lumber for additional buildings was donated by the white owner of a sawmill, and the labor for constructing the buildings was provided by black community members. By the end of the year, Jones had eighty-five students.

The school grew rapidly, and on May 17, 1913, a charter was formally granted to the Piney Woods Country Life School. Money was always scarce, but Jones adamantly refused to turn away any students because they lacked tuition. Donations from the community provided stop-gap relief. Larger donations were provided by fund-raising trips north that Jones made every summer. By 1925 Jones had to raise $30,000 to operate the school. Brick buildings were built, the curriculum was enlarged, and the Piney Woods School became a symbol of Jones's personal determination and vision. In 1954 Ralph Edwards honored Dr. Jones on the television program "This Is Your Life." As a result, $700,000 in donations were received for the Piney Woods School, and in April 1953 the Dr. Laurence C. Jones Foundation was established. When Dr. Jones died in 1975, the school had 2,000 acres of land and an endowment of over five million dollars.

Jones authored several books, among them *Piney Woods and Its Story* (1922), *The Spirit of Piney Woods* (1931) and *The Bottom Rail: Addresses and Papers on the Negro in the Lowlands of Mississippi and on Interracial Relations in the South during Twenty-five Years* (1935). In addition, he contributed numerous articles to *Pine Torch,* the monthly newspaper he founded in 1911, and which is still being published today.

Laurence C. Jones is considered one of the most important pioneers in black education in the state of Mississippi. In one of the poorest regions of the state, and against overwhelming financial and social obstacles, he founded, nurtured, and directed the Piney Woods School. He is buried there, a few feet from the cedar tree where he taught his first student.

BELLE KEARNEY (1863–1939) was born two months and five days after the Emancipation Proclamation, at her family home, Vernon Heights, in southwest Madison County, Mississippi.

Nancy Tipton Hutchinson writes in *Lives of Mississippi Authors, 1817–1967:* "After several years spent teaching in rural schools to supplement family income, Belle Kearney followed a call from Woman's Christian Temperance Union leader Frances Willard to become a traveling organizer for the group. Flaunting traditions of the day that anchored Southern women firmly in home careers, she began a fifty-year worldwide lecture circuit, advocating temperance, women's rights and, finally, her own candidacy for the United States Senate and the upper house of the state legislature."

In 1902 Kearney became the first women to address a joint session of the Mississippi legislature. In the years that followed she continued to speak out across the country for suffrage and temperance.

In 1921 Kearney ran unsuccessfully for the United States Senate post being vacated by the retirement of John Sharp Williams. Although she was soundly defeated by former governor and Senator James K. Vardaman, called the "White Chief," who had helped the Rednecks rise to power over the planter aristocracy, the *Daily Democrat-Times* said Kearney had shown that "the women in politics are as true as steel" by running a "campaign for the purification, for the elevation of Mississippi politics." In 1923 she defeated three male opponents in Madison County to win a state senatorial seat which she held for two terms.

Belle Kearney devoted most of her energies to public speaking, but she also published three books. Her autobiography, *A Slaveholder's Daughter* (1900), shows the hardness of life for the landed aristocracy after the Civil War and also provides strong insights into the development of the author's feminism. At the age of thirteen Kearney went to the Young Ladies' Academy at Canton, Mississippi, where she "began to dream dreams of graduation; afterwards of going North to a Woman's College, and later to Germany for further culture in certain branches." Her dreams were shattered when after her second year at the Academy her father had to take her home because he was unable to pay the monthly tuition of five dollars. She thought of trying to pay for her own education but knew of no women who had assumed such a responsibility. She wrote, "Industrial institutes and colleges where poor girls could work their way through were not in existence, and the doors of the State University, where tuition was free, were then open only to boys. There was nothing in Mississippi for young women except high-priced boarding schools and 'female' academies. It is humiliating to women for colleges, academies and boarding schools established for their education to be called 'female.' There is no sex in institutions of learning. The word 'woman' is strong and dignified and suggests courteous consideration. 'Female' is weak and almost insulting."

Kearney's second book, *Mama Flower* (1918), is a biography of Flora Mann Jones, the philanthropist for whom the Madison County town of Flora was named. Hutchinson notes that *Mama Flower*, like *A Slaveholder's Daugther*, "shows the childhood influence of Sir Walter Scott's romantic imagery, but its emphasis on Woman as a creature of social and political import is clearly a product of the temperance and suffrage awakenings." *Conqueror or Conquered: Or, the Sex Challenge Answered* (1921), Kearney's third book, is a novel or, as Hutchinson describes it, "a medical treatise disguised thinly in 576 pages of contrived romantic plot" in which "the book's characters expound Miss Kearney's views on sex, birth control, abortion, cigarette smoking and the 'higher life.'" After ill health forced her retirement from public life in 1931, Kearney devoted her last years to writing a continuation of the 1900 autobiography but did not complete the work before her death in 1939.

DON LEE KEITH (1940) was born in Wheeler, Mississippi, in Prentiss County. He attended the University of Mississippi before moving to New Orleans to join the staff of the *Times-Picayune*, where he worked in the capacity of reporter, editorial writer, and senior feature writer. He has twice been nominated for the Pulitzer Prize, and in 1974 he received a grant from the National Endowment for the Arts. In 1976 he became associate editor of the *Courier* in New Orleans and later served as editor-in-chief of the *New Orleans Magazine*.

During the past two decades, Keith has been the recipient of more journalism awards from the Press Club of New Orleans than any other person in the organization's history. He was twice presented with the Alex Waller Memorial Award, the club's highest distinction for writing. Other honors have come in recognition of articles ranging in topic from politics to stripteasing.

Of his relationship with Mississippi, Keith writes: "While I moved from the state of Mississippi at age twenty-one, with trips back there afterwards limited to family visits or relatively brief assignments as a journalist, almost all my values were shaped by my early life in rural Mississippi and, consequently, are probably inescapably evident in most things I write, with the exception of reportage, of course. That may be a rather immoderately roundabout way of saying what has been said by others, both with kindly and unkindly intents, that there's a little bit of Prentiss County in everything I write."

EDWIN KING (1936) was born in Vicksburg, Mississippi. He received a B.A in sociology from Millsaps College in 1958 and a masters of divinity (1961) and a masters of theology (1963) from Boston University. King has also studied at Harvard University, the University of Michigan, and the Gandhi Peace Foundation in New Delhi, India. He is a minister in the United Methodist Church and an assistant professor of sociology in the Department of Interdisciplinary Studies at the University of Mississippi Medical Center.

King has been a major activist on behalf of civil rights and civil liberties on a regional and national basis for over two decades. From 1963 to 1967 he was chaplain at Tougaloo College and worked closely with John Salter and the late Medgar Evers in the Jackson Movement campaign. King provided close links to other civil rights groups including SNCC (Student Nonviolent Coordinating Committee), CORE (Congress of Racial Equality), the Lawyer's Guild, and the National Council of Churches. In 1963 he was Aaron Henry's running mate when Henry ran for Governor of Mississippi. King also worked with Fannie Lou Hamer and Lawrence Guyot to build the Mississippi Freedom Democratic Party, served as its national committeeman at the 1964 Democratic National Convention, and was one of the founders of the Mississippi Civil Liberties Union.

"My wife, Jeannette, and I experienced the Civil Rights Movement of the 1950s and 1960s from unique perspectives—participant/observers and part of the people who would have to live with the changes," King says. "It is important to write about the period not because Mississippians, of whatever race, are so terribly different, but because other people might repeat our errors or achievements, might share our sorrows and our joys."

BEVERLY LOWRY (1938) was born in Memphis, Tennessee, and grew up in Greenville, Mississippi. She spent two years at the University of Mississippi and was graduated from Memphis State University. Of her first novel, *Come Back, Lolly Ray* (1977), a critic wrote in the *New York Times Book Review* that "what Lowry shares with that great southern tradition of fiction is an aptitude for the dramatic, a gift for metaphor and elaboration, a vision of the past abiding in and sometimes overwhelming the present." *Emma Blue,* her second novel, was published in 1978. Her third novel, *Daddy's Girl,* won the Jesse Jones Award for the best work of fiction written in 1981.

Lowry has taught creative writing at the University of Houston, and her short stories and articles have appeared in the *Black Warrior Review, Vanity Fair, Viva, Houston Review, Texas Monthly,* and *Mississippi Review* among others. Winner of a National Endowment for the Arts Fellowship in 1979 and a Guggenheim Fellowship in 1983, Lowry lives in San Marcos, Texas, and is at work on her fourth novel. She is the past president of the Texas Institute of Letters.

Lowry writes: "Growing up in Greenville meant growing up in a town the patron saint of which was a poet/scholar as well as a soldier. William Alexander Percy was our greatest hero. From the time I was in elementary school I always knew it was not only respectable to be a writer but honorable; desirable. The literary tradition in Greenville is strong. Who our next writer would be was always pondered. Teachers were on the lookout. The effect of this is invaluable. I always pay homage, whenever asked."

JOHN ROY LYNCH (1847–1939), politician, attorney, and author, was born a slave in Concordia Parish, Louisiana. In 1863 he and his family were purchased and taken to Natchez, Mississippi. Freedom came to Lynch that same year when Union forces occupied Natchez.

In his Introduction to *Reminiscences of an Active Life* historian John Hope Franklin writes: "For Lynch, the postwar years were years of discovery. He had picked up a few odds and ends of the rudiments of an education as he served his owner and guests at meals. The most valuable lesson he learned was that education was important; his mistress, he observed, became outraged when he displayed any knowledge at all. When the whites of Mississippi began to establish schools in 1865, they made no provisions for educating Negroes: and Lynch had to wait until a group of Northern teachers established a school for Negroes in 1866. It was an evening school, and Lynch attended for the four months that it remained open. After that, his education was, at best, informal—reading books and newspapers and listening to the recitations in the white school just across the alley from the photographic studio where he worked. Within a few years he had not only become quite literate but had also developed a capacity for expression that made a favorable impression on his listeners. He was developing talents and acquiring experience that would take him successively into politics, public service, the practice of law, and the pursuit of historical studies."

In Mississippi Lynch rose to prominence as a politician. He began his notable career in 1869 when he was elected to the House of Representatives of the Mississippi legislature. In 1872 he was elected Speaker of the House. At the age of twenty-six, in 1873, Lynch became Mississippi's first (and only) black member of the United States House of Representatives. When the Civil Rights Bill was before the House in June 1874, Lynch delivered his greatest speech—a plea for a bill that would open the public schools to children of all races. Lynch considered his participation in the passage of this bill in 1875 as his greatest contribution. Lynch served the House until 1883 when his Democratic opposition became too strong. He remained active in politics for the remainder of his life. In 1884 he was the first black American to deliver the keynote address before a major national political convention.

In the early 1890s Lynch began to study law, and in 1896 he passed the Mississippi bar. At the age of sixty-three he moved to Chicago where he wrote his reminiscences and practiced law. His *The Facts of Reconstruction* was published in 1913. When Lynch completed *Reminiscences of an Active Life* (published posthumously in 1970), he was already past ninety. He died in his Chicago home at the age of ninety-two after spending most of his life addressing the needs and attempting to resolve the problems of black people.

FLORENCE MARS (1923) was born and raised in Philadelphia, Mississippi, the principal town in Neshoba County. She attended Millsaps College, received a B.S. from the University of Mississippi in 1944, and worked in Atlanta during World War II. In 1948 she returned home to operate the Hereford cattle farm she inherited from her paternal grandfather, and in 1957 she bought the Neshoba County Stockyards. In addition to managing these operations, Mars has worked as a free-lance photographer. Her photographs have appeared in such publications as the *New York Times* and *Time* magazine and are used as illustrations for the book she wrote after the 1964 murder of three young civil rights workers—Andrew Goodman, James Earl Chaney, and Michael H. Schwerner—who were attempting to register black voters in her home county.

In *Witness in Philadelphia* (1977) Mars tries "to reconcile her personal outrage and shame for what occurred with some understanding of why it happened. To do this, she first recalled the milieu of her own childhood and the history of her family and neighbors; she then set these recollections against the grim circumstances of the killings. The result is the endowment of Philadelphia's tragedy with a significance that transcends the stereotyped meanness, bigotry, and hatred that kept the incident in newspaper headlines and on television screens. Mars describes what happened to a community confronted by a challenge to its most cherished beliefs and threatened with changes that its social structure was too rigid to accommodate; she reveals what it was like to be a member of this closed community, to speak out against the behavior of lifelong friends and acquaintances in a time of crisis, and to defy their efforts to silence or intimidate her."

About the author and her work Turner Catledge, also a native of Philadelphia and former editor of the *New York Times*, has written: "Florence Mars was there through it all, and in *Witness in Philadelphia* she tells what happened and why. What a witness! She witnessed with her eyes, her ears, and her heart. She saw, she heard, she felt, and through her own involvement she bore witness to qualities of courage and good will that all but evaporated in the climate of passion that flowed from an unreasoning fear of change. She is now joyously witnessing a revival of those good qualities in our town."

At the present time Florence Mars is working with her negatives and prints contemplating the publication of a book of photographs.

JAMES MEREDITH (1933), the seventh of thirteen children, was born in Kosciusko, Mississippi. His father was the son of a slave and raised Meredith to resent the white domination of southern economics. From his father, Meredith developed a strong individualism and an understanding of the economic base of racism. In his book, *Three Years in Mississippi*, Meredith states, "I have long recognized the folly of advocating a change simply because it is right, because it is humane, because it is Christian, because it is in the Constitution, or for any other nonpractical reason. I am aware of another important fact: if I were a white man, I would not give up my favored position unless there was an extremely good reason. The greatest hope for a major change in the basic status of the Negro is to convince the American whites that it is in their best interests. It is my firm conviction that the solution must result in the material improvement of both groups concerned—the oppressors as well as the oppressed."

Evidence of Meredith's awareness came early. He "perceived education as the key to destroying white domination and realized that he had to raise his scholastic record and academic goal in order to compete on an equal basis with Mississippi whites." Meredith left Mississippi at the age of sixteen to attend high school in St. Petersburg, Florida, where he felt he could get a better education. He graduated from Gibbs High School in June of 1951. Lacking money for college, he joined the United States Air Force. By the time he was nineteen, he had attained the rank of sergeant.

While in the Air Force, Meredith received numerous medals and awards and took a number of college extension courses at the University of Kansas and Washburn University, and he attended night school at New Mexico Western College. Between 1954 and 1960 Meredith was enrolled in the United States Armed Forces Institute. He completed half the courses in the United States and the other half in Japan where he attended the Far Eastern Division of the University of Maryland.

Upon leaving the Air Force, Meredith returned to Mississippi, where he enrolled with his wife in all-black Jackson State College, now Jackson State University. Meredith felt dissatisfied with the educational opportunities at Jackson State because he felt that a black state college was designed with a more limited curriculum than a corresponding white institution. Because of this, Meredith decided to enroll in the University of Mississippi. Meredith's enrollment as the first black student at the University of Mississippi was an important step in the civil rights movement in Mississippi.

Meredith graduated from the University of Mississippi in 1963, with a major in government and politics, and minors in history and French. *Three Years in Mississippi*, published in 1967, is Meredith's autobiographical account of his life from the time he left the Air Force to the time of his graduation from the University of Mississippi.

He went on to study economics at Ibadan University in Nigeria, and graduated from Columbia University Law School in 1968 with specialties in corporate, taxation, and international law. After law school he also completed the Merrill Lynch, Pierce, Fenner and Smith Financial Training School in 1969. He worked for a time with a New York stock brokerage firm, but returned to Mississippi in 1971. In recent years Meredith has taught at the University of Cincinnati and has made extensive trips to Africa to promote trade and use his experience in tree farming to teach Africans that they must replant trees they cut down to prevent destruction of fertile areas and encroachment by the desert.

ANNE MOODY (1940) was born in Centreville, Mississippi. She attended local public schools and later enrolled at Natchez Junior College. In 1963 Moody received a B.S. degree from Tougaloo College where she took part in civil rights activities, including voter registration projects and the desegregation of the Woolworth's lunch counter in Jackson. In 1964 she became a fund raiser and public speaker for the Council on Racial Equality (CORE) and was at Cornell University from 1964 to 1965 as civil rights project coordinator.

Her first book, *Coming of Age in Mississippi*, published in 1968, received the American Library Association "Best Book of the Year Award," the "Gold Medal Award" from the National Council of Catholics and Jews, and a citation from *Mademoiselle* magazine. Of it, Moody says, "*Coming of Age in Mississippi* grew out of my total life experience in Mississippi. It is a very personal account of a young girl's awakening and gradual realization of what it means to be black and living in Mississippi. It can also be said to be a case history of a rebel—someone who commits herself to a cause not because of something she has read or heard about but something she herself has experienced. That is, I think, the main reason people respond to *Coming of Age in Mississippi* the way they do—because they know that it is not some invented experience. It is real."

Senator Edward Kennedy reviewed the book for the *New York Times Book Review,* calling it "powerful and moving, a timely reminder that we cannot now relax in the struggle for sound justice in America or in any part of America." Mary Ellman in her review for the *Nation* wrote: "The book is very simply divided into sections: childhood, high school, college, and the movement. The first section, childhood, is different from and better than all the rest. Something is new here. The door is shut and the black family is inside out of white sight. This now ancient aspect of America rural southern black life begins to speak. It hits the page like a natural force, crude, and undeniable and against all principles of beauty, beautiful."

Now in its eighteenth printing *Coming of Age in Mississippi* has become a classic. It is used as a high school and college textbook in many parts of the world and has been translated into seven languages.

After leaving Mississippi, Moody lived for nine years in Europe and has since lived in New York City as a teacher, lecturer, and writer. Her second book, *Mr. Death,* was published in 1975. A sequel to *Coming of Age in Mississippi* is her forthcoming publication. *Farewell to Toosweet* covers from 1964 when she fled the Jackson-Canton area to 1974 when she came back home to see her dying mother in Centreville. She is currently working on nine manuscripts of fiction and nonfiction.

WILLIE MORRIS (1934) was born in Jackson, Mississippi, and moved in 1935 to Yazoo City, Mississippi. He attended the University of Texas where he received a degree in English and became editor of the *Daily Texan*. After graduation in 1956, he received a Rhodes Scholarship to Oxford University and studied modern history at New College until 1959. For three years (1960–63) he was editor of the *Texas Observer,* a political and literary journal based in Austin. In 1963 he was employed by *Harper's* magazine in New York. In 1967, when he was thirty-two, he became editor-in-chief of *Harper's,* substantially attracting first-rate fiction and essays, but resigned in 1971 in an editorial dispute. He has, since then, worked as a free-lance writer and lecturer, and has produced numerous articles and essays. Since his return to Mississippi, Morris has lived in Oxford and is the writer-in-residence at the University of Mississippi.

His books include *North Toward Home* (1967), *Good Old Boy* (1971), *Yazoo: Integration in a Deep-Southern Town* (1971), *The Last of the Southern Girls* (1973), *James Jones: A Friendship* (1978), *Terrains of the Heart and Other Essays on Home* (1981), *The Courting of Marcus Dupree* (1983), and *Always Stand in Against the Curve* (1983). His classic *North Toward Home* received a Houghton Mifflin Literary Fellowship Award. *The Courting of Marcus Dupree* was awarded the Christopher Medal.

In "A Sense of Place and the Americanization of Mississippi," Morris writes: "It is no accident that Mississippi produced Faulkner, the greatest of all the American novelists, and perhaps the greatest of all novelists, and Eudora Welty, and Walker Percy, and Shelby Foote, and the distinguished others. I must add that I, as a younger writer, am proud to be part of this remarkable heritage. These impulses of the imagination that gave us our literature were an expression of many things: the act of speech . . . the language of music . . . the love of place . . . the ineluctable perception of a common past . . . and at the very base of all this was that rarest and most indispensable sustenance for literature: and that is memory.

"The young people of Mississippi must learn to remember who they are, and where they come from. They must be encouraged to remember; there is a message to be carried."

LINDA PEAVY (1943) was born in Hattiesburg, Mississippi. She received a B.A. in English from Mississippi College in 1964 and an M.A. in English from the University of North Carolina at Chapel Hill in 1970. After teaching English from 1964 to 1966 at Central High in Jackson, Mississippi, and from 1966 to 1969 at Glen Oaks Senior High in Baton Rouge, Louisiana, she became an instructor in English at Oklahoma Baptist University. Since 1974 Peavy has lived with her family in Bozeman, Montana, working as a writer, editor, and lecturer. Peavy's fiction, poetry, and essays have appeared in numerous periodicals, including *Southern Exposure*, *South Dakota Review*, the *Texas Review*, *Cottonwood*, *Plainswoman*, *Crab Creek Review*, and *Memphis* magazine. In partnership with Ursula Smith, Peavy has co-authored *Women Who Changed Things* (1983), a collective biography of nine turn-of-the-century women of achievement, and *Dreams into Deeds: Nine Women Who Dared* (1985), a collective biography featuring women from the National Women's Hall of Fame. Peavy and Smith are currently writing *Women in Waiting: The Dynamics of Separation in the Westward Movement* and have written the libretto for an opera.

Peavy notes, "When I was growing up in Mississippi, evolution was a forbidden word and creation was seen as an instantaneous affair. Salvation worked the same way. At some fortuitous moment you 'got saved' and that took care of matters forever. It took years for me to alter that mind-set and realize that what was really essential was process, not product—journey, not destination. All of nature speaks to this becoming, this slow evolution that takes one from beginnings toward some largely unknown destination. Because my beginnings were in Mississippi, my journey has been different from what it would otherwise have been. A part of my personal evolution has been learning to accept, even cherish those beginnings, though raising the forbidden questions has meant that I can never return to them."

WALKER PERCY (1916) was born in Birmingham, Alabama. After the death of his parents, he and two brothers were adopted by their father's first cousin, William Alexander Percy, and raised in Greenville, Mississippi. He was graduated from the University of North Carolina in 1937 with a B.A. in chemistry and upon graduation became a student at the College of Physicians and Surgeons, Columbia University. He received his M.D., with honors, in 1941. During his internship at Bellevue Hospital in New York, Percy contracted tuberculosis and was forced in 1942 to convalesce in the Adirondacks. In 1944 he returned to Columbia to teach, but suffered a relapse, after which he retired from medicine.

While convalescing Percy read the great Russian novelists, the modern French novelists, Kierkegaard, and many of the other existentialists. He began to write and in 1961 his first novel, *The Moviegoer,* was published; in 1962 it won the National Book Award. Since then he has published articles, essays, and novels. In addition to *The Moviegoer,* Percy's fiction and nonfiction books include *The Last Gentleman* (1966), *Love in the Ruins* (1971), *The Message in the Bottle* (1975), *Lancelot* (1977), *The Second Coming* (received the 1980 Mississippi Institute of Arts and Letters Literature Award), and *Lost in the Cosmos* (1983). With each publication Percy's writing receives more international attention and praise.

In "Cinematographic Souvenir of Greenville," Percy writes: "When I attended Greenville High School in the 1930s, which was the Golden Age of the movies, it was a great thing to go to the 'show' after school . . . then they had movies in the afternoon. You would walk all the way from the old high school to the Paramount, carrying a girl's books maybe, and afterwards walk home. High school students didn't have cars in the thirties. I also remember the old Grand on Main Street near the levee. It had been an old vaudeville house, but that was before my day. They showed westerns there and I seem to remember a piano player. The balcony had the biggest rats in Greenville."

To Percy, the writing of a novel is a process of discovery, but a process with ground rules: "If you're interested in writing, you'd better enjoy reading. If you don't enjoy reading, if you prefer TV, forget it."

WILLIAM ALEXANDER PERCY (1885–1942) was born in Greenville, Mississippi, where he grew up in a secure atmosphere that was rich with music and books. His early education took place at the Sisters of Mercy convent and was supplemented by tutoring from a judge, a local priest, and the superintendent of the public school system. At fifteen, Percy was enrolled in the preparatory school at Sewanee. Disliking the uniforms that its students were required to wear, Percy took and passed the college entrance examination for the University of the South. He graduated with a B.A. in 1904 and spent the next year traveling across Europe and into Egypt.

Upon his return to the United States, Percy entered the Harvard School of Law, chiefly because he wanted to be near Boston. His interest in the law was marginal. He received his law degree in 1908 and returned to Greenville to enter practice with his father. It was during this period that Percy began to write poetry.

When World War I broke out, Percy spent two years in Europe in Herbert Hoover's Commission for Relief in Belgium. In 1916 Percy, after considerable effort, was accepted into officer's candidate school. He saw action on the front lines and returned to Greenville with the rank of captain and the Croix de Guerre.

His return to Greenville saw the advent of troubled years. In 1922 there was a resurgence of activity by the Ku Klux Klan, and Percy's stand against them, along with his father's, endangered both Percy and his family. In 1927 the Mississippi River overflowed its banks, creating the worst flood in recorded history. Because of his work in Belgium, Percy was appointed Chairman of the Flood Relief Committee and the Red Cross. He was responsible for soliciting and coordinating relief efforts within the state and from external sources. In 1929, both his parents died within a few weeks of each other. Percy was left with his father's law practice and possession of Trail Lake, 3,000 acres of some of the richest land in the South. In 1931 Percy adopted his three young cousins, Walker, LeRoy, and Phinizy Percy, after the death of their parents, and he turned his energies toward giving these orphaned boys the best opportunities he knew how to give them. Of his efforts, and of Will Percy, Walker Percy has said, "I will say no more than that he was the most extraordinary man I have ever known and that I owe him a debt which cannot be paid."

Percy's poetry was antiquated at the time of its writing. In the midst of one of history's greatest poetry revolutions, Percy persistently wrote in a Victorian vein. He was not unaware of this: "When you feel something intensely, you want to write it down—if anguish, to staunch the bleeding; if delight, to prolong the moment. When after years of pondering you feel you have discovered a new truth or an old one which suddenly for you has the excitement of a new one, you write a longish poem. To keep it free of irrelevant details and set it in some long-ago time, one, of course, you love and perhaps lived in."

Among Percy's books of poetry are *Sappho in Levkas and Other Poems* (1915), *In April Once* (1920), *Enzio's Kingdom, and Other Poems* (1924), *Selected Poems* (1930), *The Collected Poems of William Alexander Percy* (1943), and *Of Silence and Stars* (1953).

Of his 1941 memoirs, *Lanterns on the Levee,* critic Herschel Brickell of the *New York Times Book Review* wrote that it was "a work of exceptional merit and importance. The high quality of the prose would entitle it to consideration for a permanent place in our literature, and it has numerous other virtues as well." It remains Percy's major work.

Brickell wondered why a man who was only fifty-five years old was writing his autobiography. He didn't know that Percy, always frail of health, had already had a debilitating stroke. In 1942, a year after the publication of *Lanterns on the Levee,* William Alexander Percy died.

STERLING D. PLUMPP (1940) was born in Clinton, Mississippi. In 1955 his family moved to Jackson, Mississippi, where he completed school. After being selected for a scholarship, Plumpp studied for two years at St. Benedict's College and in 1968 received a B.A. in psychology from Roosevelt University. He is currently associate professor in the Black Studies Program at the University of Illinois at Chicago.

Plumpp's writings include six books of poetry, prose, and essays. In 1972 Third World Press published *Black Rituals,* a book of black psychological essays; it is a probing analysis of the black man's way of coping in a technological, urbanized, and industrialized society. His books of poetry include *Portable Soul* (1969), *Half Black, Half Blacker* (1970), *Steps to Break the Circle* (1974), *Clinton* (1976), and *The Mojo Hands Call, I Must Go* (1982). The latter, published by Thunder's Mouth Press, won the 1983 Carl Sandburg Literary Award for Poetry. In 1982 Plumpp edited a collection titled *Somehow We Survive: An Anthology of South African Writing*.

Concerning his development as a writer, Plumpp says, "When I was thirty, I found my writing voice and the ability to master techniques to reflect my inner self. The more I wrote about the South, the more tranquil my voice was. By viewing my soul through Mississippi, I could maneuver into the reservoir of my being without first having to plod through attacks against whites; I could see the survival lines of my people concealed in the many ways they did things. Though there will be other places in my life none will be home, as close and as painfully or joyfully familiar as Mississippi."

SAMUEL PRESTRIDGE (1952) was born in Columbus, Mississippi. Because his family moved throughout the South, Prestridge grew up in a number of states—Mississippi, Texas, Alabama, Georgia. His family returned to Mississippi in 1969 and he was graduated from high school in Tupelo. Prestridge received a B.A. from Mississippi College in 1974 and an M.A. from the University of Southern Mississippi in 1977. For two years Prestridge was poet-in-the-schools for the Mississippi Arts Commission. During this time he worked toward a M.F.A. at Goddard College in Plainfield, Vermont, where he studied with Donald Hall and Thomas Lux and "though I didn't get to study with him, I hung around as much as possible" with Robert Hass. In 1980 Prestridge moved to south Louisiana where he worked in the oil fields. Since his return to Mississippi in 1981 he has supported himself as a para-legal, a credit manager, and a free-lance writer. Presently he is employed by an advertising company in Jackson.

CHARLEMAE ROLLINS (1897–1979) was born in Yazoo City, Mississippi. After graduating from Western University she attended the University of Chicago and enrolled in special courses in library science at Columbia University. From 1927 to 1963 she worked at the George C. Hall branch of the Chicago Public Library where she was head of the children's department. Rollins was one of the first librarians to stress pride in black heritage. Her lifelong campaign to end the stereotyped portrayal of blacks in children's books was waged through her library work, her lecturing in children's literature at Roosevelt University, and her writing. Many of Rollins's books deal with the lives of eminent black Americans.

A noted humanitarian, she received the American Brotherhood Award of the National Conference of Christians and Jews (1952), Library Letter Award of the American Library Association (1953), Grolier Society Award (1955), Children's Reading Round Table Award (1962), Negro Centennial

Awards (1963), and Woman of the Year, Woman's National Book Association (1970).

Rollins's books include *We Build Together: A Reader's Guide to Negro Life and Literature for Elementary and High School Use* (1941), *The Magic World of Books* (1954), *Call of Adventure* (1962), *Christmas Gif'* (1963), *They Showed the Way: Forty American Negro Leaders* (1964), *Famous American Negro Poets* (1965), and *Famous Negro Entertainers of Stage, Screen, and TV* (1967). Her friendship with Langston Hughes, whom she met at a Works Project Administration writers' project sponsored by her library during the Depression, inspired her to later write *Black Troubador: Langston Hughes,* which won the 1971 Coretta Scott King Award.

When Rollins retired in 1963 the Chicago Library awarded her a meritorious plaque, and the poet Gwendolyn Brooks wrote a poem of tribute.

JAMES W. SILVER (1907) was born in Rochester, New York. When he was twelve, his family moved to the South. He attended public schools in Southern Pines, North Carolina, and graduated from the University of North Carolina in 1927. Silver received his M.A. from Peabody College in 1929 and his Ph.D. from Vanderbilt University in 1935. From 1936 to 1964 he was a professor of history at the University of Mississippi. In 1964 he joined the faculty of Notre Dame University, where he remained until 1969. Leaving Notre Dame, he taught at the University of South Florida from 1969 until his retirement in 1979.

Silver was on the campus of the University of Mississippi on September 30, 1962, when riots broke out over the admission of James Meredith, the first black to enroll in that school. In *Mississippi: The Closed Society* (1964) Silver studies the underlying causes that led to the violence of that night. The book received wide national acclaim, but Silver's reception among Mississippians was less than pleasant. In the preface to his 1984 book, *Running Scared,* Silver says, "Since the publication of my book *Mississippi: The Closed Society,* I have felt considerable anguish because a few former friends have downgraded my views to the point of challenging my common sense as well as my integrity. . . . It was a segregationist friend who remarked that inasmuch as I found it impossible to achieve eminence as a historian, I decided to become notorious."

Professor Silver is a past president of the Southern Historical Association and is the author of numerous articles and several historical studies, including *Edmund Pendleton Gaines, Frontier General* (1949).

He is retired and lives on Dunedin Beach, Florida.

ANN ODENE SMITH (1926) was born in Edwards, Mississippi, and attended Southern Christian Institute (Mount Beulah College) in her hometown. Currently she continues her teaching career which began in 1947 and is writing a book titled *Lost Horizons of Ancient Black History* which she researched in Africa.

Her early years of teaching in the rural schools of Mississippi are recorded in *God's Step Chilluns* (1981). Professor Jerry W. Ward, Jr., writes: "Ms. Smith's book deserves to be read by teachers and students in Mississippi, because it provides a springboard from which we can begin to discuss how much progress, real progress, has been made in the public school system since the 1940s. First, there is the meat of the book, its sympathetic treatment of 'raw, evil, naked, and ugly' Mississippi poverty, a condition which Hodding Carter III reminded us recently still plagues the state and the South. Second, the book is a testimony of one woman's personal war on poverty, her attempt to free rural peole who 'were truly enslaved and ensnared by ignorance, malice and the greed of the few who owned the lands and its people' through her work as a rural school teacher.

"We are humbled before the descriptions of abject poverty in Marks Chapel, Winters Burn (Canaan Chapel), Cherry Hill, Sawyers Quarter, and the bayou country. She vividly portrays the agonies of sharecropping, the humanity and ignorance of black farmers, and the abiding faith of a young teacher in the potential of black youths. *God's Step Chilluns* is a document in Mississippi history, particularly Mississippi educational history. It should be placed in school libraries. Teachers and students should read it and discuss what it reveals about change in Mississippi."

FRANK E. SMITH (1918) was born in Sidon, Mississippi. He attended the public schools of Greenwood, Mississippi, Sunflower Junior College, and the University of Mississippi, from which he received a B.A. in 1941. In 1942 he entered the army as a draftee and served in Europe with the Third Army's 243rd Field Artillery Battalion. He rose to the rank of major and received a Bronze Star.

In 1946 and 1947 Smith was managing editor of the Greenwood *Morning Star.* He was elected to the Mississippi State Senate in 1947 and in the same year became legislative assistant to United States Senator John Stennis. From 1951 through 1962 he was United States Representative from the Delta district. After his primary defeat in 1962, Smith was for ten years a director of the Tennessee Valley Authority. He was then an associate director of the Illinois Board of Higher Education and professor of public policy at Virginia Tech. In 1980 Smith returned to Mississippi to work as special assistant to Governor William Winter.

Smith was among the first of Mississippi politicians to denounce the policy of segregation. *Congressman from Mississippi*, published in 1964, is an autobiographical book in which Smith outlined his views on the then tense racial situation. Up until that point, Smith had conformed to the status quo of a Mississippi congressman. He writes, "As a condition to holding my office, I made obeisance to the 'southern way of life.' Like the rest of my colleagues from Mississippi and the South, I went on record with speeches against every civil rights measure that came up during my tenure." Still, his position seemed too liberal, and in 1962 he lost his seat.

Smith's other books include *Battle Diary: The Story of the 243rd Field Artillery Battalion in Combat* (1946), *The Yazoo* (1954), *Look Away from*

Dixie (1965), *The Politics of Conservation* (1966) and *Mississippians All* (with Audrey Warren, 1968).

In 1984 Smith was elected a Life Fellow of the Southern Regional Council. He is retired and living in Jackson, Mississippi.

ELIZABETH SPENCER (1921) was born in Carrollton, Mississippi, to a family that had lived in Carroll County since the 1830s. In 1942 she received a B.A. in English from Belhaven College, Jackson, Mississippi. Upon graduation, she attended Vanderbilt University where she received an M.A. degree. Afterwards Spencer taught at Northwest Mississippi Junior College, Senatobia, Mississippi, at Belmont College, Nashville, Tennessee, and at the University of Mississippi. While teaching at the University of Mississippi, Spencer published her first novel, *Fire in the Morning*. Since 1953 she has been a full-time writer. Spencer has received many awards for her writing including a Guggenheim Fellowship (1953), the Rosenthal Foundation Award of the American Academy of Arts and Letters (1957), the *Kenyon Review* Fellowship in Fiction (1957), the McGraw-Hill Fiction Award (1960), the Henry Bellamann Award for creative writing (1968), the Award of Merit Medal for the Short Story by the American Academy of Arts and Letters (1983), and, most recently, election to the American Academy Institute of Arts and Letters (1985).

Spencer's books include *Fire in the Morning* (1948), *This Crooked Way* (1952), *The Voice at the Back Door* (1956), *The Light in the Piazza* (1960), *Knights and Dragons* (1965), *No Place for an Angel* (1967), *Ship Island and Other Stories* (1968), *The Snare* (1972), *The Stories of Elizabeth Spencer* (1981), *Marilee* (1981), and *The Salt Line* (1984).

Of her native state Spencer writes: "Mississippi gave a wonderful cross-current to writing—when I was growing up the old had been set in its ways since the Civil War, but the new was making itself felt. Writers respond especially to this sort of tension. Then, too, there was such a wide variety of individuals, so many wildly different characters, everyone with his own story, all to be met with daily. The challenge was not where to find material but how best to use it in a modern fiction which would engage intelligence and feeling. All my early books came out of Mississippi and many still do . . . memory keeps so many things, and rather than lose them, it may even make them richer."

MILDRED D. TAYLOR was born in Jackson, Mississippi, and grew up in Toledo, Ohio, with yearly trips back to the South. Upon graduation from the University of Toledo, she spent two years in Ethiopia with the Peace Corps. Returning to the United States, she recruited for the Peace Corps before entering the School of Journalism at the University of Colorado. There, as a member of the Black Student Alliance, she worked with students and university officials in structuring a Black Studies program.

Song of the Trees (1975), Taylor's first book about the Logan family of Mississippi, won the Council on Interracial Books Award in the African American category. It was also a *New York Times* Outstanding Book of the

Year in 1975. The *Times* called it "triumphant . . . a true story and truly told." Her second book, *Roll of Thunder, Hear My Cry* (1976), won many honors including the prestigious Newbery Award from the American Library Association. It was also made into a film. A sequel, *Let the Circle Be Unbroken*, was published in 1981.

In her 1977 acceptance speech for the Newbery Award, Taylor said: "I will continue the Logans' story with the same life guides that have always been mine, for it is my hope that these books, one of the first chronicles to mirror a black child's hopes and fears from childhood innocence to awareness to bitterness and disillusionment, will one day be instrumental in teaching children of all colors the tremendous influence that Cassie's generation—my father's generation—had in bringing about the great Civil Rights Movement of the fifties and sixties. Without understanding that generation and what it and the generations before it endured, children of today and of the future cannot understand or cherish the precious rights of equality which they now possess, both in the North and in the South. If they can identify with the Logans, who are representative not only of my family but of the many black families who faced adversity and survived, and understand the principles by which they lived, then perhaps they can better understand and respect themselves and others."

MILDRED SPURRIER TOPP (1897–1963) was born on her grandfather's farm in Mason County, Illinois. Less than two years later, her grandfather loaded the whole family into his custom-built surrey and moved to Tennessee. The family moved again when she was nine, this time to Greenwood, Mississippi, where her widowed mother set up shop as a portrait photographer and her Yankee grandfather found ways to make peace with "a community comprised of some three thousand rebels." Topp attended the public schools of Greenwood and then went to Columbus to study at the Industrial Institute and College (now Mississippi State University for Women). After receiving an A.B. there in 1917, she returned to Greenwood, married, raised two children, and led what she described as "the usual life of the average woman of a small southern town—occupied with home and family, and civic, social and church affairs." Not being "the kind who collects old glass and hook rugs," however, Topp taught English at Greenwood High School from 1918 to 1922, represented Leflore County in the Mississippi legislature from 1932 to 1936, and served on the staff of the Local USO during World War II.

In 1947, at the age of fifty, Topp began writing. She claimed this happened when she discovered a ream of typing paper in the attic of her home. Unable to find any practical household uses for the paper and not being wasteful, she decided to use it for describing her childhood in Greenwood. She spent two weeks writing her autobiography, packed up the manuscript, and set off for a summer writers' workshop at the University of Colorado. There another Mississippian, Ben Ames Williams, read the manuscript and recommended its publication because the work made him "laugh for three hours." *Smile Please* was published in 1948 and became an immediate best seller. Critics described it as "the most riotous record of this year" and "a masterpiece of pure wit." Topp continued to write her reminiscences of childhood and life in a small Mississippi town in the early 1900s and published *In the Pink* in 1950. It, too, became a best seller. After the publication of these books, Topp moved from Greenwood to Oxford. She received an M.A. from the University of Mississippi in 1954 and remained there teaching composition and creative writing until her death in 1963.

GLENNRAY TUTOR (1950) was born in Kennett, Missouri, where his parents, both Mississippi natives, moved after buying a grocery store. From 1950 to 1973 Tutor's family shuttled from Mississippi to Missouri. Tutor says of this period, "The time I've spent in Mississippi equals about half of my life during those wonderful years of highways and woods and little towns and fields." In 1973 he transferred from Three Rivers College in Missouri to the University of Mississippi, graduating in 1974 with a B.A. In 1976 he completed an M.F.A. in painting with a minor in printmaking.

Although primarily a visual artist, Tutor has published stories and poems in a wide variety of publications including *Western Humanities Review*, *New Orleans Review*, *Voices International*, and *Cobblestone*.

A number of visual works by Tutor have been published in magazines and books, including the twelve charcoal illustrations in *Blooded on Arachne*, a collection of short stories by Michael Bishop. *Who Made Stevie Cry?*, also by Bishop, contains a full, wrap-a-round jacket painting by Tutor. Over one hundred of his drawings are in *Tales of the Quintana Roo* by James Tiptree Jr.

Regarding the breadth of his creative experience, Tutor says, "People should always be growing up until the moment they die. Mississippi has been a good and fertile place for me. Life supplies a thousand motivations every minute; the problem, if any, comes from trying to choose which motivation out of all of them to follow. The key to moving through this dilemma is letting feeling, above all else, lead you."

MARGARET WALKER (1915) was born in Birmingham, Alabama, the daughter of a music teacher and a minister of the Methodist Church; she grew up in Alabama, Louisiana, and Mississippi. Walker received a B.A. from Northwestern University in 1935 and an M.A. and a Ph.D. from the University of Iowa. In 1942, after working for the WPA on its Federal Writers Project, Walker began teaching at West Virginia State College in the English department. In the same year *For My People*, her first book, was published as a volume in the Yale Series of Younger Poets. In 1949 Walker joined the faculty at Jackson State University as a professor of English and later became director of the Institute for the Study of History, Life, and Culture of Black People. Her novel *Jubilee*, published in 1966, won a Houghton Mifflin Literary Fellowship Award and became an international best seller. Her other books include *Prophets for a New Day*

(1970), *How I Wrote Jubilee* (1972), *October Journey* (1973), *A Poetic Equation: Conversations Between Nikki Giovanni and Margaret Walker* (1974), and *The Daemonic Genius of Richard Wright* (1985).

Her novel *Jubilee* is an inspiring story for all people struggling for freedom and equality. In it Walker incorporated into the fictionalized life of her maternal great-grandmother actual historical events from slavery to Reconstruction.

Retired from teaching at Jackson State University, Walker is completing a collection of poems titled *This Is My Century: Black Synthesis of Time*. Her essays and public lectures are being collected by Maryemma Graham and will be published under the title *On Being Female, Black, and Free*. *Fields Watered with Blood*, a critical collection of essays on her writing, is currently being edited by Myriam Díaz-Diocaretz. The interviews of Margaret Walker are being edited and collected for publication by Dorothy Abbott.

DEAN FAULKNER WELLS (1936) was born in Oxford, Mississippi, the daughter of Dean Swift Faulkner and Louise Hale. Her father, William Faulkner's youngest brother, was killed in a plane crash before she was born.

Published in magazines and journals, Wells is the author of *The Ghosts of Rowan Oak: William Faulkner's Ghost Stories for Children*, *Belle-Ducks at The Peabody* and editor of *The Great American Writers' Cookbook*. She makes her home in Oxford, Mississippi, and with her husband, Larry Wells, operates Yoknapatawpha Press.

IDA B. WELLS (1862–1931) was born in Holly Springs, Mississippi, six months prior to the Emancipation Proclamation, the first of eight children of parents who were both slaves. When in 1878 a yellow fever epidemic killed her parents, Wells took on the task of rearing her brothers and sisters. To support them she taught school in a one-room country schoolhouse and also managed to save for further education.

In the early 1880s she went to live with her aunt in Memphis where she accepted a position as a rural school teacher in Shelby County, Tennessee.

On May 4, 1884, Wells was traveling by train to Woodstock, Tennessee, where her school was located. The conductor of the train ordered her to the smoking car. Having bought a first class ticket, she refused, and the conductor, assisted by several white passengers, removed her from the car. She got off at the next stop, returned to Memphis, and filed suit against the railroad. This was the first time a southern black had appealed to a state court since the United States Supreme Court declared unconstitutional the Civil Rights Act of 1875. She won the law suit, but when the railroad appealed, the Tennessee Supreme Court reversed the decision of the lower court.

An excerpt from Wells's diary from this period reads, "The Supreme Court reversed the decision of the lower court in my behalf . . . I felt so disappointed because I had hoped such great things from my suit for my people generally. I had firmly believed all along that the law was on our side and would, when we appealed to it, give us justice. I feel shorn of that belief and utterly discouraged, and just now, if it were possible, would gather my race in my arms and fly away with them."

During the fall of that same year, Wells passed the qualifying examinations and became a teacher in the Memphis school system. In 1887 she wrote an article about her suit against the railroad, the first of many articles to come. She invested some of her savings to become part owner of the city's only Afro-American journal, *Free Speech and Headlight.* Her articles criticizing the Memphis Board of Education for separate, inferior Negro schools led to her dismissal as a teacher in 1891. She became a full-time journalist, encouraging economic boycotts and urging blacks to leave Memphis.

Using the pen name "Iola," Wells denounced the lynching of three young, black businessmen in 1892 and as a result, her press was wrecked and her editorial offices destroyed. Wells then began work at the *New York Age* and continued to write against the inequality in the South. After Wells moved to Chicago, she published, in 1895, *A Red Record: Tabulated Statistics and Alleged Causes of Lynching in the United States 1892–1894*. This book represented the first serious statistical recording of lynchings since emancipation.

Wells was an active advocate of women's rights. She established the first black women's suffrage group, the Alpha Suffrage Club. In her demand for the right to vote, she was involved in two marches on Washington—on the eve of President Woodrow Wilson's inauguration in 1913 and at the Republican National Convention of 1918 where the women demanded inclusion of a suffrage plank in the platform.

As one of the founders of the Niagara Movement, an organization that evolved into the National Association for the Advancement of Colored People (NAACP), Wells used her voice and pen to continue speaking out for "federal anti-lynching laws, universal suffrage, quality education, and an end to discrimination and segregation."

In 1913 Wells became the first black probation officer with the Chicago Municipal Court. The poet Langston Hughes said that "her activities in the field of social work laid the groundwork for the Urban League." The Chicago Housing Authority named one of its first low-rent housing developments after her in 1941.

Ida Wells died in 1931 after an illness of two days. In 1970, nearly forty years after Wells's death, *Crusade for Justice: The Autobiography of Ida B. Wells* edited by her daughter, Alfreda M. Duster, was published.

EUDORA WELTY (1909) was born in Jackson, Mississippi. Educated in Jackson's public schools, she began writing and drawing very early, publishing poems and sketches in *St. Nicholas* magazine as early as 1920. After attending Industrial Institute and College (now Mississippi University for Women) for two years, she transferred to the University of Wisconsin, graduating with a B.A. in 1929. In 1930 she attended Columbia

University School of Business, but returned to Mississippi in 1931 when her father died. In Jackson, she worked in a variety of jobs before going to work for the WPA, traveling across the state taking photographs and writing copy for several small newspapers.

Two of her short stories "Death of a Traveling Salesman" and "Magic" were published in *Manuscript* magazine in 1936. Her first book, *A Curtain of Green*, appeared in 1941, and was a critical success. Her second volume, *The Robber Bridegroom*, appeared in 1942, and firmly established her reputation as a writer. Since the 1943 publication of *The Wide Net and Other Stories*, Welty has published *Delta Wedding* (1946), *The Golden Apples* (1949), *The Ponder Heart* (1954), *The Bride of the Innisfallen and Other Stories* (1955), *The Shoe Bird* (1964), *Losing Battles* (1970), *One Time, One Place* (1971), *The Optimist's Daughter* (1972), *The Eye of the Story* (1977), *The Collected Stories of Eudora Welty* (1980), and *One Writer's Beginnings* (1984) among others.

Welty has received great international attention and praise. Her many honors include the Pulitzer Prize, the American Book Award for fiction, the Gold Medal for the Novel by the National Institute of Arts and Letters, and the Howells Medal for Fiction by the American Academy of Arts and Letters. *One Writer's Beginnings*, a collection of 1983 lectures given at Harvard University, put her on the best-seller list. In 1984 the University Press of Mississippi published *Conversations with Eudora Welty*, interviews collected by Peggy Whitman Prenshaw.

In "Place in Fiction," she writes, "I think the sense of place is as essential to good and honest writing as a logical mind; surely they are somewhat related. It is by knowing where you stand that you grow able to judge where you are. Place absorbs our earliest notice and attention, it bestows on us our original awareness; and our critical powers spring up from the study of it and the growth of experience inside it. It perseveres in bringing us back to earth when we fly too high. It never really stops informing us, for it is forever astir, alive, changing, reflecting, like the mind of man itself. One place comprehended can make us understand other places better."

Novelist Reynolds Price says of Welty, "In all of American fiction, she stands for me with her only peers—Melville, James, Hemingway, and Faulkner—and among them, she is in some crucial respects the deepest, the most spacious, the most life-giving."

JOHN A. WILLIAMS (1925) was born in Hinds County near Jackson, Mississippi, but he grew up in Syracuse, New York, where his parents had met and married. However, following an old custom, they returned "down home" for the birth of their first child. When Williams was about one year old, his parents returned to Syracuse.

Before he finished high school, Williams joined the United States Navy (1943), serving as a hospital corpsman until his discharge in 1946. Returning to Syracuse, he completed high school, took a B.A. degree at Syracuse University, and did some graduate work. He has worked as European correspondent for *Ebony* and *Jet* magazines (1958–59) and as African correspondent for *Newsweek* (1964–65).

Williams books include *The Angry Ones* (1960), *Night Song* (1961), *Sissie* (1963), *Journey Out of Anger* (1965), *This Is My Country Too* (1965), *The Man Who Cried I Am* (1967), *Captain Blackman* (1972), *Flashbacks: A Twenty-Year Diary of Article Writing* (1973), *!Click Song* (1982), and *The Berhama Account* (1985) among others.

In *Lives of Mississippi Authors 1817–1967*, Professor Jerry W. Ward, Jr., writes: "The fact that Williams was born in the 1920s, when great numbers of blacks migrated northward in search of economic, social, and political advantages, has had a lasting impact on his work, for he is keenly aware of what it means to be the product of transplanted roots. Mississippi can claim him as one of her native sons by virtue of birth, but the enduring attitudes that give shape and substance to his writing are those formed in a northern milieu."

Williams has co-produced, written, and narrated several programs for National Educational Television. He received a grant from the National Endowment for the Arts for *!Click Song* and currently is a professor of English and journalism at Rutgers University. Additionally Williams is the chair of the board of directors for the Coordinating Council of Literary Magazines.

TENNESSEE WILLIAMS (1911–1983) was born in Columbus, Mississippi. After living his early years in various Mississippi towns, he moved with his family to St. Louis. This environment, and its effect on the young Williams, is described in his play *The Glass Menagerie* and his short story "Portrait of a Girl in Glass." Williams attended the University of Missouri from 1929 to 1931, when he was withdrawn by his father because of his failure to pass ROTC. He then worked for three years (1931–34) at the International Shoe Company in St. Louis and, as a means of escaping tedium, began to write more and more. Quitting his job, he attended Washington University before receiving a B.A. degree from the University of Iowa in 1938.

Williams revised an earlier script called "The Gentleman Caller" into *The Glass Menagerie*. It opened in Chicago on December 26, 1944 and was his first professional success. In 1945 it moved to Broadway. With this impressive start, Williams began his career as one of the world's most popular playwrights. He won two Pulitzer Prizes, one for *A Streetcar Named Desire* and another for *Cat on a Hot Tin Roof*, and four New York Drama Circle Critics Awards for these two plays, as well as for *The Glass Menagerie* and *The Night of the Iguana*. Many of Williams's plays have been made into films.

After he changed his name to "Tennessee," the first work to bear his new name was "The Field of Blue Children," printed in *Story* in September 1939. About his name change Williams writes, "I was christened Thomas Lanier Williams. It is a nice enough name, perhaps a little too nice. It sounds like it might belong to the son of a writer who turns out sonnet sequences to Spring. As a matter of fact, my first literary award was $25.00 from a Woman's Club for doing exactly that, three sonnets dedicated to Spring. I hasten to add that I was still pretty young. Under that name I published a good deal of lyric poetry which was a bad imitation of Edna Millay. When I grew up I realized this poetry wasn't much good and I felt the name had been compromised so I changed it to Tennessee Williams, the justification being mainly that the Williamses had fought the Indians for Tennessee and I had already discovered that the life of a young writer was going to be something similar to the defense of a stockade against a band of savages."

RICHARD WRIGHT (1908–1960) was born near Natchez, Mississippi, the son of a country schoolteacher mother and an illiterate sharecropper father. Because of his mother's illness and his father's eventual abandonment, his childhood was one of poverty, frequent moves from relative to relative, and interrupted schooling. His story "The Voodoo of Hell's Half Acre" was, however, published in Jackson, Mississippi, in the local black newspaper when Wright was fifteen. In 1925 he graduated from the ninth grade at Smith-Robertson Public School in Jackson at the head of his class.

Wright was a voracious reader. While working in Memphis, Wright discovered the work of H. L. Mencken and began to read some of the works mentioned in Mencken's *Prefaces*, along with a wide variety of other works. In 1927 he moved to Chicago, where he would remain for ten years. In 1932 Wright joined the American Communist Party, believing that he had finally found a group interested in the plight of the American black. He had begun writing poetry and short stories earlier, and now, on behalf of the Party, his work began to appear in such publications as *New Masses*, *Left Front*, and *Partisan Review*.

In 1937 Wright moved to New York, where he was Harlem editor of the *Daily Worker*. His first book, *Uncle Tom's Children*, was published in 1938. This was followed by his two most famous works. *Native Son*, published in 1940, is the tragic tale of a Mississippi-born black in Chicago. Its success was phenomenal, and assured Wright a place in American literature. In 1945 *Black Boy*, an autobiographical work based on his traumatic childhood in Mississippi, was released.

By 1944 Wright had left the Communist Party and in 1946, unreconciled to the continuing racism in the United States, he and his family moved to Paris, France. There he was to remain until his death. After moving to France he was active in establishing such organizations as the Society of African Culture and worked with such African leaders as Leopold Senghor, later president of Senegal, and Aime Cesaire from Martinique. Among his nonfiction works of this time are *Black Power* (1954) and *Pagan Spain* (1957).

Wright's fiction includes *The Outsider* (1953) and *Savage Holiday* (1954). In addition, three works were published posthumously—*Eight Men* (1961), *Lawd Today* (1963), and *American Hunger* (1977).

AL YOUNG (1939) was born in Ocean Springs, Mississippi, and grew up in the South, the Midwest, and on the West Coast. Educated at the University of Michigan and the University of California at Berkeley as a Spanish teacher, he continues his life-long study of human speech and language. Along the way, he has been a professional musician, disk jockey, medical photographer, railroad man, warehouseman, laboratory aide, clerk-typist, job interviewer, janitor, editor, and screenwriter. Moreover, he has taught writing and literature at such institutions as Stanford, Foothill Community College, Colorado College, the University of Washington, and the University of California at both Santa Cruz and Berkeley.

How Is Angelina? (1975), *Sitting Pretty* (1976), and *Ask Me Now* (1980) are among his most recent novels. His books of poetry—*Dancing* (1969), *The Song Turning Back Into Itself* (1971), *Geography of the Near Past* (1976), *The Blues Don't Change* (1982), *Bodies & Soul* (1981), and *Kinds of Blue* (1984) have met with critical success. Film assignments have included scripts for Dick Gregory, Sidney Poitier, Bill Cosby, and Richard Pryor. With poet-novelist Ishmael Reed, Young edits *Quilt*, an international journal devoted to multicultural writing. His work has been translated into Norwegian, Swedish, Italian, Japanese, Spanish, Polish, Russian, French, and Chinese.

Young is the recipient of the Joseph Henry Jackson Award, National Arts Council Awards for editing and poetry, a Wallace Stegner Fellowship, a National Endowment for the Arts Fellowship, the Pushcart Prize, a Fulbright Fellowship, the Before Columbus Foundation American Book Award, and a Guggenheim Fellowship.

Bodies & Soul and *Kinds of Blue* are both books of musical memoirs. The artists that inspired these essays include James Brown, Ravel, Billie Holiday, Thelonious Monk, Glenn Miller, Janis Joplin, Miles Davis, Bessie Smith, Charlie Parker, The Doors, Stevie Wonder, Rossini, Duke Ellington, John Coltrane, Sarah Vaughan, and many more.

Young writes, "I can still remember as clearly as if it were today the very first music that touched me: early songs that I sang, the first notes I ever sounded on a piano, spacious cricket concertos on summer nights, the tinkle of spoons against cups and water glasses, birdcalls, blues, spirituals, actual hollers in Mississippi fields where I picked my early share of cotton and corn and cut a little cane; my grandmother's voice and her constant humming as she went about her everyday tasks, the melodious rise and fall in the voices of Afro-Christian preachers in little tumble-down country churches, the rapid rat-a-tat of peckerwood percussion, country laments, heavy-duty juke joint fried fish and barbecue funk, jazz in all its endless guises and disguises, the swishing of leaves, the sounds of cities, the hush of streams and the roar of the ocean."